A GUIDE TO THE BIRDS OF
THE WEST INDIES

A GUIDE TO THE BIRDS OF THE WEST INDIES

Herbert Raffaele, James Wiley, Orlando Garrido,
Allan Keith, and Janis Raffaele

Principal Illustrators: Tracy Pedersen and Kristin Williams

Supporting Illustrators: Roman Company, Christopher Cox,
Cynthie Fisher, Don Radovich, Bart Rulon

Princeton University Press
Princeton, New Jersey

Plates and illustrations copyright © 1998 by Herbert Raffaele, James Wiley,
Orlando Garrido, Allan Keith, Janis Raffaele, Tracy Pedersen,
Kristin Williams, Don Radovich, Cynthie Fisher, Bart Rulon,
Christopher Cox and Roman Company

Christopher Helm (Publishers) Ltd, a subsidiary of A & C Black (Publishers) Ltd,
35 Bedford Row, London WC1R 4JH

Library of Congress Cataloging-in-Publication Data

A Guide to the Birds of the West Indies / Herbert Raffaele . . . [et
    al.] ; primarily illustrated by Tracy Pedersen, Kristin Williams
    ; with supporting illustrations by Don Radovich . . . [et al.].
        p.   cm.
    Includes bibliographical references (p.   ) and index.
    ISBN 0-691-08736-9 (cl : alk. paper)
    1. Birds--West Indies.   I. Raffaele, Herbert A.   II. Title : A Guide
    to the birds of the West Indies.
    QL668.A1P75   1998
    598'.09729--DC21   97-41790

This book has been composed in Optima

Princeton University Press books are printed on acid-free paper
and meet the guidelines for permanence and durability of the
Committee on Production Guidelines for Book Longevity of the
Council on Library Resources

http://pup.princeton.edu

Printed in the United Kingdom by Butler & Tanner Limited, Frome, Somerset

10 9 8 7 6 5 4 3 2 1

DEDICATION

To the people of the Caribbean islands and the conservation of the unique avifauna which is their heritage

The authors, artists and publishers would like to express their gratitude to the following organisations for providing sponsorship and support in the production of this book

World Wildlife Fund U.S.
National Fish and Wildlife Foundation
U.S. Fish & Wildlife Service
U.S. Forest Service

CONTENTS

CONTENTS

FOREWORD

In 1936, James Bond published his pioneering *Birds of the West Indies*, illustrated with a selection of line drawings by Earl Pool. In the course of its many revisions, color plates were added by Arthur Singer and myself. It is now my pleasure to introduce this completely new, up-to-date and comprehensive work covering the same geographical area.

Illustrations are the core of any field guide. In this new work, they are excellent and copious, showing sex, age and inter-island morphological species variation. The added value of a dozen full-page plates featuring single species endemics from as many islands is an attractive bonus in addition to the requirements of comparative illustration. There is no doubt that the opportunity to paint such singular plates was equally appreciated by the artists who had a chance to 'spread their wings' a bit.

Despite a long history of ornithological work in the area, a great deal of new information has accrued in recent years and is reflected in the text. I am particularly gratified that so much space has been given to conservation issues. I hope everyone will read this section. Island fauna are especially fragile and the pressures on them are now many. The value of this guide in promoting ecotourism may prove to be as great for the birds themselves as for the 'birder'. Posters are to be made from those plates depicting island endemics, with the aim of promoting conservation. The book royalties will be used primarily to support environmental efforts focused on local birds.

Thirty years ago, with the help of many friends, I established on Trinidad the first nature center in the West Indies. After some difficult years, it has now become a thriving place where visitors from all over the world can stay comfortably. There are trained driver-naturalists at the center, available for field trips throughout the island. Income from tourism allows us to purchase or lease additional land for protection. It also pays for the expansion of school group programs and for the support of other projects. Furthermore, we are currently planning new research facilities. This initiative should be replicated on other islands, particularly those where the need for education and support is great enough to qualify them for grants.

I am aware that all of our conservation efforts may be either too late or only a holding pattern against the onslaught of global overpopulation and what that means not only for wildlife but also for the future of mankind. We must do the best we can. I suspect that my efforts in this direction are probably of greater consequence than is my artwork.

Individuals who use this book will find it to be not only an identification guide, but a stimulating primer on the conservation of a beautiful but increasingly threatened resource. I hope their pleasure and their education will be considerable.

Don R. Eckelberry
July 1997

ACKNOWLEDGMENTS

Numerous individuals generously contributed to this book. We would like to thank the many individuals who provided us with data from their field notes or took the time to critique parts or all of the manuscript. Among these individuals are Martin Acosta, Maurice Anselme, Xiomara Aquilera Galvez, Vicente Berovides, David Blockstein, Marcel Bon Saint Come, Patricia Bradley, Paul Buckley, Wayne Burke, Jose Colon, Carlos Delannoy, Phillip Feldman, Hiram Gonzalez, Paul Hamel, Lyndon John, Nedra Kline, Susan Koenig, David Lee, Kevel Lindsay, Alejandro Llanes, David Pashley, Claude Pazis, George Reynard, Frank Rivera, Chan Robbins, Bonnie Rusk, Jorge Saliva, Fred Schaffner, Florence Sergile, Domingo Seri, Fred Sladen, P. William Smith, Lourdes Valdes Mugica, Nicola Varra, Francisco Vilella, Pascal Villard, Patricia Wainwright, Roland Wauer, and Joseph Wunderle. Special thanks in reviewing the text go to Catherine Levy, Robert Norton and Tony White.

Preparation of the artwork was an extremely laborious task involving assistance from various individuals and institutions. We extend our appreciation to Jay Sheppard and Jim Tate for critiquing illustrations; Mark Robbins, David Agro and the Academy of Natural Sciences of Philadelphia for providing specimens, facilities and critiques of the artwork; Mary Lecroy of the American Museum of Natural History, Chris Wood and Carol Spaw of The Burke Museum and William Alther and the Denver Museum of Natural History, David Willard of the Field Museum of Natural History, Steven Cardiff and Van Remsen of Louisiana State University, Dayton Baker, Lindsay Clack, Lynn Eindecker, and Curtis Robbins of the National Aviary in Pittsburgh, David Lee of North Carolina State Museum for assisting with specimens and providing access to their collections; Ralph Browning, Phil Angle and the staff of the Division of Birds, National Museum of Natural History — Smithsonian Institution for providing specimens and for the use of their collections by both the artists and authors; and to Jay Loughlin, Robin Panza, Kenneth Parkes and Stephen Rogers in the Section of Birds, with support from the Section of Botany, of the Carnegie Museum of Natural History for providing specimens, facilities and critiquing draft illustrations.

Photographic reference material was generously provided by Wayne Arndt, David Blockstein, Charles Collins, Annabelle Stockton Dod, Maurice Isaacs, Mara McDonald, Jose Ottenwalder, Yves-Jacques Ray-Millet, George Reynard, Bruce Sorrie, Guy Tudor and Wendy Van Barneveld, as well as Steve Holt and Douglas Wechsler of VIREO.

We also thank Donald Eckelberry, Arturo Kirkconnell and Robert Ridgely, Earl Shriver, Phil Smith and Sandy Sprunt Jr. for their conscientious review of illustrations; and especially to Kenneth Parkes of the Carnegie Museum who went far beyond the call of duty to assist in making skins available, critiquing illustrations and generally contributing advice throughout the entire project.

Lorraine Miller prepared the migration route maps. Authors of the island conservation write-ups are cited in the text. Margie Stump was invaluable in copying, typing, mailing and editing numerous draft manuscripts.

The Bird Banding Laboratory of the USGS Biological Resources Division generously provided access to its West Indies bird band data. The Society for Caribbean Ornithology supported this effort at many levels through the broad input of its membership and by serving as a central vehicle for communication.

Special thanks are also extended to the donor institutions which helped make this project a reality. These include the National Fish and Wildlife Foundation, U.S. Forest Service and World Wildlife Fund-U.S. for their financial contributions, and the U.S. Fish and Wildlife Service, particularly Larry Mason, for incorporating this project as an element of its Western Hemisphere Program.

INTRODUCTION

Goal

The primary goal of this guide is to promote an interest in birds among the local people of the Caribbean's islands. It is only when people appreciate and respect their birdlife that they ever come to protect it. To this end, this book has several special features. An extensive conservation section seeks to create an awareness of the plight faced by many island species. Feature plates of island endemics aim to promote pride in the unique birds of particular islands. Finally, the individual species write-ups (species accounts) of birds unique to one or a handful of islands include, when available, more comprehensive information to attract special attention to these singularly important island birds.

Beyond stimulating interest, this guide aims to go a step further by facilitating the study of West Indian birds by both novice and professional alike. The book is the first self-contained source for the field identification of all birds known to occur in the West Indies.

Far too much time has passed without islanders having an adequate reference from which to learn about their unique avian treasures. This book aims to fill that need.

Geographic Coverage

The West Indies are taken to include all islands of the Bahamas, Greater Antilles, Virgin Islands, Cayman Islands, Lesser Antilles, San Andrés and Providencia.

Omitted are Trinidad and Tobago and other islands off the north coast of South America. Though Trinidad and Tobago appear contiguous to the Lesser Antilles, their origins, and consequently their birdlife, are entirely different.

Species Coverage

The text presents accounts of 564 bird species known to occur or to have recently occurred in the West Indies. Species are included for which there are either a minimum of two specimens or photographs from the region, or a minimum of six separate sight records by reliable observers.

Five accounts address species widely considered extinct. These reputedly extinct birds are included for two reasons. Firstly, there is always the off chance that a bird thought extinct might be rediscovered after many years of going undetected. Puerto Rican Nightjar is such an example. Collected in 1888, the species went undetected for 73 years until being rediscovered in 1961. One can only hope that this will also be the case for Jamaican Petrel, which occupies remote precipices and is entirely nocturnal during its brief stint on land. Secondly, it is important to remember what we have lost. Hopefully, this book will provide a greater appreciation of what we still have, an awareness of its fragility and a recognition of the irreversibility of extinction.

Numerous other bird species have become extinct in the West Indies during historic time. At least 15 species of parrots alone fall into this category. However, all of these are known only from early chronicles and not from specimens. Extinct species chosen for inclusion in this book are those for which museum specimens exist.

Taxonomy

Much more work remains to be carried out before the taxonomy of West Indian birds is adequately understood. Recent studies are revising the tanager *Spindalis* from what was formerly considered to be one very variable species into four distinct ones. Contemporaneous research suggests that the two indigenous *Contopus* flycatchers should be split into six species, and that the Palm Crow be divided into Hispaniolan and Cuban species. Additional work is underway on several other bird groups. In general, for the purpose of this guide, the authors followed the taxonomy and use of common names proposed in the American Ornithologists' Union Checklist of North American Birds. There are a few exceptions. We divided the Lesser Antillean Pewee into three species, the Lesser Antillean, St Lucia and Puerto Rican Pewee. We based our decision upon revisions underway which we feel justify the split and have strong

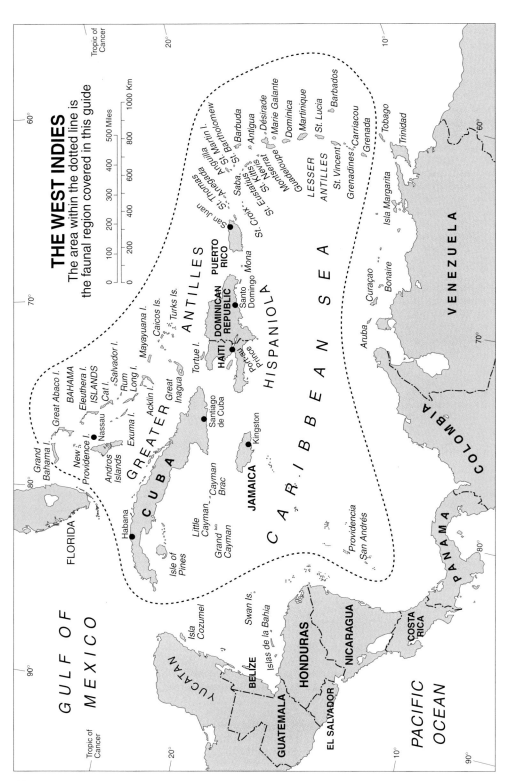

THE WEST INDIES
The area within the dotted line is
the faunal region covered in this guide

	0	100	200	300	400	500 Miles
0	200	400	600	800	1000 Km	

Tropic of Cancer

20°

10°

60°

GULF OF MEXICO

FLORIDA

Grand Bahama I.

Great Abaco I.

BAHAMA ISLANDS

Eleuthera I.

New Providence I.

Nassau

Andros Islands

Cat I.

Rum

Salvador I.

Long I.

Exuma I.

Acklin I.

Great Inagua

GREATER

CUBA

Habana

Isle of Pines

Little Cayman

Cayman Brac

Grand Cayman

Santiago de Cuba

JAMAICA

Kingston

Mayaguana I.

Caicos Is.

Turks Is.

ANTILLES

Tortue I.

HAITI

Port-au-Prince

DOMINICAN REPUBLIC

Santo Domingo

HISPANIOLA

Mona

PUERTO RICO

San Juan

St. Thomas

Virgin Is.

Saba

St. Eustatius

St. Kitts

Nevis

Montserrat

Anegada

Anguilla

St. Martin I.

St. Bartholomew

Barbuda

Antigua

Guadeloupe

Désirade

Marie Galante

Dominica

Martinique

St. Lucia

Barbados

St. Croix

LESSER ANTILLES

St. Vincent

Grenadines

Carriacou

Grenada

Tobago

Trinidad

CARIBBEAN SEA

Providencia

San Andrés

Isla Margarita

Curaçao

Bonaire

Aruba

VENEZUELA

COLOMBIA

PANAMA

COSTA RICA

NICARAGUA

HONDURAS

BELIZE

GUATEMALA

EL SALVADOR

YUCATAN

Isla Cozumel

Swan Is.

Islas de la Bahia

PACIFIC OCEAN

Tropic of Cancer

90°

80°

70°

60°

70°

80°

90°

20°

10°

12

potential to be adopted by the Union's classification and nomenclature committee. The St Lucia Nightjar has been lumped into the Rufous Nightjar on a similar basis. A few English common names were also changed to better represent certain species. An example is the substitution of the name Rose-throated Parrot for the long-standing, but inaccurate, Cuban Parrot. This change was made to eliminate the implication that this parrot is unique to Cuba when, in fact, it is a flagship species of the Bahamas and Cayman Islands avifaunas. Efforts to conserve these parrots are not enhanced by such a misnomer.

USING THE GUIDE

Species Accounts

This section differs from other recent field guides, perhaps because its primary focus is to promote usage and stimulate interest among local Caribbean inhabitants rather than serve a wholly international audience. For that reason, lengthy descriptive material on identification is omitted, particularly where we believe the plates suffice for distinguishing the species. Also reduced are details about each species' worldwide distribution. Such material is available from many other sources. Rather, emphasis has been placed on detailing the conservation status of birds and, where available, interesting information about the species in the West Indies is provided, particularly for those species unique to the islands.

Identification

Size is a basic tool in bird identification. Where length varies, because of the presence or absence of tail plumes for example, several measurements are provided.

Salient field marks are key features to look for when identifying any bird. No attempt is made to describe the species comprehensively since this is better discerned in the plates. Identification features of special importance are italicized. Whereas these usually pertain to plumage, they do sometimes include peculiar habits such as tail-bobbing.

Plumages which vary by age, sex, or season are differentiated. So are variations when a species differs substantially among islands. For species which occur in the West Indies for only a part of the year, the plumage most likely to be seen is presented first, with the least likely plumage state presented last. For example, of the various gull species which occur in the West Indies, but do not breed, immature birds occur much more regularly than adults. Consequently, the sub-adult plumages are described before those of the adult.

Similar species highlights the differences between the species being described and any others occurring within its range with which it is likely to be confused.

Local names are identified by island or island group to facilitate their appropriate usage. In the case of endemic species, or those limited to a handful of islands, all known names are included. However, for widespread species, only selected local names are presented. Local names follow the sequence: English, Spanish, French and Dutch.

Voice: The calls, songs and notes as known in the West Indies are described.

Status and Range: The worldwide range of the species is presented in general terms. No distinction is made between breeding and non-breeding parts of the range. Such information is available from many other sources.

One component of a bird's status is the extent to which it depends upon the West Indies during its life-cycle. Some species reside on a single island during their entire lives. Others may pass through the islands only during certain migratory periods.

The following terms are used to represent the overall status of each species:

Endemic: A species which is confined to a specific island or small group of islands and is found nowhere else in the world.

Year-round resident: A species which spends its entire life-cycle on a particular island or group of islands.

Breeding resident: A species which breeds on a particular island or group of islands and then migrates elsewhere during the non-breeding season.

Non-breeding resident:	A species which breeds elsewhere, but occurs on a particular island or group of islands during the non-breeding season. Sometimes referred to as a 'visitor' or 'visitant.' Other bird guides often refer to such birds as 'winter visitor.' This term has been deliberately avoided in this work since winter is not a term used on all islands and, as such, represents a bird's status from a North American perspective.
Migrant:	A species which migrates between islands or to areas outside the West Indies on a seasonal basis. Sometimes referred to as a 'transient.'
Wanderer:	A species which moves between islands at irregular intervals.

The terms used to describe the chances of observing a given species are defined below:

Common:	5 or more individuals likely to be seen daily
Fairly Common:	1–4 individuals likely to be seen daily
Uncommon:	Not likely to be seen on every trip, but can be expected at least twice per year
Rare:	Fewer than two records per year; at least one occurrence every 5 years
Very Rare:	Occurs once every 5 to 10 years
Vagrant:	Occurs less frequently than once every 10 years

These categories are based upon a skilled observer seeking the bird in the right place at the right time. In some cases, this means visiting a very specific habitat such as coastal marshes during the migration season. For birds which roost or breed communally (eg herons and terns), the status given represents the likelihood of encountering the species under more general field conditions and doesn't include flocks flying to or from a roost.

The terms have several ramifications. Firstly, some species are substantially more detectable than others. For example, every Snowy Egret in a small swamp can be located easily. However, the detection of a single Yellow-breasted Crake in that same swamp is a major undertaking. This would be the case even if crakes were substantially more abundant than herons. To address this dilemma, we have tried to indicate those species which are particularly difficult to detect. This is done either through a remark in the Comments section, or it might be obvious through noting the bird's habitat, which might be 'far out at sea.'

This issue is particularly important with regard to endangered species. The critically endangered Yellow-shouldered Blackbird might be seen during every trip to its roosting or feeding areas in Puerto Rico thus classifying it as 'locally common.' This is not to say that the total population size of the species is large. We have tried to indicate, at least for threatened and endangered species, cases where a species is classified as locally common, whereas in fact its population is small.

Misconceptions can be created by these terms when they are applied to small islands. A small island with a small pond may only sustain one pair of Pied-billed Grebes or a single Great Blue Heron. Yet these birds might be observed on every trip to the island and are thus classified as 'common.' Similarly, if that particular pond is only full seasonally, grebes may be present whenever it has water but will be absent when it is dry. We leave it to the common sense of the observer to determine how circumstances such as these apply to any particular species or island.

Comments: A pot-pourri of information about the species is contained in this section including feeding habits, flocking behavior and the altitude at which the species occurs. It is intended to provide a clearer understanding of the bird beyond its mere identification. For many species we have indicated whether or not subspecies exist and, if so, have on occasion given their scientific names. However, this has not been done for all species and other sources should be consulted for such information.

Habitat: The specific environs in which the bird is likely to be found is presented. Where birds occupy different habitats on different islands, as is the case, for example, for Yellow Warbler, such differences are noted.

Nesting: This is a very brief description of the bird's nest, nest site, egg number, egg color and breeding season. For many species, this information is fragmentary, scattered or unknown, particularly breeding season information. Hopefully, this book will stimulate increased interest in this critical aspect of every bird's life cycle — data essential for the effective conservation and management of many species.

Map: The map displays the range of the species within the West Indies. Maps are included for all species except those which occur only as vagrants in the region or are extinct. Ranges outlined by solid lines indicate that West Indian populations of the species are permanent residents within the boundaries marked, though they may move among islands within that range, for example White-cheeked Pintail. These species may also be resident outside the West Indies. This is indicated in the Range and Status section. Dashed lines indicate that the species is migratory, leaving the demarcated islands for a portion of the year. Species which breed in the West Indies but migrate elsewhere during the non-breeding season are included in this category. Maps with a combination of solid and dashed lines indicate that part of the population is sedentary while another part is migratory.

Plates

The 86 color plates depict every species for which there is an account in the text. The plumages of some birds differ noticeably from island to island, for example in the ubiquitous Bananaquit. In such cases, various island forms are illustrated. Variations in plumage between male and female, adult and immature, breeding and non-breeding birds are also depicted if important for identification purposes. For species which do not breed in the West Indies, the non-breeding plumage is illustrated more frequently than the breeding plumage.

Birds endemic to specific West Indian islands or island groups, such as the Bahamas, are illustrated in several ways. Seven plates feature the endemic birds of Cuba, Jamaica, Hispaniola and Puerto Rico. This enables anyone on these islands to become familiar with the island specialties at a glance. A dozen plates highlight individual island endemics, each representing a different West Indian island. These plates serve to illustrate the diversity of the region.

The page facing each plate contains key identifying characters and a cross-reference to the text.

BIOGEOGRAPHY

Oceanic Islands: Barriers to Dispersal

The West Indies, with Barbados and the Bahamas being major exceptions, are of volcanic origin and originally erupted from the ocean floor. This being the case, organisms that colonized these islands had to arrive by crossing open ocean, sometimes for great distances. The sea is an effective barrier to dispersal, so relatively few continental organisms have succeeded in reaching this region and becoming established. Another inhibitor to the colonization by large numbers of species is the limited number of ecological niches available on islands. An animal's niche refers to the specific set of environmental conditions that the species needs to survive. This includes the availability of food, habitat types, nest sites and shelter. Island size, elevation and distance from major landmasses from which these island's organisms have to travel, all play significant roles in the success of a colonizing species reaching the island, the diversity of niches that will be present and the ultimate success of the colonizing attempt. The vast majority of attempts fail. It is for this reason that the West Indian avifauna is not represented by a large number of species.

Diversity versus Uniqueness

What the avifauna of the West Indies lacks in diversity, it more than makes up for in uniqueness. This inverse relationship between diversity and uniqueness is generally the case for oceanic islands such as the West Indies. This is to say that the greater the distance an island is from a continent (assuming islands are of similar size and elevation), the fewer plant and animal species it will support, but the greater the distinctiveness of those species.

As an example, compare Trinidad and Tobago with Puerto Rico. Trinidad and Tobago are two sister islands lying off South America to which they were once connected by a land bridge. Their combined land mass is little more than half that of Puerto Rico, but their native avifauna totals approximately 400 species, nearly twice that of Puerto Rico's. However, all the bird species on Trinidad and Tobago, with the sole exception of an endemic guan, are found either on the South America mainland or elsewhere. Contrarily, Puerto Rico's native avifauna totals only 240 species, including 16 endemic species which, excepting two that occur in the Virgin Islands, are found nowhere else in the world.

Uniqueness: Its Values

The uniqueness of island birds is of particular interest to humankind. The simplicity of island ecosystems and the distinctive differences between organisms on adjacent islands, provide ideal conditions for the study of the evolutionary process. Indeed, the theory of evolution itself crystallized in the mind of Charles Darwin following his study of the finches on the Galapagos Islands off the coast of Ecuador.

Island organisms also provide clues to the biological history of the earth. As species evolve, the less adaptable forms are generally replaced. A few relict species such as crocodiles survive, but for the most part, scientists must be content with fossil records of this evolutionary process. In unusual circumstances, however, some of these ancient forms may be preserved as 'living fossils' through their isolation on islands.

The West Indies play such a role. For example, the Todidae is an endemic West Indian family represented by five species. However, fossil evidence from the mid-Oligocene suggests that 30 million years ago this family was fairly widespread ranging at least as widely as Wyoming in central North America. The West Indies supports approximately a dozen endemic avian genera believed to have been formerly widespread on the mainland.

Past Avifaunas

The West Indies have changed with time. As global climates fluctuated, so did the physical and biological nature of these islands. The rising and lowering sea levels in response to the warming and cooling of the earth changed the size of island masses and the degree to which dispersion of organisms was possible among island groups and from nearby mainlands. Areas that are now moist or even quite wet were much drier in the not too distant past and had vegetation that reflected that climate.

Along with the dramatic climatic and vegetative changes that occurred in the West Indies has been a shift of the composition of animal forms, many of which were unique to these islands. The extinct avifauna of the Greater Antilles is characterized by numerous species of birds of prey, often of great size, which evolved in response to the lack of mammalian predators. Among these extraordinary birds were several large owls, including a giant flightless owl (*Ornimegalonyx oteroi*), a gigantic eagle (*Aquila borrasi*) and a condor (*Antillovultur varonai*), similar in size to the present-day Andean Condor (*Vultur gryphus*) with its 3 meter (10 foot) wingspan. These raptors served as the main control agents for the many sloths and large rodents that formerly inhabited some of the islands. The absence of mammalian predators allowed several avian forms to evolve toward flightlessness, including some rails (eg *Baeopteryx cubensis*) and an ibis (*Xenicibis xympithecus*). Among other unique birds that have disappeared from the region are a small goose (*Neochen barbadiana*), snipe (*Capella* sp.), a woodcock (*Scolopax anthonyi*), a swift (*Tachornis uranoceles*) and a quail-dove (*Oreopeleia larva*).

Many of these and other species disappeared from the West Indies about 10,000 years ago as a result of climatic change and the post-glacial rise in sea level. But a second and probably more extensive wave of extinctions took place in the middle to late Holocene, from 4,500 years ago to the present, following the arrival of humans. It is suggested these extinctions were man-induced: a result of direct exploitation, habitat destruction or predation by exotic species such as rats and the mongoose. Humans also made direct use of birds — they ate them. In fact, we know of some extinct species because their remains have been found in human refuse heaps. Even though not a single specimen exists of 15 or 16 endemic parrot-like species which have disappeared from the West Indies, their former existence is evident from the logs of early explorers and descriptions by colonists who harvested these macaws, parrots and parakeets for the pot.

Aboriginal peoples had another influence on local fauna. Even before Europeans introduced exotic animals, indigenous peoples transported animals, including birds, between the islands. These animals probably served as ready sources of food during voyages, to establish sources of protein in new lands or as companions for the travelers. Regardless of the uses of these animals, their aided movements to new lands have set new challenges for biogeographers seeking to interpret the distribution patterns of birds in the West Indies.

Picturing a past Cuba with huge flightless owls shuffling through the savanna while colorful macaws and giant eagles flew overhead boggles one's imagination. So much has been lost. Yet, many of the extinctions in the distant past were natural, due to evolving ecosystems. Unfortunately, current extinction and extirpation rates, virtually all man-induced, may far exceed any that occurred in past epochs. Much more stands to be lost unless the accelerating rate of species endangerment is somehow checked.

Migration

The majority of the West Indies avifauna is migratory, meaning that the species move between different localities in a systematic way during the course of each year or during their normal life cycles. The principal group of migrants are those that breed in North America and fly southward prior to the northern winter to reside for the better part of each year in more tropical climes, then return north primarily in March and April to begin another nesting season. These migrants, commonly referred to as neotropical migrants, use several systems to achieve these long-distance movements. Most of them, particularly the songbirds, move southward within North America to the Florida peninsula and the coast of the Gulf of Mexico where they often congregate in large numbers. From there their routes diverge, some passing through the Bahamas and the Greater Antilles to the Yucatán Peninsula of Mexico, the Honduras-Nicaragua bulge or directly to the northern coast of South America. Most spread out through Mexico and Central America, diminishing in species abundance southward into northern South America and Amazonia. Some simply remain in the Bahamas or Greater Antilles and fewer still in the Lesser Antilles.

A second important migratory route, used by fewer but different species, involves birds departing from the North American coast from as far north as the Canadian Maritime

Provinces to approximately New Jersey. The route taken is then over water direct to the Lesser Antilles or to the north coast of South America. Radar studies have shown that the birds typically leave the northeastern coast of North America just after a passage of cold fronts which are followed by northwesterly winds. The birds fly southeast over Bermuda and the Sargasso Sea, rising occasionally to an altitude of 4 km (13,000'), before encountering trade winds from the east which direct them back towards the Lesser Antilles. In many cases, the birds simply overfly the Lesser Antilles completely and make landfall in South America. Particularly strong easterly winds sometimes result in Lesser Antillean landfalls. While the diversion of migrants to the Lesser Antilles may be infrequent, these islands are invaluable to exhausted, off-course migrants in need of a rest. This migration pattern is most typical of several species of sandpipers and plovers plus a few songbirds such as Blackpoll Warbler.

Likewise, the return northward is variable, with most species following a different route than that taken southbound. The great majority of songbirds which spend their non-breeding season in South America move north to the coast of the continent, but then travel westward along the coast of the Caribbean Sea and up through Central America. This results in relatively minimal northbound migration of songbirds through the Lesser Antilles.

An especially important component of the northward migration in the West Indies, particularly the Greater Antilles, is the tendency of many species to collect in flocks at favorable locations on the northwestern coasts of these islands. Staging occurs from mid-March to early April while awaiting favorable weather conditions. This phenomenon is well documented for Hispaniola and probably occurs on other islands.

Another migration pattern involves birds that breed in the West Indies and depart the islands during the non-breeding season. These few species include Sooty Tern and Antillean Nighthawk. Other species, such as Black-whiskered Vireo and Gray Kingbird, migrate off some islands but not others, and do not necessarily leave the West Indies entirely.

Austral migration is another system affecting the West Indies. This involves birds which breed in South America, but migrate north to the West Indies to spend the non-breeding season. This migration involves only a few individuals representing a handful of species and occurs almost exclusively in the southern Lesser Antilles. The most conspicuous example is Fork-tailed Flycatcher, but others include Yellow-bellied Seedeater, Blue-black Grassquit, Gray-rumped Swift and Tropical Kingbird.

A movement pattern confined to individual islands is altitudinal migration. Documentation of this phenomenon is scanty, but it is recorded from Hispaniola, Jamaica and Cuba where some flycatchers, solitaires and Antillean Siskin seasonally move to lower altitudes. Hummingbirds on St Lucia exhibit post-breeding dispersal to lower elevations, perhaps in response to the availability of nectar.

Another important pattern of bird movement which influences the West Indies is a trans-Atlantic one. While not a true migration, because of its irregularity and variation from year to year, it has an important impact, primarily in the Lesser Antilles. Formerly, Eastern Hemisphere birds carried by winds from the coast of West Africa across the Atlantic Ocean were considered isolated cases of vagrancy. However, recent field work suggests that this phenomenon is fairly routine and that some species such as Little Egret, Ruff and Black-headed Gull are to be expected regularly. To date, at least twenty species of such migrants have been found in the Lesser Antilles, especially on Barbados. Indeed, dispersal across the Atlantic by this means appears to occur often enough to account for the colonization of the Western Hemisphere by other species besides the well-documented example of Cattle Egret.

Other types of population movements which are not true migrations occur in the West Indies. Especially important are wanderings stimulated by the lack of adequate food or appropriate habitat. Small islands in particular are susceptible to dramatic fluctuations in the availability of certain resources, such as freshwater ponds which may come and go depending upon the rains. White-cheeked Pintail and White-crowned Pigeon are two species well adapted to utilizing resources while they are plentiful and then moving on once these are depleted.

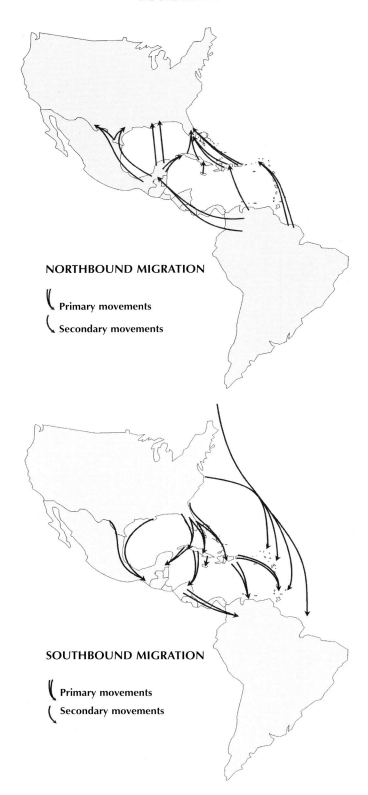

NORTHBOUND MIGRATION

Primary movements

Secondary movements

SOUTHBOUND MIGRATION

Primary movements

Secondary movements

CONSERVATION

The Problem

Growth of human populations and extensive changes in land use practices have resulted in major impacts on the earth's biological resources, especially its birdlife. Directly as a result of these human impacts, several hundred species and subspecies of birds have become extinct worldwide over recent centuries. Of particular conservation concern to the West Indies is the fact that approximately nine out of every ten of these extinct species were island forms.

Island species are particularly vulnerable for two reasons. Firstly, most species occupy very limited ranges leaving few areas to serve as safe havens where small populations might manage to survive. Secondly, island species have generally evolved in the absence of terrestrial predators such as cats, dogs, pigs, the mongoose and humans. Consequently, they often lack appropriate mechanisms with which to defend themselves and their young.

Endangerment and extinction can be part of the natural evolutionary process. However, this is only considered to be the case when naturally occurring events, such as hurricanes, are the cause for the decline. Bulldozing the last remaining stand of trees sheltering a species or releasing exotic animals that prey on the young of ground-nesting birds are hardly natural events. Not surprisingly, given the extensive development of the Caribbean over the past few centuries, virtually every bird species presently considered endangered or threatened in the West Indies has become so as the result of human-induced causes.

Principal Causes of Endangerment and Extinction

Habitat Destruction and Disturbance: Every natural habitat known to the West Indies has been significantly altered by humans. Some of these alterations are obvious, such as the cutting of lowland forest and its replacement with cattle pastures or housing developments. Others are less so, for example, the channelization of wetlands as a means of mosquito control. Some might argue that our most remote mountain forests are unaltered, but this too can be challenged. Puerto Rico's uncut Luquillo rainforest is infested with feral cats and rats which prey on native birds including the young of the endangered Puerto Rican Parrot. St Christopher's Mount Misery has suffered the affliction of the African green monkey (*Cercopethicus aethiops*) for centuries. In fact, it is often these insidious, inconspicuous changes we cause to our environment which are the most threatening because their impacts often go so long undetected.

Given the extent of development in the West Indies, it should not come as a surprise that habitat destruction and disturbance are by far the primary causes of endangerment to West Indian birds. Unless a serious attempt is made to wisely manage these development trends, through integrated planning efforts focused on each ecosystem as a whole, the list of endangered and threatened species in the West Indies will continue to grow.

Heavy deforestation in the West Indies began soon after European colonization. Lowland forests were the first to disappear followed by those of the foothills and lower mountain slopes. Timber extraction for house construction, fuelwood and furniture, along with clearing for agriculture and cattle production quickly took a heavy toll on the native vegetation. Flat islands were denuded most rapidly; those with precipitous mountains or otherwise remote localities more slowly. Nevertheless, by the late 1800s most forests of the West Indies had been felled by ax or saw, or cleared by ox or fire. The 20th century has brought the bulldozer and chainsaw as new threats to native forests along with the expansion of roads into previously inaccessible areas. Fortuitously, this has been counteracted on some islands by natural forest regeneration resulting from the use of gas and electricity as a replacement for charcoal, and by the abandonment of marginal agricultural lands resulting in a shifting of rural populations to cities.

The forests of some West Indian islands are in better shape now than they were a century ago, but others are decidedly worse off. Considering the ever-increasing threat of the chainsaw, population growth and expansive development, increased care must be taken to ensure that habitat destruction does not continue to be the single greatest threat to West Indian birdlife.

Hunting: Historically, hunting is a traditional pastime on most islands of the West Indies. It was widely practiced without adequate attention to biology of the game species hunted or controls regarding the numbers of birds taken. This has resulted in dramatic declines of formerly common species, particularly among pigeons, doves and waterfowl. This is one area in which conservation measures can benefit all involved including hunters, bird aficionados and the birds themselves.

Introduced Predators: Prior to colonization of the West Indies, either by Amerindians or Europeans, the avifauna evolved on most islands in the absence of mammalian predators. Colonization dramatically altered that situation with the introduction of black and brown rats, cats, dogs, pigs and the mongoose, among others. These non-indigenous creatures have doubtless had dramatic effects on many local bird species, particularly ground-nesters. Various seabirds, ducks, rails, doves, owls, goatsuckers and songbirds that nest on or near the ground have suffered significantly as a result of such predation. Doubtless tree-nesters have also suffered, but to a lesser extent. It is difficult to know precisely the extent to which these introduced predators have impacted local species, but it appears likely that they played major roles in the serious declines of several rail and goatsucker species.

Other Causes: Various other factors negatively impact upon the avifauna of the West Indies. Capturing wild birds for house pets or for the international bird trade has impacted native parrots particularly. The collecting of eggs for food has been detrimental to flamingos and a number of colonial nesting seabirds. Shooting of birds considered to be pests has had an impact on parrots and several other species. Shiny Cowbird, a parasite on the nests of other birds and a recently arrived species from South America, is wreaking havoc with several native orioles and other species (see Shiny Cowbird species account). Introduced bird species, primarily parrots and finches, compete with native relatives for food or nest sites. Such exotics also pose a serious threat of unknowingly introducing diseases to the islands which can decimate native bird species unadapted to foreign diseases. Chemical pollutants ranging from agricultural pesticides and herbicides to industrial and chemical wastes have notorious negative impacts on birds. Though reports of such impacts are rare in the West Indies, this does not mean such impacts have not occurred. The near absence of insect-eating birds on New Providence in the Bahamas may well be the result of intensive spraying for mosquito control. While none of these factors individually has proven to be a major factor in the decline of the West Indian avifauna, each is or has the potential to be important in species declines. They all warrant the attention of decision-makers and natural resource managers.

Island Conservation Status

There follows a series of accounts for each major West Indian island or island group describing the principal measures in place or underway for the conservation of local birds, the primary concerns faced by the island and the most pressing needs to be addressed. Each account has been prepared by a resident expert intimately knowledgable about local bird conservation concerns.

It is not intended that these accounts present a comprehensive review of conservation in the West Indies, they are far too brief for that. They are intended to convey a sense of the problems being faced today by those individuals committed to sustaining West Indian birdlife for future generations to enjoy.

It is worth highlighting a few of the central themes presented in these accounts. Salient is the need for public outreach at all levels — schools, the general public and decision-makers. The identification of public outreach and education as being the greatest need is especially noteworthy given that several Lesser Antillean islands have undertaken some of the most comprehensive bird conservation outreach campaigns conducted anywhere in the world. Most campaigns have been impressively successful as demonstrated by the remarkable recovery of the St Lucia Parrot. These advances only go to show the importance of expanding such outreach programs if local conservation objectives have any hope of being achieved.

Another theme touched upon in a number of accounts is the need to update local laws and regulations. This need, however, is not identified as being as important as the effective implementation of existing legislation. Most if not all of the islands have conservation laws to protect birds. Developing a conservation ethic and institutional capacity to implement these statutes would contribute significantly to conservation on the islands.

The setting aside of protected areas — conserving habitat — is widely regarded as important. This is not surprising considering that habitat destruction is decidedly the most important factor threatening the birdlife of the region. Illuminating is the fact that it was not regarded as the primary conservation measure needed. This suggests that Caribbean islanders believe that what is in the hearts and minds of the people is more important than what is set aside by decree, fiat or legal mandate. They lead most other nations in advancing this concept.

Antigua/Barbuda

Measures in Place: The Wild Birds Protection Ordinance enacted in 1913 provides a limited level of protection to some of Antigua/Barbuda's birds. The National Parks Act of 1984 also provides for the conservation of ecological resources of the islands. To date, only a cultural park has been created under this legislation.

The Environmental Awareness Group (EAG) was established in 1989 and is now the largest non-governmental organization involved in environmental conservation in Antigua/Barbuda. The group's objective is to create a greater awareness of the value of the natural environment and the need for conservation through planned and sensitive sustainable development.

The Biodiversity Program, which involves collaboration among various institutions, is now in its fourth year. Among its accomplishments to date is development of an ecosystem classification system. Efforts are also underway to develop a management plan for the proposed Great Bird Island Marine Sanctuary and the wider North East Coast Management Area.

Concerns and Needs: The over-riding problem facing bird conservation in Antigua/Barbuda is loss of habitat, both through degradation and total conversion. Currently, not a single area is set aside and managed specifically for bird conservation. Other major concerns are inadequate and outdated laws, poor enforcement of existing legislation, weak institutional capabilities and insufficient resources, both physical and personnel, to implement even moderate-sized initiatives.

Kevel Lindsay, Island Resources Foundation, Antigua

Bahamas

Concerns: In the perpetual quest for economic advancement our people and our leaders are increasingly lulled by our own tourism image, remaining oblivious of or forgetting that in truth, in vast areas of the Bahamas, the original natural resources have already been heavily exploited during past centuries.

The destruction of our rain forests and dry forests and the attendant extinctions of numerous species happened centuries ago, as valuable timber and barks were cut, haciendas and plantations developed with monocultures and introduced livestock, and slash and burn agriculture expanded to less arable areas. At the same time, subsistence, commercial and recreational hunting and fishing, introduction of alien species, urban sprawl, roadworks, careless tapping of fresh water, interference with natural drainage, dredging and reclamation of wetlands and tidal mangroves, pesticide spraying to eradicate mosquitoes, malaria, yellow fever and crop pests, problems of sewage and solid waste disposal and many other human intrusions have all taken a fearful toll on local biodiversity, not least the Bahamas' birdlife.

To summarize modern conservation problems of the Caribbean in general and the Bahamas in particular, all of the above needs to be recalled. These very same processes and consequences, coupled with our attitudes, traditions, cultures and indifference largely continue unabated. Rising population pressures, patterns of land ownership and new technologies only exacerbate the destruction of nature and the march towards extinction of many species.

In the past, people came to the Bahamas to live, farm and take up permanent residence. In many cases these settlers occupied the safest and best lands. The modern world brings tourism and second-home ownership. The business of accommodating large numbers of transient and semi-permanent residents brings hotels, golf courses, housing and marinas into areas formerly considered unsafe from hurricanes (beach ridges and coastal zones), unhealthy (wetlands) or unusable (too steep or inaccessible). These areas, which were often the last refuges for biodiversity in earlier centuries, are now under accelerating assault fed by greed and poverty.

The promise of ecotourism may help in some cases, but only if carried out with due care and attention. Our tourism marketing potential can easily run far ahead of the carrying capacity of our 'assets.'

Overshadowing all these problems is the absence of a conservation ethic, ignorance, sloth and indifference to conservation, and population explosion.

Needs: Our greatest needs are massive public and decision-maker education and intensified scientific research. Without these, we will not negate the problems touched upon, nor herald in a new century of restoration, and biodiversity and the quality of human life will continue to diminish.

Pericles A. Maillis, Nassau, Bahamas

Barbados

The land area of Barbados is small, covering only 425 sq km (166 sq mi). Bird habitats on the island are not extensive, and include limited mangrove (less than 0.1% of the island), seasonal ponds, isolated pockets of littoral forest and tropical moist woodland, wooded gullies, sandy beaches and sea cliffs. The predominant land uses are for cattle and sugarcane, with over half the island either in cultivation, under pasture or 'waste land.'

Concerns: Hunting as a sport persists in Barbados, having been introduced by the British several centuries ago. Hunting is not a regulated practice, and indeed some of the species protected by the Wild Birds Protection Act are shot annually including Buff-breasted Sandpiper, Hudsonian Godwit, Upland Sandpiper and Ruff. According to the U.S. Fish and Wildlife Service, populations of the former three shorebirds are all on the decline in North America. Moreover, rare visiting species such as the Eskimo Curlew are not protected by the Act. This species was regularly shot in Barbados up to the 1950s, with the last West Indian record being of a bird shot in Barbados in 1963.

Measures in Place: Wild birds in Barbados have been protected by law through the Wild Birds Protection Act since 1907. The Act was amended several times, including most recently in 1985, and outlaws the killing, wounding and harvesting of skin or feathers of the listed species. A total of 46 species are protected, including 22 migratory species (less than 20% of the migrants known from the island), and one now extirpated (the Brown Pelican, a former resident, extirpated due to habitat destruction).

Barbados has ratified the Convention on Biological Diversity and the Convention on International Trade in Endangered Species of Fauna and Flora (CITES). In addition, a National Biodiversity Action Plan is scheduled for completion in 1997.

There is a governmental initiative to amend the Wild Birds Protection Act. A Cabinet paper has been prepared for consideration which includes recommendations to increase the scope of the Act by listing more migratory species and including hunting regulations which would: (1) define the duration of the hunting season; (2) institute a system of control through bag limits; and (3) regulate the collection of data from hunters on the type and number of species killed per season. The issue of enforcement of the legislation is predicted to be an ongoing challenge.

The Government of Barbados is supporting a number of initiatives which aim to improve the conservation of the island's natural resources including birds. Most noteworthy are the feasibility study regarding establishment of a nature reserve at the island's largest remaining mangrove wetland, and the land use management study which includes potentially establishing a national park in Barbados. Both of these initiatives will address local biodiversity issues, promote the establishment of policies and regulations related to these issues and strengthen institutional capacity that will enhance the status of bird conservation in Barbados.

Needs: Protected areas need to be created which conserve habitats used by birds and provide them with safe areas to roost, feed and reproduce. Hunting regulations need to be established to control current practices, and enforcement of these regulations needs to be ensured.

The live capture of wild birds needs to be controlled especially if the practice involves endangered endemic species.

Enforcement of the Wild Birds Protection Act is required, since a number of birds covered by the Act are still being shot annually.

Barbados should ratify international agreements and conventions that promote bird conservation such as the Protocol on Specially Protected Areas in the Wider Caribbean (SPAW Protocol).

Awareness programs about the birds of Barbados need to be developed for both locals and tourists.

There is a need for detailed studies of life histories and population dynamics to better understand the status of bird populations on the island, especially rare and endangered species such as the endemic race of Yellow Warbler.

Deborah Riven Ramsey, Bridgetown, Barbados

Cuba

Cuba is recognized world-wide both for the importance of its biological diversity and the high degree to which it has been degraded. It is the only nation possessing two of the world's twelve most endangered vertebrates.

Measures in Place: From 1959 to the present, new Cuban governmental institutions, via conservation legislation, creation of protected areas and the support of research centers, have undertaken a major effort to save Cuba's biological diversity generally and native birds in particular. The effort has attempted to harmonize socio-economic development with conservation. Despite setbacks, there has been progress, highlighted by our magnificent national system of protected areas.

The most effective means of conserving threatened species is through the creation of sanctuaries or protected areas. Cuba has 73 such areas, almost all of them managed by the National Bureau for the Protection of Flora and Fauna within the Ministry of Agriculture. These areas cover 12% of the entire country and conserve representative areas of practically all of Cuba's ecosystems plus populations of all bird species in Cuba which are considered threatened or endangered.

Concerns: Deforestation began with the Spanish conquest, but accelerated dramatically upon Cuba becoming independent of Spain, when the great sugarcane plantations devastated Cuba's lowlands. Until 1900, the rate of deforestation in Cuba was approximately 0.1% per year, but in the 20th century to 1960, the rate increased to 0.7% per year. Since 1960, Cuba has remained from 15–18% forested.

In one way or another, every habitat in Cuba has been affected by humankind, whether in the form of contamination, modification, fragmentation, introduction of exotic species, degradation or total elimination. Habitat alteration, in any of its forms, has been and continues to be the fundamental threat to Cuba's avifauna. However, in a few cases over-exploitation by local communities has exacerbated this problem. This includes such activities as massive collection of eggs and young of waterbirds, the indiscriminate killing for subsistence or because of superstitions or erroneous beliefs.

With regard to all of the above as it relates to bird conservation where do we stand? As a result of so much habitat alteration and loss, a number of bird species are endangered. Refer to the list of endangered and threatened species for details (see p. 36).

Needs: An item which needs further attention is research associated with the development of management plans. Nothing is accomplished by simply declaring an area as protected and then leaving it as a 'paper park' without active management. This was precisely the problem that occurred in the case of the Ivory-billed Woodpecker. Despite declaring the area where the woodpecker was last seen, Ojito de Agua, a reserve, no measures were taken to study the bird or manage the area. Consequently, the decline of the species was not stemmed. There is decided lack of resources such as equipment, transportation and qualified technical personnel in the fields of research and management.

Of the 20 species considered threatened, only ten have been studied in enough detail to allow for the preparation of management plans. To date, only uninterrupted studies of the Rose-throated Parrot, conducted since 1987, have provided enough baseline data for the truly effective management of a threatened species. Implementation of this management plan on the Isle of Youth has resulted in recovery of the parrot population from 100 nesting pairs in 1979 to approximately 400 pairs at present.

Similar studies are underway for Sandhill Crane, Cuban Parakeet and Cuban Kite. These species are being used as 'flagships' to promote conservation of the entire habitats in which they live.

Environmental education and community participation are essential elements of these conservation plans.

Priority is given to areas which serve as 'core areas' for a threatened species or help to conserve several threatened species at once.

Increased financial support for the necessary studies and management plan development are essential.

While conserving Cuba's threatened birdlife will not necessarily result in the conservation of all the biological diversity of the island, it will conserve a large proportion including the most charismatic and beautiful species.

Dr. Vicente Berovides Alvarez, University of Habana
Lic. Xiomara Galvez Aguilera, National Bureau for the Protection of Flora and Fauna, Habana, Cuba

Dominica

Dominica is a small island with an area of 790 sq km (318 sq mi) and a human population of 71,500. The island is only 29 km (18 mi) long by 16 km (10 mi) wide. Extremely mountainous, several peaks rise precipitously to over 1230 m (4000 ft). Flatter areas are restricted mainly to small pockets along river valleys and the northeastern coast. The island's topography and physical conditions have considerably limited the rate of expansion of agriculture and the conversion of forests to non-forest uses. Consequently, Dominica has been spared the accelerated deforestation and habitat loss seen on neighboring Caribbean islands. Over 60 percent of the island is still under some form of natural vegetation cover.

Measures in Place or Underway: The Forestry and Wildlife Division of Dominica has been involved in bird conservation in general, and also in environmental education programs which aim to inform the public of the importance of birds and also to encourage an appreciation of wild birds. Strides have been made in influencing the passage of legislation aimed at the conservation and management of birds, in particular species protection, the regulation of the importation and exportation of birds and the control of hunting.

Several bird research projects are underway, including annual parrot monitoring, now in its seventh year, and seasonal research on parrot breeding biology, nesting and feeding habitats which has been carried out during the past two years.

Employees of the Forestry and Wildlife Division of Dominica patrol forested areas on a regular basis. It is the duty of the Forestry Officers to implement the provisions of the Forestry and Wildlife Act. The Division also maintains regular contact with hunters in an effort to solicit their opinions and suggestions to improve bird protection, management, policies and techniques.

A weekly environmental education program is conducted, which effectively informs and educates the public. During annual Forestry Week, television and radio programs are used to improve public awareness and to solicit public suggestions and advice on matters of protection and conservation.

In 1989, RARE Center, in collaboration with the Forestry and Wildlife Division, launched Project Sisserou in Dominica. This project was aimed at advising the public about the protection, importance and need to appreciate our two endemic parrot species.

During the past ten or more years, numerous publications have been produced such as the *New Forester*, many pamphlets, brochures, booklets and our *A–Z in Birds*.

Every year visits are made to both primary and secondary schools where various topics dealing with birds are discussed.

The revised Forestry and Wildlife Act, Chapter 60:02, deals with many aspects of bird protection and conservation. The Act details when birds should and should not be hunted. Protected birds include our two endemic parrots and our hummingbird species.

According to the Wildlife Act, no birds, dead or alive, should be exported or imported without the necessary permit from the Forestry and Wildlife Division, together with a series of veterinary documents, all of which aim to secure appropriate management and protection of local bird species. In addition to these requirements are a further set of local regulations and restrictions.

The two endemic parrot species have been routinely monitored for at least the past 16 years. During 1992 and 1993 intensive parrot counts were made at various localities on the island.

In 1994, a formal parrot research program was initiated to study the Imperial or Sisserou Parrot and the Jaco or Red-necked Parrot, both of which are endemic to Dominica. The program is intended to continue for the next two to three years. Observations of pre-laying, incubation, nestling, and fledging activities are underway.

Concerns: There are new problems such as more intensive interspecific competition between the two parrots as well as those posed by Red-necked Parrot coming into conflict with humans feeding on citrus crops. Both issues now need to be addressed.

Needs: Whereas the Forestry and Wildlife Division has some capacity to organize bird research, effectively enforce the laws, and conduct education and conservation programs, the Division's staff is limited in its capacities to conduct research and monitoring. The Division is in need of technical training at the Bachelor's and Master's degree levels and training of junior staff at the intermediate level (eg Eastern Caribbean Institute of Agriculture and Forestry [ECIAF] Rangers Certificate and Diploma Certificate courses). There is a need for continued research on the ecology of parrots and their forest habitat. There should also be national recognition of the parrots themselves as an ecotourism resource which, in combination with the backdrop of rich tropical forest, has the potential to contribute significantly to increased revenue generation and employment creation within the tourism sector.

Michael P. Zamore and Stephen Durrant, Dominica Forestry and Wildlife Division

Dominican Republic

Measures in Place or Underway: To compensate for the lack of adequate laws, the government has issued a wildlife decree which is implemented from time to time. Other measures adopted by the government are concerned with the declaration of new protected areas. During 1995, the National Park Service, in coordination with the Patronato de la Ciudad Colonial, initiated a tree planting program throughout Santo Domingo using native plants to improve the urban environment and promote the conservation of native plants and wildlife. The government is considering the creation of a separate Ministry of Natural Resources, but this has yet to be done.

Conservation efforts are also underway in the private sector. Several non-governmental organizations conduct censuses and other ornithological research. NGOs also carry out environmental education programs, principally within communities living in the buffer zones of protected areas. In this respect, a major effort is being implemented by the Grupo Ecologista Tinglar which trains local community youths to act as guides for birdwatching groups.

Concerns: The principal problem facing bird conservation in the Dominican Republic is the loss and degredation of habitats. Urban development is increasing daily and in a chaotic fashion. If we consider the endemism and inherent fragility of insular ecosystems, the effect of these human activities on our avifauna is devastating.

A second problem is the absence of adequate wildlife legislation and the weakness of the institutions responsible for implementing these laws. The Department of Wildlife, by being within the Ministry of Agriculture, lacks autonomy and any real power. An indirect consequence of this is illegal hunting and the trafficking of young birds for the pet trade, particularly parrots and parakeets. Although hunting is totally prohibited, there is evidence of intensive hunting which, because it is clandestine, is impossible to monitor.

Finally, but not least important, is the absence of an environmental education program for the entire nation. Lack of an environmental ethic is the basic cause of all the above problems.

Needs: Primary future needs include an environmental education campaign at the national level, the creation of a new law that regulates everything related to wildlife management, and ensuring that the Department of Wildlife functions independently.

Simon Guerrero, Santo Domingo, Dominican Republic

Grenada

Measures in Place: In 1994 the Government of Grenada declared the Levera area in the north of the island as a National Park so that its wildlife, mainly the birds, could be protected and preserved. The Levera area, largely undisturbed for the last 70 to 80 years, is primarily a dry tropical coastal forest. The area covers 215 hectares (530 acres) and includes an 18 hectare (45 acre) brackish lake. Trails have been made for birdwatching and guides are provided for visitors.

Grenada also has a closed season to ensure bird protection. This is between the 15th March and 15th September each year. There is also a very active society for the prevention of cruelty to animals.

Efforts are underway to protect the endemic Grenada Dove, an endangered species. Fewer than 100 birds are believed to survive in a section of the Mount Hartman Estate.

Concerns: There is a problem of poaching and shooting of game-birds in and around the lake and the dry tropical forest of Levera. Hunters use home-made slingshots (made from car inner tubes, these are silent and draw little or no attention), air rifles, and they place traps in bird nests. The main quarry are the Scaly-naped Pigeon or Ramier, doves and aquatic game birds. This is due to the lack of proper supervision by the local authorities of this vast area, and the fact that no one has ever been prosecuted.

Needs: An essential need is for bird conservation education programs on radio and television aimed at both adults and children of all ages. Outreach within our schools is also fundamental. School programs could include education tours to Levera National Park. National essay competitions on the protection of our birds might also be promoted. School holiday bird conservation projects should be developed.

There is a need to hire more wardens as only one currently exists for the conservation and protection of wildlife in the reserve.

It is also important that we establish more laws with penalties and that we enforce these laws to protect endangered species both during and outside the hunting season.

Evelyn Ross, St George's, Grenada

Guadeloupe and Martinique

[Although the text which follows refers specifically to Guadelope, many of the same constraints, problems and perceived solutions similarly apply to Martinique — the authors.]

Measures in Place: Measures in place at the regional, national and international levels include France having ratified the Convention on International Trade in Endangered Species of Fauna and Flora (1973), the Convention for the Protection and Development of the Marine Environment of the Wider Caribbean Basin (1986), the Convention for the Protection of Wetlands of International Importance Especially for Waterfowl (1986), the Convention for the Conservation of Wildlife and Natural Habitats in Europe (1990) and the Convention for the Conservation of Migratory Species of Wild Animals.

Additionally, Guadeloupe has established two protected areas. The first, established in 1987, is the Grand Cul de Sac Marin. It is a marine nature reserve consisting of coastal vegetation and mangroves and covers 3,736 hectares (9,228 acres). The second is Le Parc National de la Guadeloupe, created in 1989, which conserves 17,600 hectares (43,472 acres) of rainforest.

Guadeloupe also developed and adopted an official list of protected species in 1989.

Concerns: Hunting and the loss of wildlife habitat are the principal problems. Hunting in France is regarded as a legacy of the French Revolution of 1789 and is therefore strongly defended by an ever-increasing lobby. A great deal of damage is caused in Guadeloupe by its 2,300 hunters whose activities are neither organized nor controlled. Hunting takes place during the breeding season of certain species such as pigeons, and there are no bag limits or hunting records. Even some protected species are illegally hunted.

Habitat loss is a concern. Tourism and industrial development are responsible for substantial deforestation in wetlands, mangroves and dense forests. Pollution associated with agriculture and consumer waste is also contributing to the long-term loss of wildlife habitats.

Needs: It is important to develop and apply strict hunting regulations in conjunction with rigorous monitoring. There is a need for identifying and initiating appropriate research on endangered species. Public education and awareness programs must be implemented. In addition to these major steps, it is desirable to harmonize the control of hunting throughout the Caribbean in order to ensure the conservation of migratory birds as well as endemic species.

Maurice Anselme, National Park Service, St Claude, Guadeloupe

Haiti

Measures in Place: Bird conservation activities in Haiti are recent and embryonic even though the country's avifauna is rich and has been studied for centuries. The government of Haiti and non-governmental agencies are taking an active role to promote the protection and management of special areas in different ecosystems. The Service for the Protection of the Environment and the Ministry of Environment are jointly in charge of the protection of the country's natural patrimony. Two national parks totalling 50,000 hectares (123,500 acres) have been set aside in mountainous areas of the Massif de la Selle and the Massif de la Hotte, and will be managed by the Ministry of Environment which also coordinates the National Environmental Action Plan. The Forest and Parks Protection Technical Assistance project of the World Bank includes numerous activities associated with park management. In addition, 35 sites are listed for the protection of flora and fauna, with an emphasis on protecting native plants and birds. Legislation exists to protect migratory and native species. There are hunting regulations concerning ducks, the capture of flamingos, birds of prey and songbirds. New conservation associations and programs are in place to promote the conservation of birds and natural resources. They include production and distribution of environmental education materials, radio and television programs and other exhibits. During the last five years, a national education program focusing on environmental awareness has been initiated as well as a more environmentally sensitive curriculum within the school system.

Concerns: Birds are having a difficult time in Haiti as suitable habitat is reduced and economic problems worsen. The loss of habitat has accelerated during the past three decades. Bird conservation in Haiti faces similar problems to those found in many other developing nations. Habitat destruction due to expanding human activities associated with lumber, charcoal production and agriculture is a major problem. Many programs address economic growth without addressing environmental issues. The lack of environmental awareness and data are crucial shortcomings affecting decision-making. Reforestation programs usually focus on the monoculture of imported species which do not offer suitable habitat for birds. Few people know or appreciate the avifauna of the country and there is little value placed on programs to improve the status of birds in the countryside. Children hunt for birds with slingshots, and a substantial number of birds are taken for sport or food. As food becomes scarce and fewer children are in school for economic reasons, this problem is increasing in importance.

Needs: More official and unofficial media releases, permanent research programs and the diffusion of environmental information should be developed and maintained on a regular basis.

A protected area conservation program needs to be developed. Stewardship plans should be applied in the different ecosystems of Haiti, such as coastal zones, wetlands and the high mountains where areas of natural habitat still exist. Legislation should be established to protect all springs and ponds in the country. These zones will protect watersheds and create additional areas of suitable habitat for birds. Legislation on protected areas and deforestation needs to be enforced by governmental personnel.

Florence Sergile, Haiti-NET, Port-au Prince, Haiti

Jamaica

Measures in Place or Underway: Jamaica has forest reserves, a marine and a terrestrial park, with other Environmental Protection Areas about to be declared. The forest reserves are the responsibility of the Forest and Soil Conservation Department of the Ministry of Agriculture, while non-government groups manage the parks. The Natural Resources Conservation Authority has among its mandates the management of the country's wildlife, and is in the process of revising the Wildlife Protection Act.

Few active conservation measures are in place for the birds of Jamaica. Game-bird hunting provides one example of the application of a restricted season and bag limit for the hunting of columbids, while land controlled by some hunting clubs have become, outside of the hunting season, effective conservation areas. Other measures include the protection of one of the offshore Morant Cays by the Natural Resources Conservation Authority during the breeding season of Sooty Terns and Brown Noddies, and a small minority of owners of private properties have had their lands declared reserves, in which an attempt is made to retain

Although most research on the birds of Jamaica has been carried out by foreigners, the Gosse Bird Club, established in the late 1950s, has had a banding program in place for some years, and more recently has had success in stimulating ornithological work by young Jamaicans, resulting in five recent graduates undertaking studies which have the potential to actively contribute to bird conservation.

Concerns: The single most important threat to Jamaica's avifauna is habitat loss. In 1980–86 the deforestation rate was estimated to be 3.3% per annum (Eyre 1987); by 1994 the estimate was 5.3% per annum (WRI 1994), one of the highest deforestation rates in the world. Many laws are in place which would contain the rate of loss, but the enforcement of these laws is almost non-existent.

Without a national conservation strategy for flora and fauna, priorities are lacking, and this is compounded by a severe shortage of both people and funds to carry out conservation projects. The two shortages are most acute for work in the field where conservation ultimately must happen.

Management of parks and reserves is weak as many employees with responsibilities for conservation and land management have minimal experience with the species and habitats they are supposed to look after, and with the users of these resources.

As the formal educational system incorporates little information about endemic plants and animals, and their habitats, these studies are often neglected in the training of new teachers, and the message rarely gets through to the children. The general public is also starved of information on flora and fauna as few popular publications exist, and few items appear in the media.

Various species have been introduced into Jamaica which pose a threat as potential predators of and competitors to native birds. The most notorious is the mongoose which is implicated in the possible extinction of two bird species, the Jamaican Poor-will and the Jamaican Petrel. Since the late 1980s, the number of introduced bird species has increased from five to at least ten, as several captive species have now been discovered breeding in the wild. The most recent threat to some of Jamaica's land birds is the newly-arrived brood parasite, the Shiny Cowbird.

Needs: Conservation of habitat is the primary measure that will save the birds of Jamaica. More extensive and specific training for conservation personnel is urgently needed, so that management can begin to be tailored to priorities. At the same time, research into species and their habitats is needed to inform management decisions. This can be enhanced through the encouragement of ornithological studies at the University of the West Indies, which has taken steps in the right direction by providing a solid introduction to environmental issues in all disciplines from natural to social sciences. However, teaching and research across disciplines is still lacking, and there are a number of areas which need to be further developed to produce professionals with the skill to tackle conservation problems.

Institutional strengthening of non-government organizations is imperative if these organizations are to inform the general public, carry out educational programs and lobby for effective conservation of biodiversity. Most non-government organizations are lacking the financial and human resources to carry out the work that is necessary, such as advocacy addressed to the government and decision-makers.

Peter Vogel, University of the West Indies and Catherine Levy, Kingston, Jamaica

Netherlands Antilles: Saba, St Eustatius, St Martin

Saba

Measures in Place or Underway: The Saba Conservation Foundation is currently working with government officials to draft wildlife legislation which will afford protection for seabirds and some landbirds. This legislation should be enacted in 1997. Also pending is a proposal to establish a reserve at the top of Mt Scenery which has been submitted to the government. Approval is expected in the very near future. This elfin cloud forest reserve will protect habitat important to many of Saba's less common birds.

Concerns and Needs: Habitat loss and introduced predators, specifically cats and rats, constitute the greatest threat to bird populations on Saba. The establishment of reserves will protect vital habitat, but more vigorous predator control is needed. To date, conservation efforts have been directed toward the preservation of the marine environment, and there is little information about the avifauna available locally. Environmental education materials need to be developed and integrated into the school system.

St Eustatius

Stenapa National Parks Association, the island conservation organization, was formed two years ago. As on Saba and St Martin, first efforts have been directed towards marine conservation organization. All flora and fauna in the reserves are fully protected, but park rangers are needed to ensure enforcement. New legislation is needed which reflects the importance of bird conservation.

Environmental education materials are also needed on St Eustatius in order to generate public appreciation for birds and their habitats.

St Martin

Measures in Place or Underway: The St Maarten Nature Foundation was formed in January 1997. Marine conservation has been the focus of its first programs, but the organization recognizes the importance of bird conservation. One priority is the updating of legislation which currently protects wading birds on the French half of the island and Brown Pelicans on the Dutch side. It will be important for both of these countries to coordinate legislation in order to provide consistent protection.

Concerns and Needs: Habitat loss poses the greatest threat to birds on St Maarten. At present, there are no established reserves on the island. Areas of greatest importance need to be defined and afforded some measure of protection. Water pollution in lagoons and fresh water ponds is another significant problem. Sources of the pollution must be determined and measures taken to eliminate them. Environmental education materials are needed in order to generate public appreciation for birds and their habitats.

Mandy Walsh-McGehee, Island Conservation Effort, Saba

Puerto Rico

Measures in Place: The principal conservation measures in Puerto Rico are the laws that, in principle, protect wildlife and their habitats. The Puerto Rican Wildlife Law prohibits the destruction of all bird species found on the island along with destruction of their habitats. It also provides for the control of hunting and management of native and exotic wildlife species. The U.S. Endangered Species Act is applicable to Puerto Rico. Under this act and the Wildlife Law a plan for the management of threatened and endangered species has been approved. Most wildlife laws and regulations are implemented by the Puerto Rico Department of Natural and Environmental Resources. Several management projects are underway to conserve or enhance individual bird species or groups of species. The Puerto Rican Parrot Recovery Program is an intensive effort to restore the population of this critically endangered species. This program has existed since the late 1960s in the Luquillo rainforest of northeastern Puerto Rico. Efforts are now underway to establish a separate population of Puerto Rican Parrots in moist limestone forest in the western portion of the island. To help recover the endangered Yellow-shouldered Blackbird, a cowbird control initiative has been in place for over a decade, primarily in southwestern Puerto Rico. Waterfowl research and management projects are aimed at enhancing reproductive success of White-cheeked Pintail and West Indian Whistling-Duck.

Concerns: Most Puerto Ricans are unaware of their native wildlife. Effective bird conservation in Puerto Rico is thwarted mainly by habitat destruction due to unregulated urban development and destructive agricultural practices. Forested areas are being cleared with heavy machinery for agriculture and urban development, and wetlands are being drained and filled for housing and industrial construction. Economic incentives are given by the local government for the conversion of traditional shade coffee plantations to sun coffee monocultures with a dramatic reduction in benefits to wildlife and the disappearance of traditional coffee farming practices. Thousands of hectares of freshwater and estuarine wetlands have been drained by both governmental and private entities to create agricultural land, much of which is no longer used. Nevertheless, draining continues at high monetary and ecological costs. Importation of exotic species and their intentional or accidental release creates a threat to native birds. Laws and regulations which exist for the conservation of birds and their habitats are not enforced and, traditionally, the government is the major violator.

Needs: It is necessary to promote compliance with environmental laws. We must end forest destruction and wetland drainage and promote the protection of wetlands by the private sector and the government. Incentives must be provided for sound agricultural practices such as the farming of shade coffee instead of promoting sun coffee. Private landowners must be encouraged to protect existing natural habitats and to allow the regrowth of forest cover. The importation of exotic species must be restricted and we must promote the non-consumptive recreational use of wildlife. School curricula should include courses and field exercises about the wildlife of Puerto Rico.

Jose Colón, Ciales, Puerto Rico

St Christopher and Nevis

Measures in Place: The principal bird conservation measures in force locally are included in the National Conservation and Environmental Protection Act of 1987. They list the names of bird species protected by law and provide for the penalization of offenders with both fines and imprisonment.

Concerns: Three principal problems face bird conservation in St Christopher. These include: (1) the alteration and/or destruction of habitat in coastal areas and lower mountain slopes; (2) the proliferation of African green monkeys, which are suspected of preying on the nests of birds; and (3) a lax approach to enforcement of existing bird protection laws.

The upslope bird habitats on both islands have been increasing in size in recent years mainly due to the abandonment of agricultural lands. Contrarily, tourism development and other human settlement activities are increasingly a threat to coastal habitats, particularly those of seabirds. Such development is the primary threat to the birds of St Christopher and Nevis.

The African green monkey, introduced long ago to St Christopher, has no natural enemies on the island. It has become well established and increased its numbers to the point of becoming a pest to both agricultural crops and the nests of some bird species.

It should be noted that the practice of hunting birds has declined substantially, as reflected in the reduction of licensed firearms. The tradition whereby boys would make and use slingshots and traps to capture birds has also waned to the point where common species such as doves, honeycreepers and grassquits have become so tame that they feed and nest on porches or in garden trees close to residences.

Needs: A major bird conservation need on St Christopher and Nevis is to establish protected areas in the coastal zone. Such reserves would require effective management and law enforcement. The second important area requiring increased attention is local educational programs. There is a fundamental need to cultivate more comprehensive conservation awareness initiatives both in the schools and with the general public.

Mr. Randolph Walters, Director, Department of the Environment, St Christopher and Nevis

St Lucia

Measures in Place: The hunting season in St Lucia has not been opened since 1980 following the passage of Hurricane Allen. The current legislation is the Wildlife Protection Act of 1980. This act highlights the status of individual species including both resident and migratory birds. With our success in the conservation of the St Lucia Parrot, and the current focus on ecotourism, it is unlikely that hunting will be permitted in the near future. Nevertheless, regulations under the act are still being reviewed. St Lucia has been a leader in the Caribbean in developing environmental education programs, particularly a campaign to develop pride among the island's entire populace with respect to their unique national patrimony — the St Lucia Parrot. St Lucia established a 1500 hectare (3700 acre) Parrot Sanctuary in 1980 and has developed a nature trail program to promote ecotourism, teach local communities and schoolchildren about nature, and generate income for wildlife conservation.

Concerns: Much of our coastal habitats, especially dry forest and swamplands, are open to development. As a result, a number of important habitats for birds have been lost or are threatened. Housing, industry, tourism and agriculture have impacted endemic birds such as St

Lucia Black Finch and the St Lucia races of White-breasted Thrasher, House Wren and Rufous Nightjar. Migratory ducks, egrets, herons and sandpipers have suffered from a depletion of wetland resources.

Needs: There is a great need to increase habitat protection, particularly of coastal habitats including wetlands and dry forest. Illegal hunting, recently reported from a few remote areas, must be curtailed through more strict law enforcement. Finally, there is a need for more ecological studies of species threatened with extinction, particularly those mentioned above, to determine the measures necessary to curtail their declines.

Donald Anthony, Chief, Forestry Department, St Lucia

St Vincent and the Grenadines

Measures in Place: Since 1901, when St Vincent and the Grenadines were a colony of Britain, it was recognized that it was necessary to protect and conserve certain species of wildlife on these islands. Legislation to effect this was passed in that year, and this remained on the books until 1987.

In 1979 the islands became an independent nation and responsibility for the conservation of wildlife became the responsibility of the Department of Forestry in the Ministry of Agriculture.

The most recent legislation is the Wildlife Protection Act: S.R.O. 21 of 1987. Unfortunately, the second, third and fourth schedules of the Act are in dire need of revision.

Concerns: Apart from the inadequacy of the legislation, there are two areas of weakness which affect bird conservation in St Vincent. The first is psychological and the second is geographical. In the first case, there are few persons emotionally involved in the conservation of birds here; unfortunately these do not include the persons responsible for formulating and policing the regulations. In the second case, the nation is made up of numerous islets and cays which makes smuggling a relatively simple task, and conversely, makes policing very difficult. The indiscriminate shooting of birds and the taking of their eggs by locals and visitors, mainly yachtsmen, puts the birds in double jeopardy.

Needs: Existing legislation needs to be amended to address the problems which exist and awareness programs must be put in place to sensitize the authorities as well as the general public to the importance of the conservation of birds, both endemic and migratory.

At all ports of entry, yachtsmen should be provided with copies of bird conservation legislation, any rifles on board yachts should be 'held' until the yachts are ready to depart from the nation's waters and the yachtsmen themselves should be sensitized to the need to conserve the island's birdlife.

Special programs of awareness need to be mounted for the judiciary and the police, drawing their attention to the legislation and the rationale for the conservation of birds. General awareness programs need to be institutionalized in schools and to be presented regularly to the public by way of the mass media. The regulations to the Wildlife Protection Act need to be amended to reduce the number of species without protection or only partially protected.

For example, under Schedule II, bats are listed as vermin and are offered no protection. Under Schedule IV, Eared Dove, Zenaida Dove, Red-vented Chachalaca, Ruddy Quail-Dove and Common Ground-Dove are only partially protected, allowing hunting of these species from October to February each year. The Lesser Antillean Tanager, although fully protected, has now declined not as a result of hunting for food, but from being captured and kept as a caged bird.

It might be assumed that with legislation as old as ours, it would not be necessary at this stage to mount awareness programs; sadly, this is not the case, and the target groups need to be drawn from the lowest to the highest levels of society.

J.A.E. Kirby, Chairman, St Vincent National Trust

United Kingdom Dependent Territories: Anguilla, British Virgin Islands, Cayman Islands, Montserrat, and Turks and Caicos Islands

Measures in Place and Underway: Several conservation advances have been achieved in the five West Indian Dependent Territories thus far during the 1990s. These include (1) initiation of monitoring projects to collect data for accession to major international treaties and for drafting new local legislation to protect resident and migrant birds and their habitats; and (2) production of legislation creating national trusts which are now functioning in all of the Dependent Territories.

Regrettably, the trusts, with the exception of the Cayman Islands, are severely constrained by low levels of funding. However, following the lead of other countries of the region, the governments of the Cayman Islands and Turks and Caicos Islands have introduced an environmental tax, part of which will fund their national parks systems and possibly land acquisition. Successfully implemented, this initiative could overcome the severe funding problems faced by conservation initiatives in these small territories. Priorities for future funding are to purchase land for conservation, the implementation of conservation management plans, monitoring of threatened species and habitats, and enforcement of rules and regulations associated with protected areas.

The national trusts, thanks to a great deal of volunteer assistance, now perform vital functions in those Dependent Territories with underfunded and understaffed environmental departments. The range of trust responsibilities is broad and includes such activities as conducting educational outreach to schools and the general public, implementing scientific research and monitoring projects, advising governments, and managing parks and conservation areas. Some sites managed by national trusts are the wetland on Little Cayman which has been designated as internationally important, the Amazon parrot reserve on Cayman Brac and Little Water Cay on Turks and Caicos Islands. The trust in the British Virgin Islands is wholly responsible for protected areas while in the other Dependent Territories that responsibility is shared with government.

The Turks and Caicos Islands was the first Dependent Territory to declare a wetland of international importance under the Convention on Wetlands of International Importance. This was the 45,000 hectare (111,150 acre) Caicos Bank tidal flats and saline lagoons. The Cayman Islands declared its first site on Little Cayman in 1994 to protect the largest Red-footed Booby colony in the region. A second site, the western boundary of the Central Mangrove Wetland on Grand Cayman, is awaiting approval. Montserrat has designated a site, but disruption by the volcanic activity of Mt Soufrière has placed all projects on hold. The British Virgin Islands has yet to ratify the wetlands convention.

The British Virgin Islands, Cayman Islands and Montserrat have all introduced local legislation for the implementation of the Convention on International Trade in Endangered Species of Fauna and Flora. And all UK Dependent Territories within the region except Anguilla have ratified the Convention on the Conservation of Migratory Species of Wild Animals. The Animals Law of the Cayman Islands, revised in 1996, affords protection to all birds except White-crowned Pigeon, White-winged Dove and Blue-winged Teal. In the Turks and Caicos Islands, the Wild Birds Protection Ordinance of 1990 protects all birds except Blue-winged Teal and awards special protection to Greater Flamingo, Brown Pelican and Roseate Tern. This territory has declared 33 national parks, nature reserves and animal sanctuaries, 21 specifically to protect birds and their habitats, giving it one of the most ambitious protected area systems in the West Indies. Montserrat's Wild Birds Protection Ordinance of 1987 protects all bird species except Common Moorhen, Scaly-naped Pigeon, Zenaida Dove and Bridled Quail-Dove. Both Anguilla and the British Virgin Islands are in need of new bird conservation legislation.

Concerns and Needs: Threats to birds and their habitats mirror those encountered elsewhere. Anguilla, the Cayman Islands, British Virgin Islands and Montserrat lack sufficient protected areas. Anguilla and the Cayman Islands also suffer from severe development pressures on woodland, coastal and mangrove habitats, the costs of which are escalating rapidly. The Cayman Islands has the additional threat to nesting birds of feral cats. In the Turks and Caicos Islands, development pressures and sand mining on the large uninhabited islands and cays remain a threat, but the primary problem is how to manage and enforce laws in that territory's extensive parks system. Apart from a shortage of adequate protected areas, the British Virgin Islands has overhunting, weak laws, inadequate management and poor law enforcement.

Patricia Bradley, Author, *Birds of the Cayman Islands*

U.S. Virgin Islands

Measures in Place: The U.S. Virgin Islands conserves bird habitats under a range of protected area designations. Twenty-eight cays adjacent to St Thomas and St John are locally declared wildlife refuges. These refuges may only be visited with a permit, and visitors must be accompanied by a licensed seabird guide. Compass Point Pond and Mangrove Lagoon have been designated wildlife sanctuaries. The Virgin Islands National Park protects wildlife habitat on approximately two-thirds of St John. Buck Island, off St Croix, is under protection as a national monument. Sandy Point, Green Cay and Buck Island are federal wildlife refuges.

Several legal authorities strengthen bird conservation in the Virgin Islands. The federal Migratory Bird Treaty Act protects most bird species, while the Endangered Species Act provides special protection and recovery support for the most threatened forms. The Virgin Islands Endangered and Indigenous Species Act additionally protects 23 locally endangered birds and prohibits the importation of exotic species without a permit.

The Virgin Islands Division of Fish and Wildlife has had a monitoring and inventory program for seabirds since 1975. Other groups active in bird conservation include the St Croix Environmental Association, the Environmental Association of St Thomas and St John, The Nature Conservancy and the St John Chapter of the National Audubon Society.

Concerns: Enforcement of environmental laws is not effective. Users of natural resources usually lack a conservation ethic. There is a continuing loss and fragmentation of suitable habitat, particularly forests. Introduced exotics pose a threat to native birds as predators, as in the mongoose and feral cat, as competitors for nest sites or as carriers of disease, as is the case with introduced parrots. Seabirds are suffering from illegal egg poaching and from overharvesting of marine resources by both local and foreign enterprises.

Needs: Improved law enforcement is necessary. Increased protection must be extended to wetlands, coral reefs and seagrass beds. A territory-wide land and water use plan should be completed and implemented. Marine resources should be used in a responsible manner so as to allow for a sustainable yield. A broad-scale educational program is necessary to inform the populace of the value of conservation and the benefits of responsible consumptive use.

Dr David W. Nellis, Division of Fish and Wildlife, St Thomas, USVI

Endangered Species List

This list includes birds considered to be extinct, extirpated, endangered or threatened in the West Indies. Listed birds represent either: (1) endemic species; (2) endemic subspecies (races); or (3) any species or subspecies which is threatened or endangered throughout all or the greater portion of its range.

Where local populations are endangered or threatened, but the status of the species is stable throughout the remainder of its range, whether within or outside the West Indies, such mention is made only in the text. Examples include the Pine Warbler on Haiti and the Greater Flamingo on Hispaniola.

The following table also identifies what are believed to be the primary causes of the species' endangerment. These causes refer to both past as well as present impacts. Reference should be made to the text for more specific details about the causes of endangerment.

This list is derived from the published literature, discussions with resident West Indian bird experts and personal observation by the authors.

Extinct and Extirpated

Definition — Species and subspecies believed to no longer exist and which are represented by museum specimens.

Species	Subspecies
Jamaican Petrel	Uniform Crake (Jamaica race)
Passenger Pigeon	Hispaniolan Parakeet (Puerto Rico race)
Cuban Macaw	Puerto Rican Parrot (Culebra Island race)
Brace's Hummingbird	Burrowing Owl (St Kitts, Nevis and Antigua race)
Grand Cayman Thrush	Burrowing Owl (Marie Galante race)
	House Wren (Martinique race)
	Cuban Solitaire (Isle of Youth race)
	Puerto Rican Bullfinch (St Kitts race)
	Jamaican Oriole (Grand Cayman race)

Critically Endangered

Definition — Species and subspecies which have declined dramatically to such low population levels that their continued survival is in serious jeopardy. Active steps must be taken to ensure their survival and in some cases extinctions may have already occurred.

	Causes				
	Habitat loss	Hunting	Harvest or trade	Introduced predators	Other
Species					
Black-capped Petrel			X	X	
Hook-billed Kite (Grenada race)	X	X			
Cuban Kite	X	X			
Spotted Rail	X			?	
Eskimo Curlew		X			
Grenada Dove	X	?		X	
Puerto Rican Parrot	X	X	X	X	X[1]
St Vincent Parrot	X	X	X		
Imperial Parrot	X	X	X		
Puerto Rican Screech-Owl (Virgin Islands race)	X				X[1]
Stygian Owl (Hispaniola race)	X	X			
Jamaican Poorwill	X			X	

Species	Causes				
	Habitat loss	Hunting	Harvest or trade	Introduced predators	Other
Ivory-billed Woodpecker	X	X			
Euler's Flycatcher (Grenada race)	Unknown				
Golden Swallow (Jamaica race)	Unknown				
House Wren (Guadeloupe race)	X	X		X	
White-breasted Thrasher	X			X	
Bachman's Warbler	?				
Semper's Warbler	?			X	
Yellow-shouldered Blackbird	X				X[2]

[1]Competition with introduced species and egg predation by the Pearly-eyed Thrasher.
[2]Population decline as a result of brood parasitism by the Shiny Cowbird.

Endangered

Definition — Species and subspecies which have declined significantly to such low population levels that unless this trend is halted in the immediate future, the survival of the species will be in jeopardy.

Species	Causes				
	Habitat loss	Hunting	Harvest or trade	Introduced predators	Other
West Indian Whistling-Duck	X	X	X	X	
Zapata Rail	X			?	
Gundlach's Hawk	X	X			
Sharp-shinned Hawk (Puerto Rico race)	X			X	X[1]
Ridgway's Hawk	X				
Piping Plover	X				
Plain Pigeon	X	X		X	
Gray-headed Quail-Dove (Dominican Republic race)	X	X		X	
Blue-headed Quail-Dove	X	X		X	
Red-necked Parrot	X	X	X		
St Lucia Parrot	X	X	X		
Cuban Parakeet	X	X	X		
Bay-breasted Cuckoo	X	X			
Puerto Rican Nightjar	X			X	
Rufous Nightjar	X			X	
Fernandina's Flicker	X				
Giant Kingbird	X				
Golden Swallow (Dominican Republic race)	X				
Brown-headed Nuthatch	X				
Cuban Palm Crow	Unknown				
La Selle Thrush	X				
Yellow Warbler (Barbados race)	X				X[2]

Species	Causes				
	Habitat loss	Hunting	Harvest or trade	Introduced predators	Other
Kirtland's Warbler	X				X[3]
White-winged Warbler	X				
Gray-crowned Palm-Tanager	X				
Chat Tanager (Haiti race)	X				
Martinique Oriole					X[2]
Montserrat Oriole	X				X[2,4]
White-winged Crossbill	X				

[1] Egg and young chick predation by the Pearly-eyed Thrasher.
[2] Population decline as a result of brood parasitism by the Shiny Cowbird.
[3] Population decline as a result of brood parasitism by the Brown-headed Cowbird.
[4] Volcanic eruption.

Threatened

Definition — Species and subspecies which have experienced moderate declines or face imminent threats thus warranting specific conservation measures.

Species	Causes				
	Habitat loss	Hunting	Harvest or trade	Introduced predators	Other
White-cheeked Pintail	X	X		X	
Sharp-shinned Hawk (Hispaniola race)	X			X	
Broad-winged Hawk (Puerto Rico race)	X				
Black Rail	X			X	
Caribbean Coot	X	X		X	
Limpkin (Hispaniola race)	X	X		?	
Sandhill Crane	X	X		X	
Snowy Plover	X			X	
Double-striped Thick-Knee	X	X			
Roseate Tern	X		X	X	
White-crowned Pigeon	X	X	X	X	
Ring-tailed Pigeon	X	X			
Gray-headed Quail-Dove (Cuba race)	X	X		X	
Hispaniolan Parakeet	X	X			
Rose-throated Parrot	X		X		
Yellow-billed Parrot	X		X		
Black-billed Parrot	X		X		
Hispaniolan Parrot	X	X	X		
Stygian Owl (Cuba race)	X	X			
Least Poorwill	X			X	
White-tailed Nightjar (Martinique race)	X			X	
Bee Hummingbird	X				

Species	Habitat loss	Hunting	Harvest or trade	Introduced predators	Other
		Causes			
Hispaniolan Trogon	X				
West Indian Woodpecker (Grand Bahama race)	X				
White-necked Crow	X	X			
Forest Thrush	X	X			X[3]
House Wren (St Vincent and St Lucia races)	X	X		X	X[1]
Zapata Wren	X			?	
Cuban Solitaire	X				
Elfin Woods Warbler	X				
Green-tailed Ground Warbler (Isla Beata race)	Unknown				
Whistling Warbler	X				
Chat Tanager	X				
Black-cowled Oriole (Bahamas race)	Unknown				
Jamaican Blackbird	X				
Tawny-shouldered Blackbird (Hispaniola race)	X				X[1]
St Lucia Oriole	X				X[1,4]
Zapata Sparrow					X[2]

[1] Population decline as a result of brood parasitism by the Shiny Cowbird.

[2] Small, local populations put all three races at risk to overnight losses resulting from such natural sources as hurricanes or from human-related causes such as habitat destruction.

[3] Competition with Bare-eyed Robin and parasitism by Shiny Cowbird.

[4] Population decline as a result of pesticide spraying.

DESCRIPTIVE PARTS OF A BIRD

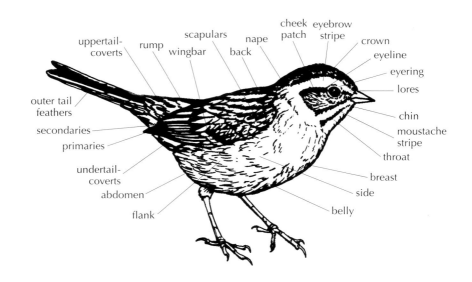

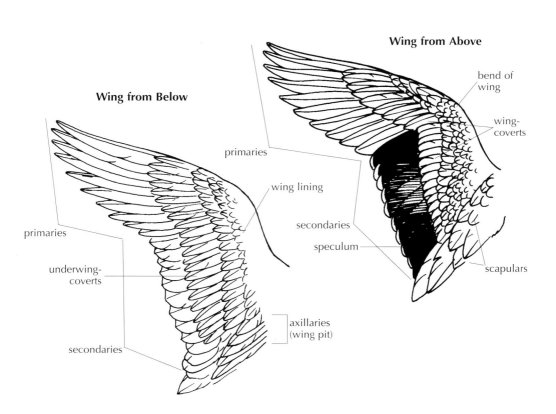

Wing from Above

Wing from Below

COLOR PLATES
1–86

PLATE 1: BOOBIES, TROPICBIRDS, FRIGATEBIRDS AND PELICANS

1 RED-FOOTED BOOBY *Sula sula*   **Page 223**
66–76 cm (26–30″).
Adult: **1a** *Brown Phase* – Brown with white hindparts. **1b** *White Phase* – White, including tail.
Immature: (Not illustrated.) Sooty brown, paler below, sometimes with a slightly darker band across breast.

2 BROWN BOOBY *Sula leucogaster*   **Page 223**
71–76 cm (28–30″).
Adult: Brown head and upperparts; white belly and abdomen.
Immature: (Not illustrated.) Like adult, but light brown on belly and abdomen.

3 MASKED BOOBY *Sula dactylatra*   **Page 222**
81–91 cm (32–36″).
Adult: White with black tail.
Immature: (Not illustrated.) Brownish head and upperparts; whitish below and on upper back and rump.

4 MAGNIFICENT FRIGATEBIRD *Fregata magnificens*   **Page 227**
94–104 cm (37–41″). Long forked tail; long slender wings with crook at wrist.
4a Adult Male: Appears all black.
4b Adult Female: Blackish overall; white breast.
4c Immature: Brownish-black; white head and breast.
4d Male Flying.

5 WHITE-TAILED TROPICBIRD *Phaethon lepturus*   **Page 221**
81 cm (32″) with tail plumes; 37–40 cm (15–16″) without tail plumes.
5a Adult: Heavy black stripes on upperwing; long tail plumes.
5b Immature: Barred back; short tail.

6 RED-BILLED TROPICBIRD *Phaethon aethereus*   **Page 221**
91–107 cm (36–42″) with tail plumes; 46–51 cm (18–20″) without tail plumes.
Adult: Red bill; black barring on back; long tail plumes.
Immature: (Not illustrated.) Barred back; short tail; black band across hindneck.

7 BROWN PELICAN *Pelecanus occidentalis*   **Page 224**
107–137 cm (42–54″). Large size. Dark; unusually shaped bill.
7a Breeding Adult: Back of head and hindneck reddish-brown.
7b Non-breeding Adult: Back of head and hindneck white.
7c Immature: Grayish-brown plumage.

8 AMERICAN WHITE PELICAN *Pelecanus erythrorhynchos*   **Page 224**
125–165 cm (49–64″). Large size. White; large orange-yellow bill.

> *Note: Illustrations not all to scale.*

PLATE 2: PELAGICS

1 GREATER SHEARWATER *Puffinus gravis*   **Page 218**
48 cm (19"). Large size. Some white on rump and hindneck; no white on forehead.
1a Above.
1b Below.

2 CORY'S SHEARWATER *Calonectris diomedea*   **Page 217**
46–53 cm (18–21"). Large size. Bill pale yellowish; mottled coloration on cheek and neck; white uppertail-coverts. Flight leisurely on bent wings.
2a Above.
2b Below.

3 BLACK-CAPPED PETREL *Pterodroma hasitata*   **Page 216**
35–40 cm (14–16"). White forehead, rump and hindneck; wrist bent; black front-edge of underwings.
3a Typical coloration above.
3b Atypical coloration. Darker.
3c Typical coloration below.

4 JAMAICAN PETREL *Pterodroma caribbaea*   **Page 217**
35–46 cm (14–18"). Sooty overall except for white rump and uppertail-coverts; legs and feet whitish-pink. Jamaica. See also Plate 83.

5 SOOTY SHEARWATER *Puffinus griseus*   **Page 218**
40–46 cm (16–18"). Medium size. Entirely dark; whitish underwings. Flight swift, direct with rapid flapping ascents and long glides close to water.
5a Above.
5b Below.

6 MANX SHEARWATER *Puffinus puffinus*   **Page 219**
30–38 cm (12–15"). Medium size. Blackish above; white below including undertail-coverts; wing linings whitish. Rocking glide flight alternated with 4–5 snappy wingbeats.
6a Above.
6b Below.

7 AUDUBON'S SHEARWATER *Puffinus lherminieri*   **Page 219**
30 cm (12"). Relatively small. Dark above; white below; dark undertail-coverts; rounded tail. Rapid wingbeats between glides.
7a Above.
7b Below.

8 BAND-RUMPED STORM-PETREL *Oceanodroma castro*   **Page 220**
19–21 cm (7.5–8"). Medium size. Head and upperparts black; narrow white rump band; square tail. In flight feet do not extend beyond tip of tail.

9 LEACH'S STORM-PETREL *Oceanodroma leucorhoa*   **Page 220**
20 cm (8"). Long pointed wings, sharply angled wrists; pale brown wing band; divided rump patch; notched tail. Flight bounding and erratic; feet do not extend beyond tail.

10 WILSON'S STORM-PETREL *Oceanites oceanicus*   **Page 220**
18–19 cm (7–7.5"). Blacker than Leach's Storm-Petrel; rounded wrists; rump patch undivided; tail square. Flight fluttery, direct with brief glides; feet extend beyond tail.

Note: Jamaican Petrel not to scale.

PLATE 3: GULLS AND SKIMMERS

1 GREAT BLACK-BACKED GULL *Larus marinus*   **Page 289**
69–79 cm (27–31"). Large size. Large yellow bill, red spot.
1a Non-breeding Adult: Black mantle; pinkish legs.
1b Second Year: (head inset) Bill pinkish, large black band near tip.
Flight of Breeding Adult and First Year: See Plate 4.

2 LESSER BLACK-BACKED GULL *Larus fuscus*   **Page 289**
53–63 cm (21–25"). Large size. Large yellow bill, red spot.
2a Non-breeding Adult: Dark gray mantle; pale yellow legs.
2b Second Year: (head inset) Bill pinkish, large black band near tip.
Flight of Breeding Adult and First Year: See Plate 4.

3 RING-BILLED GULL *Larus delawarensis*   **Page 288**
46–51 cm (18–20").
Non-breeding Adult: Black ring on yellowish bill; gray mantle; black wing tips; white head and underparts; head flecked with pale brown.
Flight of Breeding Adult and First Year: See Plate 4.

4 HERRING GULL *Larus argentatus*   **Page 288**
56–66 cm (22–26").
Non-breeding Adult: Gray mantle; pinkish legs; red spot on yellow bill; white head and underparts; head flecked with pale brown.
Flight of Breeding Adult and First Year: See Plate 4.

5 BLACK-LEGGED KITTIWAKE *Rissa tridactyla*   **Page 289**
43 cm (17"). Medium size.
Non-breeding Adult: White head, dark spot behind eye; yellow bill.
Flight of Breeding Adult and First Year: See Plate 5.

6 BLACK-HEADED GULL *Larus ridibundus*   **Page 287**
39–43 cm (15–17").
Non-breeding Adult: Thin, dark red bill, black tip; black spot behind eye; red legs.
Flight of Breeding Adult and First Year: See Plate 5.

7 BONAPARTE'S GULL *Larus philadelphia*   **Page 287**
30.5–36 cm (12–14").
Non-breeding Adult: Thin, black bill; black spot behind eye; red legs.
Flight of Breeding Adult and First Year: See Plate 5.

8 BLACK SKIMMER *Rynchops niger*   **Page 296**
40–51 cm (16–20").
Adult: Long orange bill, black tip; upperparts black; underparts white.

9 LAUGHING GULL *Larus atricilla*   **Page 286**
38–43 cm (15–17").
9a Non-breeding Adult: Head white, dark markings; dark bill; dark gray mantle; black wing tips.
9b Immature: Mottled gray-brown, whitish belly.
Flight of Breeding Adult and First Year: See Plate 5.

1a

1b

2a

2b

3

4

5

6

7

8

9a

9b

KRISTIN WILLIAMS 1991

PLATE 4: GULLS FLYING 1

1 GREAT BLACK-BACKED GULL *Larus marinus*   **Page 289**
69–79 cm (27–31"). Very large size and bill.
Breeding Adult: Black mantle. **1a** Flight Above. **1b** Flight Below.
First Year: Black bill; broad black tail band; head whitish. **1c** Flight Above. **1d** Flight Below.
Non-breeding Adult and Second Year: See Plate 3.

2 LESSER BLACK-BACKED GULL *Larus fuscus*   **Page 289**
53–63 cm (21–25"). Large size and bill.
Breeding Adult: Dark gray mantle. **2a** Flight Above. **2b** Flight Below.
First year: all mottled grayish; head brownish; black bill; broad black tail band. **2c** Flight Above.
2d Flight Below.
Non-breeding Adult and Second Year: See Plate 3.

3 HERRING GULL *Larus argentatus*   **Page 288**
56–66 cm (22–26"). Large size and bill.
Breeding Adult: Gray mantle. **3a** Flight Above. **3b** Flight Below.
First Year: Overall mottled grayish-brown; black-tipped bill, pinkish at base; blackish on tail, not in
form of band. **3c** Flight Above. **3d** Flight Below.
Non-breeding Adult: See Plate 3.

4 RING-BILLED GULL *Larus delawarensis*   **Page 288**
46–51 cm (18–20"). Medium size and bill.
Breeding Adult: Gray mantle. **4a** Flight Above. **4b** Flight Below.
First Year: Mottled grayish-brown upperwings; gray back; pinkish bill, black tip; narrow black tail
band. **4c** Flight Above. **4d** Flight Below.
Non-breeding Adult: See Plate 3.

1a

1b

1c

1d

2a

2b

2c

2d

3a

3b

3c

3d

4a

4b

4c

4d

KRISTIN WILLIAMS 1993

PLATE 5: GULLS FLYING 2

1 LAUGHING GULL *Larus atricilla*   **Page 286**
38–43 cm (15–17").
Breeding Adult: Black head; dark gray mantle; black wing tips. **1a** Flight Above. **1b** Flight Below.
First Year: Back gray; upperwings mottled brown and gray; rump white; broad black tail band.
1c Flight Above. **1d** Flight Below.
Non-breeding Adult and Immature: See Plate 3.

2 BLACK-LEGGED KITTIWAKE *Rissa tridactyla*   **Page 289**
43 cm (17").
Breeding Adult: All yellow bill; gray mantle, entirely black wing tips. **2a** Flight Above. **2b** Flight Below.
First Year: Black spot behind eye; black tail band; mantle marked with contrasting black 'W'.
2c Flight Above. **2d** Flight Below.
Non-breeding Adult: Plate 3.

3 BLACK-HEADED GULL *Larus ridibundus*   **Page 287**
39–43 cm (15–17").
Breeding Adult: Black head; red bill; gray mantle with white outer primaries tipped black above, underside of primaries blackish. **3a** Flight Above. **3b** Flight Below.
First Year: Bill cream-colored, black tip; black spot behind eye, black tail band; underside of primaries gray. **3c** Flight Above. **3d** Flight Below.
Non-breeding Adult: See Plate 3.

4 BONAPARTE'S GULL *Larus philadelphia*   **Page 287**
30.5–36 cm (12–14").
Breeding Adult: Black head; red bill; gray mantle with white outer primaries, tipped black above, underside white. **4a** Flight Above. **4b** Flight Below.
First Year: Black bill; black spot behind eye; black tail band; underside of primaries white. **4c** Flight Above. **4d** Flight Below.
Non-breeding Adult: See Plate 3.

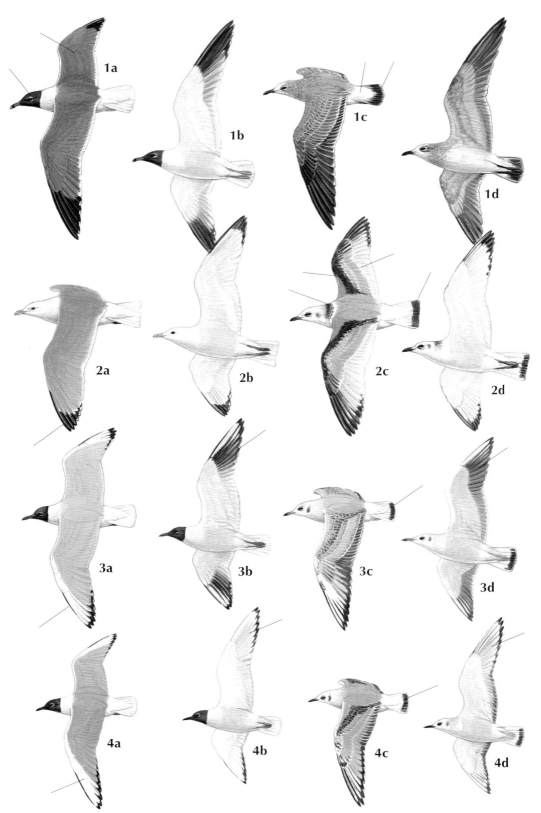

KRISTIN WILLIAMS 1995

PLATE 6: TERNS

1 CASPIAN TERN *Sterna caspia*   **Page 290**
48–58 cm (19–23"). Large size. Red bill; black crest; dark gray undersides of primaries.
1a Non-breeding: White flecks on crest.
1b Breeding: Crest entirely black.

2 ROYAL TERN *Sterna maxima*   **Page 290**
46–53 cm (18–21"). Large size. Orange-yellow bill; shaggy crest.
2a Breeding Adult: Black crown.
2b Non-breeding Adult and Immature: White forehead.

3 LEAST TERN *Sterna antillarum*   **Page 293**
21.5–24 cm (8.5–9.5"). Small size.
3a Breeding Adult: Yellow bill, black tip; white forehead.
3b Non-breeding Adult: Brown bill; head pattern less distinct. *S. a. antillarum* illustrated.

4 SANDWICH TERN *Sterna sandvicensis*   **Page 291**
41–46 cm (16–18").
4a Breeding Adult: Shaggy black crest; bill long, slender and black with conspicuous yellow tip; tail does not extend beyond folded wings when at rest.
4b Non-breeding Adult: Forecrown to above eye white.
4c: Cayenne race, *S. a. eurygnatha*. Yellow bill.

5 GULL-BILLED TERN *Sterna nilotica*   **Page 290**
33–38 cm (13–15"). Gull-like; thick black bill; shallow fork in tail.
5a Breeding Adult: Black crown and hindneck.
5b Non-breeding: Crown whitish with gray flecks. Gray spot behind eye.

6 ARCTIC TERN *Sterna paradisaea*   **Page 292**
35–43 cm (14–17").
6a Non-breeding Adult: Bill short, black; short red legs; blackish line on trailing edge of primaries.
6b Breeding Adult: Bill entirely red; white cheek pattern.
6c Immature: Incomplete black cap; indistinct shoulder bar.

7 FORSTER'S TERN *Sterna forsteri*   **Page 293**
35–42 cm (14–16.5").
7a Non-breeding Adult: Large black spot enclosing eye; silvery-white primaries; tail extends beyond folded wings when at rest.
Breeding Adult: Orange bill, black tip. **7b** Standing. **7c** Flying.

8 COMMON TERN *Sterna hirundo*   **Page 292**
33–40 cm (13–16").
8a Non-breeding Adult: Bill blackish; forehead white; shoulder with dark bar.
8b Breeding Adult: Bill red, black tip; black cap and portion of outer primaries; tail does not extend beyond wings when at rest.
8c Immature: Mantle, rump and uppertail-coverts dark gray mottled with light brownish; shoulder with dark bar.

9 ROSEATE TERN *Sterna dougallii*   **Page 291**
35–41 cm (14–16"). Very long, deeply forked tail; pale mantle and primaries; tail extends beyond wing tips when at rest.
9a Breeding Adult: Bill black with some red; black cap.
9b Non-breeding Adult: Bill blackish; forehead white past eye; indistinct dark marking on shoulder.
9c Immature: Dark forehead and crown; bill blackish; back mottled; shoulder with indistinct marks.

PLATE 7: TERNS, JAEGERS AND SKUAS

1 SOOTY TERN *Sterna fuscata*   **Page 294**
38–43 cm (15–17").
1a Adult: Blackish above; white below. Deeply forked tail, white outer feathers. White of forehead extends only to eye.
1b Immature: Entirely dark brown, flecked with white; whitish undertail-coverts and wing linings.

2 BRIDLED TERN *Sterna anaethetus*   **Page 294**
38 cm (15").
Adult: Grayish-brown above; white below; white line above and behind eye; white hindneck.
Immature: (Not illustrated.) Similar to adult; upperparts flecked with pale gray.

3 BLACK TERN *Chlidonias niger*   **Page 295**
23–26 cm (9–10").
3a Non-breeding Adult: Gray above; white below and on forecrown and hindneck; dark patch behind eye and on sides of breast.
3b Breeding Adult: Almost entirely black head and underparts.

4 BROWN NODDY *Anous stolidus*   **Page 295**
38–40.5 cm (15–16").
4a Adult: Dark brown; white cap.
4b Immature: Only forecrown white.

5 GREAT SKUA *Catharacta skua*   **Page 286**
51–66 cm (20–26"). Large size. Massive build. Mostly dark brown with golden or reddish-brown streaks on head and neck; underparts paler brown; white patch at base of primaries visible in flight.

6 SOUTH POLAR SKUA *Catharacta maccormicki*   **Page 286**
53 cm (21"). Large size. Massive build. White patch at base of primaries visible in flight.
6a *Light Phase* — Pale gray underparts, head and neck. See description under Great Skua.
6b *Intermediate Phase* — Light brown head, neck and underparts; light hindneck, sometimes a dark cap.
6c *Dark Phase* — Dark brown overall.

7 PARASITIC JAEGER *Stercorarius parasiticus*   **Page 285**
46–67 cm (18–26.5"). White patches at base of primaries visible in flight.
Adult: **7a** *Light Phase* — Dark brownish-gray above; grayish-brown cap; narrow dark breast band.
7b *Dark Phase* — Dark brown overall.
7c Subadult: Finely barred below; reddish cast to plumage.

8 POMARINE JAEGER *Stercorarius pomarinus*   **Page 284**
65–78 cm (25.5–31"). Large size. White patch at base of primaries.
Adult: Blunt, twisted central tail feathers.
8a *Light Phase* — Blackish cap; broad dark band across breast.
8b *Dark Phase* — Entirely dark brown.
8c Subadult and Immature: Heavily barred below, especially sides and underwings; central tail feathers not extended.

9 LONG-TAILED JAEGER *Stercorarius longicaudus*   **Page 285**
50–58 cm (19.5–23"). Small size.
9a Adult: Long central tail feathers, first 2–3 primaries have white bases visible in flight; cap grayish-brown; no breast band.
9b Subadult: *Light Phase* — Finely barred below; fine white barring on back. Sometimes pale head and hindneck. Central tail feathers may not be extended.
Dark Phase (Not illustrated) — Grayish-brown with darker cap; slightly paler below.

KRISTIN WILLIAMS

PLATE 8: HERONS AND EGRETS

1 LITTLE BLUE HERON *Egretta caerulea* **Page 231**
56–71 cm (22–28").
1a Adult: Uniform dark gray body.
1b Immature: White plumage; bill base grayish; greenish legs.
1c Immature Molting: Mottled with dark feathers.

2 TRICOLORED HERON *Egretta tricolor* **Page 231**
61–71 cm (24–28").
2a Adult: Gray appearance; white belly and undertail-coverts.
2b Immature: Brownish neck.

3 CATTLE EGRET *Bubulcus ibis* **Page 232**
48–64 cm (19–25"). Small size. Short, thick yellowish bill.
3a Breeding: Legs and bill reddish; tan wash on crown, breast and upper back.
3b Non-breeding: Legs black; bill yellow; tan wash reduced.

4 LITTLE EGRET *Egretta garzetta* **Page 229**
55–65 cm (22–25.5"). *White Phase* — Usually two long head plumes; bill and legs black.
Non-breeding: Lores gray-green.
Breeding: (Not illustrated). Lores reddish. *Dark Phase* — (Not illustrated.) Extremely similar to dark phase Western Reef-Heron. Gray overall.

5 SNOWY EGRET *Egretta thula* **Page 230**
51–71 cm (20–28"). Black legs; yellow feet and lores; black bill.
5a Adult.
5b Immature: Greenish-yellow band down back of legs.

6 REDDISH EGRET *Egretta rufescens* **Page 232**
69–81 cm (27–32"). Black-tipped bill, pinkish at base; ruffled neck feathers; 'dances' when feeding.
6a *Dark Phase* — Grayish overall; head and neck reddish-brown.
6b *White Phase* — White overall.
6c Immature: Bill dark; neck feathers unruffled.

7 GREAT BLUE HERON *Ardea herodias* **Page 228**
107–132 cm (42–52"). Large size.
7a *Dark Phase* — Blue-gray overall; black eyebrow stripe.
7b *White Phase* — Yellowish legs and bill.
7c Immature: Black crown.

8 GREAT EGRET *Ardea alba* **Page 229**
89–107 cm (35–42"). Large size. Yellow bill; black legs.

9 WESTERN REEF-HERON *Egretta gularis* **Page 230**
55–65 cm (22–25.5").
Breeding Adult: *White Phase* — (Not illustrated.) Extremely similar to white phase Little Egret. Two long hindneck plumes; legs dark olive-green; feet yellow; lores greenish-yellow or green; lower mandible paler than upper. *Dark Phase* — White chin and throat; lower breast and belly tinged brown; black legs; feet yellowish-green, yellow soles.
Immature: (Not illustrated.) White; variable amounts of brown feathers.

PLATE 9: HERONS, BITTERNS AND LIMPKIN

1 AMERICAN BITTERN *Botaurus lentiginosus*   **Page 227**
58–61 cm (23–24"). Black neck mark; often points bill upwards.
1a Perched.
1b Flight: Blackish wing tips.

2 LEAST BITTERN *Ixobrychus exilis*   **Page 228**
28–35 cm (11–14"). Small size. Reddish-yellow coloration; cream-colored patch on upperwing.
2a Adult.
2b Immature: Streaked breast.

3 YELLOW-CROWNED NIGHT-HERON *Nyctanassa violacea*   **Page 234**
56–71 cm (22–28").
3a Adult: Gray underparts; black and white head markings.
3b Immature: Like immature Black-crowned Night-Heron but heavier bill, grayer plumage, smaller white flecks.
Flight: Long legs extend far beyond tail.
3c Adult Flying.
3d Immature Flying.

4 BLACK-CROWNED NIGHT-HERON *Nycticorax nycticorax*   **Page 233**
58–71 cm (23–28").
4a Adult: Black crown and back; white face, underparts and head plumes.
4b Immature: Mottled brown like immature Yellow-crowned Night-Heron but thinner bill; browner; larger white flecks.
Flight: Only feet extend beyond tail.
4c Adult Flying.
4d Immature Flying.

5 LIMPKIN *Aramus guarauna*   **Page 264**
69 cm (27"). Brown plumage, white streaks; long neck and legs; long, slightly down-curved bill.

6 GREEN HERON *Butorides virescens*   **Page 233**
40–48 cm (16–19"). Small size. Dark coloration; short neck; greenish-yellow to orangish legs.
6a Adult.
6b Immature: Heavily streaked below.

1a

1b

2b

2a

3d

3c

4d

4c

3b

3a

4b

4a

5

6a

6b

TDP

PLATE 10: IBISES, SPOONBILLS, FLAMINGOS, CRANES AND STORKS

1 WHITE IBIS *Eudocimus albus*   **Page 234**
56–71 cm (22–28"). Long, down-curved bill.
1a Adult: White plumage.
1b Adult Flying: Outstretched neck; black wing tips.
1c Immature: Brown plumage; white belly and rump.

2 GLOSSY IBIS *Plegadis falcinellus*   **Page 235**
56–64 cm (22–25"). Long, down-curved bill.
2a Adult: Dark coloration.
2b Immature: Paler.

3 ROSEATE SPOONBILL *Ajaia ajaja*   **Page 235**
66–81 cm (26–32"). Spatula-like bill.
3a Adult: Pink coloration.
3b Immature: White plumage; some pink.
3c Adult Flying.

4 SCARLET IBIS *Eudocimus ruber*   **Page 235**
58.5 cm (23").
4a Breeding Adult: Bright red overall; black wing tips.
4b Immature: White; back and rump tinged pink-buff.

5 WOOD STORK *Mycteria americana*   **Page 236**
100 cm (40"). Large size. Long legs; white coloration; dark head; large bill.
5a Adult: Dark bill.
5b Immature: Yellowish bill.
Flight: Black trailing edge of wing.

6 GREATER FLAMINGO *Phoenicopterus ruber*   **Page 236**
107–122 cm (42–48"). Long legs and neck; curved bill.
6a Adult: Orangish-pink coloration.
6b Immature: Much paler.
6c Flight: Head and neck outstretched, drooping; black flight feathers.

7 SANDHILL CRANE *Grus canadensis*   **Page 265**
100 cm (40"). Large size. Long neck and legs; gray overall.
7a Adult: Bare red crown.
Immature: (Not illustrated.) Head and neck brown.
7b Flight: Neck outstretched.

From left to right: flight silhouettes of heron, Wood Stork, Sandhill Crane and ibis

1b

1a

1c

2a

2b

3b

3a

3c

6c

4a

4b

5b

5a

6a

6b

7b

7a

TBp 92

PLATE 11: PLOVERS

1 SEMIPALMATED PLOVER *Charadrius semipalmatus* **Page 269**
18.5 cm (7.25"). Brown upperparts; light orange legs; stubby bill; breast band may be incomplete.
1a Non-breeding: Dark bill.
1b Breeding: Orange bill base.

2 PIPING PLOVER *Charadrius melodus* **Page 269**
18 cm (7"). Short stubby bill; pale gray upperparts; orange legs.
2a Non-breeding: Black bill.
2b Breeding: Orange bill base.
2c Flight: White uppertail-coverts.

3 WILSON'S PLOVER *Charadrius wilsonia* **Page 268**
18–20 cm (7–8"). Single breast band; thick black bill.
3a Male: Black breast band.
3b Female: Brown breast band.

4 SNOWY PLOVER *Charadrius alexandrinus* **Page 268**
14–15 cm (5.5–5.75"). Tiny size. Slender black bill; pale coloration; dark legs.
4a Breeding: Black ear patch.
4b Immature: Lacks black in plumage.

5 COLLARED PLOVER *Charadrius collaris* **Page 268**
15 cm (5.75").
5a Adult Male: Reddish-brown hindcrown and hindneck; white forehead, throat and underparts; black band across breast; legs yellowish-pink.
Adult Female: (Not illustrated.) Thinner breast band; less reddish-brown on hindcrown and hindneck.
5b Immature: Partial breast band limited to sides of neck; no black on crown; hint of reddish-brown in plumage.

6 KILLDEER *Charadrius vociferus* **Page 269**
25 cm (10"). Two black breast bands.
6a Adult.
6b Flight: Reddish-brown rump, white wing stripe.

7 AMERICAN GOLDEN–PLOVER *Pluvialis dominicus* **Page 267**
26 cm (10"). Stocky; short bill.
7a Non-breeding: Gray coloration; contrast between dark crown and whitish eyebrow stripe.
7b Breeding: Black underparts extend to undertail-coverts.
7c Flight Below (Non-breeding): No black in wingpits; uppertail-coverts dark; no wing stripe.
7d Flight Above (Non-breeding).

8 BLACK-BELLIED PLOVER *Pluvialis squatarola* **Page 266**
26–34 cm (10–13.5"). Stocky; short bill.
8a Non-breeding: Light gray coloration; indistinct contrast between crown and eyebrow stripe.
8b Breeding: Black underparts.
8c Flight Below (Non-breeding): White uppertail-coverts and wing stripe; black wingpits.
8d Flight Above (Non-breeding).

9 NORTHERN LAPWING *Vanellus vanellus* **Page 266**
30 cm (12"). Crest; black breast band.
9a Standing.
9b Flight: White band across base of uppertail; underwings black with white linings.

1b 1a 2a 2b 2c 3b 3a 4a 4b 5a 5b 6a 6b 7a 7b 7c 7d 8a 8b 8c 8d 9a 9b

TOP

PLATE 12: SANDPIPERS 1

1 RUDDY TURNSTONE *Arenaria interpres*　　　　　**Page 277**
21–23 cm (8–9″).
1a Non-breeding: Dark breast markings; orange legs.
1b Breeding: Unusual facial markings; reddish-orange back.
1c Flight (Non-breeding): Distinctive white pattern on upperparts.

2 SOLITARY SANDPIPER *Tringa solitaria*　　　　**Page 273**
19–23 cm (7.5–9″).
2a Standing: White eyering; dark upperparts; black barring on outer tail feathers.
2b Flying Below: Underwings dark. Wingbeats deep, erratic.
Flight Above: See Plate 16.

3 COMMON SNIPE *Gallinago gallinago*　　　　**Page 283**
27–29 cm (10.5–11.5″). Long bill; striped head and back; reddish-brown tail.
Flight: See Plate 16.

4 STILT SANDPIPER *Calidris himantopus*　　　　**Page 281**
20–22 cm (8–8.5″). Greenish legs; long bill, thick at base and slight droop at tip.
4a Non-breeding: Pale eyebrow stripe.
4b Breeding: Reddish-brown ear patch.
Flight: See Plate 16.

5 RED KNOT *Calidris canutus*　　　　**Page 277**
25–28 cm (9.75–11″). Medium size. Chunky build; greenish legs; short bill.
5a Non-breeding: Gray above, white below.
5b Breeding: Orangish-red face and underparts.
Flight: See Plate 16.

6 SHORT-BILLED DOWITCHER *Limnodromus griseus*　　**Page 282**
26–30 cm (10–12″). Long straight bill. Differs from Long-billed Dowitcher by voice: whistled *tu-tu-tu*.
6a Non-breeding: Gray above; whitish below; gray breast; white eyebrow stripe.
6b Breeding: Breast and head reddish-brown; belly white.
Flight: See Plate 16.

7 LONG-BILLED DOWITCHER *Limnodromus scolopaceus*　　**Page 282**
28–32 cm (11–12.5″). Long straight bill. Differs from Short-billed Dowitcher by voice: thin *keek*.
7a Non-breeding: Similar to Short-billed Dowitcher.
7b Breeding: Reddish underparts extend to belly.

8 BUFF-BREASTED SANDPIPER *Tryngites subruficollis*　　**Page 281**
19–22 cm (7.5–8.5″). Small size.
8a Adult: Upperparts appear scaled; clean, buffy face.
8b Flight: Pure white wing linings.

9 DUNLIN *Calidris alpina*　　　　**Page 280**
20–23 cm (8–9″). Heavy bill, drooping at tip; chunky build.
9a Non-breeding: Gray wash on breast, head and upperparts.
9b Breeding: Black belly; reddish back.
Flight: See Plate 16.

1a 1b 1c
2a 2b
3
4a 4b
5a 5b
6a 6b
7a 7b
8a 8b
9a 9b

C. Fisher

PLATE 13: SANDPIPERS 2

1 SEMIPALMATED SANDPIPER *Calidris pusilla*   **Page 278**
14–16.5 cm (5.5–6.5"). Small size. Black legs; medium-length black bill.
1a Non-breeding: Grayish-brown above; whitish below.
1b Breeding: Fine breast bars; reddish-brown tints on upperparts.
Flight: See Plate 16.

2 LEAST SANDPIPER *Calidris minutilla*   **Page 278**
12.5–16.5 cm (5–6.5"). Small size. Brown coloration; yellowish-green legs; thin drooping bill.
2a Non-breeding: Brown above and on breast.
2b Breeding: More mottled with reddish-brown tints.
Flight: See Plate 16.

3 WESTERN SANDPIPER *Calidris mauri*   **Page 278**
15–18 cm (5.75–7"). Bill heavy at base, drooping at tip and longer than Semipalmated Sandpiper's.
3a Non-breeding: Grayish-brown above; whitish below.
3b Breeding: Reddish-brown scapulars, crown and ear patch.

4 BAIRD'S SANDPIPER *Calidris bairdii*   **Page 279**
18–19 cm (7–7.5"). Wings extend beyond tail.
4a Non-breeding: Brownish-gray above and on breast.
4b Breeding: Browner; faint reddish-brown tints.
Habit: Picks food rather than probes.

5 PECTORAL SANDPIPER *Calidris melanotos*   **Page 280**
20–24 cm (8–9.5"). Medium size. Yellowish-green bill and legs; sharp demarcation between streaked breast and white belly.
5a Non-breeding: Gray-brown upperparts, head and breast.
5b Breeding Male: More mottled; breast heavily streaked with black.
Flight: See Plate 16.

6 WHITE-RUMPED SANDPIPER *Calidris fuscicollis*   **Page 279**
18–20 cm (7–8"). Larger than Semipalmated and Western Sandpipers. Wings extend beyond tail; white rump.
6a Non-breeding: Darker gray than other small sandpipers.
6b Breeding: Darker brown than other small sandpipers.
Flight: See Plate 16.

7 SPOTTED SANDPIPER *Actitis macularia*   **Page 274**
18–20 cm (7–8").
Walk: Teetering.
7a Non-breeding: White underparts; orangish bill base; dark neck mark.
7b Breeding: Dark spots on underparts; orange bill with black tip.
Flight: See Plate 16.

8 SANDERLING *Calidris alba*   **Page 277**
18–22 cm (7–8.5").
8a Non-breeding: Light gray upperparts; white underparts; black mark on bend of wing.
8b Breeding: Reddish-brown head and breast.
Flight: See Plate 16.

PLATE 14: SANDPIPERS 3 AND OYSTERCATCHERS

1 HUDSONIAN GODWIT *Limosa haemastica*   **Page 276**
33–40 cm (13–16"). Long, slightly upturned bill; black tail, white at base.
1a Non-breeding: Gray overall; paler below; white eyebrow stripe.
Breeding: Dark reddish-brown below, heavily barred.
1b Flight Above (Breeding): White wing stripe and tail base.
1c Flight Below (Non-breeding): Blackish wing linings; white wing stripe.

2 MARBLED GODWIT *Limosa fedoa*   **Page 276**
40–51 cm (16–20"). Large size. Long, slightly upturned bill; no white on rump.
2a Non-breeding: Buff-colored underparts.
Breeding: Reddish-brown below, barred with black.
2b Flight (Breeding): Light primaries; cinnamon wing linings.

3 WILLET *Catoptrophorus semipalmatus*   **Page 274**
38–40 cm (15–16"). Large size. Light gray coloration; gray legs; thick bill.
3a Breeding: Finely striped head, neck and breast.
3b Flight (Non-breeding): Distinctive black and white pattern on wings.

4 LONG-BILLED CURLEW *Numenius americanus*   **Page 276**
51–66 cm (20–26"). Long, down-curved bill; unstriped head.
4a Standing.
4b Flight: Cinnamon wing linings.

5 ESKIMO CURLEW *Numenius borealis*   **Page 275**
30–35 cm (12–14"). Smaller than Whimbrel with shorter, straighter bill.
5a Standing.
5b Flight: Cinnamon-colored wing linings; dark unbarred primaries.

6 WHIMBREL *Numenius phaeopus*   **Page 275**
38–46 cm (15–18"). Large size. Long, down-curved bill; striped crown.
6a Standing.
6b Flight: Underwings barred; lacks cinnamon color.

7 AMERICAN OYSTERCATCHER *Haematopus palliatus*   **Page 270**
43–54 cm (17–21"). Black hood; long heavy bill.
7a Adult: Orange-red bill.
7b Flight: Broad white wing stripe.

PLATE 15: SANDPIPERS 4, PHALAROPES, STILTS, AVOCETS AND THICK-KNEES

1 RED PHALAROPE *Phalaropus fulicaria*   **Page 284**
21 (8").
Habit: Spins in water.
1a Non-breeding Adult: Unstreaked pale gray above; yellow spot at base of lower mandible; black smudge through eye to ear coverts. **1b Breeding Female**: Dark reddish-brown below; white facial patch.
Flight: See Plate 16.

2 WILSON'S PHALAROPE *Phalaropus tricolor*   **Page 283**
23 cm (9"). Thin straight bill.
Habit: Spins in water.
2a Non-breeding: White breast; thin dark line through eye. **Breeding Male**: (Not illustrated) Reddish-tan wash on neck. **2b Breeding Female**: Dark reddish-brown band from shoulder blending to black behind eye.
Flight: See Plate 16.

3 RED-NECKED PHALAROPE *Phalaropus lobatus*   **Page 283**
18 cm (7").
Habit: Spins in water.
3a Non-breeding Adult: Black smudge through eye; very thin, straight, black bill. **3b Breeding Adult Female**: Reddish-brown neck; golden wing-coverts. **Breeding Adult Male**: (Not illustrated.) Duller than breeding female.
Flight: See Plate 16.

4 SPOTTED REDSHANK *Tringa erythropus*   **Page 273**
30 cm (12"). Red legs and base of lower mandible. In flight, large white patch on lower back.
Non-breeding Adult and Immature: Gray above; paler below; blackish lores, paler in immature; white eyebrow stripe. **Breeding Adult**: (Not Illustrated.) Black, heavily spotted with white.

5 LESSER YELLOWLEGS *Tringa flavipes*   **Page 273**
25–28 cm (9.75–11"). Medium size. Orangish-yellow legs; bill thinner and shorter than Greater Yellowlegs.
Flight: See Plate 16.

6 GREATER YELLOWLEGS *Tringa melanoleuca*   **Page 272**
33–38 cm (13–15"). Large size. Orangish-yellow legs; long straight bill, slightly upturned.

7 BLACK-NECKED STILT *Himantopus mexicanus*   **Page 270**
34–39 cm (13.5–15.5"). Large size. Black upperparts; white underparts; long pink legs.
7a Standing. 7b Flight: Black wings; white tail extending as a V on lower back; long trailing legs.

8 RUFF (female: REEVE) *Philomachus pugnax*   **Page 281**
Male: 30 cm (12"); female: 23–28 cm (9–11"). Chunky build. Erect posture; short bill.
8a Non-breeding: Whitish bill base; buffy breast; legs pale (varying in color).
8b Breeding Male: Variably colored. Elaborately plumed breast and head.
8c Breeding Female: Variable, similar to non-breeding but darker, especially breast.
8d Flight: Long oval white patches at tail base.

9 UPLAND SANDPIPER *Bartramia longicauda*   **Page 275**
28–32 cm (11–12.5"). Short bill; small head; long neck and tail.
9a Standing. 9b Flight: Wingbeats shallow; dark primaries.

10 DOUBLE-STRIPED THICK-KNEE *Burhinus bistriatus*   **Page 266**
38–43 cm (15–17"). Large size. Plover-like; large yellow iris; whitish eyebrow stripe; striped breast.
10a Standing. 10b Flight: White wing patches.

11 AMERICAN AVOCET *Recurvirostra americana*   **Page 271**
40–51 cm (16–20"). Large size. Sharply upturned bill; black and white coloration.
11a Non-breeding: Head and neck gray.
11b Breeding (Flying): Head and neck cinnamon-colored.

PLATE 16: SHOREBIRDS FLYING

1 SOLITARY SANDPIPER *Tringa solitaria* **Page 273**
19–23 cm (7.5–9"). Dark above; bars on white-edged tail; underwings dark. Wingbeats deep; erratic. **Standing and Flying**: See Plate 12.

2 STILT SANDPIPER *Calidris himantopus* **Page 281**
20–22 cm (8–8.5"). White rump; whitish tail. **Standing**: See Plate 12.

3 COMMON SNIPE *Gallinago gallinago* **Page 283**
27–29 cm (10.5–11.5"). Zig-zag flight uttering call note. **Standing**: See Plate 12.

4 SHORT-BILLED DOWITCHER *Limnodromus griseus* **Page 282**
26–30 cm (10–12"). White rump patch extends well up back. Distinguished from Long-billed Dowitcher by voice. **Standing**: See Plate 12.

5 RED KNOT *Calidris canutus* **Page 277**
25–28 cm (9.75–11"). **Flight Above**: Barred; pale gray rump; white wing stripe. **Flight Below**: Pale gray wing linings. **Standing**: See Plate 12.

6 DUNLIN *Calidris alpina* **Page 280**
20–23 cm (8–9"). White wing stripe; white rump divided by black bar. **Standing**: See Plate 12.

7 SEMIPALMATED SANDPIPER *Calidris pusilla* **Page 278**
14–16.5 cm (5.5–6.5"). Fine white wing stripe; white rump divided by black bar. **Standing**: See Plate 13.

8 LEAST SANDPIPER *Calidris minutilla* **Page 278**
12.5–16.5 cm (5–6.5"). Dark above; very faint wing stripe. **Standing**: See Plate 13.

9 PECTORAL SANDPIPER *Calidris melanotos* **Page 280**
20–24 cm (8–9.5"). Sharp breast demarcation; fine white wing stripe; white rump divided by black bar. **Standing**: See Plate 13.

10 WHITE-RUMPED SANDPIPER *Calidris fuscicollis* **Page 279**
18–20 cm (7–8"). White rump. Fine white wing stripe. **Standing**: See Plate 13.

11 SANDERLING *Calidris alba* **Page 277**
18–22 cm (7–8.5"). White wing stripe; pale gray upperparts. **Standing**: See Plate 13.

12 SPOTTED SANDPIPER *Actitis macularia* **Page 274**
18–20 cm (7–8"). Shallow, rapid wingbeats; white wing stripe. **Standing**: See Plate 13.

13 LESSER YELLOWLEGS *Tringa flavipes* **Page 273**
25–28 cm (9.75–11"). Dark above; white uppertail-coverts. **Standing**: See Plate 15.

14 RED-NECKED PHALAROPE *Phalaropus lobatus* **Page 283**
18 cm (7"). **Flight (Non-breeding)**: White wing stripe; white stripes on back. **Standing**: See Plate 15.

15 WILSON'S PHALAROPE *Phalaropus tricolor* **Page 283**
23 cm (9"). **Flight (Non-breeding)**: White rump; dark upperparts. **Standing**: See Plate 15.

16 RED PHALAROPE *Phalaropus fulicaria* **Page 284**
21 (8"). **Non-breeding Flight of Adult**: Unstreaked pale gray above; white wing stripe. **Standing**: See Plate 15.

PLATE 17: RAILS, GALLINULES, COOTS AND JACANAS

1 ZAPATA RAIL *Cyanolimnas cerverai*   **Page 262**
29 cm (11.5"). Medium size. Near lack of stripes or spots; long green bill, red at base; red legs and iris. Cuba. See also Plate 80.

2 SORA *Porzana carolina*   **Page 261**
22 cm (8.5"). Brownish-gray plumage; stubby yellow bill. **2a Adult**: Blackish face, throat and breast. **2b Immature**: Black absent.

3 YELLOW-BREASTED CRAKE *Porzana flaviventer*   **Page 261**
14 cm (5.5"). Tiny size. Pale yellowish-brown appearance; blackish crown; white eyebrow stripe; short bill.

4 KING RAIL *Rallus elegans*   **Page 260**
38–48 cm (15–19"). Large size and long bill. **Adult**: Throat, breast and wing-coverts reddish brown; flanks and abdomen banded with black and white.

5 CLAPPER RAIL *Rallus longirostris*   **Page 259**
36 cm (14"). Primarily gray; long bill; flanks and abdomen banded with black and white.

6 SPOTTED RAIL *Pardirallus maculatus*   **Page 262**
28 cm (11"). Medium size. Long red legs; long greenish-yellow bill, red at base. **Adult**: Spotted, barred black and white body; red iris.

7 BLACK RAIL *Laterallus jamaicensis*   **Page 259**
14 cm (5.5"). Tiny size. Short black bill; white spots on back; dark reddish-brown hindneck.

8 VIRGINIA RAIL *Rallus limicola*   **Page 260**
23 cm (9"). **8a Adult**: Breast, belly and wing coverts reddish-brown; gray cheeks; black bars on flanks and abdomen; long reddish bill. **8b Immature**: Mottled gray or blackish below; bill dark. Best identified by two-note call.

9 NORTHERN JACANA *Jacana spinosa*   **Page 271**
19–23 cm (7.5–9"). Large yellow wing patches; extremely long, slender greenish toes.
9a Adult: Dark reddish-brown, except blackish head and neck; bill and forehead shield yellow.
9b Immature: Whitish below; white eyebrow stripe.

10 AMERICAN COOT *Fulica americana*   **Page 263**
38–40 cm (15–16"). **Adult**: Appears grayish-black; white bill and undertail-coverts; lacks large white frontal shield on crown as Caribbean Coot. **Immature**: (Not illustrated.) Identical to immature Carribbean Coot.

11 CARIBBEAN COOT *Fulica caribaea*   **Page 264**
38–40 cm (15–16"). **11a Adult**: Appears grayish-black; white frontal shield extending to crown; white undertail-coverts. **11b Immature**: Gray.

12 PURPLE GALLINULE *Porphyrula martinica*   **Page 263**
33 cm (13"). **12a Adult**: Bluish-purple coloration; yellow legs; bluish-white frontal shield. **12b Immature**: Golden brown; yellowish legs; bluish wings.

13 COMMON MOORHEN *Gallinula chloropus*   **Page 263**
34 cm (13.5"). White flank stripe. **Adult**: Red bill and frontal shield. **Immature**: (Not illustrated.) Gray and brown; bill lacks red.

Flight silhouette of Sora

PLATE 18: LOONS, GREBES, CORMORANTS, ANHINGA, DOVEKIE AND LARGE WATERFOWL

1 ANHINGA *Anhinga anhinga*   **Page 226**
85 cm (34"). Large size. Dark coloration; long neck and tail; long pointed bill; large whitish patches on upperwing and back. Perches with wings spread. **1a Adult Male**: Glossy black. **1b and 1c Adult Female**: Head to breast light brown. **Immature**: (Not Illustrated.) Brown above; tan below.

2 PIED-BILLED GREBE *Podilymbus podiceps*   **Page 216**
30–38 cm (12–15"). Conical bill. **2a Breeding Adult**: Black throat and bill band. **2b Non-breeding Adult**: Throat white; bill band absent. **2c Immature**: Face striped brown and white.

3 NEOTROPIC CORMORANT *Phalacrocorax brasilianus*   **Page 226**
63–69 cm (25–27"). Smaller than Double-crested Cormorant. Thinner, hooked bill; longer tail. Perches with wings spread. **3a Breeding Adult**: White edge on throat pouch. **3b Non-breeding Adult**: White throat pouch reduced or absent. **3c Immature**: Brown above; paler below.

4 LEAST GREBE *Tachybaptus dominicus*   **Page 215**
23–26 cm (9–10"). Small size. Blackish coloration; thin bill; yellow-orange iris; white wing patch (not always visible). **4a Breeding Adult. 4b Non-breeding Adult.**

5 DOUBLE-CRESTED CORMORANT *Phalacrocorax auritus*   **Page 225**
74–89 cm (29–35"). Hooked bill; perches with wings spread. **5a Breeding Adult**: Appears black; ear tufts. **5b Non-breeding Adult**: Lacks ear tufts. **5c Immature**: Brown above; paler below.

6 COMMON LOON *Gavia immer*   **Page 215**
70–100 cm (27–40"). Big, duck-like. Body sits low in water. **6a Non-breeding Adult**: Dark upperparts; long gray bill; white throat and neck. **6b Breeding Adult**: Head glossy greenish-black, body mottled black and white.

7 SNOW GOOSE *Chen caerulescens*   **Page 240**
58–71 cm (23–28"). **Adult**: **7a** *White Phase* — White; black primaries. **7b** *Dark Phase* — Bluish-gray; white head. **Immature**: **7c** *White Phase* — Grayish above; blackish bill and legs. **7d** *Dark Phase* — Brownish-gray; blackish bill and legs. **7e Adult**: *White Phase Flying* — Black wing tips.

8 GREATER WHITE-FRONTED GOOSE *Anser albifrons*   **Plate 239**
66–86.5 cm (26–34"). Medium size. **8a Adult**: White feathers frame base of pink or orange bill; belly barred with black. **8b Immature**: Uniform dark brown.

9 CANADA GOOSE *Branta canadensis*   **Page 240**
64–110 cm (25–43"). Black head and neck; white band on cheeks and throat.

10 DOVEKIE *Alle alle*   **Page 296**
21 cm (8"). Small size. Stout; short thick neck; large head; short, black, stubby bill. **10a Non-breeding Adult**: Black above; white below extending around neck; white streaks over folded wings; head black from bill to below eye and above ear. **10b Breeding Adult**: Head and breast black.

11 TUNDRA SWAN *Cygnus columbianus*   **Page 239**
122–140 cm (48–55"). Large size. Long neck; short legs. **11a Adult**: White overall; bill black, sometimes with yellow lores. **11b Immature**: Grayish-brown overall; bill pinkish.

Note: Illustrations not all to scale.

Double-crested Cormorant on the water and in flight

Dovekie

PLATE 19: WATERFOWL 1

1 **WEST INDIAN WHISTLING-DUCK** *Dendrocygna arborea*   **Page 238**
48–56 cm (19–22"). Deep brown plumage; black and white markings on abdomen.
Flight: See Plate 21.

2 **FULVOUS WHISTLING-DUCK** *Dendrocygna bicolor*   **Page 237**
46–51 cm (18–20"). Body pale yellowish-brown; white side stripe and uppertail-coverts.
Flight: See Plate 21.

3 **WHITE-FACED WHISTLING-DUCK** *Dendrocygna viduata*   **Page 238**
44 cm (17"). **Adult**: Distinctive white face. **Immature**: (Not illustrated) Paler; beige face. **Flight**: See Plate 21.

4 **BLACK-BELLIED WHISTLING-DUCK** *Dendrocygna autumnalis*   **Page 239**
46–53 cm (18–21"). Black belly; white wing patch. **Flight**: See Plate 21.

5 **WHITE-CHEEKED PINTAIL** *Anas bahamensis*   **Page 241**
38–48 cm (15–19"). Red bill mark; white cheek; green speculum, buffy borders.
Flight: See Plate 21.

6 **NORTHERN SHOVELER** *Anas clypeata*   **Page 243**
43–53 cm (17–21"). Unusually large bill. **6a Male**: Green head; white breast; reddish-brown sides.
6b Female: Mottled brown. **Flight**: See Plate 21.

7 **NORTHERN PINTAIL** *Anas acuta*   **Page 242**
Male: 69–74 cm (27–29"); female: 54–56 cm (21–22"). **7a Female and Non-breeding Male**: Mottled brown; pointed tail; long slender neck. **7b Breeding Male**: Brown head; white stripe down neck; long pointed tail. **Flight**: See Plate 21.

8 **AMERICAN BLACK DUCK** *Anas rubripes*   **Page 241**
53–64 cm (21–25"). Dark brown body; purple speculum. **8a Male**: Yellow bill.
8b Female: Greenish-black bill. **Flight**: See Plate 21.

9 **AMERICAN WIGEON** *Anas americana*   **Page 244**
46–56 cm (18–22"). Light blue bill. **9a Male**: White crown; green eye patch. **9b Female**: Brownish; gray head. **Flight**: See Plate 21.

10 **MALLARD** *Anas platyrhynchos*   **Page 241**
51–71 cm (20–28"). Blue speculum, white borders. **10a Adult Female**: Mottled brown; orange and black bill. **10b Non-breeding Male**: Similar to female, but bill greenish-black.
10c Breeding Male: Green head; yellow bill; maroon breast. **Flight**: See Plate 21.

11 **EURASIAN WIGEON** *Anas penelope*   **Page 244**
42–52 cm (16.5–20"). **11a Male**: Dark reddish-brown head; golden cream-colored crown stripe. **11b Female**: Brownish with gray head or reddish tint to head and neck. **Flight**: See Plate 21.

12 **GREEN-WINGED TEAL** *Anas crecca*   **Page 240**
33–39 cm (13–15.5"). Small size. Green speculum; no blue in forewing. **12a Female and Non-breeding Male**: Mottled brown; dark lores; whitish belly; pale patch beneath tail.
12b Breeding Male: Green eye patch; white vertical bar in front of wing. **Flight**: See Plate 21.

13 **CINNAMON TEAL** *Anas cyanoptera*   **Page 243**
38–40 cm (15–16"). **13a Female and Non-breeding Male**: Mottled brown. Similar to female Blue-winged Teal. **13b Breeding Male**: Cinnamon-colored head and underparts. **Flight**: See Plate 21.

14 **BLUE-WINGED TEAL** *Anas discors*   **Page 242**
38–40 cm (15–16"). Small size. Blue forewing. **14a Female and Non-breeding Male**: Mottled brown; light spot on lores. **14b Breeding Male**: White facial crescent. **Flight** See Plate 21.

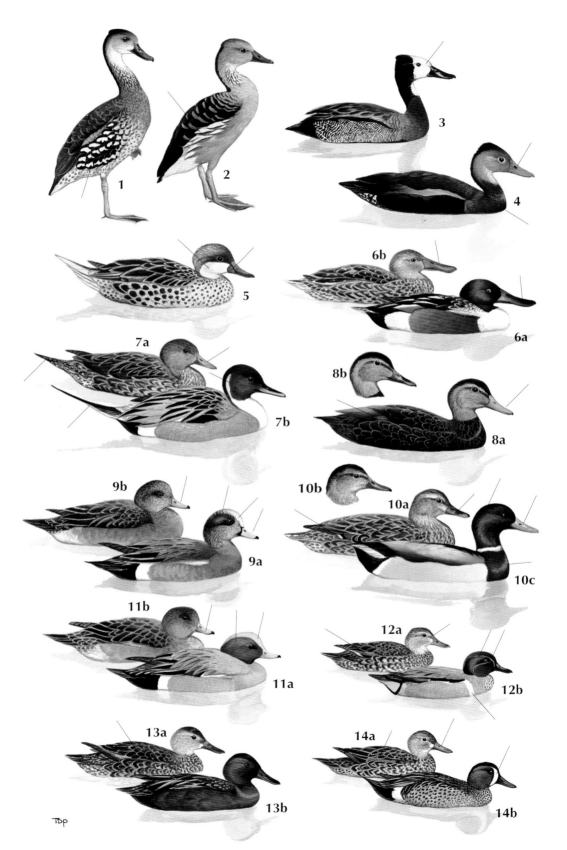

PLATE 20: WATERFOWL 2

1 GREATER SCAUP *Aythya marila* **Page 245**
38–51 cm (15–20"). **1a Male**: Head round or slightly flat-topped. **1b Female**: White feathers around bill base. **Flight**: See Plate 22.

2 LESSER SCAUP *Aythya affinis* **Page 246**
38–46 cm (15–18"). **2a Male**: Dark head, breast and tail; whitish back and flanks. **2b Female**: Brown; large white mark behind bill. **Flight**: See Plate 22.

3 RING-NECKED DUCK *Aythya collaris* **Page 245**
40–46 cm (16–18"). **3a Male**: White bill ring; black back; white vertical bar in front of wing. **3b Female**: Light bill ring; white eyering, sometimes with trailing streak. **Flight**: See Plate 22.

4 REDHEAD *Aythya americana* **Page 245**
46–56 cm (18–22"). Steep forehead. **4a Male**: Gray back; black neck; roundish red head. **5b Female**: Blue bill tipped with black. **Flight**: See Plate 22.

5 CANVASBACK *Aythya valisineria* **Page 244**
51–61 cm (20–24"). Sloping forehead profile. **5a Male**: Reddish-brown head and neck. **5b Female**: Brown head and neck. **Flight**: See Plate 22.

6 RUDDY DUCK *Oxyura jamaicensis* **Page 247**
35–43 cm (14–17"). Erect tail. **6a Breeding Male**: Reddish-brown coloration; white cheek patch; blue bill. **6b Non-breeding Male**: Brown coloration. Bill duller. **Female and Immature**: Brown plumage; single dark stripe below eye. **Flight**: See Plate 22.

7 GADWALL *Anas strepera* **Page 243**
46–57 cm (18–22.5"). White speculum. **7a Male**: Mottled gray above; rump and tail coverts black. **7b Female**: Mottled brown overall; whitish belly. **Flight**: See Plate 22.

8 MASKED DUCK *Nomonyx dominica* **Page 247**
30–36 cm (12–14"). Erect tail; white wing patch. **8a Breeding Male**: Black face; reddish-brown body. **8b Non-breeding Male, Female and Immature**: Brown; two dark facial stripes. **Flight**: See Plate 22.

9 BUFFLEHEAD *Bucephala albeola* **Page 246**
33–38 cm (13–15"). **9a Male**: White head patch. **9b Female**: Browner than male; white facial stripe. **Flight**: See Plate 22.

10 WOOD DUCK *Aix sponsa* **Page 240**
43–51 cm (17–20"). **10a Male**: Crest; unusual facial pattern. **10b Female**: Crest; asymetrical eyering. **Flight**: See Plate 22.

11 RED-BREASTED MERGANSER *Mergus serrator* **Page 247**
51–64 cm (20–25"). Crest; hooked bill. **11a Male**: Green head; dark breast; white collar. **11b Female**: Reddish-brown head and bill; whitish breast; gray back. **Flight**: See Plate 22.

12 HOODED MERGANSER *Lophodytes cucullatus* **Page 246**
40–48 cm (16–19"). Crest; hooked bill. **12a Male**: Crest has large white patch. **11b Female**: Dark plumage and bill. **Flight**: See Plate 22.

PLATE 21: WATERFOWL FLYING 1

1 BLACK-BELLIED WHISTLING-DUCK *Dendrocygna autumnalis*   **Page 239**
46–53 cm (18–21"). Upperwing with large white patch. Head and feet droop. Feet extend beyond tail. **Sitting**: See Plate 19.

2 FULVOUS WHISTLING-DUCK *Dendrocygna bicolor*   **Page 237**
46–51 cm (18–20"). Pale yellowish-brown coloration; white stripe at wing base; white rump; dark wings; reddish-brown upperwing-coverts. Head and feet droop; feet extend beyond tail. **Sitting**: See Plate 19.

3 WEST INDIAN WHISTLING-DUCK *Dendrocygna arborea*   **Page 238**
48–56 cm (19–22"). Dark overall; black and white abdomen; gray upperwing-coverts. Head and feet droop; feet extend beyond tail. **Sitting**: See Plate 19.

4 WHITE-FACED WHISTLING-DUCK *Dendrocygna viduata*   **Page 238**
44 cm (17"). White face. Wings dark above and below; no white markings except on head. Flight is heavy, feet extend beyond tail. **Sitting**: See Plate 19.

5 NORTHERN PINTAIL *Anas acuta*   **Page 242**
Male: 69–74 cm (27–29"); female: 54–56 cm (21–22"). Long slender neck; pointed tail.
5a Female and Non-breeding Male: White border on trailing edge of brown speculum; gray underwing contrasts with white belly. **5b Breeding Male**: Greenish speculum, pale tan inner border; white trailing edge. **Sitting**: See Plate 19.

6 AMERICAN WIGEON *Anas americana*   **Page 244**
46–56 cm (18–22"). White patch on forewing; green speculum; white belly.
6a Male. 6b Female. Sitting: See Plate 19.

7 WHITE-CHEEKED PINTAIL *Anas bahamensis*   **Page 241**
38–48 cm (15–19"). Red bill mark; white cheek; green speculum, pale tan borders.
Sitting: See Plate 19.

8 EURASIAN WIGEON *Anas penelope*   **Page 244**
42–52 cm (16.5–20"). White patches on forewing; green speculum; white belly; blackish flecks on wingpits. **8a Male**: Dark reddish-brown head; golden cream-colored crown stripe.
8b Female: Brownish; gray or reddish head. **Sitting**: See Plate 19.

9 NORTHERN SHOVELER *Anas clypeata*   **Page 243**
43–53 cm (17–21"). Large bill; green speculum; blue patch on forewing. **9a Male**: Green head; white breast; reddish-brown sides and belly. **9b Female**: Mottled brown. **Sitting**: See Plate 19.

10 GREEN-WINGED TEAL *Anas crecca*   **Page 240**
33–39 cm (13–15.5"). Small size. Green speculum; lacks blue in forewing.
10a Female and Non-breeding Male: Mottled brown; whitish belly. **10b Breeding Male**: Green eye patch; reddish-brown head; whitish belly. **Sitting**: See Plate 19.

11 MALLARD *Anas platyrhynchos*   **Page 241**
51–71 cm (20–28"). Blue speculum, white borders. **11a Adult Female**: Mottled brown.
11b Breeding Male: Green head; maroon breast. **Sitting**: See Plate 19.

12 CINNAMON TEAL *Anas cyanoptera*   **Page 243**
38–40 cm (15–16"). Light blue forewing; green speculum. **Breeding Male**: Cinnamon-colored head and underparts. **Female and Non-breeding Male**: (Not illustrated.) Similar to female Blue-winged Teal. **Sitting**: See Plate 19.

13 BLUE-WINGED TEAL *Anas discors*   **Page 242**
38–40 cm (15–16"). Small size. Blue forewing; green speculum.
13a Female and Non-breeding Male: Mottled brown; darkish belly. **13b Breeding Male**: White crescent on face. **Sitting**: See Plate 19.

14 AMERICAN BLACK DUCK *Anas rubripes*   **Page 241**
53–64 cm (21–25"). Dark brown body; purple speculum; white wing linings. **Sitting**: See Plate 19.

PLATE 22: WATERFOWL FLYING 2

1 GADWALL *Anas strepera*   **Page 243**
46–57 cm (18–22.5"). White speculum. **1a Male**: Mottled gray above; black rump and tail coverts; dark brown head. **1b Female**: Mottled brown; white belly. **Sitting**: See Plate 20.

2 WOOD DUCK *Aix sponsa*   **Page 240**
43–51 cm (17–20"). Long squared tail; crest; large head; bill tilted down. **2a Male**: White throat. **2b Female**: White eye patch. **Sitting**: See Plate 20.

3 BUFFLEHEAD *Bucephala albeola*   **Page 246**
33–38 cm (13–15"). **3a Male**: White head patch. **3b Female**: Browner than male; white facial stripe. **Sitting**: See Plate 20.

4 REDHEAD *Aythya americana*   **Page 245**
46–56 cm (18–22"). **4a Male**: Gray back and black neck contrast with reddish head. **4b Female**: Dull brown; white eyering; blue band around black-tipped bill. **Sitting**: See Plate 20.

5 CANVASBACK *Aythya valisineria*   **Page 244**
51–61 cm (20–24"). Elongated appearance. **5a Male**: White belly and underwings sandwiched between black breast and tail. **5b Female**: Whitish belly and underwings contrast with dark breast and tail. **Sitting**: See Plate 20.

6 RING-NECKED DUCK *Aythya collaris*   **Page 245**
40–46 cm (16–18"). Dark upperwing-coverts contrast with pale gray secondaries.
6a Male: Underparts contrast black and white. **6b Female**: Underparts contrast brown and white. **Sitting**: See Plate 20.

7 GREATER SCAUP *Aythya marila*   **Page 245**
38–51 cm (15–20"). White secondaries and inner primaries. White belly and abdomen.
7a Male: Black breast. **7b Female**: Brown breast. **Sitting**: See Plate 20.

8 LESSER SCAUP *Aythya affinis*   **Page 246**
38–46 cm (15–18"). White secondaries and black primaries. White belly and abdomen.
8a Male: Black breast. **8b Female**: Brown breast. **Sitting**: See Plate 20.

9 RUDDY DUCK *Oxyura jamaicensis*   **Page 247**
35–43 cm (14–17"). Chunky appearance; long tail; dark upperwings. **9a Breeding Male**: White cheek. **9b Female and Immature**: Cheek stripe. **Sitting**: See Plate 20.

10 MASKED DUCK *Nomonyx dominica*   **Page 247**
30–36 cm (12–14"). White wing patch; chunky body; long tail. **10a Breeding Male**: Black face; reddish-brown coloration. **10b Non-breeding Male, Female, and Immature**: Brown; two dark stripes on face. **Sitting**: See Plate 20.

11 HOODED MERGANSER *Lophodytes cucullatus*   **Page 246**
40–48 cm (16–19"). Crest; dark upperparts. **11a Male**: Small white patch on secondaries; pale forewing. **11b Female**: Small white patch on secondaries. **Sitting**: See Plate 20.

12 RED-BREASTED MERGANSER *Mergus serrator*   **Page 247**
51–64 cm (20–25"). **12a Male**: White secondaries and forewing crossed by 2 bars. **12b Female**: Secondaries white crossed by 1 bar. **Sitting**: See Plate 20.

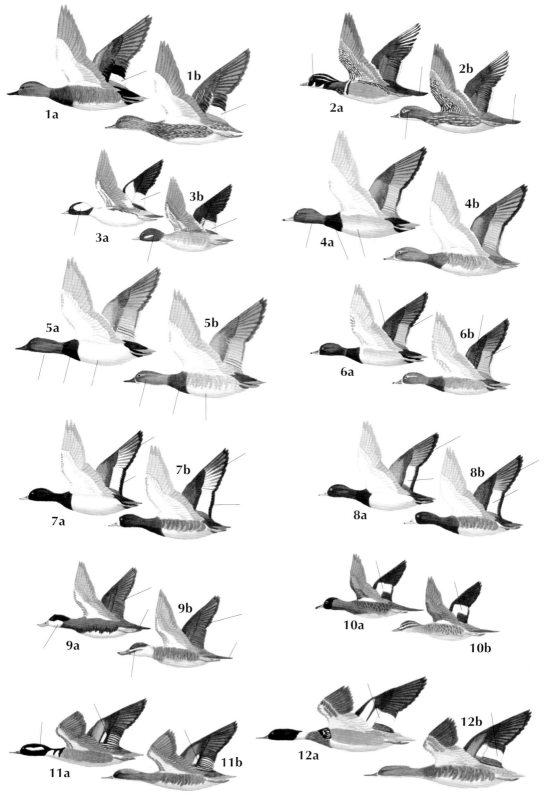

PLATE 23: RAPTORS 1

1 SHARP-SHINNED HAWK *Accipiter striatus*   **Page 251**
25–35 cm (10–14"). Small size. **1a Adult**: Upperparts dark steel-blue; finely barred reddish underparts. **1b Immature**: Brown above; streaked dark brown below. (Puerto Rico race illustrated.)
Flight: See Plate 25.

2 MERLIN *Falco columbarius*   **Page 256**
25–34 cm (10–13.5"). Small size. Underparts heavily streaked; tail barred with black.
2a Male: Dark gray above. **2b Female**: Upperparts brown. **Flight**: Pointed wings; long narrow tail; fast and agile.

3 PEREGRINE FALCON *Falco peregrinus*   **Page 256**
38–51 cm (15–20"). Large size. Dark, mask-like head pattern. **3a Adult**: Dark gray above; cream-colored with dark bars below. **3b Immature**: Brown; heavily streaked below.

4 GUNDLACH'S HAWK *Accipiter gundlachi*   **Page 252**
43–51 cm (17–20"). Medium-size. Cuba. **4a Adult**: Upperparts dark steel-blue; lightly barred gray-reddish underparts. **4b Immature**: Brown above; lighter and heavily streaked with dark brown below.
Flight: See Plate 25. See also Plate 79.

5 NORTHERN HARRIER *Circus cyaneus*   **Page 251**
46–61 cm (18–24"). Large size. White rump; long wings and tail. **5a Adult Male**: Grayish-blue.
5b Adult Female: Brown above; streaked below. **5c Flying Adult Male. Flight**: Low over ground; wings held above horizontal.

6 AMERICAN KESTREL *Falco sparverius*   **Page 255**
23–30 cm (9–12"). Small size. Usually a reddish-brown back; tail reddish with terminal black band; 2 black face bars. **Adult Male**: Blue-gray wings. **6a** Hispaniola race illustrated. **6b** Cuba, Bahamas, Jamaica race illustrated. **6c Adult Female**: Reddish-brown wings. (Hispaniola race illustrated.)

7 SWALLOW-TAILED KITE *Elanoides forficatus*   **Page 250**
51–66 cm (20–26"). **7a Perched**: Bi-colored; white head and underparts; black back, wings and long, deeply forked tail. **7b Flying.**

8 CUBAN KITE *Chondrohierax wilsonii*   **Page 250**
38–43 cm (15–17"). Large size. Robust; yellowish, massive hooked bill. Cuba. **8a Adult Male**: Dark gray; gray or finely gray barred underparts. **8b Adult Female**: Dark brown; underparts coarsely barred with reddish-brown; tan hindneck. **Immature**: (Not illustrated.) Black above; white below extending to hindneck. **Flight**: See Plate 25. See also Plate 79.

9 HOOK-BILLED KITE *Chondrohierax uncinatus*   **Page 249**
38–43 cm (15–17"). Chunky body; oversized deeply hooked bill. Plumage variable. Grenada.
9a Male. 9b Female. Flight: See Plate 25.

10 SNAIL KITE *Rostrhamus sociabilis*   **Page 251**
43–48 cm (17–19"). Broad white band across base of tail and tail coverts. Cuba.
10a Adult Male: Blackish. **10b Adult Female**: Brown above; heavily streaked below; white stripe over eye. **Immature**: (Not illustrated.) Similar to female; iris and legs paler. **Flight**: See Plate 25.

Note: Illustrations not all to scale.

PLATE 24: RAPTORS 2

1 COMMON BLACK-HAWK *Buteogallus anthracinus*   **Page 252**
51–58 cm (20–23″). Large size. Stocky, with broad wings and wide tail; long yellow legs.
Adult: One broad white tail band. **1a** (St. Vincent) Black. **1b** (Cuba) Chocolate-brown.
1c Immature: Underparts white to buffy, heavily steaked with black; several narrow pale tail bands.
Cuba and St Vincent. (St Vincent race illustrated.) **Flight**: See Plate 25.

2 BROAD-WINGED HAWK *Buteo platypterus*   **Page 253**
35–41 cm (14–16″). Medium size. Chunky. **2a Adult**: Tail boldly banded black and white; underparts
reddish-brown barring. **2b Immature**: Underparts white, heavily streaked with dark brown; tail bands
more numerous, less distinct than adult's. **Flight**: See Plate 25. (Puerto Rico race illustrated.)

3 RIDGWAY'S HAWK *Buteo ridgwayi*   **Page 253**
36–41 cm (14–16″). Medium size. Hispaniola. **3a Adult**: Dark brownish-gray above; underparts gray,
washed with brownish-red; thighs reddish-brown; tail barred black and white.
3b Immature: Underparts buffy-white, streaked pale gray and tan; tail less barred. **Flight**: See Plate
25. See also Plate 81.

4 CRESTED CARACARA *Caracara plancus*   **Page 255**
50–63 cm (19.5–25″). Large crested head; large beak; reddish facial skin. Cuba.
4a Adult: Breast whitish, barred. **Immature**: Browner; breast buffy, streaked. **4b Flight**: Contrasting
white patches near wing tips.

5 RED-TAILED HAWK *Buteo jamaicensis*   **Page 254**
48–64 cm (19–25″). Large size. **5a Adult**: Dark brown above; white below, contrasting dark belly
band. **5b Immature**: Lightly barred grayish-brown tail. **Flight**: See Plate 25.

6 TURKEY VULTURE *Cathartes aura*   **Page 248**
68–80 cm (27–32″). Large size. Dark overall; naked head. **6a Adult**: Head red.
6b Immature: Blackish head. **6c Flight**: Two-toned wings held above horizontal in broad V.

7 BLACK VULTURE *Coragyps atratus*   **Page 248**
58–68 cm (23–26.5″). Large size. Black overall; very short tail. **7a Perched**. **7b Flight**: Whitish wing
patches visible in flapping and soaring flight.

8 OSPREY *Pandion haliaetus*   **Page 249**
53–61 cm (21–24″). Large size. White underparts; dark brown above. **8a Resident Race**: White head.
8b Migratory Race: White head; dark bar behind eye. **8c Flight**: Wings bent at wrist; black wrist
patch.

1a
1b
1c
2a
2b
3a
3b
4a
4b
5a
5b
6a
6b
6c
7a
7b
8a
8b
8c

KRISTIN WILLIAMS 1992

PLATE 25: RAPTORS FLYING

1 COMMON BLACK-HAWK *Buteogallus anthracinus*   **Page 252**
51–58 cm (20–23″). Large white patch at base of primaries; long legs dangle during flap and glide flight. Cuba and St Vincent.
1a Adult. (Cuba race illustrated.)
1b Immature.
Perched: See Plate 24.

2 SHARP-SHINNED HAWK *Accipiter striatus*   **Page 251**
25–35 cm (10–14″). Short rounded wings; long narrow tail; flight rapid, alternately flapping and gliding.
Perched: See Plate 23.

3 GUNDLACH'S HAWK *Accipiter gundlachi*   **Page 252**
43–51 cm (17–20″). Short rounded wings; long narrow tail rounded at tip; flight rapid, alternating quick wingbeats with gliding. Cuba.
Perched: See Plates 23 and 79.

4 SNAIL KITE *Rostrhamus sociabilis*   **Page 251**
43–48 cm (17–19″). Broad white band across base of tail and tail coverts. Coursing flight, low to water. Cuba.
4a Adult Male.
4b Adult Female.
Perched: See Plate 23.

5 CUBAN KITE *Chondrohierax wilsonii*   **Page 250**
38–43 cm (15–17″). Large oval wings prominently barred beneath; long banded tail. Cuba.
Adult Male. (Illustrated.)
Perched: See Plate 23. See also Plate 79.

6 RIDGWAY'S HAWK *Buteo ridgwayi*   **Page 253**
36–41 cm (14–16″). Broad rounded wings; fan-shaped tail; soaring hawks show light 'wing windows'. Hispaniola.
Perched: See Plate 24. See also Plate 81.

7 HOOK-BILLED KITE *Chondrohierax uncinatus*   **Page 249**
38–43 cm (15–17″). Large oval wings prominently barred beneath; long banded tail. Grenada.
Adult Female. (Illustrated.)
Perched: See Plate 23.

8 RED-TAILED HAWK *Buteo jamaicensis*   **Page .'54**
48–64 cm (19–25″). Soars on broad rounded wings and tail.
8a Adult: Reddish tail; white underparts; dark belly band.
8b Immature: Lightly barred tail; dark belly band less distinct.
Perched: See Plate 24.

9 BROAD-WINGED HAWK *Buteo platypterus*   **Page 253**
35–41 cm (14–16″). Alternates soaring and flapping on broad rounded wings.
9a Adult: Boldly banded tail. (St Vincent, Barbados, Grenada race.)
9b Immature: Tail with finer bars; underparts streaked. (Dominica, Martinique, St Lucia race.)
Perched: See Plate 24.

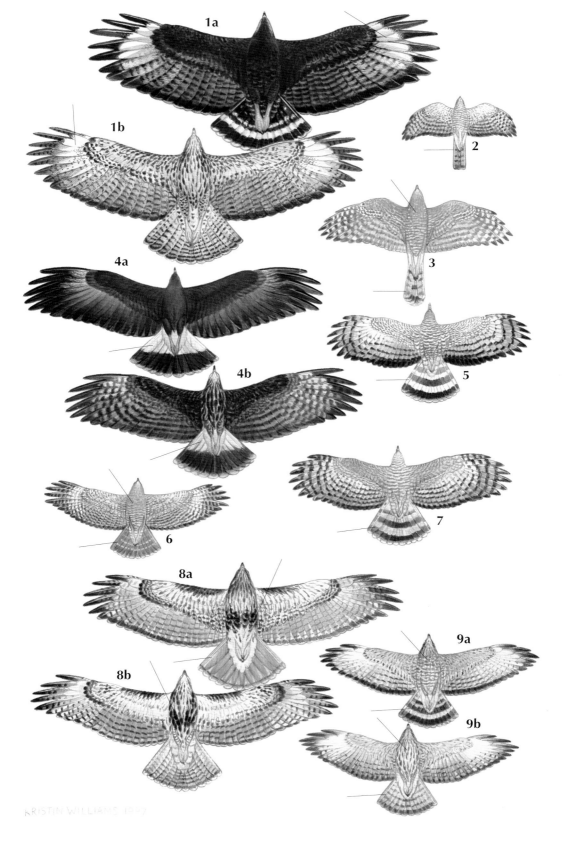

KRISTIN WILLIAMS 1997

PLATE 26: FOWL-LIKE BIRDS, CROWS, STARLINGS AND MYNAS

1 WHITE-NECKED CROW *Corvus leucognaphalus*   **Page 370**
48–51 cm (19–20"). Large size. All black; large bill. Upperparts with violet sheen. Hispaniola. See also Plate 82.

2 CUBAN CROW *Corvus nasicus*   **Page 369**
45–48 cm (17.5–19"). Large size. Black plumage, bill and legs. Bahamas and Cuba.

3 CUBAN PALM CROW *Corvus minutus*   **Page 368**
43 cm (17"). Virtually identical to Cuban Crow in field. Large size. Completely black, faint violet sheen, fading to dull brown-black in worn plumage. Cuba. See Plate 79.

4 HISPANIOLAN PALM CROW *Corvus palmarum*   **Page 369**
43 cm (17"). Virtually identical to Cuban Crow in field. Large size. Completely black, purplish and bluish sheen, fading to dull brown-black in worn plumage. Hispaniola. See Plate 81.

[JAMAICAN CROW] *Corvus jamaicensis*   **Page 370**
38 cm (15"). Not illustrated. Very similar to Cuban Crow in field. Large size. Dull black; large bill. Jamaica. See Plate 84.

5 EUROPEAN STARLING *Sturnus vulgaris*   **Page 386**
22 cm (8.5"). **5a Breeding Adult**: Glossy black; yellow bill. **5b Non-breeding Adult**: Underparts heavily flecked white; dark bill. **5c Immature**: Brownish-gray; fine stripes on breast.

6 HILL MYNA *Gracula religiosa*   **Page 387**
30 cm (12"). Brilliant orange bill; yellow wattle on hind neck; white wing patch. Puerto Rico.

7 RUFOUS-VENTED CHACHALACA *Ortalis ruficauda*   **Page 256**
55 cm (22"). Long, broad, bronze-colored tail, tipped with reddish-brown; throat red.

8 RING-NECKED PHEASANT *Phasianus colchicus*   **Page 257**
76–92 cm (30–36"). **8a Male**: Iridescent blue-green head with crest; long cinnamon tail with narrow black bars; incomplete white neck band. **8b Female**: Mottled brown; shorter tail.

9 HELMETED GUINEAFOWL *Numida meleagris*   **Page 258**
53 cm (21"). Slate-gray plumage, white spots; naked head and neck.

10 RED JUNGLEFOWL *Gallus gallus*   **Page 257**
Male: 71 cm (28"); female: 43 cm (17"). **10a Male**: Colorful plumage; red comb and wattle; large tail. **10b Female**: Smaller comb and wattle; brownish plumage.

11 NORTHERN BOBWHITE *Colinus virginianus*   **Page 258**
25 cm (10"). Chunky; brown. **11a Male**: White throat and eyebrow stripe. **11b Female**: Tan throat and eyebrow stripe.

12 CRESTED BOBWHITE *Colinus cristatus*   **Page 258**
18 cm (8"). Short tailed; long, pointed crest. **Male**: Throat and eyebrow stripe reddish-brown; crest and ear patch white; underparts spotted white. **Female**: (Not illustrated.) Lacks distinctive facial coloration of male.

13 COMMON PEAFOWL *Pavo cristatus*   **Page 258**
Male: 250 cm (100"); female: 100 cm (40"). **13a Male**: Primarily blue plumage; huge tail.
13b Female: Grayish-brown; white belly and face; greenish neck and breast; distinctive crest.

> *Note: Illustrations not all to scale.*

PLATE 27: PIGEONS AND DOVES 1

1 RING-TAILED PIGEON *Columba caribaea*   **Page 299**
41 cm (16″). Large size. Black band across tail; bluish-green hindneck. Jamaica.
1a Perched.
1b Flight.
See also Plate 83.

2 PLAIN PIGEON *Columba inornata*   **Page 298**
38–40 cm (15–16″). Pale gray-brown; reddish-brown on wings and breast; white on wing coverts.
2a Perched.
2b Flight: White band traverses wing.

3 SCALY-NAPED PIGEON *Columba squamosa*   **Page 297**
36–40 cm (14–16″). Slate-gray body, purplish-red tint upperparts visible at close range.

4 WHITE-CROWNED PIGEON *Columba leucocephala*   **Page 298**
33–36 cm (13–14″). Slate-gray body.
4a Adult Male: White crown.
Adult Female: (Not illustrated) Crown grayish-white.
4b Immature: White nearly limited to forehead.

5 ROCK DOVE *Columba livia*   **Page 297**
33–36 cm (13–14″). Color variable; white rump; black tail band (some wild birds).

6 CRESTED QUAIL-DOVE *Geotrygon versicolor*   **Page 305**
31 cm (12″). Short, distinct crest; buffy stripe beneath eye. Jamaica. See also Plate 83.

7 BLUE-HEADED QUAIL-DOVE *Starnoenas cyanocephala*   **Page 306**
30–33 cm (12–13″). Brownish-cinnamon plumage; light blue head; white facial stripe; black medallion on throat, surrounded by whitish and bluish. Cuba. See also Plate 79.

8 RUDDY QUAIL-DOVE *Geotrygon montana*   **Page 305**
25 cm (10″).
8a Male: Reddish-brown overall; buffy stripe below eye.
8b Female: Browner, less distinct facial stripe.

9 BRIDLED QUAIL-DOVE *Geotrygon mystacea*   **Page 304**
30 cm (12″). White line below eye; brown upperparts; buffy-brown underparts; reddish-brown wing patch.

10 KEY WEST QUAIL-DOVE *Geotrygon chrysia*   **Page 304**
28–30 cm (11–12″). White line below eye; reddish-brown upperparts; whitish underparts.

11 GRAY-HEADED QUAIL-DOVE *Geotrygon caniceps*   **Page 304**
28 cm (11″). Metallic purplish-blue sheen on back.
11a Hispaniola race: Distinctive white forehead.
11b Cuba race: Gray crown.

1b

2b

3

1a

2a

4b

4a

6

5

7

8b

8a

9

10

11a

11b

PLATE 28: PIGEONS AND DOVES 2

1 **WHITE-WINGED DOVE** *Zenaida asiatica*   **Page 300**
28–30 cm (11–12"). Large white wing patch; white tail tips.
1a Standing.
1b Flight.

2 **EARED DOVE** *Zenaida auriculata*   **Page 301**
22–25 cm (8.5–10").
Adult: Grayish-brown above; brown below; no white in wings or tail.
2a Standing.
2b Flight.

3 **PASSENGER PIGEON** *Ectopistes migratorius* (Extinct)   **Page 302**
41cm (16"). Pale red underparts; bluish-gray head and back; long pointed tail, white tips.

4 **MOURNING DOVE** *Zenaida macroura*   **Page 302**
28–33 cm (11–13"). Long wedge-shaped tail, fringed with white; no white on wings.
4a Standing.
4b Flight.

5 **EURASIAN COLLARED-DOVE** *Streptopelia decaocto*   **Page 299**
28–30 cm (11–12"). Gray plumage; black band around hindneck.

6 **COMMON GROUND-DOVE** *Columbina passerina*   **Page 302**
15–18 cm (5.75–7"). Tiny size.
6a Male: Bluish-gray crown and hindneck. (Jamaica race illustrated.)
6b Female: Grayer than male.
Flight: Reddish-brown wing patch. (Jamaica race illustrated.)

7 **ZENAIDA DOVE** *Zenaida aurita*   **Page 301**
25–28 cm (10–11") White band on trailing edge of secondaries; rounded tail, white tips.
7a Standing: Greater Antilles race.
7b Flight: Lesser Antilles race.

8 **CARIBBEAN DOVE** *Leptotila jamaicensis*   **Page 303**
30–33 cm (12–13"). Plump, terrestrial. White forehead, face and underparts; long red legs; underwings cinnamon-colored.
8a Standing: Grand Cayman race.
8b Flight: Jamaica race

9 **GRENADA DOVE** *Leptotila wellsi*   **Page 303**
31 cm (12"). White belly and forehead; no markings on wings. Grenada. See also Plate 29.
9a Standing.
9b Flight.

10 **SPOTTED DOVE** *Streptopelia chinensis*   **Page 300**
30 cm (12").
Adult: Hindneck black; long tail tipped white; light gray bend of wing.
Immature: (Not illustrated) Lacks neck pattern.

KRISTIN WILLIAMS 1997

PLATE 29: GRENADA DOVE

GRENADA DOVE *Leptotila wellsi*   **Page 303**
31 cm (12"). See also Plate 28.

TDP 94

PLATE 30: PARROTS 1

1 YELLOW-BILLED PARROT *Amazona collaria* **Page 311**
28–31 cm (11–12"). Green overall; bill yellow; forehead and eyering white. Jamaica. See also Plate 83.

2 ST LUCIA PARROT *Amazona versicolor* **Page 315**
42–46 cm (16.5–18"). St Lucia. See also Plate 34.
Adult: Green overall; forehead, cheeks and forecrown violet-blue; red band across throat extending down center of breast. Wings green with violet-blue primaries and red patch.

3 BLACK-BILLED PARROT *Amazona agilis* **Page 313**
26 cm (10"). Green overall; blackish bill and eyering. Sometimes red patch in wing. Jamaica. See also Plate 83.

4 ST VINCENT PARROT *Amazona guildingii* **Page 315**
41–46 cm (16–18"). Variable coloration. St Vincent. See also Plate 35.
Adult: Upperparts mostly greenish or golden-brown; forehead creamy white, shading to orange-yellow on hindneck; wings mostly black with yellow-orange patches.

5 IMPERIAL PARROT *Amazona imperialis* **Page 315**
46–51 cm (18–20"). Dominica. See also Plate 33.
Adult: Upperparts variable, mostly green, faintly edged pale gray; head dark maroon-purple; dark band on hindneck; wings green, red speculum; underparts purple-violet.

6 RED-NECKED PARROT *Amazona arausiaca* **Page 314**
33–36 cm (13–14"). Overall green; blue crown, face and chin; bright red spot on throat; red wing patch. Dominica. See also Plate 86.

PLATE 31: PARROTS 2

1 YELLOW-HEADED PARROT *Amazona oratrix*   Page 314
36 cm (14"). Large size. Yellow on head variable. Puerto Rico.
Flight: Red patch on wing; blue primaries.

2 YELLOW-CROWNED PARROT *Amazona ochrocephala*
Illustrated for comparison. Not well documented from the West Indies.

3 HISPANIOLAN PARROT *Amazona ventralis*   Page 312
28–31 cm (11–12"). Bright green overall; white forehead; dark ear spot; maroon belly. Hispaniola.
See also Plate 81.
Flight: Blue primaries and secondaries.

4 PUERTO RICAN PARROT *Amazona vittata*   Page 312
30 cm (12"). Green overall; white eyering; red forehead; two-toned blue primaries. Puerto Rico. See
also Plate 85.
4a Perched.
4b Flight.

5 RED-CROWNED PARROT *Amazona viridigenalis*   Page 313
30–33 cm (12–13"). Red forecrown; cheeks bright light green. Puerto Rico.
5a Perched.
5b Flight: Orange-red patch on wing; blue primaries.

6 ORANGE-WINGED PARROT *Amazona amazonica*   Page 313
32 cm (12.5"). Yellow cheeks and crown; blue lores and eyebrow stripe. Puerto Rico and Martinique.
Flight: Orange-red wing patch; blue primaries.

7 ROSE-THROATED PARROT *Amazona leucocephala*   Page 311
28–33 cm (11–13"). Green overall; chin, throat and lower part of face pale red; forehead and eyering white; primaries blue.
7a Cuba race.
7b Bahama race.
7c Cayman Islands race.

PLATE 32: PARAKEETS AND PARROTLETS

1 HISPANIOLAN PARAKEET *Aratinga chloroptera*   **Page 307**
30–33 cm (12–13"). Green overall; white eyering; red bend of wing. Hispaniola. See also Plate 81.
Flight: Red underwing-coverts.

2 CUBAN PARAKEET *Aratinga euops*   **Page 308**
24–27 cm (9.5–10.5"). Green overall; scattered red feathers on head, sides of neck and bend of wing.
Cuba. See also Plate 79.
Flight: Red underwing coverts.

3 BLACK-HOODED PARAKEET *Nandayus nenday*   **Page 307**
36 cm (14"). Large size. Black head; red thighs; long tail.

4 ORANGE-FRONTED PARAKEET *Aratinga canicularis*   **Page 309**
23–24 cm (9–9.5"). Medium size. Orange forehead; white eyering; blue primaries. Puerto Rico.

5 BROWN-THROATED PARAKEET *Aratinga pertinax*   **Page 309**
23–28 cm (9–11"). Yellowish-orange face; throat and breast yellowish-brown; primaries blue.
5a Adult.
5b Immature.

6 MONK PARAKEET *Myiopsitta monachus*   **Page 307**
28 cm (11"). Large size. Crown, throat and breast gray; upperparts green; flight feathers blue.

7 OLIVE-THROATED PARAKEET *Aratinga nana*   **Page 308**
30.5 cm (12"). Small size. Green; slender; long pointed tail. Dark brownish-olive underparts.
Jamaica.

8 CANARY-WINGED PARAKEET *Brotogeris versicolurus*   **Page 310**
23 cm (9"). Green; yellow band bordering wing. Puerto Rico.
Flight: Large whitish-yellow wing patch.

9 GREEN-RUMPED PARROTLET *Forpus passerinus*   **Page 310**
13 cm (5"). Small size. Green; short tail. Jamaica and Barbados.
Male: Greenish-blue rump and blue wings, particularly undersides.
Female: Lacks blue in wing; yellower on breast.

10 BUDGERIGAR *Melopsittacus undulatus*   **Page 306**
18 cm (7"). Usually green underparts (wild form) but may be blue, yellow or white; yellow head and
back barred with black.

PLATE 33: IMPERIAL PARROT

IMPERIAL PARROT *Amazona imperialis*   **Page 315**
46–51 cm (18–20″). Dominica. See also Plate 30.

PLATE 34: ST LUCIA PARROT

ST LUCIA PARROT *Amazona versicolor*   **Page 315**
42–46 cm (16.5–18″). St Lucia. See also Plate 30.

C. COX '93

PLATE 35: ST VINCENT PARROT

ST VINCENT PARROT *Amazona guildingii*   **Page 315**
41–46 cm (16–18″). St Vincent. See also Plate 30.

PLATE 36: OWLS

1 ASHY-FACED OWL *Tyto glaucops*   **Page 321**
35 cm (14″). Reddish-brown plumage; long-legged; silver-gray, heart-shaped face. Hispaniola. See also Plate 81.
1a Perched.
1b Flight.

2 BARN OWL *Tyto alba*   **Page 320**
30–43 cm (12–17″). Heart-shaped face; dark eyes.
2a White race: White face and underparts. Cuba, Jamaica, Cayman Islands.
2b Dark race: Reddish-brown face and underparts. Southern Lesser Antilles.

3 BARE-LEGGED OWL *Gymnoglaux lawrencii*   **Page 322**
20–23 cm (8–9″). Small size. Large brown eyes; beige eyebrow stripe; short tail; long bare legs. Brownish overall, speckled with white. Cuba. See also Plate 80.

4 JAMAICAN OWL *Pseudoscops grammicus*   **Page 324**
31–36 cm (12–14″). Medium size. Brown overall; short ear tufts.
Adult: Mottled yellowish-brown above; paler with dark streaks below. Jamaica. See also Plate 83.

5 PUERTO RICAN SCREECH-OWL *Otus nudipes*   **Page 321**
23–25 cm (9–10″). Small size. Underparts heavily streaked. Ear tufts usually not visible. Puerto Rico and Virgin Islands. See also Plate 85.
5a Gray Phase: Mottled grayish-brown.
5b Red Phase: Mottled reddish-brown.

6 BURROWING OWL *Athene cunicularia*   **Page 323**
23 cm (9″). Small size. Long-legged; bobs when approached.
Adult: Underparts barred. (Hispaniola race illustrated.)

7 CUBAN PYGMY-OWL *Glaucidium siju*   **Page 322**
17.5 cm (7″). Small size. Large yellow eyes; short yellow feet covered with feathers. Grayish-brown upperparts; tan underparts, spotted white. Two dark spots on back of head. Cuba. See also Plate 80.
7a Front View.
7b Rear View.

8 STYGIAN OWL *Asio stygius*   **Page 323**
41–46 cm (16–18″). Large size. Very dark coloration; conspicuous ear tufts. Cuba and Hispaniola.

9 SHORT-EARED OWL *Asio flammeus*   **Page 324**
35–43 cm (14–17″). Breast heavily streaked; yellow iris.
9a Standing.
9b Flight: Irregular; whitish underwing; black wrist patch; large buff patches on upperwing. (Puerto Rico race illustrated.)

PLATE 37: NIGHTJARS, NIGHTHAWKS, PAURAQUES AND POTOOS

1 LEAST POORWILL *Siphonorhis brewsteri*   **Page 326**
17–20 cm (6.75–8"). Small size. Darkly mottled; white neck band; narrow white tip on tail.
Hispaniola. See also Plate 81.

2 JAMAICAN POORWILL *Siphonorhis americanus*   **Page 325**
24 cm (9.5"). Small size. Mottled dark brown; narrow white chin band; reddish-brown hindneck,
spotted with black and white; tail tipped white. Jamaica. See also Plate 83.

3 WHITE-TAILED NIGHTJAR *Caprimulgus cayennensis*   **Page 328**
20–23 cm (8–9"). Reddish-brown collar. Martinique. See Tails Plate 38.
3a Male: White outer tail feathers; white throat.
3b Female: No white in tail feathers; buffy throat.

4 WHIP-POOR-WILL *Caprimulgus vociferus*   **Page 328**
23–26 (9–10"). See Tails Plate 38.
Adult Male: Blackish throat, narrow white throat stripe, 3 outer tail feathers broadly tipped white.

5 PUERTO RICAN NIGHTJAR *Caprimulgus noctitherus*   **Page 328**
22 cm (8.5"). Virtually identical to Whip-poor-will but smaller. Puerto Rico. See Tails Plate 38. See
Female, Plate 85.

6 NORTHERN POTOO *Nyctibius jamaicensis*   **Page 329**
43–46 cm (17–18"). Large size. Long tail.
6a Perched: Perches nearly upright on top of a stump or post.
6b Yellow iris appears reddish in light beam.
6c Flight: Large size; long tail.

7 RUFOUS NIGHTJAR *Caprimulgus rufus*   **Page 327**
28 cm (11"). Medium size. Dark overall; reddish-brown edge to feathers; short rounded wings. St
Lucia.

[CHUCK-WILL'S-WIDOW] *Caprimulgus carolinensis*   **Page 326**
31 cm (12"). Not illustrated. Similar to Rufous Nightjar, but less reddish-brown. See Tails Plate 38.

8 GREATER ANTILLEAN NIGHTJAR *Caprimulgus cubanensis*   **Page 327**
28 cm (11"). See Tails Plate 38.
8a Male Sitting: Mottled dark gray; breast irregularly spotted white.
8b Male Flying: Outer tail feathers broadly (Hispaniola) or narrowly (Cuba) tipped white.

9 ANTILLEAN NIGHTHAWK *Chordeiles gundlachii*   **Page 325**
20–25 cm (8–10").
9a Sitting.
9b Flying: White wing patch; erratic flight.
Call: *que-re-be-bé*.

10 COMMON NIGHTHAWK *Chordeiles minor*   **Page 325**
20–25 cm (8–10"). Nearly identical to Antillean Nighthawk.
9a Sitting.
9b Flying: White wing patch; erratic flight.
Call: *neet*.

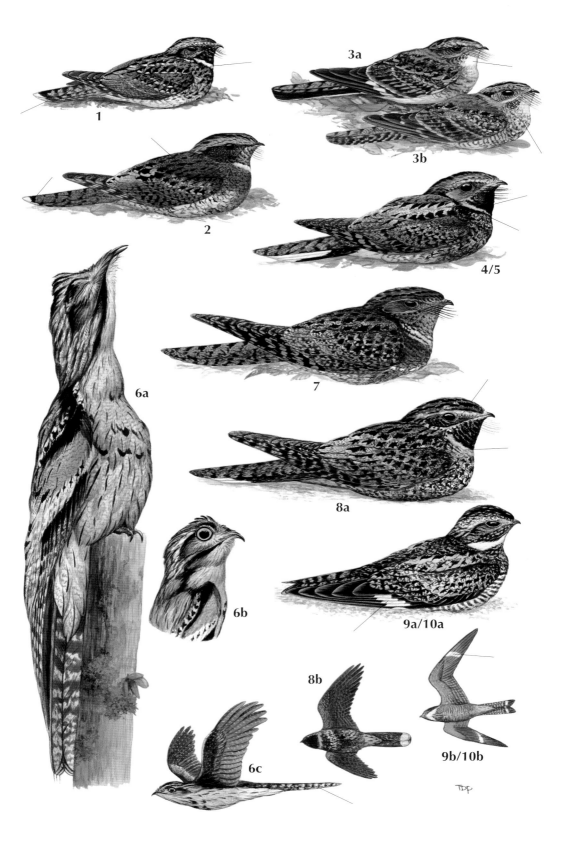

PUERTO RICAN NIGHTJAR *Caprimulgus noctitherus* Page 328
22 cm (8.5″). Puerto Rico. See also Plates 37, 85.

NIGHTJAR TAILS

Chuck-will's-widow
♂

Chuck-will's-widow
♀

St Lucia Nightjar
♂

St Lucia Nightjar
♀

*White-tailed Nightjar
uppertail*
♂

*White-tailed Nightjar
uppertail*
♀

*Greater Antillean Nightjar
Hispaniola Race*
♂

*Greater Antillean Nightjar
Cuba Race*
♂

*White-tailed Nightjar
lower tail*
♂

*White-tailed Nightjar
lower tail*
♀

Whip-poor-will
♂

Whip-poor-will
♀

Puerto Rican Nightjar
♀

PLATE 39: CUCKOOS AND ANIS

1 YELLOW-BILLED CUCKOO *Coccyzus americanus* **Page 316**
28–32 cm (11–12.5"). White underparts; long white-tipped tail; bill long and dark, down-curved, yellow at base.
Flight: Reddish-brown wing patch.

2 BLACK-BILLED CUCKOO *Coccyzus erythropthalmus* **Page 316**
30 cm (12"). White underparts; long white-tipped tail; bill long and dark, down-curved; reddish eyering.

3 MANGROVE CUCKOO *Coccyzus minor* **Page 317**
28–30 cm (11–12"). Buff-colored abdomen; black ear patch; long white-tipped tail. **Flight**: Lacks reddish-brown in wing.
3a Bahamas and Cuba race.
3b Montserrat, Guadeloupe, Dominica race.

4 HISPANIOLAN LIZARD-CUCKOO *Saurothera longirostris* **Page 318**
41–46 cm (16–18"). Large size. Pale gray breast; long white-tipped tail; straight slender bill; reddish-brown wing patch. Hispaniola. See also Plate 81.
4a whitish throat (Gonâve Island race) to **4b** dull orange throat (mainland Hispaniola race).

5 PUERTO RICAN LIZARD-CUCKOO *Saurothera vieilloti* **Page 318**
40–48 cm (16–19"). Large size. Long tail; two-toned underparts. Puerto Rico. See also Plate 85.
Adult: Gray chin and breast; cinnamon-colored belly and undertail-coverts.

6 JAMAICAN LIZARD-CUCKOO *Saurothera vetula* **Page 319**
38 cm (15"). Large size. Tail long; almost straight long bill; lower underparts pale reddish-brown; reddish-brown wing patch; red eyering. Jamaica. See also Plate 83.

7 CHESTNUT-BELLIED CUCKOO *Hyetornis pluvialis* **Page 319**
48–56 cm (19–22"). Large size. Long tail; down-curved bill; reddish underparts except for pale gray throat and upper breast; white-tipped tail. Jamaica. See also Plate 83.

8 GREAT LIZARD-CUCKOO *Saurothera merlini* **Page 317**
44–55 cm (17–22"). Large size. Long white-tipped tail. Bill long, slightly down-curved; wings dark reddish brown. Abdomen buff or pale reddish-brown. Red around eye. Bahamas and Cuba.
8a Cuba race.
8b Northern Bahamas race.

9 BAY-BREASTED CUCKOO *Hyetornis rufigularis* **Page 319**
43–51 cm (17–20"). Large size. Dark reddish-brown throat and breast; thick curved bill; reddish-brown wing patch. Hispaniola. See also Plates 40, 81.

10 SMOOTH-BILLED ANI *Crotophaga ani* **Page 320**
30–33 cm (12–13"). Entirely black; long tail; heavy parrot-like bill.

KRISTIN WILLIAMS 1996

PLATE 40: BAY-BREASTED CUCKOO

BAY-BREASTED CUCKOO *Hyetornis rufigularis*   **Page 319**
43–51 cm (17–20″). Hispaniola. See also Plates 39, 81.

KRISTIN WILLIAMS

PLATE 41: NUTHATCHES, WRENS, GNATCATCHERS, WAXWINGS AND PALMCHAT

1 PALMCHAT *Dulus dominicus* **Page 386**
20 cm (8"). Dark brown above; whitish below, heavily streaked with brown. Hispaniola. See also Plate 82.

2 CEDAR WAXWING *Bombycilla cedrorum* **Page 385**
18–18.5 cm (7–7.25"). Crest; tan plumage; yellow band on tail tip.
2a Adult.
2b Immature: Streaked underparts.

3 CUBAN GNATCATCHER *Polioptila lembeyei* **Page 373**
10.5 cm (4"). Small size. Gray above; grayish-white below; white eyering. Black crescent stripe behind eye. Long black tail, white outer feathers. Cuba.
Male: Illustrated.
Female: See Plate 80.

4 ZAPATA WREN *Ferminia cerverai* **Page 371**
16 cm (6.25"). Small size. Brown, striped with black; underparts grayish. Long bill, tail and legs. Cuba. See also Plate 80.

5 BROWN-HEADED NUTHATCH *Sitta pusilla* **Page 371**
9.5–11 cm (3.75–4.25").
Adult: Bluish-gray above; brown crown; whitish hindneck patch; dark line through eye.

6 BLUE-GRAY GNATCATCHER *Polioptila caerulea* **Page 373**
11 cm (4.25"). Similar to Cuban Gnatcatcher but bluer and lacks facial crescent. Long thin tail, white outer feathers; white underparts and eyering.
6a Breeding Male: Fine black eyebrow stripe.
6b Female: Grayer than male.

7 HOUSE WREN *Troglodytes aedon* **Page 372**
11.5–13 cm (4.5–5"). Small size. Large head.
Adult: Pale eyebrow stripe; reddish-gray above; variably dark brown to whitish below.
7a St Lucia race.
7b Grenada race.

KRISTIN WILLIAMS

PLATE 42: SWIFTS

1 WHITE-COLLARED SWIFT *Streptoprocne zonaris*   **Page 330**
20–22 cm (8–8.5"). Large size. Black coloration.
Adult: Distinctive white collar.

2 BLACK SWIFT *Cypseloides niger*   **Page 329**
15–18 cm (5.75–7"). Fairly large size. Black; slightly forked tail; at close range, white visible on forehead and eyebrow.

3 ALPINE SWIFT *Apus melba*   **Page 332**
20 cm (8"). Large size. Grayish-brown above; whitish below; dark bar across breast.

4 CHIMNEY SWIFT *Chaetura pelagica*   **Page 330**
12–14 cm (4.75–5.5"). Medium size. Dark overall; short rounded tail; pale throat visible under ideal conditions.
4a Above.
4b Below.

5 SHORT-TAILED SWIFT *Chaetura brachyura*   **Page 331**
10 cm (4"). Small size.
5a Above: Pale gray rump.
5b Below: Pale gray undertail-coverts.

6 GRAY-RUMPED SWIFT *Chaetura cinereiventris*   **Page 331**
11 cm (4.25"). Small size.
6a Above: Triangular gray rump patch.
6b Below.

7 LESSER ANTILLEAN SWIFT *Chaetura martinica*   **Page 331**
11 cm (4.25"). Small size. Tail gray, short.
7a Above.
7b Below.

8 ANTILLEAN PALM SWIFT *Tachornis phoenicobia*   **Page 332**
10–11 cm (4–4.25").
Adult: Small size. Black and white body.
8a Above: white rump.
8b Below: black breast band.

PLATE 43: HUMMINGBIRDS 1

1 PUERTO RICAN EMERALD *Chlorostilbon maugaeus* **Page 337**
9–10 cm (3.5–4"). Small size. Forked tail; no crest. Puerto Rico. See also Plate 85.
1a Male: Green overall; black tail; pinkish base of lower mandible.
1b Female: White underparts; entirely black bill; whitish tips to outer tail feathers.

2 ANTILLEAN MANGO *Anthracothorax dominicus* **Page 334**
11–12.5 cm (4.25–5"). Large size. Pale, yellowish-green upperparts.
2a Adult Male: Primarily black below; green throat.
2b Female: Whitish below and on tail tips.
2c Immature Male: Black stripe down center of whitish underparts.

3 ANTILLEAN CRESTED HUMMINGBIRD *Orthorhyncus cristatus* **Page 335**
8.5–9.5 cm (3.25–3.75"). Small size.
Adult Male: Pointed crest; underparts blackish.
3a Blue crested (Grenada, Barbados, Grenadines).
3b Green crested (remaining Lesser Antilles and Puerto Rico).
3c Female: Crest less evident; underparts pale gray.
Immature Male: (Not illustrated.) Similar to male; lacks crest.

4 GREEN MANGO *Anthracothorax viridis* **Page 334**
11.5 cm (4.5"). Large size. Entirely emerald green below; down-curved bill; rounded tail. Puerto Rico. See also Plate 85.

5 PURPLE-THROATED CARIB *Eulampis jugularis* **Page 334**
11.5 cm (4.5"). Large size. Down-curved bill; purplish-red throat; emerald-green wings.

6 GREEN-THROATED CARIB *Eulampis holosericeus* **Page 335**
10.5–12 cm (4–4.75"). Large size. Slightly down-curved bill; green breast.

7 BLUE-HEADED HUMMINGBIRD *Cyanophaia bicolor* **Page 337**
9.5 cm (3.75"). Dominica and Martinique.
7a Male: Head, throat, upper breast and tail violet-blue.
7b Adult Female: Upperparts green; bronze sheen on mantle; underparts grayish-white, flecks of green on sides.

8 RUFOUS-BREASTED HERMIT *Glaucis hirsuta* **Page 333**
12.5 cm (5"). Long down-curved bill; yellow lower mandible. Tail rounded, tipped white. Grenada.
8a Male: Upperparts dull green; underparts brown; dark forehead and crown.
8b Female: Upperparts more reddish-brown.

PLATE 44: HUMMINGBIRDS 2

1 CUBAN EMERALD *Chlorostilbon ricordii*   **Plate 336**
9–10.5 cm (3.5–4″). Medium size. Long forked tail; long thin bill, pinkish below. Bahamas and Cuba.
1a Male: Emerald green; white undertail-coverts and spot behind eye.
1b Female: Grayish underparts; sides and flanks green; white mark behind eye.

2 BEE HUMMINGBIRD *Mellisuga helenae*   **Page 340**
5.5 cm (2.25″). Small size. Short white-tipped tail. Cuba. See also Plate 80.
2a Male: Iridescent red throat, plumes extending from sides of neck in breeding season; bluish back.
2b Female: White underparts and spot behind eye; black spot on lores.

3 VERVAIN HUMMINGBIRD *Mellisuga minima*   **Page 339**
6 cm (2.5″). Small size. Green above; mostly dull white below; green sides, often with flecks on chin
and throat; straight black bill. Jamaica and Hispaniola.
3a Adult Male: Tail deeply notched. (Hispaniola race illustrated.)
3b Adult Female: Tail rounded, tipped white. (Hispaniola race illustrated.)

4 HISPANIOLAN EMERALD *Chlorostilbon swainsonii*   **Page 336**
10.5 cm (4″). Small size. Straight bill. Hispaniola. See also Plate 81.
4a Male: Green overall; black breast spot; forked tail.
4b Female: Green above; dull grayish below; tail tipped white.

5 BLACK-BILLED STREAMERTAIL *Trochilus scitulus*   **Page 338**
Male (with tail plumes): 22–24 cm (8.5–9.5″); female: 10.5 cm (4″). Jamaica. See also Plate 83.
5a Adult Male: Two long black tail feathers; crown and bill black; ear tufts.
5b Female: Underparts mostly white; short tail; outer tail feathers tipped white.

6 RED-BILLED STREAMERTAIL *Trochilus polytmus*   **Page 338**
Male (with tail plumes): 22–25 cm (8.5–10″); female: 10.5 cm (4″). Jamaica. See also Plate 83.
6a Adult Male: Two long black tail feathers; crown black; ear tufts; bill bright red, black tip.
6b Female: Underparts mostly white; short tail; outer tail feathers tipped white.

7 JAMAICAN MANGO *Anthracothorax mango*   **Page 333**
13 cm (5″). Large and dark. Jamaica. See also Plate 83.
Adult Male: Velvet-black below; cheek and sides of neck iridescent reddish-purple.
Adult Female: (Not illustrated.) Duller, pale gray on tail tip.

8 RUBY-THROATED HUMMINGBIRD *Archilochus colubris*   **Page 339**
8–9.5 cm (3–3.75″).
8a Male: Red throat; forked tail; whitish underparts; dull greenish sides.
8b Female: Green above; white below; buff-colored sides.

9 GREEN-BREASTED MANGO *Anthracothorax prevostii*   **Page 333**
12.5 cm (5″). Providencia and San Andrés.
9a Adult Male: Purple tail except central tail feathers; dark green upperparts; mix of black, green and
violet-blue underparts.
9b Adult Female: Paler.
9c Immature: Underparts lighter; black median stripe.

10 BAHAMA WOODSTAR *Calliphlox evelynae*   **Page 339**
9–9.5 cm (3.5–3.75″). Bahamas. See also Plate 45.
10a Adult Male: Deeply forked tail, with black outer and reddish-brown inner feathers.
10b Adult Female: Round reddish-brown tail and lower underparts; white throat and breast; buffy
abdomen and belly.

PLATE 45: BAHAMA WOODSTAR

BAHAMA WOODSTAR *Calliphlox evelynae*   **Page 339**
9–9.5 cm (3.5–3.75"). Bahamas. (Inaguas race.) See also Plate 44.

PLATE 46: WOODPECKERS AND PICULET

1 GUADELOUPE WOODPECKER *Melanerpes herminieri* **Page 345**
25–29 cm (10–11.5″).
Adult: Black overall; reddish wash on throat and belly. Guadeloupe. See also Plate 48.

2 CUBAN GREEN WOODPECKER *Xiphidiopicus percussus* **Page 348**
21–25 cm (8–10″). Small size. Green upperparts; yellowish underparts; noticeable crest; red patch on breast. Cuba.
Female: Black crown.
Male: See Plate 79.

3 ANTILLEAN PICULET *Nesoctites micromegas* **Page 345**
13–16 cm (5–6.25″). Tiny size. Chunky un-woodpecker-like. Hispaniola.
Adult: Olive above; paler, heavy dark spots below; yellow on crown.
Adult Female: Lacks red crown patch.
Adult Male: See Plate 82.

4 HISPANIOLAN WOODPECKER *Melanerpes striatus* **Page 346**
22–25 cm (8.5–10″). Unmarked dark buffy-olive below; white and black patches on hindneck; red crown and uppertail-coverts. Hispaniola.
Female: Smaller with shorter bill than male. Crown gray.
Male: See Plate 82.

5 JAMAICAN WOODPECKER *Melanerpes radiolatus* **Page 346**
24 cm (9.5″). Hindneck and crown red; face whitish; black upperparts; wings finely streaked with white. Jamaica.
Female: Crown brownish-olive.
Male: See Plate 83.

6 PUERTO RICAN WOODPECKER *Melanerpes portoricensis* **Page 345**
23–27 cm (9–10.5″). Upperparts blackish; rump and forehead white. Puerto Rico.
Female: Limited red on breast.
Male: See Plate 85.

7 FERNANDINA'S FLICKER *Colaptes fernandinae* **Page 349**
33–35 cm (13–14″). Large size. Yellowish-tan, black barring. Cuba.
Female: Lacks mustache stripe.
Male: See Plate 79.

PLATE 47: WOODPECKERS AND KINGFISHERS

1 IVORY-BILLED WOODPECKER *Campephilus principalis*   **Page 349**
45–50 cm (17.5–19.5"). Large size. Crest; black and white plumage; large ivory-colored bill.
1a Male: Crest red.
1b Female: Crest black.

2 WEST INDIAN WOODPECKER *Melanerpes superciliaris*   **Page 347**
26 cm (10").
2a Adult Male: Upperparts and wings barred black and white; crown to hindneck red; underparts buff-cinnamon to brownish-gray; abdomen red.
2b Adult Female: Like male; back of crown and hindneck red.
2c Immature: Crown black and hindneck red.

3 YELLOW-BELLIED SAPSUCKER *Sphyrapicus varius*   **Page 347**
20–23 cm (8–9"). White facial stripes; large white wing patch.
3a Adult Female: White throat.
3b Adult Male: Red throat.
3c Immature: Pale brown plumage.

4 NORTHERN FLICKER *Colaptes auratus*   **Page 348**
30–32 cm (12–12.5"). Black breast bar; yellow underwings and undertail; white rump, black spots on underparts.
4a Male: Black mustache stripe.
4b Female: Lacks mustache stripe.

5 HAIRY WOODPECKER *Picoides villosus*   **Page 348**
20–23 cm (8–9").
5a Adult Male: Red patch on back of head; upperparts mostly black with white on back; unbarred white outer tail feathers.
5b Adult Female: Like male; lacks red patch on head.

6 RINGED KINGFISHER *Ceryle torquata*   **Page 344**
38–41 cm (15–16").
6a Male: Wide white collar; underparts reddish-brown from breast to belly.
6b Female: Reddish-brown from lower breast to undertail-coverts; blue-gray upper breast band.

7 BELTED KINGFISHER *Ceryle alcyon*   **Page 344**
28–36 cm (11–14"). Large bill; grayish-blue crest.
7a Male: One blue breast band.
7b Female: One blue and one orange breast band.
7c Female Hovering.

PLATE 48: GUADELOUPE WOODPECKER

GUADELOUPE WOODPECKER *Melanerpes herminieri*   **Page 345**
25–29 cm (10–11.5″). Guadeloupe. See also Plate 46.

PLATE 49: TODIES AND TROGONS

1 PUERTO RICAN TODY *Todus mexicanus*   **Page 343**
11 cm (4.25"). Small size. Chunky; bright green upperparts; red throat and lower mandible; long broad bill. Yellow flanks on white underparts. Puerto Rico. See also Plate 85.
1a Adult: Red throat.
1b Immature: Lacks red throat.

2 JAMAICAN TODY *Todus todus*   **Page 343**
9 cm (3.5"). Flanks pink; abdomen and sides of breast pale yellow. Jamaica. See also Plate 83.

3 CUBAN TODY *Todus multicolor*   **Page 341**
11 cm (4.25"). Undertail-coverts yellow; flanks pink; sides of throat blue. Cuba. See also Plate 80.

4 BROAD-BILLED TODY *Todus subulatus*   **Page 342**
11–12 cm (4.25–4.75"). Belly yellow-tinted grayish-white, with pink sides; lower mandible completely red. Call a repeated whistle *terp, terp, terp*. Hispaniola. See also Plate 81.

5 NARROW-BILLED TODY *Todus angustirostris*   **Page 342**
11 cm (4.25"). Underparts as in Broad-billed Tody, but lower mandible reddish with black tip. Call a repeated two syllable *chip-chee*. Hispaniola. See also Plate 81.

6 CUBAN TROGON *Priotelus temnurus*   **Page 340**
25–28 cm (10–11"). Red belly; green back; long peculiar tail with much white on underside. Cuba. See also Plates 50, 79.

7 HISPANIOLAN TROGON *Priotelus roseigaster*   **Page 341**
27–30 cm (10.5–12"). Glossy green above; red belly; gray throat and breast. Long dark blue tail, marked with white below. Hispaniola. See also Plate 81.
7a Male: Fine black and white markings on wings.
7b Female: Lacks wing markings.

PLATE 50: CUBAN TROGON

CUBAN TROGON *Priotelus temnurus*   **Page 340**
25–28 cm (10–11″). Cuba. See also Plates 49, 79.

R.Company

PLATE 51: TYRANT FLYCATCHERS 1

1 RUFOUS-TAILED FLYCATCHER *Myiarchus validus*   **Page 358**
24 cm (9.5"). Large size. Reddish-brown tail and primaries. Jamaica. See also Plate 84.
Adult: Belly and abdomen yellow.
Immature: (Not illustrated.) Underparts whitish.

2 SAD FLYCATCHER *Myiarchus barbirostris*   **Page 357**
16.5 cm (6.5"). Jamaica. See also Plate 84.
Adult: Small size. Dark crown; yellow underparts; faint wingbars.
Immature: (Not illustrated.) Breast and throat grayish-white, only lower belly yellow.

3 GREAT CRESTED FLYCATCHER *Myiarchus crinitus*   **Page 357**
18–20.5 cm (7–8"). Bahamas and Cuba.
Adult: Upperparts greenish-brown; wings and tail reddish-brown; whitish wingbars; throat and breast
gray; belly bright yellow.

4 STOLID FLYCATCHER *Myiarchus stolidus*   **Page 359**
20 cm (8"). Medium size. Two pale white wingbars; primaries fringed with white. Throat and breast
whitish; abdomen and belly pale yellow. Jamaica and Hispaniola.

5 JAMAICAN BECARD *Pachyramphus niger*   **Page 363**
18 cm (7"). Chunky; large headed; short tail. Jamaica. See also Plates 54, 83.
5a Adult Male: Black; white mark at wing base in flight.
5b Adult Female and Immature: Reddish-brown above; pale gray below; cheeks and throat cinnamon-colored.

6 LA SAGRA'S FLYCATCHER *Myiarchus sagrae*   **Page 358**
19–22 cm (7.5–8.5"). Unusual leaning posture; flat-headed look.
Adult: Upperparts grayish to brownish-olive, with darker cap, partial collar gray; long black bill;
wings and tail with some reddish-brown; underparts grayish-white.

7 PUERTO RICAN FLYCATCHER *Myiarchus antillarum*   **Page 359**
18.5–20 cm (7.25–8"). Medium size. Upperparts dark brown; no wingbars; underparts light brownish-gray, lighter toward tail, lacks yellow wash. Puerto Rico and Virgin Islands. See also Plate 85.

8 GRENADA FLYCATCHER *Myiarchus nugator*   **Page 357**
20 cm (8"). Upperparts olive-brown; two wingbars; tail long with reddish edges to outer webs.

9 LESSER ANTILLEAN FLYCATCHER *Myiarchus oberi*   **Page 360**
19–22 cm (7.5–8.5").
Adult: Upperparts dark olive-gray; underparts yellow; tail feathers with reddish inner webs.

PLATE 52: TYRANT FLYCATCHERS 2

1 TROPICAL KINGBIRD *Tyrannus melancholicus* **Page 360**
23 cm (9"). Large size. Yellow underparts; pale gray crown; greenish back; gray facial mask.

2 WESTERN KINGBIRD *Tyrannus verticalis* **Page 360**
21–24 cm (8–9.5").
Adult: White edges to outer tail feathers; breast pale gray; belly yellow. Bahamas.

3 EASTERN KINGBIRD *Tyrannus tyrannus* **Page 361**
22–23 cm (8.5–9").
Adult: Tail black, tipped white; upperparts dark gray; head black.

4 GRAY KINGBIRD *Tyrannus dominicensis* **Page 361**
22–25 cm (8.5–10"). Gray above; pale gray-white below; distinct dark mask extending under eye.
Tail slightly notched.

5 LOGGERHEAD KINGBIRD *Tyrannus caudifasciatus* **Page 362**
24–26 cm (9.5–10"). Two-toned: dark above; white below. Crown entirely blackish; tail square with
white trailing edge except for Hispaniola and Puerto Rico birds. Large bill.
Immature: (Not illustrated) Gray above; buffy white below; buffy wing coverts.
5a Puerto Rico race.
5b Cuba race.

6 GIANT KINGBIRD *Tyrannus cubensis* **Page 362**
23 cm (9"). Large size. Massive bill; dark above; white below. Cuba. See also Plate 79.

7 FORK-TAILED FLYCATCHER *Tyrannus savana* **Page 363**
33–41 cm (13–16").
7a Adult Male: Tail in breeding plumage very long, upper half of streamers edged in white. Black
head; pale gray back; white underparts.
7b Adult Female and Immature: Duller than male; shorter tail.

8 SCISSOR-TAILED FLYCATCHER *Tyrannus forficatus* **Page 363**
31–38 cm (12–15"). Blackish wings and tail.
Adult: Head and upperparts pale gray to white; belly and undertail-coverts with pink-orange wash.
Immature: (Not illustrated.) Dull gray-brown upperparts.

1 WILLOW FLYCATCHER *Empidonax trailli* **Page 356**
15 cm (5.75"). Back grayish-olive; underparts grayish-white, very little yellow; white chin.

2 ACADIAN FLYCATCHER *Empidonax virescens* **Page 355**
12 cm (4.75"). Conspicuous yellowish eyering; 2 buffy or whitish wingbars. Throat and belly white.

3 EASTERN WOOD-PEWEE *Contopus virens* **Page 352**
16 cm (6.25"). **Adult**: Two whitish wingbars; no eyering; whitish underparts. Sides and breast dark gray, sometimes appearing as complete bar across breast.

4 WESTERN WOOD-PEWEE *Contopus sordidulus* **Page 352**
15–17 cm (5.75–6.75"). Nearly identical to Eastern Wood-Pewee; distinguish by voice.

5 EASTERN PHOEBE *Sayornis phoebe* **Page 356**
16.5–18 cm (6.5–7"). Blackish wings; no wingbars or eyering; dark upperparts; whitish underparts, pale yellow wash. **Habit**: Frequently pumps tail.

6 LEAST FLYCATCHER *Empidonax minimus* **Page 356**
13 cm (5.25"). Not well documented from the West Indies, it is presented for comparison to the more frequently recorded *Empidonax* flycatchers to emphasize the complexity of identifying this group, as a reminder that very similar vagrants to those presently known may occur, and to reiterate the importance of distinctive calls in identification. Its call note, often repeated rapidly, is a sharp 'weep' or 'wit'.

7 YELLOW-BELLIED FLYCATCHER *Empidonax flaviventris* **Page 355**
15 cm (5.75"). Upperparts olive-green; underparts yellowish, including throat. Eyering yellowish, 2 whitish or yellowish wingbars.

8 GREATER ANTILLEAN ELAENIA *Elaenia fallax* **Page 351**
15 cm (5.75"). Small size. Faint dark eyeline; 2 wingbars; bill small, pinkish base. Underparts pale gray with yellow wash; neck and breast faintly streaked gray. Jamaica and Hispaniola. **Immature**: (Not illustrated.) Lacks crown patch.

9 JAMAICAN PEWEE *Contopus pallidus* **Page 354**
15 cm (5.75"). Small size. Upperparts dark olive-gray, crown darker; underparts buffy-brown. Lower mandible orangish. Two inconspicuous (or absent) wingbars; tail notched. Jamaica. See also Plate 84.

10 JAMAICAN ELAENIA *Myiopagis cotta* **Page 350**
12.5 cm (5"). Small size. Whitish eyebrow stripe; small black bill; yellowish primary edges; no wingbars. Jamaica. See also Plate 84. **Adult**: Throat white; lower underparts pale yellow. **Immature**: Underparts pale gray, yellow on abdomen.

11 CRESCENT-EYED PEWEE *Contopus caribaeus* **Page 352**
15–16.5 cm (5.75–6.5"). Small size. Upright posture; erectile crest. Upperparts brownish-gray; underparts beige-gray, yellowish wash. White crescent behind eye. Quivers notched tail when perched. Bahamas and Cuba.

12 HISPANIOLAN PEWEE *Contopus hispaniolensis* **Page 353**
15–16 cm (5.75–6.25"). Small size. Grayish-olive upperparts; underparts gray with olive, yellow or brown wash; wingbars inconspicuous or absent; flicks tail upon lighting. Hispaniola. See also Plate 82.

13 EULER'S FLYCATCHER *Empidonax euleri* **Page 356**
13.5–14 cm (5.25–5.5"). Upperparts olive-brown; conspicuous buff or reddish-brown wingbars; underparts yellowish; grayish-olive breast band. Grenada.

14 CARIBBEAN ELAENIA *Elaenia martinica* **Page 350**
15.5–18 cm (6–7"). Two whitish wingbars; throat and lower belly whitish, light yellow wash; slight crest.

15 LESSER ANTILLEAN PEWEE *Contopus latirostris* **Page 354**
15 cm (5.75"). Small size. Upperparts brownish-olive; wings and tail black; underparts yellowish-brown.

16 PUERTO RICAN PEWEE *Contopus portoricensis* **Page 354**
15 cm (5.75"). Small size. Brownish upperparts; blackish wings and tail. Underparts buffy-brown. Puerto Rico. See also Plate 85.

17 ST LUCIA PEWEE *Contopus oberi* **Page 355**
15 cm (5.75"). Small size. Upperparts dark olive-brown; underparts reddish-brown; wings and tail black. St Lucia. See also Plate 86.

18 YELLOW-BELLIED ELAENIA *Elaenia flavogaster* **Page 351**
16.5 cm (6.5"). Upperparts grayish olive-brown; bill black above, whitish-pink below; 2 white wingbars; crest.

PLATE 54: JAMAICAN BECARD

JAMAICAN BECARD *Pachyramphus niger*   **Page 363**
18 cm (7"). Jamaica. See also Plates 51, 83.

KRISTIN WILLIAMS 1994

PLATE 55: SWALLOWS AND MARTINS

1 TREE SWALLOW *Tachycineta bicolor*   Page 365
12.5–15 cm (5–5.75″). **1a Adult**: White underparts; blue-green upperparts; notched tail.
1b Immature: Brown upperparts.

2 BAHAMA SWALLOW *Tachycineta cyaneoviridis*   Page 366
15.5 cm (6″). Bahamas. **Adult**: Deeply forked tail; greenish upperparts; white underparts.
Immature: (Not illustrated.) Less forked tail; brownish upperparts.

3 BARN SWALLOW *Hirundo rustica*   Page 368
15–19 cm (5.75–7.5″). Deeply forked tail, white spots. **3a Adult**: Underparts tan; dark reddish-brown
throat. **3b Immature**: Throat and upper breast tan; rest of underparts white.

4 CAVE SWALLOW *Pterochelidon fulva*   Page 368
12.5–14 cm (5–5.5″). Dark reddish-brown rump and forehead; pale reddish-brown ear patch, throat,
breast and sides; slight notch in tail.

5 BANK SWALLOW *Riparia riparia*   Page 367
12.5–14″ (5–5.5″). **5a Below**: Dark band across white breast. **5b Above**: Dark brown upperparts.

6 CLIFF SWALLOW *Pterochelidon pyrrhonota*   Page 367
12.5–15 cm (5–5.75″). Dark reddish-brown chin, throat and ear patch; buff-colored forehead and
rump; slight notch in tail.

7 NORTHERN ROUGH-WINGED SWALLOW *Stelgidopteryx serripennis*
                                                                                        Page 367
12.5–14 cm (5–5.5″). White underparts blend into pale brown on throat; brown upperparts.

8 GOLDEN SWALLOW *Tachycineta euchrysea*   Page 366
12.5 cm (5″). Small size. Bluish-green upperparts, golden sheen; underparts white; tail forked.
Hispaniola and Jamaica. **Immature**: (Not illustrated.) Duller above; gray breast band.

9 PURPLE MARTIN *Progne subis*   Page 364
20–22 cm (8–8.5″). Large size. **9a Adult Male**: Entirely bluish-purple. Indistinguishable from male
Cuban Martin. **9b Female and Immature**: Scaled pattern on grayish-brown breast; light gray patches
on sides of neck; indistinct border between darker breast and white belly.

10 CUBAN MARTIN *Progne cryptoleuca*   Page 364
20–22 cm (8–8.5″). Large size. Cuba. **10a Male**: Entirely bluish-purple. Indistinguishable from male
Purple Martin. **10b Female**: White belly and abdomen contrast with brown breast, sides, throat and
chin.

11 CARIBBEAN MARTIN *Progne dominicensis*   Page 365
20 cm (8″). **Adult Male**: Upperparts, head and throat blue; belly and abdomen white. **Female and
Immature**: (Not illustrated.) Underparts with brownish wash, blends gradually into white of belly.

Tree Swallow (upper) and Bahama Swallow

PLATE 56: MOCKINGBIRDS AND THRASHERS (MIMIDS)

1 CUBAN SOLITAIRE *Myadestes elisabeth*   **Page 374**
19 cm (7.5"). Olive-brown above; pale gray below. White eyering; dark mustache stripe; white outer tail feathers; bill small. Cuba. See also Plate 80.

2 RUFOUS-THROATED SOLITAIRE *Myadestes genibarbis*   **Page 375**
19 cm (7.5"). Upperparts mostly gray; throat, foreneck and undertail-coverts reddish-brown; breast light gray; outer tail feathers white.
2a St Vincent race.
2b Jamaica race.
2c Immature.

3 BROWN TREMBLER *Cinclocerthia ruficauda*   **Page 384**
23–26 cm (9–10"). Upperparts dark reddish-olive; underparts buffy-brown; bill long, down-curved near tip.
3a Dominica race.
3b Guadeloupe race.

4 GRAY TREMBLER *Cinclocerthia gutturalis*   **Page 384**
23–26 cm (9–10"). Upperparts dark olive-gray; underparts grayish-white (Martinique) or bright white (St Lucia); bill long, down-curved near tip. Martinique and St Lucia.

5 GRAY CATBIRD *Dumetella carolinensis*   **Page 381**
23 cm (9"). Gray with black cap; tail cocked slightly upwards.

6 WHITE-BREASTED THRASHER *Ramphocinclus brachyurus*   **Page 383**
20–25 cm (7.75–10"). Upperparts dark brown; underparts clear white; red iris; long, down-curved bill. Martinique and St Lucia.

7 BAHAMA MOCKINGBIRD *Mimus gundlachii*   **Page 382**
28 cm (11"). Upperparts brownish-gray, lightly streaked; underparts whitish; tail broad, almost fan-shaped in flight, tipped white.

8 SCALY-BREASTED THRASHER *Margarops fuscus*   **Page 383**
23 cm (9"). Upperparts dark grayish-brown; white underparts, heavily scaled grayish-brown; white wingbar; bill black.

9 NORTHERN MOCKINGBIRD *Mimus polyglottos*   **Page 381**
23–28 cm (9–11").
9a Adult: Gray above; grayish-white below; wings and tail marked white which shows in flight. Long tail cocked upwards.
9b Adult Flying.
9c Immature: Brownish-gray upperparts; buffy underparts.

10 PEARLY-EYED THRASHER *Margarops fuscatus*   **Page 384**
28–30 cm (11–12"). Upperparts brown; underparts white, streaked brown. White iris; large yellowish bill; large white patches on tail tip.

11 TROPICAL MOCKINGBIRD *Mimus gilvus*   **Page 382**
23–24 cm (9–9.5"). Upperparts and head gray; broad blackish eyeline; white eyebrow stripe; tail long, tipped white.
11a Southern Lesser Antilles race.
11b San Andrés race.
11c Adult Flying.

12 BROWN THRASHER *Toxostoma rufum*   **Page 383**
29 cm (11.5"). Upperparts reddish-brown; pale white wingbars; underparts buffy-white, streaked dark brown. Dark brown mustache streak; yellow-orange iris; long dark bill.

KRISTIN WILLIAMS 1997

PLATE 57: THRUSHES (MUSCICAPIDS)

1 SWAINSON'S THRUSH *Catharus ustulatus*　　　　　**Page 376**
17.5 cm (7"). Grayish-brown above; whitish below, brownish spots on breast; buff-colored eyering and lores.

2 VEERY *Catharus fuscescens*　　　　　**Page 375**
16–18 cm (6.25–7"). Upperparts reddish-brown; underparts whitish, faint spots on buffy breast; inconspicuous grayish eyering.

3 EASTERN BLUEBIRD *Sialia sialis*　　　　　**Page 374**
15–16.5 cm (5.75–6.5"). **3a Adult Male**: Upperparts bright blue; throat, breast, sides, flanks and upper belly reddish; lower belly and undertail-coverts white. **3b Adult Female**: Duller; anterior upperparts brownish-gray; whitish eyering.

4 HERMIT THRUSH *Catharus guttatus*　　　　　**Page 377**
19 cm (7.5"). Upperparts olive-brown; underparts whitish; tail reddish-brown; narrow buffy-white eyering.

5 GRAY-CHEEKED THRUSH *Catharus minimus*　　　　　**Page 375**
16–20 cm (6.25–8"). Grayish-brown above; whitish below, spots on breast and throat. Gray cheeks; no conspicuous eyering. Overlaps in plumage with Bicknell's Thrush thus cannot be distinguished safely in the field.

6 BICKNELL'S THRUSH *Catharus bicknelli*　　　　　**Page 376**
16–19 cm (6.25–7.5"). Buffy-brown upperparts; white underparts; sides of throat and breast cream-buff, spotted black; cheeks and lores grayish; tail dark reddish-brown. Overlaps in plumage with Gray-cheeked Thrush thus cannot be distinguished safely in the field.

7 WOOD THRUSH *Hylocichla mustelina*　　　　　**Page 377**
20 cm (8"). Cinnamon-colored crown; white eyering; underparts white, heavy dark spots.

8 AMERICAN ROBIN *Turdus migratorius*　　　　　**Page 378**
23–28 cm (9–11"). Upperparts grayish-brown; underparts dull red. **Adult Male**: Head and tail blackish. **Adult Female**: (Not illustrated.) Paler.

9 WHITE-EYED THRUSH *Turdus jamaicensis*　　　　　**Page 378**
23 cm (9"). **Adult**: Dark gray above; pale gray below; reddish-brown head; whitish iris; white breast bar. Jamaica. See also Plate 84.

10 LA SELLE THRUSH *Turdus swalesi*　　　　　**Page 379**
26 cm (10"). Head and upperparts slate black; white streaks on throat; lower breast and sides red; white streaks on belly. Hispaniola. See also Plate 82.

11 FOREST THRUSH *Cichlherminia lherminieri*　　　　　**Page 380**
25–27 cm (10–10.5"). Upperparts grayish-brown; underparts brown; white spots on breast, flanks and upper belly. Legs, bill and bare skin around eye yellow. **11a** Dominica race. **11b** Montserrat race.

12 COCOA THRUSH *Turdus fumigatus*　　　　　**Page 377**
23 cm (9"). St Vincent and Grenada. **Adult**: Upperparts brown; underparts paler; whitish throat patch, brown streaks.

13 BARE-EYED ROBIN *Turdus nudigenis*　　　　　**Page 378**
23 cm (9"). **Adult**: Upperparts olive-gray; underparts paler; throat white, brown streaked. Broad pale yellow eyering of bare skin; yellowish bill and feet.

14 RED-LEGGED THRUSH *Turdus plumbeus*　　　　　**Page 380**
25–28 cm (10–11"). Variable. Distinguished by gray upperparts; reddish legs and bill; eyering red; large white tail tips. **14a** *Central and western Cuba, Cayman Brac*: Reddish-brown abdomen. (Cuba race illustrated.) **14b** *Hispaniola, Puerto Rico*: Whitish abdomen; white throat; black stripes. *Bahamas, eastern Cuba*: (Not illustrated.) Gray underparts; black throat; white chin.

15 WHITE-CHINNED THRUSH *Turdus aurantius*　　　　　**Page 379**
24 cm (9.5"). Cocks tail upward. Jamaica. See also Plate 84. **Adult**: Dark gray above; paler below; white diagonal bar on wing; white chin; orange bill and legs.

PLATE 58: GRAND CAYMAN THRUSH

GRAND CAYMAN THRUSH *Turdus ravidus* (Extinct)   **Page 380**
27 cm (10.5"). Gray; red bill, eyering and legs. White abdomen and outer tail feathers.

PLATE 59: VIREOS

1 BLACK-WHISKERED VIREO *Vireo altiloquus*   **Page 393**
15–16.5 cm (5.75–6.5"). Whitish eyebrow stripe and dark eyeline; black mustache stripe. No wing-bars. **Adult**: Red iris.

2 BLUE MOUNTAIN VIREO *Vireo osburni*   **Page 391**
13 cm (5"). Robust. Gray above; pale yellow below. Large dark bill; no wingbars or eyering; iris reddish-brown. Jamaica. See also Plate 84.

3 YUCATAN VIREO *Vireo magister*   **Page 393**
15 cm (5.75"). Upperparts olive-gray; underparts white, washed with yellow. Eyebrow stripe whitish or buff; dark gray eyeline; iris brown. Cayman Islands.

4 RED-EYED VIREO *Vireo olivaceus*   **Page 392**
15 cm (5.75"). Upperparts olive; gray cap; white eyebrow stripe bordered by black eyeline and crown stripe. **Adult**: Red iris.

5 BLUE-HEADED VIREO *Vireo solitarius*   **Page 391**
12.5–15 cm (5–5.75"). Olive-green above; blue-gray head; white spectacles; 2 white wingbars. Bahamas and Cuba.

6 CUBAN VIREO *Vireo gundlachii*   **Page 389**
13 cm (5"). Small size. Bulging eyes, bordered by yellowish eyering. Olive upperparts; yellowish underparts; faint wingbars. Cuba. See also Plate 80.

7 YELLOW-THROATED VIREO *Vireo flavifrons*   **Page 391**
12.5 cm (5"). Yellow spectacles; dark iris; 2 white wingbars; yellow chin, throat and breast. Crown and back olive-green; rump gray.

8 PHILADELPHIA VIREO *Vireo philadelphicus*   **Page 392**
12.5 cm (5"). Upperparts gray-olive; crown gray; throat and upper breast pale yellow; whitish eyebrow stripe. **8a Adult**: Belly and abdomen whitish. **8b Immature**: Belly and abdomen dull yellow.

9 THICK-BILLED VIREO *Vireo crassirostris*   **Page 388**
13.5 cm (5.25"). Upperparts brownish-green; crown and hindneck grayish-green; 2 white wingbars; bright yellow spectacles. Underparts vary from **9a** entirely yellowish (central and southern Bahamas); to **9b** grayish with a tint of yellow (northern Bahamas and Cayman Islands); buff (Île Tortue). (Not illustrated.)

10 JAMAICAN VIREO *Vireo modestus*   **Page 389**
12.5 cm (5"). Jamaica. See also Plate 84. **Adult**: Dull green above; pale yellow below; 2 whitish wingbars; pinkish lower mandible; whitish iris.

11 WHITE-EYED VIREO *Vireo griseus*   **Page 387**
12.5 cm (5"). Grayish-green above; whitish below; yellow sides and spectacles, 2 white wingbars. **Adult**: White iris.

12 ST ANDREW VIREO *Vireo caribaeus*   **Page 388**
12.5 cm (5"). Upperparts olive-green; underparts whitish to pale yellow. Pale yellow stripe above bill to eye; 2 white wingbars; iris grayish-brown. San Andrés. See also Plate 86.

13 FLAT-BILLED VIREO *Vireo nanus*   **Page 390**
12–13 cm (4.75–5"). Grayish-green above; light gray below, pale yellow wash; outer tail feathers tipped white; 2 white wingbars; iris white. Hispaniola. See also Plate 82.

14 WARBLING VIREO *Vireo gilvus*   **Page 392**
12.5–15 cm (5–5.75"). Upperparts pale olive-gray; crown and hindneck slightly lighter; whitish eyebrow stripe. **14a Non-breeding Adult**: Whitish underparts. **14b Immature**: Yellowish or greenish-yellow on sides; one faint buffy wingbar.

15 PUERTO RICAN VIREO *Vireo latimeri*   **Page 390**
12.5 cm (5"). Two-toned underparts: throat and breast pale gray; belly and abdomen pale yellow. Imcomplete white eyering; brown iris. Puerto Rico. See also Plate 85.

16 MANGROVE VIREO *Vireo pallens*   **Page 388**
11.5 cm (4.5"). Olive-green above; dull yellow below and eyebrow stripe; 2 white wingbars. Reportedly occurs on Providencia.

PLATE 60: WOOD WARBLERS (EMBERIZIDS) — DARK STREAKS BELOW, NO YELLOW OR ORANGE (EXCEPT CROWN)

1 ELFIN WOODS WARBLER *Dendroica angelae*   **Page 406**
12.5 cm (5"). Puerto Rico. See also Plate 85.
1a Adult: Black and white; thin white eyebrow stripe; white patches on ear-coverts and neck; incomplete eyering; crown black.
1b Immature: Similar to adult, black replaced by grayish-green on back and yellowish-green on head and underparts.

2 BLACKPOLL WARBLER *Dendroica striata*   **Page 404**
12.5–14 cm (5–5.5").
2a Breeding Male: Black cap; white cheek.
2b Breeding Female: Grayish above; lighter below; lightly streaked sides; lacks black cap; white wingbars and undertail-coverts; pale legs.
Non-breeding Adult and Immature: See Plate 65.

3 ARROW-HEADED WARBLER *Dendroica pharetra*   **Page 405**
13 cm (5"). Jamaica. See also Plate 84.
3a Adult Male: Heavily streaked black and white above and below; 2 white wingbars.
Adult Female: (Not illustrated.) Less distinctly marked with gray.
3b Immature: Yellowish-olive above; pale yellowish below, grayish streaks; wingbars; eyering yellowish.

4 BLACK-AND-WHITE WARBLER *Mniotilta varia*   **Page 407**
12.5–14 cm (5–5.5"). Black and white, including striped crown.
4a Male: Cheek black.
4b Female: Whiter than male, particularly on cheek, throat and sides.

5 CERULEAN WARBLER *Dendroica cerulea*   **Page 405**
10–13 cm (4–5"). Two white wingbars.
5a Adult Male: Light blue head and upperparts; underparts white, sides streaked black; dark band across breast.
5b Adult Female and Immature Male: Upperparts grayish-blue; underparts dull white; yellowish tinge on throat and upper breast.
Immature Female: See Plate 65.

6 NORTHERN WATERTHRUSH *Seiurus noveboracensis*   **Page 409**
12.5–15 cm (5–5.75"). Buff-colored eyebrow stripe narrows behind eye; streaked buff-colored underparts; flecks on throat. Bobs tail.

7 LOUISIANA WATERTHRUSH *Seiurus motacilla*   **Page 409**
14.5–16 cm (5.5–6.25"). White eyebrow stripe broadens behind eye; unflecked throat; streaked whitish underparts. Bobs tail.

8 OVENBIRD *Seiurus aurocapillus*   **Page 409**
14–16.5 cm (5.5–6.5"). Upperparts brownish-olive; orange crown bordered by blackish stripes; heavily streaked underparts; white eyering.

PLATE 61: WOOD WARBLERS (EMBERIZIDS) — DARK STREAKS OR MARKINGS BELOW, YELLOW OR ORANGE IN PLUMAGE

1 PRAIRIE WARBLER *Dendroica discolor* **Page 403**
12 cm (4.75"). **Adult Male**: Bright yellow underparts; distinct black streaks on sides. Bobs tail. **Immature Female**: See Plate 65.

2 PALM WARBLER *Dendroica palmarum* **Page 403**
12.5–14 cm (5–5.5"). **Breeding**: Yellowish undertail-coverts; olive-colored rump; reddish-brown crown. Bobs tail. **Non-breeding**: See Plate 65.

3 YELLOW-THROATED WARBLER *Dendroica dominica* **Page 400**
13 cm (5"). Yellow throat; white eyebrow stripe and neck patch. **3a Breeding Adult**: Bahamas race. **3b Immature Non-breeding Male**: Bahamas race.

4 YELLOW-RUMPED WARBLER *Dendroica coronata* **Page 399**
14 cm (5.5"). Yellow rump; white throat; yellow patch on sides of breast.
4a Adult Female and Non-breeding Male: Brownish upperparts. **4b Breeding Male**: Grayish upperparts. **Immature**: See Plate 65.

5 OLIVE-CAPPED WARBLER *Dendroica pityophila* **Page 401**
12.5 cm (5"). Greenish-yellow crown; yellow throat; breast bordered by black spots. Two whitish wingbars. Bahamas and Cuba.

6 CANADA WARBLER *Wilsonia canadensis* **Page 414**
12.5–15.5 cm (5–5.75"). **Adult Male**: Black 'necklace;' bold yellow spectacles; bluish-gray upperparts. **Adult Female**: See Plate 65. **Immature**: (Not illustrated.) Olive-brown wash on upperparts.

7 MAGNOLIA WARBLER *Dendroica magnolia* **Page 398**
11.5–12.5 (4.5–5"). White tail markings. **7a Breeding Male**: Cheek black; underparts heavily striped. **7b Breeding Female**: Paler. **Non-breeding Adult and Immature**: See Plate 65.

8 CAPE MAY WARBLER *Dendroica tigrina* **Page 398**
12.5–14 cm (5–5.5"). Heavy striping on breast; yellowish rump and patch behind cheek. **8a Adult Male**: Reddish-brown cheek. **8b Adult Female**: Duller. Grayish-olive cheek. **Immature**: See Plate 65.

9 BLACK-THROATED GREEN WARBLER *Dendroica virens* **Page 399**
12.5 cm (5"). Yellowish-gray cheek. **Adult Male**: Black chin, throat, upper breast and sides. **Adult Female and Immature Male**: (Not illustrated.) Duller; chin yellowish. **Immature Female**: See Plate 65.

10 PINE WARBLER *Dendroica pinus* **Page 402**
12.5–14.5 cm (5–5.75"). **10a Adult Male:** Upperparts greenish-olive; unstreaked back; 2 white wingbars; faint breast streaks. **10b Adult Female**: Duller; browner above; grayer below. **Immature**: See Plate 65.

11 KIRTLAND'S WARBLER *Dendroica kirtlandii* **Page 402**
15 cm (5.75"). **Breeding Male**: Upperparts bluish-gray; black streaks on back; throat and belly bright yellow, black streaks on sides; inconspicuous wingbars; broken eyering; forehead and lores black. **Adult Female and Non-breeding Male**: See Plate 65.

12 BLACKBURNIAN WARBLER *Dendroica fusca* **Page 400**
13 cm (5"). **12a Adult Female, Non-breeding Male, and Immature Male**: Orange-yellow throat, breast, eyebrow stripe and sides of neck; white back stripes. **12b Breeding Male**: Orange throat and facial markings. **Immature Female**: See Plate 65.

PLATE 62: WOOD WARBLERS (EMBERIZIDS) — SIGNIFICANT BLACK OR GRAY ON FACE OR HEAD, BELOW YELLOW WITH NO OR LIGHT STREAKS

1 NASHVILLE WARBLER *Vermivora ruficapilla*　　　　**Page 396**
11.5–12.5 cm (4.5–5"). **Adult**: Head pale bluish-gray; white eyering; yellow underparts except for white belly. **Immature**: See Plate 66.

2 ORIENTE WARBLER *Teretistris fornsi*　　　　**Page 412**
13 cm (5"). Gray upperparts; yellow underparts. No wingbars nor white in plumage; yellow eyering. Long, slightly down-curved bill. Cuba. See also Plate 80.

3 WILSON'S WARBLER *Wilsonia pusilla*　　　　**Page 414**
11–12.5 cm (4.25–5"). **Adult Male**: Black cap; yellow forehead, eyebrow stripe and underparts. **Adult Female and Immature Male**: (Not illustrated.) Hint of black cap. **Immature Female**: See Plate 66.

4 KENTUCKY WARBLER *Oporornis formosus*　　　　**Page 410**
12.5–14.5 cm (5–5.75"). **Adult Male**: Yellow spectacles; black facial mark and crown; yellow underparts. **Adult Female and Immature Male**: (Not illustrated.) Duller. **Immature Female**: See Plate 66.

5 HOODED WARBLER *Wilsonia citrina*　　　　**Page 413**
12.5–14.5 cm (5–5.75"). Yellow forehead and cheeks. **5a Male**: Black hood; upperparts and wings olive-green. **5b Adult Female**: Black hood variable. See also Plate 66.

6 BACHMAN'S WARBLER *Vermivora bachmanii*　　　　**Page 394**
11–11.5 cm (4.25–4.5"). **6a Adult Male**: Large black throat and breast patch; yellow eyering, forehead, chin and belly. **6b Adult Female**: Duller; yellowish underparts; forehead and eyering. Black of breast reduced or absent; crown and hindneck gray. **Immature**: (Not illustrated.) Duller.

7 BAHAMA YELLOWTHROAT *Geothlypis rostrata*　　　　**Page 411**
15 cm (5.75"). Larger, slower than Common Yellowthroat. Heavier bill; gray cap. Bahamas. (Andros-New Providence race illustrated.) See also Plates 66, 86. **7a Male**: Black mask; yellow throat, breast and upper belly. **7b Female**: No mask; whitish eyering and eyebrow stripe; yellow throat, breast and belly.

8 COMMON YELLOWTHROAT *Geothlypis trichas*　　　　**Page 411**
11.5–14 cm (4.5–5.5"). **8a Adult Male:** Black mask; yellow throat and breast.
8b Adult Female: No facial mask; whitish eyering, usually buffy eyebrow stripe; yellow throat, breast and belly. See also Plate 66.

9 CONNECTICUT WARBLER *Oporornis agilis*　　　　**Page 410**
13.5–15 cm (5.25–5.75"). Large size. Stocky; hooded; white eyering; yellow belly to undertail-coverts which extend nearly to tail end. **9a Adult Male**: Hood bluish-gray.
9b Adult Female and Immature: Hood pale gray-brown; throat whitish. See also Plate 66.

10 MOURNING WARBLER *Oporornis philadelphia*　　　　**Page 410**
13–14.5 cm (5–5.75"). **10a Adult Male**: Hood bluish-gray; breast black. **10b Adult Female**: Hood pale gray or brownish; throat whitish; incomplete eyering. **Immature**: See Plate 66.

PLATE 63: WOOD WARBLERS (EMBERIZIDS) — BELOW YELLOW WITH LIGHT OR NO STREAKS, LITTLE OR NO BLACK OR GRAY ON HEAD

1 VITELLINE WARBLER *Dendroica vitellina* **Page 403**
13 cm (5″). Cayman and Swan Islands.
1a Adult Male: Upperparts olive-green; yellow below, faint side stripes; distinct facial pattern.
1b Immature: Crown and throat gray; facial markings buffy.
Adult Female: See Plate 65.

2 YELLOW WARBLER *Dendroica petechia* **Page 397**
11.5–13.5 cm (4.5–5.25″). Variable among islands.
Adult Male: **2a** Yellow overall; underparts with reddish streaks. Crown yellow (Bahamas and Cuba), or with varying amounts of reddish-brown, from a tinge (Jamaica, Hispaniola, Puerto Rico and Cayman Islands) (not illustrated); **2b** to a distinct cap (Anegada and most of Lesser Antilles); **2c** or entire head (Martinique).
Adult Female: See Plates 65 and 66.
Immature: See Plate 65.

3 NORTHERN PARULA *Parula americana* **Page 396**
10.5–12 cm (4–4.75″). Grayish-blue upperparts; greenish-yellow back; white wingbars; yellow breast and throat; incomplete white eyering.
3a Breeding Male: Conspicuous breast band.
3b Non-breeding Adult and Immature: Breast band faint or absent.

4 BLUE-WINGED WARBLER *Vermivora pinus* **Page 395**
12 cm (4.75″). Yellow overall; black eyeline; white wingbars.

5 PROTHONOTARY WARBLER *Protonotaria citrea* **Page 408**
13.5 cm (5.25″).
Male: Golden yellow overall; blue-gray wings and tail.
Female: See Plate 66.

6 YELLOW-HEADED WARBLER *Teretistris fernandinae* **Page 412**
13 cm (5″). Gray overall; underparts paler; yellowish head and neck. Bill long, slightly down-curved. No wingbars. Cuba. See also Plate 80.

7 ORANGE-CROWNED WARBLER *Vermivora celata* **Page 396**
11.5–14 cm (4.5–5.5″). Upperparts unmarked olive-green; greenish-yellow eyebrow stripe; thin broken yellow eyering; underparts greenish-yellow, streaked pale gray; yellow undertail-coverts. Bahamas. See also Plate 65.

8 ADELAIDE'S WARBLER *Dendroica adelaidae* **Page 401**
12.5 cm (5″). Bluish-gray upperparts; yellow throat and breast; yellow and/or white eyebrow stripe.
8a St Lucia race. **8b** Puerto Rico race.

9 YELLOW-BREASTED CHAT *Icteria virens* **Page 414**
19 cm (7.5″). Upperparts, wings and long tail olive-green; bill thick, black; lores and eyering white. Throat, breast and upper belly yellow; lower belly and undertail-coverts white.

PLATE 64: WOOD WARBLERS (EMBERIZIDS) AND KINGLETS — NO YELLOW OR STREAKS BELOW

1 AMERICAN REDSTART *Setophaga ruticilla*   **Page 407**
11–13.5 cm (4.25–5.25"). **1a Adult Male**: Black upperparts; large orange wing and tail patches.
1b Adult Female: Yellow patches in wings and tail.

2 GOLDEN-WINGED WARBLER *Vermivora chrysoptera*   **Page 395**
12.5 cm (5"). **Male**: Yellow wing patch; black throat and cheek patch.
Female and Immature: (Not illustrated.) Paler.

3 TENNESSEE WARBLER *Vermivora peregrina*   **Page 395**
11.5–12.5 cm (4.5–5"). **Breeding Male**: Upperparts bright olive-green; crown gray; white eyebrow
stripe, pale gray eyeline; underparts white. **Breeding Female**: (Not illustrated.) Similar, crown duller
and greenish; yellowish wash on breast. **Immature**: See Plate 66.

4 RUBY-CROWNED KINGLET *Regulus calendula*   **Page 372**
11.5 cm (4.5"). Upperparts olive-colored; white eyering; 2 whitish wingbars. **Male**: Concealed red
crest. **Female**: See Plate 66.

5 BLACK-THROATED BLUE WARBLER *Dendroica caerulescens*   **Page 398**
12–14 cm (4.75–5.5"). **Male:** Upperparts blue; black face; white wing spot. **Female**: See Plate 66.

6 BAY-BREASTED WARBLER *Dendroica castanea*   **Page 404**
12.5–15 cm (5–5.75"). **6a Breeding Male**: Dark reddish-brown cap and band on chin, throat and
sides; buffy neck patch. **6b Breeding Female**: Duller. **Non-breeding Adult and Immature**: See Plate 65.

7 CHESTNUT-SIDED WARBLER *Dendroica pensylvanica*   **Page 397**
11.5–13.5 cm (4.5–5.25"). **Breeding Adult Male**: Yellow cap and reddish sides.
Non-breeding Adult and Immature: See Plate 66.

8 SWAINSON'S WARBLER *Limnothlypis swainsonii*   **Page 408**
14 cm (5.5"). Upperparts dull olive grayish-brown; head brownish-gray with brown crown; whitish
eyebrow stripe; blackish line through eye; underparts whitish.

9 WORM-EATING WARBLER *Helmitheros vermivorus*   **Page 408**
14 cm (5.5"). Upperparts dull greenish-gray; head buffy with black stripes on crown and through
eyes.

10 WHISTLING WARBLER *Catharopeza bishopi*   **Page 406**
14.5 cm (5.75"). St Vincent. **10a Adult**: Blackish upperparts, hood and breast band; white eyering.
See also Plate 86. **10b Immature**: Brownish-gray upperparts, hood and breast band; white eyering.

11 PLUMBEOUS WARBLER *Dendroica plumbea*   **Page 405**
12 cm (4.75"). Guadeloupe and Dominica. **Adult**: Upperparts plain gray; white eyebrow stripe; 2
white wingbars; underparts pale gray. **Immature**: See Plate 66.

12 WHITE-WINGED WARBLER *Xenoligea montana*   **Page 415**
13.5–14 cm (5.25–5.5"). White wing patch, outer tail feathers and line above eye to forehead.
Hispaniola. See also Plate 82.

13 GREEN-TAILED GROUND WARBLER *Microligea palustris*   **Page 411**
12–14 cm (4.75–5.5"). Slender; long tail. Hispaniola. **13a Adult**: Red iris; incomplete white eyering;
lower back, rump, wings and tail greenish. See also Plate 82. **13b Immature**: Greener above; tinted
with olive below; brown iris.

14 SEMPER'S WARBLER *Leucopeza semperi*   **Page 413**
14.5 cm (5.75"). Long pale legs and feet. St Lucia. **14a Adult**: Upperparts dark gray; underparts
whitish. See also Plate 86.
14b Immature: Upperparts gray, olive-brown wash; underparts brownish-buff.

PLATE 65: WOOD WARBLERS (EMBERIZIDS) — CONFUSING PLUMAGES WITH STREAKS, SOMETIMES VERY FINE

1 CANADA WARBLER *Wilsonia canadensis*　　　　　**Page 414**
12.5–15.5 cm (5–5.75"). **Adult Female**: Gray streaks on breast; yellow spectacles.
Adult Male: See Plate 61.

2 PALM WARBLER *Dendroica palmarum*　　　　　**Page 403**
12.5–14 cm (5–5.5"). **Non-breeding**: Bobs tail. Yellow undertail-coverts; olive-colored rump; faint
eyebrow stripe. **Breeding**: See Plate 61.

3 YELLOW WARBLER *Dendroica petechia*　　　　　**Page 397**
11.5–13.5 cm (4.5–5.25"). **3a Adult Female**: Yellow overall. Faintly streaked or unstreaked below. No
reddish-brown on head. See also Plate 66. **3b Immature**: Upperparts olive-gray; underparts grayish-
white; yellow in wings. **Adult Male**: See Plate 63.

4 CAPE MAY WARBLER *Dendroica tigrina*　　　　　**Page 398**
12.5–14 cm (5–5.5"). **Immature**: Striped breast; yellowish rump; buffy patch behind cheek.
Adult: See Plate 61.

5 MAGNOLIA WARBLER *Dendroica magnolia*　　　　　**Page 398**
11.5–12.5 (4.5–5"). **Non-breeding Adult and Immature**: Pale eyebrow stripe; white eyering; gray
head. Yellow underparts, buff band nearly across breast. **Breeding Adult**: See Plate 61.

6 PRAIRIE WARBLER *Dendroica discolor*　　　　　**Page 403**
12 cm (4.75"). **Immature Female**: Bobs tail. Yellow underparts; blackish streaks on sides; whitish
facial markings. **Adult Male**: See Plate 61.

7 BLACKPOLL WARBLER *Dendroica striata*　　　　　**Page 404**
12.5–14 cm (5–5.5"). **Non-breeding Adult and Immature**: White wingbars and undertail-coverts;
faint side streaks; pale legs. **Breeding Adult**: See Plate 60.

8 YELLOW-RUMPED WARBLER *Dendroica coronata*　　　　　**Page 399**
14 cm (5.5"). Yellow rump; white throat; yellow patch on breast sides. **Immature**: Duller.
Adult and Non-breeding Male: See Plate 61.

9 BAY-BREASTED WARBLER *Dendroica castanea*　　　　　**Page 404**
12.5–15 cm (5–5.75"). **Non-breeding Adult and Immature**: Greenish-gray back; unstreaked buffy
below; white wingbars; black feet. May have pale reddish-brown wash on flanks.
Breeding Adult: See Plate 64.

10 CERULEAN WARBLER *Dendroica cerulea*　　　　　**Page 405**
10–13 cm (4–5"). **Immature Female**: Olive-green above; yellower below; 2 white wingbars. **Adult
and Immature Male**: See Plate 60.

11 VITELLINE WARBLER *Dendroica vitellina*　　　　　**Page 403**
13 cm (5"). Cayman and Swan Islands. **Adult Female**: Upperparts olive-green; entirely yellow below;
faint facial pattern; side stripes faint or absent. **Adult Male and Immature**: See Plate 63.

12 BLACK-THROATED GREEN WARBLER *Dendroica virens*　　　　　**Page 399**
12.5 cm (5"). **Immature Female**: Yellowish-gray cheek; faint side streaks.
Adult and Immature Male: See Plate 61.

13 ORANGE-CROWNED WARBLER *Vermivora celata*　　　　　**Page 396**
11.5–14 cm (4.5–5.5"). Upperparts unmarked olive-green; underparts greenish-yellow, streaked pale
gray; yellow undertail-coverts. Greenish-yellow eyebrow stripe; thin broken yellow eyering. See also
Plate 63.

14 BLACKBURNIAN WARBLER *Dendroica fusca*　　　　　**Page 400**
13 cm (5"). **Immature Female**: Yellowish throat, breast, eyebrow stripe and neck sides; white back
stripes and wingbars. **Other Plumages**: See Plate 61.

15 KIRTLAND'S WARBLER *Dendroica kirtlandii*　　　　　**Page 402**
15 cm (5.75"). **Adult Female and Non-breeding Male:** Upperparts bluish-gray, black streaks on back;
throat and belly yellow, black side streaks. Broken eyering; forehead and lores dark gray. **Breeding
Male**: See Plate 61.

16 PINE WARBLER *Dendroica pinus*　　　　　**Page 402**
12.5–14.5 cm (5–5.75"). **Immature**: Grayish-brown above; buffy-white below; 2 white wingbars;
whitish eyebrow stripe. **Adult**: See Plate 61.

PLATE 66: WOOD WARBLERS (EMBERIZIDS) AND KINGLETS — CONFUSING PLUMAGES WITHOUT STREAKED UNDERPARTS

1 CHESTNUT-SIDED WARBLER *Dendroica pensylvanica* **Page 397**
11.5–13.5 cm (4.5–5.25"). **Non-breeding Adult and Immature**: Yellowish-green above; white eye-ring; 2 yellowish wingbars. **Breeding Adult Male**: See Plate 64.

2 WILSON'S WARBLER *Wilsonia pusilla* **Page 414**
11–12.5 cm (4.25–5"). **Immature Female**: Yellow forehead, eyebrow stripe, lores and underparts. **Adult Male**: See Plate 62.

3 YELLOW WARBLER *Dendroica petechia* **Page 397**
11.5–13.5 cm (4.5–5.25"). **3a Adult Female**: Yellow overall; faintly streaked or unstreaked below. No reddish-brown on head. **3b Non-breeding Female**: Underparts with some buffy white. See also Plate 65. **Adult Male**: See Plate 63. **Immature**: See Plate 65.

4 RUBY-CROWNED KINGLET *Regulus calendula* **Page 372**
11.5 cm (4.5"). Upperparts olive-colored; white eyering; 2 whitish wingbars. **Female**: Lacks red crest. **Male**: See Plate 64.

5 TENNESSEE WARBLER *Vermivora peregrina* **Page 395**
11.5–12.5 cm (4.5–5"). **Immature**: Underparts yellowish-green; undertail-coverts white. **Breeding Male**: See Plate 64.

6 PLUMBEOUS WARBLER *Dendroica plumbea* **Page 405**
12 cm (4.75"). Guadeloupe and Dominica. **Immature**: Greenish-gray upperparts; white or buffy eyebrow stripe; 2 white wingbars. **Adult**: See Plate 64.

7 NASHVILLE WARBLER *Vermivora ruficapilla* **Page 396**
11.5–12.5 cm (4.5–5"). **Immature**: White eyering; head brownish-gray; underparts pale yellow; throat whitish or yellowish. **Adult**: See Plate 62.

8 COMMON YELLOWTHROAT *Geothlypis trichas* **Page 411**
11.5–14 cm (4.5–5.5"). **Adult Female:** No facial mask; yellow throat, breast and belly; whitish eyering, usually buffy eyebrow stripe. **Adult Male**: See Plate 62.

9 HOODED WARBLER *Wilsonia citrina* **Page 413**
12.5–14.5 cm (5–5.75"). **Adult Female**: Black hood variable. **Male and Adult Female**: See Plate 62.

10 BLACK-THROATED BLUE WARBLER *Dendroica caerulescens* **Page 398**
12–14 cm (4.75–5.5"). **Female:** White wing spot (sometimes absent) and eyebrow stripe; dull buffy underparts. **Male**: See Plate 64.

11 PROTHONOTARY WARBLER *Protonotaria citrea* **Page 408**
13.5 cm (5.25"). **Female**: Golden yellow face, throat and breast; blue-gray wings and tail. **Male**: See Plate 63.

12 KENTUCKY WARBLER *Oporornis formosus* **Page 410**
12.5–14.5 cm (5–5.75"). **Immature Female**: Yellow spectacles; gray lores; yellow underparts. **Adult Male**: See Plate 62.

13 BAHAMA YELLOWTHROAT *Geothlypis rostrata* **Page 411**
15 cm (5.75"). Larger, slower than Common Yellowthroat, heavier bill and gray cap. **Female**: No mask; whitish eyering and eyebrow stripe; yellow throat, breast and belly. **Male**: See Plates 62, 86.

14 MOURNING WARBLER *Oporornis philadelphia* **Page 410**
13–14.5 cm (5–5.75"). **Immature**: Hood pale gray or brownish; throat yellowish; eyering whitish, incomplete. **Adult**: See Plate 62.

15 CONNECTICUT WARBLER *Oporornis agilis* **Page 410**
13.5–15 cm (5.25–5.75"). **Adult Female and Immature**: Pale gray-brown hood; whitish throat; white eyering; undertail-coverts extend nearly to end of tail. **Adult Male**: See Plate 62.

PLATE 67: TANAGERS AND ALLIES (EMBERIZIDS) 1

1 ANTILLEAN EUPHONIA *Euphonia musica* **Page 417**
12 cm (4.75"). Small size. Distinctive sky-blue crown and hindneck.
Male: Variable.
1a *Puerto Rico*: Primarily dark above; rich yellow below and on rump and forehead.
1b *Hispaniola*: Primarily dark above; orangish-yellow below and on rump and forehead.
Lesser Antilles: (Not illustrated.) Prominently greenish like the female.
1c Female: Duller overall. Greenish above; yellowish-green below; rump and forehead yellowish.

2 JAMAICAN EUPHONIA *Euphonia jamaica* **Page 416**
11.5 cm (4.5"). Small size. Stubby dark bill. Jamaica.
2a Adult Male: Grayish-blue overall; belly yellow. See also Plate 84.
2b Female and Immature: Two-toned: head and underparts bluish-gray; back, wings and flanks olive-green.

3 RED-LEGGED HONEYCREEPER *Cyanerpes cyaneus* **Page 416**
13 cm (5").
3a Breeding Male: Purplish-blue body; light blue crown; black upper back, wings and tail; red legs. Underwing mostly yellow.
3b Adult Female: Dull olive-green; paler below, faint whitish streaks; legs and feet dull purple.
3c Male Flying: Underwings yellow.

4 ORANGEQUIT *Euneornis campestris* **Page 428**
14 cm (5.5"). Small size. Down-curved black bill. Jamaica.
4a Adult Male: Gray-blue; orangish-red throat. See also Plate 84.
4b Female and Immature: Crown and hindneck olive-gray; grayish-white below, faint streaks.

5 BANANAQUIT *Coereba flaveola* **Page 415**
10–12.5 cm (4–5"). Small size. Highly variable. Down-curved bill; partial yellow underparts and rump; white eyebrow stripe and white wing patch.
5a *Adult Bahamas*: White throat.
5b *Adult Puerto Rico*: Dark gray throat.
5c *Adult St Vincent*: Black upperparts; lacks eyebrow stripe; wing spot and yellow rump.
5d Immature: Yellowish eyebrow stripe.

6 SCARLET TANAGER *Piranga olivacea* **Page 419**
18 cm (7").
6a Female: Yellowish-green.
6b Non-breeding Male: Similar; wings black.
6c Breeding Male: Red overall; wings black.

7 SUMMER TANAGER *Piranga rubra* **Page 419**
18–19.5 cm (7–7.5"). Large bill.
7a Adult Male: Red overall; brighter below; wings slightly darker.
7b Female: Upperparts yellowish olive-green; underparts yellowish-orange.
Immature Male: (Not illustrated.) Similar to female; reddish tinge.

PLATE 68: TANAGERS AND ALLIES (EMBERIZIDS) 2

1 PUERTO RICAN STRIPE-HEADED TANAGER *Spindalis portoricensis*   **Page 419**
16.5 cm (6.5"). Puerto Rico.
1a Male: Black head, striped white; yellow underparts. See also Plate 85.
1b Female: Upperparts olive-brown; underparts dull whitish; gray side and flank streaks. Whitish mustache stripe.

2 HISPANIOLAN STRIPE-HEADED TANAGER *Spindalis dominicensis*   **Page 418**
16.5 cm (6.5"). Hispaniola.
Male: Yellowish underparts, reddish-brown wash; black head, striped white. See also Plate 81.
Female: (Not illustrated.) Olive-brown upperparts; underparts whitish, finely striped.

3 WESTERN STRIPE-HEADED TANAGER *Spindalis zena*   **Page 417**
15 cm (5.75").
Male: Black head, striped white.
3a Cuba race.
3b Bahamas race.
3c Female: Grayish-olive above; whitish below; 2 whitish facial stripes.

4 JAMAICAN STRIPE-HEADED TANAGER *Spindalis nigricephalus*   **Page 418**
18 cm (7"). Orangish-yellow underparts. Jamaica.
4a Male: Head black; 2 bold facial stripes. See also Plate 84.
4b Female: Upperparts olive; throat and upper breast gray.

5 BLACK-CROWNED PALM-TANAGER *Phaenicophilus palmarum*   **Page 420**
18 cm (7"). Hispaniola.
5a Adult: Crown black; throat white blending into gray breast and abdomen. Haitian race illustrated. See also Plate 82.
5b Immature.

6 LESSER ANTILLEAN TANAGER *Tangara cucullata*   **Page 416**
15 cm (5.75"). St Vincent and Grenada.
Male: Iridescent orangish-yellow above, sometimes with greenish cast; dark reddish-brown cap; wings and tail bluish-green.
6a Grenada race.
6b St Vincent race.
6c Female: Duller; greenish upperparts.

7 GRAY-CROWNED PALM-TANAGER *Phaenicophilus poliocephalus*   **Page 420**
18 cm (7"). Hispaniola.
7a Adult: Crown gray; black mask; contrast between white throat and gray breast. Haitian form illustrated. See also Plate 82.
7b Immature.

8 PUERTO RICAN TANAGER *Nesospingus speculiferus*   **Page 421**
18–20 cm (7–8"). Puerto Rico.
Adult: Olive-brown above; white below; pale brownish breast stripes; white wing spot. See also Plate 85.
Immature: (Not illustrated.) Brownish below; lacks wing spot.

9 CHAT TANAGER *Calyptophilus frugivorus*   **Page 421**
17–20 cm (6.75–8"). Mockingbird-shaped with long rounded tail. Dark brown above; mostly white below; bright yellow spot in front of eye. (Central-eastern race illustrated.) Hispaniola. See also Plate 82.

PLATE 69: ORIOLES AND ALLIES (EMBERIZIDS) 1

1 ORCHARD ORIOLE *Icterus spurius*   **Page 441**
16.5–18 cm (6.5–7"). **1a Adult Male**: Primarily black; breast, belly, lower back and bend of wing reddish-brown. **1b Female**: Grayish olive-green above, brighter on head and rump; underparts dull yellow. Two wingbars; tail bright olive-green. **1c Immature Male**: Similar to female, but black chin and throat.

2 BALTIMORE ORIOLE *Icterus galbula*   **Page 442**
18–20 cm (7–8"). **2a Adult Male**: Orange and black; white wingbar; orange tail patches.
2b Adult Female and Immature: Brownish above; orange-yellow below; 2 whitish wingbars.

3 HOODED ORIOLE *Icterus cucullatus*   **Page 441**
17.5 cm (7"). **3a Adult Male**: Orangish-yellow plumage; black throat, breast, wings, back and tail; 2 wingbars. **3b Female and Immature**: Olive-yellow overall; duller and darker above.

4 JAMAICAN ORIOLE *Icterus leucopteryx*   **Page 442**
21 cm (8"). Dull greenish-yellow; black mask and 'bib'. Jamaica and San Andrés. **4a Adult**: Large white wing patch.
4b Immature: Two cinnamon wingbars. (Jamaica race illustrated.)

5 TROUPIAL *Icterus icterus*   **Page 441**
25 cm (9.75"). Large size. Orange and black; large white wing patch; black tail.

6 MARTINIQUE ORIOLE *Icterus bonana*   **Page 441**
18–21 cm (7–8"). **Adult**: Mostly black; reddish-brown hood; reddish-orange shoulder, rump, lower belly and abdomen. Martinique. See also Plate 71.

7 YELLOW-SHOULDERED BLACKBIRD *Agelaius xanthomus*   **Page 435**
20–23 cm (8–9"). Puerto Rico. **Adult**: Glossy black; yellow shoulder patch. See also Plate 85.
Immature: (Not illustrated.) Duller; brown abdomen.

8 BLACK-COWLED ORIOLE *Icterus dominicensis*   **Page 439**
20–22 cm (8–8.5"). **8a Adult**: Black overall; distinctive yellow shoulder patch, rump and undertail-coverts extending to lower breast in Bahamas birds. (Puerto Rico race illustrated.) **8b Immature**: Upperparts mainly olive; underparts dull yellow; wings black; throat sometimes black or reddish-brown.

9 ST LUCIA ORIOLE *Icterus laudabilis*   **Page 440**
20–22 cm (8–8.5"). St Lucia. **9a Adult Male**: All black; rich orange or orange-yellow lower back, rump, belly and shoulder patch. See also Plate 86. **Female**: (Not illustrated.) Orange and yellow pattern duller. **9b Immature**: Mostly greenish; blackish throat.

10 TAWNY-SHOULDERED BLACKBIRD *Agelaius humeralis*   **Page 435**
19–22 cm (7.5–8.5"). Cuba and Haiti. **10a Adult**: Black overall; tawny shoulder patch, most conspicuous when flying. (Cuba race illustrated.) **10b Immature**: Shoulder patch smaller.

11 MONTSERRAT ORIOLE *Icterus oberi*   **Page 440**
20–22 cm (8–8.5"). Montserrat. See also Plate 72. **11a Adult Male**: Upperparts mostly black; lower back, rump, shoulder, lower breast, belly and abdomen yellowish. **11b Adult Female**: Upperparts mostly yellowish-green; underparts bright yellow. **Immature**: (Not illustrated.) Duller.

PLATE 70: ORIOLES AND ALLIES (EMBERIZIDS) 2

1 EASTERN MEADOWLARK *Sturnella magna* **Page 436**
23 cm (9"). Short tail, edged with white; yellow underparts; conspicuous black V on breast. Crown and upperparts striped. Cuba. **1a Breeding Adult**: Breast band pronounced. **1b Non-breeding Adult**: Breast band less distinct.

2 BOBOLINK *Dolichonyx oryzivorus* **Page 433**
18.5 cm (7.25"). **2a Non-breeding Adult**: Central buff crown stripe and throat; sides and abdomen streaked; pointed tail. **2b Breeding Male**: Black below; buff hindneck; white wing patches and lower back.

3 SHINY COWBIRD *Molothrus bonariensis* **Page 438**
18–20 cm (7–8"). Medium size. Conical bill. **3a Adult Male**: Glossy black, purplish sheen. **3b Adult Female**: Drab grayish-brown upperparts; lighter brown underparts.

4 BROWN-HEADED COWBIRD *Molothrus ater* **Page 439**
16.5 cm (6.5"). **4a Male**: Black body, metallic greenish sheen; brown head. **4b Female**: Brownish-gray.

5 CARIB GRACKLE *Quiscalus lugubris* **Page 438**
24–28 cm (9.5–11"). **5a Adult Male**: Black ovarall; violet, green or steel-blue sheen; iris yellowish-white; tail long, V-shaped. **5b Adult Female**: Smaller; varying amounts of glossy black; tail shorter, less V-shaped.

6 JAMAICAN BLACKBIRD *Nesopsar nigerrimus* **Page 436**
18 cm (7"). Black overall; slender pointed bill; tail short. Jamaica. See also Plate 84.

7 RED-SHOULDERED BLACKBIRD *Agelaius assimilis* **Page 434**
19–23 (7.5–9"). Cuba. **7a Male**: Scarlet shoulder patch edged yellowish. Identical to male Red-winged Blackbird. See also Plate 80. **7b Female**: Entirely black; smaller than male. **Immature Male**: (Not illustrated.) Shoulder patch reddish-brown.

8 RED-WINGED BLACKBIRD *Agelaius phoeniceus* **Page 434**
19–23 (7.5–9"). Bahamas. **8a Male**: Scarlet shoulder patch edged yellowish. Identical to male Red-shouldered Blackbird. **8b Female**: Brown above; buffy below; heavily streaked dark brown; light buffy line above eye.

9 CUBAN BLACKBIRD *Dives atroviolacea* **Page 437**
25–28 cm (10–11"). Black plumage, glossy purplish iridescence; dark iris; square tail. Bill and feet black. Cuba. See also Plate 80.

10 GREATER ANTILLEAN GRACKLE *Quiscalus niger* **Page 437**
25–30 cm (10–12"). Fairly large size. Long tail; conical, pointed bill. **Adult Male**: Glossy metallic-blue to violet-black; deep V-shaped tail; yellow iris. **Adult Female**: (Not illustrated.) Duller than male; tail with smaller V. **Immature**: (Not illustrated.) Plumage dull brownish-black; tail flat; dark iris.

11 YELLOW-HEADED BLACKBIRD *Xanthocephalus xanthocephalus* **Page 437**
21–28 cm (8–11"). **11a Non-breeding Adult Male**: Black body; orange-yellow hood; white wing patch. **11b Non-breeding Adult Female**: Upperparts grayish-brown; yellowish eyebrow stripe, throat, breast and below cheek.

PLATE 71: MARTINIQUE ORIOLE

MARTINIQUE ORIOLE *Icterus bonana*   **Page 441**
18–21 cm (7–8″). Martinique. See also Plate 69.

PLATE 72: MONTSERRAT ORIOLE

MONTSERRAT ORIOLE *Icterus oberi*   **Page 440**
20–22 cm (8–8.5″). Montserrat. See also Plate 69.

PLATE 73: FINCH-LIKE EMBERIZIDS 1

1 CUBAN GRASSQUIT *Tiaris canora*   **Page 425**
11.5 cm (4.5"). Small size. Conspicuous yellow crescent divides face and breast. Upperparts olive. Cuba.
1a Male: Face and breast black. See also Plate 80.
1b Female: Yellow less marked; face dark reddish-brown.

2 YELLOW-SHOULDERED GRASSQUIT *Loxipasser anoxanthus*   **Page 426**
10 cm (4"). Small size. Jamaica.
2a Adult Male: Two-toned: black head and underparts; yellowish wings and back. Undertail-coverts reddish-brown. See also Plate 84.
2b Adult Female: Gray below; yellowish-green above. Yellow patch on bend of wing. Undertail-coverts pale reddish-brown.

3 YELLOW-FACED GRASSQUIT *Tiaris olivacea*   **Page 425**
11.5 cm (4.5").
3a Male: Yellow throat and eyebrow stripe; black breast. (Puerto Rico race illustrated.)
3b Female and Immature: Yellowish-olive plumage; faint yellowish facial markings.

4 BLACK-FACED GRASSQUIT *Tiaris bicolor*   **Page 426**
11.5 cm (4.5").
4a Male: Black head and underparts.
4b Female and Immature: Drab brownish-olive plumage.

5 YELLOW-BELLIED SEEDEATER *Sporophila nigricollis*   **Page 424**
10.5 cm (4.5"). Grenada and the Grenadines.
5a Adult Male: Black hood; underparts yellowish-white; bill pale blue-gray.
5b Female and Immature: Upperparts olive-brown; underparts yellowish-buff; bill dark.

6 RED SISKIN *Carduelis cucullata*   **Page 443**
10 cm (4"). Puerto Rico.
6a Male: Black hood; orange-red coloration.
6b Female: Gray upperparts; light gray underparts; orange rump, wing markings and wash on breast.

7 ANTILLEAN SISKIN *Carduelis dominicensis*   **Page 444**
11 cm (4.25"). Small size. Chunky; light yellow bill. Hispaniola.
7a Male: Black head; yellowish body; tail black with 2 yellow patches. See also Plate 82.
7b Female: Olive-green above; yellowish-whitish below, streaked pale gray; 2 yellow wingbars; pale yellowish rump.

8 AMERICAN GOLDFINCH *Carduelis tristis*   **Page 444**
11–12 cm (4.25–4.75").
Non-breeding Adult and Immature: Brownish or grayish above; whitish below and on rump; black wings with white bars; often yellowish on face.
8a Non-breeding Male.
8b Non-breeding Female.
8c Breeding Male: Bright yellow overall; black cap, wings and tail.
Breeding female: (Not illustrated.) Olive above; yellowish below; black wings; white wingbars and rump.

KRISTIN WILLIAMS

PLATE 74: FINCH-LIKE EMBERIZIDS 2

1 GRASSLAND YELLOW-FINCH *Sicalis luteola*   **Page 429**
12 cm (4.75").
1a Adult Male: Upperparts pale yellow, heavily streaked blackish; underparts and rump yellow.
Female: (Not illustrated.) Duller than male.
1b Immature: Blackish streaks on breast.

2 SAFFRON FINCH *Sicalis flaveola*   **Page 429**
14 cm (5.5"). Jamaica and Puerto Rico. **Adult**: Medium size; yellow plumage; orange crown.
2a Male: Crown bright orange.
Female: (Not illustrated.) Crown yellowish-orange.
2b Immature: Yellowish breast band.

3 HOUSE SPARROW *Passer domesticus*   **Page 445**
15 cm (5.75").
3a Male: Black bib; gray crown; pale cheek.
3b Female and Immature: Brown upperparts, streaked black; buff-colored eyebrow stripe and underparts.

4 YELLOW-FRONTED CANARY *Serinus mozambicus*   **Page 444**
11.5 cm (4.5"). Yellowish breast, rump and eyebrow stripe; thick bill; dark mustache stripe. Puerto Rico.

5 VILLAGE WEAVER *Ploceus cucullatus*   **Page 445**
17 cm (6.75"). Chunky; heavy bill. Hispaniola and Martinique.
5a Male: Orange-yellow overall; black hood; red iris.
5b Female: Yellowish-green face and breast; yellow wingbars.

6 DICKCISSEL *Spiza americana*   **Page 423**
15–18 cm (5.75–7"). Yellowish eyebrow stripe and breast; reddish-brown patch at bend of wing.
6a Female and Non-breeding Male: Throat patch reduced or absent.
6b Breeding Male: Black throat patch.

7 ZAPATA SPARROW *Torreornis inexpectata*   **Page 429**
16.5 cm (6.5"). Plump; yellow underparts; white throat; dark mustache stripe. Dark reddish-brown crown; upperparts olive-gray. Wings short, rounded. Cuba. See also Plate 80.
Immature: (Not illustrated.) Darker above; lacks dark reddish-brown crown.

8 ROSE-BREASTED GROSBEAK *Pheucticus ludovicianus*   **Page 422**
19–20 cm (7.5–8").
8a Male: Black head and back; pinkish-red breast.
8b Female: Large size. White crown stripes; streaked underparts; heavy bill.

9 WHITE-WINGED CROSSBILL *Loxia leucoptera*   **Page 443**
15 cm (5.75"). Bill tips crossed; 2 broad white bars on black wings. Hispaniola.
9a Adult Male: Pale red.
9b Adult Female: Yellowish rump and breast, the latter finely streaked.

10 LESSER ANTILLEAN SALTATOR *Saltator albicollis*   **Page 422**
22 cm (8.5").
Adult: Upperparts dull green; whitish underparts, streaked olive-green. Whitish eyebrow stripe. Bill black with orange-white tip; heavy black mustache streaks.

KRISTIN WILLIAMS 1995

PLATE 75: FINCH-LIKE EMBERIZIDS 3

1 PUERTO RICAN BULLFINCH *Loxigilla portoricensis*　　　　**Page 427**
　16.5–19 cm (6.5–7.5"). Puerto Rico.
　1a Adult: Black body; reddish-brown crown, throat and undertail-coverts. See also Plate 85.
　1b Immature: Dark olive-green with reddish-brown undertail-coverts.

2 CUBAN BULLFINCH *Melopyrrha nigra*　　　　**Page 424**
　14–15 cm (5.5–5.75"). Small size. Thick, curved bill. White band on wing edge.
　2a Male: Black. Cuban race illustrated.
　2b Female: Variable. Grand Cayman race illustrated.

3 ST LUCIA BLACK FINCH *Melanospiza richardsoni*　　　　**Page 428**
　13–14 cm (5–5.5"). Pink legs and feet. Bobs tail. St Lucia.
　3a Adult Male: Plumage entirely black. See also Plate 86.
　3b Female and Immature: Contrasting gray crown, brown back; buffy below. See also Plate 86.

4 GREATER ANTILLEAN BULLFINCH *Loxigilla violacea*　　　　**Page 427**
　15–18 cm (5.75–7"). Chunky; thick bill. Orange-red eyebrow stripe, throat and undertail-coverts.
　4a Adult Male: Black overall. (Jamaica race illustrated.)
　Adult Female: (Not illustrated.) Duller black.
　4b Immature: Similar to adult. Olive-brown.

5 LESSER ANTILLEAN BULLFINCH *Loxigilla noctis*　　　　**Page 428**
　14–15.5 cm (5.5–6").
　Male (except Barbados): All black; red on chin, throat and in front of eye. Some races have red undertail-coverts.
　5a Guadeloupe — Dominica race.
　5b St Lucia race.
　5c Female, Barbados Male, and Immature: Brownish-olive above; gray below; orange undertail-coverts.

6 BLUE-BLACK GRASSQUIT *Volatinia jacarina*　　　　**Page 424**
　11 cm (4.25"). Grenada.
　6a Adult Male: Glossy blue-black; wingpits sometimes white.
　6b Adult Female: Upperparts olive-brown; underparts yellowish-buff; breast and sides heavily streaked with gray.

7 INDIGO BUNTING *Passerina cyanea*　　　　**Page 423**
　14 cm (5.5").
　Non-breeding Male: (Not illustrated.) Brown; traces of blue on wings and tail.
　7a Female: Dull brown; light breast stripes and wingbars.
　7b Breeding Male: Blue plumage.

8 BLUE GROSBEAK *Guiraca caerulea*　　　　**Page 422**
　16.5–19 cm (6.5–7.5"). Reddish-brown wingbars.
　8a Male: Blue plumage.
　8b Female: Large size. Brown plumage; heavy bill.

9 PAINTED BUNTING *Passerina ciris*　　　　**Page 423**
　13 cm (5").
　9a Male: Blue head; red underparts; green back.
　9b Adult Female and Young Male: Green above; yellowish-green below.
　Immature: (Not illustrated.) Duller than adult female; hints of green.

PLATE 76: FINCH-LIKE EMBERIZIDS 4

1 PIN-TAILED WHYDAH *Vidua macroura*   **Page 450**
Male with tail plumes: 30–33 cm (12–13"); female and non-breeding male: 11.5 cm (4.5"). Puerto Rico.
1a Breeding Male: Long tail; black and white coloration; red bill.
1b Female and Non-breeding Male: Mottled reddish-brown above; red bill; black and white facial stripes. **Immature**: (Not illustrated.) Grayish-brown above; buff-colored eyebrow stripe; bill black, pink base.

2 YELLOW-CROWNED BISHOP *Euplectes afer*   **Page 446**
11.5–12.5 cm (4.5–5"). Puerto Rico and Jamaica. **2a Breeding Male**: Yellow and black plumage.
2b Female and Non-breeding Male: Mottled brown; yellowish eyebrow stripe contrasts with dark brown eyeline; finely striped crown and breast.

3 ORANGE BISHOP *Euplectes franciscanus*   **Page 446**
12.5 cm (5"). **3a Breeding Male**: Orangish-red and black plumage.
3b Female and Non-breeding Male: Mottled brown; buff-colored eyebrow stripe; underparts, crown and breast finely striped. See also Plate 77.

4 RED AVADAVAT *Amandava amandava*   **Page 448**
10 cm (4"). **4a Breeding Male**: Deep red overall; white spots.
4b Adult Female and Non-breeding Male: Brown above; paler below; red uppertail-coverts and bill; white spots on wings; black eyeline. **4c Immature**: Wing spots buff-colored; lacks red.

5 BLACK-RUMPED WAXBILL *Estrilda troglodytes*   **Page 447**
10 cm (4"). Puerto Rico and Guadeloupe. **5a Adult**: Red bill and eyeline. **5b Immature**: Pale pinkish bill; lacks red eyeline.

6 WARBLING SILVERBILL *Lonchura malabarica*   **Page 448**
11.5 cm (4.5"). Light brown upperparts; white underparts and rump; dark tail. Puerto Rico.

7 NUTMEG MANNIKIN *Lonchura punctulata*   **Page 449**
11.5 cm (4.5"). **7a Adult**: Cinnamon hood; scalloped underparts. **7b Immature**: Cinnamon-colored above; paler below; lacks adult markings.

8 ORANGE-CHEEKED WAXBILL *Estrilda melpoda*   **Page 447**
10 cm (4"). Puerto Rico. **8a Adult**: Reddish bill and uppertail-coverts; orange cheek patch. **8b Immature**: Pale pinkish bill; lacks orange cheek.

9 BRONZE MANNIKIN *Lonchura cucullata*   **Page 448**
10 cm (4"). Puerto Rico. **9a Adult**: Black hood; grayish-brown back; white belly; flank marks.
9b Immature: Grayish-brown back; hood faint or lacking; lacks other adult markings.

10 JAVA SPARROW *Padda oryzivora*   **Page 450**
15–16.5 cm (5.75–6.5"). Puerto Rico. **10a Adult**: Gray plumage; broad pinkish-red bill; white cheek; black crown. **10b Immature**: Duller bill; buff-colored cheek; brownish body.

11 CHESTNUT MANNIKIN *Lonchura malacca*   **Page 449**
11.5 cm (4.5"). **Adult**: Black hood; cinnamon-colored back. Underparts variable: Either white with black belly or pale brown with black belly. **11a** White underparts race. **11a** Brown underparts race.
11c Immature: Cinnamon-brown above; buffy below.

PLATE 77: NEW WORLD SPARROWS (EMBERIZIDS), JUNCOS AND PIPITS

1 WHITE-CROWNED SPARROW *Zonotrichia leucophrys*   **Page 433**
18 cm (7").
1a Adult: Black and white striped crown; gray underparts.
1b Immature: Crown stripes brown and buff.

2 RUFOUS-COLLARED SPARROW *Zonotrichia capensis*   **Page 432**
15–16.5 cm (5.75–6.5").
2a Adult: Black neck band; reddish-brown hindneck; gray crown with black stripes. Often displays slight crest.
2b Immature: Duller; spotted below; lacks black or reddish-brown markings.

3 LARK SPARROW *Chondestes grammacus*   **Page 431**
15 cm (5.75").
Adult: Bold head and facial pattern; white tail corners; black breast spot.
Immature: (Not illustrated.) Head pattern mostly brown and buff; streaked underparts; tail corners white.

4 CLAY-COLORED SPARROW *Spizella pallida*   **Page 430**
12–13.5 cm (4.75–5.25").
Adult: Upperparts buff-brown; back streaked with black; rump brownish or buffy; white median crown stripe; brown check patch outlined by dark thin lines and pale lores; underparts pale buffy-gray.
Immature: (Not illustrated.) Breast finely streaked; head pattern less defined.

5 CHIPPING SPARROW *Spizella passerina*   **Page 430**
12.5–14.5 cm (5–5.75").
5a Non-breeding Adult and Immature: Crown brown (immature) or reddish-brown (adult) streaked with black; eyeline dark.
5b Breeding Adult: Bright reddish-brown crown; rump gray; gray cheek; white eyebrow stripe; black eyeline to base of black bill; underparts grayish-white.

6 LINCOLN'S SPARROW *Melospiza lincolnii*   **Page 432**
13.5–15 cm (5.25–5.75").
Adult: Upperparts grayish-olive, blackish streaks; crown brown, streaked black. Eyebrow stripe, ear patch and neck sides light gray; tail feathers narrow and pointed, outer feathers shortest.
Immature: (Not illustrated.) Eyebrow stripe buffy-white.

7 ORANGE BISHOP *Euplectes franciscanus*   **Page 446**
12.5 cm (5").
Female and Non-breeding Male: Mottled brown; buff-colored eyebrow stripe; underparts, crown, and breast finely striped. See also Plate 76.

8 GRASSHOPPER SPARROW *Ammodramus savannarum*   **Page 431**
12.5 cm (5").
8a Adult: Golden mark on eyebrow stripe; central whitish crown stripe.
8b Immature: Paler eyebrow mark; fine streaking on breast and flanks. (Hispaniola race illustrated.)

9 AMERICAN PIPIT *Anthus spinoletta*   **Page 385**
16.5 cm (6.5"). Terrestrial; thin-billed. Bobs long tail. Outer tail feathers white.
Non-breeding Adult: Buffy eyebrow stripe; blackish stripes concentrated on breast.

10 DARK-EYED JUNCO *Junco hyemalis*   **Page 433**
16 cm (6.25"). Blackish-gray; white belly and outer tail feathers; pink bill.

11 SAVANNAH SPARROW *Passerculus sandwichensis*   **Page 431**
15–19 cm (5.75–7.5"). Slender; underparts heavily streaked brown. Yellowish eyebrow stripe, sometimes buff-colored. Pale central crown stripe; dark mustache stripe.

KRISTIN WILLIAMS 1991

PLATE 78: CASUALLY OCCURRING SPECIES

1 NORTHERN GANNET *Sula bassanus*   **Page 223**
100 cm (40"). **1a Immature**: Gray upperparts; whitish flecks on wings and mantle; paler underparts.
Over 3–4 years, plumage whitens to that of adult. **1b Adult**: White; tan crown; black wing tips.

2 WHITE-WINGED TERN *Chlidonias leucopterus*   **Page 295**
24 cm (9.5"). Small size. Slightly notched tail. **Non-breeding**: Black earspot and hindcrown; white
rump; lacks dark neck mark.

3 WHISKERED TERN *Chlidonias hybridus*   **Page 294**
25 cm (10"). Small size. Slightly notched tail. **Non-breeding**: Pale gray above; black in primaries;
black hindcrown extending to eye; red legs.

4 FRANKLIN'S GULL *Larus pipixcan*   **Page 287**
37 cm (14.5"). **First Year**: White breast and underparts; gray back; partial blackish hood; white forehead; narrow black tail band.

5 BLACK NODDY *Anous minutus*   **Page 296**
34 cm (13.5"). Appears entirely blackish-brown; white on crown; long slender bill.

6 CURLEW SANDPIPER *Calidris ferruginea*   **Page 280**
18–23 cm (7–9"). Bill slightly down-curved throughout length; rump white.
Non-breeding Adult: Upperparts brownish-gray; underparts white.

7 PACIFIC GOLDEN-PLOVER *Pluvialis fulva*   **Page 267**
24 cm (9.5"). Fairly large, slender, long-legged. **Non-breeding Adult**: Golden cast to back, face, and
eyebrow stripe.

8 GRAY HERON *Ardea cinerea*   **Page 229**
90–98 cm (35–38"). Large size. Gray overall; white thighs.

9 COMMON GREENSHANK *Tringa nebularia*   **Page 272**
32 cm (12.5"). **Non-breeding**: Large size. Greenish or yellowish legs; slightly upturned bill, thicker
at base.

10 WOOD SANDPIPER *Tringa glareola*   **Page 273**
20 cm (8"). Medium size. White rump; pale yellow or greenish-yellow legs; white eyebrow stripe.

11 TOWNSEND'S WARBLER *Dendroica townsendi*   **Page 399**
13 cm (5"). Dark cheek, ringed with yellow. **Adult Male**: Black cheek, chin, throat and side streaks.
Adult Female: Slightly duller. Chin and throat yellow.

12 ORINOCO GOOSE *Neochen jubata*   **Page 239**
61–67 cm (24–26.5"). Large size. Pale gray head and neck; reddish-brown body; dark wings; white
speculum.

13 SWAMP SPARROW *Melospiza georgiana*   **Page 432**
15 cm (5.75"). **Non-breeding Adult**: Reddish-brown patches on wing-coverts and primaries; gray
central crown stripe, eyebrow stripe, cheek patch and neck sides; blackish mustache mark; white
throat.

14 NORTHERN WHEATEAR *Oenanthe oenanthe*   **Page 374**
15 cm (6"). White rump and tail patches; flicks and fans tail.
14a Breeding male: Black ear patch.
14b Female and non-breeding male: Pale reddish-brown below, white eyebrow stripe.

Note: Illustrations not all to scale.

TDP 97

PLATE 79: CUBAN ENDEMICS 1

Note: Illustrations not all to scale.

PLATE 80: CUBAN ENDEMICS 2

Note: Illustrations not all to scale.

TDP '95

PLATE 81: HISPANIOLAN ENDEMICS 1

Note: Illustrations not all to scale.

KRISTIN WILLIAMS 1992

PLATE 82: HISPANIOLAN ENDEMICS 2

Note: Illustrations not all to scale.

KRISTIN WILLIAMS

PLATE 83: JAMAICAN ENDEMICS 1

Note: Illustrations not all to scale.

KRISTIN WILLIAMS

PLATE 84: JAMAICAN ENDEMICS 2

Note: Illustrations not all to scale.

PLATE 85: PUERTO RICAN ENDEMICS (INCLUDING THE VIRGIN ISLANDS)

Note: Illustrations not all to scale.

PLATE 86: OTHER ENDEMICS

1 **BAHAMA YELLOWTHROAT** *Geothlypis rostrata*　　　　**Page 411**
　15 cm (5.75″). **1a Male. 1b Female.** (Grand Bahama – Abaco race.) Bahamas. See also Plates 62, 66.

2 **ST ANDREW VIREO** *Vireo caribaeus*　　　　**Page 388**
　12.5 cm (5″). San Andrés. See also Plate 59.

3 **SEMPER'S WARBLER** *Leucopeza semperi*　　　　**Page 413**
　14.5 cm (5.75″). St Lucia. See also Plate 64.

4 **ST LUCIA PEWEE** *Contopus oberi*　　　　**Page 355**
　15 cm (5.75″). St Lucia. See also Plate 53.

5 **WHISTLING WARBLER** *Catharopeza bishopi*　　　　**Page 406**
　14.5 cm (5.75″). St Vincent. See also Plate 64.

6 **BRACE'S HUMMINGBIRD** *Chlorostilbon bracei* (Extinct)　　　　**Page 336**
　9.5 cm (3.75″). New Providence, Bahamas.

7 **ST LUCIA BLACK FINCH** *Melanospiza richardsoni*　　　　**Page 428**
　13–14 cm (5–5.5″). **7a Male**. **7b Female**. St Lucia. See also Plate 75.

8 **RED-NECKED PARROT** *Amazona arausiaca*　　　　**Page 314**
　33–36 cm (13–14″). Dominica. See also Plate 30.

9 **ST LUCIA ORIOLE** *Icterus laudabilis*　　　　**Page 440**
　20–22 cm (8–8.5″). St Lucia. See also Plate 69.

Note: Illustrations not all to scale.

KRISTIN WILLIAMS 1996

LOONS: FAMILY GAVIIDAE

The loons are an ancient family of highly aquatic birds. The elongate bodies are specialized for an aquatic life, with their legs placed well to the rear so that they can only walk with difficulty on land. In these ways loons resemble the grebes, but loons are larger and bulkier, have thicker necks and webbed feet. They have very short tails, with moderately long necks and pointed bills, which they use to seize fish and other animals in underwater pursuit. They can dive as deep as 9 m (30') and stay submerged for up to two minutes.

COMMON LOON *Gavia immer*   Plate 18
Local Name: Somormujo (Cuba)

Identification: 70–100 cm (27–40"). A large waterbird, about the size of a goose. *Bill long, straight, broad and grayish.* **Non-breeding**: Upperparts dark brown, paler on the back; underparts grayish-white. **Breeding**: Dark head with a greenish gloss; upperparts with large white flecks. **Flight**: Head is held lower than the body, and legs extend beyond the tail. Runs over the water to take off. **Similar species**: Immature cormorants have a similar color pattern to the non-breeding Common Loon, but have a more slender bill with a hooked tip.
Voice: A repeated cackle *ha-ha-ha-ha*, with variations in tone.
Status and Range: A very rare migrant on Cuba where recorded from late November through December. Primarily recorded off the north coast. Also occurs in North America, Greenland and Western Europe.
Comments: Generally solitary. Usually in deep, open water. Dives for fish and can remain beneath the surface for substantial periods. When alarmed it either gradually submerges its body underwater or dives rapidly, not to reappear until it has swam a great distance away.
Habitat: Fresh- and saltwater aquatic habitats, mainly along coasts.

GREBES: FAMILY PODICIPEDIDAE

Unlike ducks, grebes have pointed bills, extremely short tails and flattened lobes on each toe rather than webbing that connects the toes. Grebes are more adept swimmers than most ducks, being able to dive underwater in a flash, gradually sink out of sight, or submerge until only the head remains above the surface. Grebes in the region are very rarely seen to fly, which has led to the local belief that the birds are flightless. Though they can fly, they must run some distance over the water before taking off; on land they cannot walk, but must push themselves along on their breasts. The downy young are sometimes carried on a parent's back and may remain there while the adult dives.

LEAST GREBE *Tachybaptus dominicus*   Plate 18
Local Names: Duck-and-Teal (Jamaica); Diving Dapper (VI); Diver (Jamaica, VI); Zaramagullón Chico (Cuba); Tigua (DR, PR); Ti Plonjon, Grèbe (Haiti)

Identification: 23–26 cm (9–10"). Its *small size, blackish coloration, thin bill* and *yellow-orange iris* are diagnostic. The *white wing patch* is a good field mark, but is not always visible.
Voice: A rising, reed-like *week*.
Status and Range: A common year-round resident in the Bahamas, Cuba and Jamaica, it is decidedly uncommon and local on Hispaniola and Puerto Rico and rare in the Virgin Islands and Montserrat. This grebe is a rare non-breeding wanderer to the Cayman Islands. A vagrant on Dominica. Also from south-central United States (Texas) through South America.
Comments: Generally solitary or in small family groups. Often stays among vegetation where extremely difficult to observe. When alarmed, it dives rapidly and only re-emerges among the cover of dense vegetation.

Habitat: Primarily freshwater cattail swamps and small ponds with water plants for cover. Also small temporary ponds formed after heavy rains.
Nesting: A floating nest is made among emergent vegetation. Eggs (1–7) whitish. Breeds through most of the year, but peaks from April to May and again from September to November.

PIED-BILLED GREBE *Podilymbus podiceps*   Plate 18
Local Names: Duck-and-Teal (Jamaica); Diving Dapper (VI); Diver (Cl, Grenada, St V, VI); Zara-magullón Grande (Cuba); Zaramagullón (DR); Zaramago (PR); Plonjon Fran, Grand Plongeon (Haiti); Dikbekfuut (St M); Grèbe à Bec Bigarré, Plongeon (Guad, Mart, St L)

Identification: 30–38 cm (12–15"). Note the *conical bill* of this grayish-brown duck-like bird. ***Breeding adult***: Black throat; bill with a black band. ***Non-breeding adult***: White throat; bill lacks the black band. ***Immature***: Head mottled with brown and white markings. ***Flight***: Runs over the water to take off.
Voice: A harsh cackle breaking into a distinctive *kowp, kowp, kowp*, slowing at the end.
Status and Range: Occurs throughout the West Indies as a common year-round resident on the larger islands, less common on medium-sized islands, and rare or absent from the smallest ones, due to scarcity of appropriate breeding habitat. In the southern Lesser Antilles, this grebe is a rare non-breeding resident from October to March, though it may breed on Barbados. Throughout the Western Hemisphere.
Comments: The typical grebe of West Indian ponds and lagoons. Usually solitary or in small family groups, but sometimes in loose aggregations of up to 100 individuals. Often frequents open water. If alarmed, it dives instantly and swims beneath the surface to the protection of dense aquatic vegetation.
Habitat: Primarily fresh water, but also brackish and hypersaline lagoons where fresh water is absent.
Nesting: A floating nest is constructed among emergent vegetation. Eggs (2–6) whitish. Breeds throughout the year, but primarily from March to July.

SHEARWATERS AND PETRELS: FAMILY PROCELLARIIDAE

Shearwaters are highly pelagic species, rarely coming within sight of land except to breed. Their typical pattern of flight is gliding on long, narrow wings over the waves and in the troughs, only periodically making a short series of flaps. It is this stiff-winged flight, low over the sea's surface, from which the family name is derived and which greatly aids in identification. These birds feed on small fish, squid and other organisms on or near the surface of the ocean and are equipped with special salt glands which enable them to drink salt water. In fact, shearwaters and storm-petrels are so adapted to the sea that they are obligate salt-water drinkers and apparently will die of thirst if only fresh water is available to them.

   Even during the breeding season shearwaters are not readily observed, for they nest colonially on remote islets and mountain cliffs, usually in burrows, and are only active about the nest after dark. At night the wailing cries of these birds are conspicuous and the musty odor of the nesting areas often remains long after the birds have gone. Shearwaters in the region are burrow-nesters and have legs incapable of supporting their bodies. On the ground they use their wings to propel them forward on their breasts.

BLACK-CAPPED PETREL *Pterodroma hasitata*   Plate 2
Local Names: Pampero de las Brujas (Cuba); Diablotín (DR, PR, Dominica, Guad, Mart); Chouanlasèl, Pétrel, Canard de Montagne (Haiti); Pétrel Diablotin (Guad, Mart)

Identification: 35–40 cm (14–16"). The upperparts appear black except for *white patches on the rump, hindneck and forehead*. The extent of white is variable. ***Flight***: Note the *black front-edge of the underwing*. ***Similar species***: Whiter above, especially on the forehead and rump, its faster wing-beats and high arching glides distinguish it from Greater Shearwater. Also, the Petrel's mantle is blacker, heightening the contrast with its more extensive white markings. The underwing also has a

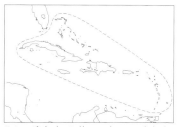

black leading edge which is absent in Greater Shearwater. In flight, the wrist is more noticeably bent than in shearwaters and the flight is more erratic.

Voice: Heard only at night around the nesting colony. Issues three distinct calls which are repeated often: (1) a drawn out *aaa-aw, eek*; (2) a drawn out *ooow, eek*; and (3) yelps like a hurt puppy (Wingate).

Status and Range: A rare and very local breeding resident in the West Indies, the only region where it is known to breed. The only significant breeding population is in southeastern Haiti (Massif de la Selle and Massif de la Hotte). A few pairs breed in mountains of the Dominican Republic (Sierra de Baoruco) and Dominica. Nested commonly on Guadeloupe into the 19th century, but long-believed extirpated. May also have nested on Martinique. Recently, Black-capped Petrels have been seen off the coast and inland on Dominica, suggesting it may still nest there. Occurs widely in the West Indies away from its breeding grounds. It is critically endangered. Populations are greatly diminished due to introduced predators and harvesting by humans. Likely to be seen only from a boat far offshore over deep water or at its remote breeding colonies. Also throughout the Gulf of Mexico, and off southeastern North America and northeastern South America.

Comments: This seabird only comes to land under the cover of darkness to breed among remote cliffs. In earlier times, fires were lit on the cliff-tops above a breeding colony on foggy, moonless nights. The disoriented petrels would crash into and around the fire whereupon they would be gathered up. Non-breeding birds occur in numbers in the Gulf Stream off the southeastern coast of the United States primarily from April to October. These birds may migrate via the Antilles Current east of the Bahamas. It has been suggested that breeding petrels may actually commute to North Carolina waters to feed. Believed to feed on squid and fish.

Habitat: Well out at sea, except when attending its nest.

Nesting: The nest is in a crevice or burrow in a steep, forested mountain cliff. On Hispaniola, they generally nest between 1500 m (5000') and 2000 m (6600'). Adults enter and leave the nest only at night and call actively while approaching the nesting cliffs. Egg (1) white. Breeds from early November to mid-May with a peak from December through February.

JAMAICAN PETREL   *Pterodroma caribbaea*   **Plates 2, 83**
Local Names: Blue Mountain Duck, Diablotín

Identification: 35–46 cm (14–18"). *Dark gray overall*, except for *white rump and uppertail-coverts*; legs and feet pinkish-white.

Status and Range: Formerly Jamaica but believed extinct. Endemic to Jamaica where it was known from the Blue and John Crow Mountains and was considered plentiful locally. Black petrels reported from Dominica may have pertained to this species. Apparently extinct as a result of predation by introduced mongoose and exploitation by humans, who harvested the chicks for food. As early as 1891, empty petrel burrows were widely found to contain mongoose.

Comments: Formerly considered a dark race (*Pterodroma hasitata caribbaea*) of Black-capped Petrel. Because of the nocturnal habits of this bird and its tendency to nest among inaccessible cliffs, the possibility remains that a small population persists in a remote part of the John Crow Mountains.

Habitat: Bred in the higher elevations of the Blue Mountains. Otherwise assumed to have ranged far offshore.

Nesting: Excavated burrows in the soil on mountain cliffs. Adults entered and left the nest only at night. Egg (1) white. It is believed that breeding occurred from October to May.

CORY'S SHEARWATER   *Calonectris diomedea*   **Plate 2**

Identification: 46–53 cm (18–21"). A large shearwater often appearing featureless at a distance. Distinguished by its *pale yellowish bill, white uppertail-coverts* which are variable in extent, and the *mottled coloration of the cheek and neck* which blend the brownish-gray of the upperparts with the whitish underparts. **Flight**: Leisurely on broad, loosely held wings, noticeably angled at the wrist. **Similar species**: The slightly smaller Greater Shearwater has a dark bill, sharply-defined black cap,

more crisply defined white uppertail-coverts and more purposeful flight. For additional guidance on distinguishing these species refer to: Bird, D. 1994. The field characters of distant Great and Cory's Shearwaters. *Birding World* 7(8): 279–282.

Status and Range: An uncommon migrant among the Bahamas primarily in May and June, but some birds occur until September. Also recorded off Cuba, Antigua, Guadeloupe, Martinique and Barbados. Its status in the West Indies is unclear due to the bird ranging far out at sea, but the species undoubtedly occurs more frequently than previously thought and likely transits the waters off virtually all of the islands. Also occurs through much of the North Atlantic, the Mediterranean Sea, off the west and south coasts of Africa, and New Zealand.

Habitat: Deep offshore waters.

GREATER SHEARWATER *Puffinus gravis*   Plate 2

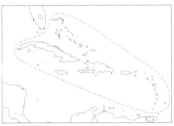

Identification: 48 cm (19"). One of the two largest shearwaters in the West Indies, it has noticeable white bands on the hindneck and rump which contrast with the distinctive black cap and dark grayish-brown upperparts. *Similar species*: Generally similar to Black-capped Petrel, but in Greater Shearwater the white of the upperparts is much reduced on the hindneck and rump and is absent on the forehead. Black-capped Petrel's mantle is blacker, increasing the contrast with its whiter upperparts. Greater Shearwater's wingbeats are much slower than those of Manx and Audubon's Shearwaters or Black-capped Petrel. See also Cory's Shearwater.

Status and Range: An uncommon non-breeding resident among the Bahamas and off Puerto Rico primarily from May to July, but could occur in any month. Likely rare through the rest of the West Indies during these same months, though under-represented in records due to its occurrence far offshore. Throughout the Atlantic Ocean.

Comments: This shearwater nests only among the small Tristan de Cunha Islands in the South Atlantic from November to April. It then migrates up the western Atlantic past the West Indies, later returning to its nesting islands primarily via the eastern Atlantic. Greater Shearwaters not yet mature enough to breed appear to be widely dispersed throughout the Atlantic Ocean.

Habitat: Well out at sea.

SOOTY SHEARWATER *Puffinus griseus*   Plate 2

Identification: 40–46 cm (16–18"). Medium-sized, blackish overall with whitish underwings. Wings long and narrow. The only all-dark shearwater routinely occurring in the Atlantic. *Flight*: Swift and direct, with rapid flapping ascents and long glides usually close to the water.

Status and Range: Apparently a rare migrant in the West Indies primarily from late May to July, but some birds occur until November. It might be expected in any month and off any island. Reported from the Bahamas, Cuba (off the northwest coast), Jamaica, Puerto Rico, Martinique, St Lucia and Barbados. The scarcity of records result from the bird occurring far offshore. Widespread throughout the oceans of the world.

Comments: Sometimes in loose flocks. A Sooty Shearwater recorded from Barbados was banded in the Falkland Islands off Argentina.

Habitat: Well out at sea.

MANX SHEARWATER *Puffinus puffinus*   **Plate 2**

Identification: 30–38 cm (12–15"). An intermediate-sized shearwater with a short tail. Blackish above and *white below,* including wing linings and undertail-coverts. **Flight**: Four or five distinctive snappy wingbeats and a rocking glide in light winds or flat seas. **Similar species**: Audubon's Shearwater is slightly smaller with a longer tail; the back and upperwings have a browner tone, the underside of the primaries are grayer and the undertail-coverts are dark. Greater Shearwater is larger, has slower wingbeats and a white rump. Manx Shearwater has a long-winged and short-tailed appearance while Audubon's Shearwater appears short-winged and long-tailed.

Status and Range: Probably a rare migrant in the West Indies primarily from November to March, but also recorded in other months. Recorded from Cuba, Hispaniola, Puerto Rico and St Vincent. The scarcity of records results from the species occurring far offshore. It likely transits the waters off all of the islands. Widespread off both coasts of the North Atlantic and eastern South America.
Habitat: Well out at sea.

AUDUBON'S SHEARWATER *Puffinus lherminieri*   **Plate 2**
Local Names: Plimico (Bahamas); Diablotin, Little Devil (Grenada, St V); Pájaro de las Tempestades (Cuba); Pampero (PR); Puffin (Haiti); Puffin d'Audubon, Puffin (Guad, Mart); Cahen (Guad, Mart, St B); Wedrego, Audubons Pijlstormvogel (Saba, St E, St M)

Identification: 30 cm (12"). A relatively small, long-tailed, blackish-brown and white shearwater, the only one regularly encountered in the West Indies. Dark blackish-brown above; white below, but with *dark undertail-coverts*. **Similar species**: The *rounded tail* and *distinctive rapid wingbeats between glides* distinguish it from dark-backed pelagic terns. Has faster wingbeats than Greater Shearwater and lacks the white hindneck and rump of this species. See also Manx Shearwater.
Voice: Highly vocal at night around the nest, when adults utter mournful, cat-like cries in flight. In their burrows, they issue a loud, distinctive *plimico* from which the local Bahaman, Puerto Rican and several other local names derive. The young utter plaintive, liquid, twittering notes.

Status and Range: A common breeding resident through most of the Bahamas primarily from March to July; it is uncommon in other months. Elsewhere in the West Indies, it is generally an uncommon and local breeding resident and is rare outside the breeding season. When not breeding, it is believed to disperse to the seas around its breeding grounds. It is not likely to be seen except from a boat far offshore. Occurs throughout the warmer oceans of the world.
Habitat: Well out at sea, often over deep water channels, except when attending its nest.
Nesting: Nests in a cliff crevice, cave, vegetation, under rocks or other cover, or digs a burrow 60–90 cm (2–3') in length. Birds enter and leave the nests only at night. One parent leaves the burrow for eight to ten days to feed while the remaining adult tends the nest. Egg (1) white. Breeds from February to July.

STORM-PETRELS: FAMILY HYDROBATIDAE

Storm-Petrels generally occur far out at sea and are the smallest of pelagic birds, being little larger than swallows. They characteristically swoop and flutter low over the water, sometimes pattering the surface with their webbed feet. This habit reputedly led to their name 'Petrel' from St Peter who doubted whether he could walk on water. Superstition has it that their presence around ships portends a storm. They nest in burrows on remote islets and are unable to walk on land; thus, they must push themselves along with their wings. In many species one parent tends the nest for days without food before being relieved by its mate. Wilson's Storm-Petrel is believed by some experts to be the most numerous bird in the world.

WILSON'S STORM-PETREL *Oceanites oceanicus*   Plate 2

Local Names: Pamperito de Wilson (Cuba); Pamperito Rabo Cuadrado (PR); Golondrina del Mar (DR, PR); Wilsons Stormvogeltje (Saba); Océanite de Wilson (Guad, Mart)

Identification: 18–19 cm (7–7.5"). A small, dark brownish-black seabird with a white rump. **Similar species**: Distinguished from the similar Leach's Storm-Petrel by being blacker; having shorter, broader and more rounded wings with less angled wrists; and a more direct flight with briefer glides reminiscent of a swallow. The rump patch is undivided and extends around to edges of the undertail-coverts; the *tail is square*, and the feet have yellow toe-webbing and extend beyond the tail. None of the above features applies to Leach's Storm-Petrel. See also Band-rumped Storm-Petrel. **Habit**: Unlike Leach's, Wilson's regularly follows boats, swooping over the wake and touching the water surface with its feet.

Status and Range: Generally a rare non-breeding resident in much of the West Indies primarily in May and June. Most frequent among the Bahamas where it is uncommon. Likely more frequent than records indicate. The scarcity of records results from the species occurring far offshore. Occurs through most of the oceans of the world.

Comments: Breeds in the subantarctic from December to February, migrating far north through most of the world's oceans in other seasons.

Habitat: Well out at sea.

LEACH'S STORM-PETREL *Oceanodroma leucorhoa*   Plate 2

Local Names: Pamperito de Tempestades (Cuba); Pamperito Rabo Horquillado (PR); Lavapiés (DR, PR); Vaal Stormvogeltje (Saba); Océanite Cul-blanc (Guad, Mart)

Identification: 20 cm (8"). A small, brownish-black seabird with a white rump. **Similar species**: Distinguished from the similar Wilson's Storm-Petrel by its longer, narrower and more pointed wings with more sharply-angled wrists; pale brown wing band; white rump patch appearing divided at close range; and *slightly forked tail*. In flight, feet do not extend beyond tail. See also Band-rumped Storm-Petrel. **Habit**: Leach's Storm-Petrel is not a follower of boats as is the Wilson's, and its flight is more erratic with deep wingbeats, often suggestive of a nighthawk.

Status and Range: A rare non-breeding resident throughout the West Indies primarily from November to June, but sometimes occurring in other months. Likely more frequent than records indicate. The scarcity of records results from the species occurring far offshore. Occurs throughout the northern oceans, as well as the South Atlantic.

Habitat: Well out at sea.

BAND-RUMPED STORM-PETREL *Oceanodroma castro*   Plate 2

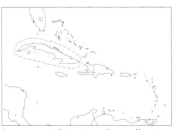

Identification: 19–21 cm (7.5–8"). Medium-sized with a black head and upperparts. Conspicuous narrow white rump band contrasts with blackish tail and underparts; *square tail*. **Flight**: Buoyant and direct, though sometimes erratic and shearwater-like with deep wingbeats. *Feet do not extend beyond tip of tail*. **Similar species**: Wilson's Storm-Petrel is smaller, has yellow webbing on its feet which protrude past tail tip in flight, frequently flutters butterfly-like when feeding and readily approaches boats. Leach's Storm-Petrel has a slightly-forked tail, buoyant flight, white rump-patch which often appears to have a notch in it and usually ignores boats.

Status and Range: Very rare off Cuba where recorded in July and December. Also recorded off Antigua. It should be expected to occur primarily from June through August. This bird's status in the

West Indies is poorly known due to the species occurring far offshore. Occurs throughout the warmer waters of the Pacific and eastern Atlantic Oceans.
Habitat: Well out at sea over deep water.

TROPICBIRDS: FAMILY PHAETHONTIDAE

As their name implies, the tropicbirds are confined to the tropical and subtropical oceans of the world. Two of the world's three species occur in this region and all are characterized by long, streamer-like central tail feathers in adult birds. Even the tails of young birds appear pointed and aid in distinguishing them from terns. When close to shore, their habit of making numerous approaches to the nesting cliffs before landing is distinctive. Tropicbirds feed primarily on squid and fish at sea, where they dive on prey from substantial heights. As their nasal openings are almost entirely blocked (as is the case with related families), excess salt filtered from the sea-water they drink passes through the mouth to the tip of the bill where the droplets are shaken off. Tropicbirds only infrequently alight on the water, and on land they shuffle around with their breasts against the ground.

WHITE-TAILED TROPICBIRD *Phaethon lepturus* Plate 1
Local Names: Scissor-tail (St V); Long-tailed (VI); Boatswain Bird (CI, Grenada, St V, VI); Bo'sun Bird (CI, Jamaica); Contramaestre (Cuba); Chirre de cola Blanca, Chirre de Altura (PR); Rabijunco (Cuba, DR, PR); Fou Pay An Ke (Haiti); Flèche en Queue (St B); Phaéton à Bec Jaune (Guad, Mart); Tropic, Geelsnavelkeerkringvogel (Saba, St E, St M); Paille en Queue (French WI)

Identification: 81 cm (31") (including tail plumes), 37–40 cm (15–16") (without plumes). **Adult**: White overall with *long tail feathers* and *heavy black stripes on the upperwing* and outermost primaries. Bill is yellow or orange. **Immature**: Barred back; short central tail feathers. The bill is yellowish and ringed with black near tip. **Similar species**: The immature differs from immature Red-billed in having coarser black barring on its upperparts and lacking a black band across the hindneck.
Voice: A raspy *crick-et*.
Status and Range: Widespread, but only a very locally common breeding resident in the West Indies primarily from March to June, though in the Bahamas birds remain through October. It is the typical tropicbird of the Bahamas, Greater Antilles and Cayman Islands, but is scarcer in the Lesser Antilles where the Red-billed Tropicbird is more abundant. Through the tropical and subtropical oceans of the world.
Comments: Best observed flying near the vertical sea cliffs it uses to breed. Aerial courtship displays are performed, the male drooping its tail as it flies before the female. Landing on the cliffs is often difficult, thus several passes are sometimes required before a successful landing is executed. It is not known where these birds migrate outside the breeding season.
Habitat: Well out at sea except when visiting sea cliffs to nest.
Nesting: Due to introduced predators, now primarily restricted to rocky crevices on sea cliffs. Egg (1) tan, heavily splotched with dark brown. Breeds primarily from March to July, but sometimes earlier.

RED-BILLED TROPICBIRD *Phaethon aethereus* Plate 1
Local Names: Rabijunco de Pico Rojo (Cuba); Chirre de Pico Colorado (PR); Tropic (Saba); Fétu en Cul (St B); Paille en Queue (Grenada, St V); Phaéton à Bec Rrouge, Paille en Queue à Bec Rouge, Cibérou, Couac (Guad, Mart); Roodsnavelkeerkringvogel (Saba, St E, St M)

Identification: 91–107 cm (36–42") (including tail plumes), 46–51 cm (18–20") (without plumes). **Adult**: White overall with *black barring on the back, long tail plumes* and a *red bill*. **Immature**: Lacks long tail plumes. The bill is yellowish, ringed with black near tip, back barred *with a black band across the hindneck*. **Similar species**: Immature White-tailed Tropicbird has bolder barring on the back and the black hindneck band is less pronounced.
Voice: A long, harsh, raspy *keé-arrr*.

Status and Range: Common in the Virgin Islands, it is generally an uncommon and very local resident on Culebra off Puerto Rico and throughout the Lesser Antilles. A vagrant off Cuba, Jamaica and Hispaniola. The Red-billed Tropicbird does not appear to undergo a regular migration, but some birds apparently disperse to seas off their breeding grounds when not nesting. Occurs through the tropical and subtropical Atlantic, northwestern Indian and eastern Pacific Oceans.

Comments: Best observed off the sea cliffs where it nests. Red-billed and White-tailed Tropicbirds use similar nest sites, but the Red-billed begins nesting earlier. Why the Red-billed is virtually absent from the Greater Antilles and the Bahamas while the White-tailed abounds is a mystery.

Habitat: Well out at sea except when visiting sea cliffs to nest.

Nesting: Rock crevices on small remote cays and sea cliffs are typical breeding sites. Egg (1) varies from whitish-buff to reddish-brown with brownish or purplish-brown blotches. Breeds primarily from January to June, but breeding has been reported from Antigua as early as late September.

BOOBIES AND GANNETS: FAMILY SULIDAE

Boobies are long-billed, sleek-plumaged birds that wander well out to sea from their colonial roosting and nesting areas. Their leisurely flapping and gliding flight, low over the water, is characteristic, as are their spectacular dives into the sea in pursuit of fish and squid. Boobies vigorously defend a small area around their nests, usually using exaggerated and stereotyped head movements in interactions with other birds. Guano deposits from some nesting populations of boobies have been harvested as an important source of fertilizer. Fossils of booby-like birds date back at least 20 million years.

MASKED BOOBY *Sula dactylatra*   Plate 1
Local Names: Booby (Jamaica); White Booby (VI); Blue-face Gannet (Grenada, St V); Pájaro Bobo Azul (Cuba); Bubí (DR); Boba Enmascarada (PR); Fou Masqué (Guad, Mart)

Identification: 81–91 cm (32–36"). **Adult**: Primarily white with a *black tail*, primaries and secondaries. **Subadult**: Similar to the adult, but upperparts with brown on head and rump and brown flecks on wing coverts. **Immature**: Head and upperparts brown with a *white hindneck*. Underparts primarily white except for throat, undertail and flight feathers. **Similar species**: The adult is distinguished from white-phased Red-footed Booby at a distance by its *dark tail*. Immature Masked differs from Brown Booby by lacking brown on the upper breast and by possessing a white hindneck. Immature Northern Gannet has a dark, rather than a yellowish, bill and is much larger.

Status and Range: A very rare and local year-round resident in the West Indies where the species is generally observed only on its breeding grounds and adjacent seas. The number of breeding pairs in the West Indies is low, estimated at 500–1,700. Known breeding areas include the southern Bahamas (Santa Domingo Cay where the colony is believed extirpated), Jamaica (Pedro and Lighthouse Cays, Morant Cays and Serranilla Cays), Puerto Rico (Monito, Alcarraza and cays off Culebra), the Virgin Islands (Cockroach and Sula Cays), Anguilla (Dog Island), Antigua (Five and Redondo Islands) and among the Grenadines. Nesting on Santa Domingo Cay has not been confirmed since the late 19th century. Very rare elsewhere in the West Indies. Masked Booby is threatened in the West Indies by habitat loss, disturbance from development and due to predation by introduced mammals. The status of the species globally appears to be stable. Occurs through the tropical and subtropical oceans of the world.

Comments: Masked Booby appears much more particular about the conditions under which it will nest than do Brown and Red-footed Boobies. As a result, it is decidedly less abundant and confined to remote areas.

Habitat: Well out at sea during the day except when attending its nest.

Nesting: Colonial. The nest is a scrape on flat ground along the edge of or near a cliff face. Eggs (1–2) white. Breeds from March to May and occasionally during September.

BROWN BOOBY *Sula leucogaster*   Plate 1
Local Names: Booby (Antigua, CI, Jamaica, VI); Pájaro Bobo Prieto (Cuba, PR); Bubí (DR); Boba Prieta (PR); Gwo Fou Gri, Fou (Haiti); Fou Brun (Guad, Mart); Bruine Boebie, Witbuikboebie (Saba, St E, St M)

Identification: 71–76 cm (28–30"). **Adult**: The entirely brown head and upperparts sharply demarcated from the white belly and abdomen are good field marks. **Immature**: Light brown on the belly and abdomen. **Similar species**: Immature Masked Booby has a white hindneck and lacks brown on the upper breast.
Voice: A hoarse *kak*.
Status and Range: A fairly common year-round resident offshore throughout the West Indies and locally abundant near its breeding grounds. Very rare or absent only from the northern Bahamas. It is the most common of the three boobies in the West Indies and generally the most likely to be seen from shore. Through the tropical and subtropical oceans of the world.
Comments: Generally seen singly or in small, loose aggregations, though sometimes occurs in numbers when feeding on large fish schools. Often rests on buoys or rocky cliffs. Flies with a series of short, unhurried flaps followed by tilting glides, often low over the sea.
Habitat: Bays, coastal areas and at sea.
Nesting: Usually colonial on remote islands or on inaccessible sea cliffs. The nest is a scrape on the ground. Eggs (1–2) white. The breeding season is prolonged and varies from year to year, but generally peaks from March to June and from September to October.

RED-FOOTED BOOBY *Sula sula*   Plate 1
Local Names: Booby (CI); Tree Booby (VI); Boba Patirroja (PR); Pájaro Bobo Blanco (Cuba, DR, PR); Fou Blanc (Haiti); Roodpootboebie (Saba); Gwo Fou Blan, Fou à Pieds Rouges (Guad, Mart)

Identification: 66–76 cm (26–30"). **Brown phase**: Primarily brown, but with distinctive *white hindparts and tail*. **White phase**: All white, including tail, with black primaries and secondaries. **Immature**: Sooty brown; paler below, sometimes with a slightly darker band across the breast. **Similar species**: Distinguished from Masked Booby at a distance by Red-footed's white tail.
Voice: A guttural *ga-ga-ga-ga*, of variable length, which trails off. Also a distinctive squawk.
Status and Range: A widespread, but very local year-round resident in the West Indies. It is abundant primarily near its remote roosting and nesting islands which are widely scattered throughout the region. Away from these colonies, it is not often seen from shore. Through the tropical and subtropical oceans of the world.
Comments: Sometimes flies low over the sea in V-shaped formation of several birds. Each evening, waves of Red-footed Boobies fly to their island roosts until the sky and trees are full of birds. The boobies call loudly as they converge on their roost. Though the Red-footed Booby typically nests on remote islands, a colony of approximately 18,000 pairs nests on the Cayman Islands (Little Cayman) in mangroves adjacent to houses. This important colony is at great risk from projected development including an enlarged airport.
Habitat: Well out at sea during the day except when attending its nest.
Nesting: Colonial, typically on remote islands. This is the only booby in the Caribbean that constructs its nest in a tree or bush. Eggs (1–2) white. Breeds primarily from April to June.

NORTHERN GANNET *Sula bassanus*   Plate 78

Identification: 100 cm (40"). **Immature**: Entirely dark gray above with whitish flecks on the wings and mantle. Paler below. Over the course of three to four years, the plumage develops to adult, with each molt increasing the extent of white feathering. The underparts and head lighten by the second year. **Adult**: Almost entirely white with a tan crown and black wingtips. **Similar species**: Immature Masked Booby has a yellowish bill; the bill color of immature Northern Gannet is dark.

Status and Range: A vagrant among the Bahamas and off Cuba. It occurs from September to May. Perhaps occurs more frequently than records indicate, but the similarity of immature birds to immature Masked Booby, and its occurrence in waters far offshore greatly reduce the potential for it being observed. Through the temperate and subarctic North Atlantic Ocean.
Comments: Immature birds are most likely to occur in the West Indies.
Habitat: Typically out to sea.

PELICANS: FAMILY PELECANIDAE

Pelicans are among the largest of all flying birds. Brown Pelican, with its 2 m (7') wingspread is actually the smallest of the living species. All pelicans are highly adapted for swimming and flying, the resident Brown Pelican preferring coastal waters, but others inhabiting large, inland lakes. It is locally believed that Brown Pelicans have a suicidal tendency and intentionally hang themselves in the forks of tree branches. Actually, this mortality is no doubt the result of the clumsiness of these large creatures, particularly young birds, among the slender branches of the mangroves rather than an intentional act on their part. Pelicans are sometimes persecuted by fishermen, who consider the bird a competitor for fish.

AMERICAN WHITE PELICAN *Pelecanus erythrorhynchos* Plate 1
Local Names: Alcatraz Blanco (Cuba); Pelícano Blanco (PR)

Identification: 125–165 cm (49–64"). The *huge size, large bill* and white coloration of this bird are distinctive. The primaries and outer secondaries are black. ***Non-breeding adult***: Bill orange-yellow; hindcrown and hindneck gray. ***Immature***: Bill gray. ***Breeding adult***: Bill orange-yellow with a knob on upper mandible; hindcrown and hindneck tan. ***Similar species***: There is the possibility of two other species of white pelican occurring as vagrants in the West Indies. Eastern White Pelican (*P. onocrotalus*) in both non-breeding and breeding plumage has a gray mark nearly the length of the bill. The immature's mantle is mottled brown. Pink-backed Pelican (*P. rufescens*) has a pinkish bill in all plumages.
Status and Range: A very rare non-breeding resident on Cuba and Puerto Rico. A vagrant elsewhere in the West Indies where reported from the Bahamas, Jamaica, Cayman Islands and St Martin. May occur in any month. Though very rare, a flock of eight birds was observed on one occasion. Through western North America to Central America.
Comments: White-plumaged pelicans in the West Indies, particularly those in the Lesser Antilles, should be observed carefully to determine that they are not Pink-backed or Eastern White Pelicans, both possible vagrants from Africa.
Habitat: Freshwater lakes and coastal bays.

BROWN PELICAN *Pelecanus occidentalis* Plate 1
Local Names: Old Joe (Jamaica); Booby (Antigua, Barbuda, Nevis, St C); Ganuche (Grenada, St V); Pelícano (DR); Pelícano Pardo (PR); Alcatraz (Cuba, DR, PR); Pélican, Blague-à-Diable (Haiti); Pélican Brun, Grand Gosier (Guad, Mart); Pelican, Bruine Pelikaan (Saba, St E, St M)

Identification: 107–137 cm (42–54"). Note the *unusual bill* and dark coloration of this large bird. ***Breeding adult***: Reddish-brown hindneck and back of head, though infrequently the hindneck remains white. ***Non-breeding adult***: White hindneck and back of head. ***Immature***: Overall grayish-brown; paler below.
Voice: Adults are silent.
Status and Range: A common year-round resident in the southern Bahamas, Greater Antilles and locally in the northern Lesser Antilles east to Montserrat. It is uncommon to rare through the rest of the West Indies with some birds wandering between islands. Migrants that breed in North America augment local numbers primarily from November to February. Also occurs through

the coastal areas of southern North America, Central America, and northern South America.

Comments: A well-known denizen of bays, docks and fishing wharfs, the Brown Pelican, when not receiving handouts, makes spectacular aerial dives for fish, its entire body sometimes disappearing beneath the surface momentarily. Fish are snared in its immense bill, the water drained, and the fish then swallowed whole. Typically in small flocks, Brown Pelicans often fly in an impressively tight formation low over the wave crests, with wingbeats in perfect unison. Brown Pelicans fly with very deliberate flaps of their huge wings and surprisingly lengthy glides. They often congregate in large mangrove roosts.

Habitat: Bays, lagoons, other protected coastal areas and calm ocean waters. Sometimes inland to freshwater reservoirs.

Nesting: Brown Pelicans nest colonially, often on offshore cays. They typically construct stick nests in trees, but sometimes near or on the ground. Eggs (2–4) white. Breeding may occur during any season and may vary from year to year.

CORMORANTS: FAMILY PHALACROCORACIDAE

Cormorants are large, long-necked birds with hooked bills. They inhabit coastal waters or inland lakes. Those of the Northern Hemisphere are primarily black, each species having distinctive coloration and form to its throat pouch. Cormorants swim with their heads cocked up and their bodies low in the water. They dive expertly in pursuit of fish.

DOUBLE-CRESTED CORMORANT *Phalacrocorax auritus* Plate 18

Local Names: Corúa de Mar (Cuba); Corúa (DR); Cormorán Crestado (PR); Gran Gozye, Cormorant (Haiti)

Identification: 74–89 cm (29–35"). Its large size, long neck, hooked bill and habit of sitting with wings spread are important characteristics. ***Breeding adult***: Totally black appearance. Small ear tufts are sometimes visible. ***Non-breeding adult***: Lacks ear tufts. ***Immature***: Brown; paler below. ***Similar species***: Generally larger-bodied than the very similar Neotropic Cormorant and with a shorter tail, especially noticeable in flight (tail length equals half of head and neck length) and slightly heavier bill. The small race of the Double-crested Cormorant from the Bahamas (San Salvador) is similar in size to Neotropic, but can be distinguished by the tail and bill proportions. For additional guidance, refer to the citation under Neotropic Cormorant. The Common Loon has a heavier bill with a pointed tip.

Voice: Generally silent away from the breeding grounds, but emits a variety of deep guttural grunts.

Status and Range: A common year-round resident on Cuba, including the Isle of Youth and on San Salvador in the Bahamas. It is generally an uncommon non-breeding resident locally elsewhere in the Bahamas and a very rare wanderer through the other islands of the Greater Antilles to the Virgin and Cayman Islands. This cormorant is a vagrant in the northern Lesser Antilles. The species is presently expanding its range eastward in the West Indies. Migrants which breed in North America are uncommon in the northern Bahamas. Also occurs widely in North America through coastal Mexico and Belize.

Comments: Usually in flocks of variable size, but sometimes singly. An excellent swimmer, it favors open water. Despite its aquatic nature, it must regularly perch in the sun with wings spread in a distinctive posture to dry its feathers which otherwise become waterlogged. Cormorants can gradually submerge their bodies underwater until only the head is above the surface or they can sink entirely out of sight. The Double-crested Cormorant on San Salvador is a small endemic race.

Habitat: Inland lakes and protected coastal waters. Generally occurs more frequently on salt water than does Neotropic Cormorant.

Nesting: A colonial nester, primarily in mangroves, it builds a platform of twigs and grasses low above the water in coastal areas. Eggs (2–4) greenish-blue with chalk-like and brownish marks at one end. Breeds from April to June and in October.

NEOTROPIC CORMORANT *Phalacrocorax brasilianus*   **Plate 18**
Local Name: Corúa de Agua Dulce (Cuba)

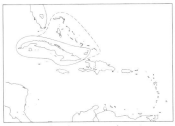

Identification: 63–69 cm (25–27"). A large, long-necked bird with a hooked bill that often sits with its wings spread. ***Breeding adult***: Black overall, the throat pouch edged with white is a good field mark. ***Non-breeding adult***: White edge on throat pouch is reduced or absent. ***Immature***: Brown; paler below. ***Similar species***: In the field, it is easily confused with Double-crested Cormorant, but has a decidedly smaller bulk, thinner bill and *longer tail*, more noticeable in flight (tail length equals head and neck length). Other differences not easily seen are the feathering in front of the eye on the Neotropic and the sharp angle to the throat patch as it rounds the bill. For additional field marks refer to: Patten, M. A. 1993. Notes on Immature Double-crested and Neotropic Cormorants. *Birding* 25(5): 343–345. The Common Loon has a heavier bill with a pointed tip.

Voice: Usually silent away from the breeding grounds, but emits a guttural grunt like a pig.

Status and Range: A common year-round resident on Cuba, including the Isle of Youth and locally in the southern Bahamas, particularly on Great Inagua. Non-breeding birds range north in the Bahamas to New Providence and Eleuthera. A vagrant on Jamaica, Puerto Rico, the Virgin Islands and the Lesser Antilles where recorded from St Barthélemy and Dominica. The species is apparently expanding its range eastward in the West Indies. Also occurs in the extreme south-central United States through Central and South America.

Comments: Formerly referred to as Olivaceous Cormorant. Displays behavior similar to that of Double-crested Cormorant.

Habitat: Both inland and coastal waters. Generally more of a freshwater bird than Double-crested.

Nesting: A platform of twigs and grasses is built in a tree or bush mainly near fresh water, but sometimes in mangroves. Typically nests in colonies. Eggs (2–4) greenish-blue with chalk-like and brownish markings at one end. Breeds primarily from May to June.

DARTERS: FAMILY ANHINGIDAE

Anhingas are wonderfully adapted for stalking fish underwater, in a manner similar to herons and egrets which hunt while wading in shallow water. Anhingas have moderately long, pointed bills which they use to skewer their prey.

ANHINGA *Anhinga anhinga*   **Plate 18**
Local Name: Marbella (Cuba, DR)

Identification: 85 cm (34"). A large, dark, long-necked bird with a long tail, pointed bill, and *large whitish patches on back and upperwing*. ***Adult male***: Mostly glossy black. ***Adult female***: Head to breast light brown. ***Immature***: Brown above; tan below. ***Similar species***: Resembles a cormorant, but neck more snake-like, tail longer, and bill longer and pointed, not hooked. **Status and Range**: A common year-round resident on Cuba, including the Isle of Youth and a vagrant elsewhere — reported from the Bahamas (Andros), the Cayman Islands (Little Cayman), Hispaniola, St Lucia and Grenada. Also occurs in southeastern North America, Central America and northern South America.

Comments: Often soars high and hawk-like, with neck extended and long tail spread. Its habit of swimming with only its slender neck and head above the surface gives it the appearance of a large snake. The Anhinga perches like a cormorant in a spread-wing posture to dry its feathers.

Habitat: Shallow, calm water bodies either fresh, brackish or saline. From large estuaries to small ponds.

Nesting: Usually colonial, often near herons, ibises and cormorants. A nest built of twigs, coarse sticks, dead leaves and lined with leaves or twigs is placed 1.5–6 m (5–20') above water or ground. Eggs (3–5) bluish-white with a chalky coating and nest-stained during incubation. Breeds from April to July.

FRIGATEBIRDS: FAMILY FREGATIDAE

The most accomplished of marine aerialists, frigatebirds have the greatest wing surface relative to their weight of any birds (the skeleton weighs only about 250 g [8 oz]). Frigatebirds cannot dive or land on the ocean as do most other seabirds. They therefore rely on their speed and agility in the air to rob other seabirds of their prey or snatch food items from the surface of the water with their long bills. Frigatebirds are confined to tropical and subtropical seas.

MAGNIFICENT FRIGATEBIRD *Fregata magnificens*   Plate 1
Local Names: Hurricane Bird, Weather Bird (Antigua, Barbuda, St E, VI); Man-o-War Bird (Bahamas, CI, Jamaica, Nevis, VI); Tijerilla, Rabijunco (PR); Rabihorcado (Cuba, PR); Tijereta (DR, PR); Sizo, Frégate (Haiti); Scissors, Ganuge (Grenada, St V); Malfini (Guad, Mart); Frégate Superbe (French WI); Amerikaanse Fregatvogel (Saba, St E, St M)

Identification: 94–104 cm (37–41"). Its *long, forked tail with long, slender, pointed wings sharply bent at the wrist* and *habit of floating motionless in the air* make it easily identifiable. **Adult male**: Generally appears entirely black in the field. During courtship, the inflatable throat pouch is bright red. **Adult female**: Blackish overall with a *white breast*. **Immature**: Dark brownish-black with a *white head and breast*. **Voice**: Silent except for guttural noises during courtship. **Status and Range**: Generally a common but somewhat local resident throughout the West Indies. Breeding grounds may serve as year-round roosts, but non-breeding birds may establish roosts some distance from the breeding grounds and sometimes wander great distances. Occurs through the tropical and subtropical waters of the Western Hemisphere, and on the Cape Verde Islands.
Comments: Notorious for stealing fish from other seabirds. It does not rest on the water; consequently, it returns each evening to a roost, often among mangroves or on an offshore islet. Occurs both singly and in large flocks of 100 or more birds. Frequently seen floating in one spot at moderate heights above calm waters with minimal wing movement as it searches for prey. The Barbuda breeding colony, estimated at 2,500 pairs, is the largest in the Caribbean.
Habitat: Over bays, inshore waters and offshore cays, sometimes penetrating well inland especially during storms.
Nesting: A stick nest is normally built in a low bush. Frigatebirds are very sensitive to disturbances while incubating and are thus confined to the most remote cays and islets. They nest colonially, usually among other seabirds. Egg (1) white. The breeding season is highly variable with egg-laying occurring from at least August to April. However, it appears to peak in November and February.

BITTERNS AND HERONS: FAMILY ARDEIDAE

Most of the members of this large, cosmopolitan family of graceful birds wade in swamps and marshes in search of fish, frogs and other prey which they spear with their long, pointed bills. Undigested matter is regurgitated in the form of pellets. The white egrets are best distinguished in the field by differences in size and coloration of the bill and legs. Bitterns inhabit dense vegetation and often 'freeze' with their bills pointed upward using their cryptic plumage to avoid detection. All birds in the heron family fly with the head drawn back with the head and neck forming an 'S' shape, a valuable field characteristic.

AMERICAN BITTERN *Botaurus lentiginosus*   Plate 9
Local Names: Ave Toro (DR); Yaboa Americana (PR); Guanabó Rojo (Cuba, DR)

Identification: 58–61 cm (23–24'). The *black neck mark* and *habit of pointing its bill upward* are good characteristics. **Flight**: *Blackish wingtips* are distinctive. **Similar species**: Immature night-herons are darker brown and lack black on the neck and wingtips. Immature Green Heron is smaller, darker and lacks a black neck mark.
Voice: A peculiar pumping sound, *oong-ka-chunk*!
Status and Range: A non-breeding resident in the West Indies primarily from October to March. It is

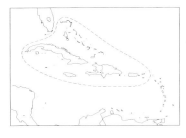

decidedly uncommon and local on the larger islands of the Bahamas and on Cuba, and is very rare in the Cayman Islands, Jamaica, Hispaniola and Puerto Rico. A vagrant in the Virgin Islands, Montserrat, Guadeloupe, Martinique and Barbados. Its similarity to immature night-herons and propensity for remaining still among dense, aquatic vegetation result in it being easily overlooked and in its frequency of occurrence being under-represented. Also throughout North and Central America.
Comments: Usually goes undetected until flushed.
Habitat: Typically thick, emergent vegetation of freshwater swamps.

LEAST BITTERN *Ixobrychus exilis*   Plate 9
Local Names: Bitlin (VI); Gaulin (Jamaica, VI); Garcita (Cuba, PR); Martinetito (DR, PR); Petit Blongios, Kio Jaune (Guad); Crabier, Ti Krabye Mang Lanmè, Martinet (Haiti)

Identification: 28–35 cm (11–14'). Distinguished by its small size and generally reddish-yellow coloration. The *cream-colored patch on the upperwing* is a good field mark in both perched and flying birds. **Adult male**: Black crown and back. **Adult female**: Dark brown crown and back. **Immature**: Paler brown crown and back; breast heavily streaked.
Voice: *Koo-koo-koo-koo*, almost a *coo*, the first syllable often higher than the others and the call accelerating slightly. Also a loud, harsh *kack*, sometimes repeated in series.
Status and Range: A common year-round resident on Cuba and Jamaica, fairly common in the Cayman Islands (Grand Cayman) and Puerto Rico, and uncommon on Hispaniola and Guadeloupe. It is uncommon to rare among the Bahamas, rare on Dominica and very rare in the Virgin Islands. The Least Bittern is a vagrant on Barbados. Also throughout much of North, Central and South America.
Comments: Solitary. Unless flushed it usually goes unnoticed among dense swamp vegetation where it often sits motionless.
Habitat: Primarily dense emergent vegetation of freshwater swamps, often with cattails, but also frequents mangrove channels.
Nesting: The nest is constructed of twigs and swamp plants above standing water. Eggs (2–5) bluish-white. Breeds from May to August.

GREAT BLUE HERON *Ardea herodias*   Plate 8
Local Names: Blue Gaulin (Jamaica); Gray Gaulin (VI); Arsnicker (Bahamas, VI); Garcilote (Cuba); Garzón, Garza Ceniza (DR); Garzón Cenizo, Garzón Blanco (white form) (PR); Krabye Nwa, Lajirond, Crabier Bleu (Haiti); Blue Heron, Amerikaanse Blauwe Reiger (St M); Grand Héron, Crabier Radar (Guad, Mart); Crabier Noir (LA)

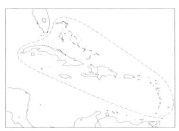

Identification: 107–132 cm (42–52"). The *largest* regularly occurring heron in the West Indies. **Dark phase**: Note its primarily gray appearance with a large, straight bill and black eyebrow stripe. **White phase**: Very rare. Entirely white with *yellow bill and legs*. Considered by some to be a separate species — Great White Heron (*Ardea occidentalis*). **Immature**: The entire crown is black, and the overall plumage is browner. **Similar species**: The white form of Great Blue Heron is distinguished from Great Egret by its larger size and *yellowish legs*. Sandhill Crane has a red crown and lacks the black eyebrow stripe. See also Gray Heron.
Voice: A deep throaty croak like a large frog *guarr*, repeated three to four times.
Status and Range: Generally a common non-breeding resident in the Bahamas, Greater Antilles and the Virgin and Cayman Islands primarily from October to April. It is uncommon in the Lesser Antilles during these months. This heron is decidedly uncommon during the remaining months in the Bahamas, Greater Antilles and the Virgin Islands. Breeding has only been confirmed on Cuba and

the Virgin Islands. The white phase is extremely rare in the West Indies. Also throughout North and Central America to northern South America.

Comments: A shy, solitary species. This heron often stands motionless in search of prey.

Habitat: Both saltwater and freshwater ponds and lagoons.

Nesting: A platform of sticks is built high in a tree in a remote swamp. Eggs (2–4) bluish. Known breeding dates include December and April through August.

GRAY HERON *Ardea cinerea*   **Plate 78**

Identification: 90–98 cm (35–38"). A very large, generally gray heron distinguished by *white thighs in all plumages*. **Similar species**: The Great Blue Heron is larger, darker, particularly on the hindneck and abdomen, and has reddish-brown thighs.

Status and Range: A vagrant on Montserrat, Martinique and Barbados. The first Gray Heron record for the West Indies was in 1959 of a bird banded in France four months earlier. Since that date, the species has been irregularly recorded, including three individuals on Barbados in 1988. This heron apparently arrives in the West Indies as a transatlantic vagrant from Africa via favorable winds. Widespread from northern Europe to Africa.

GREAT EGRET *Ardea alba*   **Plate 8**

Local Names: White Gaulin (VI); Crane (Antigua, Jamaica); Garzón (Cuba); Garza Blanca (DR); Garzón Blanco (PR); Garza Real (DR, PR); Crabier Blanc, Kòk Blan, Grande Aigrette Blanche (Haiti); Grande Aigrette, Grand Crabier Blanc (Guad, Mart); Grote Zilverreiger (Saba, St M)

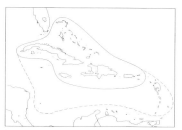

Identification: 89–107 cm (35–42"). Note its large size, *yellow bill* and *black legs*. **Similar species**: The white form of Great Blue Heron is somewhat larger and has yellowish legs. Cattle Egret resembles the Great Egret in coloration, but is much smaller, chunkier and prefers drier habitat.

Voice: A hoarse, throaty croak sounding like the winding of a large clock.

Status and Range: A common year-round resident in the Bahamas, Greater Antilles, Antigua and Guadeloupe, and an uncommon one in the Virgin Islands. It is a common non-breeding resident in the Cayman Islands, St Barthélemy and Barbados, and is generally uncommon elsewhere in the Lesser Antilles from September to April when migrants from North America augment local numbers. The species is also uncommon on San Andrés and Providencia. The Great Egret is increasing its abundance in the West Indies, and is widespread worldwide.

Habitat: Large freshwater and saltwater swamps, grassy marshes with stagnant water, river banks and turtlegrass beds in shallows behind reefs.

Nesting: A loose platform of sticks is built on a tree branch or in a shrub. Nests in wooded swamps with other species of herons in areas protected from the wind. Eggs (2–5) blue. Breeds primarily from April to June, but sometimes in other seasons.

LITTLE EGRET *Egretta garzetta*   **Plate 8**

Identification: 55–65 cm (22–25.5"). **Breeding**: *White Phase* — Overall white; usually *two long head plumes*; bill and legs black with yellow feet; lores reddish. *Dark Phase* — Gray overall, sometimes with a white chin and throat. **Non-breeding**: Grayish-green lores. **Similar species**: See Western Reef-Heron for comparisons with other white herons.

Status and Range: An uncommon breeding resident on Barbados perhaps remaining year-round. A rare wanderer or non-breeding resident on St Lucia. A vagrant on Puerto Rico, Guadeloupe and Martinique. The Little Egret was first recorded in the West Indies in 1954, the number of records increasing gradually since then. The population on Barbados now approximates 80 individuals. The species has occurred in every month, but most frequently from January to June. Up to 20 pairs now breed on Barbados. These represent the

first and only Western Hemisphere nesting records for this species. Also occurs in southern Europe, Africa and South-East Asia east to Japan.
Comments: Both white-phase and dark-phase Little Egrets occur in the West Indies. The Little Egret, native to the Eastern Hemisphere, has been observed with increasing frequency in the Western Hemisphere as far north as Newfoundland and south to Trinidad, Tobago and Suriname.
Habitat: Coastal areas, ponds and lagoons.
Nesting: Colonial with other egrets. A loosely constructed nest of twigs in mangroves. Eggs (2-3) white, laid in December (Barbados).

SNOWY EGRET *Egretta thula*   Plate 8
Local Names: White Gauldin (CI); Golden Slippers (Jamaica); Gaulin (Antigua, Nevis); White Gaulin (Jamaica, VI); Garza Real (Cuba); Garza Blanca (Cuba, PR); Garza de Rizos (DR, PR); Zegrèt Blan, Aigrette Blanche (Haiti); Aigrette Neigeuse, Aigrette (Guad, Mart); Egret, Amerikaanse Kleine Zilverreiger (St E, St M)

Identification: 51–71 cm (20–28"). Note its black legs, *yellow feet* and *lores* and thin, pure black bill. **Immature**: Legs dark in front and greenish-yellow in back. **Similar species**: Immature Little Blue Heron has a pale gray bill base, lacks yellow on the lores and has greenish legs. For more detailed guidance on identification, refer to citation under Little Blue Heron. The very rare Little Egret and Western Reef-Heron are similar. See the discussion for those species under Western Reef-Heron.
Voice: A guttural *guarr*, higher pitched and more raspy than Great Egret.

Status and Range: A common year-round resident in the Bahamas, Greater Antilles, Virgin and Cayman Islands, Antigua, Guadeloupe and Barbados, it is generally an uncommon non-breeding resident or transient elsewhere in the Lesser Antilles, though it breeds on St Martin. Migrants that breed in North America occur from October to May. The species is uncommon on San Andrés. The Snowy Egret is increasing in numbers in the West Indies. Occurs through most of the Western Hemisphere.
Comments: The species often congregates at a few preferred localities.
Habitat: Primarily freshwater swamps, but also river banks and saltwater lagoons.
Nesting: Typically a flat nest of sticks is built in mangroves on islets; often in colonies with other herons. Eggs (2–5) greenish-blue. Breeds from April to July and in October.

WESTERN REEF-HERON *Egretta gularis*   Plate 8

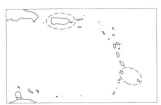

Identification: 55–65 cm (22–25.5"). Has white and dark color phases and intermediates. **Breeding adult**: *White Phase* — Overall white. Usually *two long head plumes, legs dark olive-green, feet yellow*, lores greenish-yellow or green, bill yellowish-brown, with paler lower mandible. *Dark Phase* — Overall dark gray. *White chin and throat*, lower breast and belly tinged with brown, black legs, stout bill brownish-black and *feet yellowish-green with yellow soles*. **Immature**: White with variable amounts of brown feathers; bill dull brown. **Similar species**: Snowy Egret differs from the white-phase Reef-heron in having many shaggy, fine head and breast plumes with lores ranging from bright yellow to red. The bill is usually black or blackish and is proportionately smaller and finer. Legs are usually blackish (adult) or blackish with a yellow-green stripe up the back (immature). Immature Little Blue Heron has dull yellow legs and feet, grayish lores, and a two-toned bill with gray base and dark tip. Little Egret has a proportionately smaller bill than Western Reef-Heron and always has a black bill and blacker legs. The bill of Western Reef-Heron is never entirely black and is less tapered toward the tip giving it a heavy, ungraceful appearance. The dark phase of Western Reef-Heron is very difficult to distinguish from the non-breeding plumage of Little Blue Heron or the dark phase of Little Egret at a distance. Non-breeding plumages of Snowy and Little Egrets are extremely difficult to distinguish in the field but Little Egret tends to stand more erect. It has a straighter bill that is less tapered at the tip and the upper mandible does not have a slight down-curve which is evident in direct comparison with Snowy Egret. Little Egret also has a flatter forehead than Snowy, a trait only evident in direct comparison. Finally, Snowy normally possesses bright yellow facial skin, whereas on Little Egret this is reddish during breeding plumage and generally bluish-gray or greenish-gray in non-breeding. The facial skin may sometimes turn pale yellow, but never bright yellow. For additional guidance on distinguishing these two species refer to: Massiah, E. 1996. Identification of Snowy Egret and Little Egret. *Birding World* 9(12): 434–444. For further information on separating Western Reef-Heron and Little Egret see: Dubois, P. J. and P. Yesou. 1995. Identification of Western Reef Egrets and dark Little Egrets. *British Birds* 88(7): 307–319.

Status and Range: Very rare, reported from Puerto Rico (Culebra), St Lucia and Barbados. First reported in the West Indies only in recent decades, it is appearing with increasing regularity and may soon be found to breed. It is widespread in West Africa north to western Europe.

Comments: This species' taxonomy remains problematic, since some authorities consider this heron to be a subspecies of Little Egret.

Habitat: Coastal areas, ponds and lagoons.

LITTLE BLUE HERON *Egretta caerulea*   Plate 8
Local Names: Blue Gauldin (CI); Blue Gaulin (Grenada, Jamaica, St V); Gaulin (Nevis, VI); Garza Azul (Cuba, DR, PR); Garza Blanca (immature), Garza Pinta (DR, PR); Metis Krabye Ble, Crabier Blanc (immature), Crabier Bleu (Haiti); Crabier Noir (St L); Aigrette Bleue, Petit Héron Bleu (Guad, Mart); Water Gaulin, Kleine Blauwe Reiger (Saba, St E, St M)

Identification: 56–71 cm (22–28"). The bill is grayish with a black tip. *Adult*: Identified by its *medium size* and *uniform dark gray appearance*. *Immature*: Initially entirely white; late in first year it becomes mottled with the dark feathers of adult plumage. *Similar species*: The white immature Little Blue Heron strongly resembles Snowy Egret, but is distinguished by the pale gray base to the bill, lack of yellow on the lores and greenish legs. For additional guidance on distinguishing these two species see: Kaufman, K. 1991. Summertime Blues. *American Birds* 45(2): 330–333. See also Western Reef-Heron.

Voice: A croaking, very throaty *gruuh*.

Status and Range: Generally a common year-round resident throughout the West Indies. Where it does not breed, it becomes scarce or absent in July and August. Also occurs throughout the eastern United States southward through much of South America.

Habitat: Calm, shallow freshwater and saltwater areas as well as swift-flowing rivers and streams.

Nesting: Usually colonial with other heron species in a wooded swamp. A platform of twigs is constructed high in a tree. Eggs (2–4) blue. Breeds from April to July.

TRICOLORED HERON *Egretta tricolor*   Plate 8
Local Names: Grey Gauldin (CI); Switching-neck (VI); Gaulin (Jamaica, VI); Garza Pechiblanco (DR); Garza Pechiblanca (PR); Garza de Vientre Blanco (Cuba, PR); Krabye Vant Blan, Crabier Aux Trois Couleurs, Quock (Haiti); Aigrette Tricolore, Héron Tricolore (Guad, Mart); Crabier (French LA)

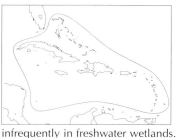

Identification: 61–71 cm (24–28"). Distinguished by its overall gray appearance, *white belly and undertail-coverts*. *Immature*: Browner.

Voice: A throaty *guarr* similar to that of Snowy Egret.

Status and Range: A common year-round resident in the Bahamas, Greater Antilles, Virgin and Cayman Islands, and San Andrés. It is generally rare in the Lesser Antilles. Occurs in much of temperate coastal North America south to northern South America.

Habitat: Mangrove swamps and saltwater lagoons, it occurs infrequently in freshwater wetlands.

Nesting: Often colonial with other heron species. The nest is a platform of sticks built on a tree limb. Eggs (3–4) bluish. Breeds from April to July.

REDDISH EGRET *Egretta rufescens*   Plate 8
Local Names: Gaulin (Jamaica); Garza Roja (Cuba); Garza Rojiza (DR, PR); Zegrèt Ble, Aigrette Bleue (Haiti)

Identification: 69–81 cm (27–32"). The *black-tipped bill, pinkish at base*, is the most conspicuous field mark in either the dark or white color phase. Other field characteristics are the ruffled appearance of the neck feathers and the bird's habit of pursuing its prey so energetically, that at times it appears to be dancing about in the water. *Dark phase*: Grayish overall; head and neck reddish-brown. *White phase*: White overall. *Immature*: Bill entirely dark; neck feathers unruffled. *Similar species*: Adult Little Blue Heron has a black-tipped bill which is gray at the base, not pink. Immature Little Blue Heron is similar to white phase Reddish Egret, but also has a gray, rather than pink, bill.

Voice: Squawks and croaks.

Status and Range: A locally common year-round resident in the Bahamas and Cuba, including the Isle of Youth, it is uncommon in the Cayman Islands (absent from Cayman Brac). This egret is irregular and local away from its breeding grounds where it is uncommon and very local on Jamaica, rare on Hispaniola and very rare on Puerto Rico. It is a vagrant in the Lesser Antilles where recorded from St Martin, Antigua, Montserrat and Dominica. Also occurs through the southern United States south to Costa Rica and on the northern coast of Venezuela.

Habitat: Primarily shallow, protected coastal waters, but also swamp edges.

Nesting: A platform of leaves and sticks is typically built in mangroves. Nesting is colonial with other herons. Eggs (2–5) pale greenish-blue. Breeds from December to April.

CATTLE EGRET *Bubulcus ibis*   Plate 8
Local Names: Cattle Gauldin (CI); Gaulin (Nevis); Cowbird, Ibis (Saba); Cattle Gaulin (VI); Tick Bird (Jamaica, Nevis); Garcita Bueyera (Cuba); Garza Ganadera (DR); Garza Africana, Garza del Ganado (PR); Krabye Gad-bèf, Grue Blanche (Haiti); Garde Boeuf (St L); Héron Garde-boeufs, Pique-boeufs, Kio Blanc (Guad, Mart); Koereiger (Saba, St E, St M); Crabier (LA); Tiqueur, Oiseau Détiqueur (French WI)

Identification: 48–64 cm (19–25"). Identified by its relatively small size and short, thick, yellowish bill, it is the *only heron of the uplands*. *Breeding*: Reddish legs and eyes; reddish-tinted bill. Tan wash on crown, breast and upper back. *Non-breeding*: Black legs and yellow bill. The tan wash is reduced. *Similar species*: Great Egret is an aquatic heron and is much larger. Its bill is yellower and longer.

Voice: Much guttural squawking around the breeding colony.

Status and Range: A common year-round resident throughout the West Indies. It is widespread in temperate and tropical portions of the world.

Comments: At dawn and dusk, these herons fly in formation to and from their roosts. Whereas other herons are rarely found away from water, the Cattle Egret is seldom found close to water except when coming to drink. This egret spread from Africa to South America and then through the West Indies in the 1950s, the result of an unusual range expansion through the Americas. As it colonized the West Indies, it apparently spread the cattle tick through the islands. Cattle Egret colonies appear to stimulate the nesting of other herons and egrets; they may well provide increased protection from predators.

Habitat: Pastures and fields where livestock are grazing or tractors are plowing. Roosts in mangroves or other densely wooded areas.

Nesting: Nesting is colonial on mangrove cays or in other wooded areas near water. The nest is a platform of twigs built in a tree. Eggs (2–4) bluish-white. Breeds primarily from April to July, but also in other seasons.

GREEN HERON *Butorides virescens*   Plate 9

Local Names: Mary Perk (CI); Water Witch (VI); Poor Joe (Bahamas, VI); Little Crabier, Kyallee (Grenada, St V); Gaulin (Jamaica, Nevis, St E, St M, Saba); Caga Leche (Cuba); Crá-Crá, Cuaco (DR); Martinete (PR); Krakra, Rakrak, Ti Krabye Riviè, Valet de Caïman (Haiti); Caiallee (St L); Héron Vert, Kio (Guad, Mart); Little Gaulin, Pond Bird, Groene reiger (Saba, St E, St M)

Identification: 40–48 cm (16–19"). *Adult*: Variable in coloration including a rare reddish-brown phase on Cuba. Note its small size, short neck, generally dark coloration and *greenish-yellow to orangish legs*. *Breeding adult*: Legs bright orange. *Immature*: Heavily streaked below. *Similar species*: The immature differs from American Bittern in being smaller, darker and lacking a black neck mark.

Voice: Upon being flushed, it calls a distinctive, piercing *skyow*. When undisturbed, the bird issues a less irritating series of *kek*, *kak* or *que* notes.

Status and Range: A common year-round resident throughout the West Indies. Occurs in much of temperate North America south to Colombia and Venezuela.

Comments: This is the small, dark, common heron of West Indian wetlands. Usually solitary, it is often discovered by its piercing call which it issues frequently. It typically perches motionless on a snag low over the water awaiting unwary prey. When surprised, it flies off, often emitting its characteristic call note.

Habitat: Any body of water from a puddle to the border of a large lagoon.

Nesting: Usually singly, though sometimes in scattered colonies, often with other herons. The nest is a platform of twigs of variable height built in a tree or bush usually in a wooded swamp. Eggs (3) greenish-blue. Breeds from April to August.

BLACK-CROWNED NIGHT-HERON *Nycticorax nycticorax* Plate 9

Local Names: Quok (Jamaica); Crabcracker (VI); Rey Congo (DR); Yaboa Real (PR); Guanabá de la Florida (Cuba, PR); Kòk Lannwit, Kòk Dlo, Coq-d'eau, Coq de Nuit (Haiti); Crabier du Nuit (St L); Bihoreau Gris, Crabier Bois, Crabier Grosse Tête (Guad, Mart)

Identification: 58–71 cm (23–28"). A medium-sized heron with a chunky appearance. *Adult*: Identified by its black crown and back and white face, underparts and head plumes. *Immature*: Brown with white flecks. *Flight*: Only the feet *extend beyond the tail*. *Similar species*: The immature is distinguished from the very similar immature Yellow-crowned Night-Heron by its browner appearance, larger white flecks on wings and upperparts, thinner bill and shorter legs. For additional guidance, refer to the citation under Yellow-crowned Night-Heron. The Limpkin is distinguished from immature Black-crowned Night-Heron by its larger size and longer, paler and slightly down-curved bill.

Voice: A distinctive *quark*, heard before sun-up and after sundown.

Status and Range: Generally an uncommon and local year-round resident on the larger islands of the Bahamas, the Greater Antilles and in the Virgin and Cayman Islands. Black-crowned Night-Heron is an uncommon to rare non-breeding resident in the Lesser Antilles from October to April when migrants that breed in North America occur widely in the West Indies. The species may breed on Barbados. It is widespread worldwide.

Comments: Nocturnal, it is usually seen at dawn or dusk. Solitary, except at the breeding colony.

Habitat: Primarily freshwater swamps though also brackish lagoons and salt ponds.

Nesting: Nesting is colonial. A bulky nest of twigs is built well up in a tree in a swamp or on a cay. Eggs (2–5) pale greenish-blue. The breeding season is quite variable ranging from as early as January to as late as July.

YELLOW-CROWNED NIGHT-HERON *Nyctanassa violacea* Plate 9

Local Names: Quok (Jamaica); Crabcracker (VI); Crab-catcher (CI, Jamaica); Rey Congo (DR); Yaboa Común (PR); Guanabá Real (Cuba, PR); Kòk Lan Nwit, Crabier Gris, Coq de Nuit (Haiti); Crabier Bois (St L); Bihoreau Violacé (Guad, Mart); Geelkruinnachtreiger (Saba, St E, St M); Crabier, Gaulin, Night Gaulin (LA)

Identification: 56–71 cm (22–28″). A medium-sized heron with a chunky appearance. *Adult*: Note the gray underparts and black-and-white head markings. *Immature*: Grayish-brown with white flecks. *Similar species*: Immature Yellow-crowned Night-Heron is very similar to immature Black-crowned Night-Heron, but has a heavier bill, grayer plumage with smaller white flecks on wings and upperparts and *longer legs which extend further beyond the tail in flight*. For additional guidance refer to: Kaufman, K. 1988. Immature Night Herons. *American Birds* 42(2): 169–171. The Limpkin is distinguished from immature Yellow-crowned by its larger size and longer, paler bill which is slightly down-curved.

Voice: A distinctive *quark* very similar to that of Black-crowned Night-Heron. It is most often heard before sun-up and after sundown.

Status and Range: Generally a common year-round resident in the Bahamas, Greater Antilles, the Virgin and Cayman Islands, and northern Lesser Antilles, it is uncommon south of Barbuda. The species is fairly common on San Andrés and Providencia. Local populations are joined from October to April by migrants that breed in North America. Also occurs in the eastern and central United States south into coastal portions of South America.

Comments: Solitary. Though mostly nocturnal, it is sometimes active during the day. Its heavy bill is adapted for eating hard-shelled crustaceans.

Habitat: Primarily mangrove swamps, but also freshwater areas and sometimes dry thickets away from water. Sometimes coastal mudflats.

Nesting: A bulky platform of twigs is constructed in a tree, sometimes far from water. Eggs (2–4) pale greenish-blue. Breeds from March to July.

IBISES AND SPOONBILLS: FAMILY THRESKIORNITHIDAE

Ibises and spoonbills are medium-sized gregarious waterbirds of shallow coastal lagoons. Ibises have distinctive down-curved bills adapted for obtaining food by probing shallow water, mud and grass for small animals, whereas bills of spoonbills are spatulate and used for catching floating prey in shallow water. Both ibises and spoonbills fly with their necks outstretched.

WHITE IBIS *Eudocimus albus* Plate 10

Local Names: Curlew (Jamaica); Cocó Blanco (Cuba, DR)

Identification: 56–71 cm (22–28″). *Adult*: The *long, down-curved reddish bill* of this fairly large white bird makes it distinctive. *Adult flight*: Note the outstretched neck and black wingtips. *Immature*: Primarily brown with a white belly and rump. *Similar species*: Glossy Ibis is entirely dark. Wood Stork is much larger and has a heavier bill. Immature Scarlet Ibis is tinged with pink on the back and rump.

Voice: A series of low, hoarse grunts and a nasal *oohh-oohh*.

Status and Range: A common year-round resident on Cuba and Hispaniola, uncommon and local on Jamaica and a rare non-breeding resident in the Bahamas. A rare wanderer to the Cayman Islands, primarily Grand Cayman, and a vagrant on Puerto Rico and Dominica. Occurs from southeastern United States to northern South America.

Comments: Typically flocks.

Habitat: Freshwater swamps, rice fields and saltwater lagoons.

Nesting: Nesting is colonial. The nest of twigs and grasses is typically built in mangroves, about 3 m (10″) above water. Eggs (3) whitish-green or yellowish-green with brownish markings, heavier at one end. Breeds from April to September.

SCARLET IBIS *Eudocimus ruber*   Plate 10

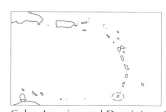

Identification: 58.5cm (23"). **Adult**: Unmistakable scarlet plumage with black wingtips. **Non-breeding adult**: Bill pinkish. **Breeding adult**: Bill blackish. **Immature**: Generally white below; brownish above. The pale *back and rump are tinged pink-buff*. **Similar species**: Immature White Ibis shows no pinkish on the rump or back.

Status and Range: A very rare wanderer to Grenada primarily from January to June, but has occurred during all months. A vagrant on Cuba, Jamaica and Dominica. Also occurs on Trinidad and much of coastal South America.

Comments: An individual Scarlet Ibis remained in Grenada for four years. There are at least five Scarlet Ibis records from Cuba in the past 40 years. These birds may well be stray escaped birds from Florida rather than natural wanderers from South America.

Habitat: Coastal swamps, lagoons and mangroves.

GLOSSY IBIS *Plegadis falcinellus*   Plate 10

Local Names: Curlew (Jamaica); Cocó Oscuro (DR); Cigueña (PR); Cocó Prieto (Cuba, DR, PR); Ibis Pechè, Ibis Noir, Pêcheur (Haiti); Coco (LA)

Identification: 56–64 cm (22–25"). **Adult**: Characterized by its entirely dark coloration and *long, down-curved bill*. **Immature**: Lighter than the adult. **Similar species**: Immature White Ibis has a white rather than dark abdomen.

Voice: A repeated grunt followed by other peculiar sounds reminiscent of a sheep.

Status and Range: Generally an uncommon and local year-round resident on Cuba, Jamaica and Hispaniola, though its numbers are increasing considerably on Cuba. It occurs very locally and irregularly on Puerto Rico where it may breed. An uncommon to rare non-breeding resident in the Bahamas and rare or a vagrant elsewhere in the West Indies. It is widespread worldwide.

Comments: Typically flocks. Apparently wanders among islands as habitat conditions warrant.

Habitat: Mud flats, marshy savannas and rice fields.

Nesting: Nesting is colonial. A simple platform of twigs is built in a small or medium-sized tree over water. Eggs (2-4) dark bluish-green or sometimes grayish-blue. Breeds primarily from June to August.

ROSEATE SPOONBILL *Ajaia ajaja*   Plate 10

Local Names: Seviya (Cuba); Cuchareta (DR); Espatil, Spatule (Haiti)

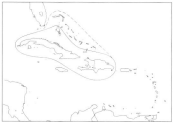

Identification: 66–81 cm (26–32"). Note its *pink coloration* and extraordinary *spatula-like bill*. **Immature**: Almost entirely white, but displays some pink.

Voice: Generally silent. On breeding grounds, emits soft grunts.

Status and Range: An uncommon and local year-round resident on Cuba and Hispaniola. In the Bahamas, it is a common year-round resident on Great Inagua, uncommon on Andros and rare or a vagrant on several other islands. It is a vagrant on Jamaica, Puerto Rico, the Virgin Islands (Anegada), the Cayman Islands (Grand Cayman), St Martin, St Barthélemy and Guadeloupe. Also occurs from the extreme southern United States through most of South America.

Comments: Typically flocks. Feeds by wading through shallow water with bill pointing downwards, waving its head back and forth, the bill straining out organisms from bottom sediments. Sometimes while feeding the head is entirely submerged. Feeds primarily on fish, but also invertebrates and plant matter.

Habitat: Primarily shallow saltwater lagoons and edges of mudflats.

Nesting: Nesting is colonial. The nest of dried grass, horse hair and feathers is built in mangroves or other shoreline trees. Eggs (2–4) dull white with dark spots. They are more heavily marked than those of White Ibis. Breeds from August to December.

STORKS: FAMILY CICONIIDAE

The storks comprise a small family of long-legged birds closely related to the ibises and spoonbills. All are large, with long necks, broad wings and short tails. The long, stout bill is usually straight. Storks are strong fliers, usually with their necks extended and legs trailing behind. They have broad wings which they use to soar on thermals. Most species are gregarious at times and may nest colonially.

WOOD STORK *Mycteria americana*   Plate 10
Local Names: Cayama (Cuba), Cocó (DR)

Identification: 100 cm (40″). Its large size, long legs, white coloration with black on wings, dark head and large bill, downcurved at the tip, are diagnostic. ***Adult***: Head bald and blackish with a black bill. ***Immature***: Head feathered and brownish with a yellowish bill. ***Flight***: Black trailing edge of wing; feet trail beyond tail. ***Similar species***: Much larger and with a much heavier bill than White Ibis. The adult plumage patterns are similar, but Wood Stork's legs are blackish, not pink, its head is dark and bare, and both primaries and secondaries are black. **Voice**: A gaspy grunt. Quite noisy on breeding grounds.

Status and Range: A rather rare year-round resident on Cuba, although found around the Birama Swamp in Granma Province, Zapata Swamp at Matanzas, locally along the coast in southern Pinar del Río Province and on some cays of the Sabana-Camagüey and Canarreos Archipelagos. This species is very rare in the Dominican Republic and is locally threatened. A vagrant on Grand Bahama in the Bahamas and on Jamaica and Dominica. Also occurs from southeastern United States to northern Argentina.

Habitat: Primarily swamps, mangroves and coastal mud flats. Also rice fields, ponds, and inland water bodies.

Nesting: In colonies, mainly in mangroves. The nest is a platform of sticks similar to that of a heron and is built in a tree. Eggs (3–5) white, larger than domestic chicken's. Breeds primarily from November to February.

FLAMINGOS: FAMILY PHOENICOPTERIDAE

The flamingos form a unique family. Feeding with their heads upside down, they filter small mollusks, crustaceans and other organisms from shallow lagoons, swallowing them with their heads still inverted, the water being strained out by the bird's specially adapted tongue and bill. They are gregarious and wary. In flight, the long thin neck is extended and the legs trail far behind the short tail.

GREATER FLAMINGO *Phoenicopterus ruber*   Plate 10
Local Names: Fillymingo (Jamaica); Flamenco (Cuba, DR, PR); Flanman, Flamant Rose (Haiti)

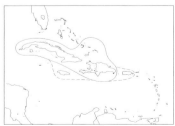

Identification: 107–122 cm (42–48″). ***Adult***: Note its *orangish-pink coloration, long legs and neck,* and *strangely curved bill.* ***Immature***: Much paler than the adult. ***Flight***: Head and neck outstretched and drooping, and flight feathers black. **Voice**: Distinctive, goose-like honks.

Status and Range: An abundant year-round resident on Great Inagua in the Bahamas where a colony of approximately 60,000 birds frequents Lake Rosa. Small colonies occur on nearby Acklins, Crooked and Caicos Islands. It is a common, but very local year-round resident on Cuba where a colony of 80,000 birds occurs at Ciego de Ávila and on Hispaniola, including Gonâve, Île-à-Vache, Saona and Beata Islands. On Hispaniola proper, it primarily occurs at Lago Enriquillo where a flock of 1,000 birds was seen in 1996. Formerly more abundant and widespread in the West Indies, particularly in the Bahamas, but has suffered severely from human persecution. Improved protection on Cuba and Hispaniola has resulted in recent increases in Greater Flamingo numbers. The species is rare and very local on Jamaica and Puerto

Rico, occurring on both islands with increased regularity, though it does not breed on either of them. Wanderers have recently occurred in the Cayman and Virgin Islands and in the northern Lesser Antilles south to St Christopher. Small numbers could occur almost anywhere in the West Indies and, should adequate habitat still exist and proper protection be provided, the birds might linger and even breed. Occurs on the north coast of South America and its offshore islands. Also Florida, the Yucatán and the Galápagos Islands, and much of the warmer portions of the Eastern Hemisphere east to Western India.

Comments: Typically flocks. Sometimes travels large distances in search of adequate habitat. Forages in shallow water, its head upside-down, filtering small organisms through its bill. Feeds on small crustaceans, mollusks and other invertebrates as well as algae and other plant matter.

Habitat: Shallow lagoons and coastal estuaries with high salinities.

Nesting: Nesting is colonial along lagoon borders. Mud is compacted into an elevated mound to form a nest. Egg (1) white. Breeds primarily from March to July.

SWANS, GEESE AND DUCKS: FAMILY ANATIDAE

The birds of this large, aquatic family are best treated by discussing the seven subfamilies that occur in the region.

Swans — In this region these very large birds, with entirely white plumage, dip for food with their long necks. They occur as vagrants.

Geese — Are intermediate between ducks and swans in size and the length of their necks. They are the most terrestrial subfamily, often feeding on grain in meadows and uplands. They occur rarely or as vagrants.

Whistling-Ducks — The largest of the ducks, they are primarily nocturnal, often grazing in wet, grassy meadows or dipping for food in shallow ponds. In flight their long legs and feet trail behind the tail, and the head is drooped, making them easily recognizable.

Dabbling Ducks — This is the best represented subfamily in the region. Dabblers only feed in shallow waters as they cannot dive and tip their heads beneath the surface, leaving their tails pointed upwards. On the other hand, dabblers can instantly take to the air when disturbed. Most have colorful iridescent patches on the secondaries, referred to as the speculum. These patches are excellent aids in identification.

Diving Ducks — These ducks frequent areas of deep open water, often diving and swimming to cover rather than taking flight when threatened. Their feet are set far back on their bodies forcing them to run over the water's surface to take flight.

Stiff-tailed Ducks — These are small, chunky ducks with short necks and stiff tails that are frequently held erect and are valuable aids in identification. They dive expertly and usually prefer to dive rather then fly to escape danger.

Mergansers — Rare in the region, these ducks have modified bills with serrate edges and a hook at the tip, adapted for catching fish. Both species that occur here are crested.

FULVOUS WHISTLING-DUCK *Dendrocygna bicolor* **Plates 19, 21**

Local Names: Chiriría Amarillenta (PR); Yaguasín (Cuba, DR); Kanna Siflè, Canard Siffleur (Haiti); Dendrocygne Fauve (Guad, Mart); Siffleur (French LA)

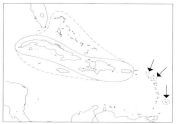

Identification: 46–51 cm (18–20"). The pale yellowish-brown coloration, *thin white stripe along the side* when sitting, *white uppertail-coverts*, long neck and erect stance are diagnostic. *Flight*: Note white uppertail-coverts and stripe at wing base. Underwing blackish; upperwing blackish with reddish-brown wing-coverts. Head and feet droop. Feet trail beyond tail. Its take-off is direct. *Similar species*: West Indian Whistling-Duck is deep brown and has dark uppertail-coverts and black and white markings on the sides and abdomen.

Voice: A squealing whistle *puteow*.

Status and Range: First recorded in the West Indies in 1943, this duck is now a common year-round resident on Cuba, locally common on Hispaniola and uncommon on Puerto Rico. It is a rare non-breeding resident in the Bahamas and a rare wanderer to the Cayman Islands, St Barthélemy, Antigua and Barbados. This duck is very rare on Jamaica and a vagrant to the Virgin Islands and the rest of the Lesser Antilles, but is extending its range southeastward in the West Indies. It is fairly difficult to observe due to its tendency to frequent dense aquatic vegetation. Occurs in five separate populations: southern United States to Mexico and the West Indies, northern South America, south-central South America, East Africa and India.

Comments: Typically flocks. It is more of a swamp-dweller than the other whistling-ducks and, unlike them, is more active during the daytime.

Habitat: Freshwater bodies with abundant water plants, especially rice fields.

Nesting: A grass nest is built in aquatic vegetation over the water or on adjacent higher ground. Rice fields are often used. Eggs (11–18) dull yellowish-white. Several females sometimes lay in the same nest forming clutches of up to 34 eggs. Breeds primarily in May and June, but sometimes extends season.

WEST INDIAN WHISTLING-DUCK   Plates 19, 21
Dendrocygna arborea

Local Names: Whistler (Antigua, Barbuda, CI, Jamaica, VI); Mangrove Duck, Night Duck (Jamaica, LA, VI); Yaguasa, Cuba Libre (Cuba); Chiriría del Caribe (PR); Yaguaza (DR, PR); Canard Siffleur, Jenjon, Gingeon (Haiti)

Identification: 48–56 cm (19–22"). Best distinguished by its deep brown coloration, white abdomen with black markings, long neck and erect stance. **Immature**: Color patterns are less distinct than in the adult. Less black on abdomen which appears as streaks rather than splotches. **Flight**: Very dark overall. Look for the mottled abdomen and gray upperwing-coverts. Head and feet droop. Feet extend beyond tail. Its take-off is direct and often silent. **Similar species**: Fulvous Whistling-Duck is yellowish-brown, has white uppertail-coverts and a white stripe along its side.

Voice: It is from this duck's shrilly whistled *chiriria* that one of its common Spanish names is derived.

Status and Range: A year-round resident through the Bahamas, Greater Antilles, the Virgin and Cayman Islands, Antigua and Barbuda. Once common, it is declining and endangered throughout its entire range. Still locally common on Cuba, it is uncommon in the Bahamas, Dominican Republic and the Cayman Islands, and rare and local on Jamaica, Puerto Rico, the Virgin Islands and Antigua. It is a vagrant elsewhere in the Lesser Antilles. The species is difficult to observe due to its nocturnal habits. This Whistling-duck's decline appears primarily due to habitat destruction and hunting. To a lesser extent, the species has suffered from introduced predators and the taking of birds to be kept as household pets.

Comments: Flocks are observed most regularly in early evening flying from mangroves or freshwater swamps where they roost during the day to nocturnal feeding grounds which include stands of royal palm and agricultural fields. The interpretation of its call as 'Cuba Libre' in Cuba has led some country people to not kill the bird.

Habitat: Mangroves, palm savannas, wooded swamps, lagoons and uplands.

Nesting: A cluster of palm fronds, a clump of bromeliads or a tree cavity appear to be typical nest sites in the Greater Antilles, but in Antigua this duck usually nests on the ground where it lines a scrape with fallen leaves and other loose vegetation. It sometimes nests in a low bush. May nest at some distance from ponds and even on offshore islands. It does not flush from the nest until the last instant and does not sound an alarm call. Eggs (4–16) white. Breeding has been recorded in virtually every month of the year and apparently varies depending on rainfall.

WHITE-FACED WHISTLING-DUCK   Plates 19, 21
Dendrocygna viduata

Identification: 44 cm (17"). **Adult**: A long-legged duck with a *distinctive white face*. **Immature**: Paler with a beige face. **Flight**: Wings are dark above and below; no white markings except on head. As with other whistling-ducks, flight is heavy with feet extending beyond tail. **Similar species**: Fulvous, Black-bellied and West Indian Whistling-Ducks are similar in profile, but all lack white on head.

Voice: A high-pitched three-note whistle.

Status and Range: A vagrant to the West Indies where recorded from Cuba, the Dominican Republic and Barbados. Last recorded in 1926. Occurs in Central and South America and Africa.

Habitat: Fresh and brackish wetlands. Generally inhabits open water.

BLACK-BELLIED WHISTLING-DUCK
Dendrocygna autumnalis

Plates 19, 21

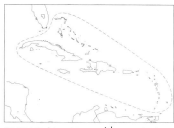

Identification: 46–53 cm (18–21"). *Adult*: The large, *white wing patch, black belly* and reddish bill and legs are good field marks. *Immature*: Much duller than the adult. Gray bill and legs. *Flight*: The upperwing has a large white patch. Head and feet droop; feet trail beyond tail. Its take-off is direct.

Voice: A characteristic shrill, chattering whistle (Pough).

Status and Range: Generally a very rare wanderer through the West Indies where reported from Andros in the Bahamas, Cuba, Jamaica, Puerto Rico, the Virgin Islands (St Croix), the Cayman Islands and the central and southern Lesser Antilles. The species appears to occur with greatest regularity on Cuba and Barbados. Occurs through the southern United States south to central South America.

Habitat: Freshwater marshes and brackish lagoons.

Nesting: Eggs (8–12) white. There is a single report from Puerto Rico of a nest with two eggs and two young in a hollow tree. It is believed to nest in Cuba.

TUNDRA SWAN *Cygnus columbianus*

Plate 18

Identification: 122–140 cm (48–55"). A huge bird with a long neck and short legs. *Adult*: White overall with a black bill, sometimes with a small amount of yellow on lores. *Immature*: Pale grayish-brown plumage; bill pinkish. *Similar species*: The Mute Swan (*Cygnus olor*), which sometimes escapes from captivity, has an orange bill with a black nob at its base.

Status and Range: A vagrant to the West Indies. Recorded from Cuba, Puerto Rico, St Thomas in the Virgin Islands and Antigua. All records to date are from December. The occurrence of Tundra Swan in the West Indies is likely the result of birds being forced further south than usual by major blizzards striking eastern North America. The species should be looked for in the West Indies following such events. Occurs through much of the northern portions of the Northern Hemisphere and straying widely elsewhere.

GREATER WHITE-FRONTED GOOSE *Anser albifrons*

Plate 18

Identification: 66–86.5 cm (26–34"). A medium-sized goose. *Adult*: Important field marks are its brownish-gray color above, white rump, *white feathers framing the base of the pink or orange bill* and *belly barred with black*. *Immature*: Appears uniform dark brown.

Status and Range: A vagrant to the West Indies. Recorded from Cuba. This goose, which breeds in the western subarctic of North America, migrates primarily down the Mississippi flyway in the center of the continent to winter along the western portion of the Gulf of Mexico and at other sites further west. Its occurrence in the West Indies, therefore, is most likely as a vagrant to Cuba. It is widespread in North America and Eurasia.

Habitat: Ponds and lagoons.

ORINOCO GOOSE *Neochen jubata*

Plate 78

Identification: 61–67 cm (24–26.5"). A large waterbird with a pale gray head and neck, reddish-brown body and dark wings with a white speculum.

Status and Range: A vagrant to the West Indies. Recorded from Barbados and Jamaica. Occurs in North-central South America.

Comments: A specimen from Jamaica, collected in 1865, has few details attached. This has led some to believe the bird was brought to Jamaica by traders. The recent occurrence of this species on Barbados suggests that it strays naturally to the West Indies.

SNOW GOOSE *Chen caerulescens*   **Plate 18**
Local Name: Guanana Prieta (Cuba)

Identification: 58–71 cm (23–28"). There are two distinct color phases. ***Adult***: *White phase* — Entirely white; *black primaries*; pink bill and legs. *Dark phase* — Bluish-gray; *white head and upperneck*; pink bill and legs. ***Immature***: *White phase* — Grayish above and blackish bill and legs. *Dark phase* — Brownish-gray overall and blackish bill and legs. ***Flight***: Its take-off is direct. **Status and Range**: A rare migrant in the northern Bahamas (Grand Bahama, Abaco and New Providence) and on Cuba. It should be looked for from October to March. A vagrant in the southern Bahamas, Puerto Rico, Virgin Islands (St Croix) and Barbados. Also occurs from northern Canada and Alaska to northern Mexico.
Habitat: Borders of freshwater ponds and swamps as well as flooded uplands. May forage in croplands.

CANADA GOOSE *Branta canadensis*   **Plate 18**

Identification: 64–110 cm (25–43"). The black head and neck with a *white band on cheeks and throat* are distinctive. ***Flight***: Dark wings with a *white band across the uppertail-coverts*. Its take-off is direct.
Status and Range: A vagrant from October to April to the Bahamas (Andros, New Providence and Eleuthera), Cuba, Jamaica, Hispaniola, Puerto Rico and the Cayman Islands. Occurs throughout much of the Northern Hemisphere.
Habitat: Borders of wetlands from saltwater lagoons to freshwater swamps including flooded uplands.

WOOD DUCK *Aix sponsa*   **Plates 20, 22**
Local Name: Huyuyo (Cuba, PR)

Identification: 43–51 cm (17–20"). ***Male***: Note its crest and unusual facial pattern. ***Female***: Identified by its crest and large, asymetrical eyering. ***Flight***: A long, squared tail and large head with bill tilted down. Its take-off is direct.
Voice: Males, when alarmed, emit a short call three to four times. Females issue a peculiar wavering note reminiscent of a woodpecker.
Status and Range: An uncommon year-round resident on Cuba, a few birds departing to breed in North America in April and returning in September. A rare migrant and non-breeding resident in the northern Bahamas from October to March. A vagrant in the Cayman Islands, Jamaica, Hispaniola, Puerto Rico, Saba and St Martin. Also occurs throughout most of eastern North America as well as the west coast.
Habitat: Canals, lagoons and impoundments.
Nesting: The nest, lined with feathers or other soft material, is in a tree cavity or dead palm, usually near the water. Eggs (6–14) bone-white. Breeds from July to October.

GREEN-WINGED TEAL *Anas crecca*   **Plates 19, 21**
Local Names: Duck-and-Teal, Teal (Jamaica); Pato de la Carolina (DR); Pato Aliverde (PR); Pato Serrano (Cuba, DR)

Identification: 33–39 cm (13–15.5"). A small duck with a green speculum and lacking blue in the forewing. ***Female and non-breeding male***: Mottled brown with dark lores, with a whitish belly and a pale patch beneath the tail. ***Breeding male***: Note the *green eye patch* and speculum, reddish-brown head and *white vertical bar in front of wing*. ***Flight***: Green speculum edged with white or buff. A surface feeder, its take-off is direct. **Similar species**: Female and non-breeding male Green-winged and Blue-winged Teals are very similar, but Green-winged Teal lacks the distinctive whitish spot on

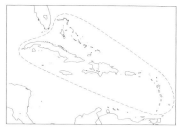

the lores and has a smaller bill, whitish belly and a pale patch beneath the tail. In flight, it lacks the blue forewing of Blue-winged Teal. It differs from the similarly-plumaged Cinnamon Teal by its smaller bill, paler belly and in flight, by the absence of blue in the forewing.
Status and Range: An uncommon non-breeding resident in the northern Bahamas and generally rare in the southern Bahamas, Greater Antilles, the Virgin and Cayman Islands and Barbados. Generally a vagrant locally in the Lesser Antilles. Occurs from October to March. It is widespread in the Northern Hemisphere.
Habitat: Shallow freshwater bodies.

AMERICAN BLACK DUCK *Anas rubripes*   Plates 19, 21

Identification: 53–64 cm (21–25"). The dark brown coloration and purple speculum are important field marks. **Male**: Bill yellow. **Female**: Bill olive, mottled with black. **Flight**: The white underwings contrast with the dark body. A surface feeder, its take-off is direct. **Similar species**: Female Mallard is lighter brown in color than American Black Duck and has white bands on either side of a blue speculum.
Status and Range: A vagrant to the West Indies. Recorded from the Bahamas (Grand Turk and perhaps San Salvador) and Puerto Rico. Occurs through eastern North America.
Comments: Though this duck resides through much of the southeastern United States during the non-breeding season, it apparently rarely strays to the West Indies. This has led some to question the veracity of records from Puerto Rico, an island well outside the bird's normal range.
Habitat: Shallow water bodies.

MALLARD *Anas platyrhynchos*   Plates 19, 21
Local Names: Duck-and-Teal (Jamaica); Pato Inglés (Cuba, DR, PR)

Identification: 51–71 cm (20–28"). A large duck with a *blue speculum bordered with white*. **Non-breeding male and immature**: Mottled brown overall with an olive-colored bill. **Adult female**: Similar, but the bill is orange with black markings. **Breeding male**: The rounded *green head, yellow bill* and maroon breast are distinctive. **Flight**: A surface feeder, its take-off is direct. **Similar species**: Northern Shoveler has a green head, like male Mallard, but has a white breast, reddish-brown sides and a noticeably longer bill. Some mergansers have green heads, but they have crests and slender, hooked bills. American Black Duck is darker than female Mallard and has a purple speculum without white edges. Female Gadwall has a white speculum and darker tail.
Status and Range: A very rare non-breeding resident from October to April in the northern Bahamas and Cuba and a vagrant on Jamaica, Hispaniola, Puerto Rico, the Virgin (St Croix) and Cayman Islands, and the Lesser Antilles where recorded from St Barthélemy, Antigua, Guadeloupe, Martinique and the Grenadines. It is often difficult to determine whether recent sightings are of wild Mallards or of birds released locally. For example, a flock was introduced on Grand Cayman in the Cayman Islands in 1983. It is widespread in North and Central America, Eurasia and parts of Africa.
Habitat: All bodies of calm, shallow water.

WHITE-CHEEKED PINTAIL *Anas bahamensis*   Plates 19, 21
Local Names: Brass Wing (Bahamas, VI); Summer Duck, White-head, White-throat (English LA); Pato de Bahamas (Cuba); Pato de la Orilla (DR); Pato Quijada Colorada (PR); Kanna Tèt Blan, Canard des Bahamas (Haiti); Bahama pijlstaart (St M)

Identification: 38–48 cm (15–19"). Note the *red bill mark* and *white cheek*. The speculum is green with buff-colored borders. **Flight**: A surface feeder, its take-off is direct.
Status and Range: A year-round resident through the Bahamas, Greater Antilles, Virgin Islands and northern Lesser Antilles from Anguilla south to Antigua. It moves among islands when conditions

warrant. Formerly common, the species has dramatically declined throughout much of its range. It is now only locally common in the Bahamas, Cuba, the Virgin Islands and Antigua; locally uncommon on Hispaniola and Puerto Rico; and uncommon to rare in most of the northern Lesser Antilles and on Barbados. A vagrant to the Cayman Islands, Jamaica, Guadeloupe and Martinique. This duck is considered threatened due to overhunting, habitat destruction and mongoose predation on nests. The Cuban population recovered dramatically following the expansion of rice plantations in 1961. Also through much of South America.

Habitat: Water bodies from fresh to hypersaline.

Nesting: A scrape is made on dry land concealed under a clump of vegetation, sometimes a great distance from water. Eggs (5–12) light tan. Breeds from February to June, but the season varies depending upon rainfall and perhaps the availability of invertebrates.

NORTHERN PINTAIL *Anas acuta*   Plates 19, 21
Local Names: Pato Pescuecilargo (Cuba, DR, PR); Kanna Pilè, Pilet (Haiti)

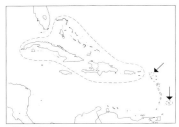

Identification: Male: 69–74 cm (27–29"); female: 54–56 cm (21–22"). *Female and non-breeding male*: Mottled brown. Identified by the noticeably pointed tail; long, slender neck; and narrow, gray bill. *Breeding male*: Note its brown head; white breast and neck stripe; and long, pointed tail. *Flight*: The long, slender neck and pointed tail characterize both sexes. The male has a greenish speculum with a buff-colored inner border and white trailing edge. The female has a browner speculum with a white trailing edge. The gray under-wing contrasts with the white belly. A surface feeder, its take-off is direct.

Status and Range: A decidedly uncommon non-breeding resident on Cuba, Hispaniola and Puerto Rico, it is rare in the Bahamas, the larger Virgin Islands, St Barthélemy and Barbados, and is a vagrant on Jamaica, the Cayman Islands and the Lesser Antilles. This is one of the first migrant ducks to arrive in the West Indies occurring as early as September and usually leaving by April. Occurs through North America to northern South America. Also Eurasia and northern Africa.

Habitat: Primarily fresh water, but also salt ponds.

BLUE-WINGED TEAL *Anas discors*   Plates 19, 21
Local Names: Teal (CI, Jamaica, St M.); Duck-and-Teal (Jamaica, St M); Pato Zarcel (PR); Pato de la Florida (Cuba, DR, PR); Sarcelle, Kanna Sasèl (Haiti); Blauwvleugeltaling (St M); Sarcelle á Ailes Bleues, Sarcelle (à ailes bl.) (Guad, Mart)

Identification: 38–40 cm (15–16"). The *blue forewing*, notice-able in flight, and the duck's small size are important field marks for both sexes in any plumage. *Female and non-breed-ing male*: Mottled brown with a green speculum. This is the Blue-winged Teal's most typical plumage while in the West Indies. *Breeding male*: Distinct white crescent on face. *Flight*: *Conspicuous blue forewing*. A surface feeder, its take-off is direct. *Similar species*: Female and non-breeding male Blue-winged and Green-winged Teal are very similar. Blue-winged Teal has a light spot on the lores, a darker belly and lacks a pale patch beneath the tail. Cinnamon Teal, a vagrant, has a larger bill, more reddish face and lacks the lore spot and dark line through the eye. For more comprehensive guidance in distinguishing females of Blue-winged Teal, Green-winged Teal, Northern Pintail, American Wigeon, Northern Shoveler, Gadwall and Mallard see: Kaufman, K. 1988. Female Dabbling Ducks. *American Birds* 42(5): 1203–1205.

Status and Range: The most common non-breeding resident duck in the West Indies, it occurs on all islands though generally less frequently in the Lesser Antilles. The species is rare on San Andrés and has yet to be recorded from Providencia. It is most abundant from October to April, but individuals may occur during any month. Recently, the species has been recorded on Puerto Rico. Occurs through North America to northern South America.

Comments: Numbers have declined sharply since the 1950s and 1960s.

Habitat: Shallow areas of both fresh- and saltwater bodies.

CINNAMON TEAL *Anas cyanoptera*   Plates 19, 21

Identification: 38–40 cm (15–16"). ***Female and non-breeding male***: Mottled brown with a green speculum. ***Breeding male***: Cinnamon-colored head and underparts. The male has red eyes in all plumages. ***Flight***: Note the light blue forewing. A surface feeder, its take-off is direct. ***Similar species***: Female and non-breeding male Cinnamon and Blue-winged Teal are very similar. Cinnamon Teal lacks the light spot on the lores and dark line through the eye, has a larger bill and a reddish tint to its plumage, most noticeable on the face. It differs from Green-winged Teal in its significantly larger bill and darker belly. In flight, Green-winged Teal lacks the blue forewing.

Status and Range: A vagrant to the West Indies. Recorded from the Bahamas, Cuba, Jamaica, Puerto Rico, the Virgin Islands, Antigua and Barbados. Occurs through much of western North America south to northern South America.

Habitat: Shallow water bodies.

NORTHERN SHOVELER *Anas clypeata*   Plates 19, 21

Local Names: Shovel-mouth (VI); Spoonbill (Jamaica, VI); Cuchareta (DR); Pato Cuchareta (Cuba, PR); Kanna Souchè (Haiti); Canard Souchet (Guad, Haiti, Mart)

Identification: 43–53 cm (17–21"). The *unusually large bill* is diagnostic. ***Male***: Green head, white breast and reddish-brown sides and belly. ***Female***: Mottled brown. ***Flight***: The blue forewing is distinctive and the speculum is green. A surface feeder, its take-off is direct. ***Similar species***: Male Mallard also has a green head, but its breast is maroon and the bill is smaller and yellow.

Status and Range: A migrant and less frequently a non-breeding resident throughout the West Indies primarily from October to May. It is common on Cuba; uncommon in the Bahamas, Hispaniola, Puerto Rico and the Cayman Islands; rare on Jamaica and very rare in the Virgin Islands. In the Lesser Antilles, the species is uncommon on Barbados, rare on Guadeloupe and Martinique and is a vagrant elsewhere. Occurs through North America south to Colombia. Also Eurasia to northern Africa.

Comments: Numbers have declined since the 1950s and 1960s.

Habitat: Fresh and brackish water bodies; rarely saline lagoons.

GADWALL *Anas strepera*   Plates 20, 22

Local Name: Pato Gris (Cuba)

Identification: 46–57 cm (18–22.5"). The *white speculum* is an important field mark in all plumages. ***Male***: Mottled gray above with *black rump and tail coverts* and dark brown head. ***Female***: Mottled brown overall except whitish belly and bill slightly orange with dark gray along the ridge. ***Similar species***: Female Mallard has a whitish tail and lacks the white speculum. Female American Wigeon has a light blue bill and green speculum.

Status and Range: A rare non-breeding resident in the Bahamas and very rare on Cuba. A vagrant on Jamaica, Hispaniola, Guadeloupe and St Lucia. Occurs from October to March. It is widespread in North America south to Guatemala.

Habitat: Usually freshwater ponds and lagoons.

EURASIAN WIGEON *Anas penelope*   Plates 19, 21

Identification: 42–52 cm (16.5–20"). *Male*: The *dark reddish-brown head* with a *golden cream-colored crown stripe* distinguish it from all other red-headed species. Breast is pinkish. *Female*: Occurs in two color phases. *Gray Phase* — Brownish overall with a gray head and light blue bill. *Red Phase* — Similar, but with a reddish tint to the head and neck. *Flight*: White patch on forewing, green speculum, white belly and blackish flecks on wingpits. A surface feeder, its take-off is direct. *Similar species*: The gray phase female is very similar to female American Wigeon, but often has a darker gray head. The red phase female is decidedly redder on the head. Both color phases of Eurasian Wigeon have blackish flecks on their wingpits, while those of American Wigeon are whitish. For additional characters on distinguishing these birds see: Harrop, A. 1994. Field Identification of American Wigeon. *Birding World* 7(2): 50–56.
Status and Range: A vagrant to the West Indies. Recorded from Hispaniola, Puerto Rico, Barbuda and Barbados. Occurs from October to February. It is widespread in Eurasia and northern Africa.
Comments: Individuals may occur in flocks of American Wigeon. A bird banded in Iceland was recovered in Barbuda.
Habitat: Usually freshwater ponds and lagoons.

AMERICAN WIGEON *Anas americana*   Plates 19, 21
Local Names: Baldpate (Bahamas); Pato Labanco (Cuba); Pato Cabecilargo (DR); Pato Cabeciblanco (PR); Kanna Zèl Blan, Siffleur Américain (Haiti); Canard d' Amérique (Guad, Mart)

Identification: 46–56 cm (18–22"). *Male*: Important field marks are the *white crown, light blue bill* and *green eyepatch*. *Female*: Brownish with a gray head and light blue bill. *Flight*: *White patch on forewing*, green speculum and white belly. A surface feeder, its take-off is direct. *Similar species*: Gadwall has a white speculum and neither sex has the pale blue bill of American Wigeon. See Eurasian Wigeon.
Status and Range: A migrant and less frequently a non-breeding resident throughout the West Indies principally from October to April. Common on Cuba, it is fairly common on Hispaniola; uncommon in the Bahamas, Puerto Rico and the Virgin and Cayman Islands; rare on Jamaica and locally rare in the Lesser Antilles including Anguilla, St Barthélemy, Guadeloupe, Dominica, Martinique and Barbados. It is very rare elsewhere in the Lesser Antilles. Occurs through North America south to northern South America.
Comments: Apparently has declined significantly throughout the West Indies since the 1950s.
Habitat: Primarily freshwater bodies, but also saltwater ponds.

CANVASBACK *Aythya valisineria*   Plates 20, 22
Local Name: Pato Lomiblanco (Cuba)

Identification: 51–61 cm (20–24"). The *sloping forehead profile* is distinctive in both sexes. *Male*: Reddish-brown head and neck. *Female*: Brown head and neck with less contrast in plumage. *Flight*: The long head and neck give the bird an elongated appearance. Its dark breast and undertail contrast with the very light belly and abdomen. A diving duck, the Canvasback runs over the water to take off. *Similar species*: Similarly-patterned Redhead lacks the sloping forehead of Canvasback.
Status and Range: A very rare non-breeding resident on Cuba from October to March, it is a vagrant in the Bahamas (Eleuthera), Jamaica, Hispaniola, Puerto Rico and Antigua. Occurs through North America irregularly to Guatemala.
Habitat: Large, relatively deep lagoons and canals with well-vegetated edges.

REDHEAD *Aythya americana*   **Plates 20, 22**
Local Name: Pato Cabecirrojo (Cuba)

Identification: 46–56 cm (18–22"). Both sexes have steep fore-heads. **Male**: *Pale gray back* and *black neck* contrast with rounded reddish head. Breast and rump are black. **Female**: Uni-formly dull brown overall. Look for the *blue bill tipped with black*. **Flight**: A diving duck, it runs over the water to take off. **Similar species**: Canvasback has a sloping forehead.
Status and Range: A very rare non-breeding resident in the Bahamas, Cuba and Barbados from November to March. A vagrant on Jamaica and Hispaniola. It is widespread in North America south to Guatemala.
Habitat: Ponds and lagoons.

RING-NECKED DUCK *Aythya collaris*   **Plates 20, 22**
Local Names: Pato Cabezón (Cuba); Cabezón (DR); Pato del Medio (PR); Kanna Tèt Nwa, Canard Tête-noire (Haiti); Fuligne (St L)

Identification: 40–46 cm (16–18"). **Male**: *White bill-ring*, black back and *white vertical bar in front of the wing* are impor-tant field marks. **Female**: Note the light bill-ring and *eyering*, sometimes with a trailing white streak between the cheek and crown. **Flight**: In both sexes, the dark upperwing-coverts con-trast with the *pale gray secondaries*. A diving duck, it runs over the water to take off.
Status and Range: A common non-breeding resident on Cuba and locally in the Bahamas (New Providence and Eleuthera). It is uncommon in the remainder of the Bahamas, Jamaica, His-paniola, Puerto Rico and the Virgin Islands; rare in the southern Bahamas, Barbados and San Andrés and generally a vagrant in the Cayman Islands and Lesser Antilles. The species occurs primarily from October to March. Occurs throughout North and Central America south to Panama.
Habitat: Confined to open freshwater areas.

GREATER SCAUP *Aythya marila*   **Plates 20, 22**

Identification: 38–51 cm (15–20"). **Male**: *Head appears smoothly rounded or slightly flat-topped*. The head's deep iri-descent green color appears black at a distance, and the bill is pale blue with a moderately wide black nail on the tip. **Female**: Note the *white feathering around the base of the bill* reaching to the forehead; dark brown sides and rump. **Flight**: Both sexes have *white secondaries and inner primaries*. A diving duck, it runs over the water to take off. **Similar species**: Adult male Lesser Scaup has a more peaked head profile, deep purple iri-descence on the head when seen in good light, a narrow black-tipped bill and white confined to the secondaries when seen in flight. Females of the two species can be distinguished by head shape and the extent of white in the primaries.
Status and Range: A very rare southbound migrant in the Bahamas, Virgin Islands (St Croix), and Barbados from September to February. The species occurs only as a vagrant on Jamaica and during its northbound migration in May. A widespread Northern Hemisphere circumpolar species.
Habitat: Deep saline waters or inland brackish ponds.

LESSER SCAUP *Aythya affinis*   Plates 20, 22

Local Names: Black Duck (Jamaica); Black Head (Jamaica, VI); Pato Morisco (Cuba); Pato Pechiblanco (PR); Pato Turco (DR, PR); Petit Fuligule (Guad, Mart); Kanna Tèt Nwa, Canard Tête-noire (Haiti, St L)

Identification: 38–46 cm (15–18"). *Male*: The dark head, breast, and tail, and whitish back and flanks are good field marks. *Female*: Brown with a large white mark behind the bill. *Flight*: In both sexes, the secondaries are white and the primaries dark. A diving duck, it runs over the water to take off. *Similar species*: The very similar Greater Scaup is distinguished by its rounder head and broader bill tip. The male's head has a greenish, rather than purplish, sheen. In flight, the secondaries and most of the primaries are white.

Status and Range: A fairly common, but local non-breeding resident in the Bahamas and Cuba, it is uncommon on Jamaica, Hispaniola, Puerto Rico and in the Cayman Islands. This duck is rare in the Virgin Islands and on San Andrés and generally very rare in the Lesser Antilles south to Barbados. Occurs primarily from November to March. Widespread throughout North America to northern South America.

Comments: Typically flocks. Numbers have declined sharply since the 1950s and 1960s.

Habitat: Bodies of open water, both fresh and saline.

BUFFLEHEAD *Bucephala albeola*   Plates 20, 22

Local Name: Pato Moñudo (Cuba)

Identification: 33–38 cm (13–15"). *Male*: Its *small size, large white head patch* and primarily white plumage are diagnostic. *Female*: Browner than the male with a distinctive white facial stripe. *Flight*: The speculum is white. The male also has a white forewing. A diving duck, it runs over the water to take off. **Similar species**: Hooded Merganser has a crested, rather than rounded, head and a slender, hooked bill. Female Hooded Merganser lacks white on the head.

Status and Range: Very rare on Cuba, the species is a vagrant in the Bahamas (Eleuthera), Jamaica and Puerto Rico. There is a questionable record from St Lucia. It should be looked for from October to March. Occurs throughout most of North America.

Habitat: Open water of bays and lagoons.

HOODED MERGANSER *Lophodytes cucullatus*   Plates 20, 22

Local Names: Pato de Cresta (Cuba); Mergansa de Caperuza (PR); Harle Couronné (Mart)

Identification: 40–48 cm (16–19"). The crest and slender bill, hooked at the tip, are distinctive of mergansers. *Male*: Crest has a *large white patch*. *Female*: Generally dark plumage and bill, the bill is dull orange near base. *Flight*: More horizontal than most ducks. The male is dark above with a small white patch on the secondaries and a pale forewing. The female is brown above with only a small white patch on the secondaries. A diving duck, it runs over the water to take off. *Similar species*: The female is similar to female Red-breasted Merganser, but is recognized by Hooded Merganser's smaller size and darker face, bill and back. It differs from the female Bufflehead by its crest; slender, hooked bill and lack of a white facial patch.

Status and Range: A very rare non-breeding resident in the Bahamas, Cuba, Hispaniola, Puerto Rico, the Virgin Islands, Martinique and Barbados. It should be looked for from November to February. Occurs through much of North America.

Habitat: Inland ponds and lagoons.

RED-BREASTED MERGANSER *Mergus serrator*   Plates 20, 22
Local Names: Pato Serrucho (Cuba); Mergansa Pechirroja (PR)

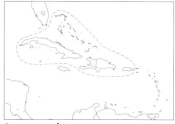

Identification: 51–64 cm (20–25"). The crest and slender, hooked bill aid identification. *Male*: Green head, white collar and dark breast. *Female*: Note the reddish-brown head and bill and whitish chin, foreneck and breast. Its back is gray. *Flight*: More horizontal than most ducks. The male's secondaries and forewing are white crossed by two dark bars. Only the female's secondaries are white and crossed by one dark bar. A diving duck, it runs over the water to take off. *Similar species*: The female differs from female Hooded Merganser by her lighter face and back and reddish bill.

Status and Range: A very rare non-breeding resident between November and March. There are records from the Bahamas, Cuba, Hispaniola, Puerto Rico and the Cayman Islands. Occurs through most of North America and Eurasia.
Habitat: Primarily open water of bays, the ocean near shore and inland lagoons.

RUDDY DUCK *Oxyura jamaicensis*   Plates 20, 22
Local Names: Blue-bill (Grenada); Rubber Duck (VI); Red Diver (Jamaica, Grenadines, VI); Diving Teal (Jamaica, VI); Pato Espinoso, Pato Rojizo (DR); Pato Chorizo (Cuba, PR); Coucouraime, Kanna Plonjon, Koukourèm, Canard Plongeur (Haiti); Canard Plongeon (LA)

Identification: 35–43 cm (14–17"). Tail often erect. *Male*: Overall reddish-brown coloration, *white cheek patch* and *blue bill*. The West Indian subspecies of the Ruddy Duck has black markings on its white cheeks. The migratory form lacks these black markings. *Female and immature*: Mostly brown with a single brown stripe below the eye. *Flight*: Appears chunky with a relatively long tail and dark upperwings. Male: White cheek. Female: Cheek stripe. A diving duck, it runs over the water to take off. *Similar species*: Female Masked Duck has two dark facial stripes rather than one.

Status and Range: A locally common year-round resident on New Providence in the Bahamas and Greater Antilles, it is uncommon and local elsewhere in the Bahamas and rare in the Virgin Islands and Barbados. A vagrant in the Cayman Islands and among the other Lesser Antilles. Migrants that breed in North America augment local populations from October to March. The resident West Indian subspecies has declined substantially in the Bahamas, Puerto Rico and the Virgin Islands to the point of being threatened on these islands. However, populations on Cuba, Jamaica and Hispaniola appear to be relatively stable. Occurs through North America to Central America.
Habitat: Predominantly deep, open freshwater bodies but also brackish lagoons.
Nesting: The nest is built over water in emergent swamp vegetation. Eggs (4–12) white and very large. Breeds from June to August.

MASKED DUCK *Nomonyx dominicus*   Plates 20, 22
Local Names: Squat Duck, Duck-and-Teal (Jamaica); Pato Agostero (Cuba); Pato Criollo (DR); Pato Enmascarado (PR); Croube, Kanna Zonbi, Canard Masqué (Haiti); Erismature Routoutou (Guad, Mart); Canard Routoutou, Canard Zombie (LA)

Identification: 30–36 cm (12–14"). Erect tail; white wing patch. *Breeding male*: Note the black face, reddish-brown coloration and blue bill. *Non-breeding male, female and immature*: *Two brown facial stripes; white wing patch*. *Flight*: Chunky, with a long tail and conspicuous white patch on the secondaries and portion of forewing in all plumages. Its take-off is direct. *Similar species*: Female Ruddy Duck has only one dark facial stripe and lacks a white wing patch.
Status and Range: A fairly common, but local year-round resident on Cuba; uncommon on Jamaica, Hispaniola and St Lucia and rare on Puerto Rico, Marie Galante off Guadeloupe, Martinique and Barbados. Masked Duck is a very rare wanderer elsewhere in the West Indies. It breeds locally in the Greater Antilles, is known to breed on Martinique and St Lucia and is suspected to breed on Guadeloupe. Its numbers apparently fluctuate in the West Indies; however, the species appears to

have declined on several islands and is now considered threat-ened. The causes are primarily habitat destruction and, to a lesser extent, hunting and egg predation by rats. Occurs from Mexico south through South America.

Comments: Frequents thick, aquatic vegetation and is easily overlooked.

Habitat: Freshwater swamps and canals with much floating vegetation and rice fields.

Nesting: The nest is built among swamp vegetation over or near the water. Eggs (8–18) (the latter presumably by two females)

beige. Breeds from May to August.

AMERICAN VULTURES: FAMILY CATHARTIDAE

This small Western Hemisphere family contains only seven species, all of which are large birds with unfeathered heads and necks. They are excellent soarers and all feed primarily on carrion. Only two species occur in the West Indies.

BLACK VULTURE *Coragyps atratus*   **Plate 24**

Identification: 58–68 cm (23–26.5"). A large, black bird with a very short tail. *Flight*: Conspicuous white wing patches. Flight is labored, alternating rapid spurts of flapping with brief glides. Wings held horizontal. Soars at altitude. *Similar species*: Turkey Vulture lacks white wing patches, has a longer tail and rocks as it soars, flapping only occasionally, with its wings held well above the hor-izontal. Adult Common Black-Hawk has a broad, white tail band.

Status and Range: A vagrant to the West Indies. Recorded from the Bahamas (Bimini), Cuba, Jamaica and Grenada. Occurs through the southern United States to northern Chile and northern Argentina.

Habitat: Primarily open lowlands, including urban areas.

TURKEY VULTURE *Cathartes aura*   **Plate 24**

Local Names: Crow, Carrion Crow (Bahamas); John Crow (CI, Jamaica); Aura Tiñosa (Cuba, DR, PR); Malfini Karanklou, Vautour (Haiti)

Identification: 68–80 cm (27–32"). Its large size, blackish col-oration and small bare head are diagnostic. Distinctive soaring flight with its dark two-toned wings held well above the horizon-tal in a broad V. *Adult*: Head red, noticeable only at close range. *Immature*: Head blackish. *Similar species*: See Black Vulture.

Voice: Mute, but young and even adults make some noises at the nest, by expelling air, producing a hissing whistle and other unusual sounds.

Status and Range: A common and widespread year-round res-ident on Cuba and Jamaica, it is common, but local, in the large northern Bahama Islands (Grand Bahama, Abaco and Andros), northeastern Hispaniola and south-western Puerto Rico. Migratory individuals apparently augment local numbers in the Bahamas and Cuba. In the Cayman Islands, the species is a rare non-breeding resident on Cayman Brac and a rare wanderer to Grand Cayman. It is a vagrant in the Virgin Islands (St Croix). Occurs throughout most of the Western Hemisphere.

Comments: Feeds on carrion and sometimes assembles in great numbers on cloudy days. Often sun-bathes on exposed perches, with wings outstretched. Has remarkable senses of sight and smell. There is uncertainty as to whether or not Turkey Vulture was introduced to some islands such as His-paniola and Puerto Rico or extended its range naturally.

Habitat: Open areas at all elevations including scrublands, open forests, cane fields, pasturelands, towns and garbage dumps.

Nesting: Lays its eggs in a shallow depression usually under vegetation on the ground, inside a crevice formed by large boulders or on a cliff ledge, between sea level to high elevations. Eggs (1–2) whitish or grayish with brown spots. Breeds primarily from February to April, but breeding may occur year-round.

OSPREYS: FAMILY PANDIONIDAE

The single species of this family occurs throughout the world, except for South America which it only visits during migration. The Osprey is well adapted for capturing fish, having spine-studded soles to its feet and large claws for gripping its slippery prey. It captures fish by hovering and then plunging, feet first, with half-closed wings, often submerging completely. Partially as a result of pesticide contamination, Osprey numbers declined to dangerously low levels in the 1960s and 1970s. Many populations have shown good recoveries after some of the more potent chemicals were banned.

OSPREY *Pandion haliaetus*   Plate 24

Local Names: Fish Eagle (Jamaica); Sea Eagle (VI); Fish Hawk (CI, Jamaica, LA, VI); Aguila de Mar (PR); Guincho (Cuba, DR, PR); Malfini Lanmè, Malfini de Mer (Haiti); Malfini la Mer (St L); Balbuzard Pêcheur, Aiglon, Gligli Montagne (Guad, Mart); Visarend (Saba, St E, St M); Malfini de la Mer (French LA)

Identification: 53–61 cm (21–24"). The more widespread migratory race (*P. h. carolinensis*) is identified by its white head with a dark bar behind the eye, and by the contrast of its primarily white underparts and dark upperparts. The resident race (*P. h. ridgwayi*) has a whiter head with only a trace of an eyestripe. **Flight**: The wings are characteristically bent at the wrist, and the bird appears white below with a dark wrist patch.
Voice: A series of abbreviated piercing whistles.
Status and Range: A non-breeding resident throughout the West Indies primarily from September to April. It is common in the Bahamas, Greater Antilles and the Virgin and Cayman Islands and is uncommon through the Lesser Antilles. The resident race breeds commonly among the southern Bahamas north to Exuma and Cat Island and on Cuba's offshore cays and in the mangroves of Zapata Swamp. The migratory form now also breeds on Cuba and there is a single breeding record from St Lucia. Non-breeding birds may linger through August when they are joined by arrivals from the north. The migratory race is relatively rare in the southern Bahamas where the resident race abounds. Occurs worldwide.
Comments: Both races sometimes breed in mixed pairs on Cuba. This is the only fish-eating hawk in the West Indies.
Habitat: Calm bodies of fresh or salt water including mangroves, lagoons, lakes, impoundments and canals.
Nesting: The large, bulky nest of twigs typically is constructed in a tree or on a rocky promontory. Eggs (3) white, creamy white, or shades of light tan with drab brownish blotches. Breeds from April to June.

KITES, EAGLES, HAWKS AND ALLIES: FAMILY ACCIPITRIDAE

Members of the Accipitridae occur on all continents except Antarctica and have even reached many of the most isolated oceanic islands. These predatory birds glide more frequently than the falcons and are further distinguished by their rounded, rather than pointed, wings. Most species are persecuted because a few forms take poultry or other livestock. Actually, because they also take vermin and pest insects, the economic value of these species generally far outweighs any losses resulting from depredation of domestic stocks.

HOOK-BILLED KITE *Chondrohierax uncinatus*   Plates 23, 25

Local Names: Mountain Hawk, Merlion, Gree-gree

Identification: 38–43 cm (15–17"). A chunky hawk with an oversized, *deeply hooked bill*; *large oval wings prominently barred beneath*; and a *long, banded tail*. Plumage is variable with several basic patterns. **Adult male**: *Light phase* — Typically dark gray with gray or finely gray-barred underparts. **Adult female**: *Light phase* — Typically dark brown with reddish-brown barring below and a tan hindneck. **Adult**: *Black phase* — Solid black, but tail with one broad white band. Sexes alike.
Immature: *Light phase* — White cheeks, hindneck and underparts; breast, thighs and tail barred.
Immature: *Black phase* — Dark blue above, dark brown wings flecked with white and with a

streaked breast. **Flight**: Several rapid flaps followed by a tilting glide; soars infrequently.
Voice: A musical two–three note whistle. Also a shrill scream.
Status and Range: A critically endangered year-round resident in extreme southwest and northeast Grenada where 15–35 birds were estimated to survive in 1987. Its endangerment appears to have resulted primarily from habitat loss, though shooting of birds apparently also played a role. Also occurs from Mexico south to northern Argentina.
Comments: A very sluggish bird, it feeds on forest-dwelling tree snails. On Grenada, it is known to feed on only two snail species. The subspecies of Hook-billed Kite on Grenada is endemic.
Habitat: Mainly dry scrubland of southwestern Grenada, but also in mountain forests.
Nesting: A bulky stick nest is built high in a tree. Eggs (2–3) buffy-white with spots. Breeds from March to July.

CUBAN KITE *Chondrohierax wilsonii*   Plates 23, 25, 79
Local Names: Gavilán Caguarero, Gavilán Sonso, Gavilán Babosero

Identification: 38–43 cm (15–17″). A large, robust hawk, with a massive, *yellowish hooked bill*; large *oval wings prominently barred beneath*; and a *long, banded tail*. **Adult male**: Typically dark gray with gray or finely gray-barred underparts. **Adult female**: Generally dark brown; underparts coarsely barred; reddish; tan hindneck. **Immature**: Bi-colored black above and white below, white extending in a band around hindneck. **Similar species**: Broad-winged Hawk's banded tail is shorter and broader, and the underwings unbarred.

Voice: Unknown.
Status and Range: Endemic to Cuba where it is the rarest raptor and is on the verge of extinction. Formerly much more widespread, including parts of western Cuba, but now confined to northeastern Cuba in the extreme north of Oriente Province, between Moa and Baracoa, and perhaps to parts of Holguín and Guantánamo Provinces. Cuban Kite is critically endangered due to habitat destruction and alteration, including the apparent reduction of tree snails, its primary food, and by being erroneously shot as a predator on chickens.
Comments: A sluggish bird that feeds in the forest understory, primarily on the colorfully-marked *Polymita* tree snails, which are exploited by people who sell them to collectors and tourists. Cuban Kite does not extract the snail in the same manner as the Snail Kite, but pierces the shell with its massive bill and removes the animal through the hole. It also feeds on slugs. A tame bird, it is not shy of humans. Unfortunately, this trait makes it a very easy target for farmers who erroneously believe that this hawk periodically takes their chickens. Some authorities consider Cuban Kite to be a race of Hook-billed Kite.
Habitat: Among tall trees of forests bordering rivers below 500 m (1640′).
Nesting: Unknown.

SWALLOW-TAILED KITE *Elanoides forficatus*   Plate 23
Local Name: Gavilán Cola de Tijera (Cuba)

Identification: 51–66 cm (20–26″). A bi-colored kite with a long, *deeply forked tail*. The *white head* and underparts contrast with the black back, wings and tail.
Voice: High *ke-wee-wee*, *hewee-we*, the first note short.
Status and Range: A rare migrant on Cuba and very rare in the northern Bahamas and Cayman Islands (Grand Cayman). More regular migrating southward from August to October, with a few birds remaining until January. Less frequent moving northward from February to June. A vagrant on Jamaica. Numbers are increasing in the Cayman Islands. Also occurs through southeastern North America and Central and South America.
Comments: When hunting, glides slowly, low to ground, with steady wings, but the tail is constantly balancing. Feeds mainly on reptiles, frogs and insects. On migration, often soars to more than 500 m (1640′), often in small flocks.
Habitat: Coastal swamps, savannas and river mouths.

SNAIL KITE *Rostrhamus sociabilis* Plates 23, 25
Local Name: Gavilán Caracolero

Identification: 43–48 cm (17–19"). Note the *broad, white band across the base of tail and both the upper- and undertail-coverts*; slender bill conspicuously hooked. Iris, lores, base of bill, and legs red. *Adult male*: Blackish. *Adult female*: Brown above and white below, heavily streaked with brown. Note the white eyebrow stripe. *Immature*: Similar to the female, but iris and legs paler. *Similar species*: Northern Harrier has white only on rump (not on tail) with long, narrow wings and a gliding, tilting flight, rather than the broad wings and heavy flapping flight of the Snail Kite.

Voice: A rasping ratchet-like, *ge-ge-ge-ge*.
Status and Range: A common year-round resident on Cuba, particularly in Zapata Swamp, but uncommon on the Isle of Youth and some cays including Santa María, Romano and Coco. After a drastic decline in the 19th century, populations are now increasing and this kite is widespread in appropriate habitat because of the establishment of reservoirs and rice fields. Also occurs from southern North America through South America.
Comments: Forages by slowly flying over marshes with an active, flapping flight. Feeds solely on the freshwater apple snail (*Pomacea*).
Habitat: Freshwater marshes, open swamps, reservoirs, rice fields and canals.
Nesting: Nests in loose colonies. The nest is a compact platform of sticks built 1–2.5 m (3–8') above water in clumps of vegetation or occasionally on a dead tree stump. Eggs (2–3) cream-colored, spotted or blotched with brown. Breeds from March to July.

NORTHERN HARRIER *Circus cyaneus* Plate 23
Local Names: Aguilucho Palido (PR); Gavilán Sabanero (Cuba, DR), Gavilán de Ciénaga (DR, PR); Gwo Malfini Savann (Haiti); Busard Saint-Martin (Guad, Haiti, Mart)

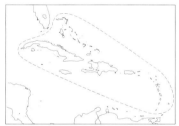

Identification: 46–61 cm (18–24"). The large size, long wings and tail, and particularly the *white rump* identify this hawk. *Adult male*: Grayish-blue. *Adult female*: Brown above and white below, heavily streaked with brown. *Immature*: Brown above; entirely reddish-brown below with dark brown streaks on the breast. *Flight*: Usually low over the ground with a series of heavy flaps and distinctive tilting glides, *the wings held well above the horizontal*. Occasionally soars. *Similar species*: Snail Kite has more expansive white markings at base of tail and rump, broader wings and a more labored flight.

Status and Range: A decidedly uncommon and local non-breeding resident primarily from October to April in the Bahamas, Cuba, Hispaniola and Puerto Rico. Uncommon only as a migrant in the Cayman Islands and rare in the Virgin Islands. In the Lesser Antilles, it is a rare migrant on Anguilla, St Martin, Dominica and Barbados, and is very rare or a vagrant on the remaining islands. Occurs through North America south to northern South America. Widespread in Eurasia.
Habitat: Marshes, swamps, open savannas and rice fields.

SHARP-SHINNED HAWK *Accipiter striatus* Plates 23, 25
Local Names: Gavilancito (Cuba); Guaraguaíto de Sierra (DR); Halcón de Sierra (PR); Emouchet, Malfini Mouche (Haiti)

Identification: 25–35 (10–14"). A *small* forest hawk with short, rounded wings, a small head and a long, *narrow, squared-off tail, boldly barred with black*. *Adult*: Dark steel-blue above; narrow reddish bars below. *Female*: Much larger than the male. *Immature*: Brown above; buffy below, streaked with dark brown. *Flight*: The short, rounded wings and long, narrow tail are characteristic. Sharp-shinned Hawks fly rapidly through the forest alternately flapping and gliding. *Similar species*: On Cuba, Gundlach's Hawk is much larger and more robust. Adult Broad-winged Hawk has a similar color pattern, but is much larger, chunkier, and has a shorter tail and broader wings.
Voice: A leisurely, high-pitched *que-que-que-que*, similar to that of North American birds, but much slower.

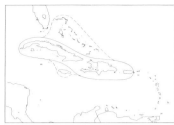

Status and Range: A common, but increasingly local year-round resident on Cuba and Hispaniola; its numbers are declining on the latter island. It is rare and very local on Puerto Rico. Migrants which breed in North America reside in the Bahamas from February to April where they are common on Grand Bahama, uncommon on Andros and New Providence, and rare elsewhere. Small numbers of migratory non-breeding birds also occur on Cuba, Jamaica and perhaps on the other Greater Antilles. A vagrant in the Virgin Islands (St John). The Puerto Rican race (*A. s. venator*) is best seen in Toro Negro and Maricao forests. That subspecies has declined dramatically in the Sierra de Luquillo and Carite forests and is now endangered due to habitat loss, introduced predators, particularly rats, and egg and chick predation by the Pearly-eyed Thrasher. The Hispaniolan race (*A. s. striatus*) is threatened as a result of habitat destruction and predation. Also occurs through North, Central and South America.

Comments: In early morning, performs soaring display flights. Feeds almost exclusively on small birds. Like Hispaniola and Puerto Rico, Cuba sustains an endemic race (*A. s. fringilloides*).

Habitat: Mature forests, mainly in hills and mountains. Migrant birds apparently occur in coastal forests on Cuba.

Nesting: Nest is a platform of twigs placed high in a tree or palm. Eggs (3–4) light brown spotted with dark brown. Breeds from March to June.

GUNDLACH'S HAWK *Accipiter gundlachi* Plates 23, 25, 79
Local Names: Gavilán Colilargo, Gavilán Rabilargo, Halcón

Identification: 43–51 cm (17–20"). A *chunky, medium-sized* forest hawk with relatively short, rounded wings and a *long, narrow tail*, rounded at the tip and boldly barred with black. **Adult**: *Upperparts dark steel-blue; underparts lightly barred with gray-red*. **Immature**: Brown above; lighter and heavily streaked with dark brown below. **Flight**: Rapid flaps followed by brief glides. **Similar species**: Similar in form to the much smaller Sharp-shinned Hawk, but tail round-tipped in flight. Broad-winged Hawk is more robust with a broad tail and flies by soaring, rather than by flapping and gliding.

Voice: Loud, harsh cackling *kek-kek-kek-kek-kek*. Also a wailing squeal.

Status and Range: Endemic to Cuba where rare, but widely distributed. Most frequently found around Casilda, Gibara and Zapata Swamp. Also Cayo Coco. It is considered an endangered species due primarily to habitat destruction and, to a lesser extent, human persecution. The status of this bird is difficult to determine due to its secretive behavior.

Comments: Feeds primarily on small- to medium-sized birds, including doves and pigeons. Females are larger than the males and, consequently, take larger prey. Reputedly, females generally hunt in more open areas whereas males hunt more frequently among forest undergrowth. Apparently a significant predator on poultry, Gundlach's Hawk is persecuted in rural areas. There are two subspecies.

Habitat: Forest borders, swamps, wooded coasts, mangroves and mountains below 800 m (2600').

Nesting: Nest of branches and twigs, with bark lining, is built 7–20 m (23–65') in a fork of a tall tree beneath the canopy. Eggs (2–4) grayish-white. Breeds primarily from March to June, but sometimes as early as January.

COMMON BLACK-HAWK *Buteogallus anthracinus* Plates 24, 25
Local Names: Crab Hawk (St V); Gavilán Batista (Cuba); Crabier (St L)

Identification: 51–58 cm (20–23"). A *large, stocky, relatively inactive chocolate-brown* (Cuba) or *black* (St Vincent) hawk with *broad wings*. **Adult**: *One broad white tail band*. **Immature**: Underparts white to buffy, heavily streaked with black; tail has several narrow pale bands. **Flight**: A large, *white patch at base of primaries is visible*, more so in Cuban than St Vincent birds. Note its *wide tail* and *long, yellow legs* which dangle in flight. **Similar species**: Immature Red-tailed Hawk is distinguished from immature Common Black-Hawk by its narrower wings and tail, lack of buffy underwing patches, less distinctive tail bands and typical soaring flight, rather than Black-hawk's alternating flapping and gliding flight. Immature Broad-winged Hawk is smaller and has shorter wings which

are much paler beneath. Black Vulture lacks the broad white tail band.

Voice: A nasal whistling *ba-tis-taa* or *ba-tis-taa-ooo*. Also a harsh *haaaah*.

Status and Range: A common and widely distributed year-round resident on Cuba and uncommon on St Vincent. A vagrant on Puerto Rico, St Lucia, the Grenadines and Grenada. Also occurs from southern North America to northern South America.

Comments: Sometimes soars like a *Buteo*, particularly at mid-day, but more often uses an alternating flapping and gliding flight. Feeds chiefly on crabs, amphibians and crayfish. The Cuban form is sometimes treated as a separate species, Cuban Black-Hawk (*Buteogallus gundlachii*), because of morphological and vocal differences.

Habitat: On Cuba, inhabits cays, coastal forests and open areas near swamps and beaches. On St Vincent, found in mountain forests.

Nesting: Constructs a large stick nest at moderate height or high in a tall tree. Eggs (1–3) white to olive-beige, spotted with pale purple at one end. Breeds from April to June.

RIDGWAY'S HAWK *Buteo ridgwayi*   Plates 24, 25, 81
Local Names: Gavilán, Guaraguaíto (DR); Ti Malfini Savann (Haiti)

Identification: 36–41 cm (14–16″). **Adult**: Distinguished by its dark brownish-gray upperparts, *underparts gray washed with brownish-red, thighs reddish-brown* and tail barred black and white. **Adult male**: Grayer than female with bright reddish-brown bend of wing. **Adult female**: Browner overall with drab brown bend of wing. Note the lighter breast with more barring, gray belly with a reddish-pink tint and the more heavily barred tail. **Immature**: Underparts buffy-white with pale gray and tan streaks; tail less distinctly barred. **Flight**: Soars on broad wings with a fan-shaped tail. The wings display light patches. **Similar species**: Considerably smaller than Red-tailed Hawk which, as an adult, has a reddish tail.

Voice: Shrill calls of three basic types: (1) *kleeah*, used in self-assertive and aggressive contexts; (2) *weeup*, given in food exchanges and displays; (3) a whistled squeal, given during high-intensity interactions.

Status and Range: Endemic to Hispaniola and adjacent islands, including Gonâve, Grande Cayemite, Île-à-Vache and Beata. Once locally common on Hispaniola, but with extensive habitat destruction, populations are declining to the point where the species is endangered. It may presently be most abundant on Hispaniola's offshore islands. On the Haitian mainland, confined to the Massif du Nord. There is a single record from the island of Culebra off Puerto Rico.

Comments: Often allows close approach before flying. Feeds on lizards, snakes, rats, bats, amphibians, insects and small birds. Apparently replaces the similarly-sized Broad-winged Hawk on Hispaniola.

Habitat: Forested foothills, including wet limestone hills and mixed savannah-woodland-palm habitat.

Nesting: Nest is a bulky structure of sticks and epiphytes, lined with downy feathers and built high in a tree or palm. Eggs (2–3) chalky cream, heavily marked with orange-red mottling. Breeds from March to June.

BROAD-WINGED HAWK *Buteo platypterus*   Plates 24, 25
Local Names: Chicken Hawk (Antigua, Grenada), Chicken-eater (Dominica, Grenada, St L, St V); Guaraguao (Cuba); Guaraguao de Bosque (DR, PR); Gree-gree (Grenada); Manger-poulet, Petite Buse (Mart); Malfini (Haiti, Mart, St L)

Identification: 35–41 cm (14–16″). A medium-sized, chunky soaring hawk. **Adult**: *Tail boldly banded with black and white*; underparts with reddish-brown barring. **Immature**: Underparts white, heavily streaked with dark brown and tail bands more numerous, but less distinct than the adult's. **Similar species**: Red-tailed Hawk is much larger and has a white breast with a band of dark streaks

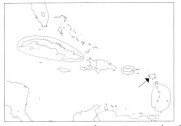

across the belly. In flight, Broad-winged Hawk flaps more often than Red-tailed Hawk. Sharp-shinned and Gundlach's Hawks have a similar color pattern, but have long, narrow tails rather than fan-shaped ones, and fly with a rapid spurt of wingbeats alternating with short glides, rather than by soaring. Cuban Kite has a long, banded tail and heavily barred underwings.

Voice: A thin, shrill squeal *pweeeeeeeeee.*

Status and Range: A widely distributed year-round resident throughout most of its irregular range in the West Indies. On Cuba, locally common, particularly in Oriente Province and Zapata Swamp. A few migrants that breed in North America supplement local birds in western Cuba from August through May. This species has apparently declined considerably on Cuba due to deforestation. Rare and very local on Puerto Rico (mainly in the Sierra de Luquillo, Carite and Río Abajo forests) where threatened with extirpation due to the impacts of habitat loss. It is uncommon on St Christopher and is a common resident on Antigua and from Dominica south to Grenada. A vagrant on Jamaica and Barbados. Also occurs through North and Central America and northern South America.

Comments: Feeds mainly on invertebrates, amphibians, reptiles and small birds. Performs soaring display flights high above the forest, during the morning, especially in the breeding season. Five subspecies reside in the West Indies.

Habitat: Generally dense broadleaved, mixed and plantation forests at all elevations, less frequently in open woodlands. During migration, also in open country. On Antigua, frequents open woodlands and occurs in urban areas and towns.

Nesting: A small, bulky nest of sticks and leaves, lined with bark strips and other vegetation, is typically built at 6–30 m (20–100') in a tree and is concealed among epiphytes. Eggs (2–4) dull white, creamy white or bluish-white, usually marked with brown. Breeds from January to June.

RED-TAILED HAWK *Buteo jamaicensis*   Plates 24, 25

Local Names: Fowl Hawk (Nevis); Chicken Hawk (Jamaica, LA, VI); Gavilán de Monte (Cuba); Guaraguao (DR); Guaraguao Colirrojo (PR); Malfini Ke Rouj, Gros Malfini (Haiti); Roodstaartbuizerd (Saba, St E, St M)

Identification: 48–64 cm (19–25"). A large hawk most often seen soaring on broad, rounded wings and tail. *Adult*: Dark brown above and white below, it is distinguished by its contrasting *dark belly band* and *reddish tail. Immature*: Faintly barred grayish-brown tail with more heavily streaked underparts. *Similar species*: Immature Broad-winged Hawk is smaller, has broad tail bands and flaps more in flight. Immature Red-tailed differs from immature Common Black-Hawk by its narrower wings and tail, absence of buffy patches on the underwings, less defined tail bands and its soaring flight. The smaller Ridgway's Hawk has a barred tail.

Voice: A sharp, raspy *keeer-r-r-r* slurring downward, sounding somewhat like a rusty hinge.

Status and Range: A common year-round resident on the larger islands of the northern Bahamas (Andros, Grand Bahama and Abaco), Greater Antilles, the Virgin Islands, St-Barthélemy, Saba, St Christopher and Nevis, and rare on St Eustatius. A vagrant elsewhere in the Bahamas and on Guadeloupe, St Lucia and Montserrat, and probably extirpated on St Martin. Prehistoric remains from Barbados. It is widespread from Alaska to Panama.

Comments: Feeds mainly on introduced rodents, lizards, snakes, birds and large invertebrates. Some of the densest populations in the West Indies are in interior forests, including rain forests, unlike in North America where the largest concentrations are in open, drier areas.

Habitat: Widespread in open country, woodlands, forests, towns and even urban areas in lowlands and mountains.

Nesting: A large, bulky stick nest is built high in a tree or on a cliff face. Eggs (2–3) dull white, unmarked or faintly spotted. Breeds from January to July.

CARACARAS AND FALCONS: FAMILY FALCONIDAE

The swift-flying falcons do not characteristically soar or glide as do the other hawks and vultures. They can further be distinguished in flight from other hawks by their pointed wings and long, narrow tails. Caracaras differ in being broad-winged, heavier-bodied birds that feed, to some degree, on carrion.

CRESTED CARACARA *Caracara plancus*   Plate 24
Local Name: Caraira (Cuba)

Identification: 50–63 cm (19.5–25″). A distinctive raptor with a *large, crested head* and large beak with *reddish facial skin*. **Adult**: Breast whitish and barred. **Immature**: Browner overall; breast buffy and streaked. **Flight**: Contrasting *white patches* near wing tips. Flies more like a crow than a hawk.
Voice: A harsh rattling *ca-ca-ca-ca*.
Status and Range: A rare and local, but widespread year-round resident on Cuba particularly in the central portion of the island, Zapata Swamp, the Isle of Youth (especially in the northwest) and cays of both coasts. A vagrant on Jamaica. Also occurs in the southwestern United States through South America.
Comments: Often on the ground with vultures. Walks swiftly and sometimes chases vultures from a carcass. A versatile feeder on birds, lizards and other animals and, to a lesser extent, on carrion.
Habitat: Semi-arid open country, including palm savannas, cut-over areas and pastures.
Nesting: Builds a bulky, crude nest of twigs, vines and other vegetation, generally in a cabbage palm, but sometimes high among bromeliads in a tall tree. Eggs (1–3) white to medium brown, heavily spotted with dark brown. Breeds from February to December. Some individuals breed twice a year.

AMERICAN KESTREL *Falco sparverius*   Plate 23
Local Names: Sparrow Hawk (Jamaica); Bastard Hawk (VI); Killyhawk (CI, LA, VI); Killy-killy (Jamaica, LA, VI); Cuyaya (DR); Falcón Común (PR); Cernícalo (Cuba, DR); Grigri Fran, Faucon (Haiti); Grigri Poulet (St L); Crécerelle d'Amérique, Gligli, Grigri (Guad, Mart); Amerikaanse Torenvalk (Saba, St E, St M)

Identification: 23–30 cm (9–12″). Its small size, reddish-brown back (except in the dark phase of the Cuban race *F. s. sparveroides* which is dark gray), reddish tail with a broad, black terminal band and two black facial bars are distinctive. The underparts vary between races from white to reddish-brown. **Adult male**: Blue-gray wings. **Adult female**: Reddish-brown wings. **Immature**: Dark breast streaks.
Voice: A high-pitched *killi-killi-killi* from which some of its common names are derived.
Status and Range: Generally a common year-round resident in the Bahamas, Greater Antilles, Virgin Islands and Lesser Antilles south to St Lucia, it is rare further south and on San Andrés. The resident race of the southern Bahamas is expanding its range northward and has also colonized Jamaica in recent decades where it is now common and widespread. Kestrels that breed in North America migrate to the Bahamas, Cuba and the Cayman Islands where they remain as non-breeding residents from October to April. Occurs throughout the rest of the Western Hemisphere.
Comments: Frequents high, exposed perches from which it searches for prey. It is from this habit that 'Cernícalo', the local Cuban and Dominican Republic name, is derived. Cernícalo is a modification of Tsar Nicholas, a formerly 'high-perched' monarch. Three West Indian races include *F. s. sparveroides* on Cuba, the Bahamas and Jamaica; *F. s. dominicensis* on Hispaniola; and *F. s. caribearum* on Puerto Rico, the Virgin Islands and the Lesser Antilles. Only the Cuban race has two color phases, one very dark and the other extremely light.
Habitat: Dry, open lowland areas with adequate perches and nest sites. Also forest edges in the mountains, towns and even cities.
Nesting: The eggs are laid in a cavity in a tree or building or on a cliff edge. Eggs (2–4) tan flecked with brown. Breeds from January to August. Some pairs raise two broods per year.

MERLIN *Falco columbarius* Plate 23
Local Names: Pigeon Hawk, Bird Hawk (Jamaica); Halconcito de Palomas (Cuba); Falcón Migratorio (PR); Halcón (DR, PR); Grigri Mòn, Emerillon (Haiti); Grigri Morne (St L); Faucon Émerillon, Gligli, Grigri (Guad, Mart); Smelleken (Saba, St E, St M)

Identification: 25–34 cm (10–13.5"). This small falcon is distinguished by its upperparts: dark gray in the male and dark brown in the female. Underparts are heavily streaked and the tail is barred with black. When perched, note its pale tan eyebrow stripe. *Flight*: Its great speed and agility; pointed wings and long, narrow tail aid identification.
Voice: A repeated warble-like call, rarely given in the West Indies.
Status and Range: A migrant throughout the West Indies primarily in October, it is somewhat scarcer as a non-breeding resident through the intervening months until March. It occurs rarely as early as August and as late as May. Generally, during migration, it is common in the Bahamas, uncommon in the Greater Antilles, the Virgin and Cayman Islands, and on San Andrés and Providencia, and is rare in the Lesser Antilles. Occurs through North America to northern South America. Also Eurasia.
Habitat: Coastal lakes and lagoons where shorebirds abound, as well as woodlands and forests.

PEREGRINE FALCON *Falco peregrinus* Plate 23
Local Names: Duck Hawk (Jamaica); Halcón Peregrino (PR); Halcón de Patos (Cuba, DR); Slechtvalk (St M); Peregrin (St L); Faucon Pélerin, Malfini (Guad, Mart)

Identification: 38–51 cm (15–20"). Its *large size*; *pointed wings*; long, narrow tail and *rapid pigeon-like flight* identify it on the wing. When perched, its *mask-like head pattern* is distinctive. *Adult*: Dark gray above; cream-colored with dark bars below. *Immature*: Brown above; underparts cream-colored with heavy brown streaks.
Voice: A rough *kack-kack-kack-kack*. Also a series of interrupted and discordant notes.
Status and Range: A decidedly uncommon to rare and local non-breeding resident throughout the West Indies primarily from October to April. One breeding record exists for Cuba and another for Dominica. Occurs worldwide.
Habitat: Offshore cays and rocks, and areas with abundant shorebirds, seabirds or waterfowl prey. It sometimes occurs inland including woodlands, forests and in cities on high buildings and church steeples where it feeds on Rock Doves. Peregrines often frequent the same localities year after year.

CURASSOWS AND GUANS: FAMILY CRACIDAE

The chachalacas are large, chicken-like birds, often with colorful feather crests, rattles or knobs on their heads. Their flight is heavy and direct on broad, rounded wings. Chachalacas have strong legs and large feet, which are used to scratch for food on the ground. They are forest-dwellers and are agile in trees. Although fossils are known from France and the United States, the chachalacas are now primarily restricted to the Neotropics.

RUFOUS-VENTED CHACHALACA *Ortalis ruficauda* Plate 26
Local Name: Cocrico (St V)

Identification: 55 cm (22"). A large, long-tailed chicken-like bird. Note its olive-brown upperparts; gray head and hindneck; *long, broad, bronze-colored tail tipped with reddish-brown*; gray underparts; reddish-brown flanks and undertail-coverts and bare red throat.
Voice: Calls loudly repeating its local names *cocrico, cocrico* ... and *chachalaca, chachalaca* ...
Status and Range: An uncommon year-round resident in the Grenadines (Union Island and formerly

Bequia). Believed introduced to the Grenadines in the late 17th century from Tobago. Native to Colombia and Venezuela.
Comments: Primarily forages on the ground, but sometimes found low in trees. Diet includes small fruits, berries and young shoots.
Habitat: Scrub and woodlands.
Nesting: The nest is a small flimsy structure of sticks built in a bush or small tree at low to moderate heights above ground. Eggs (2–3) pale yellow-white. Breeds from March to July.

PARTRIDGES, GROUSE, TURKEYS AND QUAIL: FAMILY PHASIANIDAE

This family includes a variety of primarily gregarious, terrestrial birds that fly strongly for short distances when pressed. The quails are characterized by their small size and short tails. Junglefowl, pheasants and peafowl are much larger birds, the males possessing very long tails and brightly colored plumage.

RED JUNGLEFOWL *Gallus gallus*   Plate 26
Local Names: Female: Gallina; Male: Gallo (DR, PR)

Identification: Male: 71 cm (28″); Female: 43 cm (17″). *Male (Rooster)*: Resplendently plumaged with a red comb and wattle on head and a long, bushy tail. *Female (Hen)*: Smaller comb and wattle; brownish plumage.
Voice: A universally recognized *cockadoodledoo*. Also a variety of clucks and other notes. Chicks give a soft, characteristic call note *pee-o*.
Status and Range: This well-known, introduced bird is found in a wild state very locally in the Dominican Republic at Los Haitises and in the Sierra de Baoruco, as well as on Puerto Rico among the haystack hills, and on Mona Island and possibly Culebra. It is also feral in the Grenadines. Domesticated birds are common on farms throughout the West Indies. Introduced throughout the world. Native to South-East Asia.
Habitat: Dry and moist forests.
Nesting: A scrape is made on the ground, sometimes lined with twigs. Eggs (fewer than 10) white or light brown.

RING-NECKED PHEASANT *Phasianus colchicus*   Plate 26
Local Name: Faisán (Cuba)

Identification: 76–92 cm (30–36″). A large chicken-like bird with a long, pointed tail. *Male*: Brown above with black mottling, *iridescent blue-green head with crest*, red face wattle, long cinnamon-colored tail with narrow black bars and an *incomplete white band around the neck*. Reddish-brown breast. *Female*: Mottled brown with a shorter tail.
Voice: The male's territorial call is a loud, harsh *kok-cack*.
Status and Range: Introduced fairly widely in the West Indies, but has failed to survive on most islands. Ring-necked Pheasant is common on Eleuthera in the Bahamas, where it has been introduced at Hatchet Bay and it is locally common on Cuba in the northern portion of the Isle of Youth. Widely introduced in the Western Hemisphere. Native to Asia.
Nesting: Nesting has not been described in the West Indies. Generally a scrape is made on the ground under protective cover and is sparsely lined with plant material. Eggs (8–14) pale brown.

COMMON PEAFOWL *Pavo cristatus*　　　**Plate 26**

Identification: Male: 250 cm (100"); Female: 100 cm (40").
Male (Peacock): Body primarily blue with a magnificent, huge tail that can be raised into a broad fan. **Female (Peahen)**: Principally grayish-brown with a white belly and face, greenish neck and breast and a distinctive crest.
Voice: A loud scream, *My Arm!*
Status and Range: Introduced in the 1950s to Little Exuma in the Bahamas where it is now fairly common, but secretive in the wild. This species has been widely introduced in the West Indies as a garden and farmyard bird, but is not known to be feral outside of Little Exuma. Native to India and South-East Asia.
Nesting: Two chicks observed in July on Little Exuma.

CRESTED BOBWHITE *Colinus cristatus*　　　**Plate 26**
Local Name: Quail (Grenadines)

Identification: 18 cm (8.0"). A small, short-tailed quail with a *long, pointed crest*. **Male**: Throat and eyebrow stripe reddish-brown, crest and ear patch white and underparts spotted with white. **Female**: Lacks the distinctive facial coloration of the male. Crest brown. **Similar species**: Northern Bobwhite lacks the pointed crest plume.
Voice: A loud, melodious whistle similar to call of Northern Bobwhite, sounding like a repeated *coo-kwee*.
Status and Range: Introduced to the Grenadines (Mustique), Puerto Rico and the Virgin Islands (St Thomas), but has been extirpated from the latter two islands. Its status in the Grenadines is uncertain. Native to Guatemala south to northern South America and northeastern Brazil.
Habitat: Cultivated areas, hedgerows and scrubland.

NORTHERN BOBWHITE *Colinus virginianus*　　　**Plate 26**
Local Names: Quail (Bahamas, Barbados, VI); Cordoniz (DR); Codorniz (Cuba, PR); Kay, Caille (Haiti)

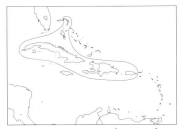

Identification: 25 cm (10"). A chunky, brown bird resembling a small chicken scampering about in the underbrush. Often does not flush until nearly underfoot when it bursts from cover. **Male**: White throat and eyebrow stripe. **Female**: Tan throat and eyebrow stripe. **Similar species**: Crested Bobwhite has a long, pointed crest.
Voice: A clear whistled rendition of its name *bob-white* or *bob, bob-white*.
Status and Range: A common year-round resident on Cuba, including the Isle of Youth. Introduced and now common in the Bahamas (New Providence, Abaco and Andros), uncommon on Hispaniola and rare and local on Puerto Rico. Introductions on other islands have been unsuccessful. Introduced to portions of the West Indies. Native to Cuba and much of temperate North America south to Guatemala.
Comments: Ground dwelling, in flocks. The birds on Cuba represent an endemic race.
Habitat: Scrubland and pasture with ample cover.
Nesting: It nests on the ground in a clump of grass. Eggs (10–18) dull white. Breeds from May to July.

HELMETED GUINEAFOWL *Numida meleagris*　　　**Plate 26**
Local Names: Guinea Torcaz (PR); Guinea (Cuba, DR); Pentad Maron, Pintade, Sauvage (Haiti)

Identification: 53 cm (21"). Distinguished by its unusual body shape, dark gray feathering with white spots, and nearly naked head and neck.
Voice: A wild, maniacal, cackling call.

Status and Range: Introduced in the West Indies centuries ago and now occurring very locally in the wild state on some islands. Fairly common locally in the Dominican Republic among the foothills of the Sierra de Baoruco. Rare on Cuba (including the Isle of Youth), Puerto Rico, the Virgin Islands (St Croix), St Martin (Isle Pinel) and Barbuda. Most birds receive handouts from local farmers and are somewhat domesticated. However, truly wild populations also exist. Native to central East Africa.

Comments: Ground dwelling in small flocks. Flushes with a burst of whirring wings. Roosts in trees and bushes.

Habitat: Primarily dry scrubland.

Nesting: The nest is a scrape on the ground. Eggs (fewer than 15) light buff-colored.

RAILS, GALLINULES AND COOTS: FAMILY RALLIDAE

Rails are chicken-like, marsh-dwelling birds. They are secretive, primarily nocturnal and are much more frequently heard than seen. Playing tapes of their calls from the edge of a marsh is an excellent way to discover their presence. They rarely flush, preferring to run for cover, but when they do fly, they quickly settle back among dense vegetation in which they hide. Their flight appears labored, with legs dangling conspicuously. Rails have long toes and either long or short bills. Those with short, thick bills are often called crakes. Gallinules and coots are larger than rails and are more aquatic (the coots being most at home in the water). They resemble ducks, but have a distinctive bill with a frontal shield and, when swimming, characteristically jerk their heads.

BLACK RAIL *Laterallus jamaicensis*   Plate 17
Local Names: Black Crake (Jamaica); Gallinuelita Prieta (Cuba); Gallito Negro (PR)

Identification: 14 cm (5.5″). Note its tiny size, short black bill, white spots on its back and dark reddish-brown hindneck. **Similar species**: The downy young of gallinules, coots and other rails are black, but lack these field marks.

Voice: A *ki-ki-kurr*, the first two syllables being high-pitched whistles. The defense call is an emphatic and irregularly pulsing cackle. Typically only calls well after dark.

Status and Range: A rare and local breeding resident on Hispaniola, a rare non-breeding resident on Cuba and very rare and local on Jamaica and Puerto Rico, primarily from October to March. Recorded on Cuba in nearly every month of the year; thus, it may breed, but this has yet to be corroborated. Formerly a breeding resident on Jamaica and Puerto Rico. A vagrant in the Bahamas (Eleuthera) and Antigua. The endemic Greater Antillean race of Black Rail has declined most likely from habitat loss and disturbance and from introduced predators. Occurs through the eastern and central United States south to western South America.

Comments: Shy and usually active only after dark, the Black Rail is easily overlooked. It runs rather than flies when disturbed and rarely leaves the cover of marsh grasses, thus it is far more often heard than seen.

Habitat: Wet grassy marsh edges, both saline and fresh.

Nesting: The cup-shaped nest is often hidden amidst, and supported by, a mat of dead marsh grass. Eggs (7) buff-white with fine reddish-brown spots.

CLAPPER RAIL *Rallus longirostris*   Plate 17
Local Names: Marsh Hen (VI); Mangrove Hen (Jamaica, VI); Pond Shakee (LA); Gallinuela de Manglar (Cuba); Gallinuela de Mangle (DR); Pollo de Mangle (PR); Rato, Rateau, Râle d'eau (Haiti); Râle Gris, Pintade (Guad, Mart)

Identification: 36 cm (14″). A primarily gray, chicken-like bird recognized by its long bill and habit of stalking among mangrove roots. The upperparts are mottled gray and black, the cheek is gray and the breast is grayish with variable amounts of tan on the throat and belly. **Similar species**: Common

Moorhen, which is also chicken-like and found in mangroves, has a much shorter bill than Clapper Rail. Virginia Rail is much smaller, is only likely to be found in freshwater marshes and has a different voice. King Rail is very similar to Clapper, but tends to have a more reddish-brown neck and wings, more distinct barring on flanks and abdomen and is primarily found in freshwater marshes. Uniform Crake is smaller, has a reddish-brown coloration and a short, greenish bill.

Voice: The call is a loud, grating series of *kek* notes slowing at the end. The cackle of one rail often sets off a chorus of others.

Status and Range: A common year-round resident in the Bahamas, Cuba and Puerto Rico; locally so on Jamaica, Hispaniola, the Virgin Islands and Barbuda and rare and local on St Christopher, Guadeloupe and Martinique. It is a vagrant on Barbados. Occurs through the coastal United States south through South America.

Comments: Far more often heard than seen. It is most active at dawn and dusk.

Habitat: Salt marshes and mangroves.

Nesting: The nest is a platform of sticks built among mangrove roots. Eggs (5–9) creamy white and spotted. Breeds in April and May.

KING RAIL *Rallus elegans*   **Plate 17**
Local Name: Gallinuela de Agua Dulce (Cuba)

Identification: 38–48 cm (15–19″). A large rail about the size of a small hen. Bill long and slender. *Flanks and abdomen strongly banded with black and white*. **Adult**: Throat, breast and wing coverts reddish-brown; upperparts mottled brown and black. **Immature**: Grayer; lacks reddish-brown coloration. Chicks are black with the entire bill pale white. **Similar species**: Difficult to distinguish from Clapper Rail, which is less reddish, especially on wings and neck, has less distinct barring on flanks and abdomen and occurs primarily in mangroves. Virginia Rail is much smaller and usually has a redder bill and wings.

Voice: Like that of Clapper Rail, but shorter, more musical and resonant: a repeated *ta-ta-ta...*, not descending.

Status and Range: A fairly common year-round resident on Cuba, including the Isle of Youth. A vagrant on Jamaica. Occurs through eastern North America and the interior of Mexico.

Comments: Most active at dawn and dusk. Feeds on fruits, insects, crustaceans and snails. Far more often heard than seen.

Habitat: Freshwater wetlands with tall, dense vegetation such as sawgrass marshes, plant-choked canals, rice plantations and flooded sugarcane fields. Sometimes brackish marshes.

Nesting: An elaborate nest of plant materials is built on elevated ground, on a mound of plant material or under a bush. Eggs (5–11) beige with spots. Breeds from June to September.

VIRGINIA RAIL *Rallus limicola*   **Plate 17**
Local Name: Gallinuela de Virginia (Cuba)

Identification: 23 cm (9″). **Adult**: Breast, belly and wing-coverts reddish-brown; upperparts mottled brown and black. Note the *gray cheeks*. It has black bars on the flanks and abdomen and a long, reddish bill. *Best identified by its two-note call*. **Immature**: Mottled gray or blackish below; the bill is dark. **Similar species**: About half the size of King and Clapper Rails and usually with redder bill and wings.

Voice: A metallic two-syllabled *kid-ick*, *kid-ick* or *ticket-ticket* and a series of descending grunts.

Status and Range: A rare non-breeding resident from September to April on Grand Bahama in the Bahamas and very rare on Cuba. A vagrant elsewhere in the Bahamas and Puerto Rico. Occurs through southern Canada to South America.

Comments: Most active at dawn and dusk. Elusive and difficult to detect. When pursued, it runs

silently though the grass, rarely flushing in a weak, fluttering flight, with its long legs dangling.
Habitat: Primarily freshwater marshes and canals with dense vegetation, but also brackish and salt-water wetlands.

UNIFORM CRAKE *Amaurolimnas concolor*   Not illustrated
Local Names: Red Rail, Wood Rail, Water Partridge

Identification: 26 cm (10"). ***Adult***: A *uniformly reddish-brown* rail with a *yellowish-green bill* and reddish legs. ***Immature***: Duller and darker; throat and breast streaked white; yellow iris, not red as in adult. ***Similar species***: Clapper Rail is larger and lacks the short, greenish bill and overall reddish-brown coloration.
Voice: A series of clear whistles, loudest in the middle, then speeding up and fading away: *tooeee, toooeee, tooooeee, tooooeee, tooee, tooee-tuee-tui*. Also a sharp, nasal *kek* and low, clear whistles (Styles and Skutch).
Status and Range: Formerly a year-round resident on Jamaica.
Extirpated sometime after 1881, presumably because of predation by the introduced mongoose. Occurs from southern Mexico, south into South America.
Comments: Said to have been very sluggish, preferring to run rather than take cover and, when flushed, flew heavily for a short distance.
Habitat: Dense cover of wooded swamps and the edges of streams, it was apparently more of a 'land rail' than other West Indian species. Also occurred at fairly high altitudes. An endemic subspecies inhabited Jamaica.

SORA *Porzana carolina*   Plate 17
Local Names: Gallinuela Chica (Cuba); Gallito (DR, PR); Ti Rato (Haiti); Soraral (St M); Râle de Caroline, Marouette de Caroline, Rale (Guad, Mart, St L)

Identification: 22 cm (8.5"). A relatively small brownish-gray rail with a distinctive *stubby, yellow bill*. ***Adult***: Blackish face, throat and breast. ***Immature***: Black absent.
Voice: A clear, descending whinny and a plaintive, rising whistle *ker-wee*.
Status and Range: A non-breeding resident throughout the West Indies primarily from October to April, this species is common on Cuba and fairly common in the Bahamas. It is uncommon and local, but occurs regularly on Jamaica, Hispaniola, Puerto Rico and the Virgin and Cayman Islands, and is generally rare in the Lesser Antilles and on San Andrés. Occurs through North, Central, and northern South America.
Comments: Secretive. Much more often heard than seen.
Habitat: Primarily rice fields, canals and freshwater swamps with dense vegetation. Also mangroves.

YELLOW-BREASTED CRAKE *Porzana flaviventer*   Plate 17
Local Names: Twopenny Chick (Jamaica); Gallinuelita (Cuba); Guineíta (DR); Gallito Amarillo (DR, PR); Ti Rato Jòn (Haiti)

Identification: 14 cm (5.5"). Very rarely seen well, it is distinguished by its tiny size and pale yellowish-brown appearance. When seen well, note the blackish crown, white eyebrow stripe and small bill. ***Flight***: The feet dangle and the head droops.
Voice: A *tuck* of medium pitch and strength and a high-pitched, softly whistled *peep*.
Status and Range: An uncommon and local year-round resident on Cuba, Jamaica and Puerto Rico; it is rare on Hispaniola. Also from southern Mexico south through South America.
Comments: Typically observed only by wading in the shallow water of a swamp edge. It will flush a short distance before again dropping into the vegetation.

Habitat: Freshwater swamps and canals with borders of short grass or other water plants.
Nesting: The nest is woven atop a floating plant. Eggs (3–5) pale cream-colored and lightly spotted with brown or lavender. Breeds from March to June.

ZAPATA RAIL *Cyanolimnas cerverai* Plates 17, 80
Local Names: Gallinuela de Santo Tomás, Gallinuela Sin Cola

Identification: 29 cm (11.5"). A medium-sized rail distinguished by its *near lack of stripes or spots, long green bill with red at the base*, and red legs and iris. **Similar species**: Spotted Rail is much more heavily marked with spots and bars.
Voice: A low, repeated call resembling the call of Bare-legged Owl or like a bouncing ball, *cutucutu-cutucutu-cutucutu.* Also other short sounds of different tones, including a short *kuck-kuck* that resembles Limpkin's call.
Status and Range: Endemic to Cuba where it is rare and very locally confined to the area north of Santo Tomás in Zapata Swamp and nearby Treasure Lake. This rail is endangered, most likely as a result of periodic burning of the swamp and perhaps due to introduced predators.
Comments: Zapata Rail is the only species in its genus. It is flightless, or nearly so, with completely unknown habits. The species is named after Fermín Cervera, a taxidermist who discovered it where the other famous endemics from Santo Tomás in the Zapata Swamp — Zapata Wren and Zapata Sparrow — were discovered. This rail is secretive and few have seen it. It calls when water levels are high, from November to February. Found together with Spotted and King Rails, whose voices are quite different. Only six birds have been collected, five of which are in North American museums with the remaining one at the University of Havana on Cuba. For many years, this species was thought to be restricted to the territory north of Santo Tomás. During the 1980s, it was also found at Treasure Lake.
Habitat: Freshwater sawgrass savannas with scattered tussocks of bushes.
Nesting: The only nest ever reported was in a sawgrass hummock and constructed about 60 cm (2') above the water level. Eggs (3) white. Breeding is known to occur in September and October and is believed to also take place in December and January.

SPOTTED RAIL *Pardirallus maculatus* Plate 17
Local Names: Gallinuela Escribano (Cuba); Gallito Manchado (DR)

Identification: 28 cm (11"). A medium-sized rail with long, red legs and long, *greenish-yellow bill, red at the base*. **Adult**: Spotted and barred black and white body. Red iris. **Immature**: Browner with less spotting. **Similar species**: Zapata Rail lacks the heavy spotting and barring.
Voice: A peculiar high, guttural grunt that sounds much like a pig. Also an accelerating *tuk-tuk-tuk-tuk* a bit like a bouncing ball and not dissimilar to the typical call of Zapata Rail.
Status and Range: A rare and local year-round resident on Cuba and Hispaniola. On Cuba, it is found in the Zapata Swamp, some ricefields in Habana Province and reported from Lanier Swamp on the Isle of Youth. On Hispaniola, confined to northeastern Dominican Republic. Very rare and local on Jamaica where it has only been recorded from the Black River Morass. Its status on the island is unclear, though the possibility exists that this rail is a rare breeding resident. Spotted Rail is critically endangered in the West Indies due to habitat destruction and alteration. The possible impact of the mongoose and other introduced predators on its survival is difficult to surmise. Also occurs through Mexico and Central and South America.
Comments: Generally solitary and very secretive. Much more often heard than seen. On Cuba, best found in marshy areas north of Santo Tomás at Zapata Swamp, where endemic Zapata Rail also occurs. A distinct race (*P. m. inoptatus*) inhabits the West Indies.
Habitat: Freshwater swamps with emergent vegetation in which it can hide. Also rice fields.
Nesting: The nest has not yet been found on Cuba or Jamaica. In Central America, the nest is constructed of grass. Eggs (3–7) white or cream-colored with small reddish-brown or bluish-gray spots, a bit smaller than those of Clapper Rail. The breeding season is unknown.

PURPLE GALLINULE *Porphyrula martinica* **Plate 17**

Local Names: Blue-pate Coot (Jamaica); Gallareta Inglesa (PR); Gallareta Azul (Cuba, DR, PR); Poule Sultane, Poul Dlo Tèt Ble, Poule d'eau à Cachet Bleu (Haiti); Cascamboi (St L); Gallinule Violacée, Poule d'eau à Cachet Vert, Talève Violacée (Mart); Kascamiol (Grenada, St V)

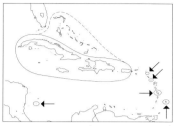

Identification: 33 cm (13"). ***Adult***: The *bluish-purple plumage*, *yellow legs* and bluish-white frontal shield are good field marks. ***Immature***: Golden brown. Note the bluish wings and *yellowish legs*. ***Similar species***: The immature lacks the flank stripe of Common Moorhen and is more tan with bluish wings. **Voice**: A high-pitched, melodious *klee-klee* and many cackling and guttural notes.

Status and Range: A common year-round resident on Cuba and Hispaniola and decidedly uncommon on Jamaica, Puerto Rico, the Cayman Islands and San Andrés. In the Bahamas, it is an uncommon migrant on some larger northern islands (Grand Bahama, Andros and New Providence) from August to October and March to May. It is rare and local among the remainder of the Bahamas during these months. Purple Gallinule occurs even less frequently in the Bahamas as a non-breeding resident from November to February. A rare resident on St-Barthélemy, Montserrat, Martinique and Barbados, it is a vagrant among the other Lesser Antilles and in the Virgin Islands. Occurs from the southeastern United States through Central and South America.

Habitat: Rice fields and freshwater swamps with dense, water plants.

Nesting: A low nest of vegetation is constructed among cattails or rice grass. Eggs (3–12) pinkish-buff colored and spotted. Breeds from July to September.

COMMON MOORHEN *Gallinula chloropus* **Plate 17**

Local Names: Red Seal Coot (CI, Grenada, Jamaica, Nevis, St V); Water Hen (Grenada, Jamaica, St V); Water Fowl (Grenada, St V, VI); Water hoen (Saba, St M); Gallareta Común (PR); Gallareta Pico Rojo (Cuba, DR); Poul Dlo Tèt Rouj (Haiti); Poule d'eau (St. L); Gallinule-d'eau (Guad, Mart); Poule d'eau à Cachet Rouge, Gallinute-d'eau (Guad, Haiti, Mart)

Identification: 34 cm (13.5"). ***Adult***: Note the *red bill tipped with yellow, red frontal shield* and *white line down the flank*. ***Immature***: Gray and brown, it lacks the red bill, but displays the white flank stripe. ***Similar species***: Clapper Rail has a much longer bill. Immature Purple Gallinule is more tan, lacks a flank stripe and has bluish wings. **Voice**: A variety of clucks and cackles, the most common being a piercing laugh-like cackle slowing at the end *ki-ki-ki-ki-ka-, kaa, kaaa*.

Status and Range: Generally a common year-round resident throughout the West Indies. Occurs worldwide.

Comments: A fairly conspicuous waterbird, it is not particularly shy, often straying from dense vegetation at the pond edge to swim in calm, open water. It swims with a characteristic bobbing motion of the head.

Habitat: All swamps and canals with water plants. Also mangroves, lakes and rice fields.

Nesting: The nest is usually a bulky mass of plant material suspended over water. Eggs (3–9) grayish-tan, lightly spotted. Breeds the year round, but peaks from May to September.

AMERICAN COOT *Fulica americana* **Plate 17**

Local Names: White Seal Coot (Jamaica); Water Fowl (VI); Gallareta de Pico Blanco (Cuba); Gallareta Pico Blanco (DR); Gallinazo Americano (PR); Poul Dlo Jidèl, Judelle, Poule d'eau à Cachet Blanc (Haiti); Poule d'eau (St L); Amerikaanse Meerkoet (St M); Foulque d'Amérique (Guad, Mart)

Identification: 38–40 cm (15–16"). ***Adult***: Grayish-black with a *white bill* and undertail-coverts. ***Immature***: Paler than the adult. ***Flight***: It runs over the water to take off. ***Similar species***: In the field, the lack of the white frontal shield extending onto the crown distinguishes it from Caribbean Coot. Immatures are virtually identical.

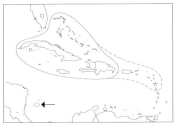

Voice: A variety of croaks and cackles.

Status and Range: An uncommon breeding resident in the Bahamas, Cuba, Jamaica, Hispaniola and occasionally the Cayman Islands, primarily from May to August. Migrants that breed in North America augment local numbers from September to April making the species common throughout the Bahamas, Greater Antilles and Cayman Islands during these months. This species is uncommon and occasionally breeds in the Virgin Islands and is rare or a vagrant in the Lesser Antilles from October to May. It is an uncommon migrant on San Andrés. Widespread in the Western Hemisphere.

Comments: Often flocks. Swims with a bobbing motion of the head. Dives proficiently.

Habitat: Principally open freshwater areas with much submergent vegetation.

Nesting: A nest of dried grass and aquatic plants is built on the ground among vegetation, mangrove roots or as a floating nest. Eggs (6–12) beige and heavily spotted. Breeds primarily from March to June.

CARIBBEAN COOT *Fulica caribaea*   Plate 17

Local Names: White Seal Coot (Jamaica); Water Fowl (VI); Gallareta del Caribe (Cuba); Gallareta Pico Blanco (DR); Gallinazo Antillano (PR); Poul Dlo Tèt Blan, Poule d'eau à Cachet Blanc (Haiti); Foulque à Cachet Blanc (Guad, Mart)

Identification: 38–40 cm (15–16"). Identified by its grayish-black coloration, white undertail-coverts and particularly by the *white frontal shield extending well up onto the crown*. **Immature**: Paler than the adult. **Flight**: It runs over the water to take off. **Similar species**: American Coot has a white bill, but lacks the white frontal shield extending onto the crown. Immatures are virtually identical.

Voice: A variety of croaking and cackling sounds.

Status and Range: An uncommon and local year-round resident on Hispaniola and Puerto Rico, it is a rare resident on Jamaica and the Virgin Islands. Some individuals doubtless wander among islands in response to habitat conditions. This species is generally a rare wanderer in the Lesser Antilles with a few recent breeding records on Antigua, Martinique and Guadeloupe, including Marie-Galante. It is suspected of breeding on Barbados. Caribbean Coot appears to be a very rare non-breeding transient on Cuba. This species has apparently diminished greatly throughout the West Indies because of hunting, habitat degradation and due to introduced predators. It is considered threatened. Also occurs on the southeastern tip of the United States, Venezuela, Trinidad and Curaçao.

Comments: Typically flocks. Swims with a bobbing head motion. Dives proficiently. Recent interbreeding with American Coots has been observed on several islands.

Habitat: Primarily open freshwater bodies.

Nesting: A floating nest is constructed. Eggs (4–8) white with spots. Breeds year-round with peaks from April to June and September to November.

LIMPKINS: FAMILY ARAMIDAE

The Limpkin is the sole member of this Western Hemisphere family. It dwells primarily in swamps, wading among the vegetation in search of snails. Limpkins are solitary, largely nocturnal and often roost in trees.

LIMPKIN *Aramus guarauna*   Plate 9

Local Names: Clucking Hen (Jamaica); Guareao (Cuba); Carrao (DR, PR); Gran Kola, Poule-à-jolie (Haiti)

Identification: 69 cm (27"). A large, long-legged and long-necked wading bird, it is entirely brown with white streaks in its plumage. The long, slightly down-curved bill is distinctive. **Similar species**: Limpkin

could be confused with young night-herons, but can be distinguished by its larger size and longer, paler, down-curved bill.

Voice: A loud, piercing *carrao* which gives rise to its local Spanish names.

Status and Range: A common year-round resident in a few of the northern Bahamas (Andros and Eleuthera), Cuba and locally on Jamaica, particularly in cockpit country. The Limpkin is uncommon on Hispaniola and is generally rare, but widely distributed, among the other islands of the Bahamas. It is extirpated from Puerto Rico. The Hispaniolan subspecies is considered threatened due to habitat loss, hunting and possibly the impact of introduced predators. Also occurs in the extreme southeastern United States, and from southern Mexico through most of South America.

Comments: A secretive bird, most active at dawn and dusk, it is often located by its call. Limpkins on Hispaniola and (formerly) Puerto Rico are noted for their reluctance to fly. This has led to the suggestion that they may have been evolving towards flightlessness.

Habitat: Grassy freshwater swamps, marshes, lakes, rice fields, wooded floodplains of rivers and upland wet forests.

Nesting: A loose platform nest on or low above the ground is built in a thick tangle of vegetation, usually near water. Eggs (7–8) pale creamy-buff or olive-buff and spotted with brown. Breeds from June to October.

CRANES: FAMILY GRUIDAE

Cranes are large, long-legged and long-necked birds that have wing-spans of up to 2.4 m (8'). Most inhabit grasslands or marshy areas. The bill is straight and rather long. The wings are broad with a short tail. The legs are long and the tibiae is partly bare; the hind toe is elevated. Sexes are alike. Cranes are gregarious, except in the breeding season. Most are migratory. Cranes fly with their long neck and legs extended, often soaring to great heights on broad wings. An elaborate 'dance' display is performed by both sexes of the pair, which also give a 'unison call', usually during morning nest exchanges. Cranes have a long fossil history extending back to 40 million years. Today, several crane species are threatened with extinction.

SANDHILL CRANE *Grus canadensis*   Plate 10
Local Name: Grulla

Identification: 100 cm (40"). A very large bird with long legs and a long neck. ***Adult***: Gray with a bare red crown. Its call is unmistakable. ***Immature***: Head and neck brownish; body gray mottled with brown. ***Similar species***: Great Blue Heron lacks the red crown and has a whitish face and black eyebrow stripe. Immatures have an entirely black crown.

Voice: A high-pitched, trumpet-like call *curroo-curroo* ... repeated any number of times. It can be heard from well over 1 km (0.6 miles) away.

Status and Range: A rare and local year-round resident on Cuba. Found in Zapata Swamp, Guayaberas Swamp in Sancti Spíritus, the vicinity of Júcaro in Camagüey, El Marquéz and the northwestern part of the Isle of Youth (La Reforma, Los Indios and Siguanea). It is considered threatened as a result of habitat loss, hunting and introduced predators. Occurs through North America.

Comments: Typically in flocks of fewer than ten individuals, rarely as many as thirty. Pairs form during the breeding season. Sometimes after the rainy season they visit roads and puddles to feed on fish, reptiles, frogs, mice and large insects. Courtship involves an impressive dance in which birds prance, hop and flutter high in the air. The Cuban Sandhill Crane is an endemic subspecies (*G. c. nesiotes*).

Habitat: Marshes with emergent vegetation, swamp borders, open areas, edges of pine barrens and natural savannas.

Nesting: The nest is built on bare or grassy ground in open savannas or surrounded by shallow water. It is quite large with interwoven grasses. Eggs (2) creamy beige-greenish with dark spots. Eggs are laid in March and April with chicks fledging in June and July.

THICK-KNEES: FAMILY BURHINIDAE

The thick-knees are fairly large, long-legged upland birds that inhabit open country and pastures. They are typically shy. When disturbed, thick-knees swiftly run away but, if pressed, will make a short, yet strong, flight. Their large, yellow eyes are an adaptation to their crepuscular and nocturnal habits.

DOUBLE-STRIPED THICK-KNEE *Burhinus bistriatus*   Plate 15
Local Names: Búcaro (DR); Kòk Savann, Poul Savann, Courlis de Terre (Haiti)

Identification: 38–43 cm (15–17"). A *large, plover-like bird* with a *large, yellow iris*; *whitish eyebrow stripe*; and a *striped breast*. *Flight*: Conspicuous *white wing patches*. Its camouflaged plumage makes the species difficult to detect. *Similar species*: Much larger than all plovers.
Voice: A loud, rattling *ca-ca-ca-ca-ca-ca-ca-ca!*, rising in volume, then descending in pitch and fading away. Usually calls at dusk, dawn and during the night.
Status and Range: Formerly a common year-round resident on Hispaniola, but now uncommon and local because of hunting and habitat destruction. It is considered threatened. Also occurs through Central and South America.
Comments: Secretive. Primarily nocturnal and ground dwelling. Feeds on insects, worms, mollusks and sometimes small lizards and small rodents. Generally found in pairs or family groups. Kept by people to eat roaches and other household vermin.
Habitat: Semi-arid open country, savannas, plantations and rice fields.
Nesting: Does not build a nest, but lays its well-camouflaged eggs on the ground. Adults vigorously defend eggs and chicks. Eggs (2) tan, marked with maroon. Breeds in April and May.

PLOVERS AND LAPWINGS: FAMILY CHARADRIIDAE

Plovers are chunky birds. Except for the Killdeer, all species in the region frequent the water's edge. They have relatively shorter bills, necks and legs than the similar-appearing sandpipers. These surface-feeding birds also have a distinctive broadening at the bill tip which sandpipers lack. Six West Indian species have neck or breast markings.

NORTHERN LAPWING *Vanellus vanellus*   Plate 11

Identification: 30 cm (12"). Easily distinguished by its *crest*, which is present in all plumages and the *broad, black breast band*. *Immature*: The crest and black and white color pattern are less conspicuous. *Flight*: White band across base of upper tail with black patch at tip, rounded wingtips, contrasting white wing linings and black flight feathers, rounded wingtips.
Status and Range: A vagrant to the West Indies. Recorded from Paradise Island in the Bahamas, Puerto Rico, Martinique and Barbados. Apparently a transatlantic wanderer from Africa on favorable winds. Occurs throughout Eurasia to northern Africa.

BLACK-BELLIED PLOVER *Pluvialis squatarola*   Plate 11
Local Names: Lapwing (Jamaica); Pluvial Cabezón (Cuba); Playero (DR); Playero Cabezón (PR); Plivye Kòt Nwa, Pluvier, Bécasseau (Haiti); Pluvier Argenté, Pluvier Gris, Pluvier Grosse Tête (Guad, Mart); Soldier Bird, Zilver Plevier (St M, Saba)

Identification: 26–34 cm (10–13.5"). *Non-breeding*: Note the large size, stocky build, short bill, light mottled-gray coloration and indistinct contrast between gray crown and whitish eyebrow stripe. *Breeding*: *Black underparts*. *Flight above*: The white uppertail-coverts, white tail with dark bars and distinct white wing stripe are good field marks. *Flight below*: *Black wingpits*. *Similar species*: The very similar American and Pacific Golden-Plovers occur more typically in fields than

along water edges. The Black-bellied is larger with a larger bill and is grayer in non-breeding plumage. In breeding plumage, note Black-bellied's light crown and hindneck. It has *white, rather than dark, undertail-coverts* and lighter flecks above.
Voice: A single, plaintive *klee* and also a *klee-a-lee.*
Status and Range: Generally a common non-breeding resident in the West Indies from August to May; a few birds also occur in June and July. Occurs worldwide.
Comments: Typically in loose flocks.
Habitat: Tidal mudflats and other coastal water edges.

AMERICAN GOLDEN-PLOVER *Pluvialis dominica* Plate 11
Local Names: Pluvial Dorado (Cuba); Playero Americano (DR); Playero Dorado (PR); Plivye Savann (Haiti); Pluvier Bronzé (Guad, Mart); Pluvier Doré (Haiti, Guad, Mart); Kleine Goud-plevier (St E, St M)

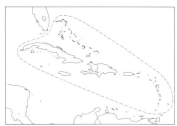

Identification: 26 cm (10″). *Non-breeding*: Fairly large and stocky with a short bill, mottled gray coloration and a distinct contrast between dark crown and whitish eyebrow stripe. *Breeding*: Black underparts with a golden cast on mottled upperparts. *Similar species*: Very similar to the more common Black-bellied Plover, but American Golden-Plover frequents fields rather than water edges. In non-breeding plumage, American Golden-Plover is darker above, particularly on the crown which highlights the white eyebrow stripe. In breeding plumage, which is rarely seen in the West Indies, note the black underparts extending to the undertail-coverts and the golden flecks on the upperparts. *Flight above*: Distinguished from Black-bellied Plover by the dark tail and uppertail-coverts and the absence of a white wing stripe. *Flight below*: Lacks the black wingpits of the Black-bellied. See also Pacific Golden-Plover.
Voice: A variety of calls including a single, loud whistle and a soft, warbled *cheedle-wur*, sometimes given as a loud whistle.
Status and Range: Generally a rare southbound migrant throughout the West Indies, primarily from August to November and very rare during its return north principally in March and April. It occurs annually in large numbers on Barbados. Widespread worldwide.
Comments: Typically flocks. Usually occurs in uplands, unlike other regularly occurring West Indian plovers.
Habitat: Primarily upland fields, golf courses and plowed fields. Also tidal flats.

PACIFIC GOLDEN-PLOVER *Pluvialis fulva* Plate 78

Identification: 24 cm (9.5″). A fairly large, slender, long-legged plover. *Non-breeding adult*: Note the golden cast to the back, face and eyebrow stripe. *Breeding*: Black below; mottled black and yellowish-brown above. *Similar species*: Very similar to American Golden-Plover, but more slender and longer-legged. Non-breeding Pacific Golden-Plovers are decidedly yellower on the back, face, eyebrow stripe and breast. Breeding American Golden-Plovers have a broad, white patch edging the breast whereas this is a slender stripe in the Pacific. Black-bellied Plover generally occurs along water edges, is larger, has a larger bill and is grayer in non-breeding plumage. In breeding plumage, note its white undertail-coverts, light crown and hindneck and paler flecks on its upperparts. For additional guidance on identification refer to: Golley, M. and A. Stoddart. 1991. Identification of American and Pacific Golden Plovers. *Birding World* 4(6): 195–204; and Dunn, J. L., J. Morlan and C. P. Wilds. 1987. Field Identification of forms of Lesser Golden-Plover. *Proceedings of the 4th International Identification Meeting, International Birdwatching Center Eilat*, pp. 28–33.
Status and Range: A vagrant on Barbados. Likely overlooked due to its close similarity to American Golden-Plover and to being considered of the same species until recently. Occurs through Asia, Australia and the South Pacific. Also the United States (Alaska and California).

COLLARED PLOVER *Charadrius collaris*   **Plate 11**
Local Name: Little Ploward (Grenada)

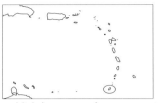

Identification: 15 cm (5.75"). ***Adult male***: Distinct *reddish-brown hindcrown and hindneck*. Further distinguished by its white forehead, throat and underparts and black band across breast. *Legs pinkish*. ***Adult female***: Shows a thinner breast band and is less reddish-brown. ***Immature***: Partial breast band limited to sides of neck, no black on crown and only a hint of reddish-brown in plumage. ***Flight***: *No wing stripe*. ***Similar species***: Semipalmated Plover is slightly larger, has a stubbier bill and *white hindneck*, lacks reddish-brown on the upperparts and has a white wing stripe in flight.
Voice: A sharp, metallic whistle *peet* or *peep-peep* and a cricket-like *chitit*.
Status and Range: An uncommon to rare breeding resident on Grenada and perhaps in the Grenadines (Mustique). A rare wanderer to Barbados and a vagrant on St Martin, St Christopher and St Lucia. Also occurs in Central and South America.
Habitat: Salt flats, coasts and river banks.
Nesting: Nests on sand or mudflats. Eggs (2) buffy with small black spots (January–September).

SNOWY PLOVER *Charadrius alexandrinus*   **Plate 11**
Local Names: Frailecillo Blanco (Cuba); Corredor (DR); Playero Blanco (PR); Pond Bird, Strandplevier (St M); Pluvier à Collier Interrompu, Collier (Guad, Mart)

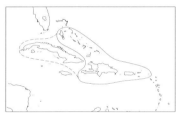

Identification: 14–15 cm (5.5–5.75"). Distinguished by its tiny size, pale coloration, *slender black bill*, dark neck marks and *blackish or dark legs*. ***Breeding***: Black ear patch. ***Immature***: Lacks black plumage markings of adults. ***Similar species***: Piping Plover has relatively shorter, stubbier bill and orangish legs.
Voice: A weak whistle similar to calling someone's attention.
Status and Range: A common year-round resident in the southern Bahamas north to San Salvador; also common on Hispaniola and Anguilla. It is an uncommon year-round resident in the northern Bahamas (Andros, Exuma and Eleuthera), Puerto Rico (extremely local in the southwest), the Virgin Islands (Anegada), St Martin and St-Barthélemy. Snowy Plover is a very rare breeding resident on Cuba, dispersing after nesting, perhaps to other islands. A vagrant on Jamaica, in the Cayman Islands and from Antigua in the Lesser Antilles southward. This plover may move among islands, particularly smaller ones, after breeding. The race of Snowy Plover native to the West Indies and North America (*C.a. nivosus*) is considered threatened due to habitat degradation and introduced predators. Widespread worldwide.
Habitat: Primarily beaches and lagoon borders with extensive salt flats.
Nesting: The nest is a depression in the sand, sometimes lined with shell fragments. Eggs (3) sand-colored with scrawled markings. Breeds from January to August.

WILSON'S PLOVER *Charadrius wilsonia*   **Plate 11**
Local Names: Thick-billed Plover (Jamaica); Little Ploward, Nit (LA); Sand Bird (LA, VI); Titere Playero (Cuba); Cabezón (DR); Playero Marítimo (PR); Kolye Fran, Bécassine (Haiti); Pond Bird, Dikbekplevier (St M); Pluvier de Wilson, Collier (Guad, Mart)

Identification: 18–20 cm (7–8"). The broad, breast band and long, thick, black bill are good field marks. ***Male***: Black breast band. ***Female and immature***: Brown breast band. ***Similar species***: Semipalmated Plover is smaller and has a much shorter, stubbier bill and orange legs, whereas Wilson's are pinkish.
Voice: The call is an emphatic raspy whistle *pete*, *whit*, or *wheet*. Also a quick two to three syllabled *ki-ki-ki*.
Status and Range: A common year-round resident in the Bahamas, Greater Antilles, Virgin Islands and on some of the northern Lesser Antilles, including St Martin, St-Barthélemy, St Christopher, Antigua and Barbuda. Numbers decline in some areas, such as on Cuba and Puerto Rico, from September to March when the birds are not breeding. It uncommonly ranges to the

Cayman Islands and is an uncommon year-round resident in the Grenadines. Elsewhere in the Lesser Antilles Wilson's Plover is either rare or a vagrant. Occurs through warmer coastal areas of the Western Hemisphere.

Habitat: Primarily the borders of salt ponds.

Nesting: The nest is a depression in the sand sometimes lined with bits of shell. Eggs (2–4) light buff-colored, splotched. Breeds primarily from March to July.

SEMIPALMATED PLOVER *Charadrius semipalmatus*　　　　Plate 11

Local Names: Frailecillo Semipalmeado (Cuba); Playero (DR); Playero Acollarado (PR); Kolye Janm Jòn, Collier à Pattes Jaunes (Haiti); Becasse a Collier (St L); Pond Bird, Ring Neck, Amerikaanse bontbekplevier (St M); Pluvier Semipalmé, Collier (Guad, Mart)

Identification: 18.5 cm (7.25"). Identified by its brown upperparts, dark breast band, stubby bill and *orange legs*. Sometimes the breast band is incomplete and shows only as bars on either side of the breast. **Non-breeding**: The bill is dark and may lack orange at the base. **Breeding**: Orange base of bill. **Similar species**: Piping Plover is much paler above. Wilson's Plover is larger with a much larger bill and pinkish legs. Collared Plover is smaller with a more slender bill, dark hindneck, reddish-brown on the upperparts and lacks a white wing stripe in flight. **Voice**: The call note is a plaintive *weet*. Also a questioning whistle *tee-weet*.

Status and Range: Generally a common non-breeding resident through most of the West Indies from August to May, though uncommon on Cuba. Most frequent in the region during its southward migration in September and October. A few individuals occur during June and July. Occurs through the Western Hemisphere.

Comments: Typically flocks, often with other shorebirds.

Habitat: Tidal flats.

PIPING PLOVER *Charadrius melodus*　　　　Plate 11

Local Names: Frailecillo Silbadór (Cuba); Playerito (DR); Playero Melódico (PR)

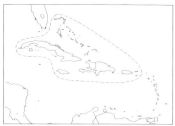

Identification: 18 cm (7"). Distinguished by its pale gray upperparts, *short stubby bill*, and *orange legs*. **Non-breeding**: Black bill. The breast band may be partial or absent. **Breeding**: The base of the bill is orange; the breast band may be partial or complete. **Flight**: Note the white uppertail-coverts and black spot near the tip of the tail. **Similar species**: Distinguished from Snowy Plover by its relatively shorter, stubbier bill and lighter legs. The similar Semipalmated Plover is browner above.

Voice: A thin, whistle *peep* and *pee-lo*.

Status and Range: A fairly common non-breeding resident in the northern Bahamas (Exuma, Eleuthera, Andros and New Providence), it is rare elsewhere in the Bahamas, the Greater Antilles and Virgin Islands (St Croix) primarily from late August to March. Piping Plover is a vagrant in the Lesser Antilles south to Barbados. This plover is endangered primarily due to habitat loss and degradation of its breeding grounds in North America. Occurs primarily in Canada and the United States.

Habitat: Recently dredged spoils and sandy water edges, both fresh and saline. Also offshore cays.

KILLDEER *Charadrius vociferus*　　　　Plate 11

Local Names: Tilderee (Jamaica); Soldier Bird (St E, St M, VI); Titere Sabanero (Cuba); Ti-ito (DR); Playero Sabanero (PR); Kolye Doub, Collier Double, Chevalier de Terre (Haiti); Pluvier Kildir, Double Collier (Guad, Mart); Pond Bird, Killdeerplevier (St E, St M)

Identification: 25 cm (9.75"). Immediately identified by *two black bands* on the breast. **Flight**: The reddish-brown rump is conspicuous.

Voice: A plaintive, high-pitched *kee* and *dee-de* reminiscent of its name.

Status and Range: A common year-round resident in the Bahamas and Greater Antilles, less so in the Virgin Islands. Southbound migrants, some remaining as non-breeding residents, augment local numbers primarily from September to March. Killdeer is generally an uncommon non-breeding resident in the Cayman Islands, northern Lesser Antilles south to St-Barthèlemy and on Barbados and San Andrés. It is rare to very rare elsewhere in the Lesser Antilles. Occurs from North America south to western South America.
Habitat: Wet fields, short grass, mudholes and the edges of freshwater ponds.
Nesting: The nest is a slightly lined depression on the ground. Eggs (3–4) pale buff-colored and heavily splotched. Breeds from March to October.

OYSTERCATCHERS: FAMILY HAEMATOPODIDAE

The oystercatchers form a small family of stout, coastal birds with large, brightly colored bills. Their bills are unusual in that they are laterally compressed, an adaptation for opening bi-valves, their chief food. These mollusks are sometimes immersed in water before being swallowed.

AMERICAN OYSTERCATCHER *Haematopus palliatus*   Plate 14
Local Names: Whelkcracker (St M, VI); Ostrero (Cuba, PR); Caracolero (DR, PR); Casseur de Burgau (St B); Amerikaanse scholekster (St M); Huitrier d'Amérique, Huitrier (Guad, Mart)

Identification: 43–54 cm (17–21"). Note its large size, *black hood* and *long, heavy bill*. **Adult**: Orange-red bill; pinkish legs. **Immature**: Dull pinkish bill, dark at tip. Gray legs. **Flight**: Broad, white wing stripe and uppertail.
Voice: A loud, emphatic, coarsely whistled *wheep*.
Status and Range: A fairly common, but very local year-round resident in the southern and central Bahamas, Puerto Rico, the Virgin Islands and Guadeloupe (Petite Terre). Rare and local, primarily outside the breeding season, but also a spotty breeder in the northernmost Bahamas, Cuba, Hispaniola and the Lesser Antilles. It is a vagrant on Jamaica and likely breeds more widely in the West Indies than is presently known. Also occurs on the east coast of the United States south along both coasts of Mexico and Central and South America.
Comments: Restricted exclusively to a relatively scarce habitat type occupied by no other bird species in the West Indies except, perhaps, Ruddy Turnstone.
Habitat: Typically stony beaches and rocky headlands of offshore islands and cays.
Nesting: The nest is a scrape in sand, pebbles or coral rubble on a remote coastal beach or islet. Eggs (1–3) buff-colored, spotted with dark brown. Breeds from May to July.

STILTS AND AVOCETS: FAMILY RECURVIROSTRIDAE

These are noisy, gregarious wading birds with very long legs. They occur in open, shallow wetlands.

BLACK-NECKED STILT *Himantopus mexicanus*   Plate 15
Local Names: Cap'n Lewis (Jamaica); Soldier, Crackpot Soldier, Pète-pète (LA); Tell Tale (CI, VI); Redshank (LA, VI); Cachiporra (Cuba); Zancudo (DR); Viuda (DR, PR); Pèt-pèt, Echasse (Haiti); Bécasse (St B); Echasse d'Amérique (Guad, Mart)

Identification: 34–39 cm (13.5–15.5"). Note its relatively large size; *long, pink legs*; *black upperparts and white underparts*. **Flight**: Black wings above and below, white underparts, tail and lower back, extending as V on back.

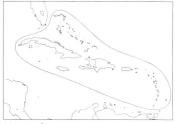

Voice: A loud raucous series of notes *wit, wit, wit, wit, wit.*
Status and Range: Widespread year-round throughout the West Indies. A common breeding resident from March to October in the southern and central Bahamas, Greater Antilles and the Virgin and Cayman Islands. It sometimes becomes scarce outside the breeding season. An uncommon to rare breeding resident in the northernmost Bahamas (Grand Bahama, Andros and Abaco) and generally an uncommon one among the northern Lesser Antilles south to Guadeloupe. It is rare among the Lesser Antilles farther south. Widespread in the Western Hemisphere.
Comments: Typically flocks. A conspicuous, noisy shorebird occurring in a wide range of water bodies.
Habitat: Mudflats, salt ponds and open mangrove swamps.
Nesting: The nest, built near water, is a platform of grass and twigs. Eggs (3–7) olive-green with large splotches. Breeds primarily from late April to August and occasionally in September and October.

AMERICAN AVOCET *Recurvirostra americana*   Plate 15
Local Name: Avoceta (Cuba, PR)

Identification: 40–51 cm (16–20"). Good field marks are its large size, *sharply upturned bill* and black and white coloration. ***Non-breeding***: Head and neck gray. ***Breeding***: Head and neck cinnamon-colored.
Voice: A high-pitched, melodious *klee.*
Status and Range: A very rare non-breeding resident in the Bahamas and Cuba primarily from July to January and in April. A vagrant on Jamaica, Puerto Rico, the Virgin and Cayman Islands, Antigua and Barbados. Though American Avocet occurs very infrequently and irregularly in the West Indies, it sometimes occurs in surprising numbers. In June of 1995, over 150 birds were seen, one flock alone containing nearly 50 individuals. Also through western North America to Guatemala.
Habitat: Shallow wetland borders.

JACANAS: FAMILY JACANIDAE

Jacanas are inhabitants of tropical swamps, ponds and lake edges, particularly where there are waterlilies. With their extremely long toes, jacanas are able to walk on the floating vegetation without sinking. However, they can swim and will dive to escape danger. The flight of jacanas is slow and labored. Unusual among birds, the male is smaller than the female and it is the male which incubates the eggs and cares for the young. In some species the female has several mates, also unusual among birds.

NORTHERN JACANA *Jacana spinosa*   Plate 17
Local Names: River Chink, Pond Coot (Jamaica); Gallito de Río (Cuba); Gallito de Agua (DR); Médecin, Chevalye Dore, Poul Dlo Dore, Jacana, Poule d'eau Dorée (Haiti)

Identification: 19–23 cm (7.5–9"). A chicken-like bird with large, *yellow wing patches* and *extremely long, slender, greenish toes.* ***Adult***: Body deep reddish-brown, except blackish head and neck. *Bill and forehead shield yellow.* ***Immature***: Whitish below; white eyebrow stripe. ***Flight***: Low over water with shallow wingbeats and dangling legs; characteristically raises its wings after landing, displaying yellow undersides.
Voice: A sharp repeated cackle, especially in flight. Also rasping, chattering and clacking notes.
Status and Range: A common year-round resident on Cuba, Jamaica and Hispaniola. A vagrant on Puerto Rico. Occurs through southern North America and Central America.

Comments: Very active and noisy. Food consists of mollusks, small fish, crustaceans, insects and aquatic seeds, which it seeks while walking slowly over floating plants. Unusual among birds in that the male alone incubates the eggs.

Habitat: Freshwater bodies with large-leaved floating vegetation.

Nesting: Builds a small nest of plant material among dense, floating aquatic vegetation. Eggs (3–4) buffy brown, heavily scrawled with black. Breeds from April to September.

SANDPIPERS, PHALAROPES AND ALLIES:
FAMILY SCOLOPACIDAE

The sandpipers are the second most numerous family in the West Indies and the second most difficult group to identify at the species level. Of the many species that occur here, all but the Willet are transients from their breeding grounds, primarily in the far north. The sandpipers are characterized by their long legs and necks and thin, pointed bills. Most wade in shallow water, or on wet flats where they probe in the mud for invertebrates. They are highly gregarious and often occur in mixed feeding assemblages which aids their identification. Several species remain in the region late enough to be seen in their breeding plumage. In all species that occur here, with the notable exception of the Ruff, both sexes have similar plumages.

COMMON GREENSHANK *Tringa nebularia*   Plate 78

Identification: 32 cm (12.5"). **Non-breeding**: Identified by its relatively large size, *greenish or yellowish legs* and *slightly upturned bill*, thicker at the base. **Breeding**: Breast heavily flecked with black. **Flight**: A *white V extends from the uppertail-coverts onto the back* as in the dowitchers. **Similar species**: Greater Yellowlegs has orangish-yellow legs and lacks the white V on its back.

Status and Range: A vagrant in the West Indies. Recorded from Puerto Rico and Barbados. This shorebird may well be transiting the Atlantic Ocean from Africa much more regularly than records indicate, but could be going undetected beause of its relatively close similarity in appearance to the commonly occurring Greater Yellowlegs. Widespread in the Eastern Hemisphere.

GREATER YELLOWLEGS *Tringa melanoleuca*   Plate 15

Local Names: Snipe (VI); Zarapico Patiamarillo Grande (Cuba); Playero Grande con Patas Amarillas (DR); Playero Guineilla Mayor (PR); Gwo Bekasin Janm Jòn, Bécasse à Pattes Jaunes (Haiti); Pied Long (St L); Pond Bird, Grote Geelpootruiter (St M); Grand Chevalier, Clin, Clin-clin (Guad, Mart)

Identification: 33–38 cm (13–15"). Its large size, *orangish-yellow legs* and long, straight bill aid identification. **Flight**: Dark above with white uppertail-coverts. **Similar species**: It often occurs with the more common Lesser Yellowlegs, allowing size comparison. Greater Yellowlegs has a relatively longer, thicker bill that often appears slightly upturned and two-toned, being paler at the base. Its sharp three to four note call is distinctive. Upland Sandpiper has a shorter bill and typically occurs in grasslands, rather than mudflats. See also Common Greenshank and Spotted Redshank.

Voice: A loud, irritating whistle of three to four notes *cu-cu-cu*, or *klee-klee-cu*.

Status and Range: A non-breeding resident throughout the West Indies, it is generally common during its southbound migration from August to October. Greater Yellowlegs is less common from November to May and rarely occurs in June and July. Overall, it occurs in smaller numbers than Lesser Yellowlegs. Occurs through the Western Hemisphere.

Comments: Typically flocks.

Habitat: Mudflats and shallows of both freshwater and saltwater bodies.

LESSER YELLOWLEGS   *Tringa flavipes*   **Plates 15, 16**

Local Names: Snipe (VI); Zarapico Patiamarillo Chico (Cuba); Playero con Patas Amarillas (DR); Playero Guineilla Menor (PR); Bekasin Janm Jòn, Bécassine à Pattes Jaunes (Haiti); Pied Jaune (St L); Petit Chevalier, Patte Jaune (Guad, Mart); Pond Bird, Kleine Geelpootruiter (Saba, St M); Pattes Jaunes (French WI)

Identification: 25–28 cm (9.75–11″). Its medium size, distinctive *orangish-yellow legs* and thin, straight bill help identify this sandpiper. *Flight*: Dark above with white uppertail-coverts. *Similar species*: The thinner, shorter bill and one to two note call are the best characteristics for distinguishing it from Greater Yellowlegs. Upland Sandpiper has a shorter bill and typically occurs in grasslands, rather than mudflats. See also Wood Sandpiper and Spotted Redshank.
Voice: A one (usually) or two note call *cu-cu*, softer and more nasal than that of Greater Yellowlegs.

Status and Range: A non-breeding resident throughout the West Indies, it is generally common during migration from August to October and March to May. From November to February generally uncommon, and particularly rare during June and July when most Lesser Yellowlegs are on their breeding grounds far to the north. Occurs through the Western Hemisphere.
Comments: Typically flocks, often together with Greater Yellowlegs.
Habitat: Mudflats and shallows of both freshwater and saltwater bodies.

SPOTTED REDSHANK   *Tringa erythropus*   **Plate 15**

Identification: 30 cm (12″). In all plumages, the *red legs and base of lower mandible* and, in flight, the *large white patch on the lower back* are distinctive characteristics. *Non-breeding adult and immature*: Gray above; paler below. Note its *blackish lores*, paler in immatures and the white eyebrow stripe. *Breeding adult*: Black; heavily spotted with white. *Similar species*: Both Greater and Lesser Yellowlegs have yellow, not red, legs and lack red at the base of the bill.
Status and Range: A vagrant in the West Indies. Recorded from Barbados. Likely a wanderer from Africa which crosses the Atlantic Ocean using favorable winds. Occurs through Eurasia south to central Africa.
Habitat: Shorelines, tide pools and marshes.

WOOD SANDPIPER   *Tringa glareola*   **Plate 78**

Identification: 20 cm (8″). A slender, medium-sized sandpiper with an entirely *white rump, pale yellow or greenish-yellow legs* and a conspicuous white eyebrow stripe. *Flight*: Note the *pale gray underwings*. *Similar species*: Solitary Sandpiper has a black mark down the center of its rump with white on either side; also lacks a conspicuous eyebrow stripe, but has a relatively more noticeable white eyering and darker wing linings. Lesser Yellowlegs has gray, rather than brown, upperparts and lacks a distinctive eyebrow stripe. *Similar species*: See Solitary Sandpiper.
Status and Range: Rare on Barbados where it has occurred several times in recent years and has remained through the non-breeding season. Apparently arrives via transatlantic movements on favorable winds. Occurs throughout the Eastern Hemisphere.

SOLITARY SANDPIPER   *Tringa solitaria*   **Plates 12, 16**

Local Names: Zarapico Solitario (Cuba); Playero Solitario (DR, PR); Bekasin Dlo Dous, Bécassine Solitaire, Chevalier à Aile Noire (Haiti); Dos Noir (St L); Chevalier Solitaire, Pond Bird, Amerikaanse Bosruiter (St M); Grande Aile, Aile Noire (Guad, Mart)

Identification: 19–23 cm (7.5–9″). Note its *white eyering*, dark upperparts, black barring of the outer tail feathers and dark greenish legs. *Flight*: Entirely dark above with heavy bars on its white-edged tail. Underwings entirely dark. *The wingbeats are distinctively deep and erratic.*

Habit: Frequently bobs its tail. **Similar species**: Wood Sandpiper has an entirely white rump and a more conspicuous eyebrow stripe, while Solitary Sandpiper has a relatively more noticeable white eyering and darker wing linings.
Voice: A hard, emphatic series of whistles when alarmed *weet-weet-weet*. Also a soft *pip* or *weet* when undisturbed.
Status and Range: A non-breeding resident throughout the West Indies, it is generally an uncommon southbound migrant in September and October and even less frequent as a resident from November to May, though its numbers may not decline significantly on Cuba and Hispaniola. There are records year round; scarcer in the Lesser Antilles. Occurs through the Western Hemisphere.
Comments: Generally occurs singly.
Habitat: Freshwater edges.

WILLET *Catoptrophorus semipalmatus* Plate 14
Local Names: Laughing Jack (CI); Tell-bill-willy (Grenada, VI); Zarapico Real (Cuba); Chorlo (DR); Playero Aliblanco (PR); Bekasin Zèl Blanch, Bécasse à Aile Blanche (Haiti); Chevalier Semipalmé, Aile Blanche (Guad, Mart, St L)

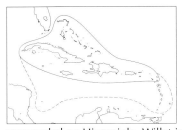

Identification: 38–40 cm (15–16″). Distinguished by its large size, light gray coloration, gray legs and thick bill. **Breeding**: Fine black stripes on head, neck and breast. **Non-breeding**: More uniformly gray. **Flight**: The *black and white wing pattern* is diagnostic.
Voice: A sharp *chip-chip-chip*. Also a loud, piercing whistle and other sharp, whistling calls.
Status and Range: A year-round resident in the Bahamas, Greater Antilles and Cayman Islands where it is common from August to November when the resident breeding population is augmented by migrants from the north. Breeding is as yet unrecorded on Hispaniola. Willet is uncommon from December to April and rare in other months. It is generally an uncommon year-round resident in the Virgin Islands and on Antigua and is also suspected of breeding on Anguilla, St Martin and Barbuda. Elsewhere in the Lesser Antilles it is regarded as a non-breeding resident ranging from common on St Barthélemy, Guadeloupe and Martinique to uncommon on Barbados and rare on the remaining islands. Willet is common on Providencia and uncommon on San Andrés. Widespread in the Western Hemisphere.
Habitat: Primarily tidal flats, but occurs on borders of both saltwater and freshwater bodies.
Nesting: The nest is a slightly lined depression in the sand. Eggs (4) buff-colored and heavily splotched. Breeds from April to July.

SPOTTED SANDPIPER *Actitis macularia* Plates 13, 16
Local Names: Weatherbird (English LA); Zarapico Manchado (Cuba); Playerito Manchado (DR); Playero Coleador (PR); Bekasin Zèl Tranble (Haiti); Becasse (St L); Chevalier Branlequeue (Guad, Haiti, Mart); Chevalier Grivelé, Batmar, Branle Queue (Guad, Mart); Tip-up, Dipper, Amerikaanse Deverloper (Saba, St E, St M)

Identification: 18–20 cm (7–8″). **Non-breeding**: Field marks are its white underparts with a dark mark on the side of the neck and the orangish base of the bill. **Breeding**: Distinct *dark spots on the underparts* and *orange bill with a black tip*. **Flight**: Very *shallow, rapid wingbeats* and shows a white wing stripe. **Habit**: A distinctive *teetering walk*.
Voice: A whistle *we-weet*.
Status and Range: Generally a common non-breeding resident throughout the West Indies from August to May though less common from December to February. It is rare in June and July. Occurs through the Western Hemisphere.
Comments: Not generally found on mudflats with other shorebirds and does not typically flock.
Habitat: Water edges of mangroves, coastlines, streams and rice fields.

UPLAND SANDPIPER *Bartramia longicauda* **Plate 15**
Local Names: Cotton-tree Plover (Grenada, St V); Ganga (Cuba, PR); Maubèche des Champs, Poule Vergenne (Guad, Mart)

Identification: 28–32 cm (11–12.5"). The orangish-yellow legs; thin, relatively short bill; small head and long, slender neck and long tail help identify this sandpiper. Its occurrence in grasslands, rather than along water edges, and relatively solitary behavior aid identification. **Habit**: Often perches on posts. **Flight**: Dark primaries, long tail and stiff, shallow wingbeats like those of Spotted Sandpiper are distinctive. **Similar species**: Both Lesser and Greater Yellowlegs have longer bills and typically occur on mudflats, rather than in grasslands. Buff-breasted Sandpiper has a shorter neck, legs and bill, and is unstreaked below.

Status and Range: A rare migrant in the Bahamas, Puerto Rico and some of the Lesser Antilles including St Barthélemy, Montserrat, Guadeloupe, Dominica and Barbados from August to early October and decidedly less frequent during its return north in April and May. It is very rare on Cuba and the Cayman Islands during both migrations and is a vagrant elsewhere in the West Indies and on all islands outside the migration periods. Occurs through most of the Western Hemisphere.
Habitat: Grasslands, pastures and open savannas.

ESKIMO CURLEW *Numenius borealis* **Plate 14**

Identification: 30–35 cm (12–14"). A small curlew most readily distinguished in flight when its *cinnamon-colored wing linings* and *dark, unbarred primaries* are visible. **Similar species**: Eskimo Curlew is noticeably smaller with a shorter and straighter bill than the very similar Whimbrel. Also has a less conspicuously striped crown and a buffier breast.
Status and Range: A vagrant in the West Indies. There are records from Puerto Rico, Guadeloupe, Barbados, the Grenadines (Carriacou) and Grenada. The species is critically endangered and now near extinction primarily due to overhunting. It was, perhaps, always a rare migrant in the region from late August to early November, except on Barbados where it regularly occurred in American Golden-Plover flocks. Formerly Eskimo Curlew bred in abundance in northwestern Canada and migrated the length of the hemisphere to central Argentina and back each year. It was hunted by the tens of thousands for food and sport on the western plains of the United States primarily from 1870 to 1900, after which time the bird became relatively scarce. Believed extinct for a number of years, the population is presently estimated at no more than a few dozen birds. Occurs from northwestern Canada and Alaska to southern South America.
Comments: Unwary and curious.
Habitat: Grasslands and plowed fields, sometimes mudflats.

WHIMBREL *Numenius phaeopus* **Plate 14**
Local Names: Zarapico Pico Cimitarra Chico (Cuba); Playero Picocorvo (PR); Kouli, Courlis (Haiti); Tivi-tivi (St L); Curlew, Regenwulp (St M); Courlis Corlieu, Bec Crochu (Guad, Mart)

Identification: 38–46 cm (15–18"). Distinguished by its relatively large size, striped crown and *long, down-curved bill*. **Flight**: Underwings are barred and lack cinnamon color. **Similar species**: See other curlews.
Voice: A hard, rapid whistle *whip-whip-whip-whip* or *kee-kee-kee-kee*, not as raspy as the call of Greater Yellowlegs. Also other calls.
Status and Range: Generally an uncommon to rare, but regular migrant throughout the West Indies. On Jamaica and Puerto Rico, the Whimbrel is sometimes common very locally; however, somewhat peculiarly, it is very rare on Cuba. Whimbrel occurs in all months being most frequent in September and least abundant in June and July. Widespread worldwide.
Comments: The Eurasian subspecies which sometimes occurs in the West Indies has an inverted V of white feathers from the rump up the center of the back.
Habitat: Ponds, swamps and marshes.

LONG-BILLED CURLEW *Numenius americanus*   **Plate 14**

Identification: 51–66 cm (20–26"). A large shorebird with an extremely *long, down-curved bill*. It is mottled cinnamon-brown above and paler below and has bluish legs and *diagnostic cinnamon wing linings visible in flight*. **Similar species**: Whimbrel is smaller and has stripes on the crown. Also, its overall coloration is grayer.
Status and Range: A vagrant in the West Indies. Old records from Cuba and Jamaica and recent sightings from Puerto Rico, the Virgin Islands (St Croix) and Antigua. May occur in any month. This species breeds in the prairies of central North America, migrating outside the breeding season to the western and Gulf coasts. The bird's numbers declined substantially during the 1900s as its nesting habitat dwindled. This decline reduces the chance of stray birds occurring in the West Indies. Primarily occurs from western and central North America to Guatemala.
Habitat: Mudflats, lagoons, wetlands, sandbars and shorelines.

HUDSONIAN GODWIT *Limosa haemastica*   **Plate 14**
Local Names: Avoceta Pechirroja (Cuba); Playero (DR); Barga Aliblanca (PR); Barge Hudsonienne (Guad, Mart)

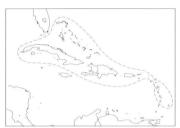

Identification: 33–40 cm (13–16"). Note the long, slightly *upturned bill* which is pinkish at the base and the *black tail* with a *white base*. **Non-breeding**: Gray overall; paler below with a white eyebrow stripe. **Breeding**: Dark reddish-brown below, heavily barred. Female paler. **Flight above**: White wing stripe and base of tail. **Flight below**: *Blackish wing linings* and *white wing stripe*.
Status and Range: Uncommon on Barbados and very rare in the Bahamas, Cuba, Hispaniola, Puerto Rico, the Virgin Islands, St Martin, St Barthélemy, Antigua, Guadeloupe (including Marie-Galante), Dominica, Martinique and St Lucia during southward migration primarily in September and October. Hudsonian Godwit breeds very locally in northern Canada and Alaska and then undertakes an extraordinary migration south, primarily over the Atlantic Ocean to spend the non-breeding season in southern South America. It is believed that large numbers pass over the West Indies at this time without stopping. The return migration northward is more westerly, apparently along the Central American coast. Occurs through the Western Hemisphere.
Habitat: Grassy freshwater pond edges and mudflats.

MARBLED GODWIT *Limosa fedoa*   **Plate 14**
Local Names: Avoceta Parda (Cuba); Playero (DR); Barga Jaspeada (PR)

Identification: 40–51 (16–20"). The large size, *absence of white on the rump* and long, slightly *upturned bill* identify this species. **Non-breeding**: Buff-colored underparts. **Breeding**: Reddish-brown underparts barred with black. **Flight above**: Cinnamon-colored overall with blackish primary wing-coverts. **Flight below**: *Cinnamon-colored wing linings* with paler flight feathers.
Status and Range: A vagrant or very rare migrant on Cuba, Jamaica, Hispaniola, Puerto Rico, the Virgin and Cayman Islands and in the Lesser Antilles where recorded from St Christopher, Guadeloupe, Martinique, Barbados, the Grenadines (Carriacou) and Grenada. Occurs from late August to early April. Ranges through North and Central America.
Habitat: Mudflats and marshy areas.

RUDDY TURNSTONE *Arenaria interpres*   Plate 12
Local Names: Revuelvepiedras (Cuba); Playero Turco (DR); Playero Turco (PR); Eriys, Tournepierre (Haiti); Calico (St L); Pond Bird, Steenloper (St M); Pluvier Fajou, Tournepierre à Collier, Pluvier des Salines (Guad, Mart)

Identification: 21–23 cm (8–9"). ***Non-breeding****: Dark breast markings; orange legs.* ***Breeding****: Unusual black and white facial markings* and a *reddish-orange back.* ***Flight****:* Distinctive white pattern on upperwings, back and tail.
Voice: A variety of calls including a loud, nasal *cuck-cuck-cuck*, increasing in volume.
Status and Range: Generally a common non-breeding resident throughout the West Indies in all months except June and July when it is uncommon. Widespread worldwide.
Comments: Typically forms looser flocks than most other sandpipers. Its English name derives from its distinctive foraging behavior of overturning small stones in search of invertebrate prey.
Habitat: Mudflats, pond edges and both sandy and rocky coasts.

RED KNOT *Calidris canutus*   Plates 12, 16
Local Names: Playero Pechirrojo (DR); Playero Gordo (PR)

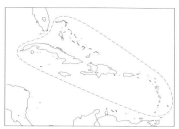

Identification: 25–28 cm (9.75–11"). In all plumages, its medium size, chunky build, usually *greenish legs* and relatively short bill distinguish this sandpiper. ***Non-breeding****:* Gray above; white below. ***Breeding****:* Orangish-red face and underparts. ***Flight above****:* Note the white wing stripe and pale gray, barred rump. ***Flight below****:* Pale gray wing-linings.
Voice: A soft hoarse two-note *chunt, chunt*, sounding something like a chuckle or rattle.
Status and Range: Generally rare through the West Indies in September and October during its southbound migration. It occurs even less frequently while migrating northward in March and April. There are records from every month of the year. A vagrant in the Lesser Antilles except on Barbados where it occurs regularly. Red Knot breeds only in the high Arctic but migrates great distances, some birds spending the non-breeding season in the southernmost portions of South America, Africa and Australia. This species apparently flies long distances between stops, many birds likely overflying the West Indies, particularly while migrating southward. Widespread worldwide.
Habitat: Sandy tidal flats.

SANDERLING *Calidris alba*   Plates 13, 16
Local Names: Zarapico Blanco (Cuba); Playerito Blanquito (DR); Playero Arenero (PR); Bécassine Blanche, Bekasin Blan (Haiti); Bécasseau Sanderling, Gros Maringouin Blanc (Guad, Mart); Pond Bird, Drieteen Strandloper (St E, St M)

Identification: 18–22 cm (7–8.5"). ***Non-breeding****:* This is the lightest-colored of the sandpipers, with white underparts and *light gray upperparts*. It often has a *black mark* on the bend of the wing. ***Breeding****:* Reddish-brown head and breast. ***Flight****:* Conspicuous white wing stripe.
Voice: A distinctive *whit*.
Status and Range: Generally a fairly common non-breeding resident throughout the West Indies from September to April, and rare from May to August. Widespread worldwide.
Habitat: Primarily sandy beaches where flocks advance and retreat rapidly with each wave.

SEMIPALMATED SANDPIPER *Calidris pusilla*   Plates 13, 16
Local Names: Zarapico Semipalmeado (Cuba); Playerito (DR); Playerito Gracioso (PR); Z'aloutte (Guad); Ti bekasin Janm Nwa, Bécassine à Pattes Noires (Haiti); Bécasseau Semi-palmé, Maringouin, Alouette (Guad, Mart); Maringouin (Haiti, Mart); Pond Bird, Kleine Grijze Strandloper (St E, St M)

Identification: 14–16.5 cm (5.5–6.5"). In all plumages, identified by its *small size, black legs* and *medium-length black bill.* This is the principal small sandpiper one should know well and against which all others should be compared. ***Non-breeding***: Grayish-brown above; whitish below. ***Breeding***: Finely barred upper breast and reddish-brown tints on upperparts. ***Female***: The bill is slightly longer and more drooped at the tip than the male's. ***Flight***: Fine white wing stripe and white rump divided by black bar. ***Similar species***: See Western, White-rumped, Least and Baird's Sandpipers. For additional information refer to: Viet, R. R., and L. Jonsson. 1987. Field Identification of Smaller Sandpipers within the Genus *Calidris. American Birds* 41(2): 212–236.
Voice: A soft chatter on take-off. Also a fairly deep, somewhat hoarse *cherk.*
Status and Range: Generally a common non-breeding resident through most of the West Indies from August to May; a few occur in June and July. During the peak of its southward migration from August to October, it is probably the most abundant shorebird in the West Indies. Widespread worldwide.
Comments: Typically in large flocks.
Habitat: Mudflats and borders of still water from puddles to salt ponds.

WESTERN SANDPIPER *Calidris mauri*   Plate 13
Local Names: Zarapico Chico (Cuba); Playerito (DR); Playerito Occidental (PR); Ti bekasin bèk long, Maubèche (Haiti); Pond Bird, Alaskastrandloper (St M); Bécasseau d'Alaska (Guad, Mart)

Identification: 15–18 cm (5.75–7"). Bill relatively long, heavy at base, narrower and drooping at tip. Only distinguished with certainty by its voice and when the scapulars are reddish-brown in August and September before the molt into non-breeding plumage is completed. ***Non-breeding***: Grayish-brown above; whitish below. ***Breeding***: Note the reddish-brown crown, ear patch and scapulars. ***Similar species***: The relatively long bill, heavy at base and down-curved at tip, helps distinguish Western Sandpiper from the very similar Semipalmated Sandpiper. However, these species overlap substantially with regard to this character. See also White-rumped and Baird's Sandpipers.
Voice: In flight, a *kreep,* coarser and more querulous than that of Semipalmated Sandpiper (Pough).
Status and Range: A non-breeding resident throughout the West Indies primarily from September to March, but occurs in all months. The species is probably fairly common through much of the region, but is often overlooked due to its similarity to the more common Semipalmated Sandpiper with which it often occurs. Ranges through North and Central America, and northern South America. Also Siberia.
Comments: Western generally feeds in deeper water than Semipalmated.
Habitat: Borders of still water, particularly mudflats.

LEAST SANDPIPER *Calidris minutilla*   Plates 13, 16
Local Names: Zarapiquito (Cuba); Playerito (DR); Playerito Menudo (PR); Ti bekasin piti (Haiti); Recuit (St L); Bécasseau minuscule, Ricuit (Guad, Mart); Pond Bird, Amerikaanse Kleinste Strandloper (St M, Saba)

Identification: 12.5–16.5 cm (5–6.5"). Note its *tiny size* and *yellowish-green legs.* Its brown coloration, streaked breast and thin bill with a slightly drooping tip also help in identification. ***Non-breeding***: Brown above and on breast; white belly and abdomen. ***Breeding***: Plumage more mottled and with reddish-brown tints. ***Flight***: Dark above with a very faint wing stripe. ***Similar species***: Its yellowish-green legs distinguish it from all other small sandpipers.

Voice: A thin, soft whistle *wi-wi-wit*. Also an almost whinny-like trill that drops both in pitch and volume *tr-tr-tr-tr-tr-tr*.
Status and Range: Generally a common migrant from August to October and April to May and an uncommon to rare non-breeding resident from November to March through most of the West Indies. It is least frequent in June and July. Widespread in the Western Hemisphere.
Comments: Typically flocks, often with Semipalmated Sandpipers.
Habitat: Borders of still water, particularly coastal mudflats.

WHITE-RUMPED SANDPIPER *Calidris fuscicollis*   Plates 13, 16

Local Names: Zarapico de Rabadilla Blanca (Cuba); Playerito (DR); Playero Rabadilla Blanca (PR); Bekasin ke blan, Bécassine queue blanche (Haiti); Becasse (St L); Pond Bird, Bonaparte's Strandloper (St M); Bécasseau à croupion blanc (Guad, Mart)

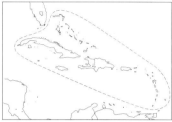

Identification: 18–20 cm (7–8"). The *white rump* distinguishes this from other small sandpipers in flight. *Non-breeding*: Brownish-gray above and on upper breast, appearing hooded. *Breeding*: Browner with reddish-brown tints on crown, upper back and ear patch. *Similar species*: It is distinctly larger than Semipalmated and Western Sandpipers and is darker gray in non-breeding plumage and darker brown in breeding plumage. The breast is also more heavily streaked and, when standing, the wings extend beyond the tail. Best distinguished from Baird's by its entirely white rump.
Voice: A distinctive mouse-like squeak, *peet* or *jeet*. Also a thin, high-pitched trill.
Status and Range: Generally an uncommon to rare migrant southbound through the West Indies from August to October and a rarer northward migrant in March and April. There are a few records from November to February. The species is easily overlooked and this doubtless accounts for the absence of records from some of the Lesser Antilles. Widespread in the Western Hemisphere.
Comments: This sandpiper regularly occurs on tidal flats with other shorebirds.
Habitat: Rice fields, mudflats and borders of still water.

BAIRD'S SANDPIPER *Calidris bairdii*   Plate 13

Identification: 18–19 cm (7–7.5"). The similarity of this infrequently occurring sandpiper to many other species requires that it be identified with extreme care. *Non-breeding*: Brownish-gray above and on breast. *Breeding*: Browner and with faint reddish-brown tints. *Similar species*: Baird's Sandpiper is distinguished from Semipalmated and Western by its larger size and wings extending noticeably beyond the tail. White-rumped and Baird's Sandpipers are similar in these characteristics and are best separated in flight. Baird's white rump is divided into lateral patches by a dark central stripe. In White-rumped Sandpiper, the white patch is continuous. Baird's has a buffier breast than most similar sandpipers. It also picks for food rather than probes. For additional guidance on distinguishing immature Baird's and White-rumped Sandpipers refer to: Alstrom, P. 1987. The Identification of Baird's and White-rumped Sandpipers in Juvenile Plumage. *Birding* 19(2): 10–13.
Status and Range: Generally a very rare migrant to the Virgin (St Croix) and Cayman (Grand Cayman) Islands, Dominica, St Lucia, the Grenadines (Mustique) and Barbados, the only West Indian islands from which it has been recorded. Its status is poorly known since it is easily overlooked due to its strong similarity to other more common sandpipers. It should primarily be expected during its southbound migration in September and October and to a lesser extent on its northward return in March and April. Widespread in the Western Hemisphere.
Comments: Typically occurs singly or in small groups, unlike other sandpipers which are more gregarious.
Habitat: Primarily upper edges of inland wetland habitats including dry edges among vegetation. Often occurs some distance from water.

PECTORAL SANDPIPER *Calidris melanotos*   Plates 13, 16

Local Names: Grassbird (VI); Zarapico Moteado (Cuba); Playerito (DR); Playero Manchado (PR); Bekasin Fal Nwa, Bécassine à Poitrine Noire (Haiti); Pond Bird, Amerikaanse Gestreepte Strandloper (St M); Bécasseau à Poitrine Cendrée, Dos Rouge (Guad, Mart)

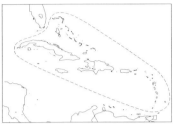

Identification: 20–24 cm (8–9.5"). Its medium size, *yellowish-green bill and legs*, and *sharp demarcation between the heavily-streaked breast and white belly* are good field marks. Males are often noticeably larger than females. **Non-breeding**: Gray-brown upperparts, head and breast. **Breeding male**: More mottled; breast heavily streaked with black. **Flight**: Sharp breast demarcation. Also a fine white wing stripe and white rump divided by black bar.

Voice: A low, harsh *krip*.

Status and Range: Generally an uncommon southbound migrant from August to early November through the West Indies, though rare on Cuba and reportedly some of the Lesser Antilles. It is rare during northward migration in March and April and is even less frequent in other months. After nesting in the Arctic portions of North America and Siberia, most Pectoral Sandpipers migrate southward over the western Atlantic Ocean, many birds probably overflying the West Indies on the way to their non-breeding grounds in southern South America. The northward migration generally passes most of the West Indies. Sometimes large flocks numbering in the thousands stop to rest in the West Indies during passage. Widespread in the Western Hemisphere and also Asia south to Australia.

Comments: Typically flocks, but not in association with other sandpipers.

Habitat: Wet meadows and grassy areas including golf courses after heavy rains.

DUNLIN *Calidris alpina*   Plates 12, 16

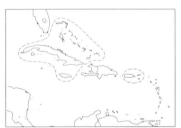

Identification: 20–23 cm (8–9"). Note the heavy bill, distinctively drooping at the tip and short-necked hunched appearance. **Non-breeding**: Gray wash on the breast, head and upperparts. **Breeding**: Characteristic *black belly* and reddish back. **Flight**: White wing stripe and white rump divided by black bar. **Similar species**: Curlew Sandpiper, a vagrant, is differentiated from Dunlin, while both are in non-breeding plumage, by its entirely white rump. Refer to citation under Curlew Sandpiper for additional information.

Voice: Flight call a distinctive harsh, nasal *tzeep*.

Status and Range: A rare non-breeding resident in the Bahamas; very rare on Cuba, Jamaica, Puerto Rico and the Virgin Islands and a vagrant in the Cayman Islands, St Christopher, Dominica and Barbados. Occurs from late August to April. Widespread through the Northern Hemisphere.

Habitat: Borders of still water, particularly mudflats.

CURLEW SANDPIPER *Calidris ferruginea*   Plate 78

Identification:18–23 cm (7–9"). Note the *bill is slightly down-curved throughout its length* and, in flight, the *white rump*. **Non-breeding adult**: Upperparts brownish-gray; underparts white. **Breeding male**: Reddish-brown overall. **Female**: A bit duller. **Immature**: Back nearly black; underparts white with tan breast. **Similar species**: Non-breeding Dunlin lacks the white rump, and its bill is down-curved only at the tip. For additional information on distinguishing Curlew Sandpiper from Stilt Sandpiper and Dunlin, refer to: Kaufman, K. 1990. Curlew Sandpiper and its I.D. Contenders. *American Birds* 44(2): 189–192.

Voice: A soft *chirrup*.

Status and Range: Very rare, but regular on Barbados and a vagrant elsewhere in the West Indies where recorded from Puerto Rico, the Virgin Islands (Virgin Gorda), Antigua, Dominica, the Grenadines (Carriacou) and Grenada. Should be looked for during migration in September, October and April until June. Widespread in the Eastern Hemisphere.

Comments: One record from Barbados was of a bird banded fourteen days earlier in Belgium. Curlew Sandpiper breeds only in the high Arctic of central Asia, but migrates widely through Europe, Africa, Asia and Australia.
Habitat: Mudflats, marshes and beaches.

STILT SANDPIPER *Calidris himantopus*   **Plates 12, 16**
Local Names: Zarapico Patilargo (Cuba); Playero Zancudo (DR); Playero Patilargo (PR); Pond Bird, Stelstrandloper (St M); Bécasseau à Échasses, Chevalier Pied-vert (Guad, Mart)

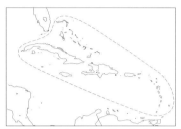

Identification: 20–22 cm (8–8.5″). Difficult to identify. The best field marks are its *dull greenish legs*, whitish eyebrow stripe and *long bill, thick at the base with a slight droop at the tip*. **Non-breeding**: Grayish above; whitish below. Look for the pale eyebrow stripe. **Breeding**: Reddish-brown ear patch and heavily barred underparts. **Flight**: *White rump* and whitish tail. **Similar species**: Dowitchers have a longer, straighter bill.
Voice: A very soft, unmusical and unabrasive *cue*.
Status and Range: Generally uncommon in the West Indies, though common locally on Hispaniola, Puerto Rico and the Virgin Islands primarily during its southbound migration from late August to early November. It occurs as a non-breeding resident in all months, but least frequently in June and July. Ranges through most of the Western Hemisphere.
Comments: Typically in large flocks.
Habitat: Mudflats and shallow lagoons.

BUFF-BREASTED SANDPIPER *Tryngites subruficollis*   **Plate 12**
Local Name: Bécasseau Roussâtre (Guad, Mart)

Identification: 19–22 cm (7.5–8.5″). **Adult**: *Upperparts have a scaled look*. It is further identified by the large dark eye framed by a pale eye-ring on a *clean buffy face*; a thin, black bill; underparts buff with spots on sides extending from breast to lower belly; *yellow legs and feet* and short tail not extending beyond folded wings at rest. **Flight**: *White wing linings*. **Similar species**: Upland Sandpiper is larger, has proportionately longer neck, legs and bill and is streaked below.
Status and Range: Very rare among the Lesser Antilles during southbound migration from September to early November and rarer still northbound·in April. A vagrant in the Bahamas (New Providence), Cuba, Hispaniola, Jamaica, Puerto Rico and the Virgin Islands (St Croix). Occurs through much of the Western Hemisphere.
Comments: Sometimes migrates with American Golden-Plovers. Both are most likely to be found after easterly storms. Migrates between Arctic North America and southern South America.
Habitat: Fields, pastures and areas with short grass, including golf courses.

RUFF *Philomachus pugnax*   **Plate 15**

Identification: Male: 30 cm (12″); Female: 23–28 cm (9–11″). **Non-breeding**: Best distinguished by its fairly chunky build, erect posture, whitish around base of the bill, buffy breast which is sometimes scaled in appearance and the relatively short and slightly drooped bill. Some individuals possess white feathering on the head. The legs are often pale varying from dull yellow to orange, green or brown. **Breeding male**: Extreme variability among males, but all are easily distinguished by the elaborate breast and head feathers which can be white, black, reddish or a combination thereof. **Breeding female**: Variable. Similar to non-breeding birds, but darker, particularly on the breast. **Flight**: The long, oval *white patches at the base of the tail* are a good field mark.
Status and Range: A rare, but regular migrant on Barbados and generally a vagrant elsewhere in the West Indies where recorded from Jamaica, Puerto Rico, the Virgin Islands, Antigua, Barbuda,

Montserrat, Guadeloupe, St Lucia, St Vincent and Grenada. Most regular in September and October when stray migrants occur, but recorded from August to May. Widespread in the Eastern Hemisphere.
Comments: Typically feeds sluggishly, often in the company of yellowlegs.
Habitat: Mudflats and borders of ponds and lagoons.

SHORT-BILLED DOWITCHER *Limnodromus griseus*   Plates 12, 16
Local Names: Zarapico Gris (Cuba); Playero Pico Largo (DR); Chorlo Pico Corto (PR); Bekasin Bèk Long, Bécasseau (Haiti); Pond Bird, Kleine Grijze Snip (St M); Bécasseau Roux, Bécasseau (Guad, Mart)

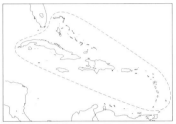

Identification: 26–30 cm (10–12"). The *very long, straight bill* is distinctive. *Non-breeding*: Gray above and whitish below with a pale gray breast and white eyebrow stripe. *Breeding*: Variable. The form that occurs in the West Indies (*L. g. griseus*) has a pale reddish-brown head and breast blending to white on the belly. The breast is finely barred and flanks heavily barred. *Flight*: *White patch extending well up the back*. *Habit*: Feeds with *vertical thrusts* of the bill. *Similar species*: See Long-billed Dowitcher.
Voice: In flight, a soft, rapid whistle *tu-tu-tu*, harsher when the bird is alarmed.
Status and Range: Generally a fairly common, but local non-breeding resident in the Bahamas, Greater Antilles, Cayman Islands and Barbados from August to April, and rarely from May to July. It is uncommon in the Virgin Islands and uncommon to rare in most of the Lesser Antilles. Dowitchers in the West Indies are most likely this species unless very carefully identified as Long-billed. Widespread in North and Central America, and northern South America.
Comments: Typically flocks.
Habitat: Primarily tidal mudflats.

LONG-BILLED DOWITCHER *Limnodromus scolopaceus*   Plate 12
Local Names: Zarapico Gris Piquilargo (Cuba); Playero Pico Largo (DR); Chorlo Pico Largo (PR)

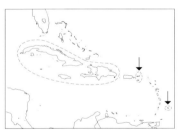

Identification: 28–32 cm (11–12.5"). Bill very long and straight. *Non-breeding*: Gray above, paler below and with white eyebrow stripe. *Breeding*: Reddish breast, belly and abdomen. The breast is finely barred and the flanks are moderately barred. *Flight*: A white patch extends well up the back. *Habit*: Feeds with vertical bill thrusts. *Similar species*: Very difficult to distinguish from Short-billed Dowitcher. Safely identified in the field only by voice. In non-breeding Long-billed Dowitcher, the gray of the breast tends to be darker, more even and extends lower onto the belly than in Short-billed Dowitchers that occur in the West Indies (*L. g. griseus*). In breeding plumage, Long-billed has reddish underparts to the lower belly whereas Short-billed is typically white on the belly. For additional information on identification of dowitchers in breeding plumage refer to: Jaramillo, A. and B. Henshaw. 1995. Identification of Breeding Plumaged Long- and Short-billed Dowitchers. *Birding World* 8(6): 221–228, and Wilds, C.P. and Mike Newlon. 1983. The Identification of Dowitchers. *Birding* 15(4, 5): 151–165.
Voice: A thin, high pitched *keek*, singly or in series.
Status and Range: Its status in the West Indies is uncertain as both dowitchers were until recently considered a single species. There are records from Cuba, Jamaica, Hispaniola, the Virgin and Cayman Islands, St Christopher and Barbados. Indications are that it is a very rare migrant. Occurs from North America south to Guatemala. Also northeastern Asia.
Comments: Dowitchers observed in the West Indies should be presumed to be Short-billed unless identified with certainty to the contrary. Dowitchers in freshwater habitats should be examined carefully since Long-billed favors that habitat. Though this species breeds in the high Arctic of western North America and Siberia, most Long-billed Dowitchers migrate to the southern United States and Mexico to pass the non-breeding season.
Habitat: Primarily shallow fresh and brackish water, but also tidal mudflats.

COMMON SNIPE *Gallinago gallinago*   **Plates 12, 16**
Local Names: Becasina (Cuba, DR, PR); Guineíto (DR); Bekasin Fran (Haiti); Watersnip (St M); Bécassine des Marais, Bécassine (Guad, Mart)

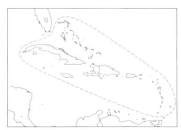

Identification: 27–29 cm (10.5–11.5"). The *long bill* and *striped head* and back are good field marks. The tail is reddish-brown. **Flight**: It usually bursts from cover in a zig-zag flight uttering its call note.
Voice: A somewhat variable guttural squawk when flushed.
Status and Range: A fairly common non-breeding resident in the Bahamas, Cuba and Hispaniola, it is uncommon on Jamaica, Puerto Rico and the Virgin and Cayman Islands and generally so through the Lesser Antilles. Common Snipe occurs primarily from October to April. Widespread in the northern Hemisphere.
Habitat: Grassy freshwater edges and grassy or muddy savannas.

WILSON'S PHALAROPE   *Phalaropus tricolor*   **Plates 15, 16**
Local Name: Falaropo de Wilson (PR)

Identification: 23 cm (9"). Note the thin, straight bill. **Non-breeding**: Totally white breast and *thin, dark gray mark through the eye*. **Breeding male**: Reddish-tan wash on neck. **Breeding female**: Dark reddish-brown band starting at the shoulder and blending into black behind the eye. **Flight**: Dark upperparts; white rump. **Habit**: *Spinning* in the water to stir up food is a certain field mark of phalaropes. **Similar species**: See also Red and Red-necked Phalaropes.
Status and Range: A rare migrant and less frequently a non-breeding resident between August and May on Barbados and very rare on Jamaica, Puerto Rico and the Virgin and Cayman Islands. It is a vagrant in the Bahamas, Hispaniola, Antigua, Guadeloupe, Martinique and Grenada. most of central and western North America to South America. Occurs from most of central and western North America to South America.
Comments: Phalaropes swim more than other shorebirds.
Habitat: Primarily shallow ponds and lagoons.

RED-NECKED PHALAROPE *Phalaropus lobatus*   **Plates 15, 16**
Local Name: Zarapico Nadador (Cuba)

Identification: 18 cm (7"). **Non-breeding adult**: Distinguishing marks include a black cap above a white forehead, *broad black bar through the eye* and ear-coverts and *very thin, straight black bill*. **Breeding adult female**: Black cap, dark *back streaked with white or pale-buff* and a warm reddish-brown neck and golden wing-coverts. **Breeding adult male**: Duller than female. **Immature**: Similar to the non-breeding adult. **Flight**: White wing stripe and white stripes on the back. **Similar species**: Non-breeding Wilson's Phalarope has a thin, gray eyestripe, rather than a broad, black bar, and has a longer bill and no white stripes on back. See also Red Phalarope.
Status and Range: A very rare migrant in the Bahamas, Cuba and Hispaniola from October to January and a vagrant northbound in April and May. Red-necked Phalarope is also a vagrant on Jamaica and Puerto Rico. The scarcity of records results from the species occurring far at sea. Widespread in the Arctic and the Atlantic, Pacific and Indian Oceans.
Habitat: Usually remains far out at sea; on ponds and lagoons when it occurs on land.

RED PHALAROPE *Phalaropus fulicaria*   **Plates 15, 16**
Local Name: Zarapico Rojo (Cuba)

Identification: 21 cm (8"). ***Non-breeding adult***: *Unstreaked pale gray above,* underparts white, bill stout and black except for *yellow spot at base of lower mandible,* hindcrown blackish and *broad, black bar through the eye to ear-coverts.* **Breeding female**: Entirely *dark reddish-brown below* with a conspicuous *white facial patch.* **Breeding male**: Dull orangish-brown below with a less distinct whitish facial patch. ***Non-breeding adult in flight***: Unstreaked pale gray above with a conspicuous white wing stripe. **Similar species**: Red Phalarope is stockier than either Red-necked or Wilson's Phalaropes and has a shorter and thicker bill, *no stripes on the back* in any plumage and a noticeable wing stripe in flight. Non-breeding Wilson's Phalarope has a dark cap, but a plain white face unlike the other two species; it also has an unmarked back, a *white rump patch* and *no wing stripe in flight.*
Status and Range: Apparently a very rare migrant in the West Indies. Reported from Cuba, the Virgin Islands and Antigua between October and January. This species probably occurs more frequently than records indicate; the scarcity of records result from the birds occurring far out at sea. Occurs in the Arctic and through the Atlantic and Pacific Oceans.
Habitat: Usually remains far out at sea; on ponds and lagoons when it occurs on land.

SKUAS, GULLS, TERNS AND SKIMMERS:
FAMILY LARIDAE

This family consists of several distinctive subgroups.
  Jaegers and Skuas — In this region jaegers and skuas are found over the open ocean and are rarely seen from land. They are predatory birds, with hooked bills, often harassing gulls and terns and forcing them to drop their catches. The name jaeger is derived from the German work *Jager,* meaning hunter. Their flight is very swift and direct like that of a falcon, and there is a sharp bend at the angle of the wing. The bases of the primaries form a distinctive white patch. Several species have dark color phases, but these are very rare in the region. The long central tail feathers in adult jaegers are diagnostic in each species; skuas lack these.
  Gulls and Terns — The gulls and terns form a cosmopolitan subfamily that primarily frequents coastal waters, rivers and large lakes. Gulls are more robust than terns, with broader wings and fan-shaped tails. Adults are usually a combination of white, gray and black, whereas immatures, which may take several years to develop adult plumage, are principally mottled brown. Terns are slim birds of graceful flight, often with long, notched tails; black about the head and with thin, pointed bills. Unlike gulls, which feed off the surface, many terns hover and dive into the water after fish. Both terns and gulls are quite gregarious and generally nest in colonies.
  Skimmers — This very distinctive subgroup contains only three species with widely separated ranges. They are characterized by having the lower mandible substantially longer than the upper one. Both the upper and lower mandibles form two blades with the sharp edges facing one another. The birds feed by plowing the surface of calm waters with the lower bill and snapping up fish and other organisms.

POMARINE JAEGER *Stercorarius pomarinus*   **Plate 7**
Local Names: Estercorario Pomarino (Cuba); Middelste Jager (Saba); Labbe Pomarin (Guad, Mart)

Identification: 65–78 cm (25.5–31"). The largest jaeger, heavy-bodied with white base to primaries which flashes in flight. There are two color phases with much intermediate variation. **Adult**: The central tail feathers can be long, but are usually twisted to give a spoon-like appearance. *Light phase* — Blackish cap and a *broad, dark band across the breast. Dark phase* — Less frequent; entirely dark ranging from brown to black, perhaps slightly paler below. **Subadult and immature**: Usually *heavily barred below,* especially along the sides under the wings. Most birds develop pale bellies as they approach adult plumage. Central tail feathers may not extend beyond rest of tail. **Similar species**: Parasitic Jaeger is smaller, has a more buoyant flight with a slightly faster wingbeat and lacks heavy barring on the sides. Long-tailed Jaeger is smaller still. Adults have very long, pointed tail feathers,

no breast band and a graceful tern-like flight. For additional guidance on distinguishing juveniles, refer to: Olsen, Klaus M. 1987. Identifying juveniles of the smaller skuas. Proceedings of the 4th International Identification Meeting, International Birdwatching Center Eilat, pp. 34–40.

Status and Range: Apparently an uncommon non-breeding resident from October to May in the West Indies, especially over deep water at sea east of the Lesser Antilles and, to a lesser extent, in the Bahamas. The scarcity of records results from the species occurring far out at sea. Widespread through the Arctic and most oceans of the world.

Habitat: Generally far offshore. Occasionally seen close to land harassing gulls and terns.

PARASITIC JAEGER *Stercorarius parasiticus* Plate 7
Local Name: Estercorario Parasítico (Cuba)

Identification: 46–67 cm (18–26.5"). A small jaeger with a strong, direct flight. All color phases in flight show white patches at base of primaries. *Adult*: *Light phase* — Dark brownish-gray above; whitish below; distinct *grayish-brown cap*; and *narrow, dark band across upper breast*. *Adult*: *Dark phase* — Dark brown overall; perhaps slightly paler below. *Subadult*: *Finely barred below* and often has a *reddish cast to overall plumage*. Pointed tips to central tail feathers may protrude from tip of tail. *Similar species*: Pomarine Jaeger is decidedly larger, has a more labored flight and has heavily barred sides. Long-tailed Jaeger is smaller, has a more graceful flight and the adults have long central tail feathers. Immature and subadult Long-tailed Jaegers without long central tail feathers cannot be distinguished reliably by any single trait. For additional information on distinguishing juveniles, refer to citation under Pomarine Jaeger.

Status and Range: Apparently an uncommon migrant and rare non-breeding resident widely present in the West Indies from August to May. Recorded off the western Bahamas, Cuba, Jamaica (Morant Cays), Hispaniola, the Virgin Islands, Guadeloupe, Dominica, Martinique, Barbados, St Vincent, the Grenadines and Grenada. The scarcity of records results from the species occurring far out at sea. Widespread through the Arctic and most oceans of the world.

Comments: Often harasses terns and other small seabirds.

Habitat: Usually far offshore.

LONG-TAILED JAEGER *Stercorarius longicaudus* Plate 7
Local Names: Estercorario Rabero (Cuba); Labbe à Longue Queue (Guad, Mart)

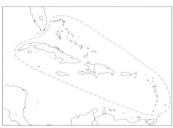

Identification: 50–58 cm (19.5–23"), including 15–25 cm (6–10") tail. The *smallest* jaeger. Adults have no dark phase as do Pomarine and Parasitic Jaegers. A distinct dark phase does occur in immatures. *Adult*: A distinct grayish-brown cap, *no breast band* and *back and secondaries grayish contrasting with darker primaries*. All adults have elongated central tail feathers, but only the first two or three primaries have white bases, so the white wing-flash in flight is less noticeable than in other jaegers. *Subadult*: *Dark phase* — Much less frequent; nearly uniform grayish-brown with a darker cap and slightly paler beneath. Central tail feathers may not be extended. *Light phase* — Finely barred below and fine white barring on back. Some have a pale head and hindneck and blue legs. Central tail feathers may not be extended. *Flight*: Graceful and tern-like. Will follow boats. *Similar species*: See Parasitic Jaeger and citation under Pomarine Jaeger.

Status and Range: Apparently a very rare migrant through the West Indies primarily from August to October and March to May. Reported off the Bahamas, Cuba, Jamaica, Hispaniola, the Cayman Islands, Guadeloupe, Dominica, Martinique and Barbados. A few birds remain off the Lesser Antilles from November through February. Likely more frequent than records indicate. The scarcity of records

results from the species occurring far out at sea. Widespread in the Arctic, the Atlantic Ocean and the western Pacific Ocean.
Habitat: Far offshore.

SKUA *Catharacta spp.* **Plate 7**

Identification: 51–66 cm (20–26"). A large, bulky, powerful and high-flying, gull-like predatory seabird. Great Skua (*C. skua*) is mostly dark brown with reddish-brown highlights to the feathers and golden or reddish-brown streaks about the head and neck. Underparts are a paler reddish-brown. The adult may have an indistinct dark cap, but immatures often lack this. Base of primaries is white, producing a wing patch in flight. South Polar Skua (*C. maccormicki*) is slightly smaller and has three color phases. The dark phase is very like the above description, but has noticeably darker underparts and lacks the reddish tones to its plumage. The intermediate phase has a light brown head, neck and underparts, often displaying a noticeable light hindneck and may have a distinct dark cap. The light phase has pale gray underparts, head and neck. For additional guidance on skua identification refer to: Gantlett, S. and S. Harrap. 1992. Identification forum: South Polar Skua. *Birding World* 5(7): 256–270.
Status and Range: Few records, but not as rare as previously believed. Skuas likely occur through the West Indies. There are several sight reports that might apply to either Great or South Polar Skua from November to May from the Caribbean Sea, off Cuba, Hispaniola, Puerto Rico, the Virgin Islands, St Barthélemy, Guadeloupe and Dominica. South Polar Skua is probably an annual migrant through the eastern West Indies from the southern Atlantic. The scarcity of records results from skuas occurring far at sea. Occurs primarily in the subarctic and temperate North Atlantic Ocean.
Comments: The taxonomy of the skuas is far from settled, the worldwide number of species variously considered to be from three to six. Specialists often cannot agree on the identity of specimens; thus extreme care should be exercised in making field identifications, if that is even attempted. Great and South Polar Skuas are the only *Catharacta* species documented from the Northern Hemisphere. The extent to which skuas occurring in the West Indies pertain to one species or the other remains to be determined. Birds banded in Europe have been recovered in Guyana waters just outside the West Indies.
Habitat: Far offshore.

LAUGHING GULL *Larus atricilla* **Plates 3, 5**
Local Names: Mauve (Grenada); Booby, Gullie, Laughing Bird, Davy (LA); Sea Gull (LA, VI); Galleguito (Cuba); Gaviota Gallega (PR); Gaviota Cabecinegra (DR, PR); Mòv Tèt Nwa, Pigeon de Mer (Haiti); Pigeon la Mer (St L); Mouette Atricille (Guad, Mart); Mauve à Tête Noire (Guad, Haiti, Mart); Lachmeeuw (Saba, St E, St M)

Identification: 38–43 cm (15–17"). ***Breeding adult***: The black head together with the dark gray mantle and black wingtips are distinctive. The bill is reddish. ***Non-breeding adult***: Similar, but there is a diffuse gray mark on the rear of the white head, and the bill is black. ***Immature***: Mottled gray-brown except for whitish belly. ***First year***: White rump, gray sides and back including a broad, black tail band. Upperwing mottled brown and gray. ***Second year***: Partial hood, some spotting on tail and a slaty mantle. ***Similar species***: Adult Black-headed Gull has a *paler gray mantle, white primaries*, red bill and legs and gray undersides to the primaries. First year Black-headed Gull has a narrow, black tail band, black ear-spot and two-toned bill. Adult Bonaparte's Gull is smaller and has a pale gray mantle and white in the primaries, with the immature possessing a narrow tail band and pale underwing-coverts. See also Franklin's Gull.
Voice: A squawky, somewhat variable *caw* and *caw-aw*. Also a laugh-like *ka-ka- ka-ka-ka-ka-ka-kaa-kaa-kaaa-kaaa.*
Status and Range: A widespread year-round resident in the West Indies, it breeds locally. Generally common from April to September, the species becomes irregular and rare throughout most of the West Indies during the remainder of the year. Overall its numbers are increasing in the West Indies. Occurs through the tropical, subtropical and portions of the temperate Western Hemisphere.
Comments: This is the commonest gull in the West Indies and should be learned well to serve as a basis of comparison to other gull species.
Habitat: Calm bays, coastal waters and offshore islets.

Nesting: A well-woven nest is made on the ground or in a crevice on a rocky offshore cay. Eggs (3–4) grayish-brown with large splotches. Breeds from May to July.

FRANKLIN'S GULL *Larus pipixcan*   Plate 78

Identification: 37 cm (14.5"). *First year*: Note the narrow, black tail band; white breast and under-parts; gray back; *partial blackish hood* and *white forehead*. *Non-breeding adult*: Similar to breeding plumage, but with only a *partial black hood* and *whitish forehead*. *Breeding adult*: Black head, slaty mantle and *wingtips having a black bar bordered with white on both sides*. *Similar species*: Similar to Laughing Gull in all plumages, but first year and non-breeding adult Franklin's Gulls have a more distinctive partial black hood with a white forehead. First year birds are also differentiated by their white underparts. Breeding adult Franklin's Gull has white in the wingtips, whereas those of Laugh-ing Gull are entirely black. For additional details on identification of juvenile Franklin's Gull without white in the wing tips see: Lehman, P. 1994. Franklin's vrs. Laughing Gulls — A 'New' Problem Arises. *Birding* 26(2): 126–127.
Status and Range: A vagrant in the West Indies where reported from Hispaniola, Puerto Rico, St Barthélemy and Guadeloupe. Records range from late August through January though it may occur in later months. Ranges through much of North and Central America and western South America.
Habitat: Bays and estuaries.

BLACK-HEADED GULL *Larus ridibundus*   Plates 3, 5
Local Names: Gaviota Cabecinegra (PR); Mouette Rieuse (Guad)

Identification: 39–43 cm (15–17"). *First year*: Note its black ear-spot; two-toned bill (cream-colored at the base and black at the tip); narrow, black tail band and *gray undersides to primaries*. *Non-breeding adult*: Similar to the immature, but *bill is reddish* with a black tip, mantle is pale gray and outer primaries are white, tipped with black. *Breeding adult*: Similar to the non-breeding adult, but head is black and bill red. *Similar species*: Bonaparte's Gull is slightly smaller, has a black bill and lacks pale gray undersides to its primaries at any age. See also Laughing Gull and the reference: Kauf-man, K. 1993. Identifying the Common Black-headed Gull. *American Birds* 47 (5): 1156–1159.
Status and Range: A rare and local non-breeding resident on Puerto Rico (where regular only in San Juan harbor), the Virgin Islands (St Thomas and St Croix), Guadeloupe and Barbados. A vagrant in the Bahamas (Eleuthera and Grand Turk), Cuba, Antigua, St Lucia and Grenada. It occurs from November to June. Numbers are increasing throughout the West Indies. Widespread through much of Eurasia to northern Africa and the Philippines. Local in North America.
Comments: Black-headed Gulls which occur in the West Indies tend to be subadults. Adult plumage is reached at about two years of age.

BONAPARTE'S GULL *Larus philadelphia*   Plates 3, 5
Local Name: Galleguito Chico (Cuba)

Identification: 30.5–36 cm (12–14"). *First year*: Note the black ear-spot; thin, black bill; narrow, black tail band and *whitish undersides to primaries*. *Non-breeding adult*: Similar to the immature, but mantle is pale gray, tail and outer primaries are white and legs are red. *Breeding adult*: Similar to the non-breed-ing adult, but the head is black. *Similar species*: Black-headed Gull is slightly larger; the adult has a red bill and gray undersides to primaries. Adult Laughing Gull has a dark mantle and black primaries. First year Laughing Gull has a broader tail band and darker underwing-coverts. See also Black-legged Kittiwake.
Status and Range: An uncommon non-breeding resident on Cuba and locally on Abaco and Eleuthera in the Bahamas from August to April. Rare elsewhere in the Bahamas and on Barbuda, and a vagrant on Hispaniola, Puerto Rico, Antigua and Martinique. Widespread in northern Atlantic and Pacific Oceans.
Comments: Bonaparte's Gulls which occur in the West Indies tend to be subadults. Adult plumage is reached at about two years of age.
Habitat: Coastal areas, harbors, lagoons and at sea.

RING-BILLED GULL *Larus delawarensis* Plates 3, 4
Local Names: Gallego Real (Cuba); Gaviota Piquianillada (PR); Mòv Bèk Jòn, Goéland (Haiti); Goéland à Bec Cerclé (Guad, Mart)

Identification: 46–51 cm (18–20"). *First year*: Mottled grayish-brown wings; gray back. *Tail has a broad, black band* and the bill is pinkish with a black tip. *Second year*: Upperparts and mantle mostly gray in sharp contrast to black primaries which may have only a single white spot at wingtip. The tail is densely mottled with pale gray subterminal marks showing a partial band with white at the base, and the bill is greenish with a black band. *Non-breeding adult*: Field marks are its *yellowish bill with a black band* and its yellowish-green legs. Also note its gray mantle, black wingtips with white spotting and white head and underparts, the head flecked with pale brown. *Breeding adult*: Similar to non-breeding adult, but white head and underparts are unspotted. *Similar species*: Distinguished from Herring Gull by its smaller size, proportionately more delicate head and bill and yellowish-green or grayish-green legs (not pink) even in subadult plumages. Herring Gull may have a black bill tip, but almost never has a true *ring* on the bill.

Status and Range: A fairly common, but local non-breeding resident in the northern Bahamas and Puerto Rico, it is uncommon in the southern Bahamas, Cayman Islands and Barbados, rare on Cuba, Jamaica, Hispaniola and the Virgin Islands and generally rare in the Lesser Antilles south to St Vincent. It occurs in all months, but primarily from December to March. Numbers are increasing throughout the West Indies and elsewhere in the bird's range. Widespread in North America.

Comments: Ring-billed Gulls wandering to the West Indies are primarily subadults. Adult plumage is reached at about three years of age.

Habitat: Coastal areas, harbors, lagoons and bare, open ground from parking lots to grassy fields. Often frequents urban areas. It seldom occurs far at sea.

HERRING GULL *Larus argentatus* Plates 3, 4
Local Names: Gallego (Cuba), Gaviota del Norte (DR), Gaviota Argéntea (PR); Mòv, Mauve (Haiti); Goéland Argenté (Guad, Mart); Zilvermeeuw (Saba, St M)

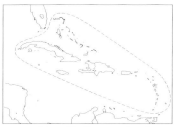

Identification: 56–66 cm (22–26"). A large gull with a large bill. *First year*: Back and wings heavily streaked grayish-brown, bill pinkish at base and black at tip, tail without clear band; legs pink. *Second year*: Variable amounts of gray on back and wings, outer primaries black and bill pinkish with a pale gray band beyond nostril. *Third year*: Tail white with a broad, black band and bill yellowish with dark band. *Non-breeding adult*: Heavy yellow bill with red spot near tip of lower mandible; head and underparts white, the head flecked with pale brown; gray mantle and pink legs. *Breeding adult*: Head and underparts white. *Similar species*: Lesser Black-backed Gull is slightly smaller and the adult has a dark grayish-black mantle and yellowish legs. (See Lesser Black-backed Gull for additional information.) Great Black-backed Gull is larger and has a massive bill, and the adult has jet black back and wings. See also Ring-billed Gull.

Status and Range: Generally an uncommon and local non-breeding resident in the Bahamas, Cuba and the Cayman Islands from September to May and rare from June to August. It is rare on Jamaica, Hispaniola, Puerto Rico and the Virgin Islands and generally occurs very rarely in the Lesser Antilles from October to March. Herring Gull numbers are increasing in the West Indies. Widespread throughout the Northern Hemisphere.

Comments: Herring Gulls wandering to the West Indies are primarily subadults. Adult plumage is reached at about four years of age.

Habitat: Coastal areas, harbors and lagoons.

LESSER BLACK-BACKED GULL *Larus fuscus*   Plates 3, 4

Identification: 53–63 cm (21–25"). A large gull with a large bill. *First year*: Overall mottled grayish, but head brownish in contrast. *Second year*: Bill pinkish with a large black band near tip. Dark gray back; broad, black tail band; white rump and brownish-gray wings with no white spots at tip. *Non-breeding adult*: Dark grayish-black mantle, *pale yellow legs*, mottled brown head and neck and yellow bill with red spot near tip. *Breeding adult*: Similar to non-breeding adult, but head and neck are white. *Similar species*: Adult Great Black-backed Gull is larger, has a jet black mantle and pink legs. First and second year birds are distinguished by their larger size and massive bill. Adult Herring Gull has a paler mantle and pink legs, with first and second year birds having a less pronounced white rump patch. For more information on distinguishing Lesser Black-backed Gull see: Post, P. W. and R. H. Lewis. 1995. The Lesser Black-backed Gull in the Americas: Occurrence and Subspecific Identity; Part I. *Birding* 27(4): 282–290, and Part II. *Birding* 27(5): 370–381.

Status and Range: Very rare in the West Indies from November to April where it might occur on any island with appropriate habitat. To date, recorded from the Bahamas (New Providence and Abaco), Puerto Rico, the Virgin Islands (St Croix), St Martin, St Barthélemy, Antigua and Barbados. Occurrence increasing in the West Indies as well as in eastern coastal North America. Primarily occurs through Europe, western Asia and portions of Africa.

Comments: Wanderers to the West Indies tend to be subadults. Adult plumage is reached at about four years of age. Often congregates with other species of gulls.

Habitat: Beaches and protected bays.

GREAT BLACK-BACKED GULL *Larus marinus*   Plates 3, 4

Identification: 69–79 cm (27–31"). Identified in all plumages by its *very large size and bill*. *First year*: Mottled grayish-brown above and below; head white with pale flecks on rear and hindneck; bill black and tail has a broad, black band. *Second year*: Bill pinkish with large black band near tip, rump patch white and mantle with black blotches. *Non-breeding adult*: Black mantle, pink legs, pale flecks on head and yellow bill with red spot near tip. *Breeding adult*: Similar to non-breeding adult, but the head is entirely white.

Similar species: See Herring and Lesser Black-backed Gulls.

Status and Range: Rare on Puerto Rico from October to March and a vagrant elsewhere in the West Indies where recorded from the Bahamas, Cuba, Hispaniola, St Barthélemy and Barbados. Numbers are increasing in the West Indies. Widespread in the coastal North Atlantic Ocean.

Comments: Wanderers to the West Indies tend to be subadults. Adult plumage is reached at about four years of age.

BLACK-LEGGED KITTIWAKE *Rissa tridactyla*   Plates 3, 5

Identification: 43 cm (17"). A medium-sized gull. *First year*: White head with a black ear-spot. In flight, *wings and mantle boldly marked with a contrasting W* from wingtip to wingtip. Also has a black bill and terminal tail band. *Non-breeding adult*: Field marks are its *yellow bill* and white head with a black mark behind the eye, sometimes extending to the back of head. The mantle is gray and the wingtips black with no white in them. *Breeding adult*: Similar to non-breeding adult, but the head is entirely white. *Similar species*: First year is distinguished from immature Bonaparte's Gull by its black half collar on the hindneck and, in flight, by the white trailing edge of the secondaries.

Status and Range: Very rare in the Bahamas and a vagrant off Cuba, Hispaniola, Jamaica, the Virgin Islands, Guadeloupe and St Lucia from December to March. Likely to occur more frequently than records indicate, but goes unobserved due to occurrence far out at sea. Widespread in the Arctic and the temperate oceans of the Northern Hemisphere.

Comments: Wanderers to the West Indies tend to be subadults. Adult plumage is reached at about four years of age.

Habitat: Far offshore; may associate with other gulls and terns.

GULL-BILLED TERN *Sterna nilotica*   Plate 6
Local Names: Gullie (VI); Gaviota de Pico Corto (Cuba); Gaviota Piquigorda (PR); Fou Bèk Nwa (Haiti); Fou (St L); Sterne Hansel (Guad, Haiti, Mart)

Identification: 33–38 cm (13–15"). A chunky gull-like tern. Note the proportionately *heavy black bill*, broader wings than other terns and *very shallow fork to the tail*. **Breeding adult**: Black crown and hindneck. **Non-breeding adult**: Crown whitish with pale gray flecks. Distinct *gray spot behind eye*. **Immature**: Back and scapulars are mottled with grayish and bill is brownish.
Voice: Raspy three-syllabled *za-za-za* or a two-syllabled *cay-wek, cay-wek*.
Status and Range: An uncommon breeding resident in the Bahamas from April through August. It is uncommon and local on Hispaniola, Puerto Rico, the larger Virgin Islands and off Anguilla on Sombrero Island during those same months. In September, these terns disperse and occur rarely on Cuba, Jamaica, the Cayman Islands and the Lesser Antilles south to Barbados and St Vincent through March. Widespread, but local in most tropical and temperate oceans of the world.
Habitat: Freshwater and brackish habitats near the coast as well as coastal bays and lagoons, salt flats and fields.
Nesting: Nest is a shell-lined scrape in sand, coral or matted vegetation in small, loose colonies. Eggs (2–4) buffy-white with numerous dark brown markings at the broad end. Breeds from May to July.

CASPIAN TERN *Sterna caspia*   Plate 6
Local Names: Gaviota Real Grande (Cuba), Gaviota Real (DR); Gaviota de Caspia (PR)

Identification: 48–58 cm (19–23"). Identified by its relatively *large size*; black crest; long, *stout, red bill* and *dark gray underside to primaries*. **Non-breeding adult**: Crest flecked with white. **Breeding adult**: Crest entirely black. **Immature**: Tail barred with brownish-black and bill orange-red. **Similar species**: Royal Tern is distinguished by its smaller size, orange-yellow bill, pale underside to its primaries and, in non-breeding plumage, by its white forehead.
Status and Range: Generally a rare non-breeding resident locally in the southern Bahamas, Cuba, Jamaica, Hispaniola and Barbados. Very rare on Puerto Rico and the Cayman Islands. A vagrant in the northern Bahamas, on St Croix in the Virgin Islands and in the Lesser Antilles where recorded from St Christopher, Antigua, Dominica, Martinique and St Lucia. May occur during any month. Occurs through North and Central America, northern South America, Eurasia, Africa and Australia.
Habitat: Coastal areas, harbors and lagoons.

ROYAL TERN *Sterna maxima*   Plate 6
Local Names: Egg Bird, Gaby, Sea Gull (LA); Gullie (VI); Sprat Bird (CI, LA); Gaviota Real (Cuba, DR, PR); Fou Bèk Jòn, Sterne, Pigeon de Mer (Haiti); Sterne Royale (Guad, Mart); Foquette (Guad, Mart, St B); Mauve (Guad, Mart, St L); Koningsstern (Saba, St E, St M)

Identification: 46–53 cm (18–21"). A *large tern* with an *orange-yellow bill*, the top and back of head with elongated black feathers forming a shaggy crest. **Breeding adult**: Crown entirely black. **Non-breeding adult and immature**: Forehead white. **Similar species**: See Caspian Tern.
Voice: A harsh, high-pitched *kri-i-ik*, very similar to a parakeet.
Status and Range: A common, but local year-round resident in the Bahamas, Greater Antilles and the Virgin and Cayman Islands and generally fairly common in the Lesser Antilles and on San Andrés. Despite its year-round abundance, Royal Tern

breeds only very locally in the West Indies. Migrants augment local numbers primarily from October through April. Occurs through the southern United States south to much of coastal South America. Also the west coast of Africa.

Habitat: Coastal areas, harbors and lagoons.

Nesting: Nesting is generally in colonies on small cays. The nest is a scrape on a sandy beach or in a rock depression. Eggs (1–2) white to pale buff-colored, spotted with brown. Breeds from April to July and is irregular as to location and number of pairs.

SANDWICH TERN *Sterna sandvicensis*   Plate 6

Local Names: Gaviota de Pico Amarillo (Cuba); Gaviota Pico Agudo (DR); Gaviota Piquiaguda (PR); Sterne Caugek (Guad, Mart); Grote Stern (St E, St M)

Identification: 41–46 cm (16–18"). A relatively large tern. **Breeding adult:** Field marks are its very pale gray coloration, appearing white at a distance, *shaggy black crest* and a *long, slender black bill with a conspicuous yellow tip.* (See Comments regarding the yellow-billed form.) Tail does not extend beyond folded wings when at rest. **Non-breeding adult:** Similar to breeding plumage, but forecrown to above eye is white. Cap is often white flecked with black. **Immature:** Like the adult but back, rump, scapulars and uppertail-coverts pale gray mottled with brown, gray or blackish.

Status and Range: A common year-round resident in the Bahamas and Cuba and uncommon on Puerto Rico, the Virgin Islands, and possibly off Anguilla on Sombrero Island. Outside the breeding season it ranges to other islands where it is a common non-breeding resident on Jamaica, St Barthélemy and Antigua primarily from October to March; uncommon on Hispaniola, St Martin, Guadeloupe, Martinique and Barbados; rare on Dominica, St Lucia, St Vincent and Grenada and very rare in the Cayman Islands and elsewhere in the Lesser Antilles. Occurs through tropical, subtropical and temperate coastal portions of the Atlantic Ocean.

Comments: The South American form, Cayenne Tern (*S. s. eurygnatha*), considered by some authorities to be a separate species, has identical plumage characters, but the entire bill is dull yellow. Cayenne Terns interbreed with Sandwich Terns at large colonies in Bonaire and Curaçao off Venezuela and in smaller colonies off Puerto Rico and in the Virgin Islands.

Habitat: Coastal areas, harbors and lagoons.

Nesting: The nest is a simple scrape on a sand bar or in coral rubble. Eggs (1–2) buffy-white, finely spotted or speckled and scrawled with dark brown markings. Breeds from May to July.

ROSEATE TERN *Sterna dougallii*   Plate 6

Local Names: Gullie (VI); Gaviota Rosada (Cuba); Palometa (DR, PR); Fou Blan, Sterne (Haiti); Petite Fouquette (St B); Carita (St L); Dougalls Stern (St M); Sterne de Dougall, Petite Mauve (Guad, Mart); Mauve Blanche (Guad, Haiti, Mart)

Identification: 35–41 cm (14–16"). Distinguishing characteristics are its very long, deeply forked tail, *pale gray mantle and primaries, tail extending well beyond wing tips when at rest and underside of primary feather tips with little or no blackish coloration.* **Breeding adult:** Bill black with some red; cap black. **Non-breeding adult:** Bill blackish, indistinct dark marking on the shoulder and forehead white past the eye. **Immature:** Dark forehead and crown, bill blackish, back mottled and shoulder with indistinct marks. **Similar species:** Adult Common Tern's mantle is darker gray and primary wing feathers have noticeable blackish on the underside. Immature Common Tern has a distinct black shoulder mark. Roseate Tern flies with faster, deeper wingbeats than Common Tern. Roseate Terns in the Caribbean have much more red in the bill than individuals from North America. This has led to their frequent misidentification as Common Terns. Non-breeding Forster's Tern has a black eye patch. For additional field marks, see references under Forster's Tern. See also Arctic Tern.

Voice: Its raspy *krek* and soft two-syllabled *tu-ick* call notes differ noticeably from the harsh *kee-arr-r* of Common Tern.

Status and Range: Widespread, but generally uncommon to rare and very local in the West Indies primarily from April to September. The species is common only in the Virgin Islands. Small breeding colonies are found from the Bahamas south through the Greater Antilles, principally off southwestern Puerto Rico and the Virgin Islands and more sparsely south through the Lesser Antilles. Absent from the Cayman Islands. The Virgin Islands and islets off southwestern Puerto Rico support the largest population of Roseate Terns in the tropical Atlantic totalling approximately 2,500 pairs. The subspecies of the Roseate Tern native primarily to the Atlantic Ocean (*S. d. dougallii*) has declined dramatically in the north temperate zone. Similar evidence of the bird's decline in the West Indies is not available, but there are known pressures of habitat disturbance, egg collecting and rat predation. Subspecies in the West Indies and as a whole are considered threatened. Occurs worldwide throughout tropical and subtropical seas, but declining generally.

Comments: Some Roseate Terns from the West Indies spend non-breeding season along coast of Brazil.

Habitat: Coastal areas, harbors and lagoons.

Nesting: Nest is in a sand or coral scrape, or in a rock depression, usually in colonies on an offshore cay. The birds choose different sites in different years, though fidelity to a general nesting area is strong. Eggs (1–3, rarely four or more when a nest is shared by several females) greenish-gray to buff, heavily spotted with dark brownish-purple. Breeds from May to July.

COMMON TERN *Sterna hirundo*   Plate 6

Local Names: Gullie (VI); Gaviota Común (Cuba, DR, PR); Fou Bèk Rouj, Sterne Pierre (Haiti); Sterne Pierregarin, Petite Mauve (Guad, Mart); Visdief (Saba, St M)

Identification: 33–40 cm (13–16″). **Breeding adult**: Distinguishing marks are its black cap, *red bill with black tip* and *partly black outer primaries (black color can be seen in flight);* tail does *not* extend beyond tips of folded wings while at rest. **Non-breeding adult**: Bill blackish, *shoulder with distinct dark bar* and forehead white past the eye. **Immature**: Forehead white; bill blackish; mantle, rump and uppertail-coverts dark gray mottled with light brownish and primaries and *shoulder black*. **Similar species**: Immature Roseate Tern has a paler mantle, less black in primaries, a darker bill and a less distinct black shoulder mark. Common Tern's flight is slower with shallower wingbeats than that of Roseate. Non-breeding Forster's Tern has a black patch around the eye. For additional distinguishing characters, see references under Forster's Tern. See also Arctic Tern.

Voice: A strong *kee-arr-r* particularly in defense of the nest.

Status and Range: A rare breeding resident in very small numbers in the Bahamas and Cuba. Earlier reports of breeding from Puerto Rico, the Virgin Islands, St Martin and Saba likely pertain to the Roseate Tern. Migrants which breed in North America are uncommon to rare, but have been reported from most of the West Indies. Occurs primarily from May through October though recorded in all months of the year. Widespread worldwide.

Habitat: Coastal areas, harbors and lagoons. Migrates far out at sea.

Nesting: Nests in a scrape or on bare rock lined with seaweed or grasses. More aggressive toward intruders at nests than Roseate Tern, which helps distinguish them in large mixed colonies. Eggs (2–3) whitish to pale buff with brownish spots. Breeds from May to July.

ARCTIC TERN *Sterna paradisaea*   Plate 6

Local Name: Gaviota del Artico (PR)

Identification: 35–43 cm (14–17″). **Non-breeding adult**: Identified by the *blackish line along the trailing edge of primaries*; a *short, black bill* and short, red legs. **Breeding adult**: Bill entirely blood red. Underparts gray; cheek patch white. **Immature**: Incomplete black cap and indistinct shoulder bar. The tail is shorter than the adult's. **Similar species**: Non-breeding Arctic Tern is distinguished from Common, Roseate and Forster's Terns by proportionately smaller all-black bill, shorter legs when seen at rest, rounded head and a 'neckless' appearance in flight. For additional field marks, see citation under Forster's Tern.

Status and Range: A rare non-breeding migrant on Puerto Rico from June to October. A vagrant on Cuba and the Virgin Islands (St Croix and St John). Apparently under-reported due to its similarity to Roseate and Common Terns and the occurrence of Arctic Tern far out at sea. Widespread but local worldwide.

Comments: A circumpolar breeder in the Northern Hemisphere; migrates to Southern Hemisphere oceans including the Antarctic.

Habitat: Generally far offshore, but regularly rests among Roseate Terns at their breeding colonies.

FORSTER'S TERN *Sterna forsteri*   Plate 6
Local Name: Gaviota de Fórster (Cuba)

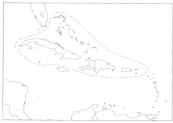

Identification: 35–42 cm (14–16.5"). **Non-breeding adult**: Note the *silvery-white primaries, large black spot enclosing the eye* and *forked tail extending beyond folded wings* while at rest. **Breeding adult**: *Bill orange* with black tip. **Immature**: Similar to the non-breeding adult, but has a shorter tail and some black in primaries. **Similar species**: See Common, Roseate and Arctic Terns. Also see: Wilds, Claudia P. 1993. The Identification and Aging of Forster's and Common Terns. *Birding* 25(2): 94–108; and Kaufman, K. 1987. Terns Overhead. *American Birds* 41(2): 184–187.

Status and Range: A decidedly rare migrant and less frequently a non-breeding resident in the Bahamas, Cuba and the Cayman Islands from November to April. It is very rare on Hispaniola, Puerto Rico and the Virgin Islands, and is a vagrant on Jamaica and the Lesser Antilles where recorded from Antigua, Montserrat and St Vincent. Widespread in North America south to Costa Rica.

Habitat: Coastal areas, harbors and lagoons.

LEAST TERN *Sterna antillarum*   Plate 6
Local Names: Spratt Gull (LA); Egg Bird (CI, VI); Gaviotica (Cuba); Gaviota Chiquita (DR); Gaviota Chica (PR); Pigeon de Mer (Haiti); Fou (St L); Sterne des Antilles, Petite Mauve, Petite Sterne (Guad, Mart); Dwergstern (St E, St M)

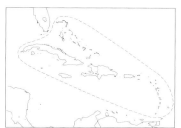

Identification: 21.5–24 cm (8.5–9.5"). The smallest tern in the West Indies. **Breeding adult**: Besides its small size, other field marks are its black crown, *V-shaped white forecrown, pale yellow bill with black tip* and yellow legs. **Non-breeding adult**: Head pattern less distinctive; bill brown. **Adult flight**: Wings white with outer two primaries black. **Immature**: Black bill, hindcrown, eyestripe and bar on shoulder; back and crown whitish flecked with black.

Voice: A chattering *kip* or *kipic* and an inquisitive high-pitched note of *zreeep* are very characteristic.

Status and Range: Generally a common, but local breeding resident in the Bahamas, Greater Antilles, Cayman Islands, St Martin, Antigua and Barbuda primarily from May to August. It is an uncommon and local breeding resident in the Virgin Islands and several of the other northern Lesser Antilles south to St Christopher. Least Tern is a migrant or a wanderer among the more southern Lesser Antilles where it is uncommon on Guadeloupe, Martinique and Barbados, rare on Dominica and very rare elsewhere. Migrants that breed in North America pass through the West Indies from September to March. Birds which breed in the West Indies appear to spend these same months at sea in the southeastern Caribbean Sea and in the Atlantic Ocean off Guyana. The race of Least Tern inhabiting the West Indies, *S. a. antillarum*, also breeds on both coasts of the United States where some local populations are considered endangered. While human disturbance and introduced predators have doubtless impacted the West Indian population, the limited information available on the bird's status in the Caribbean does not warrant this tern being classified as threatened. Though human impacts have been negative in some areas, human activities have unexpectedly created new nesting habitat in others. Widespread and local in North America.

Comments: Nesting Least Terns suffer predation by mongoose and dogs (St Croix), monkeys (St Christopher) and disturbance from humans.

Habitat: Coastal areas, harbors and lagoons.

Nesting: Nest is a scrape in a wide variety of habitats from industrial sites to barely above highwater line on a sand bar, coral rubble spit or dried mudflat, either as single pairs or in loose colonies. Eggs (1–2, rarely 3) buff-white spotted with chocolate brown. Breeds from April to July.

BRIDLED TERN *Sterna anaethetus*   Plate 7

Local Names: Hurricane Bird (LA); Booby (VI); Egg Bird (Bahamas, LA, VI); Gaviota Oscura (DR); Gaviota Monja (Cuba, DR, PR); Mauve (Guad); Fou Gri, Oiseau Fou (Haiti); Thoirou (St L); Sterne Bridée, Touaou (Guad, Mart); Dongue (Guad, Mart, St B); Brilstern (Saba, St M)

Identification: 38 cm (15"). **Adult**: *Grayish-brown above* and *white below, white hindneck* and *white line above and behind eye*. **Immature**: Similar to the adult, but upperparts flecked with pale gray. **Similar species**: Sooty Tern is blacker above, lacks a white hindneck and the white on the forehead does not extend behind the eye.

Voice: A puppy-like *yep* or whining *yerk*. Also a continuous *ah-ah-ah ...*

Status and Range: Generally a fairly common, but local breeding resident throughout the West Indies occurring from April to August. It is observed only infrequently in other months. Seen easily on its breeding islets, otherwise typically observed only from a boat at sea. Occurs through all of the tropical and subtropical seas of the world.

Habitat: Far offshore.

Nesting: The nest is a concealed scrape under vegetation, an overhanging rock or in a crevice on an islet or cay; nests in small groups or loose colonies. Egg (1) pale buffy-gray and marked with numerous fine dark brown spots. Breeds from April to July.

SOOTY TERN *Sterna fuscata*   Plate 7

Local Names: Booby (VI); Egg Bird (Bahamas, LA, VI); Gaviota Monja Prieta (Cuba); Gaviota Monja (DR); Gaviota Oscura (DR, PR); Fou Nwa, Sterne Noire, Oiseau Fou (Haiti); Twado (St L); Sterne Fuligineuse, Touaou (Guad, Mart); Bonte Stern (Saba, St E, St M)

Identification: 38–43 cm (15–17"). **Adult**: *Blackish above* and *white below* with a deeply forked tail, white outertail feathers and *white of the forehead extends only to the eye*. **Immature**: Dark brown overall with whitish spots on mantle and wings, tail less deeply forked than the adult's and whitish undertail-coverts and wing linings. **Similar species**: Bridled Tern has a *white line from the forehead to behind the eye* and a *white hindneck*.

Voice: Call note is a distinctive, plaintive *wide-a-wake* or *wacky-wack*.

Status and Range: Generally a common breeding resident throughout the West Indies from May to August. It is rare in other months. Away from its breeding islets usually seen only from a boat at sea. Occurs through the tropical seas of the world.

Comments: Very aerial; does not dive. Some birds nest at other widely dispersed colonies of the Gulf-Caribbean region. One of the most abundant of the world's tropical seabirds.

Habitat: Far offshore.

Nesting: Nest is a scrape on a coral rubble beach or under overhanging vegetation, mostly in large, gregarious colonies. Egg (1) buff-colored and marked with dark brown spots. Breeds from April to August.

WHISKERED TERN *Chlidonias hybridus*   Plate 78

Identification: 25 cm (10"). A small tern with a slightly notched tail. **Non-breeding**: Primarily pale gray above with ample black in the primaries. The rear portion of the crown is black extending to the eye, and the legs are red. **Breeding**: The black crown and dark gray underparts highlight the bird's white cheek. Birds in breeding plumage are much less likely to be observed in the West Indies. **Similar species**: Non-breeding Black Tern is decidedly darker above and has a dark patch on the side of its neck. Non-breeding White-winged Tern's whitish rump contrasts with its darker back.

Status and Range: A vagrant on Barbados. Apparently a transatlantic wanderer carried on favorable winds from Africa. Occurs through the tropical and temperate Eastern Hemisphere.

Habitat: Inland freshwater bodies, but also calm coastal areas.

WHITE-WINGED TERN *Chlidonias leucopterus*   Plate 78

Identification: 24 cm (9.5"). A small tern with a slightly notched tail. **Non-breeding**: Note the black ear-spot and rear portion of the crown, white rump and absence of a dark neck mark. **Breeding**: Primarily black except for the white tail and rear portion of the body. The wings are pale gray with black underwing linings, and the legs are red. Breeding plumage is much less likely to be seen. **Similar species**: Non-breeding Black Tern has a gray rump, dark mark on the side of the neck, dark legs and darker wings especially the upper forewing.

Status and Range: A vagrant in the West Indies. Reported from the Bahamas (Great Inagua), the Virgin Islands (St Croix) and Barbados. A transatlantic wanderer, likely from Africa via favorable winds. Occurs through the tropical and temperate Eastern Hemisphere.

Habitat: Inland freshwater bodies.

BLACK TERN *Chlidonias niger*   Plate 7
Local Names: Gaviota Prieta (Cuba); Gaviota Negra (DR); Gaviota Ceniza (PR)

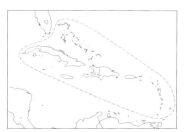

Identification: 23–26 cm (9–10"). **Non-breeding adult**: *Gray above*. The forecrown, hindneck and underparts are white except dark patches at sides of breast. Note the *dark patch behind the eye*. **Breeding adult**: *Head, breast and belly black*. **Immature**: Like the adult, but upperparts washed with brownish and sides washed with grayish. **Flight**: *Buoyant and slightly erratic*. Often hovers. **Similar species**: See Whiskered and White-winged Terns.

Status and Range: A fairly common migrant on Jamaica and Puerto Rico, it is uncommon on Antigua and Barbados and rare in the Bahamas, with the exception of Eleuthera where uncommon. Black Tern is rare on Cuba and Hispaniola. It is very rare or absent elsewhere in the West Indies. Occurs from April to November. Widespread, but local from North America and western Eurasia south to South America and Africa.

Habitat: Fresh and brackish ponds and rice fields. Often stays well out at sea during migration.

BROWN NODDY *Anous stolidus*   Plate 7
Local Names: Booby, Blackbird (LA); Booby Blackbird (VI); Egg Bird (Bahamas, LA, VI); Gaviota Boba (Cuba); Cevero (DR); Cervera (PR); Fou Tèt Blan, Sterne Grise (Haiti); Catbird (Saba); Minimie (St B); Mwen (Grenada, StV); Noddi Brun (Guad, Mart); Moien (Guad, Mart, St L); Bruine Noddy (Saba, St M)

Identification: 38–40 cm (15–16"). **Adult**: Entirely dark brown except *silvery-white forecrown fading to brown on hindneck*. **Immature**: Similar to the adult, but only forecrown white. **Similar species**: See Black Noddy.

Voice: A harsh *karrk*.

Status and Range: Generally a locally common and widespread year-round resident throughout the Bahamas, Greater Antilles, Virgin Islands and Lesser Antilles. A vagrant in the Cayman Islands. Away from its breeding islets, it is usually seen only from a boat at sea. Occurs through the tropical and subtropical seas of the world.

Habitat: Far offshore.

Nesting: Nests in loose, though sometimes large, colonies on offshore cays. The nest can be in a bare rock depression or crevice sparingly decorated with pebbles, shells or feathers; on flotsam situated on steep cliff walls; in an elaborately constructed seagrass and twig nest situated in a tree or low bush or on sparsely vegetated flat ground. Egg (1) pale buffy-white, sparsely marked at the large end with reddish-brown. Breeds from April to August.

BLACK NODDY *Anous minutus* Plate 78

Identification: 34 cm (13.5"). Appears entirely blackish-brown with a white crown. *Immature*: White on crown limited to a broad well-demarcated band on forehead. *Similar species*: Very similar to Brown Noddy, but with a longer, thinner bill; white of the crown extends farther down the hindneck; neck is noticeably more slender and underwings are darker. Best distinguished by voice or by direct comparison with Brown Noddy.
Voice: Sharp, dry nasal cackles, chatters and squeaky notes. Also a plaintive, piping whistle *wheeeaeee* with rising inflection (Styles and Skutch).
Status and Range: A vagrant in the West Indies where recorded from Puerto Rico, the Virgin Islands (French Cap), off Anguilla on Sombrero Island and Barbados. In 1997 approximately 40 Black Noddies were seen off southwestern Puerto Rico and about 20 individuals off Culebra. These sightings suggest the species may now be breeding locally in the West Indies. The population in Aruba off Venezuela is increasing, which may result in more frequent West Indian occurrences. Occurs through much of the tropical and subtropical Atlantic and Pacific Oceans.
Habitat: Well offshore and around rocky islets.

BLACK SKIMMER *Rynchops niger* Plate 3
Local Name: Pico de Tijera (Cuba, DR, PR)

Identification: 40–51 cm (16–20"). Unmistakable scissor-like *black and orange bill* with the lower mandible being much longer than the upper. *Adult*: Black above; white below. *Immature*: Upperparts mottled blackish-brown.
Status and Range: Generally a very rare migrant from November to April in the Bahamas, Cuba, Hispaniola, Puerto Rico and the Virgin Islands. A vagrant on Jamaica, the Cayman Islands and Grenada. Occurs through much of coastal North, Central and South America.
Comments: Often nocturnal. This bird has the unique habit of plowing the surface of the water with its lower mandible in search of prey. Occurrences of Black Skimmer in the Lesser Antilles in particular may well be of vagrants from South America rather than from North America.
Habitat: Calm coastal waters, harbors and lagoons.

DOVEKIE *Alle alle* Plate 18

Identification: 21 cm (8"). A small, stout seabird with a *short, thick neck*; large head and short, black *stubby bill*. *Non-breeding adult*: Black above and white below with the *white extending well around the neck*, white streaks over folded wings and head black from bill to below eye and above ear. *Breeding adult*: Head and breast entirely black. *Flight*: Wingbeats are blurringly rapid, reminiscent of a huge beetle.
Status and Range: A vagrant in the West Indies. Reported from Cuba and the Bahamas (Grand Bahama) from October to December. Only likely to occur following major winter storms striking eastern North America. Dovekie in the West Indies is likely under-reported due to its occurring far offshore. Occurs through the subarctic portion of the North Atlantic south to coastal mideastern United States and Western Europe.
Habitat: Far out to sea unless blown ashore; then most likely on large bodies of water.

PIGEONS AND DOVES: FAMILY COLUMBIDAE

The pigeons are a cosmopolitan family. Most are plump in general form and gregarious in habit, though some, such as the quail-doves in the West Indies, are solitary. A clapping or whirring sound of the wings is often conspicuous as they take flight and most species are strong fliers. There is clear definition between pigeons and doves, the latter are generally smaller and longer-tailed. Many species raise several clutches of young per year.

ROCK DOVE *Columba livia*   Plate 27
Local Names: Pigeon (Jamaica); Paloma Casera (PR)

Identification: 33–36 cm (13–14"). Very variable. The natural coloration is a combination of black, gray and white, including a *black tail band* and *white rump*.
Voice: A varied assortment of gentle cooing notes.
Status and Range: Introduced through much of its range, including the West Indies where a common year-round resident in the northern Bahamas, Greater Antilles, the Virgin and Cayman Islands, and in most large towns of the Lesser Antilles. It is semi-feral and may be entirely feral, locally, on Puerto Rico and perhaps on other islands. Rarely occurs in forests or more remote habitats occupied by other large pigeons. Introduced through most of the Western Hemisphere. Native to temperate regions of the Eastern Hemisphere.
Habitat: Typically a tame resident of city streets and populated rural areas.
Nesting: A nest is constructed on a building, bridge or other available ledge, or in a rock crevice or tree. Eggs (2) white. Breeds year-round.

SCALY-NAPED PIGEON *Columba squamosa*   Plate 27
Local Names: Red Head (VI); Blue Pigeon, Mountain Pigeon (LA); Torcaza Morada (Cuba); Paloma Rubia (PR); Paloma Turca (DR, PR); Ranmye Kou Wouj (Haiti); Ramier (Dominica, Grenada, Guad, Haiti, Mart, St L, St V); Pigeon à Cou Rouge, Ramier Cou Rouge (Guad, Mart); Grote Blauwe Duif (Saba, St E, St M)

Identification: 36–40 cm (14–16"). *Adult*: At a distance this pigeon appears entirely slate-gray. At close range the head, neck and breast have a purplish-red tint. *Immature*: More reddish-brown than the adult. *Similar species*: Scaly-naped Pigeon lacks the white on the head of White-crowned Pigeon and is much larger and darker than the doves. Plain Pigeon is much lighter purplish-red on the wings and abdomen, and shows a white leading edge to its wing. In flight, it displays a conspicuous white band across the upperwing.
Voice: The distinctive common call heard frequently in the early morning is an emphatic *cruu, cruu-cru-cruuu* with the heaviest accent on the fourth syllable. The very soft first syllable is separated by a pause. The last three syllables sound like *Who are you!*
Status and Range: A year-round resident through much of the West Indies, it is common on Puerto Rico, the Virgin Islands and many islands of the Lesser Antilles. It is fairly common in the Cordillera Central and other remote mountain forests of the Dominican Republic. On Haiti, it is also fairly common in the Massif de la Hotte and uncommon in the Massif de la Selle. Scaly-naped Pigeon is rare elsewhere on Hispaniola. On Cuba, it is uncommon in the east and rare in the west. It is rare among some of the Lesser Antilles, including St Martin, St Eustacius, Antigua and Barbuda, due to lack of available habitat or hunting pressures. Vagrant on Jamaica. Overall, this pigeon has declined widely in the West Indies because of intensive hunting. Locally, on Puerto Rico, this species has experienced a population increase, likely resulting from the regeneration of secondary forests from abandoned agricultural lands. Also occurs on islands off Venezuela.
Comments: Primarily arboreal, it will feed opportunistically on the ground such as on dairy farms or following forest destruction by hurricanes. Usually occurs individually or in small flocks. Most frequently observed flying high over the forest canopy.

Habitat: Typically mountain forests. On some islands, it ranges into well-wooded lowlands; on St Christopher and Barbados it occurs in towns and villages.
Nesting: A frail stick nest is constructed in a tree, among palm fronds or even on a bromeliad. It is sometimes built atop an abandoned rat nest. On uninhabited islands, apparently nests on the ground. Eggs (2) glossy white. Breeds year-round, but principally from March to June.

WHITE-CROWNED PIGEON *Columba leucocephala* Plate 27
Local Names: Blue Pigeon (LA); Bald Pate (CI, Jamaica, LA, VI); White Head (St M, VI); Torcaza Cabeciblanca (Cuba); Casquito Blanco, Paloma Coronita (DR); Paloma Cabeciblanca (PR); Pigeon à Couronne Blanche, Ramier Tête-blanche (Guad, Mart); Ranmye Tèt Blan, Ramier à Tête Blanche (Haiti, French WI); Witkruinduif (St M)

Identification: 33–36 cm (13–14"). The body appears entirely dark gray except for the *white crown*. **Male:** Crown clear white. **Female:** Crown is grayish-white. **Immature:** Grayish-white of crown nearly limited to forehead. **Similar species:** The slightly larger Scaly-naped Pigeon appears entirely dark gray at a distance, but has a dark rather than a white crown.
Voice: *Cruu, cru, cu-cruuu,* which sounds like 'Who took two.' A bit faster and less deliberate than Scaly-naped Pigeon, with the second syllable having a characteristic rising inflection. Also a distinct low purring sound.

Status and Range: A common breeding resident generally remaining year-round in the Bahamas, Cuba, Jamaica and Antigua and locally common on Hispaniola, Puerto Rico, the Virgin Islands, San Andrés and Providencia. It is uncommon in the Cayman Islands, Anguilla and St Barthélemy and rare on St Martin and Guadeloupe. This pigeon is a very rare wanderer elsewhere in the Lesser Antilles south to the Grenadines. Formerly abundant throughout most of its range, this species has declined dramatically and is now threatened due to the impacts of habitat loss, severe over-hunting, harvesting of nestlings for food and introduced predators. Birds move among islands under certain stressful conditions and in regular seasonal movements. Also occurs in the United States (Florida Keys) and islands off Mexico and Belize.
Comments: A highly gregarious, arboreal species typically occurring in flocks. Single roosts and breeding colonies on Cuba support hundreds of thousands of White-crowned Pigeons. Similar large colonies existed until recently on Hispaniola. This species is a powerful flyer often commuting 45 km (28 miles) or more in each direction between its roosting and feeding grounds.
Habitat: Primarily coastal woodlands and mangroves when breeding, but also well inland into the mountains as they follow available food resources in the non-breeding season.
Nesting: White-crowned Pigeon is generally a colonial nester, though on Antigua and Barbuda individual pairs commonly nest by themselves. A flimsy twig nest is built, typically in mangroves or dry scrub, but also in large trees around towns and on Barbuda, in holes of cliffs. Eggs (2) glossy white. Breeds primarily from March to August, but sometimes as late as September. Nesting seasons differ from area to area depending on local food conditions.

PLAIN PIGEON *Columba inornata* Plate 27
Local Names: Blue Pigeon (Jamaica); Torcaza Boba (Cuba); Paloma Ceniza (DR); Paloma Sabanera (PR); Ramier Ceniza, Ramye Miyèt, Ramier (Haiti)

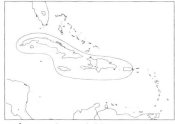

Identification: 38–40 cm (15–16"). Paler than the other large arboreal pigeons, with more brown in the plumage, *white edge to the wing-coverts,* and reddish-brown on wings and breast. **Immature:** Darker and browner than the adult. **Flight:** A thin, *white band across the wing.* **Similar species:** Distinguished from Scaly-naped Pigeon, when perched, by the purplish-red color on the wing and abdomen, and by the white band on the leading edge of the wing. White-winged Dove is smaller, browner and has a much more noticeable white wing band. Ring-tailed Pigeon has a banded tail and lacks white in the wing.
Voice: A deep, deliberate *whoo, wo-oo* or *who, oo-oo* and other variations.

Status and Range: Confined to the Greater Antilles where it is a common but local year-round resident on Hispaniola, particularly in the Dominican Republic, and rare and local on Cuba, (including Cayo Romano), Jamaica and Puerto Rico. The Puerto Rican population, believed to have declined to fewer than 100 birds in the 1970s, has expanded to perhaps several thousand individuals. Overall, however, the species has declined dramatically throughout its range and is considered endangered due to habitat loss, hunting and predation by introduced mammals.

Comments: Arboreal, typically in flocks. Surprisingly tame.

Habitat: Primarily savannas, open woodlands, coastal scrub, dry limestone forests and forest edges in the lowlands, but also occurs in open woodlands in the mountains to moderate elevations. On Puerto Rico, virtually confined to the latter habitat through the latter half of the 1900s, but recently appears to be recolonizing coastal areas.

Nesting: A fragile stick nest is built in bamboo clumps, clusters of vines or palm fronds. Egg (1) dull white, but three clutches may be raised in a season. Breeds year-round, but primarily from February to June.

RING-TAILED PIGEON *Columba caribaea* Plates 27, 83
Local Name: Ringtail

Identification: 41 cm (16″). Note its large size, *black band across the uppertail, bluish-green hindneck* and absence of white in the wings. **Adult male**: Bluish-gray above; head and underparts pinkish. **Adult female**: Slightly duller and browner than the male. **Immature**: Brownish-gray with reddish-brown fringes on upperwing and head feathers and underparts pale reddish-orange. **Similar species**: No other West Indian pigeon has a banded tail. Plain Pigeon has white on wing and lacks the greenish hindneck.

Voice: Call a throaty *cru-cru-crooooo*, last note lower. Also a mournful, soft *uhu-cooo*, repeated, the last syllable being louder and more emphatic.

Status and Range: Endemic to Jamaica where it is fairly common locally, particularly in Cockpit Country and the Blue and John Crow Mountains. Illegal hunting and forest destruction have reduced this from an abundant species to one which is threatened.

Comments: Arboreal, foraging on fruits and seeds most often in canopy. Typically occurs in small flocks. Record for Puerto Rico most certainly in error. Formerly, hunters lit fires under fruiting trees as smoke reputedly attracted the birds.

Habitat: Chiefly forested inland hills and mountains from 300–600 m (1000–2000′) above sea level. Descends to lower elevations in cooler months.

Nesting: The nest is a crude platform of twigs with a bed of leaves and bark constructed among dense foliage high in a tall tree deep in the forest. Eggs (2) white. Breeding is believed to occur from late February to August.

EURASIAN COLLARED-DOVE *Streptopelia decaocto* Plate 28
Local Names: Tórtola (Cuba); Tourterelle Turque (Guad)

Identification: 28–30 cm (11–12″). A medium-sized dove, overall gray, with dark primaries and a *black collar around hindneck*. **Similar species**: The domestic Ringed Turtle-Dove (*Streptopelia risoria*) (not illustrated) is best distinguished by its two-syllable, throaty call whereas that of Eurasian Collared-Dove is three syllables and less throaty. Eurasian Collared-Dove is also larger and browner with gray, rather than whitish, undertail-coverts; much darker primaries and a long tail which is either rounded or squared, not pointed. For a more complete discussion of distinctions between these two species refer to: Smith, P. W. 1987. The Eurasian Collared-Dove Arrives in the Americas. *American Birds* 41(4): 1370–1379.

Voice: Call a repeated three-syllabled, *kuk-kooooo00ó-kook*, with brief pauses between phrases. Also a harsh, nasal *mew*, similar to a loud Gray Catbird call, given in flight or upon landing.

Status and Range: Introduced to New Providence in the Bahamas in 1974, it is now a common year-round resident in the northern Bahamas (New Providence, Abaco, Bimini, Grand Bahama, Andros and several of the Berry Islands) and is still expanding its range. It apparently spread to Cuba from the Bahamas in the 1980s and is now fairly common locally around Havana and at the extreme western tip of the Guanahacabibes Peninsula. This dove is a common resident in the Cayman Islands, likely the result of a separate introduction. Introduced to Guadeloupe in 1976, the species is locally common, including on nearby Les Saintes. It is now locally common on Martinique where first reported in 1994. A few individuals have been reported from St Christopher, Nevis, Montserrat and Dominica; nesting has been recorded on the latter two islands. It can be expected that the entire West Indies will soon be colonized by birds from the existing populations. Native to Asia and Europe.

Comments: Forages for seeds on the ground. Sometimes takes discarded human food. Readily comes to feeding stations. Sometimes mistaken for Ringed Turtle-Dove which occurs in a semi-domesticated state in several rural and urban areas on Puerto Rico, the Virgin Islands and elsewhere. However, this bird has not been known to establish itself in the wild in any country where it has been released.

Habitat: Urban areas.

Nesting: The nest is an unlined platform of twigs constructed in a bush, tree, palm or on a building ledge. Eggs (2) white. On Cuba, it breeds primarily from March to August.

SPOTTED DOVE *Streptopelia chinensis*　　　　　　　　　**Plate 28**

Identification: 30 cm (12"). ***Adult***: The *black hindneck spotted with white*, long tail broadly tipped with white and light gray bend of the wing distinguish this dark dove. ***Immature***: Lacks the neck pattern. ***Similar species***: Mourning Dove has a more sharply pointed tail and lacks a spotted black collar.

Voice: A coarse *ooo-hoo-ooo-hurrrrp*, with a rising inflection.

Status and Range: Very local around Estate Canaan in the Virgin Islands (St Croix) resulting from releases in 1964. It bred in small numbers in the wild before Hurricane Hugo struck St Croix in 1989. Its present status is unknown. Introduced to many parts of the world. Native to South-East Asia.

Nesting: A frail twig platform nest is built in a tree from near ground level to 6 m (20') high. Eggs (2) glossy white. Breeds from April to July.

WHITE-WINGED DOVE *Zenaida asiatica*　　　　　　　　**Plate 28**

Local Names: Lapwing (Jamaica); White-wing (CI, Jamaica); Paloma Aliblanca (Cuba); Aliblanca (DR); Tórtola Aliblanca (PR); Barbarin, Toutrèl Zèl Blan (Haiti).

Identification: 28–30 cm (11–12"). Note the *large, white central wing patch*, both when perched and in flight. Tail tips white. ***Similar species***: Zenaida Dove has a white band on the trailing edge of the secondaries. Mourning Dove has no white in its wing. White-winged Dove is more arboreal than either of these species. Plain Pigeon has a much less distinct white band transversing its wing and is a much larger bird.

Voice: *Coo-co, co-coo* or *coo-co, co-co-coo* on a single pitch, which sounds like 'Two bits for two.' Also a distinctive yodel-like cooing modulating between two notes.

Status and Range: Generally a common year-round resident in the southern Bahamas, Cuba (more so in the east), Jamaica, Hispaniola, Grand Cayman in the Cayman Islands, San Andrés and Providencia. It is uncommon in the northern Bahamas and on Puerto Rico and rare in the Virgin Islands (St Croix and St John) and the remaining Cayman Islands. Vagrant on Saba. The species is expanding its range eastward through the West Indies. Occurs through southern North America, Central America and the central portion of South America's west coast.

Comments: Usually flocks. Primarily arboreal in forested areas, but a ground-dweller in urban areas with scattered trees, where it frequently feeds with Zenaida Doves and Common Ground-Doves.

Habitat: Arid scrubland, mangrove swamps, open woodlands and urban gardens. Primarily coastal, but sometimes in the mountains.

Nesting: This dove breeds colonially, building a frail nest of twigs and grasses at low to moderate height. Eggs (2) white. The breeding season varies from year-round in urban areas to being concentrated from April to June in arid zones.

ZENAIDA DOVE *Zenaida aurita*   **Plate 28**
Local Names: Seaside Dove (Grenada); Pea Dove (CI, Jamaica); Wood Dove (Barbados, Nevis); Mountain Dove (Grenada, LA, VI); Guanaro (Cuba); Rolón (DR); Tórtola Cardosantera (PR); Toutèl Wouj, Grosse Tourterelle (Haiti); Tourterelle à Queue Carrée, Toutrelle, Tourterelle (Guad, Mart, French WI); Zenaida Treurduif (Saba, St E, St M)

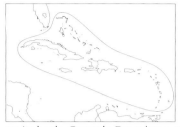

Identification: 25–28 cm (10–11"). The *white band on the trailing edge of the secondaries* coupled with the rounded tail with white tips is distinctive. Greater Antillean and Bahaman birds have entirely reddish-brown underparts. Zenaida Doves in the Lesser Antilles, except for the northernmost islands, have a whitish abdomen and undertail-coverts. **Similar species**: Mourning Dove has no white in the wing and has a longer, pointed tail. White-winged Dove has a large, white central wing patch. Eared Dove's tail is shorter and lacks white tips, and it has a darker abdomen and fewer black spots on its back. Grenada Dove has a white forehead, whiter belly and lacks black spots on its back.
Voice: A gentle cooing, almost identical to that of Mourning Dove, *coo-oo, coo, coo, coo*, the second syllable rising sharply. On Jamaica, rendered as 'Mar-y boil brown rice.'
Status and Range: A common year-round resident throughout the West Indies, although slightly less abundant in the southern Lesser Antilles where Eared Dove is more common. Also occurs on the southern coast of the United States (Florida), the coast of the Yucatan Peninsula and its offshore islands.
Comments: Typically feeds on seeds on the ground, but sometimes takes seeds and fruits from trees. A popular game species throughout its range. Mourning Dove occurs primarily in settlements whereas Zenaida Dove occurs primarily in the country in the Dominican Republic. This situation is almost the reverse on Puerto Rico where Zenaida Dove abounds in many settled areas. Zenaida Dove may be displaced locally by colonization of White-winged Dove, as appears to be the case on Grand Cayman in the Cayman Islands.
Habitat: Primarily open coastal areas, gardens and hotel grounds. Also open woodlands, scrub thickets and pine woods with dense understory. Occurs in suitable habitat into the mountains, but less frequent at higher elevations.
Nesting: The nest is a thin platform of twigs built in a bush or tree, though sometimes on the ground. Eggs (2) white. The breeding season is variable, occurring year-round in urban areas, from February to June in moist and wet habitats and from April to June in arid zones. May have up to six broods per year.

EARED DOVE *Zenaida auriculata*   **Plate 28**
Local Names: Trinidad Ground Dove (Grenada); Tourterelle Ortolan (St L, St V, French WI)

Identification: 22–25 cm (8.5–10"). **Adult**: Grayish brown above with a few small black spots on scapulars, sides of neck golden with a metallic purple patch, *underparts brown all the way to undertail-coverts* and *reddish-brown tips* to outer feathers of short tail. Lacks white in wings or tail. **Similar species**: Zenaida Dove has a proportionately longer tail with white tips, a white band on the trailing edge of secondaries, pale lower belly and more noticeable black spots on its back.
Voice: A soft *ooa-oo, u-ooa-oo*, like Zenaida Dove but shorter.
Status and Range: A fairly common year-round resident on southern St Lucia and common on St Vincent, the Grenadines and Grenada. Very local on Barbados. Two records from Martinique. This dove has only recently colonized St Lucia, Barbados and St Vincent. Also widespread in South America and its coastal islands.
Comments: Sometimes occurs in large flocks. Forages on the ground, but perches in trees. Formerly called Violet-eared Dove.
Habitat: Semi-arid brushlands primarily in lowlands.
Nesting: The nest is loosely built of sticks in shrubs, trees and palms at varying heights. Eggs (2) white. Breeds from December to September.

MOURNING DOVE *Zenaida macroura*   **Plate 28**
Local Names: Paloma, Long-tail, Pea Dove (Jamaica); Paloma Rabiche (Cuba); Tórtola, Fifi (DR); Tórtola Rabilarga (PR); Rabiche (DR, PR); Toutrèl Ke Fen, Tourterelle, Queue-fine (Haiti)

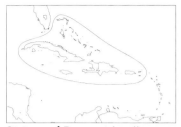

Identification: 28–33 cm (11–13″). Its *long, wedge-shaped tail* fringed with white is distinctive. Lacks white in wing. *Male*: Purplish sheen on sides of neck and hindneck. *Female*: Reduced purplish iridescence on neck. *Immature*: Browner than the adult, heavily spotted with black and lacks iridescence. *Similar species*: Zenaida and White-winged Doves have white wing markings. Spotted Dove has a black hindneck spotted with white and a less pointed tail.
Voice: A mournful cooing almost identical to that of Zenaida Dove, *coo-oo, coo, coo, coo*, the second syllable rising sharply.
Status and Range: A locally common year-round resident in the Bahamas and Greater Antilles. This dove is a common transient in the Cayman Islands. There is a questionable report from St Lucia. Its numbers and range are increasing in the West Indies, likely the result of forest clearing and agricultural expansion. Occurs through North and Central America.
Comments: A ground feeder, usually in flocks except when adults pair to breed.
Habitat: Primarily lowland open country, dry coastal forests and agricultural lands, often near bodies of fresh water. Also agricultural areas in mountains.
Nesting: A nest of twigs and grasses is constructed at low to medium height in a bush or tree, though at times on the ground. Eggs (2) white. Breeds from March to August.

PASSENGER PIGEON *Ectopistes migratorius*   **Plate 28**
Local Names: Paloma Mensajera, Paloma Migratoria (Cuba)

Identification: 41 cm (16″). Large, with pale red underparts; bluish-gray head and back and a long, pointed tail with white-tipped outer feathers. *Female*: Duller and browner than the male. *Similar species*: Similar in shape to a Mourning Dove, but much larger and with a longer, pointed tail. Upperparts and especially head darker and more grayish.
Status and Range: Extinct. Vagrant on Cuba during the middle of the 19th century. This bird suffered one of the most dramatic and best-documented extinctions in history. Formerly North America's most abundant bird, centuries of habitat fragmentation coupled with over-harvesting led to its rapid decline in the late 1880s and extinction in 1914. Apparently stragglers occurred on Cuba more often than suggested in the literature. Gundlach, a famous Cuban ornithologist of the late 1800s, mentions only two examples. Both were of birds found in Havana and prepared by him. Formerly ranged through much of North America.

COMMON GROUND-DOVE *Columbina passerina*   **Plate 28**
Local Names: Tobacco Dove (Bahamas); Duppy Bird (Jamaica); Grounie (Nevis); Ground Dove (CI; Jamaica, LA); Tojosa (Cuba); Rolita (DR, PR); Zòtolan, Ortolan (Haiti); Colombe à Queue Noire, Z'otolan, Ortolan (Guad, Mart, St L); Musduifje (Saba, St E, St M)

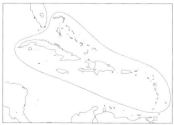

Identification: 15–18 cm (5.75–7″). The only *tiny* dove in the West Indies. Moderate variation in plumage among islands. *Male*: A bluish-gray crown and hindneck; pinkish tint on underparts. *Female*: More uniformly gray overall. *Flight*: Flashes a reddish-brown wing patch.
Voice: A monotonous, often repeated call either of single or double notes, *coo, coo, coo, coo...* or, *co-coo, co-coo, co-coo...* or, *hoop, hoop, hoop...* in staccato fashion.
Status and Range: A very common year-round resident throughout the West Indies. Also occurs through the southern United States, Mexico, Central America and northern South America.
Comments: Primarily ground dwelling, it sometimes seeks refuge in trees.
Habitat: A wide range of lowland habitats except heavily wooded areas.

Nesting: A nest of rootlets, grasses or twigs is built in a bush, tree or on the ground. This dove sometimes nests in cavities. The nest is often constructed atop the nest of a Bananaquit or other small bird. Eggs (2) glossy white. Breeds year-round with a peak in May and June.

GRENADA DOVE *Leptotila wellsi*   Plates 28, 29
Local Names: Whistling Dove, Mountain Dove

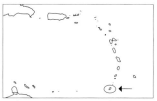

Identification: 31 cm (12"). **Adult**: Distinguishing characteristics are its unmarked gray-brown upperparts, white forehead to crown, buffy cinnamon-colored breast, *white belly, no markings on wings* and outer tail feathers tipped with white. **Flight**: Cinnamon-colored underwings. **Similar species**: Resembles Caribbean Dove which does not occur on Grenada. It is duller and slightly smaller than Zenaida Dove which has a spotted back, lacks a white forehead and does not have as white a belly.

Voice: A distinctive, descending *hoooo*, repeated at eight-second intervals virtually like clock-work. Reputedly, only the male calls.

Status and Range: A very rare endemic restricted to the southwestern peninsula of Grenada where best found around Mount Hartman Estate and Halifax Harbor. Formerly occurred on nearby offshore islands. Due to habitat loss, it is now critically endangered. Total population may be less than 100. Hunting and the introduced mongoose may have also contributed to its decline.

Comments: Primarily terrestrial. Closely related to Gray-fronted Dove (*L. rufaxilla*), which has a wide Central and South American distribution and with which it has often been considered conspecific.

Habitat: Lowlands and hillsides with mature dry scrub forest. It appears to favor a mixture of closed canopy, dense scrub and large areas of bare ground.

Nesting: The nest is a platform of twigs constructed in a tree, palm or bush up to 4 m (13') above the ground. Eggs (2) white. Breeding is known to occur from December to February and in July. It apparently varies according to rainfall and consequently differs in various parts of the island.

CARIBBEAN DOVE *Leptotila jamaicensis*   Plate 28
Local Names: Ground-Dove (San Andrés); White-belly (CI, Jamaica)

Identification: 30–33 cm (12–13"). A *plump, ground-dwelling* dove, with a *white face and underparts* and *long, red legs*. Note its *cinnamon-colored underwings*, gray crown, iridescent purplish-red hindneck and white-tipped outer tail feathers. **Adult male**: Bright iridescence on neck. **Adult female**: Neck iridescence slightly reduced. **Immature**: Duller, with pale reddish-brown fringes to most covert feathers. Neck and breast dull brown or pale reddish-brown. **Similar species**: Other ground-dwelling, woodland doves have darker underparts. Resembles Grenada Dove with which it does not overlap in range.

Voice: Call is a high-pitched, plaintive *cu-cu-cu-oooo* 'Who cooks for you?', or 'What's that to you-oo?,' with the last note drawn out, more strongly accented, descending and broken into two syllables.

Status and Range: A locally common year-round resident on Jamaica, but in the Cayman Islands, an uncommon resident on Grand Cayman and rare on Cayman Brac. Fairly common on the western side of San Andrés. Introduced to the Bahamas (New Providence) in an effort to restock that island with birds after the hurricanes of the late 1920s and now an uncommon and local resident. Also occurs in southeastern Mexico and on adjacent islands, and islands off northern Honduras.

Comments: Relatively tame; usually walks to cover rather than flies. Forages under cover of bushes or shrubs and walks about rapidly, pumping head and bobbing tail. Feeds primarily on seeds. Somewhat variable through its range: San Andrés race (*L. j. neoxena*) is smaller than the Jamaican race (*L. j. jamaicensis*); former is also duller, with less vivid iridescence on the neck and with a pink wash on the breast. The Grand Cayman race (*L. j. collaris*) is like the Jamaican form, but is generally slightly smaller.

Habitat: Primarily lowlands and foothills from open areas and gardens to dense secondary forests.

Nesting: Nests in dense bushes, occasionally on the ground. Eggs (2) white. Breeds from March to May.

KEY WEST QUAIL-DOVE *Geotrygon chrysia*   **Plate 27**
Local Names: Barbiquejo (Cuba); Perdiz Grande (DR, PR); Perdrix Grise, Pèdri Vant Blan (Haiti)

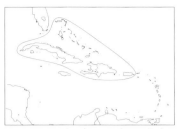

Identification: 28–30 cm (11–12"). Note the *white line under the eye, reddish-brown back and wings* and primarily white underparts. **Female**: Less iridescence on hindneck and upper back. **Similar species**: Bridled Quail-Dove has browner upperparts and is much darker below. Ruddy Quail-Dove has more reddish-brown underparts and a duller streak below the eye.
Voice: A moan on one pitch, gradually increasing in volume and then fading rapidly. Very ventriloquial. Similar to the call of Bridled Quail-Dove.
Status and Range: A fairly common year-round resident locally in the northern Bahamas, Cuba and Hispaniola, but uncommon in the southern Bahamas (Caicos Islands) and locally on Puerto Rico. These islands comprise the entire range of the species.
Comments: A ground dweller, it is often heard deep among dense vegetation where it is very difficult to see.
Habitat: Dense woods and scrubby thickets with ample leaf litter, primarily in arid and semi-arid zones, but also in moist and wet mountain forests with undisturbed understory.
Nesting: Reported to nest in low undergrowth, among bromeliads or on the ground. The nest is a loose platform of twigs. Eggs (2) buff-colored. Breeds from February to August.

BRIDLED QUAIL-DOVE *Geotrygon mystacea*   **Plate 27**
Local Names: Marble Dove (Antigua); Wood Dove (LA); Marmy Dove (Antigua, LA, VI); Wood Hen (LA, Saba); Partridge (Nevis, St E, VI); Perdiz de Martinica (PR); Colombe à Croissants, Perdrix Croissant (Guad, Mart, St L)

Identification: 30 cm (12"). The *white streak below the eye, brown upperparts* (except for crown and neck) and reddish-brown limited to a patch on the wing are good field marks. Underparts buffy-brown. **Female**: Less iridescence on hindneck and upper back. **Similar species**: Key West Quail-Dove has reddish-brown upperparts and is whitish below rather than brown. Ruddy Quail-Dove is entirely reddish-brown.
Voice: A mournful *who-whooo*, on one pitch or descending towards the end, getting loudest in the middle of the second syllable and then trailing off. Sometimes the first syllable is omitted. Similar to the call of Key West Quail-Dove.
Status and Range: Generally an uncommon to rare year-round resident in the Lesser Antilles (absent from Anguilla, St Martin, Barbados, St Vincent, the Grenadines and Grenada) and on the larger, forested Virgin Islands, though possibly extirpated from St Croix as a result of Hurricane Hugo in 1989. It is extremely rare and local on Puerto Rico including the island of Vieques. These islands comprise the entire range of the species.
Comments: Primarily ground dwelling, it is very secretive, thus being much more frequently heard than seen.
Habitat: Dense mountain forests with thick undergrowth, though locally in coastal forests.
Nesting: A flimsy nest of twigs is usually built at a low height. Several nests are constructed before one is settled upon as a nest site. Eggs (2) pinkish-buff. Breeds primarily from May to July and to a lesser extent from October to December.

GRAY-HEADED QUAIL-DOVE *Geotrygon caniceps*   **Plate 27**
Local Names: Camao, Azulona (Cuba, DR); Perdiz Coquito Blanco (DR); Perdrix Gris (Haiti)

Identification: 28 cm (11"). A pigeon-like ground-dwelling dove, with a metallic purplish-blue sheen on the back. Hispaniolan birds have a distinctive white forehead; those in Cuba have a completely gray crown. Bill and legs reddish. Displays a peculiar balance of the neck and tail while walking or perching. **Similar species**: All other quail-doves on Cuba and Hispaniola have facial stripes and are browner.

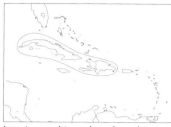

Voice: A continuous, low *uup-uup-uup-uup* without pauses. On Hispaniola, changes to a prolonged *coo-o-o*.

Status and Range: A year-round resident known only from Cuba and Hispaniola. On Cuba, it is uncommon and very local, mainly in the western and central portions of the island. On Hispaniola, this species is known only from the Dominican Republic where it is rare and very local in the Cordillera Central, Sierra de Baoruco and Sierra de Neiba. It may actually be fairly common in a few localities, but is difficult to find. The endemic subspecies on Hispaniola is considered endangered due to habitat loss, hunting and introduced predators, while the subspecies on Cuba is threatened due to the same factors.

Comments: Forages for seeds on the ground alone or in pairs. Typically calls from a branch. On Cuba, it associates more with Blue-headed and Ruddy Quail-Doves than with Key West Quail-Dove.

Habitat: Humid soils with plenty of decayed leaves. On Cuba, either at low elevations in wet forests bordering swamps or at middle altitudes in dense, moist woods. In the Dominican Republic, occurs primarily in dense mountain forests and coffee plantations, but is known from near sea level near Bayahebe outside of Parque del Este.

Nesting: A nest of twigs and leaves is built in a bush or tangle of vines at a height of 1–3 m (3–10'). Eggs (usually 1, but sometimes 2) beige and oval. Breeds from January through August.

RUDDY QUAIL-DOVE *Geotrygon montana*   Plate 27

Local Names: Red Partridge (Jamaica); Partridge (CI, LA); Mountain Dove (Grenada, St V); Boyero (Cuba); Perdiz Colorada (DR); Perdiz Pequeña (PR); Pèdri Fran (Haiti), Colombe Rouviolette, Perdrix Rouge, Grise (Guad, Mart); Perdrix Rouge (Haiti, French WI)

Identification: 25 cm (10"). **Male**: Predominantly reddish-brown with a conspicuous light buff stripe beneath the eye. **Female**: Browner, less reddish and with a less conspicuous facial stripe than the male. **Similar species**: Bridled and Key West Quail-Doves have white stripes beneath the eye and neither have the overall reddish-brown plumage of Ruddy Quail-Dove. Crested Quail-Dove is (obviously) crested and has a gray head and gray underparts.

Voice: A mournful *coo* gradually fading in strength and sometimes in pitch, like blowing across the mouth of a bottle. Very ventriloquial.

Status and Range: A fairly common year-round resident on Puerto Rico, it is locally common on Cuba, Jamaica and Hispaniola and is uncommon on the large, forested islands of the Lesser Antilles, including Antigua, Guadeloupe, Dominica, Martinique, St Lucia, St Vincent and Grenada. It is less common among the Lesser Antilles where it is hunted. It is very rare in the Virgin Islands (St John and St Croix). Also occurs through Central America and much of South America.

Comments: Ground-dwelling, it is much more often heard than seen.

Habitat: Primarily dense forests and plantations of shade coffee in the hills and mountains, but also locally on the coast.

Nesting: A loose nest of twigs and leaves is usually constructed low in a bush or tree, but sometimes on the ground. Eggs (2) light buff-colored. Breeds from February to August.

CRESTED QUAIL-DOVE *Geotrygon versicolor*   Plates 27, 83

Local Names: Mountain Witch, Blue Dove, Blue Partridge

Identification: 31 cm (12"). A plump, ground-dwelling dove, with a *short but distinct crest, primarily gray head and underparts, bronze-colored hindneck* and *reddish-brown upper back and much of wings*. It has a conspicuous *buffy stripe beneath the eye*. **Adult female**: Neck and belly paler and browner than the male. **Immature**: Duller with reddish-brown edges to most feathers. **Similar species**: Ruddy Quail-Dove is reddish-brown with no gray on head and breast, and it lacks a crest.

Voice: A mournful two to three syllabled *woof-woo-wooo*, the first note sharp with the following notes softer and lower in pitch.

Status and Range: Endemic to Jamaica where it is fairly common locally, particularly in the Blue Mountains and Cockpit Country.

Comments: Searches for food on the forest floor and along trails and road edges. Conspicuously pumps head and bobs tail while walking. Typically flushes only a short distance into dense vegetation.
Habitat: Wet forest undergrowth of the mountains and limestone hills.
Nesting: The nest is a coarse platform of twigs built in forest undergrowth, close to or on ground. Eggs (2) buff. Breeds from March to June.

BLUE-HEADED QUAIL-DOVE *Starnoenas cyanocephala* Plates 27, 79
Local Names: Perdiz, Paloma Perdiz

Identification: 30–33 cm (12–13"). The largest of the Cuban quail-doves. A brownish-cinnamon bird that blends with dead leaves. The conspicuous light blue head and white facial stripe combined with a handsome black medallion on the throat, surrounded by whitish and bluish, makes this dove unmistakable. Throat and around eyes black.
Voice: Two similar notes like *uuuu-up, uuuu-up*, the last syllable rising and stopping quickly.
Status and Range: This jewel of the Cuban avifauna is endemic. Previously rather common, this species had already undergone a noticeable decline by the middle of the 19th century. It is now fairly rare and very local and is considered endangered. Its numbers have decreased steadily as a result of hunting and deforestation. The introduced mongoose likely also contributed to its decline. Primarily a bird of the lowlands, it also occurs at moderate elevations. Principal areas where it still occurs include the Guanahacabibes Peninsula, Pinares de La Güira in San Diego and in the vicinity of Zapata Swamp (Bodega Vieja, Molina and Soplillar). Very rare on the Isle of Youth.
Comments: Usually in pairs on the ground, where it forages mainly on seeds, berries and snails. It is shy and when alarmed takes off quickly, producing a peculiar sound in flight in a manner similar to European Partridge *Perdix perdix*. This doubtless led to its local name, 'Perdiz,' which is Spanish for partridge. Sometimes perches on a limb where it calls incessantly. The meat is excellent, which is another reason for its decline. Stick traps called 'casillas' are used locally to trap the bird. *Starnoenas* is a monotypic genus.
Habitat: Deciduous forests with a dense canopy, open understory and stony forest floor, particularly with ample leaf litter.
Nesting: The nest is built roughly of twigs and leaves, either on the ground or low to it, in a stump cavity, the fork of a branch among the roots of trees and sometimes among tangled vines. Eggs (2) white. Breeds primarily from April to July.

PARAKEETS, MACAWS AND PARROTS:
FAMILY PSITTACIDAE

The parrots form a distinctive family typical of warmer climates. They are easily recognized by their raucous calls, large heads and extremely heavy bills, which are often used to assist them in their movements among branches. Most species in the region are gregarious and primarily green. Those referred to as parakeets are distinguished by their long, pointed tails and smaller size. Flight is direct, with rapid, shallow wingbeats. Many of the species occurring in the region have been introduced, primarily as a result of caged birds escaping. Brown-throated Parakeet (Virgin Islands) and Green-rumped Parrotlet (Jamaica) are long established, but the remaining introductions were apparently made during the late 1950s and 1960s.

BUDGERIGAR *Melopsittacus undulatus*   Plate 32
Local Name: Periquito de Australia (PR)

Identification: 18 cm (7"). The typical pet shop parakeet or 'budgie' is widely known. Its natural coloration is green below with a yellow head and back heavily barred with black; however, varieties in a wide range of other colors have been bred.

Voice: A sharp screech.

Status and Range: A regular escapee on Puerto Rico in the San Juan area, particularly around Río Piedras. It may now breed, but there is as yet no evidence of this. Small flocks also recorded in the Cayman Islands (Grand Cayman), and it is an occasional escapee on Jamaica where recorded around Kingston and in the Dominican Republic where there are records from Santo Domingo and on Guadeloupe. Native to Australia.

Habitat: Short grass.

MONK PARAKEET *Myiopsitta monachus* Plate 32
Local Names: Perico Monje (PR); Conure Veuve, Perruche Souris (Guad)

Identification: 28 cm (11″). A fairly large parakeet, primarily green, with a *gray crown, throat and breast* and a long, pointed tail. The flight feathers are blue.

Voice: An unusually loud and raucous series of squawks.

Status and Range: Introduced to Puerto Rico, probably during the 1950s, it is common around El Morro in Old San Juan, the Isla Grande Reserve in Santurce and on the campus of the University of Puerto Rico in Río Piedras. It is also fairly common in the Luquillo Beach-Fajardo area and uncommon elsewhere on the coast. The species is expanding its range on the island. A feral breeding population exists in the Cayman Islands in George Town on Grand Cayman. Monk Parakeet is rare on Guadeloupe where there is one active nest site. There is one record from the Virgin Islands (St Croix). The population on Eleuthera in the Bahamas, first recorded about 1980, appears to be extirpated. Native to south-central South America.

Comments: Typically in close flocks. Feeds on a wide variety of seeds, fruits and flowers, both in trees and on the ground.

Habitat: Coastal areas including palm groves, lawns and urban areas with ornamental trees.

Nesting: Unique in the parrot family, it constructs a large, sometimes huge, stick nest, often at the base of palm fronds. The nest is communal and contains separate chambers for the various pairs of parakeets. Eggs (5–8) white. The breeding season has yet to be determined.

BLACK-HOODED PARAKEET *Nandayus nenday* Plate 32
Local Name: Periquito Caperuzado (PR)

Identification: 36 cm (14″). A large, primarily green, parakeet distinguished by its *black head*, red thighs and long tail.

Voice: Raucous squawks.

Status and Range: Rare and local on Puerto Rico where it was introduced probably in the early 1970s. The species occurs in very small numbers primarily along the northeastern coast. There is one record for St Croix in the Virgin Islands. Native to central South America.

Habitat: Sparse woodlands, palm groves and pastures with thickets.

Nesting: There are no nesting records from Puerto Rico.

HISPANIOLAN PARAKEET *Aratinga chloroptera* Plates 32, 81
Local Names: Perico (DR); Perico Dominicano (PR); Perruche, Perich (Haiti)

Identification: 30–33 cm (12–13″). A large parakeet. Bright green overall, with a long, pointed tail, white eyering and a *red edge along the bend of the wing*. **Flight**: *Red underwing-coverts*. **Similar species**: Hispaniolan Parrot is more robust, larger and with a shorter tail. Olive-throated Parakeet lacks red on the bend of the wing.

Voice: Screeching flight and perch calls, much simpler than those of Hispaniolan Parrot.

Status and Range: Endemic to Hispaniola, including its off-shore islands, Hispaniolan Parakeet is locally common in undisturbed habitat, but elsewhere is rapidly declining and reduced in distribution. In the Dominican Republic, it still occurs in good numbers in the Sierra de Baoruco and Sierra de Neiba, particularly at middle elevations between 900 and 1800 m (3000–6000'). Recently extirpated from Los Haitises. On Haiti, it is common in the Massif de la Selle and the la Citadelle area in the Massif du Nord. It is uncommon elsewhere on Haiti. Introduced to Puerto Rico where it occurs very locally, primarily in the southwest. Also introduced to Guadeloupe where it is very local in distribution. The species is threatened as a result of habitat loss and hunting.

Comments: Feeds mostly on fruits and seeds. Travels and forages in flocks, often feeding on corn and other crops, for which they are destroyed by farmers. As has been the pattern throughout the West Indies, parakeet populations have declined more rapidly than have parrot populations. The subspecies of Hispaniolan Parakeet (*A. c. maugei*) endemic to Puerto Rico and Mona Island became extinct at the turn of the 19th century, the last specimen being taken in 1892.

Habitat: Forested mountains and lowlands.

Nesting: Nests in tree cavities and arboreal termite nests. Eggs (3–4) white. Breeds from February to June.

CUBAN PARAKEET *Aratinga euops*   Plates 32, 79
Local Names: Catey, Periquito (Cuba)

Identification: 24–27 cm (9.5–10.5"). Almost entirely green with a long, pointed tail and some scattered red feathers on head, sides of neck and bend of the wing. **Flight**: Red under-wing-coverts. **Similar species**: Smaller and slimmer than Rose-throated Parrot. The long, pointed green tail, which is paler underneath, makes this bird unmistakable.

Voice: A loud and characteristic *crick-crick-crick* repeated mainly when flying. While perched or feeding, it emits a low whisper-like sound.

Status and Range: Endemic to Cuba where it has declined and now has a patchy distribution. It remains fairly common in Zapata Swamp, Trinidad Mountains, Sierra de Najasa and in the eastern part of the island, especially south of Moa and around La Melba. With the exception of Zapata Swamp, the parakeet is now absent from the western provinces. In Central Cuba, it occurs in Guasimal, Trinidad, Peralejo and Camagüey (Najasa). Found in the eastern provinces of Holguín, Santiago de Cuba and Guantánamo. Formerly common throughout Cuba and on the Isle of Youth, it disappeared from most of its former range by the late 1800s. Now endangered, the principal cause of its decline has been habitat destruction followed by the taking of birds as pets and the shooting of birds as crop pests.

Comments: Its demand as a pet is not as high as Rose-throated Parrot. It is able to learn several words. Mainly eats a wide variety of seeds and fruits. Usually quiet while foraging in groups, blending easily among the vegetation due to its green coloration. Contrarily, it is noisy in flight. The species seems somewhat nomadic, ranging widely in search of favored fruiting trees.

Habitat: Woodlands, forest edges, riverine forests, savannas with cabbage palms and tree stumps near swamps.

Nesting: Does not build a nest, but prefers the empty holes of woodpeckers, particularly Cuban Green Woodpecker, or dead palms without fronds. However, unlike Hispaniolan Parakeet, it only infrequently uses arboreal termite nests, preferring active ones to those which are abandoned. Eggs (2–5) white, almost round and with a little luster. Usually nests from March to August.

OLIVE-THROATED PARAKEET *Aratinga nana*   Plate 32
Local Name: Parakeet

Identification: 30.5 cm (12"). A *small, green, slender parakeet* with a *long, pointed tail. Dark brownish-olive underparts*; pale eyering and bill. **Similar species**: The two native parrots, Yellow-billed and Black-billed, are more robust with short, squared tails. Olive-throated Parakeet has a more

PARAKEETS, MACAWS AND PARROTS

erratic, rapid flight than the native parrots. Hispaniolan Parakeet has red on the bend of the wing.

Voice: A screeching *creek, creek* or a high-pitched *screet*.

Status and Range: A common and widespread year-round resident on Jamaica. Recently reported from the Dominican Republic in the lower elevations of the Sierra de Baoruco. It has yet to be determined whether these birds are of Jamaican or Central American stock. Also occurs in Mexico and Central America.

Comments: Typically forages and roosts in small flocks. Feeds on a wide variety of fruits and seeds, resulting in it periodically becoming a pest to cultivated crops. Jamaican farmers consider it the greatest pest of the island's parrots. *Aratinga nana nana* is an endemic subspecies, sometimes considered a full species.

Habitat: Scrub, woodlands, forests, croplands and gardens in both moist and dry areas of the coast, hills and lower mountains.

Nesting: Nests in arboreal termite nests or tree cavities. Eggs (3–5) white. Breeds from March to June.

ORANGE-FRONTED PARAKEET *Aratinga canicularis*   Plate 32
Local Name: Periquito Frentianaranjado (PR)

Identification: 23–24 cm (9–9.5"). A medium-sized green parakeet with an *orange forehead, white eyering* and a long, pointed tail. The primaries are blue. ***Immature***: Smaller orange forehead patch.

Voice: Raspy squawks, not as harsh as those of Monk Parakeet.

Status and Range: Introduced to Puerto Rico, probably in the 1960s, this species is locally uncommon at Cabezas de San Juan near Fajardo where it occurs in small numbers. Native to Mexico and Central America.

Habitat: Wooded pastures and urban areas with ornamental trees.

Nesting: The nest has not yet been found on Puerto Rico.

BROWN-THROATED PARAKEET *Aratinga pertinax*   Plate 32

Identification: 23–28 cm (9–11"). A fairly large, green parakeet with a *yellowish-orange face and forehead* and a long, pointed tail. The throat and breast are dull yellowish-brown. The primaries are blue.

Voice: Raucous squawks.

Status and Range: A fairly common resident on St Thomas in the Virgin Islands particularly the eastern end, this species was introduced in the 1800s, apparently from Curaçao. Elsewhere in the Virgin Islands, it is reported from Tortola and there are a few sightings from St John. In the mid-1970s, a few birds bred on the eastern tip of Puerto Rico and it also occurred on nearby Culebra and Vieques; the bird's present status on these islands is uncertain, but there are no confirmed sightings since 1982 on Puerto Rico and 1976 on Culebra and Vieques. This parakeet is uncommon on Saba where there appear to be two separate populations, one at Wall's Bay and the other in the Bottom. It is also uncommon on Dominica. Recently recorded from Guadeloupe and Martinique. Native to Panama, northern South America and its adjacent islands.

Habitat: On St Thomas, wooded thickets in the hills.

Nesting: Excavates a nest chamber in an active termite nest or uses an existing cavity in a palm. Eggs (4–7) chalky white. Breeds from March to July.

CUBAN MACAW *Ara tricolor*   Plate 79
Local Name: Guacamayo

Identification: 50 cm (20"). A large, parrot-like bird, with a long tail and massive bill. Head red with yellow on crown and neck. Back reddish and feathers edged with greenish-yellow. Rump, uppertail- and undertail-coverts, primaries and secondaries are blue. Side of head, neck and underparts are orange-red.
Status and Range: This beautiful bird was endemic to Cuba and the Isle of Youth. It was probably not rare during Columbus' time, but declined rapidly thereafter. Cuban Macaw became extinct during the last decade of the 19th century on Cuba and earlier on the Isle of Youth.
Comments: In former days, its feathers were used as ornaments in foreign countries. It was said that Spanish soldiers shot them for target practice and it was also hunted for food. Formerly known as *Ara tricolor*, this name is now given to the extinct Hispaniolan Macaw, of which no specimens are known. Some authorities suggest both macaws be united as one species.
Habitat: Forests bordering swamps.

GREEN-RUMPED PARROTLET *Forpus passerinus*   Plate 32
Local Names: Parakeet, Guiana Parrolet (Jamaica)

Identification: 13 cm (5"). A *very small, short-tailed, green* parrot with a pale bill. *Male*: Greenish-blue rump and wings, particularly the undersides. *Female*: Lacks blue in the wing and has a yellower breast.
Voice: A shrill, squeaky chattering *swee-swee-swee* or *swee-swee-swee-sweetie* when flock lands. Flight call a repeated *phil-íp* or *tsup-tsup*. Often twitters while feeding or resting.
Status and Range: A common and widespread year-round resident on Jamaica where its range has steadily increased since the 1918 introduction near Old Harbour. Rare on Barbados where introduced during the early 1900s and unsuccessfully introduced on Martinique. Native to northern South America.
Comments: Forms chattering flocks that fly rapidly in close formation with much tilting. Feeds on a wide variety of flowers, fruits, buds and grass seed. It is sometimes a pest on grain crops such as corn.
Habitat: Mostly open country, particularly drier lowlands and hills to 500 m (1625'), but occurs at all elevations on Jamaica.
Nesting: Nests in tree cavities and eaves of houses. Eggs (4–7) white. Breeds from April to July.

CANARY-WINGED PARAKEET *Brotogeris versicolurus*   Plate 32
Local Name: Periquito Aliamarillo

Identification: 23 cm (9"). A small parakeet, though larger than a budgerigar, that when perched appears entirely green with the exception of its ivory-colored bill and a *yellow band bordering the wing*. The tail is long and pointed. *Flight*: The wings flash a large *whitish-yellow triangular patch* that is unmistakable.
Voice: High-pitched squawks.
Status and Range: Probably introduced to Puerto Rico during the 1950s, this parakeet is locally common on the island. It is the most successful of the introduced psittacines on Puerto Rico and can be seen in flocks of over 1,000 birds. Recently recorded from the Dominican Republic where its status is unknown. Native to northern and central South America.
Comments: Flocks move about feeding on seasonal fruits and sometimes cause damage to farmer's crops.
Habitat: Woodlands along the coast, low hills and the foothills of higher mountains. Also towns and urban areas.
Nesting: Three nests have been found, all excavated within termite nests located in trees or palms.

ROSE-THROATED PARROT *Amazona leucocephala*   Plate 31
Local Names: Bahama Parrot (Bahamas); Cayman Islands Parrot (CI); Cuban Parrot, Loro, Cotorra, Perico (Cuba)

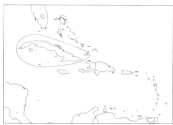

Identification: 28–33 cm (11–13"). A pigeon-sized parrot, green overall, with *chin, throat and lower part of face pale red. Forehead and eyering white* and primaries blue. Coloration is variable between islands. Often appears black in flight. *Similar species*: Hispaniolan Parrot, with which it does not overlap in range, has white restricted to the forehead and lacks red on the throat, upper breast and cheeks.

Voice: Very noisy, especially when perched in a flock. In flight, a harsh *squawk-squawk*. Vocalizations vary considerably among populations. In captivity, they easily learn to repeat words.

Status and Range: Native only to the Bahamas, Cuba and the Cayman Islands. In the Bahamas, it occurs only on Abaco and Great Inagua where it is fairly common. With protection, it has substantially increased in numbers on Abaco over the past 20 years. In 1995, it was estimated that approximately 800–1,100 parrots were present on Abaco. On Cuba, it is locally common in Guanahacabibes Peninsula, Zapata Swamp, Sierra de Najasa and some mountains of Oriente Province. Populations decreased dramatically on the Isle of Youth in the 1950s, but are now recovering. The parrot is fairly common in the Cayman Islands (Grand Cayman and Cayman Brac), but is at risk due to habitat destruction by humans and hurricanes and by harvesting for pets. Overall, the species has declined dramatically throughout its range and is considered threatened.

Comments: Parrots are desirable pets everywhere and Rose-throated Parrot is no exception. More than deforestation, the capture of fledglings has caused a considerable decrease of local populations. This is exacerbated by the destruction of nesting sites through felling of dead palms to obtain young birds. On Cuba and other Caribbean islands, this practice is forbidden, but clandestine collecting continues. These parrots usually gather in large flocks, splitting into pairs during the breeding season. Mainly eats fruits and seeds of many types of shrubs and trees, including oranges and other citrus. Sometimes a nuisance to farmers. Presently divided into five subspecies including two on Cuba, two in the Cayman Islands and one in the Bahamas.

Habitat: Strictly forests, but at all elevations.

Nesting: Mainly uses old woodpecker nest holes and dead palms that have lost their foliage. The Abaco population in the Bahamas has the unique behavior of nesting in limestone crevices in the ground. Eggs (3–4) white, almost round. Breeds from March to July.

YELLOW-BILLED PARROT *Amazona collaria*   Plates 30, 83
Local Name: Parrot

Identification: 28–31 cm (11–12"). Green overall, with a *yellow bill* and *white forehead band and eyering*. Look for the bluish forecrown and ear-coverts, maroon throat and base of tail and blue primaries and secondaries. Wingbeats shallow, below plane of back. *Similar species*: Black-billed Parrot has a dark bill and lacks maroon on the throat. Olive-throated Parakeet is smaller, with a long, pointed tail.

Voice: A high-pitched *tah-tah-eeeeep* when perched. A bugling *tuk-tuk-tuk-taaah* in flight which is lower pitched and the last syllable more drawn out than in Black-billed Parrot.

Status and Range: Endemic to Jamaica. It is locally common and widespread, more so than Black-billed Parrot. Particularly found in Cockpit Country, Mount Diablo and John Crow Mountains. A flock is established at Hope Gardens in Kingston. This parrot is declining as a result of collecting for the pet trade and habitat destruction. It is considered threatened.

Comments: A wary bird. Usually in pairs or small flocks. Feeds in the treetops on numerous types of seeds, fruits, berries and buds. Sometimes a pest to gardens and plantations. Appears confined to closed forests during the breeding season, but spreads out to feed in more open areas when not breeding.

Habitat: Primarily mid-elevation wet forests of hills and mountains.

Nesting: Nests high in a tree cavity, abandoned woodpecker hole or rock crevice. Eggs (2–4) white. Breeding believed to occur primarily from March to July, but nestlings reported as late as October.

HISPANIOLAN PARROT *Amazona ventralis*   Plates 31, 81
Local Names: Cotorra (DR); Cotorra Dominicana (PR); Jako, Jacquot, Perroquet (Haiti)

Identification: 28–31 cm (11–12"). Distinguished by its *bright green* overall, with a *white forehead*, dark ear-spot and maroon belly. *Flight*: Bright blue primaries and secondaries are visible. The flight is duck-like with rapid wingbeats, and the wings move below the plane of the back. *Similar species*: Resembles Rose-throated Parrot, but white restricted to the forehead and no red on throat, upper breast or cheeks. Their ranges do not overlap. Hispaniolan Parakeet is smaller with a long, pointed tail.
Voice: Loud bugling calls in flight; perch calls consist of loud squawkings and screeches.
Status and Range: Endemic to Hispaniola, including Grande Cayemite, Gonâve, Saona and Beata Islands. It was formerly common throughout the main island, but is now much reduced in numbers to the point of being extirpated or uncommon in most areas. This parrot is still locally common only in major forest reserves such as Parque del Este, Los Haitises, Jaragua and Bermudez/Ramirez. Hispaniolan Parrot occurs sparsely in Santo Domingo. The species is considered threatened due to habitat loss, hunting and harvesting for the pet trade. Introduced to Puerto Rico where locally common, especially in the western and north-central parts of the island.
Comments: Usually travels in pairs or flocks of up to several hundred birds. Normally feeds on seeds and fruits at middle to high levels in trees. Forms small to large foraging flocks that sometimes depredate crops, whereupon birds are shot or poisoned. Often roosts at higher elevations, descending to lower altitudes to feed. In great demand in the local and international pet trade, which has negatively affected most populations. Despite legislation and some vigorous efforts to curb that trade, parrots are still being harvested throughout the island. Trade is partly driven by the high price which these birds command on the international market.
Habitat: On Hispaniola, found at all elevations in forests, woodlands and scrub wherever suitable fruits and seeds are available and it is not heavily persecuted. On Puerto Rico, occurs in forests and woodlands of foothills.
Nesting: Nests in a tree cavity or, occasionally, a pothole in cliffs. Eggs (2–4) white. Breeds from February to June.

PUERTO RICAN PARROT *Amazona vittata*   Plates 31, 85
Local Names: Puerto Rican Amazon, Cotorra de Puerto Rico

Identification: 30 cm (12"). Identified by its *white eyering, red forehead* and *two-toned blue primaries*. *Similar species*: The very similar Red-crowned Parrot has more extensive red on the crown and an orange-red wing patch.
Voice: A wide variety of raucous squawks including a distinct bugling call which is issued only in flight.
Status and Range: The endemic Puerto Rican Parrot is critically endangered and is one of the rarest birds in the world. In 1975, only 13 parrots were known to survive in the wild, all in the rain forest of the Luquillo Mountains, in addition to eight birds in captivity. By 1989, the wild parrot population had increased to 48 birds, but Hurricane Hugo, which swept across Puerto Rico on September 18 of that year, nearly devastated the population, reducing it to approximately 20 to 22 birds. As of August 1996, Puerto Rican Parrot numbers 44 wild birds and 87 in captivity. The captive flock is split between aviaries in the Luquillo mountains and Río Abajo. The Puerto Rican Parrot's decline has been due to several factors. Principal among these was the cutting of lowland forests which destroyed most of the parrot's native habitat, particularly the huge old trees that contained rotten cavities essential for nesting. Parrots were also routinely shot by farmers as crop pests and were regularly collected and sold as pets. Other lesser factors affecting the parrot are the arboreal Brown or Roof Rat, the predatory Pearly-eyed Thrasher which preys on untended eggs and chicks, a warble fly (family Muscidae) which infests nestlings, and the Red-tailed Hawk. An endemic subspecies which formerly inhabited Culebra is now extinct.
Habitat: Formerly, most forested areas of mountains and lowlands. Presently, mid-elevation wet forests of eastern Puerto Rico which retain suitable nesting and feeding habitat.

Nesting: A large, deep tree cavity is used for nesting. Eggs (3–4) white. Breeds from late February through early June.

BLACK-BILLED PARROT *Amazona agilis*   Plates 30, 83
Local Name: Parrot

Identification: 26 cm (10"). Entirely green with a *blackish bill and eyering*. Flight feathers primarily blue. Some individuals have a *red patch in the wing* visible in flight. The base of the tail is red, and the wingbeats are shallow below the plane of the back. *Similar species*: Yellow-billed Parrot has a yellow bill, white eyering and maroon throat. Its wingbeats are slightly slower and deeper than those of Black-billed Parrot. Olive-throated Parakeet is smaller with a long, pointed tail.
Voice: Perched calls include *rrak* and *muh-weep* whereas its flight bugle is *tuh-tuk*. Also a sharp screech. Its calls are higher pitched than those of Yellow-billed Parrot.
Status and Range: Endemic to Jamaica. Fairly common in undisturbed habitat, particularly Mount Diablo and Cockpit Country. It is more scarce in eastern Jamaica. Sometimes found with Yellow-billed Parrot, but is less widely distributed. This parrot is threatened primarily as a result of habitat destruction and collecting for the pet trade.
Comments: Occurs both in pairs and flocks. Usually feeds high in treetops on fruits, berries, blossoms, nuts, seeds and occasionally plantains. Black-billed Parrot is smaller than Yellow-billed and has a substantially thinner bill. This suggests that the species may avoid competition by using different food resources.
Habitat: Mid-level moist forests of hills and mountains.
Nesting: Uses abandoned woodpecker holes and cavities in trees. Eggs (2–4) white. Breeds from March to June.

RED-CROWNED PARROT *Amazona viridigenalis*   Plate 31
Local Name: Cotorra Coronirroja

Identification: 30–33 cm (12–13"). Note the *red forecrown* and bright light green cheeks. *Flight*: *Orange-red wing patch* and blue primaries. *Similar species*: Puerto Rican Parrot has red only on the forehead and lacks the orange-red wing patch. The habitats of these two species are not known to overlap.
Voice: A distinct call, not nearly as raspy and raucous as most parrots, *keet, kau- kau-kau-kau.*
Status and Range: Introduced to Puerto Rico probably in the late 1960s, the species occurs in small numbers very locally around the coast. Near Salinas, as many as 40 birds have been reported in a single flock. Native from Mexico to northern South America.
Habitat: Lowland moist forests and scrub.
Nesting: Nests in a tree cavity. Eggs (2) white. Breeds from March to June.

ORANGE-WINGED PARROT *Amazona amazonica*   Plate 31
Local Name: Cotorra Alianaranjada (PR); Aourou (Mart)

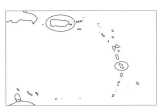

Identification: 32 cm (12.5"). Green overall. Identified by *yellow cheeks and crown* and blue lores and eyebrow stripe. *Flight*: Orange-red wing patch and blue primaries.
Voice: The call, *kweet, kweet, kweet, kweet* is higher pitched, weaker and less raucous than most other parrots in the West Indies.
Status and Range: Introduced to Puerto Rico probably in the late 1960s and to Martinique more recently, this species probably breeds on both islands. It is uncommon in metropolitan San Juan in small numbers and is unrecorded elsewhere on Puerto Rico. The species is moderately widespread

in central Martinique where breeding occurred in 1994. Native to Trinidad, Tobago and northern and central South America.
Habitat: Lowland second-growth forests.
Nesting: The nest is unknown on Puerto Rico.

YELLOW-HEADED PARROT *Amazona oratrix* **Plate 31**
Local Name: Cotorra Cabeziamarilla

Identification: 36 cm (14″). A large, primarily green parrot, it has *yellow on the head* which may cover most of the face or the entire head from the neck up. *Flight*: Red wing patch and blue primaries. *Similar species*: Several related parrots, specifically Yellow-crowned Parrot (*A. ochrocephala*) and Yellow-naped Parrot (*A. auropalliata*) were formerly lumped with Yellow-headed Parrot as a single species. Consequently, little attention was paid to differentiating them in the field. Yellow-crowned is distinguished by the presence of yellow only on its forecrown, whereas Yellow-naped has yellow confined to the hindneck. Yellow-crowned Parrot is illustrated to assist in identification even though its presence in the West Indies has not been confirmed.
Voice: Raucous squawks.
Status and Range: Introduced to Puerto Rico probably in the early 1970s, it is rare but known to breed. The species occurs very locally in small numbers along the north coast. Native to Mexico and Belize.
Habitat: Lowland second-growth forests.
Nesting: On Puerto Rico, a nest was located in a royal palm cavity. Eggs (2–4) white.

RED-NECKED PARROT *Amazona arausiaca* **Plates 30, 86**
Local Names: Jaco, Perroquet, Parrot

Identification: 33–36 cm (13–14″). Overall green with a blue crown, face and chin; *bright red spot on the throat* and a red wing patch. It is the smaller of the two parrots on Dominica.
Voice: The flight call is a two-syllable *rrr-eee*, like a drawn out hiccup. This call is also given while perched. Territorial counter-calls of Imperial Parrot include a variety of rolling trills, growls, squawks and chattering.
Status and Range: Endemic to Dominica where it is critically endangered, but increasing in numbers and expanding its range as a result of strict protection, law enforcement and education. From a low of about 150–300 individuals in 1980, approximately 1,000 birds now survive as estimated by the Forestry and Wildlife Division of Dominica. Considered locally common in the Northern Forest Reserve. Highest concentrations are in northeastern forests (Bense to Marigot Heights). Red-necked Parrot has become re-established in the south of the island after suffering severely from the ravages of Hurricane David in 1979 and Hurrican Allen in 1980. In recent years the parrot has extended its feeding and roosting range coastwards and is regularly seen in secondary forest and dry evergreen associations at elevations of 250 m (820′) or lower throughout the northern half of the island. Formerly, principal causes of its endangerment included habitat destruction, hunting for food, capturing of birds for local pets and the international pet trade and hurricanes. Beginning in the 1970s, Dominica has undertaken major efforts to conserve this parrot. Habitat destruction by humans and natural causes remain as the most critical threats.
Comments: Forages in the canopy on berries, nuts and seeds and occasionally is an agricultural pest on oranges and grapefruits. Pairs and family units are observed from June to September and form larger flocks of 15 or more birds in subsequent months until pairing to nest. Red-necked Parrot overlaps in range with Imperial Parrot in several forests of Dominica. The Syndicate Estate in the Morne Diablotin Forest Reserve and the section of the Northern Forest Reserve adjacent to that estate are two of the best areas for viewing the parrot.
Habitat: Moist primary rain forests, generally at mid-elevations (300–500 m) where it overlaps to some extent with Imperial Parrot. Overall, Imperial Parrot tends to occupy higher elevations than Red-necked Parrot.
Nesting: Nests in a tree cavity, predominantly in *Sloanea*, *Decryodes* and *Amanoa*. Eggs (2) white. Breeds from February to June, but primarily March to May. Typically raises two young per brood.

ST LUCIA PARROT *Amazona versicolor*   **Plates 30, 34**
Local Name: Jacquot

Identification: 42–46 cm (16.5–18"). *Adult*: Field marks are its mostly green upperparts and underparts; *violet-blue forehead, cheeks and forecrown*; *red band across throat extending down the center of the breast* and green wings with *violet-blue primaries* and a *red patch*. **Status and Range**: Endemic to St Lucia, it is uncommon and local. Critically endangered primarily as a result of habitat destruction, hunting and capturing parrots for local pets and the international pet trade. Reduced to approximately 100 birds in the wild during the late 1970s, the population has rebounded to about 300 individuals in 1990. This increase is due to an extraordinary public education program begun in the 1970s by the St Lucia Forestry Department.
Comments: Feeds in the forest canopy on a wide variety of fruits, seeds and flowers. May travel considerable distances to feed on favorite fruiting trees. Roosts deep in the forest, flying out to the forest edges to forage during the day.
Habitat: Primarily moist forests in mountains. Also secondary forests and cultivated areas.
Nesting: Nests in a cavity in a tall tree. Eggs (2) white. Breeds primarily from February to May.

ST VINCENT PARROT *Amazona guildingii*   **Plates 30, 35**
Local Name: Parrot

Identification: 41–46 cm (16–18"). A large, dramatically patterned parrot, variable in coloration, with two major color phases — one predominantly green and one golden-brown. Intermediates between the two occur. *Adult*: Upperparts mostly dull greenish or golden brown, *creamy white forehead shades to orange-yellow on hindcrown*, violet-blue cheeks and *black wings with yellow-orange patches which are conspicuous in flight*. Tail is orange at base with a wide central band of violet and a broad yellow tip. *Immature*: Plumage greener overall.
Voice: The flight call is a loud, somewhat un-parrot-like *gua, gua, gua* ... Reputedly, there is some variation between the parrot's calls on the east and west sides of the island.
Status and Range: An uncommon endemic to St Vincent where it is critically endangered. Occurs primarily in the upper reaches of the Buccament, Cumberland and Wallilibou valleys. From 440 to 500 birds were estimated to survive in 1988. Occasionally breeds near the eastern windward coast. The species is endangered primarily as a result of clearing mature forests for agriculture and the selective cutting of nest trees for charcoal, thus reducing suitable habitat for the parrot. The local government is striving to reduce the taking of chicks and the practice of 'wing-shooting' adults as a means of supplying the local and foreign pet trade. Hunting has also been a factor in this parrot's decline.
Comments: Feeds in the forest canopy primarily on a wide variety of fruits, seeds and flowers. Flocks in some valleys appear isolated to the extent that their calls and ratios of color phases differ.
Habitat: Mature moist mountain forests.
Nesting: Nests in a cavity high up in a tall tree, typically a gommier (*Dacryodes excelsa*). Eggs (2) white. Breeds primarily from March to June, but eggs are sometimes laid as early as January.

IMPERIAL PARROT *Amazona imperialis*   **Plates 30, 33**
Local Name: Sisserou

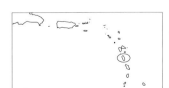

Identification: 46–51 cm (18–20"). A large, dark-colored parrot. *Adult*: Upperparts mostly green, edged with pale gray; head dark maroon-purple; dark violet band on hindneck which appears black in low light; wings green with red speculum and primaries dull violet-blue. The tail is dull reddish-brown with a greenish-blue tip, and underparts from breast to abdomen are purple-violet.
Voice: The flight call is a distinctive, trumpeting, metallic *eeeee-er* that descends at the end. Also shrieks, squawks, whistles and bubbly trills while perched. More shrill and metallic than Red-necked Parrot.
Status and Range: Critically endangered. Endemic to Dominica where it is uncommon and local. An estimated 300 birds survive, primarily on the northeast and southeast slopes of Morne Diablotin

above 500 m (1600') in the Northern Forest Reserve. Population numbers are difficult to ascertain because of the bird's secretive nature and the largely inaccessible areas they inhabited in the past, Causes of its endangerment primarily included habitat destruction, hunting for food, capturing birds for local pets and the international pet trade, and the hurricanes of 1979 and 1980. Since the 1970s, Dominica has taken major steps to conserve this parrot and the man-made threats mentioned above have been largely eliminated. Currently natural disasters such as hurricanes and competition with Red-necked Parrot for nest cavities constitute the primary threats.

Comments: Cryptic for an Amazon parrot; does not form noisy flocks, but usually stays in family groups of two to four birds which move quietly about the forest in the underside of the canopy feeding on various fruits.

Habitat: Mid- and high elevation wet forests. It generally occurs at higher elevations than Red-necked Parrot, although in foraging for food the Sisserou frequently descends to lower elevations where it interacts with Red-necked Parrot.

Nesting: Nests in cavities high up in tall trees, primarily *Sloaena*. Eggs (2) white. Breeds from February to July with a peak from March to May with fledging occurring from late July to early August. Typically raises only one young per brood.

CUCKOOS, ROADRUNNERS AND ANIS:
FAMILY CUCULIDAE

Cuckoos are slender birds with long tails and long, thin bills that are somewhat down-curved. They are very slow and deliberate in their movements among the branches and their flight is direct. Many species, though not those in this region, are brood parasites, laying their eggs in the nests of other birds. The anis, which are confined to the tropics and subtropics of this hemisphere, form an unusual assemblage of three species within the Cuculidae. All are black with a characteristic heavy bill and have the unique communal nesting habit described for the Smooth-billed Ani.

BLACK-BILLED CUCKOO *Coccyzus erythropthalmus*   Plate 39
Local Names: Primavera de Pico Negro (Cuba); Pájaro Bobo Pico Negro (DR)

Identification: 30 cm (12"). Slender with a long, white-tipped tail; white underparts; long, dark, down-curved bill; reddish eyering and wing-coverts entirely gray-brown. **Similar species**: The very similar Yellow-billed Cuckoo lacks a truly red eyering, has reddish-brown in the primaries and more conspicuous white markings under the tail. Mangrove Cuckoo has a black ear patch and buff-colored lower underparts. Immature Black-billed Cuckoos in September and October may have some yellow in the bill, have a yellowish eyering and even have some reddish-brown in their primaries. These birds can be distinguished from Yellow-billed Cuckoo by their pale gray undertails which lack distinctive white spots.

Voice: A series of three to four notes *cu-cu-cu-cu.*

Status and Range: A regular, but rare migrant on Cuba and Hispaniola, very rare in the northern Bahamas (New Providence, Andros and Grand Bahama) and a vagrant on Jamaica, Puerto Rico, the Cayman Islands and in the Lesser Antilles on Antigua, Dominica, St Lucia and Barbados. Occurs from September to November and April to May. Likely more regular in the Bahamas than records indicate. Ranges from eastern North America to northern South America.

Habitat: Scrublands, mangrove forests and both dry and moist forests in the lowlands.

YELLOW-BILLED CUCKOO *Coccyzus americanus*   Plate 39
Local Names: May Bird (Jamaica); Rain Crow (LA); Rain Bird (Jamaica, LA); Arrierito (Cuba); Pájaro Bobo Piquiamarillo (PR); Primavera (Cuba, DR); Ti Tako Vant Blan (Haiti); Coulicou à Bec Jaune (Guad, Mart); Geelsnavelkoekoek (St E, St M)

Identification: 28–32 cm (11–12.5"). Distinguished by its completely white underparts and absence of black on the cheek. It has a long, white-tipped tail and long, down-curved bill that is yellow at the base. **Flight**: The *reddish-brown wing patch* is diagnostic. **Similar species**: Mangrove Cuckoo has

a black ear patch and a buff-colored abdomen. Black-billed Cuckoo lacks yellow in the bill and reddish-brown in the wing.
Voice: A throaty *ka-ka-ka-ka-ka-ka-ka-ka-ka-kow, kow, kow, kow* (or *kowp, kowp, kowp* at end). The volume increases initially, then remains constant. The call slows substantially during the final syllables.
Status and Range: A rather uncommon breeding resident from May to August on Cuba, Hispaniola and Puerto Rico and rarely on Jamaica and the Virgin Islands. May possibly breed in the Bahamas and has bred in the northern Lesser Antilles on St Martin. During September and October, it migrates southward joined by birds from North America. The returning northbound migration occurs in March and April. Very few birds occur from November to February in the West Indies. During migration, these cuckoos sometimes pass through the West Indies in large concentrations. As a migrant, this cuckoo is common in the southern Bahamas, Cuba, Hispaniola and Puerto Rico; uncommon in the northern Bahamas, the Cayman Islands and Jamaica; rare in the Virgin Islands and varies from uncommon to rare through the Lesser Antilles. Occurs from the United States to South America.
Habitat: Lowland scrub and dry forests, generally not at higher elevations.
Nesting: A flimsy, cup-shaped nest of twigs and dried grass is usually constructed low in a bush. Eggs (2–5) blue. Breeds from April to July.

MANGROVE CUCKOO *Coccyzus minor*   Plate 39
Local Names: Sour-sop Bird (Antigua); Old Man Crackers (Jamaica); Cat Bird, Coffin Bird (LA); Mani Coco (VI); Rainbird (CI, Grenada, Jamaica, VI, LA); Cowbird (Jamaica, LA); Arrierito (Cuba); Primavera, Pájaro Bobo (DR); Pájaro Bobo Menor (PR); Ti Tako (Haiti); Cuckoo Manioc, Cou-cou Maicoc (Grenada, St V); Coulicou Masqué, Gangan, Coucou Manioc (Guad, Mart, St L); Mangrovekoekoek (St M)

Identification: 28–30 cm (11–12"). Note the *black ear patch* and buff-colored abdomen. The bird is slender with a long, white-tipped tail and long, down-curved bill that is yellow at the base. *Flight*: Direct with short glides. No reddish-brown in wings. *Similar species*: All other cuckoos lack the black ear patch. Yellow-billed and Black-billed Cuckoos have white underparts. All Lizard-Cuckoos are much larger.
Voice: Similar to that of Yellow-billed Cuckoo, but slower and more nasal.
Status and Range: Generally a fairly common year-round resident thoughout the West Indies, though on Cuba it occurs primarily in the east where it is uncommon and confined to a few coastal localities and cays. It also occurs on the southeastern tip of the United States, in Central America and northern South America.
Comments: Arboreal and not very active, this inconspicuous bird is usually located by its call.
Habitat: Usually dry scrub, but also mangroves, shade coffee plantations and most areas with substantial forests or thickets except for high mountains.
Nesting: Builds a flimsy stick nest in a tree. Eggs (2–3) blue. Breeds from February to June.

GREAT LIZARD-CUCKOO *Saurothera merlini*   Plate 39
Local Names: Rain Crow, Big Rain Crow, Kataw (Bahamas); Arriero, Tacó, Guacaica (Cuba)

Identification: 44–55 cm (17–22"). A large cuckoo with a long, tapered tail; tail feathers tipped with large, white spots. Bill long and only slightly down-curved. Wings dark reddish-brown on Cuba and lacking the reddish tint in the Bahamas. Brownish or grayish upperparts with a buff or pale reddish-brown abdomen. Red around eye. *Similar species*: The three other cuckoos on Cuba and the Bahamas (Mangrove, Yellow-billed and Black-billed) are much smaller and have relatively shorter, more curved bills.
Voice: Two typical calls. One is short and loud with a guttural resonance, *tacóó...tacóó*. The other is long, loud and increases in strength, *ka-ka-ka-ka-ka...* the

latter is faster, longer and louder than the similar call of Mangrove Cuckoo.

Status and Range: Unique to Cuba and the Bahamas. It is common and widespread throughout Cuba, including the Isle of Youth, and the larger cays north of Camagüey Province. In the Bahamas, it is uncommon and limited to Andros, Eleuthera and New Providence.

Comments: Generally solitary and very tame on Cuba, but very secretive in the Bahamas. This bird is not as large as it looks due to its very long tail. It glides more than flies, but is capable of flying quite long stretches. While foraging, the tail dangles down. Sometimes descends to the ground when pursuing prey and runs with tail straight, resembling a mongoose, especially when crossing roads. Feeds on a wide variety of prey, including fruits, but mainly lizards, small snakes, frogs and sometimes mice. The female is larger than the male which may result in some differences in feeding habits between the sexes. Some country people claim that boiling this species in soup improves a person's appetite. It is also believed that the bird calls on the hour. Four subspecies are recognized.

Habitat: Wooded areas at all altitudes, but mainly in bushy country with plenty of vines and dense vegetation.

Nesting: The cup-shaped nest, which is rather small for such a large bird, is well hidden among dense vegetation not high above the ground. Eggs (3) white with a shiny luster. Breeds from April to October.

PUERTO RICAN LIZARD-CUCKOO *Saurothera vieilloti* **Plates 39, 85**
Local Names: Pájaro Bobo Mayor, Pájara Boba, Pájaro de Lluvia (PR)

Identification: 40–48 cm (16–19"). Its large size, very long tail and two-toned underparts are good field marks. *Adult*: Gray on chin and breast; cinnamon-colored belly and undertail-coverts. *Immature*: Cinnamon wash, rather than gray, on the breast. *Similar species*: Mangrove Cuckoo is much smaller and has a black ear patch.

Voice: An emphatic *ka-ka-ka-ka...* of long duration gradually accelerating and becoming louder, sometimes with altered syllables at the end. Also soft *caws* and other call notes.

Status and Range: A fairly common though inconspicuous endemic to Puerto Rico occurring at all elevations. A single specimen, apparently a stray bird, is known from the Virgin Islands (St Thomas).

Comments: More often heard than seen, this species is quite inactive, often sitting quietly among dense vegetation showing little alarm at one's approach. Its diet consists entirely of animal matter, primarily small lizards, but also large spiders and insects. Locally it is often called the 'Pájaro de Lluvia' (Rain Bird) because its call is believed to forecast rain.

Habitat: The haystack hills of the north coast, shade coffee plantations, all mountainous areas with thick forests and the dry coastal forests in the vicinity of Guánica.

Nesting: The nest is a loose structure built of sticks and leaves. Eggs (2–3) white. Breeding appears to occur throughout the year based on the limited data available.

HISPANIOLAN LIZARD-CUCKOO **Plates 39, 81**
Saurothera longirostris
Local Names: Pájaro Bobo, Tacot (DR); Tako (Haiti)

Identification: 41–46 cm (16–18"). The large size; *pale gray breast*; long tail with white tips and a straight, slender bill identify it. Has a reddish-brown wing patch. Throat varies from whitish (Gonâve Island) to dull orange (mainland Hispaniola). *Similar species*: Bay-breasted Cuckoo has a dark reddish-brown breast.

Voice: A prolonged throaty *ka-ka-ka-ka-ka-ka-ka-ka-kau-kau-ko-ko* in descending tones. Also a guttural *tuc-wuh-h*.

Status and Range: Endemic to Hispaniola, including Saona, Gonâve and Tortue Islands, where it is common. Occurs from sea level to elevations above 1200 m (4000')

Comments: Often seen moving deliberately through the vegetation where it pursues lizards and larger insects. It forages from the understory to the forest canopy.

Habitat: Widely distributed in forested and wooded areas, including plantations of shade coffee.

Nesting: A well-hidden rough structure of twigs, situated at a moderate height. Eggs (2–3) white. Breeds from March to June.

JAMAICAN LIZARD-CUCKOO *Saurothera vetula* **Plates 39, 83**
Local Names: Old Woman Bird, May Bird, Rain Bird, Ring Tail, Sawdering

Identification: 38 cm (15″). A rather large, long-tailed bird with a very long, almost *straight bill*. The lower underparts are a pale reddish-brown. Has a *reddish-brown wing patch* and red eyering. Tail feathers have large, white tips. *Similar species*: Chestnut-bellied Cuckoo is larger, has a down-curved bill and lacks the reddish-brown wing patch and red eyering. Mangrove and Yellow-billed Cuckoos are smaller; the former has a black ear patch and the latter shows uniform white underparts.
Voice: Rapid, low, trailing *cak-cak-cak-ka-ka-ka-k-k* (Downer and Sutton). Higher pitched, faster and longer in length than that of Chestnut-bellied Cuckoo.
Status and Range: Endemic to Jamaica where common, but less so than Chestnut-bellied Cuckoo. Widespread; most common at Mona and Ferry River, but also frequent at Mount Diablo, Cockpit Country, Hardwar Gap, John Crow Mountains and Mandeville. Infrequent above 1200 m (3900′).
Comments: Moves slowly through the understory peering here and there and feeding on a wide range of animal matter from insects to lizards. It sometimes probes for its prey. More often heard than seen.
Habitat: Primarily moist or wet mid-elevation forests, second-growth woodlands and wooded ravines.
Nesting: A shallow nest of loose twigs lined with leaves is constructed among dense vegetation at a low to medium height. Eggs (3–4) dull white. Breeds from March to August.

CHESTNUT-BELLIED CUCKOO *Hyetornis pluvialis* **Plates 39, 83**
Local Names: Old Man Bird, Hunter, Rain Bird, May Bird

Identification: 48–56 cm (19–22″). A large, long-tailed bird with a *down-curved bill*. Note its primarily *reddish underparts*, except for the pale gray throat and upper breast. Tail feathers broadly tipped with white. *Similar species*: Jamaican Lizard-Cuckoo is smaller, with a nearly straight bill, reddish-brown wing patch and pale reddish-brown lower underparts. Mangrove and Yellow-billed Cuckoos are much smaller and lack the dark reddish-brown belly.
Voice: A throaty, accelerating *quawk-quawk-ak-ak-ak-ak-ak*, slower, deeper and shorter than that of Jamaican Lizard-Cuckoo. Also a soft *qua*.
Status and Range: Endemic to Jamaica where common in mountain forests.
Comments: Feeds on a wide array of animal prey, including insects, lizards, bird nestlings and eggs and small mammals. Moves slowly through the forest, sometimes running along tree limbs. More often heard than seen.
Habitat: Open, wet forests at mid-elevations. Also open woodlands, dense second-growth forests and gardens generally between 400–1500 m (1300–4900′). Infrequent in the lowlands, mostly in the non-breeding season.
Nesting: A twig nest is built in a bush or tree. Eggs (2–4) white. Breeds from March to June.

BAY-BREASTED CUCKOO *Hyetornis rufigularis* **Plates 39, 40, 81**
Local Names: Cúa, Tacot (DR); Tako Kabrit, Tacot Cabrite (Haiti)

Identification: 43–51 cm (17–20″). A large, active cuckoo distinguished by its *dark reddish-brown throat and breast* and thick, curved bill. Also has a reddish-brown wing patch and a very long tail with white feather tips. *Similar species*: Hispaniolan Lizard-Cuckoo has a pale gray breast.
Voice: A strong *cua*, followed by a guttural, accelerating *u-ak-u-ak-ak-ak-ak-ak- ak.ak*.
Status and Range: Endemic to Hispaniola, including Gonâve Island, where it is rare. In the Dominican Republic, its distribution has become very local and it has declined to the point of endangerment,

in part because of habitat destruction and also due to being hunted for medicinal purposes.
Comments: Retiring. Feeds on insects, lizards, frogs, small mammals and bird eggs and nestlings. Believed by some local people in the Dominican Republic to cure arthritic and other body pains.
Habitat: Primarily low to moderate elevations in dry deciduous forests, but also found locally from arid lowlands to mountain rain forests.
Nesting: A nest is constructed at a low to moderate height in a bush or dense tree. Eggs (2) dirty white. Breeds from March to June.

SMOOTH-BILLED ANI *Crotophaga ani*   Plate 39
Local Names: Crow (Bahamas); Black Arnold (CI); Old Witch (Grenada); Black Parrot, Tick Bird, Savanne Blackbird (Jamaica); Black Witch (VI); Old Arnold (CI, VI); Garrapatero (PR); Judío (Cuba, DR, PR); Boustabak, Bout-de-tabac (Haiti); Grote Ani (St E); Merle Corbeau (Grenada, St L); Ani à Bec Lisse, Bilbitin, Merle, Juif (Guad, Mart)

Identification: 30–33 cm (12–13"). A large, entirely black bird with a very heavy, *parrot-like bill*. Its conspicuous long, flat tail helps distinguish it. **Flight**: Straight, with rapid, but shallow wing strokes followed by short glides.
Voice: A very loud and conspicuous squawky whistle *a-leep*.
Status and Range: A common year-round resident in the Bahamas, Greater Antilles, Virgin and Cayman Islands and Providencia. Its status in the Lesser Antilles is variable ranging from being common on Dominica, St Vincent and Grenada; uncommon on Martinique and Guadeloupe; and rare or absent on the remaining islands. Smooth-billed Ani is rare on San Andrés. Also occurs on the southeastern tip of the United States, and from southwest Costa Rica through most of South America.
Comments: Typically in small, noisy flocks. Often lands clumsily. Numbers seem to fluctuate significantly on small islands, being absent for a time, recolonizing and then disappearing again.
Habitat: A wide range of open lowland habitats with scattered trees or bushes.
Nesting: Smooth-billed Ani, along with the other two members of its genus, is unique in the bird world in building a bulky nest which is sometimes used communally by several females. Twenty or more eggs are regularly found in a single nest with groups of four to five eggs being laid in layers separated by leaves. Only the top layer of eggs hatch. The eggs are sky blue with a chalky white coating that is easily scratched off. Apparently breeds year-round.

BARN OWLS: FAMILY TYTONIDAE

The barn owls form a small family of widely distributed birds. They have a heart-shaped facial disk, long legs and exhibit habits very similar to the typical owls. Barn owls are highly nocturnal and primarily depend on their acute sense of hearing to locate prey. More fossil than living species are known, including gigantic flightless forms.

BARN OWL *Tyto alba*   Plate 36
Local Names: Jumbie Bird (LA); Patoo, Kritch Owl, Scritch Owl, White Owl (Jamaica); Screech Owl (CI, Jamaica, LA); Jumpy Bird (Grenada, St C, St V); Lechuza Común, Lechuza Blanca (DR); Lechuza (Cuba, PR); Frize, Fresaie (Haiti); Chat-huant (LA)

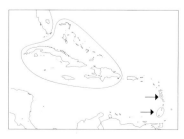

Identification: 30–43 cm (12–17"). A large nocturnal owl with a flat, heart-shaped face and large dark eyes. Birds in the Greater Antilles (*T. a. furcata*) are pale colored, with light orange-brown upperparts and mostly white underparts. Lesser Antillean birds (*T. a. insularia*) are much darker, with dark grayish-brown upperparts, pale brown head and buffy underparts.
Similar species: Jamaican Owl is smaller and much darker, with ear tufts. Ashy-faced Owl is darker overall and its heart-shaped face is silver-gray, rather than white.
Voice: A loud, hissing screech, as well as loud, clicking sounds.

Status and Range: A common year-round resident on Cuba, Jamaica, Hispaniola and Dominica; uncommon in the Bahamas and the Cayman Islands and rare on St Vincent, the Grenadines and Grenada. Small numbers of birds that breed in North America occur in the Bahamas, Cuba, Jamaica and Hispaniola and as a vagrant on Puerto Rico from October to March. It is widespread worldwide.
Comments: Nocturnal. Sometimes perches on fence posts, especially in rice fields.
Habitat: A wide range of relatively open areas from the coast to the mountains including rice fields, dry scrublands, open woodlands and human settlements.
Nesting: No nest is built. The eggs are usually laid in a cavity of a dead tree, a palm on a cave ledge or in a church steeple. Eggs (2–8) white. Breeds in all months, but primarily from August to April.

ASHY-FACED OWL *Tyto glaucops*   Plates 36, 81
Local Names: Lechuza Común (DR); Frize (Haiti)

Identification: 35 cm (14"). A reddish-brown, long-legged owl, with a *silver-gray, heart-shaped face*. **Similar species**: Barn Owl has a white facial disk and underparts.
Voice: A hissing cry, prefaced by a series of high-pitched, ratchety clicks.
Status and Range: Endemic to Hispaniola where it is fairly widespread and common locally. In the Dominican Republic, it is common particularly in and around Santo Domingo, los Haitises, the southeastern portion of the island and throughout the Barahona Peninsula, especially in coastal forests south of Barahona near limestone cliffs where it likely nests.
Comments: Nocturnal. Feeds on rodents, bats, lizards, frogs and birds.
Habitat: Open woodlands, scrub and dry and moist forests.
Nesting: The nest is formed of an accumulation of prey remains on a ledge, in a sinkhole or cave. Eggs (4–7) white, unmarked. Breeds from January to June.

TYPICAL OWLS: FAMILY STRIGIDAE

The typical owls are nocturnal birds of prey (though some may be seen abroad during the day) that complement the hawks which are daytime predators. They are characterized by a distinctive facial disk, a large head with the eyes directed forward and silent flight. Owls swallow their food whole and regurgitate bones, feathers and insect wings in a compact pellet.

PUERTO RICAN SCREECH-OWL *Otus nudipes*   Plates 36, 85
Local Names: Cuckoo Bird (VI); Múcaro de Puerto Rico, Múcaro Común (PR)

Identification: 23–25 cm (9–10"). The only small owl on Puerto Rico and the Virgin Islands. Grayish-brown above, white below marked with heavy brown streaks. Some birds are decidedly more reddish-brown than others. A rare gray phase inhabits dry forests. Ear tufts are not noticeable except when the bird is alarmed.
Voice: Usually a tremulous trill, though sometimes it chatters, whoops or emits a maniacal laugh.
Status and Range: Endemic to Puerto Rico where it is common and in the Virgin Islands where it is very rare. Its distribution is limited by the availability of trees with adequate roosting and nesting cavities. This owl is probably extirpated from Vieques where it was reported only once, but it may occur in small numbers on Culebra. Recorded in the Virgin Islands from St Thomas, St John, St Croix, Virgin Gorda, Tortola and possibly Guana Island. The subspecies endemic to the Virgin Islands, Vieques and Culebra is critically endangered primarily due to habitat loss and likely also to predation on its eggs by the Pearly-eyed Thrasher.
Comments: Completely nocturnal and is seen during the day only when flushed from a dense thicket or tree cavity in which it roosts. However, the species actively calls in the evening and early morning. Calling birds are attracted by imitating a squeaking mouse. Puerto Rican folklore suggests

that this owl feeds on coffee beans and that it can be used as a cure for asthma. There is no scientific support for either of these contentions.

Habitat: All types of forests from wet and wooded areas of the mountains to isolated dense tree stands on the coast.

Nesting: In a tree cavity. Eggs (2) white. Breeds from April to June.

BARE-LEGGED OWL *Gymnoglaux lawrencii*　　　　Plates 36, 80
Local Names: Sijú Cotunto, Cotunto, Cuco

Identification: 20–23 cm (8–9″). A plump, rather small owl with a big head; very large, *dark brown eyes*; a conspicuous beige eyebrow stripe; short tail and long, naked, greenish legs. Brownish overall, speckled with white. **Similar species**: In size and appearance much like a Burrowing Owl but has whiter underparts which are streaked, rather than barred, and has dark eyes. Also its habitat is completely different since Burrowing Owl lives in open areas and occurs on or near the ground. Cuban Pygmy-Owl is smaller with yellow eyes and feathered legs.

Voice: The most distinctive call is a *cu-cu-cu-cucucu*, given in a low and repeated sequence reminiscent of the sound of a bouncing ball. The female sometimes gives a harsh, plaintive scream that resembles the call of female Stygian Owl.

Status and Range: Endemic to Cuba and the Isle of Youth where it is rather common. Rare on Cayo Romano, Cayo Coco and probably on Guajaba and Sabinal.

Comments: Strictly nocturnal. During the day, it hides in holes and cavities of trees or in caves. Usually occurs in pairs. Flies only short distances on short, rounded wings. Feeds mainly on large insects including moths and also on frogs and rarely small birds. A separate race inhabits the Isle of Youth.

Habitat: Strictly woods or large tree plantations close to woods.

Nesting: Like Cuban Pygmy-Owl, the Bare-legged Owl does not build a nest, but takes advantage of cavities in broken tree limbs, trees and dead palms without foliage, as well as abandoned woodpecker holes. Also nests in caves, sheltered areas and crevices. Eggs (usually 2) white, similar to those of Cuban Pygmy-Owl, but a bit larger. Breeds from January to June.

CUBAN PYGMY-OWL *Glaucidium siju*　　　　Plates 36, 80
Local Names: Sijú Platanero, Sijú Sijucito

Identification: 17.5 cm (7″). The smallest raptor in Cuba. No bigger than a ground-dove, but much plumper with a big head and large yellow eyes. Very short, yellow feet covered with feathers, but very large for the bird's size. The short tail is often twitched sideways. Two dark spots on the back of the head resemble eyes. The underparts are white speckled with tan. There are two color phases: grayish-brown upperparts and cinnamon-brown upperparts. **Similar species**: Burrowing Owl is much larger, primarily terrestrial and has long, unfeathered legs. Bare-legged Owl has dark eyes and bare legs.

Voice: Usually a low and sporadically repeated *uh, uh, uh...*, syllables short and rather plaintive. The male, especially during breeding season, gives the most peculiar and unusual call *hui-hui-chiii-chiii-chi-chi-chi...*, increasing in strength. Very atypical of an owl.

Status and Range: Endemic to Cuba and the Isle of Youth where it is rather common. Rare in some of the large cays north of Camagüey (Coco and Romano).

Comments: A tame owl active both day and night. Usually found in pairs, but the individuals keep somewhat distant from one another. It flies short distances on stubby, rounded wings. Has the peculiar habit of turning its head almost completely around, showing the spots that mimic eyes on the back of the head. Feeds mainly on lizards and large insects, including moths. A local race (*G. s. vittatum*) occurs on the Isle of Youth.

Habitat: Woods and tree plantations.

Nesting: Nests in natural cavities in trees or abandoned holes of woodpeckers. Eggs (3 to 4) white, almost round, with very little luster. Breeds primarily from December to April.

BURROWING OWL *Athene cunicularia* **Plate 36**
Local Names: Cuckoo Bird (Bahamas); Sijú de Sabana (Cuba); Cucu (DR); Koukou, Chouette à Terrier (Haiti)

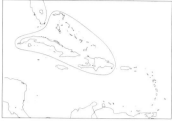

Identification: 23 cm (9″). A small, long-legged owl, most readily distinguished by its habits of often being out in broad daylight, standing on open ground or perched on a low post. Conspicuously bobs when approached. *Adult*: Mottled brown and white overall, barred underparts. *Immature*: Buffy below rather than heavily barred. *Flight*: Rapid and low to ground; usually flies a short distance and frequently hovers. *Similar species*: No other small owl in the Bahamas or on Hispaniola. Cuban Pygmy-Owl is much smaller, arboreal and has short, feathered legs. Bare-legged Owl has whiter, streaked rather than barred underparts, and dark eyes.

Voice: A soft, high-pitched, two-note *coo-coooo*. When alarmed, gives a clucking chatter.
Status and Range: A fairly common year-round resident through most of the Bahamas, though declining on Grand Bahama and New Providence. A locally common year-round resident in western Cuba, particularly in southeastern Pinar del Río, La Fé, Cortés, La Palma, Matanzas and Jauco, but also Guantánamo, Isle of Youth and several cays of the Sabana-Camagüey Archipelago. A common year-round resident in the western half of Hispaniola, including Gonâve and Beata Islands. Extirpated from St Christopher, Antigua and Marie-Galante off Guadeloupe. Possibly still present on Nevis. Occurs through North, Central and South America.
Comments: Nocturnal when not breeding. Feeds on insects, large spiders, lizards, frogs and small birds.
Habitat: Open scrubby areas, sandy pine savannas and pastures. Sometimes golf courses. In the Dominican Republic, occurs in mountain limestone ravines up to 600 m (2000′).
Nesting: Singly or in scattered colonies, the nest is a 1–2.5 m (3–8′) deep burrow in sandy soil. Earth excavated by owls makes a large mound at the entrance and is used by the adults as a look-out point. Eggs (3–8) glossy white. Breeds from December to July.

STYGIAN OWL *Asio stygius* **Plate 36**
Local Names: Lechuza Orejita (DR); Siguapa (Cuba, DR); Maitre-bois, Mèt Bwa, Chouette (Haiti)

Identification: 41–46 cm (16–18″). Identified by its *large size*, *very dark coloration* and conspicuous *ear tufts*. *Similar species*: All other West Indian owls are smaller, lighter colored and lack or have very short ear tufts.
Voice: Generally silent; occasionally gives one loud, abrupt *hu!*, as if to scare someone. During the breeding season, the male calls with a low-pitched *fool* repeated at regular intervals, and the female answers with a higher-pitched *niek*.
Status and Range: A rare year-round resident on Cuba where there are extensive forests and woodlands, including La Güira, Pinar del Río and Topes de Collantes. Generally very rare on Hispaniola, including Gonâve Island, though it is locally uncommon in portions of the Dominican Republic such as Parque Bermudez/Ramirez in the Cordillera Central and pine forests of the southwest. The Cuban subspecies is endangered and the Hispaniolan race critically so, primarily due to forest destruction, but also hunting. It is possible that the demise of most of the two island's native mammal faunas, a likely food source for this owl, also has hastened its decline. Also occurs from Mexico to South America.
Comments: Secretive and difficult to detect on Hispaniola, whereas much more easily located on Cuba where it is more vocal. Feeds on large insects, small crabs, reptiles and small rodents. Stygian Owl has been persecuted by local people who believe it has supernatural powers and can transform itself into a witch. Its call is considered a bad omen.
Habitat: Dense deciduous and pine forests, from semi-arid to humid and from sea level to mountains.
Nesting: On Cuba, reported to nest high in trees in a hawk-like nest. Eggs (perhaps 2) white. Breeds from April to May on Hispaniola. The breeding season is unknown on Cuba.

SHORT-EARED OWL *Asio flammeus*   **Plate 36**
Local Names: Cárabo (Cuba); Lechuza de Sabana (DR); Múcaro Real (PR); Chat-huant (Haiti)

Identification: 35–43 cm (14–17"). Tan below; heavy streaking on the breast is reduced on the abdomen. Note its yellow iris and distinct facial disk. Most easily identified by its large size and habits of perching on posts and flying low over fields. *Flight*: Alternately flaps and glides in a somewhat erratic pattern. This owl shows conspicuous black wrist patches on whitish underwings and large buff patches on the upperwings. **Voice**: A short, emphatic *bow-wow*. Also a distinct noise produced by clapping its wings together beneath its body.
Status and Range: A locally common year-round resident on Cuba and Hispaniola and uncommon on Puerto Rico, the species has increased dramatically in recent decades on the former two islands. Decidedly rare in the Cayman Islands. A vagrant on Grand Turk in the Bahamas, the Virgin Islands and St Barthélemy. It is widespread worldwide.
Comments: Most active at dawn and dusk, it has the distinctive habit of flying low over open areas in search of prey. Sometimes observed on fence posts or low bushes, it takes cover under the latter during the day. West Indian birds appear not to vary among islands, but differ from continental forms in plumage and vocalizations. This has led to the suggestion that the West Indian form be considered a separate species.
Habitat: Open country in the lowlands including pastures, short-grass marshlands, savannas, rice fields and citrus plantations.
Nesting: The nest is in a scrape under a bush or thick clump of grass. Eggs (3–4) white. Breeding is primarily from April to June, but has been recorded as early as December.

JAMAICAN OWL *Pseudoscops grammicus*   **Plates 36, 830**
Local Names: Brown Owl, Potoo, Patoo

Identification: 31–36 cm (12–14"). A *medium-sized brown owl with short, but obvious ear tufts*. **Adult**: Mottled yellowish-brown above; paler with dark streaks below. **Immature**: Lighter than the adult. **Similar species**: Barn Owl is paler with a heart-shaped face and without ear tufts.
Voice: A guttural *whogh*; occasionally a high-pitched quiver *whoooo*, usually heard at dusk and before dawn. A high *wheee-eee* is said to be produced by immatures (Downer and Sutton).
Status and Range: An endemic genus and species to Jamaica where it is common and widespread primarily from the coast to mid-elevations and infrequently in high mountains.
Comments: Entirely nocturnal and arboreal. Regularly returns to same roost. Feeds on beetles, mice, lizards and tree frogs. Takes smaller prey than Barn Owl and is more of a forest species.
Habitat: Forests, woodlands, forest edges, gardens and infrequently, open, park-like areas.
Nesting: Nests in a tree cavity or fork of branches concealed by bromeliads and other foliage. Eggs (2) white. The breeding season is uncertain, but is believed to occur from December to June.

GOATSUCKERS (NIGHTJARS): FAMILY CAPRIMULGIDAE

The nightjars are sometimes called 'goatsuckers' from the ancient myth that at night these birds used their gaping mouths to rob goats of their milk, causing the udders to dry up and the animals to go blind. This myth was long ago shown to have no foundation. Rather the birds use their huge, bristled mouths to engulf nocturnal insects on the wing. During the day, most species are inactive and rest on the ground or lengthways on a branch where their mottled plumage serves as perfect camouflage.

COMMON NIGHTHAWK *Chordeiles minor*   **Plate 37**

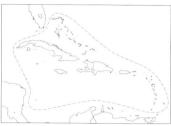

Identification: 20–25 cm (8–10"). Virtually identical to Antillean Nighthawk which has tan, rather than blackish, wing linings and which is sometimes buffier below and paler above, but these are not consistent field marks. Identified with certainty only by its call.
Voice: A distinctive, nasal *neet*.
Status and Range: A migrant throughout the West Indies moving southward in September and October and northward in April and May. The abundance of the species is unclear in the West Indies due to it being distinguishable from the more common Antillean Nighthawk only by its call and by the fact that both species are nearly silent in September and October. Clearly its presence tends to be underestimated. It occurs throughout the Western Hemisphere.
Comments: Exhibits same behavior and occurs in same habitats as Antillean Nighthawk.

ANTILLEAN NIGHTHAWK *Chordeiles gundlachii*   **Plate 37**
Local Names: Pirra-ma-dick (Bahamas); Rickery-Dick (CI); Gimme-me-bit (Jamaica); Piramidig (LA); Mosquito Hawk (LA, VI); Querequeté (Cuba); Querebebé (DR); Querequequé (PR); Peton-vwa, Peut-on-voir (Haiti)

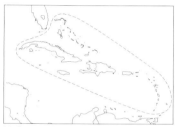

Identification: 20–25 cm (8–10"). A dark hawk-like bird with slender, pointed wings distinguished by a conspicuous *white wing patch* and erratic flight. **Male**: Note a narrow white band near the tail tip. **Female**: Lacks the white tail band. **Similar species**: Nearly identical to Common Nighthawk which has blackish wing linings while those of Antillean are tan. Common Nighthawk is sometimes whiter below and darker above, but these are not consistent field marks. Distinguished with certainty only by its call. All other birds of this family in the West Indies, such as nightjars and poorwills, lack a white wing patch.
Voice: A loud, raspy, distinctive rendition of its local names *que-re-be-bé*.
Status and Range: A common breeding resident in the Bahamas, Cuba, Cayman Islands, Jamaica and Hispaniola from May to August, but occurring as early as March and as late as October. It is only a locally common breeding bird on Puerto Rico and the Virgin Islands during the same months. Nighthawks are rare migrants through the Lesser Antilles where both Antillean and Common may well occur. Probably spends the non-breeding season in South America.
Comments: Typically seen in numbers foraging for flying insects high over open areas at dawn or dusk. It may be abroad during daylight when the weather is overcast. Sometimes seen sitting on country roads at night.
Habitat: Open areas such as fields, pastures, pine barrens, savannas and coastal fringes.
Nesting: Nests in a scrape on the ground among leaves, sand or gravel. Eggs (1–2) with a bluish or greenish tint and heavily marked with gray or brown. Breeds from May to July.

JAMAICAN POORWILL *Siphonorhis americanus*   **Plates 37, 83**
Local Name: Jamaican Pauraque

Identification: 24 cm (9.5"). A *small* nightjar mottled dark brown with a narrow, white chin band, a *reddish-brown hindneck spotted with black and white* and rather long legs. **Male**: Long tail tipped with white. **Female**: Similar to the male, but has buffy rather than whitish tail markings, which are substantially narrower. **Similar species**: Antillean Nighthawk is larger, has a conspicuous white band on its wing, flies high and has a distinctive call. Chuck-will's-widow is even larger and reddish-brown and has proportionally a much shorter tail. Northern Potoo is much larger with no white chin band.
Status and Range: Endemic to Jamaica where perhaps extinct. Only four specimens are known, the last collected in 1866. All were from the lowlands on the southern side of the island. Considered

critically endangered, its decline probably resulted from introduction of the mongoose and destruction of the bird's lowland forest habitat.

Comments: Nocturnal. Possibly still survives in dry limestone forests, such as in the Hellshire Hills. The Jamaican iguana, which had been considered extinct, was recently 'rediscovered' there. Puerto Rican Nightjar, which once ranged through Puerto Rico's lowlands, was also considered extinct until rediscovered in the dry limestone forests of southwestern Puerto Rico. Jamaican Poorwill should be sought in the little-studied dry limestone regions of Jamaica using taped vocalizations of close relatives to encourage a response. Probably fed by pursuing medium-sized insects in flight beneath the forest canopy.

Habitat: Probably open, dry forests in semi-arid lowlands.

LEAST POORWILL *Siphonorhis brewsteri*   **Plates 37, 81**
Local Names: Torico (DR); Grouiller-corps, Gouye-kò (Haiti)

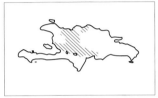

Identification: 17–20 cm (6.75–8″). A small, darkly mottled nightjar, the smallest in the West Indies. *Adult*: Has a *distinct white neck band* and *narrow, white terminal band on the tail*. *Immature*: More buffy than the adult. *Flight*: Like a giant moth, erratic and floppy, moving between trees. *Similar species*: Greater Antillean Nightjar is larger and darker. Chuck-will's-widow is much larger and more reddish-brown in color. Both lack a white terminal tail band. **Voice**: A guttural repetition of its local name *torico, torico*. Also a rising whistle.

Status and Range: Endemic to Hispaniola, including Gonâve Island. Found in the scrublands of southwestern Dominican Republic, particularly the scrub limestone forests on the north slope of the Sierra de Baoruco, near sea level between Oviedo and Pedernales and likely throughout Jaragua National Park south of Barahona. On Haiti, occurs between Arcahaie and Montruis north of Port-au-Prince. At least formerly numerous in scrubby woods on Gonâve Island (near Pointe-a-Raquette). It is somewhat common locally, although it was formerly believed extinct. The species is considered threatened likely as a result of habitat destruction and introduced predators. The true status and local distribution of the species is poorly known.

Comments: Entirely nocturnal. Formerly called Least Pauraque. The downy young look like a fluffy ball of white cotton and appear to mimic a round, whitish cactus which grows on its nesting grounds. In fact, the first nestling discovered was by a botanist collecting cacti. The bird was thought to be a cactus until it moved.

Habitat: Semi-arid areas of cactus and thorn scrub up to 450 m (1500′) often in association with pine forests.

Nesting: The nest is a depression in the leaf litter on the ground, generally at the base of a tree. Eggs (2) dull white evenly spotted with gray and brown. Breeds from April to July.

CHUCK-WILL'S-WIDOW *Caprimulgus carolinensis*   **Plates 37, 38**
Local Names: Guabairo Americano (Cuba); Don Juán (DR); Guabairo Mayor (PR); Chouette, Petonvwa (Haiti)

Identification: 31 cm (12″). A large nightjar, mottled reddish-brown overall, the breast primarily blackish with a white throat band. *Male*: White inner webs of three outer tail feathers. *Female*: Outer tail feathers tipped with buff and blend to dark. *Similar species*: Greater Antillean Nightjar is smaller, darker, less reddish and has white breast spots. Whip-poor-will is smaller, grayer and has a black throat. Least Poorwill is much smaller, less reddish-brown and lacks a white terminal tail band. Rufous Nightjar would be indistinguishable in the field from Chuck-will's-widow, but their ranges do not overlap. Rufous Nightjar is slightly more reddish-brown.

Voice: A clear, whistled rendition of its name with the first syllable weakest *chuck-will's-wid-ow*. It seldom calls in the West Indies.

Status and Range: A non-breeding resident from September to May, the species is common on Hispaniola; uncommon in the Bahamas, Cuba, Jamaica and Saba and rare on Puerto Rico and the

Virgin and Cayman Islands. It is a vagrant on St Martin, St Barthélemy and Barbuda. Occurs from eastern North America to northern South America.

Comments: Entirely nocturnal. It is rarely flushed during the day from among dense thickets. The bird is sometimes seen at night along country roads.

Habitat: Woodlands and occasionally at cave entrances, from the coast to mid-elevations.

RUFOUS NIGHTJAR *Caprimulgus rufus*   Plate 37
Local Names: Cent-coups-de-couteau, Jacques-pas-papa-pouw

Identification: 28 cm (11"). A medium-sized nightjar. Dark overall with reddish-brown edges to feathers and short, rounded wings. This is the only nightjar known from St Lucia. **Similar species**: Would be indistinguishable in the field from Chuck-will's-widow which is not known from so far south. Rufous Nightjar is slightly more reddish-brown.

Voice: Vigorous loud calls recalling its local names; emphasis is on the last syllable. Calls most frequently at dusk and only during the breeding season.

Status and Range: A locally common resident in northeastern St Lucia only from Grand Anse south to Dennery. May also occur at Anse la Raye. This nightjar likely occurs year-round. Its population size is now very small and its range greatly restricted. The subspecies is endangered as a result of habitat destruction and predation by introduced predators. Also occurs from Costa Rica south through north-central South America to northern Argentina and southern Brazil.

Comments: Nocturnal. Much of its range coincides with high concentrations of the fer-de-lance, a poisonous snake. While formally considered a separate species, St Lucia Nightjar (*C. otiosus*), it is now thought to be a long-winged race of this predominantly South American species.

Habitat: Relatively undisturbed dry scrub forests.

Nesting: Nests in a scrape on the ground. Eggs (2) white with light brown spots. Breeds in May and June.

GREATER ANTILLEAN NIGHTJAR   Plate 37
Caprimulgus cubanensis
Local Names: Guabairo (Cuba); Pitanguá (DR); Petonvwa, Chouette (Haiti)

Identification: 28 cm (11"). Mottled dark gray overall; *breast irregularly spotted with white*. **Male**: Outer tail feathers broadly (Hispaniola) or narrowly (Cuba) tipped with white. **Female**: Lacks white in tail feathers. **Similar species**: Smaller, darker and less reddish than Chuck-will's-widow which lacks the white breast spots. Antillean Nighthawk, much more likely to be seen, is characterized by a bold white band on the outer wing. Least Poorwill is smaller and paler. Whip-poor-will is smaller, paler, browner and has more white on the face, neck and tail.

Voice: A plaintive, frequently repeated *gua-by-ro* reflecting various local names.

Status and Range: Unique to Cuba and Hispaniola. A common and widespread year-round resident in parts of Cuba, including Zapata and Lanier Swamps, Isle of Youth and Cayo Coco. Formerly considered a rare year-round resident on Hispaniola, but has increased. Now fairly common in the western Dominican Republic, including Puerto Escondido, la Leonor, Restauración, Iguana Arriba, Sierra de Neiba, Jarabacoa, Galindo and Loma de Cabrera.

Comments: Nocturnal. At night, perches at the edge of roads in wooded areas. Feeds primarily on insects that it captures in flight. Some authorities separate the Hispaniolan population (Hispaniolan Nightjar, *C. ekmani*) from Cuban birds (Cuban Nightjar, *C. cubanensis*) on the basis of color and voice differences.

Habitat: On Cuba, moderately dense forests, particularly bordering wooded swamps and rivers. On Hispaniola, various forest types, especially semi-arid forests.

Nesting: The nest is a shallow scrape on the ground. Eggs (2) greenish-gray and heavily marked. Breeds from April to July.

WHIP-POOR-WILL *Caprimulgus vociferus*   **Plates 37, 38**
Local Name: Guabairo Chico (Cuba)

Identification: 23–26 cm (9–10"). *Adult male*: Mottled grayish-brown with a *blackish throat; narrow, white throat stripe* and three *outer tail feathers broadly tipped with white*. *Adult female*: Duller with a *buff throat stripe* and outer tail feathers narrowly tipped with buff. *Similar species*: Chuck-will's-widow is larger, more reddish-brown in color and lacks black on the throat. Greater Antillean Nightjar is noticeably larger, darker, grayer and has less white on the face, neck and tail.
Voice: A repeated *whip-poor-will*, with an accent on the first syllable. Calls more frequently at dawn than dusk, although usually not vocal in the West Indies.
Status and Range: A vagrant in western Cuba and Jamaica. Widespread in North America and through Central America south to Panama.
Comments: Nocturnal.
Habitat: Dry, open woodlands.

PUERTO RICAN NIGHTJAR   **Plates 37, 38, 85**
Caprimulgus noctitherus
Local Names: Guabairo, Guabairo Pequeño de Puerto Rico

Identification: 22 cm (8.5"). A small, cryptically plumaged goatsucker. Mottled gray, brown and black. Black throat edged with a pale band. *Male*: White throat band and portion of outer tail feathers. *Female*: Buff-colored throat band and tips of outer tail feathers. *Similar species*: Distinguished from Chuck-will's-widow by its distinctly smaller size, less reddish-brown plumage and by the greater amount of white in the tail of the male. It lacks the white wing mark of Antillean Nighthawk.
Voice: An emphatic, whistle *whip, whip, whip*... normally two to fifteen in a sequence. Also emphatic clucking. Very bright or very dark nights are poor for calling.
Status and Range: Endemic to Puerto Rico where it is locally common only in and around Guánica State Forest. The species occurs sparingly in other localities on Puerto Rico's southwest coast ranging from Guaniquilla to El Combate. Its distribution appears to be limited both by the lack of suitable habitat and the presence of nest and chick predators, specifically the feral cat and mongoose. These factors have caused the endangerment of this nightjar.
Comments: Puerto Rican Nightjar becomes active after dark, sallying from a perch to pursue nocturnal flying insects beneath the forest canopy. It calls throughout the year, particularly at dusk and before dawn, enabling one to locate this elusive bird. Calling is most active from November to May, decreasing with egg-laying. Believed by scientists to be extinct for over 70 years, Puerto Rican Nightjar was rediscovered in 1961 following the taping of a mysterious call. Before its rediscovery, the bird was only known from a specimen taken in 1888 and some subfossil cave deposits. Despite the lack of awareness by scientists about this nightjar's status, local people had known it well.
Habitat: Mature, dry semi-deciduous forests 7–10 m (23–33') in height with open understory and dense leaf litter.
Nesting: Nesting is directly on dense leaf litter of the forest floor beneath a bush. Eggs (1–2) buffy-brown splotched with darker markings, particularly around the broad end. Breeds from late February to early July. The male primarily incubates the eggs.

WHITE-TAILED NIGHTJAR *Caprimulgus cayennensis*   **Plates 37, 38**
Local Names: Engoulevent Coré, Cohé, Coré

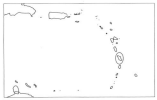

Identification: 20–23 cm (8–9"). Both sexes' wingtips fold over the rump and *do not* reach to tip of its rounded tail when at rest. *Adult male*: Note its *reddish-brown collar*, distinct white eyeline, *white outer tail feathers* and a white bar on the outer four primaries. *Adult female*: Duller than the male and lacks the collar, white outer tail feathers and white outer primaries. *Similar species*: Antillean Nighthawk has conspicuous white wing patches in flight.
Voice: A high whistle.
Status and Range: A very rare and local year-round resident in southern Martinique and on Caravelle

Peninsula from where there are only a few reports since 1980. A vagrant on Puerto Rico and Barbados. This nightjar is threatened on Martinique apparently as a result of habitat destruction and introduced predators. It is the only nightjar known from Martinique. Also occurs from Costa Rica through northern South America.

Comments: Nocturnal. May be seen sitting on country roads at night.

Habitat: Grassy fields.

Nesting: The nest is a scrape on gravelly soil, usually under sparse cover. Eggs (1–2) buffish-pink, uniformly spotted or scrawled with light brown or gray. Breeds from January to July.

POTOOS: FAMILY NYCTIBIIDAE

The potoos are chunky, neotropical relatives of the nightjars. The plumage is soft and fluffy, with cheek feathers modified as bristles on the sides of the wide gape. These odd-looking birds hawk flying insects, carrying their prey back to the original perch to consume it. Potoos are solitary, nocturnal and found in forested and woodland habitats. During the day, they typically perch in a very upright position atop a stump or on a tree branch.

NORTHERN POTOO *Nyctibius jamaicensis*   Plate 37
Local Names: Patoo (Jamaica); Don Juan Grande, Bruja, Lechusa (DR); Chat-huant, Chanrouan Ke Long (Haiti)

Identification: 43–46 cm (17–18"). A large, *long-tailed* nocturnal bird best identified by its habit of perching nearly upright on the end of a stump or post. Though the iris is yellow, it appears reddish in a beam of light. **Immature**: Paler than the adult. **Similar species**: Distinguished from nightjars and poorwills by its conspicuously longer tail and larger size.

Voice: A guttural *kwah, waugh, waugh, waugh, kwaah* (Dod). Also a hoarse *waark-cucu.*

Status and Range: A fairly common year-round resident on Jamaica where widespread primarily below 1000 m (3300'). Generally rare on Hispaniola, including Gonâve Island. In the Dominican Republic, it is regular in the southwest (Puerto Escondido, Barahona and la Descubierta) and also in the eastern interior (Hato Mayor, Almirante and Hoyón). A vagrant on Mona and Desecheo Islands off Puerto Rico. Also occurs from Mexico to Costa Rica.

Comments: Very cryptically plumaged, it allows a close approach. Arboreal. Feeds on moths, beetles and other insects, for which it sallies from a perch, in a manner similar to flycatchers. May use the same perch for months. Jamaica and Hispaniola each has an endemic subspecies.

Habitat: Arid and humid forests and scrublands adjacent to open areas. Also palm groves, pastures and cattle corrals. On Jamaica, also golf courses.

Nesting: The nest is a mere indentation atop a stump or broken branch at a moderate 7 m (23') height. Egg (1) white, spotted. Reportedly breeds from February to November on Jamaica and from April to July on Hispaniola.

SWIFTS: FAMILY APODIDAE

Seven species of this unique, cosmopolitan family occur in the West Indies. Swifts are the most aerial of land birds pursuing flying insects on the wing throughout the day without landing to rest. Even copulation occurs in flight. They are propelled extremely rapidly by shallow flaps of their stiff, bowshaped wings. One species is reported to hold the speed record for all birds, an amazing 322 km per hour (200 miles/h). Swifts use saliva in the construction of their nests.

BLACK SWIFT *Cypseloides niger*   Plate 42
Local Names: Swallow, Black Swallow, Rain Bird (Jamaica, VI, Dominica, St L); Vencejo Negro (Cuba, DR, PR); Hirondelle de Montagne, Chiksol (Haiti); Hirondelle Morne (St L); Oiseau de la Pluie, Gros Martinet Noir (Guad, Haiti, Mart); Martinet Sombre, Hirondelle (Guad, Mart)

Identification: 15–18 cm (5.75–7"). A *fairly large, black* swift with a *slightly forked tail*. At close range, white visible on forehead and eyebrows. *Similar species*: White-collared Swift is larger, with white on neck. All other swifts regularly occurring are somewhat or decidedly smaller, with shorter tails, a more darting flight and quicker wingbeats. Flight more rapid and darting than that of swallows or martins; holds wings below horizontal in gliding flight.
Voice: Mostly silent, but occasionally gives a soft *tchip, tchip* when flying.

Status and Range: Widespread in the West Indies. A locally common year-round resident on Jamaica and Hispaniola, but rare and local on Cuba. Black Swift is a common breeding resident from approximately April through September on Guadeloupe, Dominica and Martinique; uncommon on Puerto Rico, St Lucia and St Vincent and rare on Montserrat, Barbados and Grenada. These birds then migrate south during which time they are infrequently observed among the Virgin Islands and Lesser Antilles. A vagrant in the Cayman Islands. Also occurs in Central America, western North America, Guyana and Columbia.
Comments: Aerial. Often in flocks, feeding on insects high in the air. Where Black and White-collared Swifts occur on the same island, the former occur at higher elevations than the latter. Being a powerful long-distance flier, it may be found during breeding season on islands where it may not breed, such as on Barbados and St Lucia.
Habitat: Mountains; less frequently lowlands and coastal areas.
Nesting: Usually in small colonies. The nest is a shallow cup of moss placed in a crevice or shallow nook in a steep rock face in mountains, often near or under a waterfall. Egg (1) white. Breeds from March to September.

WHITE-COLLARED SWIFT *Streptoprocne zonaris*   Plate 42
Local Names: Rain Bird, Ringed Gowrie (Jamaica); Vencejo de Collar (Cuba, DR); Golondrina (DR); Oiseau de la Pluie, Zouazo Lapli Kou Blan (Haiti)

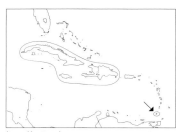

Identification: 20–22 cm (8–8.5"). A large, black swift. *Adult*: Has a distinctive *white collar*. *Immature*: Pale collar. *Similar species*: All other regularly occurring swifts are smaller and lack a white collar. Alpine Swift is a vagrant and is white below with a dark breast band.
Voice: A high-pitched *screee-screee* or rapid *chip-chip-chip-chip*.
Status and Range: A common year-round resident on Jamaica and Hispaniola, including Tortue Island. However, it is declining on Haiti. On Cuba, a fairly common year-round resident locally in the eastern mountains and Sierra del Escambray. An uncommon wanderer to Grenada. A vagrant on Puerto Rico (Vieques), Saba, St Christopher and Martinique. Also occurs from Mexico to South America.
Comments: Aerial. Rapid flight, with spectacular swoops and aerobatics. Typically in flocks of up to 200 birds, foraging for flying insects at all heights above the forest.
Habitat: Primarily over foothills, mountain valleys and forests, including open areas. Less regularly over lowlands, particularly during bad weather.
Nesting: A shallow nest of mud and moss is attached to a cliff, behind waterfalls or in dead palms. Eggs (2) white. Breeds in May and June.

CHIMNEY SWIFT *Chaetura pelagica*   Plate 42
Local Name: Vencejo (DR)

Identification: 12–14 cm (4.75–5.5"). A medium-sized, *dark swift*, with *pale brown on the chin and throat*. The short, rounded *tail is barely visible in flight*. *Similar species*: White-collared and Black Swifts are larger; the former with a distinct white ring around the neck, the latter with a more conspicuous tail which is slightly forked.
Voice: Loud, rapid, twittering in flight.
Status and Range: An uncommon migrant in the Cayman Islands, decidedly uncommon and local

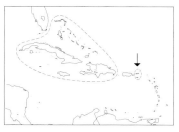

in the Bahamas and very rare on Cuba, Jamaica, Hispaniola and the Virgin Islands (St Croix). Southward migration is from August to October and northward in April and May. Occurs from eastern North America to northern South America.
Habitat: Forages above cities and towns. Also above open fields and woodlands.

SHORT-TAILED SWIFT *Chaetura brachyura* Plate 42
Local Name: Rain Bird (St V)

Identification: 10 cm (4"). A small swift, distinguished by its *pale gray rump and undertail-coverts* that contrast with its blackish plumage. The *tail is very short*. **Similar species**: Other small Lesser Antillean swifts are more uniform in color and have longer tails. Wings are longer than those of Lesser Antillean Swift. Black Swift is distinctly larger.
Voice: A soft, wheezy, twittering in flight.
Status and Range: A common breeding resident on St Vincent from March to September, from where it apparently departs after breeding. A vagrant in the Virgin Islands (St Croix), Barbados and possibly Puerto Rico and Grenada. Also occurs from Panama to central South America.
Comments: Aerial. Like other swifts, usually appears in flocks that forage on flying insects. That Short-tailed Swifts might leave St Vincent after breeding is curious considering all populations of the species outside the West Indies are reputed to be year-round residents. Interestingly, Short-tailed Swifts breeding in nearby Trinidad were found to nest primarily in manholes underground.
Habitat: Over towns, open areas and forests in lowlands and hills.
Nesting: The nest is a half-cup of twigs glued with saliva to a vertical surface of a chimney or cave. Eggs (3–6) white. Breeds from March to September.

GRAY-RUMPED SWIFT *Chaetura cinereiventris* Plate 42
Local Names: Rain Bird, Oiseau de la Pluie

Identification: 11 cm (4.25"). A small swift, mostly black upperparts with a *triangular gray rump patch*. Note its black, *longish tail*, yielding a slender appearance and gray underparts. **Similar species**: Short-tailed Swift has a noticeably shorter, stubbier tail and pale gray undertail-coverts. Lesser Antillean Swift has a *short, gray* tail.
Voice: A thin, high-pitched twitter.
Status and Range: Locally common on Grenada; possibly a year-round resident, but probably only seasonal. Primarily occurs in mountains, but also found at Halifax Harbor in lowlands. A vagrant on Hispaniola. Also occurs on Trinidad and Tobago, through most of South America and in southern Central America.
Habitat: Typically over forests.
Nesting: Nests in hollow trees or caves and possibly in chimneys as in South America. The nest is constructed of twigs bound together by saliva and glued to the wall of the nest cavity. Eggs (2–4) white. Breeds from March to May.

LESSER ANTILLEAN SWIFT *Chaetura martinica* Plate 42
Local Names: Chique-sol, Petit Martinet Noir, Hirondelle (Guad, Mart, St L)

Identification: 11 cm (4.25"). A small swift, upperparts dull brownish-gray overall with a gray rump, underparts dark gray and *tail gray and short*. **Similar species**: Gray-rumped Swift is nearly identical, but does not overlap in range. Its long tail is black and its underparts are lighter. Short-tailed Swift has greater contrast in its plumage, a shorter tail and longer wings.

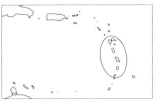

Status and Range: A fairly common year-round resident on Dominica, Martinique, St Lucia and St Vincent. Uncommon on Guadeloupe. A vagrant on Nevis. These islands compose the entire range of the species.
Comments: Aerial and highly gregarious, often in flocks of 20 to 40 individuals.
Habitat: Primarily over mountain forests, but also over lowland forests and open areas.
Nesting: The nest is a half-cup of twigs glued with saliva to a verticle surface of a hollow tree or cave. Eggs (3) white. Breeds in May and June.

ALPINE SWIFT *Apus melba*   Plate 42

Identification: 20 cm (8"). A large swift, grayish-brown above and whitish below with a *dark bar across the breast*. **Similar species**: Black Swift and White-collared Swift are both black overall including underparts, except for a white collar on the latter. Antillean Palm Swift is much smaller.
Status and Range: A vagrant on Barbados, St Lucia, Guadeloupe and Desecho Island off Puerto Rico. Alpine Swifts in the West Indies apparently are transatlantic wanderers probably blown off course during their migration between Europe and West Africa and assisted in their flight to the Caribbean by favorable winds. Its usual range is southern Europe, southwestern Asia and Africa.
Comments: Aerial. Usually among other swifts foraging for flying insects.
Habitat: Open areas and fields.

ANTILLEAN PALM SWIFT *Tachornis phoenicobia*   Plate 42
Local Names: Swallow (Jamaica); Vencejito de Palma (Cuba); Vencejito (Cuba, DR); Jolle-jolle, Petit Rolle, Hirondelle, Ti Irondèl (Haiti)

Identification: 10–11 cm (4–4.25"). **Adult**: A small black and white swift identified by its *white rump* and *black breast band*. **Immature**: Buffy below, rather than white. **Similar species**: Bank Swallow lacks the white rump. It also has shorter, broader wings and a slower, less darting flight. Alpine Swift is much larger.
Voice: A constantly emitted, faint high-pitched twitter.
Status and Range: A common year-round resident on Cuba, including the Isle of Youth, Jamaica and Hispaniola, including Saona, Beata and Île-à-Vache. A vagrant on Puerto Rico. Primarily occurs in lowlands, but sometimes in mountains. Occurs to at least 1700 m (5500') on Hispaniola. These islands comprise the entire range of the species.
Comments: Aerial. Forages in flocks for flying insects, its only food, with very rapid, erratic, bat-like flight, gliding between flapping spurts. Usually forages low over ground, no higher than 20 m (65').
Habitat: Open cultivated areas, sugarcane plantations, edges of palm savannas and even urban zones.
Nesting: Colonial. A globular nest of plant fibers, feathers and other materials is glued together with saliva and generally attached to palm fronds or even thatched roofs of tobacco sheds. Eggs (2–5) white. Breeds from March to April.

HUMMINGBIRDS: FAMILY TROCHILIDAE

The members of this large, Western Hemisphere family are particularly abundant in the tropics. Most are brilliantly iridescent, but appear black in poor light. They characteristically have long, pointed bills for probing into flower corollas from which they obtain insects and suck nectar with their long, tubular tongues. These diminutive creatures feed by hovering before blossoms with wings beating nearly 50 times per second. This gives them the appearance of a large bee. In fact, the smallest hummingbird in the world, indeed the world's smallest bird, is called the Bee Hummingbird. It is endemic to Cuba and 14 of these mites weigh but one ounce. Hummingbirds are very aggressive, particularly around their feeding territories.

RUFOUS-BREASTED HERMIT *Glaucis hirsuta* Plate 43

Local Names: Brown Hummingbird, Brown Doctor Bird, Brown Breast, Colibri Balisier, Doctor Bird

Identification: 12.5 cm (5"). *Long down-curved bill with yellow lower mandible* is diagnostic. Tail rounded and tipped with white. *Male*: Upperparts dull green, underparts brown, with dark brown forehead and crown. *Female*: Upperparts more reddish.
Voice: A high *sweep*, sometimes repeated. Less frequently a *sweep, swee-swee.*
Status and Range: A fairly common year-round resident on Grenada in mountains above 450 m (1500'). Rare in lowlands. Also occurs from tropical South America north to Panama.
Habitat: Mountain forests, forest edges and banana, cocoa and nutmeg plantations. Frequents flowering *Heliconia.*
Nesting: Nest usually is a loose cup attached to the underside of a *Heliconia* leaf, fern or palm frond, often overhanging running water. The male often frequents the vicinity of the nest early in the nesting cycle. Breeding activity is high early in the rainy season apparently so that adequate food will be available for developing nestlings. The same nest may be used to raise several consecutive broods. Eggs (2–3) white. Breeds from December to August.

GREEN-BREASTED MANGO *Anthracothorax prevostii* Plate 44

Identification: 12.5 cm (5"). *Adult male*: Note its dark green upperparts and a mixture of black, green and violet-blue underparts. Tail purple except for central tail feathers. *Adult female*: Slightly paler than the male. *Immature*: Green above; underparts white or brownish-white with a black median stripe.
Status and Range: A common resident on Providencia and San Andrés. Also occurs from Mexico through much of Central America to Venezuela.
Habitat: Primarily open coastal areas with scattered trees and bushes, including around human habitations.

JAMAICAN MANGO *Anthracothorax mango* Plates 44, 83

Local Names: Black Hummingbird, Mango Hummingbird, Doctor Bird

Identification: 13 cm (5"). A *large* hummingbird distinguished by its *entirely black underparts* and *reddish-purple cheek and sides of neck. Adult male*: Brilliant iridescence; underparts velvet-black. *Adult female*: Duller than the male, especially underparts and tail tipped with pale gray. *Immature male*: Similar to the adult female, except throat deep blue. *Similar species*: Much darker than other Jamaican hummingbirds, which also lack the purplish cheek.
Voice: A series of sharp, raspy tics *tic-tic-tic...*
Status and Range: Endemic to Jamaica where widespread and common, particularly in coastal and lowland areas, but also in the mountains.
Comments: Feeds on insects and nectar of flowers of trees, cacti and shrubs. The only Jamaican hummingbird that feeds extensively at cactus flowers. It also extracts insects from spider webs.
Habitat: Forest edges, banana plantations and gardens.
Nesting: Builds a nest of densely woven silky fibers and cobwebs, camouflaged with flecks of lichens and secured to branches above 2 m (7'). Eggs (2) white. Breeds year-round.

ANTILLEAN MANGO *Anthracothorax dominicus*   **Plate 43**
Local Names: Zumbador Grande (DR); Zumbador Dorado (PR); Quanga Négresse, Oiseau-mouche, Wanga Nègès (Haiti)

Identification: 11–12.5 cm (4.25–5″). A large hummingbird with pale, yellowish-green upperparts and a black, down-curved bill. **Adult male**: *Primarily black below* with a green throat. **Female**: Whitish below and on tips of tail. **Immature male**: Black stripe down center of whitish underparts. **Similar species**: Female Hispaniolan and Puerto Rican Emeralds are smaller, have paler lower mandibles and greener outer tail feathers. Green-throated Carib has a green rather than black breast.
Voice: An unmusical, thin trill that is quite loud. Also sharp, chipping notes.
Status and Range: A common year-round resident throughout Hispaniola at all elevations including its offshore islands and common on Puerto Rico where most frequent on the drier southern coast and the haystack hills of the north to 250 m (800′). Nearly absent from the east coast. It is increasingly rare among the Virgin Islands and has been extirpated from most of them. These islands comprise the entire range of the species.
Habitat: Clearings and scrub in both arid and moist areas. Also gardens and shade coffee plantations.
Nesting: A deep, downy cup-shaped nest is often coated with spider webs and lichens and is built on a branch 2–10 m (7–33′) above the ground. Eggs (2) white. Breeds from March to August.

GREEN MANGO *Anthracothorax viridis*   **Plates 43, 85**
Local Names: Puerto Rican Mango, Zumbador Verde, Colibrí Verde, Zumbador Verde de Puerto Rico, Zunzún Verde, Zunzún Verde de Puerto Rico

Identification: 11.5 cm (4.5″). Both sexes can be readily distinguished by their relatively large size; entirely emerald green underparts; down-curved, black bill and rounded tail. **Similar species**: Puerto Rican Emerald, which occurs in the same habitat, is much smaller and has a forked tail.
Voice: The call, a trill-like twitter, is infrequently heard. When angered, issues loud, harsh rattling or chattering notes. The call note is a hard *tic*.
Status and Range: Endemic to Puerto Rico, this is the common large hummingbird of the central and western mountains. It is decidedly uncommon in the Luquillo Mountains of eastern Puerto Rico. Green Mango is irregularly seen on the coast, particularly in the western portion of the island.
Comments: As is the case with all five resident hummingbirds on Puerto Rico, this species feeds to a large extent on animal matter, primarily insects and spiders. It also relies on nectar for sustenance and can be reliably found at flowering *Heliconia*. Formerly, when tobacco was grown on Puerto Rico, this hummer was erroneously blamed for eating the seeds.
Habitat: Mountain forests and coffee plantations.
Nesting: The cup-shaped nest is coated with lichens. Eggs (2) white. Breeding is not well studied, but has been recorded in October, December, February, April and May. As is typical with hummingbirds, the male does not attend the nest or help feed the young.

PURPLE-THROATED CARIB *Eulampis jugularis*   **Plate 43**
Local Names: Ruby-throat, Colibri Rouge (St L); Colibri Madère, Fou-fou d'Espagne, Falle Rouge (Guad, Mart); Doctor Bird (Saba, St E)

Identification: 11.5 cm (4.5″). In all plumages, the throat often appears black, except in good light. **Adult**: A large hummingbird with a down-curved bill distinguished by its emerald green wings, and purplish-red throat and breast. **Male**: Moderately down-curved bill. **Female**: Has a longer and more sharply down-curved bill than the male. **Immature**: Bill shorter, scattered brown feathers on the upperparts with some orange feathering on the throat.
Voice: A sharp *chewp*, repeated rapidly when agitated.
Status and Range: Limited to the Lesser Antilles where it occurs widely. A fairly common year-round

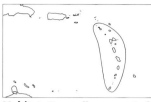

resident on St Barthélemy, Saba, Guadeloupe (including Marie-Galante), Dominica, Martinique, St Lucia, St Vincent and Grenada, it is uncommon on St Eustatius, St Christopher, Nevis, Antigua and Montserrat. A vagrant in the Virgin Islands (St Croix and St John), Barbuda, Barbados and the Grenadines (Bequia).

Comments: The differences in bill length and shape between the male and female suggest interesting partitioning of food resources that is as yet unstudied.

Habitat: Generally mountain forests and banana plantations; occasionally and seasonally at sea level.

Nesting: A cup-shaped nest is hung in a fork of a small branch, often high above the ground, but ranging in height from 3–18 m (10–60'). Eggs (2) white. Breeds from January to July.

GREEN-THROATED CARIB *Eulampis holosericeus*   Plate 43

Local Names: Green Doctor Bird (LA); Doctor Brushie (Antigua, Barbuda); Doctorbird (Antigua, Barbuda, LA, VI); Green Hummingbird (Grenada, St V); Zumbador de Pecho Azul, Zumbadorcito Crestado (PR); Colibri Vert (St L); Colibri Falle Vert, Falle Vert (Guad, Mart)

Identification: 10.5–12 cm (4–4.75"). Its large size, slightly down-curved bill and *green breast* are important field marks, though the breast often appears black in poor light. The blue breast mark is discernible only under ideal conditions. **Similar species**: Male Antillean Mango has a black breast.

Voice: A sharp *chewp* and a loud wing rattle (Wetmore).

Status and Range: A common year-round resident throughout the Lesser Antilles, Virgin Islands and northeastern Puerto Rico to as far west as San Juan. Rare elsewhere along Puerto Rico's coast. These islands comprise the entire range of the species.

Habitat: Gardens and rain forests at all elevations in the Lesser Antilles, though less frequent in the mountains on Guadeloupe. Appears to prefer dry terrain on Martinique. On Puerto Rico, primarily coastal.

Nesting: The downy, cup-shaped nest has lichens lining the exterior and is built in the fork of a twig 2–9 m (7–30') above the ground. Eggs (2) white. Generally breeds from March to mid-July.

ANTILLEAN CRESTED HUMMINGBIRD   Plate 43
Orthorhyncus cristatus

Local Names: Doctor Brushie (Antigua, Barbuda); Doctor Bird (Antigua, Barbuda, PR, LA); Little Doctor Bird (LA, PR, VI); Zumbador Crestado (PR); Coulibri (Grenada, St V); Colibri Huppé, Fou-fou (Guad, Mart, St L)

Identification: 8.5–9.5 cm (3.25–3.75"). Its tiny size is an important field mark. **Adult male**: *Pointed crest*; underparts blackish. **Female**: Crest less evident; underparts pale gray. **Immature male**: Similar to adult male, but lacks the crest. **Similar species**: Female Puerto Rican Emerald lacks a crest and is whiter below than female Antillean Crested.

Voice: A combination of emphatic notes usually including a *pit-chew* like a ricocheting bullet.

Status and Range: A common year-round resident throughout the Lesser Antilles, Virgin Islands and on Puerto Rico's northeastern coast. Its range is expanding on Puerto Rico. The species is known only from these islands.

Comments: Its diet shifts from nectar to insects and spiders during the dry season in dry scrub habitat.

Habitat: Primarily lowland openings, gardens, forest edges and especially arid habitats, but also mountain forests.

Nesting: The nest is a tiny cup of cotton or fine fibers with lichens coating the exterior and firmly bound together with spider webs. It is built 0.6–2 m (2–7') above the ground in a tree, bush or vine. Eggs (2) white. Breeds year-round, but primarily from January to August.

CUBAN EMERALD *Chlorostilbon ricordii* **Plate 44**

Local Names: Emerald Hummingbird, Hummingbird, God Bird (Bahamas); Zunzún, Zumbador, Zumbete, Pica Flor (Cuba)

Identification: 9–10.5 cm (3.5–4"). Note its medium size; long, forked tail; slim body and long, thin bill, pinkish below. *Male*: Emerald green, white undertail-coverts and spot behind eye sometimes appears black in field. *Female*: Grayish underparts; sides metallic green with a conspicuous white mark behind the eye. Less iridescent upperparts and tail less deeply forked. *Similar species*: Female Ruby-throated Hummingbird has a darker bill and less white behind the eye than female Cuban Emerald. Brace's Hummingbird, known only from New Providence, is slightly smaller and has a longer and more curved bill that is blacker on the lower mandible.

Voice: A short, penetrating, squeaking twitter usually emitted while taking off.

Status and Range: Known only from Cuba and the Bahamas. A common year-round resident throughout Cuba, including the Isle of Youth, and on many keys. In the Bahamas, common on Grand Bahama, Abaco and Andros, but absent elsewhere.

Comments: Feeds on nectar and invertebrates, especially spiders or insects caught in their webs. Also takes flying insects. Emeralds are solitary, but several individuals might gather at a flowering plant. Very pugnacious and territorial, it chases other hummingbirds and even larger birds away from flowers. Cuban Emerald has been seen to attack even vultures near its nest. Contrarily, it is sometimes so tame as to land on flowers in a person's hand. Males have a particularly noisy flight.

Habitat: All habitats from the coast to mid-elevations, especially woods, swamp edges, gardens and shrubby vegetation, particularly on keys.

Nesting: The nest is a small cup of cotton, downy feathers, lichens, hairs and other soft materials, built in the fork of a twig usually within 3 m (10') off the ground. Only the female broods the eggs. Eggs (2) white, oblong. Breeds year-round.

BRACE'S HUMMINGBIRD *Chlorostilbon bracei* **Plate 86**

Identification: 9.5 cm (3.75"). A small green hummer with a long, slightly down-curved bill. *Similar species*: Cuban Emerald, which does not typically occur on New Providence, is slightly larger with a shorter, straighter bill that is paler on the lower mandible than in Brace's Hummingbird.

Status and Range: Extinct. Formerly endemic to the Bahamas. Known from only one specimen collected in 1877 on New Providence in the Bahamas.

Habitat: Thought to be undisturbed forests.

HISPANIOLAN EMERALD *Chlorostilbon swainsonii* **Plates 44, 81**

Local Names: Zumbador, Zumbador Verde, Zumbaflor (DR); Wanga Nègès Mòn, Ouanga Négresse, Colibri (Haiti)

Identification: 10.5 cm (4"). A *straight-billed, tiny* hummingbird. *Male*: Green overall, dull *black breast spot*, deeply forked tail and lower mandible mostly pinkish. *Female*: Green above, dull grayish below with metallic green sides and outer tail tips whitish. *Similar species*: Female Antillean Mango is larger, has reddish-brown outer tail feathers and a darker bill. Vervain Hummingbird is similar to female Hispaniolan Emerald, but is much smaller and has a shorter, darker bill. Female Ruby-throated Hummingbird has a darker bill and a bit less white behind the eye than female Hispaniolan Emerald.

Voice: A series of sharp, metallic tics *tic-tic-tic...*

Status and Range: Endemic to Hispaniola where it is common in the mountains, but rare at low elevations to which it ranges during the non-breeding season. Found in nearly all parts of the Dominican Republic. Considered threatened on Haiti (Massif de la Selle and Massif de la Hotte) because of habitat destruction.

Habitat: Moist forests and shade coffee plantations in mountains, hills and limestone karst. Also in clearings.
Nesting: A cup-shaped nest, constructed of moss, plant materials and cobwebs and speckled with lichens, is built 1–2 m (3–7') off the ground. Eggs (2) white. Breeds from April to June.

PUERTO RICAN EMERALD *Chlorostilbon maugaeus* Plates 43, 85
Local Names: Zumbadorcito de Puerto Rico, Colibrí, Fork-tailed Hummingbird, Zumbador, Zumbadorcito, Zunzún

Identification: 9–10 cm (3.5–4"). One of Puerto Rico's two small hummingbirds, it is identified by its small size, *forked tail* and lack of a crest. **Male**: Green above and below with a black tail and a pinkish base of lower mandible. **Female**: Similar to male, but has white underparts, an entirely black bill and the outer tail feathers have whitish tips. Its tail may be forked, notched or even-edged. **Similar species**: The tiny Antillean Crested Hummingbird, confined primarily to Puerto Rico's northeastern coast, often has a noticeable crest and a rounded tail. The other hummingbird of the mountains on Puerto Rico is the Green Mango, which is distinguished by its larger size, down-curved bill and rounded tail. Female Ruby-throated Hummingbird often has a noticeable white spot behind the eye. This is reduced or absent in female Puerto Rican Emerald. Female Puerto Rican Emerald also has a bright green forehead and crown, rather than grayish-brown with a tint of green. It has greenish, rather than dull brownish-gray sides, a shorter bill and usually a black bar under and behind the eye. Female Ruby-throated Hummingbird sometimes has black lores and black beneath the eye, but usually not behind the eye.
Voice: A series of *tic* notes given at various speeds and a thin, rapid trill with a high-pitched buzz at the end.
Status and Range: Puerto Rican Emerald is endemic to Puerto Rico where it is common in the mountains, but also occurs irregularly on the coast, particularly the drier south coast.
Comments: In the mountains, females primarily inhabit shady areas whereas males frequent more exposed, sunnier sites, usually at greater heights above the forest floor. These differences are not so marked in dry areas where both sexes inhabit shaded localities. The two sexes exhibit differential feeding preferences. The female feeds heavily on insects and spiders it gleans from the limbs and leaves of trees whereas the male forages most actively on the nectar of blossoms.
Habitat: Primarily mountain forests and edges including shade coffee plantations, but also lowland wooded areas and even mangroves.
Nesting: A tiny cup-shaped nest of fine fibers is coated with lichens and built in the fork of a twig. Eggs (2) white. Breeds primarily from February to May, but also irregularly through the year.

BLUE-HEADED HUMMINGBIRD *Cyanophaia bicolor* Plate 43
Local Names: Colibri Tête Bleue, Frou-frou Bleu (male in Martinique), Colibri Falle Blanc, Fou-fou Feuille Blanc (female in Martinique)

Identification: 9.5 cm (3.75"). **Male**: *Head, throat, upper breast and tail violet-blue.* **Female**: Shiny green above with a bronze sheen on mantle, grayish white below with flecks of green on sides and a blackish ear patch.
Voice: Shrill, metallic notes, rapidly descending in pitch. Also a metallic *click-click-click* (Tyrrell).
Status and Range: A common year-round resident known only from the mountains of Dominica and Martinique. Usually occurs from 500 to 1200 m (1600–4000'), though occasionally in lowlands where flowers are in bloom.
Comments: Feeds primarily on nectar and insects in the forest understory.
Habitat: Moist open areas in mountain forests, along mountain streams and wooded edges of fields.
Nesting: The nest is a small, deep cup constructed of plant materials, covered with lichens and bound to a twig by cobwebs. It is usually low to the ground, built at approximately 2.5 m (8') and sheltered under a large leaf. Eggs (2) white. Breeds from February to May.

BLACK-BILLED STREAMERTAIL *Trochilus scitulus*   **Plates 44, 83**

Local Names: Eastern Streamertail, Doctor Bird, God Bird, Jamaican Doctor Bird, Long-tail, Long-tailed Doctor Bird, Scissors-tail

Identification: Male (with tail plumes) 22–24 cm (8.5–9.5"); Female 10.5 cm (4"). Similar to Red-billed Streamertail, but slightly smaller, more blue-green in color and with a *completely black bill*. **Adult male**: Distinguished by its *two long, black tail feathers* and *entirely black bill*. Also note its *black crown and ear tufts*. **Female**: Green above and white below with green spots on sides. The tail is short with white outer tips; the *bill totally black*. **Immature male**: Lacks streamers of the adult male.

Voice: Similar to Red-billed Streamertail, including the vibrating hum produced in flight by the adult male's elongated streamers.

Status and Range: An endemic genus and species to Jamaica. Common, but occurs only in the extreme eastern part of the island. Found from Port Antonio and Morant River eastward through the John Crow Mountains. Overlaps with Red-billed Streamertail between the Blue and John Crow Mountains.

Comments: Feeds on small insects and nectar from many types of plants. Sometimes feeds through holes pierced in flower corollas by Bananaquits if the corolla is too long for the hummingbird's bill and tongue to reach the food. Courtship of Black-billed and Red-billed Streamertails consists of elaborate displays by the male and is unusual compared to most hummingbirds in that the female, rather than the male, initiates courtship. The local name 'Doctorbird' has several possible derivations, the most likely dates back to the Amerindians, who associated the hummingbird with tobacco, one of their important medicinal plants, hence the name.

Habitat: Humid forests, banana plantations and gardens.

Nesting: The nest is built at 3–4 m (10–13') in second-growth forest. It is similar to that of Red-billed Streamertail, but built of coarser materials such as tiny twigs, branches and roots, rather than delicate fibers, and is more loosely constructed. Eggs (2) white. Breeds from October to March.

RED-BILLED STREAMERTAIL *Trochilus polytmus*   **Plates 44, 83**

Local Names: Western Streamertail, Doctor Bird, Long-tailed Hummingbird, Scissors-tail, God Bird, Jamaican Doctor Bird

Identification: Male (with tail plumes) 22–25 cm (8.5–10"); Female 10.5 cm (4"). **Adult male**: Easily identified by its *two long* (13 cm), *black tail feathers* (absent in molt) and *red bill tipped with black*. The body and head are metallic green, with a *black crown* and conspicuous *ear tufts*. **Female**: Note the short tail and outer feathers with white tips. The body is metallic green above, primarily white below, with green spots on the sides. The bill, with red confined to base, sometimes appears black in the field. **Immature male**: Similar to adult male, but lacks tail streamers. Tail is tipped with green. **Similar species**: Distinguished from Black-billed Streamertail by its partially red bill.

Voice: A loud, metallic *ting* or *teet* and a prolonged *twink-twink-twink...* or *think-think-think...* dropping in pitch at the end. Agitated male gives a loud single-note *zeet* call. In flight, the male's scalloped tail streamers create a high whining hum.

Status and Range: An endemic genus and species to Jamaica where it is the most abundant and widespread resident bird. It is absent only from the extreme eastern portion of Jamaica including the John Crow Mountains.

Comments: Formerly combined with Black-billed Streamertail as a single species. However, the two species differ in their call, courtship flight, bill color and bill width. The two species overlap in range only between the Blue and John Crow Mountains, bordered by Port Antonio in the north and the Morant River in the south. Hybrids occur in this area of contact. Feeds on nectar and small insects.

Habitat: Primarily middle and high elevation forests, but also in gardens and parks; seasonal along the coast.

Nesting: A compact cup-shaped nest is built low in a bush at forest edge and constructed of plant materials bound with cobwebs and camouflaged with lichens. Eggs (2) white. Breeds year-round mainly from October to March. Up to three broods may be raised in one season.

BAHAMA WOODSTAR *Calliphlox evelynae*   **Plates 44, 45**
Local Names: Hummingbird, God Bird (Bahamas)

Identification: 9–9.5 cm (3.5–3.75"). **Adult male**: Greenish above with a *deeply forked tail with black outer and reddish-brown inner feathers*. Reddish-violet throat, white breast and lower underparts reddish-brown. **Adult female**: White throat and breast and a *rounded, reddish-brown tail and lower underparts*. **Immature**: Similar to female.
Voice: A sharp *tit, titit, tit, tit, titit*, often speeding up into a rapid rattling sound. Song a dry, rhythmic *prítitidee, prítitidee, prítitidee* (Brudenell-Bruce).
Status and Range: A common year-round resident throughout the Bahamas to which it is endemic. It is less common on islands which it co-inhabits with the Cuban Emerald.
Comment: Males on the Inaguas in the southern Bahamas have violet feathers on the forehead as well as the throat.
Habitat: Gardens, scrub, woodlands, forest edges, clearings and mixed pine forests.
Nesting: A tiny, well-constructed cupped nest of plant materials is camouflaged with bark and built from 0.6–4 m (2–13') above ground in the fork of a sapling, bush or tree. Eggs (2) white. Breeds year-round.

RUBY-THROATED HUMMINGBIRD *Archilochus colubris*   **Plate 44**
Local Name: Colibrí (Cuba)

Identification: 8–9.5 cm (3–3.75"). **Male**: Red throat, moderately forked tail and whitish underparts with dull greenish sides are important field marks. **Female**: Green above, white below and duller on the breast and abdomen with buff-colored sides. The bill is dark. The tail is rounded and tipped with white. There is a small white spot behind the eye. **Similar species**: Female Ruby-throated Hummingbird is similar to several West Indian hummers. Female Cuban and Hispaniolan Emeralds both have a paler bill, a more conspicuous white stripe behind the eye and greenish sides. See Puerto Rican Emerald.
Voice: A peculiar twitter, similar to the squeak of a mouse, *cric-cric*.
Status and Range: A rare migrant to the northern Bahamas and Cuba in March and April and very rare on those islands from November to February as a non-breeding resident. A vagrant in the Cayman Islands (Grand Cayman), Jamaica, Hispaniola and Puerto Rico. Occurs through much of eastern North America and Central America.
Habitat: Large gardens, wood edges and clusters of trees.

VERVAIN HUMMINGBIRD *Mellisuga minima*   **Plate 44**
Local Names: Little Doctorbird, Bee Hummingbird, Little Bee Hummingbird (Jamaica); Zumbadorcito, Zumbaflor (DR); Ouanga Négresse, Sucé-fleurs, Zwazo-mouch, Wanga Nègès, Suce-fleur (Haiti)

Identification: 6 cm (2.5"). A *tiny* hummingbird that is green above and predominantly whitish below with a *straight black bill*. The chin and throat are sometimes flecked; sides and flanks are dull green. **Adult male**: Tail deeply notched. **Adult female**: Tail rounded and tipped with white. **Immature male**: Similar to the adult female, except chin and throat flecked with gray, and white tips on outer tail feathers not so sharply defined. **Similar species**: Much smaller than other hummingbirds in its range. Female Hispaniolan Emerald has a longer, paler bill.
Voice: A loud, rhythmic song of high-pitched, metallic squeaks.
Also an extended throaty buzz.
Status and Range: A common and widespread year-round resident known only from Jamaica and

Hispaniola, including the nearby islands of Île-à-Vache, Gonâve, Tortue, Saona and Catalina. One record from Puerto Rico.

Comments: More often heard than seen. Often hovers at food source with tail cocked up. The second smallest bird in the world; an adult weighs 2.6 g (0.1 oz). Its egg weighs 0.37 g (0.01 oz) and a hatchling 0.32 g (0.01 oz).

Habitat: All open areas with small flowers. Present in open woodlands and shade coffee plantations, but absent from dense forests.

Nesting: Often built low to the ground in a bush, the tiny nest is a cup of fine fibers covered with lichens, cobwebs and bark. Eggs (2) white. Breeds year-round, but chiefly from December to May.

BEE HUMMINGBIRD *Mellisuga helenae* Plates 44, 80

Local Names: Pájaro Mosca, Zunzuncito, Trovador, Zumbete, Zumbadorcito, Colibrí, Zumbador, Pájaro Mosca Cubano

Identification: 5.5 cm (2.25″). The world's smallest bird. Tail short, tipped with white. *Male*: A bit smaller than Vervain Hummingbird. Its characteristic iridescent red throat has plumes extending around the side of the neck during the breeding season. Back is iridescent blue and green. *Female*: Whitish below with an inconspicuous white spot behind the eye and a black spot on lores. *Similar species*: Distinguished from all other hummingbirds in Cuba by its diminutive size and very short tail.

Voice: A twitter, long and quite high. Also low warbling notes. Its song is somewhat similar to that of Cuban Grassquit.

Status and Range: Endemic to Cuba and formerly the Isle of Youth. It has a spotty distribution, including Habana, Sierra de Anafe, Guanahacabibes Peninsula, Zapata Swamp, Moa, Mayarí and the coast of Guantánamo. Now rare and localized. Formerly much more common and widespread. A vagrant on Providenciales in the Bahamas. The species is threatened apparently as a result of habitat alteration and destruction.

Comments: In flight, makes a peculiar noise like a bumble bee. It is quite tame and solitary. Males like to perch high on bare twigs of trees and may use the same perch for years. In Zapata Swamp, one male used the same three perches for three years. When flowers are scarce, it feeds on insects as well. Tends to feed at horizontal flowers, whereas Cuban Emerald feeds at vertical ones. The red throat appears differently colored depending on the light. When displaying, the male flies straight up in the air and descends abruptly. It is chased by Cuban Emeralds.

Habitat: Primarily coastal forests and forest edges, but also mountain valleys, forests of the interior, swamplands and gardens.

Nesting: The nest is a very small cup of cotton, grass, hair and other soft vegetable materials, similar in shape to that of Cuban Emerald but smaller. It is built on a twig approximately 2.5 m (8′) above the ground. Eggs (2) white. Breeds primarily in March and April, but also in other months.

TROGONS: FAMILY TROGONIDAE

Trogons are pantropical, brightly colored birds that have many unusual anatomical features. All are short-necked with small, weak feet; short, rounded wings and long tails. They are strictly arboreal, usually solitary and found in forests. The flight of trogons is undulating and rapid, but not prolonged. They feed by darting from their perch and snatching insects from the air or from foliage, or small fruits from a stem.

CUBAN TROGON *Priotelus temnurus* Plates 49, 50, 79

Local Names: Tocoloro, Tocororo, Toroloco, Guatiní

Identification: 25–28 cm (10–11″). The *red belly, green back, blue crown* and short, broad bill and *long, peculiar tail* with much white on the underside make this bird unmistakable. Perched, it also has a distinctive posture.

Voice: Very varied. Most commonly a repeated call that sounds much like several of its local names, *toco-toco-tocoro-tocoro...* Also emits a low and short mournful call that makes it difficult to locate.

Status and Range: Endemic to Cuba where it is widely distributed and common. It is uncommon on the Isle of Youth and rare on three of the largest keys north of Camagüey Province (Guajaba, Romano and Sabinal).

Comments: This beautiful trogon is the national bird of Cuba. Though inactive, its size, bright colors and distinctive voice make it easy to find. Feeds mainly on flowers, but also on buds and fruits. Usually found in pairs. The trogon's flight is rather short and noisy. It hovers while feeding, much like a flycatcher.

Habitat: Wet and dry forests at all altitudes. Primarily shady areas.

Nesting: Does not build a nest, but usually uses the abandoned holes of woodpeckers or natural cavities in trees. Eggs (3–4) white with a slight bluish tinge. Breeds primarily from May to August.

HISPANIOLAN TROGON *Priotelus roseigaster* **Plates 49, 81**
Local Names: Papagayo, Cotorrita de Sierra, Piragua, Loro (DR); Caleçon Rouge, Pic de Montagne, Dame Anglaise, Demoiselle Anglaise, Kalson Wouj (Haiti)

Identification: 27–30 cm (10.5–12"). Identified by its glossy green upperparts, *red belly*, yellow bill and gray throat and breast. Note its long, dark blue tail heavily marked with white below. *Male*: Wings with fine black and white barring. *Female*: Lacks fine wing markings.

Voice: *Toca-loro; coc, ca-rao* or *cock-craow*, repeated several times, early in the morning, especially during breeding season. Also cooing and puppy-like whimpering sounds.

Status and Range: Endemic to Hispaniola. In the Dominican Republic, found in the Cordillera Central, Sierra de Neiba, Sierra de Baoruco and the Cordillera Septentrional, where it is still locally common in undisturbed habitat. During the non-breeding season, descends to lower elevations (Ebano Verde and Las Cruces de Puerto Escondido). Still abundant in parts on Haiti (Massif de la Hotte), but declining and considered threatened. Populations have been considerably reduced throughout its range because of habitat destruction.

Comments: A relatively inactive bird. Typically occurs in pairs, the two individuals calling regularly to one another. Due to ventriloquial nature of its call, this bird is frequently difficult to locate. Feeds mainly on insects, but also small lizards and fruits, which it sometimes takes on the wing. It is dependent upon large, mature trees for nesting cavities.

Habitat: Mountain forests, including mature pine and broadleaf forests, above 300 m (1000'). Local in coastal mangroves.

Nesting: Nests in tree cavities, often the abandoned nest of a Hispaniolan Woodpecker. Eggs (2) pale green. Breeds from March to July.

TODIES: FAMILY TODIDAE

The todies are most closely related to the motmots and more distantly to kingfishers. Though the family is now confined to the Greater Antilles, it is believed to have originated from a Central American stock now extinct. Fossil evidence indicates that the family once extended northward well into North America. Todies have a voracious appetite; a captive specimen ate about 40% of its body weight in insects each day. The average number of insects caught by a single bird in the Luquillo Mountains of Puerto Rico was 1.8 per minute, from dawn through to dusk. Todies have one of the highest rates of feeding young ever recorded in an insectivorous bird.

CUBAN TODY *Todus multicolor* **Plates 49, 80**
Local Names: Pedorrera, Cartacuba, Barrancarríos

Identification: 11 cm (4.25"). A distinctive small, stubby, primarily green bird with a big head, no neck, large flat bill and red throat. The *flanks are pink, sides of throat blue* and *undertail-coverts yellow*. *Flight*: It makes a characteristic rattling with its wings.

Voice: When perched, sometimes repeats a peculiar short *tot-tot-tot-tot*. The most characteristic call is a soft *pprreeee-pprreeee*, that gave origin to its common name, 'Pedorrera.'

Status and Range: This endemic bird is common and widely distributed on Cuba, including the Isle of Youth and the four large cays north of Camagüey Province (Cayo Coco, Guajaba, Romano and Sabinal).

Comments: Usually in pairs. A rather inactive bird that searches for prey from a perch. It then flits up to glean its prey from twigs and undersides of leaves. Its main food consists of caterpillars, spiders and insects. Rarely, it will eat small fruits.

Habitat: Wooded and semi-wooded areas, forests, stream edges and areas with earthen embankments at all elevations.

Nesting: Digs a tunnel about 0.3 m (1') in length with a chamber at the end in a clay embankment, though sometimes uses a rotten trunk or tree cavity. The walls of the tunnel and the egg chamber are covered with a thick glue-like substance mixed with grass, lichen, algae, small feathers and other materials that probably act as a sealant. Eggs (3–4) white. Breeds primarily from March to June.

BROAD-BILLED TODY *Todus subulatus*   Plates 49, 81
Local Names: Barrancolí, Barranquero, Colibrí (DR); Perroquet de Terre, Kolibri Fran, Colibri (Haiti)

Identification: 11–12 cm (4.25–4.75"). Bright green above with a red throat, grayish-white below and tinted yellow with pink sides. *Lower mandible entirely reddish.* **Immature**: Lacks red on throat; breast streaked with pale green. **Similar species**: Narrow-billed Tody is whiter below and usually has a black-tipped bill, but this is not always the case. It is best distinguished by voice.

Voice: A monotonous, often repeated, whistle *terp, terp, terp,* uttered in a complaining tone. A single-note call of the same tone contrasts with the Narrow-billed Tody's two-note call.

Status and Range: Endemic to Hispaniola, including Gonâve Island, where it is primarily common in the lowlands.

Comments: Perches with tail pointed down and broad bill pointed up at an angle of 45 degrees, actively turning its head to watch for insects. It captures its prey in quick flight on whirring wings, with an audible snap of its bill. It is less active than Narrow-billed Tody and forages higher in the vegetation among the outer, less dense foliage.

Habitat: Semi-arid areas from the lowlands to 1700 m (5600') in virgin and second-growth forests, including pine, as well as scrub, shade coffee plantations and some mangroves. Not found in dense rain forests. Often occupies vegetated ravines and areas with earthen embankments.

Nesting: Digs a 30–60 cm (1–2') tunnel in a soil bank, with a nest chamber at the end. Eggs (3–4) white. Breeds from April to June.

NARROW-BILLED TODY *Todus angustirostris*   Plates 49, 81
Local Names: Barrancolí, Chi-cuí, Pichuí (DR); Tete-seche, Kolibri Mòn, Colibri, Chicorette (Haiti)

Identification: 11 cm (4.25"). A tiny, chunky bird with brilliant green upperparts, red throat, whitish underparts tinted with yellow and pinkish sides. *Lower mandible reddish, usually with a black tip.* **Immature**: Lacks red on throat; breast streaked with pale green. **Similar species**: Broad-billed Tody is grayish-white below and has an entirely red lower mandible. Since Narrow-billed Tody sometimes lacks the black tip on the lower mandible, it is best distinguished by voice.

Voice: Call note a frequently repeated, two-part *chip-chee,* accented on the second syllable. Also a chattering, trilly *chippy-chippy-chippy-chip,* dropping in pitch, but not in tone.

Status and Range: Endemic to Hispaniola where common primarily in mature broadleaved forests of the humid uplands. Considered threatened on Haiti because of rapid habitat destruction.

Comments: It is almost exclusively insectivorous, but occasionally eats tiny lizards. It captures food by sallying from an exposed perch to grab its food from vegetation while in flight. During flight, the wings make a strange, whirring rattle typical of all todies. In the Dominican Republic, its range overlaps with Broad-billed Tody at low elevations.

Habitat: Generally confined to dense, wet forests, including pine, chiefly at high elevations, but found locally at lower elevations, as at los Haitises, the northeastern lowlands, and dry lower mountains and limestone forests. Primarily occurs in ravines and near earthen embankments. Frequents both shade and sun coffee plantations.

Nesting: Excavates a tunnel in a soil bank to 30 cm (14") with a nest chamber at the end. Eggs (3–4) white. Breeds from April to June.

JAMAICAN TODY *Todus todus*   **Plates 49, 83**
Local Names: Rasta Bird, Robin, Robin Redbreast

Identification: 9 cm (3.5"). A chunky, diminutive bird. *Bright green above* with a *red throat* and a *long, broad, reddish bill.* The flanks are pink and the abdomen and sides of breast are pale yellow.

Voice: Almost silent during the non-breeding season. Calls include a loud *beep* and a rapid guttural 'throat-rattling' given during territorial displays while perched.

Status and Range: Endemic to Jamaica where it is widespread and common from the coast to the mountains.

Comments: Uses a sit-and-watch foraging strategy as do other todies. Catches prey on the wing, usually taken from undersides of leaves, often with a noticeable wing rattle. Usually forages in the understory 1–5 m (3–16') above the ground. Feeds on relatively large insects and their larvae and occasionally fruit.

Habitat: All forest types, from arid to wet.

Nesting: Excavates a burrow in an earth bank or a rotten tree trunk with a nest chamber at the far end. Eggs (1–4) white. Breeds from December to July.

PUERTO RICAN TODY *Todus mexicanus*   **Plates 49, 85**
Local Names: San Pedrito, Medio Peso, Papagayo

Identification: 11 cm (4.25"). A diminutive, chunky forest bird. It is the only small species on Puerto Rico, other than the hummingbirds, that is primarily bright green. The red throat; long, broad, red bill; *yellow flanks* and short, non-hovering flights of about one meter readily distinguish this species. ***Immature***: Lacks the bright red throat and has a shorter bill.

Status and Range: Puerto Rican Tody is a common and widespread endemic to Puerto Rico from the coast to the mountains.

Comments: It is difficult to see, but is often heard. When perched, this tody has the habit of pointing its bill upward and with rapid, jerky movements of the head, scans the undersurface of leaves for insects. On spying its prey, the tody sallies out, snaps up the morsel and proceeds to a new perch all in one short, curved arc. The bird depends almost exclusively on this method of procuring its food. Todies normally forage low to the ground and are most active on sunny mornings after rain. There are also peaks of activity in March and September.

Habitat: Forested areas, including damp forests of hills and mountains, shade coffee plantations and dense thickets in the arid lowlands of the south coast.

Voice: A loud, nasal *beep* or *bee-beep* is characteristic. Wing rattles in flight using the narrow-tipped primaries, mostly during courtship and territorial nest defense.

Nesting: Excavates a curved burrow in an earth bank with a terminal nest chamber, but twice as many burrows are abandoned as are actually used. The parents are sometimes assisted in raising their nestlings by one or two additional adults, probably offspring from a previous brood of the nesting pair. This assistance increases the number of offspring which eventually fledge. Eggs (1–4, the average is 2.3) shiny white, with breeding occurring primarily from March to July.

KINGFISHERS: FAMILY ALCEDINIDAE

The kingfishers are a cosmopolitan family with only two representatives in the region. They are a distinctive group characterized by their large heads and long, pointed bills and often brilliant coloration. Many feed on fish and hover similar to Ringed and Belted Kingfishers. Kingfishers excavate nesting burrows in clay banks.

RINGED KINGFISHER *Ceryle torquata*   Plate 47
Local Names: Martin-pêcheur à Ventre Roux, Cloche, Pie, Cracra (Guad, Mart)

Identification: 38–41 cm (15–16"). **Male**: Note its *crest, wide white collar, reddish-brown underparts* from breast to belly and white abdomen. **Female**: Reddish-brown from lower breast to undertail-coverts; *blue-gray upper breast band*. **Flight**: Both sexes have *distinctive reddish underwing-coverts*. **Similar species**: Belted Kingfisher is smaller, lighter-billed and has a *white* lower belly and underwing-coverts.
Voice: A harsh rattle.
Status and Range: A fairly common year-round resident on Dominica and Martinique though uncommon and local on Guadeloupe. A vagrant on Puerto Rico and Montserrat. Also occurs from the south-central United States (Texas) south through South America.
Comments: Often shy; may roost for long periods during mid-day.
Habitat: Edges of large streams, lakes and reservoirs.
Nesting: Sometimes colonial. Nests in a burrow excavated in a bank; tunnel may be 2 m (7') long. Eggs (3–5) white. Breeds from April to August.

BELTED KINGFISHER *Ceryle alcyon*   Plate 47
Local Names: Sally Benjamin (St E); Kingfisherman (CI, VI); Kingfisher (Jamaica, St E); Pájaro del Rey (PR); Martín Pescador (Cuba, DR, PR); Martin-pêcheur d'Amérique, Martin-pêcheur, Pie (Guad, Mart); Bandijsvogel (Saba, St E, St M)

Identification: 28–36 cm (11–14"). Field marks are its *large bill, grayish-blue crest, rattling call* and *habit of diving* for fish. **Male**: Blue breast band. **Female**: Single blue and one orange breast band. **Similar species**: Ringed Kingfisher is larger, heavier billed, and has more extensive reddish-brown underparts and reddish underwing-coverts.
Voice: A loud rattle.
Status and Range: Generally a fairly common non-breeding resident throughout the West Indies from September to April, with records from every month. Occurs through North, Central and northern South America.
Comments: It frequents conspicuous perches and often hovers before plunging into the water after prey.
Habitat: Calm bodies of water, both saline and fresh.

WOODPECKERS AND ALLIES: FAMILY PICIDAE

As the name of the family aptly implies, woodpeckers use their chisel-like bills not only to bore into trees in search of insects, but also to excavate nest holes. These birds have unusually long tongues for extracting insects from deep cavities. Most species have two hind toes which help support them and the stiff tail serves as an additional prop while climbing. Males of most species have red markings about the head. Drumming on trees serves to define territories. Cavities excavated by woodpeckers provide very important nest sites for other birds including parrots, flycatchers and Bahama Swallow, amongst others.

ANTILLEAN PICULET *Nesoctites micromegas*   Plates 46, 82
Local Names: Carpintero de Sierra, Carpintero Bolo (DR); Charpentier Camelle Charpentier-bois, Sèpantié Moutangn, Sèpantye Bois, Charpentier (Haiti)

Identification: 13–16 cm (5–6.25″). A *tiny, chunky, atypical woodpecker* that taps tree trunks or branches occasionally and criss-crosses its way along twigs and vines. **Adult**: Olive above and pale yellowish with heavy dark spots below. Yellow on crown. **Adult male**: Bright red patch in center of crown. **Adult female**: Slightly larger than the male and lacks red patch on crown. **Immature**: Duller green above with a duller yellow crown; abdomen more barred.
Voice: A staccato, woodpecker-like *kuk-ki-ki-ki-ke-ku-kuk*, surprisingly loud for this diminutive bird. Both sexes call.
Status and Range: Endemic to Hispaniola where common especially in the east. Also on Gonâve Island. Occurs at highest elevations in the Baoruco Mountains, but in the Cordillera Central occurs primarily in pines below 300 m (1000′). Considered threatened by habitat destruction on Haiti.
Comments: The only piculet in the West Indies, it was originally described in error from Brazil.
Habitat: Dry and humid forests, including pines mixed with some broadleaved trees, thorn forests and dense second-growth, both in mountains and lowlands, particularly semi-arid areas and mangroves. Occurs from sea level to at least 1800 m (5900′) elevation.
Nesting: The nest is in a cavity in a palm, tree or post at a height below 5 m (16′). Eggs (2–4) white. Breeds from March to July.

GUADELOUPE WOODPECKER *Melanerpes herminieri*   Plates 46, 48
Local Names: Pic de Guadeloupe, Tapeur, Tapé, Toto-bois

Identification: 25–29 cm (10–11.5″). **Adult**: Black overall with a reddish wash on the throat and belly, most noticeable in breeding season. Feet are grayish-blue. **Male**: The *bill is about 20% longer than the female's.* **Immature**: Duller. **Flight**: Direct, unlike most other members of the genus which have undulating flight.
Voice: Unlike other *Melanerpes*, sexes can be determined by call intonation, which is a slightly longer, higher pitched and more of a shriek in the male's *Wa-uh* than the female's *Wa-ah* call. A staccato *Cht-cht-cht-cht-cht-cht-cht-cht* is also emitted by both sexes.
Status and Range: Endemic to Guadeloupe where it is common; more numerous on Basse-Terre than Grande-Terre. It is absent from Guadeloupe's offshore island. Vagrant on Antigua.
Comments: Birds from southern Basse-Terre are slightly larger and blacker than those from northern and eastern Grande-Terre. Often shy and retiring; not so conspicuous as many other *Melanerpes*. Feeds primarily on insect larvae which are pecked from dead trees. It also feeds on fruits and sometimes tree frogs. The pair remains on its territory year-round. Its principal predator is the introduced rat. Clearcutting and dead tree removal are major threats.
Habitat: Elevation from sea level to the tree line at 1000 m (3300′). It is found in every habitat type including semi-deciduous forests on igneous ground and evergreen forests on Basse-Terre. Also mangrove, swamp and semi-deciduous forests on clay ground on Grande-Terre, but is unevenly distributed.
Nesting: An excavated cavity in a dead tree trunk, branch or coconut palm. Eggs (3–5) white. Incubation is 14–16 days, with the young staying in the nest for 33–37 days. Breeds from February to the end of August.

PUERTO RICAN WOODPECKER   Plates 46, 85
Melanerpes portoricensis
Local Name: Carpintero

Identification: 23–27 cm (9–10.5″). Note the red throat and breast, white rump and forehead and blackish upperparts. **Adult male**: Underparts primarily red with buffy sides. **Adult female and immature:** Less red on the underparts than the adult male. **Flight**: Undulating as with most woodpeckers.
Voice: A wide variety of calls, the most common being *wek, wek, wek-wek-wek- wek-wek...*

becoming louder and faster as it proceeds. Other vocalizations include *kuk* notes like a hen and *mew* notes. Drumming is infrequent and not very loud.

Status and Range: Endemic to Puerto Rico where it is the only common woodpecker and Vieques where it is rare.

Comments: The species often forms small congregations of two to five or more birds. Wood-boring larvae, ants and earwigs are among its principal foods, although seeds and fruits are regularly eaten. Females tend to forage higher in trees than do males and they more frequently glean for prey, taking prey items from the tree surface. Males tend to pick and probe more than females.

Habitat: From coastal plantations to mountain forests. However, it appears to be most common in hills and lower mountains including areas where shade coffee is grown.

Nesting: Drills a nest cavity high in a palm or tree. Both parents care for the young. Eggs (4) white. Breeds primarily from January to April.

HISPANIOLAN WOODPECKER *Melanerpes striatus*   Plates 46, 82
Local Names: Carpintero (DR); Sèpantié, Charpentier, Sèpantye Fran (Haiti)

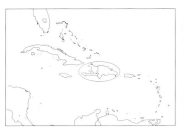

Identification: 22–25 cm (8.5–10"). A conspicuous medium-sized woodpecker. *Unmarked dark buffy-olive below* and greenish-yellow above with pale black bars. Note the *white and black patches on hindneck, red hindcrown and uppertail-coverts* and whitish to yellow eye. **Male**: Distinctly larger and longer billed than the female. **Similar species**: Yellow-bellied Sapsucker is smaller, has contrasting black and white facial markings and upperparts and a conspicuous white wing patch. **Voice**: Strong, variable vocalizations including a loud, rolling call interrupted with throaty noises. Call notes *wup* (alarm-aggression) and *ta-a*. Short *bdddt* with three to five distinct notes. Drumming signals given in vicinity of nest.

Status and Range: Endemic to Hispaniola where common and widespread. Also on Beata Island. This is possibly the most widely distributed of Hispaniola's endemic birds.

Comments: Hispaniolan Woodpecker has a number of interesting traits including the large difference in bill size between the sexes (male's bill 20% longer than female's), its tendency to form noisy social groups and its habit of often nesting colonially with up to a dozen pairs in a single tree.

Habitat: Most numerous in hilly, partly cultivated and partly wooded areas and in palms scattered among cultivated fields. From wooded swamps, mangroves and scrub on the coast to humid mountain forests. Absent only where trees are lacking.

Nesting: Excavates a cavity in a live or dead palm or tree, a live cactus or a telephone pole. Reputed to even nest in cliff burrows. Nesting often colonial. Eggs (4–6) white. Breeds mainly from February to July, but to some extent throughout the year.

JAMAICAN WOODPECKER *Melanerpes radiolatus*   Plates 46, 83
Local Name: Woodpecker

Identification: 24 cm (9.5"). Distinguished by its *red hindcrown and hindneck, whitish face*, black upperparts and wings finely streaked with white. Olive-gray below; yellow to red patch on abdomen. **Male**: Red crown. **Female**: Brownish-olive crown. **Similar species**: Yellow-bellied Sapsucker is smaller, with a bold black and white facial pattern, black breast band and a large white wing patch. **Voice**: Both male and female drum loudly in the breeding season. A loud, rollicking *chee-ee-urp* cry, similar to that of Olive-throated Parakeet. The call is a variable, single note or given in a rapid series of three or more *churp-chur-churp* notes.

Status and Range: Endemic to Jamaica where it is widespread and common at all elevations. The only woodpecker on Jamaica, except for the uncommonly occurring Yellow-bellied Sapsucker.

Comments: Chips away rotten wood in search of insects and larvae. Flight undulating.

Habitat: From coastal coconut groves to forested mountain summits, including both dry and wet forests, forest edges, woodlands, shade coffee plantations and gardens.

Nesting: Excavates a hole in a tall dead tree usually 5–10 m (16–33') above ground. Its home range overlaps those of neighboring pairs; however, it defends the area around its nest site. Two to three broods may be raised in one year. The male does most of the nest cavity excavation and broods the eggs and young at night. Both sexes tend the nest during the day. Eggs (3–5) white. Breeds primarily from December to August.

WEST INDIAN WOODPECKER *Melanerpes superciliaris*   **Plate 47**
Local Names: Red-head (CI); Carpintero Jabado (Cuba)

Identification: 26 cm (10"). **Adult male**: Upperparts and wings barred black and white, *crown to hindneck red*, underparts buff-cinnamon to brownish gray and abdomen red. **Adult female**: Like the male, except only the back of crown and hindneck are red. **Immature**: Red confined to back of crown.

Voice: The most typical call is a distinctive loud, high-pitched *krruuu-krruu-kruu...*, frequently repeated. Also has several short, low-pitched calls, usually given between mates, including a *carrah-carrah-carrah...*

Status and Range: Known only from the Bahamas, Cuba and the Cayman Islands. A common and widespread resident on Cuba, including the Isle of Youth and many offshore cays. In the Bahamas, it is common on Abaco, uncommon on San Salvador and is apparently extirpated from Grand Bahama. In the Cayman Islands, this woodpecker is limited to Grand Cayman where it is fairly common. The Grand Bahama race is considered threatened due to habitat loss.

Comments: Where this woodpecker co-exists with Rose-throated Parrot, the parrot often uses the abandoned woodpecker cavities for its own nest.

Habitat: Primarily dry forests, scrub, forest and swamp edges, coastal forests and palm groves. On Abaco, it inhabits settled areas.

Nesting: Excavates a nest hole in a tree, palm or cactus. Eggs (2–6) white. Breeds from January to August.

YELLOW-BELLIED SAPSUCKER *Sphyrapicus varius*   **Plate 47**
Local Names: Sapsucker, Spanish Woodpecker (Jamaica); Carpintero Pechiamarillo (PR); Carpintero de Paso (Cuba, DR); Charpentier, Sèpantye Nwa, Pic Américain (Haiti)

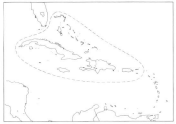

Identification: 20–23 cm (8–9"). Identified in all plumages by the *large, white wing patch* which shows as white wing-coverts in flight. **Adult**: Red forehead and crown, rarely black. Note its *black and white facial pattern* and black breast band. **Adult male**: Red throat. **Adult female**: White throat. **Immature**: Plumage pale brown with light spots above and lighter below. Faint facial stripes. **Similar species**: Smaller than most of the more common woodpeckers, from which it is further distinguished by its large white wing patch and striking head pattern. The similarly-sized Cuban Green Woodpecker has greenish upperparts and a distinctive all-red crown. Hairy Woodpecker lacks a breast bar and white wing patch and the male has red on the back of its head, rather than on the forehead. Hispaniolan and Jamaican Woodpeckers are larger, lacking the black and white facial pattern, and the large white wing patch.

Voice: Mostly silent in the West Indies, but occasionally gives a soft *mew*. Most often detected by its tapping on tree trunks.

Status and Range: A non-breeding resident in the West Indies, primarily from October to April, it is common in the Bahamas and Cuba and uncommon on Jamaica, Hispaniola, the Cayman Islands and San Andrés. Rare on Puerto Rico and the Virgin Islands and a vagrant on St Martin, St-Barthémeny and Dominica. Yellow-bellied Sapsucker may be more common than reported as it is quiet and retiring and thereby easily overlooked. Occurs through North and Central America.

Comments: Drills a series of holes horizontally in a live tree. Feeds on sap and insects attracted to the sap. Often returns to the same feeding trees.

Habitat: Forests, forest edges, woodlands and gardens in coastal and mountain areas.

CUBAN GREEN WOODPECKER
Xiphidiopicus percussus
Local Names: Carpintero Verde, Guasusa, Jorre Jorre, Ruán, Tajá

Plates 46, 79

Identification: 21–25 cm (8–10″). A small woodpecker with a noticeable *crest, green on the upperparts*, yellowish underparts, a white face with a black stripe behind the eye and a *red patch on the breast*. *Male*: Red crown. *Female*: Black crown. *Immature*: Duller than the adult, with more barring and a darker forehead. *Similar species*: Yellow-bellied Sapsucker is the same size, but does not have green in its plumage.
Voice: The typical call is a short, low and harsh *jorr-jorr-jorr…* Also a higher pitched and shorter *eh-eh-eh*.
Status and Range: Endemic to Cuba, including the Isle of Youth and several of the cays of both coasts. Common and widespread, it is perhaps the most abundant of Cuba's woodpeckers. West Indian Woodpecker is also common on Cuba, but is not found in deep woods, at high altitudes or in mangroves as is Cuban Green Woodpecker.
Comments: Usually in pairs. Forages on dead branches where it pecks for insects under bark or in crevices. Five races: *percussus* is common on Cuba; *insulaepinorum* on the Isle of Youth; *gloriae* on Cayo Cantiles in the Canarreos Archipelago; *cocoensis* on Cayo Coco and nearby cays in the Sabana-Camagüey Archipelago and *monticola* in the eastern zone of the island.
Habitat: Many forest types including wet and dry, open and dense, in both mountains and lowlands; also in mangroves.
Nesting: Drills a nest cavity in either a live or dead tree. Both parents attend the young. Eggs (3–4) white and very smooth, a bit smaller than those of the other local woodpeckers. Breeds from February to August.

HAIRY WOODPECKER *Picoides villosus*
Local Names: Spanish Woodpecker, Sook (Bahamas)

Plate 47

Identification: 20–23 cm (8–9″). *Adult male*: Red patch on back of head, upperparts mostly black with *white on back* and underparts mostly white, black eyeline and mustache stripe on an otherwise white face, and unbarred *white outer tail feathers*, the tail feathers having black spots in subspecies on Grand Bahama and Abaco. *Adult female*: Like the male, but lacks a red head patch. *Immature*: Similar to adults, but has reddish patch on crown. *Similar species*: Yellow-bellied Sapsucker has a large white wing patch and lacks a black breast bar.
Voice: A loud *keek*.
Status and Range: A fairly common year-round resident limited to several of the northern Bahamas (Grand Bahama, Abaco, Andros and New Providence). Vagrant on Puerto Rico (Mona Island). Occurs through North and Central America.
Comments: Shy; usually found in pairs. Tends to drum loudly. Two endemic subspecies inhabit the Bahamas: *P. v. piger* on Grand Bahama and Abaco and *P. v. maynardi* on New Providence and Andros. Both of these subspecies are among the smallest races of Hairy Woodpecker.
Habitat: Primarily in pine woods; may forage in other woodlands.
Nesting: Nests in a dead tree cavity, sometimes a palm. Eggs (3–4) white. Breeds from March to July.

NORTHERN FLICKER *Colaptes auratus*
Local Names: Black-heart (CI); Carpintero Escapulario (Cuba)

Plate 47

Identification: 30–32 cm (12–12.5″). A fairly large woodpecker characterized by a conspicuous *black bar across the breast, yellow underwings and undertail*, beige underparts with black spots, a large *white rump patch spotted with black* and a red patch on hindneck. *Adult male*: Black mustache stripe. *Adult female*: Lacks mustache stripe. *Immature*: Paler. *Similar species*: Fernandina's Flicker appears similar when viewed from the rear, but lacks the red hindneck and white rump. Northern Flicker's black breast bar is diagnostic.
Voice: Northern Flicker's call is a long cackle *pic-pic-pic-pic-pic-pic-pic*. It can only be confused

with that of Fernandina's Flicker. Makes a softer and lower call, when in pairs, that seems to pronounce the name *fli-quer, fli-quer*. From the nest, it gives a short, high *ee-ee-ee* call.

Status and Range: A fairly common year-round resident in the Cayman Islands (Grand Cayman) and locally on Cuba in the Sierra del Rosario, Zapata Swamp and Topes de Collantes. It is uncommon elsewhere on Cuba where the endemic subspecies (*C. a. chrysocaulosus*) is decreasing due to deforestation. The Cayman Islands race is also endemic (*C. a. gundlachi*). Occurs widely in North America.

Comments: Primarily arboreal, but sometimes forages and dust bathes on the ground.

Habitat: Any areas with trees including forests, woodlands, mangroves and gardens.

Nesting: Excavates a hole rather high in a tree or palm. Sometimes uses a branch cavity. Eggs (4–6) white, very smooth. Breeds mainly in April and May, but ranges from January to August.

FERNANDINA'S FLICKER *Colaptes fernandinae* Plates 46, 79

Local Names: Carpintero Churroso, Carpintero Hediondo, Carpintero de Tierra, Carpintero Hormiguero

Identification: 33–35 cm (13–14"). The largest Cuban wood-pecker except for Ivory-billed. Almost entirely yellowish tan with fine black barring. No red on the head. Underwings yellow. **Male**: Black mustache stripe. **Female**: Lacks mustache stripe. **Similar species**: Northern Flicker has a black patch on the breast. It also has black spots rather than bars on the underparts and a gray rather than tan crown. Fernandina's Flicker is the only woodpecker in Cuba that has zebra-like stripes all over its body.

Voice: A loud *pic-pic-pic-pic-pic-pic*, slightly slower and deeper pitched than Northern Flicker. During breeding season, even from its nest, gives a loud, short *ch-ch-ch*, with a nasal resonance. Its call may be mistaken for the cackling of Gundlach's Hawk.

Status and Range: Endemic to Cuba where it is rare and locally distributed. It is the rarest woodpecker after the Ivory-billed. In the west, found in the Sierra del Rosario, especially at Soroa. Also found at Zapata Swamp and Bermejas in Matanzas Province. It is less rare in the central provinces and on Camagüey, but has not been found east of Holguín. It may occur on cays north of Camagüey. A vagrant in the Bahamas (Grand Bahama). Fernandina's Flicker is endangered due to habitat loss.

Comments: Forages mainly on the ground for insects, worms, grubs and seeds, especially where trees are sparse and the ground is covered with leaf litter. It also visits dusty trails and even lawns. Usually found in pairs during the breeding season; otherwise remains solitary with the exception of evenings, when the pair roosts together. Appears to displace Northern Flicker as Cuba's ground-dwelling woodpecker. Sometimes occurs in colonies of up to 15 pairs.

Habitat: Savanna edges and open forests with scattered trees and dense leaf litter.

Nesting: Excavates a cavity in a dead palm, often a cabbage palm, usually relatively close to the ground. The same nest may be used in successive years. Eggs (4–5) white, similar to those of Northern Flicker. Breeds from March to June.

IVORY-BILLED WOODPECKER *Campephilus principalis* Plate 47

Local Name: Carpintero Real

Identification: 45–50 cm (17.5–19.5"). By far the *largest* West Indian woodpecker, as big as a crow with a *prominent crest, black and white plumage* and *a large ivory-colored bill*. **Male**: Red crest. **Female**: Black crest.

Voice: A soft, toy trumpet-like call *tut-tut-tut-tut;* rather unusual for the bird's large size.

Status and Range: On the verge of extinction. During the 1800s, Ivory-billed Woodpecker was found in several areas on Cuba, including the west, and as recently as the late 1980s, was very locally distributed in the district south of Moa (Ojito de Agua). It also formerly occurred through the southeastern United States.

Comments: After the disappearance of the North American race, the remaining Cuban individuals constituted the last of the species. This population was feared to consist of no more than three or four pairs in the late 1980s and has possibly succumbed to extinction since it was undetected in several comprehensive field surveys in the early 1990s. However, there are still reports of its survival in remote, unstudied areas. The bird's large size, rapid deforestation of the island, local persecution, localized distribution and need for large dead trees in which to nest have all contributed to its decline. It fed by peeling off big pieces of bark with its strong bill in search of insects. Aboriginal peoples used its bill as adornments and for trophies. More recently, the bill was prized by hunters. **Habitat**: Pine woods, mixed with deciduous forests.
Nesting: Excavates a cavity of considerable size in a large tree. Eggs have not been found on Cuba, only fledglings.

TYRANT FLYCATCHERS: FAMILY TYRANNIDAE

The tyrant flycatchers are a large Western Hemisphere family predominantly inhabiting South America. Most species are dull plumaged with a colorful crown patch that is usually concealed. Many species typically sit on exposed perches from which they sally forth to snare flying insects. Their broad bills, with bristles at the base, are well adapted for this purpose. A few species feed heavily on berries. Flycatchers are poor songsters, even in the breeding season. Some are extremely aggressive, particularly in the breeding season when they attack all birds, even large hawks and herons, that intrude into their territories.

JAMAICAN ELAENIA *Myiopagis cotta* Plates 53, 84
Local Names: Sarah Bird, Yellow-crowned Elaenia

Identification: 12.5 cm (5"). A small flycatcher distinguished by its *whitish eyebrow stripe, small black bill, yellowish primary edges* and lack of wingbars. **Adult**: Note its hidden orange-yellow crown patch that is sometimes exposed if the bird is excited, white throat and pale yellow lower underparts. **Immature**: Underparts pale gray, becoming yellow on abdomen; lacks a crown patch. **Similar species**: All other flycatchers typical of Jamaica lack the whitish eyebrow stripe and yellowish primaries.
Voice: A rapid, high-pitched *ti-si-si-sip* or *si-sip*, the last note lower than the rest.
Status and Range: Endemic to Jamaica where uncommon, but widespread from lowlands to high mountains.
Comments: Rather cryptic and easily overlooked. Forages for insects primarily by sallying out and picking them off nearby vegetation while in flight. Rarely feeds on fruits. Found at many levels within a forest, but typically from 4–8 m (13–26') above the ground.
Habitat: Most frequent in wet forests at moderate elevations. Also open woodlands, scrublands, shade coffee plantations and dry forests.
Nesting: The well-concealed, cupped nest is built of plant materials. Eggs (3) dull creamy white or buffy, moderately spotted with reddish-brown to blackish, with spotting concentrated around the broad end. Breeds from March to June.

CARIBBEAN ELAENIA *Elaenia martinica* Plate 53
Local Names: Whistler (LA); Top-knot Judas (CI); Pea Whistler (Nevis, LA, VI); Juí Blanco (PR); Piole (St L); Elénie Siffleuse, Siffleur, Siffleur Blanc (Guad, Mart); Cheery-Cheer, Kleine Grijze Vliegenvanger (Saba, St E, St M)

Identification: 15.5–18 cm (6–7"). Olive-gray above with *two whitish wingbars, throat and lower belly whitish with a light yellowish wash*, breast pale gray and bill dark with a pinkish lower mandible. Suggestion of slight crest and displays whitish-yellow crown patch when agitated. **Similar species**: Yellow-bellied Elaenia (only on St Vincent and Grenada) has a yellower belly, a more distinctive crest and is larger. Pewees have less conspicuous wingbars and lack whitish lower

bellies. Puerto Rican Flycatcher is larger and lacks wingbars and a yellow wash on the belly. Lesser Antillean Flycatcher is larger and lacks wingbars.

Voice: This elaenia calls well into the day. It has a repetitious *jui-up, wit-churr*. The last syllable is softest and appears to be caused by rattling of the bill. Song is a longer drawn-out *pee-wee-reereeree*.

Status and Range: Generally a common and widespread year-round resident in suitable habitat in the Cayman and Virgin Islands, Puerto Rico and the Lesser Antilles. Rare on Providencia and San Andrés. Also occurs on islands off the Yucatan and Belize, as well as Trinidad, Aruba, Curaçao and Bonaire.

Habitat: Woodlands, scrub and forests. Primarily in dry lowlands, but occurs in mountains on islands which it co-inhabits with Yellow-bellied Elaenia.

Nesting: The nest is a flimsy, shallow cup of twigs built in a shrub or tree to 9 m (30') above the ground. Eggs (2–3) pinkish-orange with dark markings at the broad end. Breeds primarily from January to September.

YELLOW-BELLIED ELAENIA *Elaenia flavogaster*   Plate 53
Local Names: Top-knot Pippiree, Johnny Head (Grenada, St V)

Identification: 16.5 cm (6.5"). Head and upperparts grayish olive-brown and bill black above, whitish pink below. It is further identified by brown wings with *two white wingbars*. Often *raises crest* slightly. Lower underparts pale yellow. **Similar species**: Caribbean Elaenia is smaller, has a less prominent crest and has less yellow on the belly.

Voice: A harsh, drawn-out *creup* or *creup-wi-creup*. Both members of a pair often sing together.

Status and Range: A fairly common year-round breeding resident on St Vincent, the Grenadines and Grenada. Widespread from central Mexico to southern Brazil.

Comments: Generally found in pairs; noisy from early morning well into day. Primarily feeds on small berries, but also sallies for insects.

Habitat: Primarily lowland forest edges, open woodlands, scrub and gardens.

Nesting: The nest is a shallow cup of fine plant material bound with spider webs, lined with feathers. Lichens and moss are scattered on its exterior. It is constructed in the fork of a twig at varying heights above the ground. Eggs (2–3) cream-colored, heavily spotted with red or brown, particularly at the broad end. Breeds primarily from April to June, but also in other months.

GREATER ANTILLEAN ELAENIA *Elaenia fallax*   Plate 53
Local Names: Sarah Bird (Jamaica); Maroíta Canosa (DR); Chitte Sara, Ti Chit Sara, Siffleur (Haiti)

Identification: 15 cm (5.75"). A small, rather non-descript flycatcher. Field marks include a *faint dark eyeline, two distinct wingbars* and a *small bill with a pinkish base*. Underparts pale gray, washed with yellow. Neck and breast faintly streaked with gray. White crown patch usually concealed. **Immature**: Lacks crown patch. **Similar species**: Jamaican Elaenia has a whitish eyebrow stripe, small black bill and no wingbars. Jamaican and Hispaniolan Pewees are much darker below and lack wingbars. Sad Flycatcher is slightly larger and has a heavier black bill. Stolid Flycatcher is much larger, with the yellow of the underparts being more distinct and it is a lowland bird. Eastern Wood-Pewee has a darker breast and lores and lacks an eyeline.

Voice: A harsh *pwee-chi-chi-chiup*, *see-ere*, *chewit-chewit* (Downer and Sutton). Also a trill sung at dawn.

Status and Range: A locally common year-round resident known only from the mountains of Jamaica and Hispaniola.

Comments: Inconspicuous and silent in non-breeding season. Sallies from its perch to take prey off leaves and twigs. Forages from near the ground to high in the canopy. Feeds on both fruits and insects. It most frequently forages in pairs, but is a regular participant in mixed species flocks in pines on Hispaniola.
Habitat: Pine forests on Hispaniola, open country with scattered trees and wet forests all at high elevations.
Nesting: The nest is a moss cup with a feather lining built either high in a tree or near the ground in a bush. Eggs (2) lightly spotted. Breeds in May and June.

WESTERN WOOD-PEWEE *Contopus sordidulus*   Plate 53
Local Name: Bobito (Cuba)

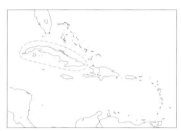

Identification: 15–17 cm (5.75–6.75"). Nearly identical to Eastern Wood-Pewee. Only accurately distinguished by voice (see description under Eastern Wood-Pewee).
Voice: A nasal, descending *peeyee* or *peeer*.
Status and Range: A very rare migrant on Cuba and a vagrant on Jamaica in September and October. Primarily occurs from western North America to northern South America.
Comments: Generally migrates southward from western North America through Central America, a few birds irregularly straying eastward of this route into the West Indies.
Habitat: Woodlands and river groves.

EASTERN WOOD-PEWEE *Contopus virens*   Plate 53
Local Name: Bobito de Bosque (Cuba)

Identification: 16 cm (6.25"). ***Adult***: Identified by *two whitish wingbars* and whitish underparts washed with dark gray on sides and breast, sometimes appearing as a complete bar across breast. Generally lacks an eyering, but may show a hint of one. Other distinguishing features include a dull orange lower mandible, moderately-notched tail and relatively long wings, extending halfway down the tail. The undertail-coverts are sometimes yellowish. ***Immature***: Buff-colored wingbars. ***Similar species***: Accurately distinguished from the very rare Western Wood-Pewee only by voice. Western Wood-Pewee may have darker underparts and a darker lower mandible. Greater Antillean Elaenia is paler on the breast with pale lores and a dark eyeline. All resident West Indian pewees are darker and buffier below and either lack or have inconspicuous buff-colored wingbars. Willow Flycatcher has paler wingbars and Acadian Flycatcher is greener above and yellower below.
Voice: A plaintive whistle *pee-a-wee*, slurring down, then up.
Status and Range: A rare migrant through the Bahamas, Cuba, Cayman Islands, Providencia and San Andrés. A vagrant on Jamaica, the Virgin Islands (St Croix) and Barbados. Most frequently recorded as a southbound migrant in September and October, less so northbound in March and April. There are a few December and January records. Occurs through eastern North America to Central and northern South America.
Comments: Easily overlooked due to close resemblance to more common species.
Habitat: Mixed and coastal woodlands, forests, forest edges, scrub, open areas and gardens.

CRESCENT-EYED PEWEE *Contopus caribaeus*   Plate 53
Local Names: Flycatcher, Tity (Bahamas); Bobito Chico, Pitibobo (Cuba)

Identification: 15–16.5 cm (5.75–6.5"). A small flycatcher, the size of a sparrow, but with an upright posture. Often shows an erectile crest. Brownish-gray upperparts, darker on the head, with beige-gray underparts, sometimes with a yellowish tinge. Shows a *conspicuous white crescent behind the eye*. Lacks wingbars. ***Habit***: *Flicks its tail upon landing*. ***Similar species***: Wood-Pewees do not have the white crescent behind the eye and have whitish wingbars. La Sagra's Flycatcher is larger, lacks

the white eye crescent and has dark reddish-brown edged tail feathers. *Empidonax* flycatchers have conspicuous white wing-bars and eyerings.

Voice: A prolonged, thin whistle that resembles the sound made by a bullet cutting through the air. Sometimes emits a feeble *vi-vi* note that could be confused with one of the calls of La Sagra's Flycatcher. On Cuba, the dawn song is a high-pitched, weak, squeaky whistle consisting of two phrases, usually given sequentially, *eeah, oweeeah*. In the Bahamas, the song is similar, but has a third *dee-dee* phrase (Reynard *et al.*). The dawn song is repeated every three or four seconds, while daytime songs are given less frequently.

Status and Range: This is the common resident pewee of the northern Bahamas and Cuba, which together make up its entire range. In the Bahamas, it is limited to Grand Bahama, New Providence, Abaco, Andros, Eleuthera and Cat Island. On Cuba, it occurs widely from the coast to moderate elevations including the Isle of Youth and many keys on both coasts.

Comments: Typically uses a low perch from which it flies to catch insects on the wing. Small insects constitute its main food, but it will also eat fruits. It has the habit of returning to the same perch or a nearby one after each sally for food. Relatively tame, it is easily approached. Formerly it was treated, with its counterparts on Jamaica and Hispaniola, as Greater Antillean Pewee. Five subspecies of Crescent-eyed Pewee are recognized.

Habitat: Pine forests, woods, forest edges, tree plantations, brushy scrub and swamp edges as well as mangroves. In the Bahamas, it is found in pine forests from February to July, where it apparently breeds.

Nesting: Builds a small, finely made cupped nest similar to a hummingbird's, but larger, located on a branch or in the fork of a twig. Constructed of roots, hair, dried grass, lichens and other soft matter and lined with small feathers and plant materials. Eggs (2–4) with dark dots, crowned at the broad end with lilac or grayish dots. Believed to breed in the Bahamas from February to March. On Cuba, begins breeding in March, but the breeding season is not well known.

HISPANIOLAN PEWEE *Contopus hispaniolensis*   Plates 53, 82
Local Names: Maroita (DR), Pipirete Tèt Fou (Haiti)

Identification: 15–16 cm (5.75–6.25"). A small flycatcher with grayish-olive upperparts, darker on the head. Underparts gray with olive, yellow or brown wash; wingbars inconspicuous or absent. Lower mandible pale at base. **Habit**: *Flicks its tail upon landing.* **Similar species**: Stolid Flycatcher is substantially larger and has white wingbars. Greater Antillean Elaenia is much paler below and has two distinct wingbars.

Voice: A strong, mournful *purr, pip-pip-pip-pip* (Wetmore and Swales). The dawn song is a loud, rapid-fire volley *shurr, pet-pit, pit-pit, peet-peet* with the paired syllables successively rising in pitch (Reynard *et al.*).

Status and Range: Endemic to Hispaniola where it is common and widespread from the coast to the mountains, occurring to at least 1800 m (6000'). Also on nearby Gonâve Island and a vagrant on Mona Island located between Hispaniola and Puerto Rico. A vagrant in the Bahamas where two individuals were observed on Providenciales following the passage of Hurricane Floyd over Hispaniola in September 1987.

Comments: A tame bird, it flies from its perch to catch small insects, its principal food, on the wing. Frequently returns to the same perch. Also feeds on small fruits. It generally perches low above the ground. In pine forests, this pewee regularly forages in mixed species flocks.

Habitat: Various, including pine and broadleaf forests, forest edges, shade coffee plantations and orchards at all elevations.

Nesting: A fine cupped nest of lichens, moss and rootlets is constructed 3–5 m (10–16') off the ground in the fork of a twig. The female constructs the nest and incubates the eggs, but both sexes feed the young. Eggs (2–4) creamy white with a pinkish tint, heavily marked with reddish-brown and grayish spots and blotches concentrated around the broad end or the middle of the egg. Breeds from May to June.

JAMAICAN PEWEE *Contopus pallidus*   **Plates 53, 84**
Local Names: Willie Pee, Little Tom Fool, Stupid Jimmy

Identification: 15 cm (5.75"). A small flycatcher with dark olive-gray upperparts, darker on head. Underparts buffy brown. Lower mandible orangish; wingbars absent or very indistinct. The tail is slightly notched. **Habit**: *Flicks its tail upon landing.* **Immature**: Underparts gray, lower mandible yellowish-white and wingbars reddish-brown. **Similar species**: Stolid Flycatcher is larger and has two white wingbars. Greater Antillean Elaenia is much paler below and has two distinct wingbars. Eastern Wood-Pewee is whiter below with distinct wingbars, and it does not normally flick its tail upon landing.

Voice: A plaintive *pee* at varying tonal levels (Downer and Sutton). Also, during the daytime, a rising and then falling *oéeoh* (Reynard *et al.*). The dawn song consists of two alternating phrases *paléet*, *weeléeah* (Reynard *et al.*).
Status and Range: Endemic to Jamaica where common and widespread at high and mid-elevations. Infrequently occurs in lowlands outside the breeding season.
Comments: Feeds primarily by capturing small insects in the air, for which it sallies from an exposed perch. Jamaica's three *Myiarchus* flycatchers also sally for insects, but these are snatched from leaf surfaces, a practice rarely executed by the Jamaican Pewee. It usually forages from 2–9 m (7–30') above the ground, though sometimes much higher. Openings in the forest beneath the canopy are most frequented and, to a lesser extent, forest edges. Eastern Wood-Pewee reputedly forages vertically upward, typically returning to the same perch, and its flights are shorter. Foraging by the Jamaican Pewee is horizontal via lengthier sorties, with the bird regularly moving to a different perch.
Habitat: Primarily mid-elevation forests and, to a lesser extent, high mountain forests. Also forest edges.
Nesting: Apparently builds a small, cup-shaped nest of finely woven plant material. Breeding primarily occurs in high and mid-elevation forests from April to June.

PUERTO RICAN PEWEE *Contopus portoricensis*   **Plates 53, 85**
Local Name: Bobito

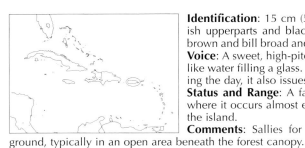

Identification: 15 cm (5.75"). A small flycatcher with brownish upperparts and blackish wings and tail. Underparts buffy brown and bill broad and flat with pale base to lower mandible.
Voice: A sweet, high-pitched trill, sometimes rising up the scale like water filling a glass. The dawn song is a repetitive trill. During the day, it also issues some warbling phrases.
Status and Range: A fairly common endemic to Puerto Rico where it occurs almost exclusively in the western two-thirds of the island.
Comments: Sallies for insects from a perch low above the ground, typically in an open area beneath the forest canopy.
Habitat: Moist forests and woods at primarily moderate to low elevation; less frequent in drier habitats near sea level and in mangroves.
Nesting: The nest is a cup of lichens, moss and fine plant materials with thin bark camouflaging the exterior. Eggs (2) cream-colored with dark markings at the broad end. Breeds from March to June.

LESSER ANTILLEAN PEWEE *Contopus latirostris*   **Plate 53**
Local Names: Tombé Levé, Loulou Fou, Gobe-mouches, Mouche Rolle Gobe- mouche (Guad, Mart, French WI)

Identification: 15 cm (5.75"). A small flycatcher. Upperparts brownish-olive, wings and tail black, underparts yellowish-brown and bill broad and flat with pale base to lower mandible.
Voice: An emphatic rising *pree-e-e* and a high-pitched and repeated *peet-peet-peet*.
Status and Range: A fairly common, but somewhat local year-round resident known only with certainty from Guadeloupe, Dominica and Martinique. There are sporadic reports of the species existing high in the mountains on St Christopher.

2

Comments: Perches low and sallies for insects. Formerly the Puerto Rican and St Lucia Pewees were considered races of Lesser Antillean Pewee.
Habitat: Primarily mountain forests and woods, sparingly in drier forests and scrub near sea level and in mangroves.
Nesting: The nest is a cup of lichens, leaves and moss built on a twig of a tree or bush. Eggs (2) cream-colored with dark reddish-brown markings around the egg's mid-section.

ST LUCIA PEWEE *Contopus oberi*   Plates 53, 86
Local Name: Gobe-Mouche

Identification: 15 cm (5.75"). A small flycatcher with dark olive-brown upperparts and *reddish-brown underparts*. Note its *black wings and tail* and *broad, flat bill with pale base to lower mandible*.
Voice: An emphatic rising *pree-e-e* and a high-pitched *peet-peet-peet*.
Status and Range: A fairly common endemic resident on St Lucia.
Comments: Perches low and sallies for insects. Generally occurs in openings in the forest understory.
Habitat: Primarily in moist forests at higher altitudes; scarce at lower altitudes and in drier habitats.
Nesting: The nest is a cup made of leaves, lichens and moss placed on a branch. Eggs (2) dark cream-color heavily spotted with brown (Danforth). Breeds in May and June.

YELLOW-BELLIED FLYCATCHER *Empidonax flaviventris*   Plate 53
Local Name: Bobito Amarillo

Identification: 15 cm (5.75"). Distinguished by its olive-green upperparts and *yellowish underparts including the throat*. Eyering broad and yellowish, two whitish or *yellowish wingbars* and *lower mandible pale orange*. **Similar species**: About the size and shape of a pewee, but with conspicuous wingbars and distinct eyering. Acadian Flycatcher has less yellow below and a white throat.
Voice: Practically silent during migration. Call note a strong, ascending *pee-wee*.
Status and Range: A very rare and irregularly occurring southbound migrant on Cuba during September and early October. Even rarer northbound in April. Vagrant on Jamaica. Occurs through North and Central America.
Comments: Voice is one of the best characters to separate *Empidonax* flycatchers in the field, but unfortunately during their short stay in the West Indies these birds are usually silent. Most *Empidonax* flycatchers in the West Indies are infrequent migrants that occur primarily during their southbound migration. They mingle with warblers, pewees, thrushes and other passerines. Sometimes they remain in an area two or three days before continuing their journey.
Habitat: Forests, woodlands, tree clumps, river and swamp edges and gardens.

ACADIAN FLYCATCHER *Empidonax virescens*   Plate 53
Local Name: Bobito Verde (Cuba)

Identification: 12 cm (4.75"). Note the conspicuous yellowish eyering and two buffy or whitish wingbars. Most of lower mandible is yellowish. Throat and belly are white. **Similar species**: Similar in size to Eastern Wood-Pewee, but has greener upperparts and more yellowish underparts. Yellow-bellied Flycatcher is yellower below, particularly on the throat. Willow Flycatcher has less yellow below and a less conspicuous eyering. However, these differences are minimal. See notes under Willow Flycatcher.

Voice: Virtually always silent as a migrant. Call note a soft *weet*.

Status and Range: A rare, southbound migrant on Cuba and the northern Bahamas in September and October and rare northbound in April. Vagrant in the Cayman Islands. It is the least rare of the four *Empidonax* flycatchers that pass through the West Indies. Occurs from North America to northern South America.

Comments: Overlaps in habitat use with other *Empidonax* flycatchers during migration. On the breeding grounds, most species can be separated by habitat preference and voice.

Habitat: Open woodlands, forest edges, tree clumps and gardens.

WILLOW FLYCATCHER *Empidonax trailli* Plate 53
Local Name: Bobito de Traill (Cuba)

Identification: 15 cm (5.75″). Back grayish-olive and underparts grayish-white with almost no yellow. White chin. Lacks a noticeable eyering and has whitish wingbars. **Similar species**: Similar in size and coloration to Eastern Wood-Pewee which has heavier, whitish wingbars. Acadian Flycatcher is a bit yellower below, has a more conspicuous eyering and a greener back. Other migrant flycatchers such as Alder (*E. alnorum*) and Least (*E. minimus*) may occur in the West Indies. In the field, Alder is indistinguishable from Willow Flycatcher except by call and Least Flycatcher nearly so. Consequently, it is ill advised to attempt to identify most *Empidonax* as to species based solely upon plumage characters. For additional guidance on *Empidonax* identification refer to: Witney, B., and K. Kaufman. 1985. The *Empidonax* challenge. Part I: Introduction. *Birding* 17(4): 151–158. Also by the same authors: (1985) Part II: Least, Hammond's and Dusky Flycatchers. *Birding* 17(6): 277–287; (1986) Part III: Traill's Flycatcher and the Alder/Willow problem. *Birding* 18(3) 153–159; (1986) Part IV: Acadian Yellow-bellied and Western Flycatchers. *Birding* 18(6) 315–327.

Voice: A characteristic *fi-bi-o*, something of a cross between a whistle and a buzz. Also a harsh *fitz*.

Status and Range: A very rare migrant on Cuba, including the Isle of Youth, and Jamaica from mid-September to mid-October. Occurs in North and Central America.

Habitat: River and swamp edges, woodlands, tree clumps and gardens.

EULER'S FLYCATCHER *Empidonax euleri* Plate 53

Identification: 13.5–14 cm (5.25–5.5″). Note the *conspicuous buff or pale reddish-brown wingbars*, underparts yellowish with *grayish-olive breast band*, whitish eyering and olive-brown upperparts.

Voice: A murmuring *pee, de-dee-dee-dee-dee*, the first note higher pitched than the others.

Status and Range: Formerly a very rare resident on Grenada where found near Grand Etang. Possibly extirpated; no reliable reports since 1950. Very little is known about this bird on Grenada. It is believed the species was a year-round resident since the island race was endemic. This flycatcher subspecies is critically endangered, but the cause is not known. Also occurs on Trinidad and in tropical South America.

Comments: Sallies for insects from a low perch. Frequently flicks tail up and down with a jerky motion.

Habitat: Primarily moist mountain forests.

Nesting: The nest has not been found on Grenada. On Trinidad, it is a deep cup of grass built on a branch or sometimes in a tree cavity. Eggs (2–3) cream-colored with reddish-brown spots. Breeds from May to July.

EASTERN PHOEBE *Sayornis phoebe* Plates 53
Local Name: Bobito Americano (Cuba)

Identification: 16.5–18 cm (6.5–7″). Diagnostic field marks are a *dark head with no eyering, black-ish wings with no wingbars* and longish dark *tail which it frequently pumps*. Underparts whitish with pale yellow wash, especially in September and October.

Status and Range: A very rare southbound migrant on Cuba and in the Bahamas where recorded from Grand Bahama, Bimini, Eleuthera and Great Inagua. Occurs from mid-September to February. Also found through eastern and central North America.
Habitat: Woodland edges, fence lines and hedgerows. Often associated with fresh water.

SAD FLYCATCHER *Myiarchus barbirostris*   Plates 51, 84
Local Names: Little Tom Fool, Dusky-capped Flycatcher

Identification: 16.5 cm (6.5"). **Adult**: Distinguished by its relatively small size, *dark crown, yellow underparts,* except for the chin and throat and *faint wingbars.* **Immature**: Breast and throat grayish-white. Only the lower belly is yellow. **Similar species**: Stolid Flycatcher is larger, has more distinct wingbars and whiter edges to primaries, lacks yellow on the breast, has a less distinct crown pattern and a distinctive call. The tail and primaries of the larger Rufous-tailed Flycatcher are distinctly reddish brown. Greater Antillean Elaenia is smaller and has a finer bill.
Voice: An emphatic *pip, pip-pip.* Sometimes *pip-pip-pireee,* rising at the end (Downer and Sutton).
Status and Range: Endemic to Jamaica where widespread and common.
Comments: Typically perches at 3–9 m (10–30') above the ground and sallies to snatch small insects from leaves, sometimes taking two or three per sortie. Often returns to the same perch.
Habitat: Primarily forests and woodlands from lowlands to middle elevations, more scarce in semi-arid lowland areas. Less frequent in fairly open forests at higher elevations. Its range contracts to middle elevations outside of the breeding season.
Nesting: Nest is constructed of vegetation in a diverse array of cavities from woodpecker holes to house eaves. Eggs (3–4) heavily spotted. Breeds from April to June.

GREAT CRESTED FLYCATCHER *Myiarchus crinitus*   Plate 51
Local Name: Bobito de Cresta (Cuba)

Identification: 18–20.5 cm (7–8"). **Adult**: Upperparts greenish-brown, *wings and tail with reddish-brown,* whitish wingbars, throat and breast gray, and belly bright yellow. **Similar species**: Tropical Kingbird is much paler on the throat and has a pale gray crown. La Sagra's Flycatcher has yellow confined to the abdomen and undertail-coverts, has a plaintive rather than harsh call and perches at a 45 degree angle, rather than nearly erect.
Voice: A loud, harsh *wheeep* with a rising inflection.
Status and Range: A rare migrant and non-breeding resident on Cuba from as early as September through April. A very rare migrant in the northern Bahamas and a vagrant on Hispaniola (Dominican Republic) and Puerto Rico. It is widespread in North America south to northern South America.

GRENADA FLYCATCHER *Myiarchus nugator*   Plate 51
Local Names: Loggerhead, Sunset Bird, Pippiree Gros-téte

Identification: 20 cm (8"). Good field marks are its olive-brown upperparts, *dark brown head* with slightly erectile crest, black bill with pinkish lower mandible, *two pale brown wingbars,* primaries with reddish edges and *long tail with conspicuous reddish edges to outer webs.*
Voice: A loud *quip* or harsh *queuk.*

Status and Range: A common year-round resident known only from St Vincent, the Grenadines and Grenada at all elevations.
Comments: Formerly considered conspecific with *M. tyrannulus*, the Brown-crested or Rusty-tailed Flycatcher. Like other flycatchers in this genus, it sallies into the open, often returning to the same perch, and flicks its tail.
Habitat: Open areas around settlements and lowland scrub, especially near palms.
Nesting: Nests in tree cavities and sometimes human-made structures such as open pipes. Eggs (2–4) creamy white, heavily spotted. Breeds from March to October.

RUFOUS-TAILED FLYCATCHER *Myiarchus validus*   Plates 51, 84
Local Names: Big Tom Fool, Big Head Bob

Identification: 24 cm (9.5"). Large, with a distinctive *reddish-brown tail and primaries*. The belly and abdomen are yellow. *Immature*: Underparts whitish. **Similar species**: Its larger size and reddish-brown primaries distinguish it from both Sad and Stolid Flycatchers. Great Crested Flycatcher, not yet recorded on Jamaica, has less reddish-brown wings and whitish wingbars.
Voice: A fast, rolling, descending *pree-ee-ee-ee-ee*, rather like the neigh of a horse. Also a *chi- chi-chiup* (Downer and Sutton).
Status and Range: Endemic to Jamaica where it is fairly common, primarily at mid-elevations and less frequently in high mountains and lowlands.
Comments: Often perches beneath the forest canopy among dense vegetation from which it sallies for prey. Habitat differs from that of similar Stolid Flycatcher, which is found mainly in arid woodlands, mangroves and scrub. Feeds on fruits and insects, including cicadas, moths and butterflies.
Habitat: Various forest types, but primarily moist forests and, to a lesser extent, dry scrub and secondary forests.
Nesting: A nest of grass and leaves is built in a shallow cavity in a tree or stump. Eggs (3–5) cream-colored, heavily marked with brown and black particularly at the broad end. Breeds from April to July.

LA SAGRA'S FLYCATCHER *Myiarchus sagrae*   Plate 51
Local Names: Tom Fool (Bahamas, CI); Bobito Grande (Cuba)

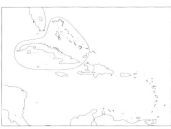

Identification: 19–22 cm (7.5–8.5"). A medium-sized flycatcher, with an unusual leaning posture and a flat-headed appearance. It has a long, usually all-black bill and two inconspicuous white wingbars. **Adult**: Upperparts grayish to brownish-olive, with the *rump cinnamon-colored* during the breeding season and gray in non-breeding plumage. The crown is dark, the breast and sides of the neck gray, underparts grayish-white and undertail-coverts dingy yellowish, but difficult to detect in the field. *Wings and tail with a small amount of reddish-brown*. The crest is held erect when agitated. **Immature**: Upperparts reddish-brown; underparts grayish. **Similar species**: Best distinguished from other *Myiarchus* flycatchers by voice and by habit of perching at a 45 degree angle rather than nearly erect. Crescent-eyed Pewee is smaller, lacks reddish-brown in the tail and has a conspicuous white eyespot. Cuban Solitaire has a mustache stripe, white eyering and white outer tail feathers. For additional information on identification of La Sagra's Flycatcher see: Smith, P. W., and D. S. Evared. 1992. La Sagra's Flycatcher. *Birding* 24(5): 294–297.
Voice: Song, usually given at dawn and more often during the breeding season, is a two-syllabled whistle *tra-hee*. The call is a short, plaintive whistled *huit*.
Status and Range: A common year-round resident in the northern Bahamas, Cuba including the Isle of Youth, and the Cayman Islands (Grand Cayman). It is generally uncommon in the southern Bahamas and absent from Turks & Caicos. These islands comprise the entire range of the species.
Comments: Typically forages in the understory, mainly by snatching prey during hovering flights. Feeds

primarily on caterpillars, katydids and other insects, but also eats fruits. Formerly combined with Stolid Flycatcher, but differences in vocal behavior distinguish it from other *Myiarchus* flycatchers.
Habitat: Pine woods, mixed woodlands, dense thickets, mangroves and forests at all elevations.
Nesting: Nest is a cup-shaped structure of hair, feathers, plant fibers and other soft materials, built in a cavity of a trunk, broken tree limb or bamboo stalk. Eggs (4) white with a yellowish wash and grayish-purple spots at the broad end. Breeds from April to July.

STOLID FLYCATCHER *Myiarchus stolidus* Plate 51
Local Names: Tom Fool (Jamaica); Manuelito (DR); Louis, Pipirite Gros-tête, Pipirit Gwo-tèt, Alouette Huppée (Haiti)

Identification: 20 cm (8"). A medium-sized flycatcher *with two pale white wingbars* and primaries heavily fringed with white. Throat and breast whitish, abdomen and belly pale yellow and bill black and moderately heavy. The brown tail has reddish-brown inner webs. **Similar species**: Sad Flycatcher is smaller, has less distinct wingbars, the yellow of the belly extends up to the breast, and it shows a more distinct crown pattern. The call also differs. Rufous-tailed Flycatcher is larger, lacks wingbars and has reddish-brown primaries. Pewees and elaenias are substantially smaller, whereas kingbirds are larger and more robust.
Voice: A prolonged, rolling *whee-ee-ee, swee-ip, bzzrt* (Downer and Sutton). Also a plaintive *jui* on Hispaniola.
Status and Range: A common year-round resident throughout Jamaica and Hispaniola and its adjacent islands (Gonâve, Tortue, Grande Cayemite and Beata). These islands comprise the entire range of the species.
Comments: An active bird easily approached. Feeds on insects, which it typically captures on the wing by snatching them from a twig or leaf. Also feeds on fruits, which are plucked while hovering.
Habitat: Lowland forests and forest edges, including arid woodlands, scrub and mangrove forests. Less frequent in edges of wet mid-elevation forests. On Hispaniola, also in pine woods.
Nesting: Nests in cavities in anything from trees to houses. Eggs (3–4) pale yellow, heavily spotted with dark brown especially at the broad end. Breeds from April to June.

PUERTO RICAN FLYCATCHER *Myiarchus antillarum* Plates 51, 85
Local Names: Stolid Flycatcher, Juí de Puerto Rico (PR)

Identification: 18.5–20 cm (7.25–8"). A medium-sized flycatcher with dark brown upperparts and head, faint wingbars and light brownish-gray underparts, becoming lighter toward the tail and without a yellow wash. *The call is the best field mark*. **Similar species**: Caribbean Elaenia is smaller, has two wingbars and a conspicuous yellow wash on the belly. Loggerhead Kingbird is much larger, with a distinctly two-toned body pattern and larger bill.
Voice: The most characteristic call is a plaintive whistle *whee*, from which the bird's Spanish name is derived. Also a dawn song, *whee-a-wit-whee*, the two middle syllables of which are unmusical and sometimes sung independently during the day.
Status and Range: A common year-round resident on Puerto Rico, fairly common on Vieques and rare on Culebra. Among the Virgin Islands, it is uncommon on St John and rare on St Thomas, Virgin Gorda and Tortola. These islands comprise the entire range of the species.
Comments: This inconspicuous and inactive bird would easily go unnoticed except for its distinctive call which reveals its presence. Puerto Rican Flycatcher was formerly lumped with several other West Indian flycatchers under the name Stolid Flycatcher. In 1967, Dr. Wesley Lanyon determined the Puerto Rican population to be distinct, based on differences in vocalizations. Puerto Rican Flycatcher was nearly extirpated from Puerto Rico after a hurricane struck the island in 1928, but the species has since recovered. It has declined in the Virgin Islands as a result of habitat destruction.
Habitat: Wooded areas, including mangrove borders, arid scrub, coffee plantations, the haystack hills and mountain forests, except for the higher slopes.

Nesting: A nest of plant stems, lined with finer materials, is built in a tree cavity or open stump. Eggs (3–5) yellowish-white with spots concentrated at the broad end. Breeds from late April to July.

LESSER ANTILLEAN FLYCATCHER *Myiarchus oberi*　　**Plate 51**
Local Names: Loggerhead (Nevis); Gros Tête (St L); Arbitre (Guad); Gobe-mouches Huppé (Mart); Tyran Janeau, Siffleur, Siffleur Huppé (Guad, Mart); Pipiri Gros-tête (French LA)

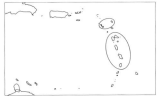

Identification: 19–22 cm (7.5–8.5"). **Adult**: Distinguished by dark olive-gray upperparts, *mostly yellow underparts* from upper belly to undertail-coverts, and *tail feathers with reddish inner webs*. **Immature**: Brighter reddish edges to wings and tail which fade with aging. **Similar species**: Caribbean Elaenia is smaller and has whitish wingbars.
Voice: A loud, plaintive whistle *peeu-wheeet*. Also short whistles *oo-ee, oo-ee* or *e-oo-ee*.
Status and Range: A common year-round resident on Barbuda, St Christopher, Nevis, Dominica, Martinique and St Lucia. It is rare on Guadeloupe. These islands comprise the entire range of the species.
Comments: Formerly lumped with Stolid Flycatcher (*M. stolidus*) of the Bahamas and Greater Antilles.
Habitat: Primarily edges of dense woodlands, forests and tree plantations at or above 100 m (330'). Much less often in lower altitude second growth or scrub.
Nesting: A loose nest of plant fibers, feathers and plant down is built in a tree cavity. Eggs (3–4) creamy buff, heavily spotted and scrawled with purplish-brown and violet-gray. Breeds from March to July.

TROPICAL KINGBIRD *Tyrannus melancholicus*　　**Plate 52**
Local Name: Yellow Pippiree

Identification: 23 cm (9"). Fairly large, with primarily *yellow underparts*, pale gray crown, greenish back and gray facial mask. Typically the orange crown patch is concealed. **Similar species**: Western Kingbird has white in outer tail feathers and a smaller bill. Great Crested Flycatcher is much darker and browner above.
Voice: Similar to that of Gray Kingbird, but the call is a softer and less emphatic *pip- pri-pip-pri-pip-pri...*
Status and Range: A rare and irregular migrant on Grenada, remaining to breed in some years and not occurring at all in most years. Recorded from all months. Vagrant on Cuba. Occurs through the southern United States to South America.
Habitat: Open, semi-arid scrubland.
Nesting: The nest is a bulky bowl of twigs usually built near the end of a branch of a large tree or shrub. Eggs (2–3) glossy white with chocolate brown or purplish markings that are heavier at the broad end and finer near the narrow end.

WESTERN KINGBIRD *Tyrannus verticalis*　　**Plate 52**

Identification: 21–24 cm (8–9.5"). **Adult**: Head and hindneck pale with a dark gray line through the eye, *pale gray upper breast, yellow belly* and with *conspicuous white edges to outer tail feathers*. **Similar species**: Tropical Kingbird has a larger bill and lacks white in the outer tail feathers.
Status and Range: A very rare migrant, primarily in October and November, in the northern Bahamas south to Eleuthera. A vagrant on Cuba. There are records as late as early January. It is widespread in western North America south to Costa Rica.

EASTERN KINGBIRD *Tyrannus tyrannus* **Plate 52**
Local Name: Pitirre Americano (Cuba)

Identification: 22–23 cm (8.5–9"). **Adult**: *Upperparts dark gray* and *head and tail black.* Note its white underparts, two indistinct wingbars and *tail with a terminal white band.* The rarely seen crown patch is orange-red. **Similar species**: Loggerhead Kingbird has a heavier bill, a *brownish-gray back* washed with olive, a yellow wash on the lower bell, and much less white on tail tip. Gray Kingbird has *gray upperparts* with a dark facial mask and lacks a white tail band. Giant Kingbird is larger, has a heavier bill, darker crown, lacks a white tail band and is found only on Cuba. Immature Fork-tailed Flycatcher has a pale gray back.

Status and Range: An uncommon migrant in western Cuba, including the Isle of Youth, and the Cayman Islands (Grand Cayman). Rare in the northern Bahamas, eastern Cuba, Jamaica and San Andrés and a vagrant in the southern Bahamas (Providenciales), Puerto Rico, St Christopher and Dominica. Occurs most regularly as a southbound migrant in September and October, less frequently northbound in April and early May. The range includes North America south to central South America.

Habitat: Semi-open woodlands including gardens in urban areas. Often perches in tall trees.

GRAY KINGBIRD *Tyrannus dominicensis* **Plate 52**

Local Names: Fighter (Bahamas); Pitiwick, Rain Bird (LA); Chichery (VI); Pippiree, Hawk-beater (Grenada, St V); Petchary (Jamaica, VI); Petigre (DR); Pitirre (Cuba, PR); Pipirit, Titiri (Haiti); Pipiri (Mart); Piritata (Nevis); Grive d'hivernage (St B); Pipirite (St L); Pipirite, Tyran Gris (Grenada, Guad); Chincherry (Saba, St E); Grote Grijze Vliegenvanger (Saba, St E, St M)

Identification: 22–25 cm (8.5–10"). Gray above, pale gray-white below with a distinct *dark mask* extending under the eye and a slightly notched tail. The small yellow-orange patch on crown is rarely visible. **Similar species**: Loggerhead Kingbird has a dark crown extending below the eye, distinct voice and no notch in the tail. Eastern Kingbird has a white-tipped tail and darker upperparts, including most of head. Northern Mockingbird cocks its longer tail upward and has distinct white wing and tail patches.

Voice: Call is a loud, emphatic *pi-tirr-ri.* The song is a more musical, six-syllabled variation *pi-ti-rée, pi-ti-rro* of the call. Also a sharp *peet, burr,* and *tirré.*

Status and Range: One of the most conspicuous and common species throughout the West Indies. It is a year-round resident from Hispaniola east through the Lesser Antilles. However, most breeding birds from the Bahamas, Cuba, Jamaica and the Cayman Islands migrate off-island from November to March. Some birds leave the Lesser Antilles as well, apparently for northern South America. It is possible that these are replaced by migrants from Cuba and vicinity. It also occurs in northern South America and coastal southeastern United States.

Comments: Feeds primarily on large insects captured on the wing by sallying from its perch. Gray Kingbird often returns to the same perch and batters the insect before eating it. Some birds take advantage of street lights to feed at night on the attracted insects. Gray Kingbirds may form large, temporary communal roosts, composed of dozens or hundreds of birds. It is very aggressive, earning some of its common names by attacking much larger birds including hawks and frigatebirds.

Habitat: Mountains and lowlands, in open areas with scattered trees. Usually on exposed perches, such as telephone lines and bare tree tops.

Nesting: An open nest crudely constructed of twigs and usually sparsely lined with finer materials is built in trees, shrubs and human-made structures at varying heights. Eggs (2–4) pink to reddish, heavily marked at one end with irregular blotches. Breeds mainly from April to June.

LOGGERHEAD KINGBIRD *Tyrannus caudifasciatus* Plate 52

Local Names: Tom Fighter (CI); Loggerhead (Jamaica); Pitirre Guatíbere (Cuba); Manjuila (DR); Clérigo (PR); Tête Police, Pipirit Chandèl (Haiti)

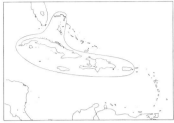

Identification: 24–26 cm (9.5–10"). Dark above and white below, this flycatcher is distinctively two-toned. *Crown entirely blackish*, with a rarely seen yellow or orangish crown patch. The *square tail* has a white trailing edge except for Hispaniola and Puerto Rico populations. The bill is large. **Immature**: Gray above; buffy-white below with buffy wing-coverts. **Similar species**: Gray Kingbird has a lighter crown with only ear-coverts dark, rather than a dark crown. It also has a notched tail and distinctive voice. Eastern Kingbird is smaller, with a smaller bill, blacker back and with more white on the tip of the tail; also lacks a yellow wash on the lower belly. Loggerhead Kingbird has a much larger bill than any of the *Myiarchus* flycatchers. Giant Kingbird is larger in size with a larger bill, paler crown and the white terminal tail band is inconspicuous.

Voice: Calls variable, but usually a loud, mallet-like chattering, with *bzze-beep* or *bee-beep* elements in them, such as *joú-bee-beep*. Song a bubbling, repeated *p-p-q* in breeding season. Also a distinctive, loud, ascending dawn song. Mostly silent outside breeding season.

Status and Range: A common and widespread year-round resident through the northern pine-forested Bahamas (Grand Bahama, Abaco, Andros and New Providence), the Greater Antilles and the Cayman Islands, but it has been absent from Little Cayman in recent years. These islands comprise the entire range of the species.

Comments: Typically occurs in more forested areas than Gray Kingbird. On islands from which Gray Kingbirds depart for a portion of the year, the Loggerhead expands its habitat use. Commonly sallies from its low perch to capture insects, usually by plucking them off a leaf or twig rather than in mid-air like the Gray Kingbird. Fruits and small lizards are also eaten. Usually on exposed perches, such as posts, tree branches and telephone wires.

Habitat: Dry and wet woodlands, pine and broadleaf forests, shade coffee plantations, mangrove swamps and open areas with scattered trees from the lowlands to mid-elevations.

Nesting: An unlined, cup-shaped nest of twigs, stems and grasses is built in a tree or shrub at various heights above the ground. Typically the nest is in the fork of a twig on an outer branch. Eggs (2–4) tinted reddish-brown with darker brown and violet markings at the broad end. Breeds principally from February to July, but some nesting has been noted from November to January.

GIANT KINGBIRD *Tyrannus cubensis* Plates 52, 79

Local Name: Pitirre Real (Cuba)

Identification: 23 cm (9"). The largest West Indian kingbird with a *very large bill*. Upperparts dark, especially the crown, and underparts white. Typically the orange crown patch is not visible. **Similar species**: Loggerhead Kingbird is smaller in bill and size, has a white tail band and a darker crown. Eastern Kingbird is smaller, has a finer bill, paler crown and white tail band.

Voice: A chatter resembling that of Loggerhead Kingbird, but louder, longer, deeper and a bit harsher. Also a call of four distinct syllables.

Status and Range: Endemic to Cuba, including the Isle of Youth. Formerly also the Bahamas (Great Inagua and Caicos Islands). On Cuba, it is rare and local in distribution. Most abundant around Moa (Ojito de Agua). Giant Kingbird is endangered with its decline apparently due to deforestation.

Comments: Perches high in trees on exposed branches from which it sallies after prey. It is sluggish and, unlike other kingbirds, may sit with its belly resting on its perch. A large prey item may be flipped in the air, sometimes several times, to accommodate it properly in the bill. Giant Kingbird feeds on large insects, lizards and fledglings of other birds and also consumes significant amounts of fruit. Usually found in pairs.

Habitat: Forests and woodlands near rivers and swamps. Also pine barrens mixed with hardwoods and semi-open woodlands with tall trees.

Nesting: Builds a cupped nest of roots, dried grass and small twigs, without a lining, high in a tree between forked twigs of a horizontal branch. Eggs (2–3) white with a brownish tinge and with scattered grayish speckles confined to one end. Breeds from April to June.

SCISSOR-TAILED FLYCATCHER *Tyrannus forficatus*   Plate 52

Identification: 31–38 cm (12–15"). A pale flycatcher with a *conspicuously long tail*. Wings and tail blackish. *Adult*: Head and upperparts pale gray to white, belly and undertail-coverts with a *pink-orange wash* and *axilars reddish*. *Immature*: Dull gray-brown upperparts and small reddish axilar patch. *Similar species*: Fork-tailed Flycatcher has a black cap and is white below, rather than pinkish orange.
Status and Range: A vagrant in the West Indies from late October to December when recorded from the Bahamas (Grand Bahama, Abaco and San Salvador), western Cuba, Hispaniola and Puerto Rico. Its typical range encompasses Central North America south to Panama.

FORK-TAILED FLYCATCHER *Tyrannus savana*   Plate 52
Local Names: Scissor-tail (Grenada); Bobito de Cola Ahorquillada (Cuba)

Identification: 33–41 cm (13–16"). *Adult male*: Note its black head, *pale gray back*, blackish-brown wings and white underparts. *Tail in breeding plumage is very long* with upper half of streamers edged in white; shorter during molt. *Adult female and immature*: Like the male, but duller with a shorter tail. *Similar species*: Eastern Kingbird is rather like immature Fork-tailed, but has a *dark gray back*. Scissor-tailed Flycatcher lacks the black cap and has a pinkish-orange wash below in adult plumage.
Status and Range: A very rare, local and irregularly occurring migrant on Grenada primarily in July and August. Frequents the vicinity of the airport. A vagrant in the Grenadines (Carriacou), Barbados, St Lucia, St Barthélemy, St Martin, the Cayman Islands, Jamaica and Cuba. Its primary range includes Central and South America.
Comments: Grenada birds, which appear to be have overshot their primary non-breeding grounds in Venezuela and Trinidad, apparently migrate to Argentina and Chile to breed. Such an austral migration is unusual among West Indian birds.
Habitat: Open savannas.

COTINGAS: FAMILY COTINGIDAE

Cotingas are a diverse group of arboreal neotropical birds, ranging in size from small hummingbird (7.6 cm [3"]) to crow (48 cm [19"]) size. Some have brilliant plumages, which they use in spectacular courtship displays. Voices are variable, ranging from loud, bell-like calls to grunting sounds; some have beautiful musical qualities, whereas others sound 'metallic'. Only one species occurs in the West Indies.

JAMAICAN BECARD *Pachyramphus niger*   Plates 51, 54, 83
Local Names: Judy (male), Mountain Dick (female), Kissidy, Rickachay, London City, Rickatee, Weaver Bird

Identification: 18 cm (7"). A heavy set, *large-headed, stubby-billed* and *short-tailed* bird which behaves like a flycatcher. *Adult male*: Entirely black, it shows a white mark at the base of the wing in flight. *Adult female and immature*: Generally reddish-brown above and pale gray below; cheeks and throat cinnamon-colored. *Similar species*: Jamaican Blackbird is sleeker, with a longer, thinner and more pointed bill and a smaller head than the similarly-colored adult male Becard.
Voice: Two hoarse *queecks* followed by a very musical, syncopated, not clearly defined, *Co-ome and tell me what you hee-ear*. The phrase gradually rises in pitch and then falls on the last two syllables.

Status and Range: Endemic to Jamaica where widespread and locally fairly common.
Comments: Moves slowly beneath the canopy, often hovering to take prey from twigs, although it also hawks for insects and gleans insects and fruit. The Becard may range to lower elevations outside the breeding season. Although well-represented in mainland tropics, it is the only member of the cotinga family in the West Indies.
Habitat: Primarily tall open forests and forest edges in the hills and lower mountains, but also in closed forests, woodlands, pastures with trees and gardens at mid-elevations.
Nesting: The nest is a spectacularly large mass of plant material suspended from a tree branch, sometimes above the canopy, but also at lower heights within woodland or in an open area. The entrance to the interior chamber is from below. More than one brood may be raised per season. Eggs (3) dull white, heavily marked with dark gray, concentrated at the broad end. Breeds from March to June.

SWALLOWS: FAMILY HIRUNDINIDAE

The swallows are the most distinctive family in the huge order of perching birds. Of cosmopolitan distribution, they are characterized by their short, broad bills and long, pointed wings, and their habit of feeding on flying insects on the wing. Swallows are very gregarious and can often be seen in large numbers over fields and marshes or perched on wires. Though they resemble swifts, the two families are not closely related. Swifts are distinguished by their much longer wings, shallower wing strokes and more rapid flight.

PURPLE MARTIN *Progne subis*   Plate 55
Local Name: Golondrina Azul Americana (Cuba)

Identification: 20–22 cm (8–8.5"). A large swallow. ***Adult male***: Entirely bluish purple. ***Adult female and immature***: Note the scaled pattern on its grayish-brown breast, light gray patches on sides of neck and an indistinct border between the darker breast and whitish belly. ***Similar species***: The male is indistinguishable from Cuban Martin in the field. Female Cuban Martin has darker brown markings on the breast, throat and chin, which are more sharply defined from the white belly. Female Caribbean Martin has a brown wash on the breast, rather than a scaled pattern.
Voice: Gurgling, which includes a high *twick-twick*. Also when chasing each other, pairs emit a high, melodious warble. Calls are very similar to those of other martins.
Status and Range: Common on Cuba and the Cayman Islands (Grand Cayman) and uncommon in the Bahamas as a southbound migrant, primarily from mid-August to mid-October; also a rare northbound migrant, primarily in March. Infrequent in other months. Vagrant on Jamaica, Hispaniola, Puerto Rico and the Virgin Islands. Occurs from North America to eastern South America.
Comments: On Cuba, often mixes with resident Cuban Martins before continuing its journey. There is a single record of an entirely dark male martin nesting with what was apparently a female Caribbean Martin on St Croix in the Virgin Islands. Whether the male was a Purple or Cuban Martin was undetermined.
Habitat: Towns and open areas.

CUBAN MARTIN *Progne cryptoleuca*   Plate 55
Local Name: Golondrina Azul (Cuba)

Identification: 20–22 cm (8–8.5"). A large swallow. ***Male***: Bluish-purple overall, with some concealed white feathers on the belly. ***Female***: White belly and abdomen contrast sharply with the brown breast, sides, throat and chin. ***Similar species***: The male is impossible to separate from Purple Martin in the field. In the hand, Cuban Martin has concealed white feathers on the belly and a slightly more forked tail. Female Purple Martin has paler brown markings on the breast, throat and chin which blend gradually into a whitish belly. Both sexes of Caribbean Martin are more similar to female Cuban Martin in their underparts pattern, but the white below is restricted to the lower belly

and abdomen, whereas in Cuban Martin it extends to the upper belly. Also, female Caribbean Martin has less contrast between the white and dark of the underparts. **Voice**: Gurgling, which includes a high-pitched *twick-twick*, similar to the sound made by a taut cable or wire when someone makes it vibrate. Also a strong, melodious warble. The calls are slightly distinct from those of Caribbean and Purple Martins. **Status and Range**: A common breeding resident on Cuba, including the Isle of Youth, and Cayo Coco, where it arrives in February (earliest date: 21 February) and departs in October (latest date: 21 October). Vagrant in the Bahamas (Eleuthera). It is believed to migrate to South America outside the breeding season, but this is not confirmed.

Comments: Sometimes individuals mingle with flocks of Purple Martins migrating south. Unless collected, it is practically impossible to determine if males flying over other Caribbean islands are Cuban or Purple Martins. The non-breeding range is unknown, but is presumably in South America. Classified by some as a subspecies of Caribbean Martin.

Habitat: Cities, towns and rural areas. Also swamp borders and open habitats, particularly in the lowlands, but sometimes in the mountains.

Nesting: Usually colonial, but sometimes solitary. Nests in the abandoned holes of woodpeckers, atop palm trunks, holes in dead mangroves and in the shelter of cliffs and caves near coasts. Also nests under bridges, in buildings, church towers and even in cavities of air conditioners. Builds its nest with mud, leaves, grass and vegetable fibers, cemented with saliva to form a compact cup. Eggs (4–6) white. Breeds from March to July.

CARIBBEAN MARTIN *Progne dominicensis*   Plate 55

Local Names: Purple Swallow (Grenada, St V); Swallow (Jamaica, LA, VI); Golondrina Grande (DR); Golondrina de Iglesias (PR); Hirondelle à Ventre Blanc (Haiti); Hirondelle (Guad, Mart, St L); Gale Bird, Caraïbische Zwaluw (Saba, St M, St E)

Identification: 20 cm (8"). A bi-colored martin. **Male**: Upperparts, head and throat blue; belly and abdomen white. **Female and immature**: Similar to the adult male, but blue of underparts replaced by a brownish wash that blends somewhat gradually into white of belly. **Similar species**: Female Cuban Martin has white underparts extending to the upper belly, whereas in Caribbean Martin the white extends only to the lower belly. Female Caribbean Martin has less of a contrast between the white and dark of the underparts. Female Purple Martin has a scaled pattern on the breast, rather than a wash.

Voice: Gurgling, which includes a high *twick-twick*. Also a melodious warble and a gritty *churr*. Very similar to the calls of Cuban and Purple Martins.

Status and Range: A fairly common breeding resident in much of the West Indies from January to September. However, it is a vagrant in the southern Bahamas (Great Inagua, Mayaguana and Grand Turk) and the Cayman Islands and absent from the northern Bahamas and Cuba. It also occurs on Tobago and is thought to migrate to South America from October to December.

Habitat: Primarily towns, open areas, freshwater bodies and coastal sites with rock promontories.

Nesting: A simple nest of twigs, leaves and other plant materials is constructed in a crevice of a cliff, building or tree. One was found in the exhaust pipe of an oil barge. Eggs (2–6) white. Breeds from February to August.

TREE SWALLOW *Tachycineta bicolor*   Plate 55

Local Names: Golondrina de Arboles (Cuba); Golondrina Migratoria (DR); Golondrina Vientri-blanca (PR)

Identification: 12.5–15 cm (5–5.75"). **Adult**: Blue-green above, *entirely white underparts* and slightly notched tail identify this swallow. The wing linings are pale gray. **Immature**: Brown upperparts. **Similar species**: Bahama Swallow has a deeply forked tail and white wing linings. Golden Swallow has a more forked tail, longer wings and a more graceful flight.

Voice: Mostly silent in the West Indies, but sometimes twitters.

Status and Range: A common non-breeding resident on Cuba and locally common in the Cayman Islands primarily from November to May, but occurring from September to June. The species is an uncommon migrant in the northern Bahamas and Jamaica and is rare on Hispaniola, Puerto Rico and the Virgin Islands (St Croix). It is very rare in the southern Bahamas. The species occurs through North America to northern Central America.
Habitat: Swamps, marshes, rice fields and other wetlands.

GOLDEN SWALLOW *Tachycineta euchrysea* Plate 55
Local Names: Swallow, Rain Bird (Jamaica); Golondrina Verde (DR); Oiseau de la Pluie, Jolle-Jolle, Irondèl Vèt, Hirondelle Verte (Haiti)

Identification: 12.5 cm (5"). **Adult**: A *small* swallow. *Iridescent bluish-green upperparts* with a *golden sheen, white underparts* and moderately forked tail. The Hispaniolan race is much duller than the Jamaican race. **Female**: Duller than the male and grayish on the breast. **Immature**: Duller above; gray breast band. **Similar species**: Tree Swallow has a shallower tail notch, relatively shorter wings and is less graceful in flight. Bahama Swallow, which it does not overlap in range, has a more deeply forked tail and no golden sheen on its upperparts.
Voice: A soft twittering *chi-weet* during the breeding season.
Status and Range: An uncommon year-round resident on Hispaniola in the high mountains of the Sierra de Baoruco, Sierra de Neiba and Cordillera Central. An increasingly rare and very local resident on Jamaica in Cockpit Country where it was last reported with certainty in 1989. It was formerly common on Jamaica into the late 1800s in the Blue Mountains and central highlands. The endemic Hispaniolan race is considered endangered and the race on Jamaica critically so. The reason for this swallow's decline on Hispaniola appears to be habitat destruction, specifically of high altitude pine forests. The causes of its decline on Jamaica are unknown. Hispaniola and Jamaica comprise the entire range of the species.
Comments: Graceful, often seen foraging over pine forests or perched with several other individuals in large, dead pine snags.
Habitat: On Hispaniola, mainly in relatively open country and pine forests of high mountains, but also over rain forests. On Jamaica, occurs over open areas, such as sugarcane fields on the northern fringe of Cockpit Country.
Nesting: In old woodpecker holes and other tree cavities, especially standing dead trees, under house eaves and possibly in caves. Eggs (3) white. Breeds from April to June.

BAHAMA SWALLOW *Tachycineta cyaneoviridis* Plate 55
Local Name: Golondrina de Bahamas (Cuba)

Identification: 15.5 cm (6"). **Adult**: Dark greenish above, wings blue, *underparts white including wing linings* and with a *deeply forked tail*. **Female**: Slightly duller than the male. **Immature**: Brownish upperparts and tail less forked. **Similar species**: Tree Swallow has a slightly notched tail and pale gray wing linings.
Voice: A metallic *chep* or *chi-chep* (Brudenell-Bruce).
Status and Range: Endemic to the Bahamas where common on Grand Bahama, Abaco and Andros. It may now be extirpated as a breeding bird on New Providence. Outside the breeding season, this swallow moves to more open habitats and sometimes to other islands of the Bahamas. Sites where it is most readily seen include the pond at San Andros Airport, Lucays National Park on Grand Bahama and along the Great Abaco Highway. It is a vagrant in eastern Cuba.
Habitat: Pine forests, towns, clearings and near cliffs.
Nesting: Often nests in a tree cavity in a pine forest. Sometimes under eaves of buildings. Appears to depend entirely on cavities for nesting. Eggs (3) white. Breeds from April to July.

NORTHERN ROUGH-WINGED SWALLOW
Stelgidopteryx serripennis
Local Names: Golondrina Parda (Cuba); Golondrina (DR)

Plate 55

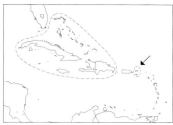

Identification: 12.5–14 cm (5–5.5"). Entirely brown above, this swallow is identified by its white underparts blending into pale brown on the throat.

Status and Range: Generally a rare southward migrant and rarer non-breeding resident and northbound migrant through the Bahamas, Cuba, Jamaica, Hispaniola and the Cayman Islands from August to April. It is very rare in the Virgin Islands, primarily occurring on St Croix and is a vagrant on Guadeloupe. Its numbers appear to vary from year to year. It occurs through North and Central America.

Comments: Often in the company of other swallows.
Habitat: Open fields and wetlands.

BANK SWALLOW   Riparia riparia
Local Names: Golondrina de Collar (Cuba), Golondrina Parda (PR); Hirondelle de Rivage (Guad, Mart)

Plate 55

Identification: 12.5–14 cm (5–5.5"). The *dark band* across the white breast coupled with dark brown upperparts are diagnostic in all plumages. ***Similar species***: Antillean Palm Swift has a white rump and longer, narrower wings. Its flight is more rapid and darting.

Status and Range: A southbound migrant through the West Indies primarily from September to December and a northbound migrant in April and May. There are records of migrants and non-breeding residents for every month except July. Uncommon in the Bahamas, Cuba, Puerto Rico, the Virgin and Cayman Islands, Barbados and San Andrés, the species is generally rare through most of the West Indies, though still unrecorded from a few of the Lesser Antilles. It is widespread nearly worldwide.

Comments: Typically in association with other swallows on utility wires.
Habitat: Primarily open areas along the coast during migration.

CLIFF SWALLOW   Pterochelidon pyrrhonota
Local Names: Golondrina de Farallón (Cuba); Hirondelle à Front Blanc (Guad); Hirondelle Blanc (St L)

Plate 55

Identification: 12.5–15 cm (5–5.75"). Distinguished by its *dark reddish-brown chin, throat and ear patch* along with a *buff-colored forehead and rump* and with only a slightly notched tail. ***Similar species***: Cave Swallow has a darker forehead and a much paler ear patch and throat.

Voice: A short, melodious note repeated while pursuing insects in flight.

Status and Range: A southbound migrant from late August to early December, returning northward from late March to early May, the species is uncommon in the Cayman Islands, Barbados and San Andrés; rare in the Bahamas, Cuba, Virgin Islands, Guadeloupe, Dominica and St Lucia and very rare to a vagrant elsewhere in the West Indies. It is widespread in the Western Hemisphere.

Comments: The absence of Cliff Swallow records from Jamaica, Hispaniola and Puerto Rico is likely due to it being overlooked in localities where the very similar Cave Swallow is common.
Habitat: Primarily along the coast during migration.

CAVE SWALLOW *Pterochelidon fulva*　　　　　　　　**Plate 55**
Local Names: Swallow, Rain Bird (Jamaica); Golondrina de Cuevas (Cuba, DR, PR); Irondèl Falèz, Hirondelle Fauve (Haiti)

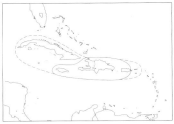

Identification: 12.5–14 cm (5–5.5"). The dark reddish-brown rump and forehead, pale reddish-brown ear patch, throat, breast and sides and slightly notched tail distinguish this swallow. **Similar species**: Cliff Swallow has a dark reddish-brown throat and ear patch and a lighter forehead.
Voice: A chattering or twittering. Also a rather musical call note *twit* is common.
Status and Range: A common breeding resident through the Greater Antilles. It is present year-round on Jamaica, Hispaniola and Puerto Rico, but on Cuba most birds depart from September to February when not breeding. It is a rare migrant in the Cayman Islands and Virgin Islands where it primarily occurs on St Croix. It is a vagrant on Martinique, St Lucia, St Vincent and the Grenadines. It also occurs in the extreme south-central United States and Mexico.
Comments: Typically in large flocks, which often perch together on utility wires or forage on the wing for tiny insects.
Habitat: Principally over fields, wetlands, around cliffs and in towns.
Nesting: The nest is constructed of mud in a cave mouth, on a building or under a ledge or bridge. Eggs (2–5) white with markings of various colors concentrated at the broad end. Breeding is colonial from March to July.

BARN SWALLOW *Hirundo rustica*　　　　　　　　**Plate 55**
Local Names: Swallow (VI); Golondrina Cola de Tijera (Cuba); Golondrina del Norte (DR); Golondrina de Horquilla (PR); Irondèl Ke Long (Haiti); Hirondelle Roux (St L); Hirondelle Rustique, Hirondelle de Cheminée, Hirondelle (Guad, Mart); Christmas Bird, Boerenzwaluw (Saba, St E, St M)

Identification: 15–19 cm (5.75–7.5"). **Adult**: Note its primarily *tan underparts*, dark reddish-brown throat and *deeply forked tail* with white spots. **Immature**: Throat and upper breast tan, remainder of underparts white and tail less deeply forked.
Voice: A thin, unmusical *chit*.
Status and Range: Generally a common migrant throughout the West Indies primarily from September to October and April to May, though individuals occur during every month. It is widespread globally.
Comments: Typically in flocks zigzagging over fields or perched on utility wires. Feeds on small flying insects.
Habitat: Open areas over fields and swamps, primarily along the coast during migration.

JAYS, MAGPIES AND CROWS: FAMILY CORVIDAE

Crows, the largest of passerines, are found almost world-wide, being absent only from New Zealand and most of the other islands of the Pacific Ocean. Crows in the West Indies are primarily black with strong bills. They are typically gregarious, aggressive, strong fliers and lack a musical song. The apparent intelligence of crows is well-demonstrated in their varied feeding behaviors. Some species drop mollusks or nuts from the air onto a hard surface to crack the shells.

CUBAN PALM CROW *Corvus minutus*　　　　　　　　**Plates 26, 79**
Local Names: Cao Pinalero (Pinar del Río); Cao Ronco (Camagüey)

Identification: 43 cm (17"). A *large, completely black* bird, with a faint violet sheen fading to dull brown-black in worn plumage. Its nostrils are completely covered by bristles. **Similar species**: Slightly smaller than Cuban Crow and appears to have a shorter neck in flight. *Best identified by its distinctive voice.*

Voice: A harsh *craaao*, with an initial abrupt rise in pitch, then leveling off and falling slightly at the end of the phrase. Several calls are usually given in series.
Status and Range: Endemic to Cuba where it is rare and very local. It is confined to two lowland regions on Cuba: the northwestern part of the Sierra de Los Organos in Pinar del Río Province (El Francisco, La Manaja, Asiento Viejo and Los Acostas) and the Camagüey Province (San Miguel, Jimaguayú, El Jardín, San Pablo, La Panchita, El Delirio, Santa Rosa and Tayabito). It is greatly outnumbered by the Cuban Crow. Considered endangered, the causes of its decline are unknown.
Comments: Social, usually seen in small groups. Typically arboreal, but may forage on the ground. Feeds on fruit, seeds, invertebrates and lizards. Formerly Hispaniolan and Cuban Palm Crows were considered one species, Palm Crow (*C. palmarum*). However, the two populations are now considered different species, based on distinct differences in their voices, plumages and tarsus and bill sizes.
Habitat: Forests, scrub and palm savanna.
Nesting: Nest is a rough platform of twigs usually built high in a palm tree. Eggs (3–4) pale green, evenly speckled or blotched with olive-brown and dark brown. Breeds from March to May.

HISPANIOLAN PALM CROW *Corvus palmarum* Plates 26, 81
Local Names: Cao (DR, Haiti); Ti Kaw (Haiti)

Identification: 43 cm (17″). A *large, completely black* bird, with a purplish and bluish sheen fading to dull brown-black in worn plumage. *Flight*: Wings appear shorter than those of White-necked Crow and it flies with a steadier flapping. Characteristically flicks tail downward. *Similar species*: Considerably smaller than White-necked Crow, which is a much more robust bird. *Best identified by its distinctive and less variable voice*.
Voice: A harsh nasal *aaar*, with the vowel sound as in the word 'fast'. Usually given in a series of several calls.
Status and Range: A common resident endemic to Hispaniola. In the Dominican Republic, found in the mountain pine forests of the Cordillera Central and Sierra de Neiba and irregularly at lower elevations, such as around Lago Enriquillo. On Haiti, known from Etang Saumâtre, Artibonite, Mirebalis, Le Selle and other localities, but absent from the Massif de la Hotte.
Comments: Usually seen in small- to medium-sized groups of up to 50 birds, foraging on the ground or in trees. Feeds on fruit, seeds, insects, snails and lizards. Formerly considered to be a single species with the Cuban Palm Crow.
Nesting: The nest is crudely constructed of twigs built high in a palm or pine tree. Eggs (3–4) pale green, evenly speckled or blotched with olive-brown and dark brown. Breeds from March to May.

CUBAN CROW *Corvus nasicus* Plates 26, 79
Local Names: Cao Montero, Cao (Cuba)

Identification: 45–48 cm (17.5–19″). A large, noisy black crow with a purple sheen, a black bill and legs and conspicuous nostrils. *Similar species*: Cuban Palm Crow is a bit smaller, appears to have a shorter neck in flight and has a very different voice. However, it is rare and localized.
Voice: Much louder and noisier than parrots, especially when gathered in large flocks. Characteristically a high call with a nasal quality, *caah-caaah*. Also gobbling, reminiscent of a turkey, and diverse guttural phrases similar to parrot calls. Trained, it can repeat words, but not so well as parrots.
Status and Range: A common year-round resident on Cuba, including some cays north of Camagüey and the southern part of the Isle of Youth. In the Bahamas, limited to only a few of the most southern islands where it is common on North and Middle Caicos, rare on Providenciales and a vagrant on Grand Turk. These islands comprise the entire range of the species.
Comments: Usually gathers in flocks, particularly when bad weather approaches. During the

breeding season, separates into pairs. Omnivorous, it feeds on fruits, seeds, corn, plantains, reptiles, frogs and other items.

Habitat: Primarily thin forests, but also palm plantations, treed borders of swamps, croplands and garbage dumps. Formerly, strictly a forest bird, but recently has begun to frequent human settlements near forests.

Nesting: Although a large structure, the nest is difficult to find as it is usually built high among palm fronds. It is constructed of sticks, twigs, dried leaves, feathers and other soft materials. Eggs (4) greenish with brownish-violet spots. Breeds primarily in April and May.

WHITE-NECKED CROW *Corvus leucognaphalus* Plates 26, 82
Local Names: Cuervo (DR); Corneille, Kaw (Haiti)

Identification: 48–51 cm (19–20″). *Large, entirely black*, with a large bill. Upperparts violet sheen; the white at the base of the neck cannot be seen except in display. **Similar species**: Best distinguished from the smaller Hispaniolan Palm Crow by its more variable voice. Also note its less direct, occasionally soaring, flight.

Voice: A wide variety of vocalizations, including a *caw* and clucking, gurgling, bubbling and laugh-like calls and squawks.

Status and Range: Endemic and locally common on Hispaniola, including Gonâve and Saona Islands, but rapidly declining and considered threatened because of habitat alteration and hunting. Extirpated from Puerto Rico since 1963. Prehistoric remains from the Virgin Islands (St Croix).

Comments: Feeds mainly on fruits and seeds, but also takes vertebrates and large insects. Forms large foraging flocks that sometimes leave the forest to raid crops. It is also considered a game bird. Recent sightings of crows on Puerto Rico have proven to be escaped exotics. Due to its rapid decline on Hispaniola, and with the recovery of habitat and improvement in wildlife conservation on Puerto Rico, consideration should be given to reintroducing White-necked Crow in its former range.

Habitat: Primarily moist uplands, including limestone hills, but occurs from semi-arid scrublands and open lowlands with scattered trees to mountain pine forests.

Nesting: A crude nest of sticks is built in a tree or palm. Eggs (3–4) greenish-blue with dark markings. Breeds from February to June.

JAMAICAN CROW *Corvus jamaicensis* Plates 26, 84
Local Names: Jabbering Crow, Jamming Crow, Jamicrow

Identification: 38 cm (15″). *Large, entirely dull black*, with a *large bill*. **Flight**: Slow and labored. **Similar species**: The only crow on Jamaica. All other black birds on Jamaica are considerably smaller.

Voice: A loud *craa-craa* as well as semi-musical jabbering.

Status and Range: Endemic to Jamaica where locally common. It may be expanding its range on the island. Most often encountered in Cockpit Country and John Crow Mountains; less so in Moneague and Worthy Park.

Comments: Commonly in pairs, sometimes in small flocks. Characteristically perches on high, bare limbs of tall trees. Works through epiphytes and tree crevices searching for invertebrates and frogs. Also takes bird eggs and fruits.

Habitat: Primarily mid-elevations in undisturbed wet limestone forests. Less frequent in disturbed wooded areas and park-like country at mid-elevations.

Nesting: A crude platform of sticks and other plant material is built high in a tall tree. Eggs (3) pale greenish-blue, greenish-white or yellowish-green, marked with dark brown and olive-brown. Breeds from April to June.

NUTHATCHES: FAMILY SITTIDAE

The nuthatches are plump, short-tailed, arboreal birds. Their short legs, long toes and strong claws are adaptations for climbing on tree trunks and branches, and even allow these small birds to walk upside-down on the underside of branches. Unlike woodpeckers, nuthatches do not use their tail as a support when climbing. Their flight is undulating. The name nuthatch is related to the birds' nut-eating habits. Thick-shelled nuts are opened by wedging them in a bark fissure and hammering them with the robust bill.

BROWN-HEADED NUTHATCH *Sitta pusilla*   Plate 41

Identification: 9.5–11 cm (3.75–4.25"). Diagnostic field marks are its *bluish-gray upperparts, brown crown*, dark brown line through the eye and *white hindneck patch*. The underparts are whitish.
Voice: A weak, fast, squeaky high-pitched chatter.
Status and Range: A very rare and local year-round resident on Grand Bahama in the Bahamas, its population has been declining dramatically since the 1960s. Considered endangered due to habitat destruction. It is widespread in the southeastern United States.
Comments: Climbs up and down old pine trunks and along limbs, often upside down, in small groups or singly, gleaning for insects. The endemic subspecies on Grand Bahama differs from other races primarily in voice and, to a lesser extent, in appearance.
Habitat: Limited to pine barrens.
Nesting: Nests in a tree cavity or stub at a low height. Eggs (3–5) creamy white, heavily spotted with shades of red-brown.

WRENS: FAMILY TROGLODYTIDAE

Wrens are typically plump, active birds, with a short tail that can be cocked above the back. They usually feed on or near the ground, moving with agility through the undergrowth. Typically solitary. Although inquisitive, wrens only infrequently leave cover. They fly with rapid wingbeats. One of their most notable features is their spectacularly beautiful songs. Polygamy is frequent in some species.

ZAPATA WREN *Ferminia cerverai*   Plates 41, 80
Local Name: Fermina

Identification: 16 cm (6.25"). Sparrow-sized, brown in color and striped with black except for the underparts which are grayish. Tail, bill and legs long. Wings short and round. *Similar species*: House Wren is smaller, less heavily barred above and does not occur in sawgrass marshes.
Voice: One of the best songsters in the West Indies. The typical song is high, strong and very musical, starting with a low guttural note and transforming into a warble that sounds similar to a canary. Usually repeats its song three times before falling silent for a period. The intervals between songs are much shorter during the breeding season. Sings nearly year-round, but is silent during harsh weather. The wren also has several harsh notes and sharp *chips* of various tones. Its alarm call is peculiar. Both sexes sing, but the female's song is shorter and thinner.
Status and Range: Endemic to Cuba and one of the island's most famous birds. Constitutes one of the three endemic species, the other two being Zapata Rail and Zapata Sparrow, found primarily if not only in Zapata Swamp. Occurs in a limited area north of Santo Tomás on both sides of Zanja (ditch) 'La Cocodrila' where it is rare and extremely localized. The extent of its range in the marshes is unknown; however, it can still be found near the Hatiguanico River and apparently has expanded its range in Zapata Swamp to include Hato de Jicarita and an area 8 km (5 miles) west of the road from Jagüey to Playa Larga. Zapata Wren is threatened as a result of its extremely limited habitat, which is periodically burned. The introduced mongoose may also have influenced its decline.

Comments: Highly secretive, the species was unknown to scientists until 1926. Practically impossible to find unless located by its song. Drops its tail while singing. Hides in grass tussocks and bushes. When alarmed, it tries to disappear silently, walking through the grass rather than flying. Flies only short distances. Feeds on insects, spiders, caterpillars, small snails, lizards and berries.
Habitat: Strictly sawgrass marshes.
Nesting: The first nest of the Zapata Wren was discovered on June 12, 1986, with four nests having been found to date. The nest is built about 1 m (3') above the ground and is well-concealed among green sawgrass, where it is woven into a globular structure with a side entrance, very similar to nests of grassquit and bullfinch. The nest is lined with feathers. Eggs (2) white. The eggs are laid at one-day intervals. Breeding occurs from January to July.

HOUSE WREN *Troglodytes aedon*   Plate 41
Local Names: Godbird (Grenada); Rock Bird, Wall Bird (LA); Rossignol (Guad, St L); Oiseau Bon Dieu (French WI)

Identification: 11.5–13 cm (4.5–5"). A small, active brown bird with a large head relative to the rest of its body. *Adult*: Reddish-gray above with a *pale eyebrow stripe* and variably dark brown to whitish below. The throat is also variably pale or brown, bill is either all dark or with lower mandible yellow and *wings and tail are heavily barred with black*. **Similar species**: Zapata Wren is larger, more heavily barred, and only occurs in sawgrass marshes. **Voice**: A bursting, gurgling warble unlike any other resident landbird in the West Indies; dialects vary slightly among islands. Also a sharp chatter.
Status and Range: A common year-round resident on Dominica, locally so in the lowlands of Grenada, uncommon on St Vincent and rare and local on St Lucia where it is confined to northeastern dry coastal scrub between Louvet and Marquis. Not reported on Guadeloupe since 1973 and believed extirpated from Martinique where not recorded since 1900. The St Lucia and St Vincent races are threatened. The causes of the decline of all races are due to hunting, predation by rats and the mongoose and habitat destruction from charcoal burning. On St Lucia, the impact of the mongoose may have been less because the native boa (*Constrictor orophias*) keeps the mongoose in check in limited areas. Brood parasitism by the Shiny Cowbird also threatens the St Lucia and St Vincent races. Vagrant in western Cuba. Migrants from North America are very rare in the northern Bahamas. It occurs through most of the Western Hemisphere.
Comments: A bird of low vegetation and undergrowth. Lesser Antillean forms do not cock their tails like North American birds. Darker-plumaged birds are reputed to occur in moist upland forests with lighter ones occurring in lowland coastal areas. Each island has or had an endemic subspecies. The taxonomy of the complex is not well settled. Some authorities give specific rank, e.g. Antillean House Wren (*T. martinicensis*) to Lesser Antillean birds collectively, or even to separate Lesser Antillean island populations.
Habitat: From moist upland forests to arid lowland coastal areas and human settlements.
Nesting: A twig nest is built in a cavity in banks or vegetation, occasionally well above ground. Eggs (2–6) whitish, heavily speckled brownish-red. Breeds from May to August.

MUSCICAPIDS: FAMILY MUSCICAPIDAE

The muscicapids are a very large and diverse family represented in this region only by the thrushes. The thrushes are a distinctive subgroup, cosmopolitan in range, of which the local species are typical. They generally have long legs, an erect posture and feed on both berries and insects, often on the ground. Many are good songsters.

RUBY-CROWNED KINGLET *Regulus calendula*   Plates 64, 66

Identification: 11.5 cm (4.5"). Note its tiny size, olive-colored upperparts, *bold white eyering* and two whitish wingbars. *Male*: Usually a concealed red crest. *Female*: Lacks red crest.
Status and Range: A very rare non-breeding resident in the northern Bahamas from October to

March. A vagrant on Cuba, Jamaica and Hispaniola (Dominican Republic). It is widespread in North America to northern Central America.
Comments: Generally occurs in low, scrubby vegetation through which it actively hops and flits in search of tiny insects.

BLUE-GRAY GNATCATCHER *Polioptila caerulea*　　　　Plate 41
Local Names: Rabuita (Cuba); Cat Bird, Chew Bird, Spain-Spain, Cotton Bird (English speaking islands)

Identification: 11 cm (4.25"). A small, gray, active bird with a *long, thin tail* and *white outer feathers*, often cocked upward. Note its white underparts and conspicuous *white eyering*. **Male**: Note its bluish tint to upperparts and fine black eyebrow stripe during breeding season. **Female**: Paler, lacks eyebrow stripe. **Similar species**: It is smaller, slimmer and with a longer tail than a warbler. On Cuba, it may be confused with Cuban Gnatcatcher, but it lacks the black facial crescent. The songs are also very different: Blue-gray Gnatcatcher has a soft imperceptible song and a peculiar call note, whereas Cuban Gnatcatcher has a relatively loud, melodious song.
Voice: Usually detected by its voice, which is a mew-like call, similar to that of Gray Catbird, and usually of two syllables, *zpee-zpee*. Occasionally gives a soft whisper-like song.
Status and Range: A common year-round resident on the larger islands of the Bahamas, augmented primarily from September to November by southbound migrants from North America which occur on the smaller islands as well. It is a common non-breeding resident on Cuba, including the Isle of Youth, from September through April and is uncommon during those months in the Cayman Islands. It occurs from North America south to Honduras.
Habitat: Scrubland on all islands. Also mangroves in the Cayman Islands. On Cuba, occurs in all lowland and mid-elevation habitats from forests to gardens.
Nesting: A cup-shaped nest is built low either in a bush, the fork of a tree branch or sometimes a small palm. Eggs (3) bluish-green, spotted. Breeds from March to June.

CUBAN GNATCATCHER *Polioptila lembeyei*　　　　Plates 41, 80
Local Name: Sinsontillo

Identification: 10.5 cm (4"). A small, slender bird with a long, black tail with white outer feathers, often cocked upward. Gray above and grayish-white below with a white eyering. Note the *black crescent stripe* extending from the eye to behind the ear. **Female**: Paler. **Similar species**: Can only be confused with Blue-gray Gnatcatcher which lacks the black facial crescent. Cuban Gnatcatcher is also a bit thinner and smaller, more nervous and has a louder, melodious song.
Voice: Despite its small size, it has a loud and melodious song. The song begins with a whistle repeated about four times, followed by a trill and a thin varied whisper, *pss-psss-psss-psss-tttiizzzt-zzzz-ttizzz-tzi-tzi-tzi*. Reminiscent of Zapata Wren, but softer. It also has a number of other calls.
Status and Range: Endemic to Cuba where it is common in the east, absent in the west and patchily distributed in between. It is common on the southern coast of the eastern provinces (Granma, Santiago de Cuba and Guantánamo) and the arid coasts of the north (environs of Holguín-Gibara) around Bayamo and in Camagüey and Ciego de Ávila provinces (Nuevitas and Playa Santa Lucía). It is locally common east of Sierra de Najasa, southern Camagüey and the larger cays north of Camagüey (Coco, Romano, Guajaba and Sabinal). This gnatcatcher is also locally distributed along the arid southern coast of Sancti-Spíritus province (Casilda and Trinidad).

Comments: The local name is derived from its resemblance to Northern Mockingbird in both appearance and song. Pairs sometimes travel with their offspring. It is a tame and active bird, which forages incessantly for insects among the lower branches of vegetation. Blue-gray Gnatcatcher on Cuba generally forages among the mid-level or high branches. While foraging, it tends to raise its tail almost vertically above its back.

Habitat: Fairly dense coastal thorn-scrub, but sometimes inland from the coast in similar vegetation.

Nesting: The cup-shaped nest is built in the fork of a twig in a low spiny bush and is constructed of horse hair, fur, vegetable fibers and small leaves with an outside layer of cobwebs, lichens and other soft materials. It is similar to, and not much larger than, a hummingbird's nest. Eggs (3–5) white with some spots at one end. Breeds from March to June.

NORTHERN WHEATEAR *Oenanthe oenanthe*　　　　**Plate 78**

Identification: 15 cm (6"). An active ground-dwelling bird distinguished in all plumages by its *white rump and tail patches* and its habit of *flicking and fanning its tail*. **Female and non-breeding male**: Pale reddish-brown below; grayish-brown above with a white eyebrow stripe. **Breeding male**: Gray upperparts with a black ear patch.

Status and Range: A vagrant in the West Indies where recorded from the Bahamas (Andros and Eleuthera), Cuba, Puerto Rico and Barbados. Likely reaches the West Indies as a transatlantic wanderer when birds migrating from Europe to Africa get blown off-course to the West Indies by favorable winds. The primary range includes much of the Eastern Hemisphere as well as parts of northern Canada and Alaska.

EASTERN BLUEBIRD *Sialia sialis*　　　　**Plate 57**

Identification: 15–16.5 cm (5.75–6.5"). **Adult male**: Note its *bright blue upperparts* including tail and wings; *reddish throat, breast, sides, flanks and upper belly* and white lower belly and undertail-coverts. **Adult female**: Duller with a whitish eyering. **Immature**: Grayish-blue above flecked with white and breast and upper belly whitish with conspicuous gray ringlets.

Voice: Call note is a clear whistle *chur-lee*.

Status and Range: A vagrant in the Bahamas (Eleuthera), western Cuba and the Virgin Islands (St John). It is widespread in eastern North America.

Comments: Feeds on insects and berries often on or near the ground.

Habitat: Field edges and open country with hedgerows.

CUBAN SOLITAIRE *Myadestes elisabeth*　　　　**Plates 56, 80**
Local Name: Ruiseñor

Identification: 19 cm (7.5"). Plain-colored, with the appearance of a flycatcher, it is olive-brown above and pale gray below. Field marks include a *white eyering, dark mustache stripe, white outer tail feathers* and a small bill. **Similar species**: La Sagra's Flycatcher has the hint of a crest and lacks an eyering and white outer tail feathers. None of the flycatchers possesses a mustache stripe.

Voice: Its flute-like song is very high pitched and can be heard from a long distance. The song is melodious and quite varied, but difficult to describe. It is similar to the sound of rubbing a wet finger against the rim of a fine porcelain cup. The solitaire sings for most of the year, but less so in certain months, especially March. Sporadically gives a short whistle-like call.

Status and Range: Endemic to Cuba where it is common, but quite local. In western Cuba, it is found only in Sierra de los Organos, Sierra del Rosario and Sierra de la Güira. In the east, it is more widely distributed, being found in Sierra Maestra, Sierra del Magüey, Sierra de Moa, Toa and Baracoa. A race endemic to the Isle of Youth was extirpated in the 1930s. Cuban Solitaire is considered threatened believed to be due to habitat loss.

Comments: An excellent songster. Inactive; when not foraging, tends to sit for long periods in the tops of trees. Cuban Solitaire is difficult to find unless it sings, and even then, its ventriloquial song makes it difficult to spot. Feeds by sallying out from a branch like a flycatcher and sometimes hovering to take insects and especially small fruits of various kinds, including ripe palm nuts. When foraging, may descend close to the ground on slopes of hills, but is mainly found on high branches of the canopy. Each territory is occupied by a pair. Any flycatcher-like bird should be carefully examined since it could prove to be a solitaire.

Habitat: Dense and humid forests of the hills and mountains.

Nesting: The cup-shaped nest is constructed of fine fibers covered with moss, lichens and plant down and is hidden in a moist rock crevice among ferns and mosses. The nest is sometimes built in a tree cavity. Eggs (3) pale green, heavily spotted with brown. Breeds from February to April.

RUFOUS-THROATED SOLITAIRE *Myadestes genibarbis*   Plate 56

Local Names: Solitaire, Fiddler (Jamaica); Mountain Whistler (Jamaica, St V.); Jilguero (DR); Mizisyen, Oiseau Musicien (Haiti); Siffleur Morne (St L); Solitaire à Gorge Rousse, Siffleur de Montagne, Solitaire Siffleur (Mart); Siffleur Montaigne, Soufriere Bird (St V)

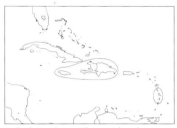

Identification: 19 cm (7.5"). Mostly gray above with a white chin. Note its *reddish-brown throat, foreneck and undertail-coverts*; light gray breast; yellow feet and tail with white outer feathers which become visible when fanned in flight. On St Vincent, it is black above with olive uppertail-coverts.

Voice: A hauntingly beautiful minor-key whistle, most often heard at dawn.

Status and Range: A fairly common year-round resident on Jamaica, Hispaniola, Dominica, Martinique, St Lucia and St Vincent. However, its numbers are much reduced on Haiti due to habitat loss. These islands comprise the entire range of the species.

Habitat: Dense, moist mountain forests.

Nesting: A cup-shaped nest is usually made in a crevice and covered by vegetation or may be located in the center of a tree fern or bromeliad. Eggs (2) bluish-white or blue with white spots. Breeds from April to August.

VEERY *Catharus fuscescens*   Plate 57

Local Name: Tordo Colorado (Cuba)

Identification: 16–18 cm (6.25–7"). *Upperparts reddish-brown*, rarely olive-brown. Underparts whitish with *faint spots* on a buffy breast. Has an inconspicuous grayish eyering. **Similar species**: More reddish-brown above and more lightly spotted below than other migrant thrushes.

Status and Range: A rare migrant in the northern Bahamas, Cuba, Jamaica and Hispaniola, and very rare in the southern Bahamas and Cayman Islands. A vagrant in the Virgin Islands (St John), St Christopher, Providencia and San Andrés. Occurs in September and October and in April and May. Its range includes North, Central and South America.

Comments: A shy, ground dweller.

Habitat: Open forests, woodlands with substantial undergrowth, scrub and gardens.

GRAY-CHEEKED THRUSH *Catharus minimus*   Plate 57

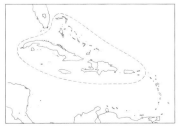

Identification: 16–20 cm (6.25–8"). Grayish-brown above and whitish below, with spots on the breast and throat. Distinguished by its *gray cheek* and lack of a conspicuous eyering or any reddish-brown coloration. **Similar species**: The extremely similar Bicknell's Thrush has paler lores, more buffy-brown upperparts, a buffy wash on its breast and more yellow on the lower mandible. These birds are too similar to separate accurately in the field. Refer to citation under Bicknell's Thrush for additional information on distinguishing these species. Swainson's Thrush has a distinct buff-colored eyering and Veery has much finer spots below and more reddish-brown upperparts. Hermit Thrush has a reddish-brown tail.

Status and Range: The status of this thrush in the West Indies is presently unclear following the splitting of Bicknell's Thrush from it in 1995. It appears that Gray-cheeked Thrush is a rare migrant in western Cuba where it far outnumbers Bicknell's. Its status in eastern Cuba, Hispaniola, Puerto Rico and the Virgin Islands remains to be determined. Gray-cheeked Thrush reports from the northern Bahamas may well pertain to this species, and there is a specimen from the southern Bahamas. This thrush is probably a rare migrant on Jamaica and the Cayman Islands. A bird captured on Martinique was carefully identified as a Gray-cheeked Thrush. Reports of Gray-cheeked Thrush from Providencia and San Andrés may well be accurate. It occurs in North and Central America and northern South America.

Comments: Feeds on the ground.

Habitat: Forests and woodlands.

BICKNELL'S THRUSH *Catharus bicknelli*   Plate 57

Identification: 16–19 cm (6.25–7.5"). Field marks are its buffy-brown upperparts, white underparts and sides of throat and breast cream-buff, boldly spotted with black. Also distinguished by its grayish cheeks and lores and dark reddish-brown tail. **Similar species**: Gray-cheeked Thrush is generally slightly larger and some birds are grayer above with darker lores, a whiter breast and pinkish rather than yellow on the lower mandible, but there is overlap in these characters. Overall, these birds are too similar to separate accurately in the field. For additional guidance on distinguishing these species see: Curson, J. 1994. Identification Forum: Separation of Bicknell's and Gray-cheeked Thrushes. *Birding World* 7(10): 359–365; Parkes, K.C. 1995. Identification of Bicknell's Thrush. *Birding World* 8: 316–317; and Smith P. W. 1996. More thoughts on Bicknell's Thrush. *Birding* 28: 275–276. Swainson's Thrush has a distinct eyering. Veery is more finely spotted below and more reddish-brown above. Hermit Thrush has a reddish-brown tail.

Voice: Song a high-pitched *chook-chook, wee-o, wee-o, wee-o-tee-t-ter-ee*, slurring downward. Call a harsh, slurred whistle. Generally silent in the West Indies.

Status and Range: An uncommon migrant and non-breeding resident on Hispaniola from late September to early May where it is most abundant in the Sierra de Baoruco of the Dominican Republic. It is likely a rare migrant in the Bahamas, particularly the southernmost islands, in eastern Cuba and on Jamaica from September to November and March to May. A vagrant on Puerto Rico and the Virgin Islands. It also occurs in northeastern North America.

Comments: Typically shy and wary. Searches for invertebrates and fruits on the ground. Formerly considered a subspecies of Gray-cheeked Thrush, from which it can be distinguished mainly by differences in song. Unfortunately, this feature is of little use in the West Indies. Many West Indian specimens formerly regarded as Gray-cheeked Thrushes have been found to be Bicknell's, with the exception of most specimens from western Cuba.

Habitat: Broadleaf forests, generally at higher elevations. Also woods or gardens with large trees which provide substantial shade.

SWAINSON'S THRUSH *Catharus ustulatus*   Plate 57
Local Name: Tordo Olivado (Cuba)

Identification: 17.5 cm (7"). Grayish-brown above and whitish below, with brownish spots on the breast and a *buff-colored eyering* and lores giving it a spectacled appearance. **Similar species**: Distinguished from Veery and Gray-cheeked and Bicknell's Thrushes by its conspicuous eyering. Hermit Thrush has a less conspicuous eyering and a reddish-brown tail.

Status and Range: A rare migrant on Cuba, Jamaica and the Cayman Islands and very rare in the northern Bahamas. It occurs from September through November and March into May. Its abundance fluctuates from year to year. Its range includes North, Central and South America.

Comments: Feeds on the ground, but also forages in palms with ripe fruits and nuts. Swainson's Thrush is very shy and flies out of sight very quickly. During migration, birds may remain at one site for two or three days.
Habitat: Open woods and tree clumps with much leaf litter and little undergrowth. Also gardens.

HERMIT THRUSH *Catharus guttatus*   Plate 57

Identification: 19 cm (7.5"). Note its *olive-brown upperparts, reddish-brown tail* and whitish underparts with a buffy wash. Large spots on the breast form streaks from the sides of throat to flanks. *Narrow buffy-white eyering.* **Similar species**: Swainson's, Bicknell's and Gray-cheeked Thrushes and Veery all lack the contrasting dark back and reddish-brown tail.
Status and Range: A very rare non-breeding resident in the northern Bahamas from October to April. Vagrant on Cuba. It is widespread in North America south to Guatemala.
Comments: Forages on the ground.
Habitat: Forest thickets.

WOOD THRUSH *Hylocichla mustelina*   Plate 57
Local Name: Tordo Pecoso (Cuba)

Identification: 20 cm (8"). Distinguished by its *cinnamon-colored crown, conspicuous white eyering* and *white underparts with heavy dark spots*. **Similar species**: No other thrush is so heavily spotted or has such a reddish-brown crown. Ovenbird is smaller and its cinnamon-colored crown is bordered by black stripes.
Voice: Emits short *pit-pit-pit* notes. During migration, seldom sings its melodious three to five syllabled song with the last syllable trilled.
Status and Range: A rare migrant on Cuba and very rare in the northern Bahamas. A vagrant in the southern Bahamas, Jamaica, Hispaniola, Puerto Rico and the Cayman Islands. It occurs primarily from mid-September to November and in March and April. A few birds may remain on Cuba from December through February. It occurs through North and Central America.
Comments: Feeds on the ground.
Habitat: Tree plantations and large gardens.

COCOA THRUSH *Turdus fumigatus*   Plate 57
Local Names: Mountain Grieve (Grenada); Grive des Cacaos (St V)

Identification: 23 cm (9"). *Adult*: Upperparts entirely rich brown; paler below. W*hitish throat patch with brown streaks*; dark bill. **Similar species**: Bare-eyed Robin has a yellow eyering, yellowish bill and more white on its lower belly.
Voice: A series of loud, musical phrases, each short and differing from one another, with a brief pause between each. Sometimes issues a plaintive, four-note call, the first two notes higher, the last two lower. Also a *weeo, weeo, weeo*.
Status and Range: A fairly common year-round resident on St Vincent and Grenada. More often found in mountains and higher elevation plantations, than in lowlands where Bare-eyed Robin is more common. It is widespread in South America.
Comments: Primarily forages on the ground for invertebrates and berries.
Habitat: Forests, cacao plantations and croplands with scattered trees.
Nesting: The nest is a bulky cup of grass, rootlets and other plant material lined inside with mud and covered outside with moss. Eggs (1–3) mostly greenish-blue with reddish-brown spots. Breeds primarily from November to June.

BARE-EYED ROBIN *Turdus nudigenis* **Plate 57**

Local Names: Yellow-eyed Grieve (Grenada); Merle à Lunettes, Grive à Paupières, Grive Chat (Mart); Grieve à Lunettes (Mart, St L)

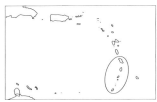

Identification: 23 cm (9"). *Adult*: Identified by its plain olive-gray upperparts, paler underparts and *white throat with brown streaks*. Its *broad, pale yellow eyering of bare skin* and yellowish bill and feet are good field marks. *Immature*: Paler than the adult; buffy spots on wings form bars. *Similar species*: Forest Thrush has scaled underparts. Cocoa Thrush lacks an eyering, has a dark bill and is darker on the lower belly.
Voice: Song is a loud, liquid, variable *cheerily cheer-up cheerio*, especially at dawn. Also a squeaky '*miter-ee*.'
Status and Range: A fairly common year-round resident on Martinique (first recorded in 1951), St Lucia, St Vincent, the Grenadines and Grenada, it is slowly expanding its range northward through the Lesser Antilles. An introduction attempt on Barbados failed. It is widespread in South America.
Comments: Typically arboreal, but also forages on the ground. Feeds on insects, worms, seeds and fruits. Regularly seen along forested road edges. It is very aggressive towards other thrushes and is suspected to have played a role in the near extirpation of Forest Thrush from St Lucia.
Habitat: Primarily lowlands, both in drier and moderately moist open woodlands, plantations, second growth and forest borders.
Nesting: The nest is a large cup of plant material lined with mud. Often has two broods. Eggs (1–3) deep bluish-green with reddish-brown spots. Breeds from late April to August.

WHITE-EYED THRUSH *Turdus jamaicensis* **Plates 57, 84**

Local Names: Glass-eye, Shine-eye, Fish-eye, Long Day Bird, Long Day Hopping Dick

Identification: 23 cm (9"). *Adult*: Dark gray above and pale gray below, it is distinguished by its *reddish-brown head*, conspicuous *whitish iris* and *white breast bar*. *Immature*: Throat unstreaked; breast boldly streaked. *Similar species*: White-chinned Thrush has a dark throat, reddish iris, orange legs and bill and a conspicuous white wing mark.
Voice: The musical song consists of repeated phrases like that of Northern Mockingbird, but louder and less variable. A whistled *hee-haw* is typically included. Also other high-pitched, harsh call notes.
Status and Range: Endemic to Jamaica where fairly common in mountains.
Comments: A secretive bird, it often forages among dense vegetation for fruits and invertebrates at all levels from forest floor to treetops. A few birds range to lowland valleys during the non-breeding season.
Habitat: Wet forests from their lowest elevations at approximately 100 m (325') to mountain summits. Also shade coffee plantations and other wooded areas at moderate elevations.
Nesting: The bulky, cup-shaped nest of plant material is built in a tree. Eggs (2) pale bluish-green, heavily speckled. Breeds from April to June.

AMERICAN ROBIN *Turdus migratorius* **Plate 57**

Local Names: Zorzal Migratorio (Cuba); Mirlo Norteamericano (PR)

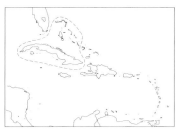

Identification: 23–28 cm (9–11"). Easily identified by its *primarily dull red underparts*. *Male*: Blackish head and tail. *Female*: Paler. *Similar species*: Red-legged Thrush has a reddish bill and legs and a gray breast.
Status and Range: A rare non-breeding resident from October to April in the northern Bahamas and Cuba. Numbers vary from year to year; sometimes occurring in flocks when North America experiences harsh winters. A vagrant on Jamaica, Hispaniola and Puerto Rico. It occurs from North America south to Guatemala.

Comments: Forages primarily on the ground for invertebrates and berries.
Habitat: Open woodlands, gardens, parks and open scrub.

LA SELLE THRUSH *Turdus swalesi*   Plates 57, 82
Local Names: Zorzal de la Selle, Cho-cho (DR); Ouèt-ouèt Lasèl, Kouèt-kouèt Nwa, Merle (Haiti)

Identification: 26 cm (10"). Note its *grayish-black head and upperparts*, with a few white streaks on throat. *Red lower breast and sides* with a broad, *white streak on belly*. **Similar species**: Red-legged Thrush is paler above, lacks red below, and has red legs and white on the tail. Chat Tanager is smaller and has white underparts. **Voice**: A series of deliberate *tu-re-oo* and *cho-ho-cho* calls (Dod), continued indefinitely. Also a loud *wheury-wheury-wheury* alarm call and gurgling notes.
Status and Range: Endemic to Hispaniola. Locally common on Haiti in the Massif de la Selle above 1400 m (4500'). Rare in the Dominican Republic where it occurs in the Sierra de Baoruco (Loma de Toro, Zapotén and Pie Pol), the Sierra de Neiba and the Cordillera Central in the vicinity of Alto Bandera. Endangered throughout its range because of habitat destruction.
Comments: Forages mostly on the ground for earthworms, insects and fruits, where it runs in spurts, then abruptly pauses. Sings from exposed perches at dawn, but nearly impossible to find during the middle of the day. There are two distinct subspecies.
Habitat: Low dense vegetation and wet forests, including pines in high mountains.
Nesting: A bulky nest, largely of moss, is built at low or moderate height above the ground in a shrub or tree. Eggs (2–3) greenish-blue, spotted. Breeding has been reported from May to July.

WHITE-CHINNED THRUSH *Turdus aurantius*   Plates 57, 84
Local Names: Hopping Dick, Jumping Dick, Twopenny Chick, Chick-me-Chick, Chap-man-chick

Identification: 24 cm (9.5"). **Adult**: Dark gray above and paler below, it is identified by a *conspicuous white diagonal bar on wing, white chin, orange bill and legs* and habit of cocking its tail upward. **Immature**: Breast darker brownish-gray; abdomen streaked. **Similar species**: White-eyed Thrush has a whitish iris, brown legs and bill and lacks white in the wing.
Voice: Variable. A musical song in the breeding season, a shrill whistle *p'lice, p'lice* and a repeated chicken-like clucking (Downer and Sutton).
Status and Range: Endemic to Jamaica where common and widespread.
Comments: Forages primarily on ground for a wide range of prey including slugs, lizards, insects, berries and even frogs, mice and small birds. Some White-chinned Thrushes move to lower elevations during the non-breeding season. This species is more tolerant of disturbed vegetation than is White-eyed Thrush.
Habitat: Primarily forests, woodlands, road edges, cultivated areas and gardens in mountains at middle and high elevations. Less frequent in lowlands, but of regular occurrence there.
Nesting: The nest is a coarse cup, built in a shrub, tree or at the base of a palm frond. Eggs (2–3) dull whitish to pale greenish, spotted. Breeds from May to July.

GRAND CAYMAN THRUSH *Turdus ravidus*   Plate 58
Local Name: Thrush

Identification: 27 cm (10.5"). A gray thrush with a red bill, eyering and legs and a white abdomen and outer tail feathers.
Voice: A quiet, prolonged series of warbled notes.
Status and Range: Extinct. Endemic to Grand Cayman in the Cayman Islands from where it was last reported in 1938. Common when first described in 1886, it was already very rare and local in the early 1900s, though 13 specimens were collected in 1916. Its final haven was dense forest at the eastern end of the island. The causes of the species' demise are unknown. Habitat destruction probably played a primary role. Major hurricanes in 1932 and 1944 could have proven the final blow to this thrush's already decimated population.
Habitat: Forests.
Nesting: Unknown.

RED-LEGGED THRUSH *Turdus plumbeus*   Plate 57
Local Names: Bahama Thrush (Bahamas); Old Thruss (CI); Zorzal Real, Zorzal de Patas Coloradas (Cuba, PR); Chua-chuá, Cigua Calandra (DR); Ouèt-ouèt (Haiti)

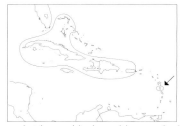

Identification: 25–28 cm (10–11"). Very variable among islands, but always distinguished by its gray upperparts, *reddish legs and bill, red eyering* and large, white tail tips. Underparts range from almost entirely gray with a black throat and white chin in the Bahamas and eastern Cuba, to a reddish-brown abdomen in central and western Cuba and the Cayman Islands (Cayman Brac) and a white throat with black stripes and a whitish abdomen on Hispaniola and Puerto Rico. *Similar species*: American Robin and Chat Tanager both lack the red bill and legs. La Selle Thrush is darker above, has a red breast and sides and lacks red legs and white on the tail.
Voice: Call notes include a low *wéecha* and a rapid, high-pitched *chu-wéek, chu-wéek, chu-wéek* (Rolle). Alarm call a loud *wheet-wheet*. The song is a melodious, but monotonous series of one to three syllabled phrases similar to that of Pearly-eyed Thrasher, but a bit more musical and with shorter pauses between phrases.
Status and Range: A common and widespread year-round resident throughout most of its range. Found in the northern Bahamas (Grand Bahama, Abaco, Andros, New Providence and Cat Island) and Cuba, including the Isle of Youth. Also on Hispaniola (including Gonâve, Tortue and Saona Islands), Puerto Rico and Dominica. Fairly common in the Cayman Islands (Cayman Brac), but rarely seen during the non-breeding season. These islands comprise the entire range of the species.
Comments: Typically seen in the early dawn as it darts from roadsides. Forages mainly on the ground for invertebrates among leaf litter. Also eats fruits and small vertebrates. A conspicuous and aggressive bird during the breeding season, but secretive at other times. It is absent from Jamaica where it appears to be replaced ecologically by White-chinned Thrush.
Habitat: Woodlands and forests at all elevations, scrub, thick undergrowth, gardens and shade coffee plantations.
Nesting: The nest is a bulky mass of leaves lined with grass and other material, usually from 3–9 m (10–30') up in a tree, but sometimes in a palm, on a stump or under the eaves of a house. Eggs (3–4) pale greenish-blue, heavily speckled with reddish-brown. Breeds from January to September, but peaks from April to July.

FOREST THRUSH *Cichlherminia lherminieri*   Plate 57
Local Names: Yellow-legged Thrush (Dominica); Grive à Pattes Jaunes (Guad); Mauvis (St L)

Identification: 25–27 cm (10–10.5"). Upperparts grayish-brown and *underparts brown with white spots on breast, flanks and upper belly* giving it a scaled effect. *Legs, bill and bare skin around eye yellow*. *Similar species*: Resembles Pearly-eyed Thrasher in size, but is browner and its tail lacks white spots. Scaled underparts distinguish it from Bare-eyed Robin.

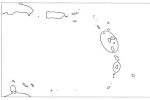

Voice: A soft, musical pattern of clear notes.

Status and Range: An uncommon resident on Montserrat, Guade-loupe and Dominica and rare on St Lucia. These islands comprise the entire range of the species. Forest Thrush has declined, proba-bly due to habitat loss, competition with Bare-eyed Robin, brood parasitism by Shiny Cowbird, being hunted by humans as a favored food and perhaps due to predation by the mongoose and other introduced predators.

Comments: A shy, unique genus of thrush restricted to the Lesser Antilles. Sings from a concealed perch. Feeds on insects and berries from ground level to tree canopy.

Habitat: Moist mountain forests.

Nesting: A bulky, cup-shaped nest is built usually not far above the ground in a bush or tree. Eggs (2–3) greenish-blue. Breeds in April and May.

MOCKINGBIRDS, THRASHERS AND ALLIES (MIMIC THRUSHES): FAMILY MIMIDAE

The habit of several species to mimic other birds gives this Western Hemisphere family its name. Mimids appear very much like thrushes, but are typically more slender with longer tails and with more lengthy, down-curved bills.

GRAY CATBIRD *Dumetella carolinensis*   **Plate 56**

Local Names: Blue Thrush, Blue Thrasher (Bahamas); Zorzal Gato (Cuba)

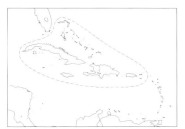

Identification: 23 cm (9"). An entirely gray bird with a *black cap, reddish-brown undertail-coverts* and a long tail often cocked slightly upwards.

Voice: A distinctive soft cat-like *mew*. Alarm note is a *pert-pert-pert*. Song is a series of disconnected phrases including *mews*, imitations and pauses.

Status and Range: A common migrant and non-breeding resi-dent in the Bahamas, Cayman Islands and Providencia, and uncommon on Cuba, Jamaica and San Andrés. It is rare on His-paniola and a vagrant on Puerto Rico and Anguilla. Occurs pri-marily from October through April. It is widespread in North and Central America south to Panama.

Comments: Moderately shy and more often heard than seen. Generally forages near or on the ground.

Habitat: Thickets and dense undergrowth.

NORTHERN MOCKINGBIRD *Mimus polyglottos*   **Plate 56**

Local Names: English Thrasher (Bahamas); Nightingale (CI, Jamaica); Sinsonte (Cuba); Ruiseñor (DR, PR); Rosiyol, Rossignol (Haiti)

Identification: 23–28 cm (9–11"). Gray above and grayish white below, it is distinguished by *wings and tail conspicuously marked with white* which shows clearly in flight and the *long tail often cocked upward*. **Immature**: Brownish-gray upperparts; buffy underparts. **Similar species**: Gray Kingbird lacks white wing and tail patches and does not cock its shorter tail. Bahama Mockingbird is larger, lacks white in the wings and has a white-tipped rather than a white-edged tail.

Voice: A clear, melodious series of phrases, each phrase repeated several times. Alarm call a loud *tchack*. Also an angry growl-like call. Sometimes incorporates calls and song phrases of other species in its own repertoire. Sings at night as well as during the day.

Status and Range: A common resident throughout the Bahamas, Greater Antilles and the Virgin and Cayman Islands. Introduced to New Providence at about the turn of the 20th century, it now outnumbers the native Bahama Mockingbird. An introduced population on Barbados is now extirpated. It primarily occurs in lowlands, but also at lower elevations in mountains. It also occurs from southern Canada to southern Mexico.

Habitat: Open country with scattered bushes or trees, including semi-arid scrub, open mangrove forests, gardens, parks and settled areas.

Nesting: The nest is a coarse open cup of twigs, lined with finer plant material, and built in a bush or tree. Eggs (3–4) pale bluish-green, with heavy splotches at the broad end. Breeds from January to July.

TROPICAL MOCKINGBIRD *Mimus gilvus*   Plate 56

Local Names: Pickaro, Peckow (Grenada); Nightingale, Grieve Blanche, Pierre-fouillé (la Désirade); Pied Carreau (Grenada, St L); Pié Fouillé (Guad, la Désirade); Grive des Savanes, Moqueur des Savanes (Guad, Mart)

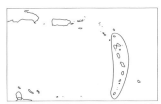

Identification: 23–24 cm (9–9.5"). Field marks include gray upperparts and head; broad, *blackish eyeline*; white eyebrow stripe; wings darker than the back and two wingbars. *Tail is long and conspicuously tipped with white*. **Similar species**: The ranges of Bahama and Northern Mockingbirds do not overlap with this species.
Voice: Repeated couplets of musical whistles and phrases lasting several seconds. Less likely than Northern Mockingbird to incorporate songs of other species. Also a harsh *chuck* alarm call, similar to that of Northern Mockingbird.

Status and Range: A fairly common year-round resident on Guiana Island off the northeastern coast of Antigua, Guadeloupe, Dominica, Martinique, St Lucia, St Vincent, the Grenadines, Grenada and San Andrés. On Guadeloupe, the species is very local at the extreme eastern end of the island. It is expanding its range northward from Dominica. This range expansion is likely due to human alteration of the landscape creating more favorable conditions for the mockingbird throughout the islands. It is widespread in Central and South America.

Habitat: Open areas around human dwellings, dry lowland scrub and agricultural areas.

Nesting: A rough cup-nest is built in a bush or tree. Eggs (2–4) grayish-green, heavily marked with reddish-brown. Believed to begin breeding as early as February and lasting to July. A second breeding cycle occurs from September to November.

BAHAMA MOCKINGBIRD *Mimus gundlachii*   Plate 56

Local Names: Spanish Nightingale, Salt Island Nightingale, Hill's Mockingbird (Jamaica); Sinsote Prieto, Sinsote Carbonero (Cuba)

Identification: 28 cm (11"). Its upperparts are brownish-gray with fine streaks; underparts whitish with dark streaks on sides. Field marks include its large size and *long, broad tail almost fan-shaped in flight, tipped with white*. Two white wingbars are not conspicuous in flight. **Similar species**: Northern Mockingbird is smaller and shows *conspicuous white in wing and on the sides of tail in flight*. Pearly-Eyed Thrasher has darker upperparts, a pale bill and a white iris.
Voice: The song is a series of phrases, each repeated several times before the bird changes to a new one. It is more melodious, but less variable than that of Northern Mockingbird. Does not mimic other birds.

Status and Range: Generally a common year-round resident in the Bahamas. This mockingbird is also common in the cays of northern Cuba and in the Hellshire Hills area of southern Jamaica. These islands comprise the entire range of the species.

Comments: Bahama Mockingbird appears to inhabit taller, denser vegetation than does Northern Mockingbird.

Habitat: Semi-arid scrub, woodlands and near human habitation.

Nesting: A rough cup-shaped nest is built in a bush. Eggs (2) cream-white with reddish-brown spots and blotches concentrated at the broad end. Breeds from February to June.

BROWN THRASHER *Toxostoma rufum* **Plate 56**
Local Name: Sinsonte Colorado (Cuba)

Identification: 29 cm (11.5"). Upperparts including long tail are reddish-brown. Also note the pale white wingbars, *buffy-white underparts boldly streaked with dark brown,* dark brown mustache streak, yellow-orange iris and long, dark bill.
Status and Range: Vagrant. Wanderers irregularly reach the Bahamas where reported from Harbour Island, Grand Bahama and Cuba during October and November, when the species is undergoing its southward migration to non-breeding quarters in the southeastern United States. It is widespread in North America.
Comments: Forages on the ground by tossing aside leaf litter. Also frequents low vegetation.
Habitat: Dense undergrowth.

WHITE-BREASTED THRASHER *Ramphocinclus brachyurus* **Plate 56**
Local Names: Moqueur Gorge-blanche, Gorge Blanche (Mart); Gorge Blanc (St L)

Identification: 20–21 cm (7.75–8.25") Martinique; 23–25 cm (9–10") St Lucia. *Adult*: Note its *dark brown upperparts,* entire underparts clear white, *red iris* and long, slightly down-curved bill. Often droops its wings and may twitch or flick wings when excited or curious. *Immature*: Entirely warm dark brown, developing a creamy white patch on the breast as it gets older. *Similar species*: Gray Trembler is gray above, has a longer bill and a white iris.
Status and Range: A local and increasingly rare year-round resident known only from Martinique and St Lucia. On Martinique, found at Presqu'île de la Caravelle. On St Lucia, restricted to the east coast from Petite Anse south to Anse Pouvert and Frigate Island Reserve, an area with high concentrations of the poisonous snake, the fer-de-lance. Formerly common and widespread, it is now critically endangered as a result of habitat destruction by encroaching farmers and charcoal burners. The world population may be less than 150 pairs. Other threats include the Pearly-eyed Thrasher, rats, the mongoose, boa constrictors and Bare-eyed Robin which has colonized St Lucia and is very aggressive towards other thrush-like birds. Juvenile White-breasted Thrashers spend much time on the ground before fledging where they are noisy and exposed to terrestrial predators.
Comments: Primarily forages on the ground tossing aside leaf litter in search of small invertebrates, particularly insects. Feeds to a lesser extent on berries, fruits and even small lizards and tree frogs. The White-breasted Thrasher is the only member of its genus. It has two subspecies.
Habitat: Dense thickets of semi-arid wooded stream valleys and ravines.
Nesting: A rough cup-shaped nest is built 2–5 m (7–16') above ground. Eggs (2) unmarked greenish-blue. Breeds from April to August.

SCALY-BREASTED THRASHER *Margarops fuscus* **Plate 56**
Local Names: Black-billed Thrush (Antigua, Saba, St E); Grieve (St L); Spotted Grieve (St V); Grivotte (Mart); Moqueur Grivotte, Grive Fine (Guad, Mart)

Identification: 23 cm (9"). This species is distinguished by *white underparts heavily scaled* with grayish-brown from throat to belly, one *whitish wingbar, black bill,* yellow-brown iris and tail tipped with white. *Similar species*: Pearly-eyed Thrasher is larger and has a large, *yellowish bill* and no wingbars.
Voice: Repeats phrases in a manner similar to Tropical Mockingbird, but with less vigor.
Status and Range: Generally a fairly common year-round resident from Saba and St Barthélemy south to St Vincent. Rare and local on Grenada and possibly extirpated on St Eustatius, Barbuda and Barbados. A vagrant in the Grenadines. These islands comprise the entire range of the species.
Comments: Arboreal and retiring, but not especially shy. Feeds primarily on fruits.
Habitat: Both moist and semi-arid forests and woodlands.
Nesting: A rough cup-shaped nest is built in a tree. Eggs (2–3) greenish-blue. Breeds in May and June.

PEARLY-EYED THRASHER *Margarops fuscatus* **Plate 56**
Local Names: Jack Bird, Paw-paw Bird, Black Thrasher (Bahamas); Mango Bird (Nevis); Wall-eyed Thrush (VI); Sour-sop Bird (Nevis, VI); Zorzal Pardo (DR, PR); Louis Jo, Pie Voleuse (St B); Grive-corossol, Truche, Moqueur Corossol, Grosse Grive (Guad, Mart)

Identification: 28–30 cm (11–12"). Upperparts are brown and *underparts white, streaked with brown.* Also has a distinctive *white iris,* a *large, yellowish bill* and large, white patches on the tail tip. **Similar species**: In the Bahamas, Bahama Mockingbird has a darker bill and eye and paler upperparts. In the Lesser Antilles, Scaly-breasted Thrasher is smaller, has a smaller, black bill and one whitish wingbar. Forest Thrush is browner and lacks white tail spots.
Voice: A series of one to three syllabled phrases (e.g. *pío-tareeu-tsee*) with fairly lengthy pauses separating them. Often sings well into the day and during clear nights. Also many raucous call notes, including a guttural *craw-craw* and a harsh *chook-chook*.
Status and Range: A common year-round resident throughout most of its discontinuous range. It occurs in the southern and central Bahamas north to Exuma and Cat Island and appears to be spreading northward. It is almost unrecorded on Hispaniola, but is common on adjacent Beata Island. Also common on Puerto Rico, the Virgin Islands and the Lesser Antilles south to St Lucia with the exception of Martinique where it is uncommon. A vagrant on Jamaica and Barbados. Outside the West Indies it also occurs on Bonaire.
Comments: Arboreal. Normally feeds on fruits, invertebrates and small vertebrates, but this extraordinarily aggressive species also eats the eggs and young of other birds. It competes with other birds for cavity nest sites.
Habitat: Thickets, woodlands and forests at all elevations from mangroves and coastal palm groves to mountain tops. Also urban areas.
Nesting: A bulky twig nest is usually constructed in a cavity, though occasionally open nests are placed in a bush or tree. On Mona Island off Puerto Rico, this thrasher nests in caves. Eggs (2–3) glossy deep blue. Breeds from December to September.

BROWN TREMBLER *Cinclocerthia ruficauda* **Plate 56**
Local Names: Grive Trembleuse, Trembleur Brun, Cocobino (Guad, Mart); Trembleur (Mart, St L)

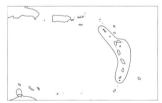

Identification: 23–26 cm (9–10"). Distinguished by its dark reddish-olive upperparts, buffy underparts, *very long bill which is slightly down-curved near tip* and yellow iris. **Habit**: Typically droops wings and trembles as it searches for food or when aroused. Frequently cocks its tail up over its back. **Similar species**: Gray Trembler is noticeably grayer above and whiter below.
Voice: A series of semi-melodic phrases; also harsh call and alarm notes.
Status and Range: Known only from the Lesser Antilles where it is a fairly common year-round resident on Saba, Guadeloupe and Dominica; uncommon on St Christopher, Nevis, Montserrat, St Lucia and St Vincent and rare on Martinique and Grenada. A vagrant in the Virgin Islands (St Thomas), St Eustatius and Antigua.
Comments: Arboreal. Tosses vegetation aside with its bill as it forages for invertebrates. Formerly lumped by taxonomists with Gray Trembler as a single species. The genus is endemic to the West Indies.
Habitat: Wet forests on most islands, although occurs in secondary forests and drier woodlands. On St Lucia, found only in dry forests or scrub.
Nesting: Nests in a cavity of a tree or builds a domed nest of grass with a side entrance, usually in a palm. Eggs (2–3) greenish-blue. Breeds in March and April.

GRAY TREMBLER *Cinclocerthia gutturalis* **Plate 56**
Local Names: Moqueur Trembleur, Grive Trembleuse, Trembleur Gris (Mart); Trembleur (St L)

Identification: 23–26 cm (9–10"). Upperparts dark olive-gray, underparts grayish-white (Martinique) or bright white (St Lucia), *bill very long and slightly down-curved near tip* and white iris. **Habit**: Typ-

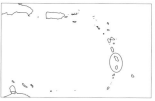

ically droops wings and trembles as it searches for food or when aroused. Often cocks tail over its back. ***Similar species***: Brown Trembler is browner above and darker below. White-breasted Thrasher has a *red iris*, a proportionately shorter bill and is *dark brown above*.
Voice: Wavering, whistled phrases; also harsh scold and call notes.
Status and Range: A fairly common year-round resident on Martinique and St Lucia which account for the entire range of the species. Occurs at all elevations.
Comments: Arboreal. Often uses its long bill to tear apart clusters of dry leaves and vegetation in search of invertebrates. Recently separated taxonomically from Brown Trembler. The genus, composed of just two trembler species, is endemic to the West Indies.
Habitat: Mature moist forests, usually at higher elevations. Less often in second growth, dry scrub and open woodlands.
Nesting: A domed nest with a side entrance is built of dry grass, often in a palm, but sometimes nests in a tree cavity. Eggs (2–3) greenish-blue. Breeds in March and April.

WAGTAILS AND PIPITS: FAMILY MOTACILLIDAE

Motacillids are characterized by slender, pointed bills; short necks; slender bodies and long legs, feet and tails. They walk or run rather than hop, and spend most of their time on the ground. All have a strong undulating flight. Motacillids occur world-wide except in the extreme north and some oceanic islands. Most are rather gregarious except in the breeding season.

AMERICAN PIPIT *Anthus spinoletta*   Plate 77

Identification: 16.5 cm (6.5"). A thin-billed, long-tailed *terrestrial* bird with a habit of regularly *bobbing its tail* while walking. Upon taking flight, it displays conspicuous *white outer tail feathers*. ***Non-breeding adult***: Note the *buffy eyebrow stripe*, two faint wingbars and pinkish-buff underparts (October and November) or pale gray underparts (January through March) with blackish stripes concentrated on the breast.
Status and Range: A very rare non-breeding resident in the Bahamas south to San Salvador and a vagrant on Jamaica, Providencia and San Andrés from October to March. As yet unrecorded from Cuba where the species almost certainly occurs. It is widespread across North America and Eurasia.
Habitat: Open fields and sandy areas.

WAXWINGS: FAMILY BOMBYCILLIDAE

There are only three species in this family, all of which have crests and possess red, waxy structures on the tips of their secondaries. They are arboreal and feed primarily on berries, though they sometimes sally after insects in flycatcher fashion. Only one is found in this area.

CEDAR WAXWING *Bombycilla cedrorum*   Plate 41
Local Name: Picotero del Cedro (Cuba)

Identification: 18–18.5 cm (7–7.25"). The *crest* and *yellow-tipped tail* distinguish this tan bird. ***Immature***: Streaked below.
Voice: A clear, short, high-pitched trill. Also an unmusical *che-che-check*.
Status and Range: A rare non-breeding resident, varying greatly in numbers from year to year. Most frequent on Cuba where it is sometimes fairly common from October to April. Rare on Jamaica and the Cayman Islands primarily from December to April, very rare widely in the Bahamas and a

vagrant on Hispaniola, Puerto Rico, the Virgin Islands, Guadeloupe and Dominica. It occurs through North and Central America to Panama.
Comments: Typically flocks in trees with ripe berries.
Habitat: Mountain rain forests to lowland cultivated edges and urban gardens.

PALMCHATS: FAMILY DULIDAE

The Dulidae consists of but one species, the Palmchat of Hispaniola. This family is probably more closely related to the waxwings (Bombycillidae) than to any other passerines. Palmchats are arboreal, noisy and gregarious, even to the point of building a communal nest.

PALMCHAT *Dulus dominicus*   **Plates 41, 82**
Local Names: Cigua Palmera, Cigua de Palma (DR); Oiseau Palmiste, Lesklav, Zouazo Palmis (Haiti)

Identification: 20 cm (8"). A conspicuous flocking bird of the treetops. Dark brown above; underparts whitish and *heavily streaked with brown.*
Voice: Quite noisy, particularly around its nest, producing an array of strange call notes.
Status and Range: Endemic to Hispaniola, including Gonâve and Saona Islands. Common, conspicuous and widespread in lowlands to mid-elevations. The Palmchat may be experiencing nest parasitism by the Shiny Cowbird.
Comments: This is the national bird of the Dominican Republic. It feeds primarily on fruits and berries. Palmchat is the only member of its genus and family making it very special both from an evolutionary and taxonomic standpoint. Palmchat and the todies are the only endemic bird families in the West Indies.
Habitat: Primarily royal palm savannas, but also other open areas with scattered trees. Absent from dense forests.
Nesting: The nest is a large structure of twigs, placed high in a palm, tree or on a pole. Palms which do not have fronds overlapping with those of other trees are usually selected for nesting. Its nest is built and occupied by several pairs, with each nest chamber having a separate entrance. The inner chamber is lined with shredded bark upon which eggs are laid. Large nests may be up to 2 m (7') in width. Eggs (2–4) white, heavily spotted with dark purplish-gray, especially at the broad end. Breeds from March to June.

STARLINGS AND ALLIES: FAMILY STURNIDAE

A large Eastern Hemisphere family, with a few species having been introduced to this hemisphere. They are stocky birds with long, conical bills and usually a somewhat iridescent breeding plumage.

EUROPEAN STARLING *Sturnus vulgaris*   **Plate 26**
Local Names: Starling (Jamaica); Estornino (Cuba, PR)

Identification: 22 cm (8.5"). A glossy black bird with a short tail. ***Breeding adult***: *Bill yellow.* ***Non-breeding adult***: *Underparts heavily flecked with white spots*; dark bill. ***Immature***: *Brownish-gray with fine breast stripes.* ***Flight***: *Straight, unlike other black birds in the region. The wings are distinctively swept back.*

Voice: A wide variety of whistles, squeaks and raspy notes. The species is a good imitator.
Status and Range: Introduced to Jamaica around 1903, it is fairly common, but local. European Starlings are also a fairly common breeding bird on Grand Bahama and the Biminis in the Bahamas. A few birds occur rarely in the Bahamas and eastern Cuba from October to March. Whether the birds recorded on Cuba are migrants from Jamaica or North America, the latter also an introduced population, remains to be determined. Recorded for the first time on Puerto Rico in 1973 and the Virgin Islands (St Croix) in 1982, the species appears not to have taken hold on these islands. Recorded from the Cayman Islands (Cayman Brac) in 1992. Also introduced to North America, it is native to Eurasia and North Africa.
Comments: Typically flocks and often feeds on the ground. An aggressive species, the European Starling is a potential threat to native species with which it might compete, particularly for nest sites. It has been observed displacing Jamaican Woodpeckers from an active nest cavity.
Habitat: Primarily open lowland areas, including pastures and gardens.
Nesting: Builds a nest in a cavity or at the base of a palm frond. Eggs (5–7) pale light blue and slightly glossy. Breeds from April to June.

HILL MYNA *Gracula religiosa*   Plate 26
Local Name: Maina de Colinas

Identification: 30 cm (12″). This entirely black bird is identified by its brilliant *orange bill, yellow wattle on its hindneck* and white wing patch.
Voice: A rich, somewhat plaintive, three-syllabled whistle accented on the second note. One of the best mimics in the bird world.
Status and Range: Introduced to Puerto Rico apparently in the late 1960s, it is an uncommon and very local resident along the north and east coasts. It is native to India east through South-East Asia and Indonesia.
Habitat: Open woodlands with dead snags.
Nesting: The nest is built in a tree cavity. Eggs (2–5) glossy light blue, spotted with reddish-brown, dark brown and black. Breeds from February to June.

VIREOS: FAMILY VIREONIDAE

Vireos are typically dull olive-green birds that resemble warblers, but have thicker bills, hooked at the tip. They are sluggish in their movements, carefully inspecting twigs and the undersides of leaves for insects as they move among the branches.

WHITE-EYED VIREO *Vireo griseus*   Plate 59
Local Names: Vireo de Ojo Blanco (Cuba); Julián Chiví Ojiblanco (PR)

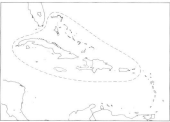

Identification: 12.5 cm (5″). Grayish-green above, whitish below, with *yellow* sides and *spectacles* and *two white wingbars*. **Adult**: *White iris*. **Immature**: Duller; dark iris. **Similar species**: Thick-billed and Yellow-throated Vireos also have yellow spectacles. However, the former is entirely pale yellow below and the latter has a much yellower chin, throat and breast. Both have a dark iris. Pine Warbler lacks distinct spectacles and has finely streaked sides. Jamaican Vireo has a pinkish bill, paler yellow sides and lacks yellow spectacles. Cuban Vireo lacks yellow spectacles and has only faint wingbars.
Voice: A loud, slurred three to seven syllabled song, such as *chip-a-tee-weeo-chip*, repeated with variations. More rapid and less emphatic than that of Thick-billed Vireo. Alarm a churring note. Call a *pick*.

Status and Range: Generally an uncommon non-breeding resident in the Bahamas, Cuba and the Cayman Islands, it is rare on Jamaica and Puerto Rico and very rare on Hispaniola and the Virgin Islands (St John). Occurs primarily from October through March, though there are records as early as September and as late as July. Occurs from southeastern North and Central America south to Panama.
Comments: Solitary. Usually in dense vegetation low to the ground where it moves about slowly. These traits, plus the bird's drab appearance and similarity to more common species, result in it being easily overlooked.
Habitat: Undergrowth, scrub, coastal thickets and brushy woodlands.

THICK-BILLED VIREO *Vireo crassirostris*   Plate 59
Local Names: Chick-of-the-village (Bahamas); Shear-bark (CI); Vireo de Bahamas (Cuba); Oiseau Canne, Zwazo Kann (Île Tortue)

Identification: 13.5 cm (5.25"). The plumage is variable between birds on different islands, but is generally distinguished by its brownish-green upperparts, grayish-green crown and hindneck, blackish lores, dark iris, *two white wingbars* and *bright yellow spectacles*, sometimes broken around the eye. The underparts vary from being entirely yellow in the southern Bahamas to being grayish with a tint of yellow in the northern Bahamas and Cayman Islands to being entirely buff on Île Tortue. **Immature**: Lacks blackish lores. **Similar species**: White-eyed Vireo has a smaller and thinner bill and is whitish on the throat, breast and belly. The adult has a *white iris*. Yellow-throated Vireo has a bright yellow chin, throat and breast which is coupled with a white belly and abdomen. It also has an olive-green rather than grayish crown and lacks black lores. Mangrove Vireo, which reportedly occurs on Providencia, lacks grayish-green on the crown and hindneck. It is illustrated on Plate 59 merely for comparison.
Voice: Bubbly and variable *chik-didle-wer-chip*, very similar to the song of White-eyed Vireo, but slower and less emphatic. On Providencia, the call is limited to a chatter.
Status and Range: A common year-round resident in the Bahamas, Hispaniola (where it is known only from Île Tortue), the Cayman Islands and Providencia. It is an uncommon migrant in coastal north-central Cuba during October where it occurs locally near Rancho Velez and on several nearby cays. It also occurs on islands east of Nicaragua.
Comments: More often heard than seen, it is usually located by its call. As with all vireos, this can be quite a challenge when the bird is sitting motionless, singing among dense leaves, as it often does. Recently extirpated from Little Cayman. Thick-billed Vireos in Providencia have such a different song that some experts suggest that they belong to a separate species.
Habitat: Undergrowth, woodland edges and bushes.
Nesting: The nest is a round cup usually suspended in a branch fork of a bush. Eggs (2–3) whitish or pale buffy with heavy spotting. Breeds from April to July.

MANGROVE VIREO *Vireo pallens*   Plate 59

Identification: 11.5 cm (4.5"). Dull yellow eyebrow stripe and underparts. Olive-green above, with two white wingbars. **Similar species**: Thick-billed Vireo has a grayish-green crown and hindneck that contrasts with its brownish-green upperparts.
Status and Range: It is believed that former reports of Thick-billed Vireo from Providencia were misidentifications. Providencia records of that species likely pertain to Mangrove Vireo. It also occurs from Mexico to Costa Rica.
Habitat: Mangroves.

ST ANDREW VIREO *Vireo caribaeus*   Plates 59, 86

Identification: 12.5 cm (5"). Note its olive-green upperparts, pale yellow stripe above bill to eye, grayish-brown iris, whitish to pale yellow underparts and two white wingbars.
Voice: Different from other vireos in having three different song patterns: a repetitive chatter of a single syllable from two to twenty or more times; a two-syllabled song repeated one to fifteen times *se-wi, se-wi, se-wi ...*; and a three-syllabled call, variable in its composition. Both sexes utter a single

contact note while foraging.

Status and Range: Endemic to San Andrés where it is fairly common in the southern third of the 52 sq. km (17 sq. miles) island. This vireo has the smallest natural range of any West Indian bird species.

Comments: The most active forager of the West Indian vireos, St Andrew's stalks insects among leaves and twigs from near ground level up to 10 m (33') in the trees. It may eat a greater proportion of insects to fruits than most other vireos, but this remains to be corroborated.

Habitat: Mangroves, bushes and scrubby pasture.

Nesting: The nest is a deep cup built in the fork of a twig 1–2 m (3–7') above the ground in a shrub or tree. The interior is lined with fine grass. The exterior is covered with moss and leaf parts with a few whole leaves attached to the bottom. Both sexes care for the eggs and young. Eggs (2) glossy white with small brown spots, particularly at the broad end. Breeds from May to July.

JAMAICAN VIREO *Vireo modestus*   Plates 59, 84
Local Names: White-eyed Vireo, Sewi-sewi

Identification: 12.5 cm (5"). Distinctively *flicks tail up*. **Adult**: Dull green above and pale yellow below, it is distinguished by *two whitish wingbars, pinkish lower mandible* and *whitish iris*. **Immature**: Identified by a dark iris, grayer head and the yellow of the underparts confined to a central stripe. **Similar species**: White-eyed Vireo has brighter yellow sides and flanks, a dark bill and yellow spectacles. Immature Arrow-headed Warbler is similar to immature Jamaican Vireo, but the warbler has a pale yellowish eyering, a dark eyeline and bill, and flicks its tail down, rather than up. Blue Mountain Vireo is larger, has a dark iris and lacks wingbars. Red-eyed Vireo lacks wingbars.

Voice: Repeats the same phrase for several minutes before changing to a new refrain. Typically the phrases are rapid and high-pitched, a common one being its local name, *sewi-sewi*, or others such as *twee-weet-weet-wuu* or *pee-eu*. Also a loud, rapid scolding *chi-chi-chi-chi-chi*.

Status and Range: Endemic to Jamaica where widespread and common from the most arid to the most humid regions at all elevations.

Comments: Active, but secretive, keeping to dense vegetation at all heights. Feeds primarily on small insects and to a lesser extent on fruit.

Habitat: Frequents most forests, forest edges and thickets, particularly in the arid lowlands. Absent from mangroves and cultivated woodlands.

Nesting: The nest is a hanging cup of fern, moss or bromeliad stalks and camouflaged with lichens, built in the fork of a twig. Eggs (2–3) white with dark brown spots and blotches primarily at the broad end. Breeds from April to June.

CUBAN VIREO *Vireo gundlachii*   Plates 59, 80
Local Names: Juan Chiví, Chichinguao, Ojón

Identification: 13 cm (5"). A small bird, chunkier than a warbler and with a larger bill. *Bulging eyes*, bordered by a *smudgy yellowish eyering*. Olive upperparts and yellowish underparts with faint wingbars. **Similar species**: Can be separated in the field from Yellow-throated, Blue-headed and White-eyed Vireos by its lack of conspicuous wingbars. Black-whiskered Vireo, which possesses a somewhat similar song, has a whitish eyebrow stripe, black eyeline and a dark mustache stripe. Red-eyed Vireo has a white eyebrow stripe bordered by a black eyeline and crown stripe and lacks an eyering.

Voice: A high, oft-repeated call from which its local name 'Juan Chiví' is derived: *wi-chiví, wi-chiví, wi-chiví...* A guttural alarm note, *Shruo*, very similar to call of other vireos, particularly Yellow-throated.

Status and Range: Endemic to Cuba, including the Isle of Youth, and keys on both coasts where it is common and widespread in appropriate habitat.
Comments: Usually found in pairs, which work through their territory while foraging. Often joins mixed flocks, especially with Yellow-headed Warblers or Oriente Warblers. Rather sluggish and does not fly long distances because of its short, rounded wings. Usually detected by its distinctive song. Typically forages at low heights above the ground.
Habitat: Brushlands, forest edges and dense scrub and thickets primarily in the lowlands, but also in the hills and mountains.
Nesting: Few nests have been found, since they are well hidden among thick vegetation, tangles and vines. The nest is a pendant structure built in a twig with grass, horse hair, plant fibers, animal fur, rootlets, small feathers and cobwebs. Eggs (3) white with small brown or pale purple spots, concentrated at the wider end. Breeds from April to June.

PUERTO RICAN VIREO *Vireo latimeri*   Plates 59, 85
Local Names: Bien-te-veo, Julián Chiví, Latimer's Vireo

Identification: 12.5 cm (5"). Distinguished by its *two-toned underparts* — throat and breast pale gray, belly and abdomen pale yellow — and by its *incomplete white eyering* and brown iris. **Similar species**: Black-whiskered Vireo has a black mustache stripe and whitish eyebrow stripe. Songs differ.
Voice: The common call is a melodious whistle usually of three to four syllables, which is repeated, with pauses between refrains, for several minutes. A new phrase is then sung continuously for some time. Usually at least one syllable is strongly accented. A rattling *chur-chur-churr-rrr*, somewhat like a chattering laugh, is reported to serve in courtship and as a scolding note. Its contact note is a *tup, tup* and it also issues a hoarse, grating, cat-like *mew*.
Status and Range: Endemic to western Puerto Rico where it is a common resident. Puerto Rican Vireo does not occur east of Loíza Aldea, Caguas and Patillas. Most common in the haystack hills of the north coast and in the more heavily forested valleys among the hills of the south coast. It also commonly occurs in the mangroves of Torrecilla-Piñones, but is unknown from other mangroves.
Comments: Puerto Rican Vireo forages at all levels, but more frequently near the ground. Feeds primarily on insects, but eats some plant matter. Its scolding call attracts other birds, especially Bananaquits, Puerto-Rican Stripe-headed Tanagers and grassquits. Like other vireos, rather inactive and would be difficult to locate without its frequent calling.
Habitat: Forests of all types and at all elevations including mangroves, dry coastal scrub, moist limestone hills and wet mountain forests. Also shade coffee plantations. Avoids open areas.
Nesting: The nest is a deep cup of coarse grass or twigs, lined with finer grass and camouflaged on the outside with spider egg sacks, green moss and other vegetation. Built in the fork of a twig at a low to moderate height in a shrub or tree. Eggs (3) with a pale pinkish hue, speckled with fine reddish-brown spots which sometimes form a ring around the broad end of the egg. Breeds from March to June.

FLAT-BILLED VIREO *Vireo nanus*   Plates 59, 82
Local Names: Cigüita Juliana (DR); Chit je blan (Haiti)

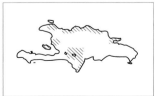

Identification: 12–13 cm (4.75–5"). Grayish-green above and light gray below, washed with pale yellow. Note the *outer tail feathers with narrow white tips, two white wingbars* and *white iris*. **Similar species**: Black-whiskered Vireo has a mustache stripe, other facial markings and lacks wingbars. Female Antillean Siskin is finely streaked below and has a paler, heavier bill.
Voice: A chattering, high-pitched *weet-weet-weet-weet-weet-weet-weet*. Also a slower version, often repeated.
Status and Range: Endemic to Hispaniola, including Gonâve Island, where uncommon and local in distribution.
Comments: Moves about slowly in low bushes, sometimes foraging on the ground. Feeds on fruits and insects, sometimes pursuing these in flight.

Habitat: Primarily lowlands in semi-arid scrub and undergrowth. Also occurs in moist hilly country. Absent from mountains.
Nesting: The nest, of plant material, is cup-shaped and built in a bush. It is sometimes held together with horse hair. Eggs (2) white, unmarked or only lightly marked with gray at one end. Breeds from February to June.

BLUE MOUNTAIN VIREO *Vireo osburni*　　　　**Plates 59, 84**

Identification: 13 cm (5"). A *robust gray* vireo lacking facial markings, with a relatively *large, dark bill* and *without wingbars or an eyering*. Pale yellow below; iris reddish-brown. ***Immature***: Yellow of underparts confined to belly and undertail-coverts. **Similar species**: Jamaican Vireo has conspicuous white wingbars and is considerably smaller, and the adult has a white iris. Black-whiskered and Red-eyed Vireos are larger, with distinct facial markings.
Voice: A trilling or bubbling whistle, only descending slightly in tone. Alarm call a harsh *burr*, descending in pitch at end.

Status and Range: Endemic to Jamaica where uncommon. Found primarily in the Blue and John Crow Mountains, Cockpit Country and Mount Diablo.
Comments: Secretive, foraging within dense foliage where heard more often than seen. Feeds on seeds and insects.
Habitat: Mainly humid and moist mountain forests, but also upland woods and shade coffee plantations down to approximately 100 m (330').
Nesting: The nest is a dangling moss cup at low to moderate height in a sapling or tree. Breeding is believed to occur primarily from March to July, but details of its eggs, clutch size and nesting habits have not been described.

BLUE-HEADED VIREO *Vireo solitarius*　　　　**Plate 59**
Local Name: Verdón de Cabeza Azul (Cuba)

Identification: 12.5–15 cm (5–5.75"). Olive-green above with a *blue-gray head, white spectacles* and *two prominent white wingbars*. **Similar species**: Cuban Vireo lacks the white spectacles, blue-gray head and conspicuous wingbars.
Voice: Short, garbled two- to three-syllabled phrases.
Status and Range: A very rare non-breeding resident in the northern Bahamas and Cuba from September to April. A vagrant on Jamaica. It is widespread in eastern North America.
Comments: Similar in behavior to other vireos. Easily overlooked due to its habits and similarity to more common species.
Habitat: Low, dense bushes and shrubs.

YELLOW-THROATED VIREO *Vireo flavifrons*　　　　**Plate 59**
Local Names: Verdón de Pecho Amarillo (Cuba), Julián Chiví Gargantiamarillo (PR)

Identification: 12.5 cm (5.5"). Note its *yellow spectacles,* two *white wingbars* and dark iris. The *chin, throat and breast are yellow*, the crown and back are olive-green and the rump gray. **Similar species**: White-eyed Vireo has a white chin, throat and breast. Thick-billed Vireo is usually entirely yellow below; it also has black lores and a grayish crown. Pine Warbler has less yellow on the face and has streaked sides. Cuban Vireo lacks distinctive yellow spectacles and conspicuous wingbars.
Voice: Song a wheezy *chee-wee, chee-woo, u-wee, chee-wee....* Call a scolding *chi-chi-chur-chur-chur-chur-chur* (Brudenell-Bruce).

Status and Range: Locally common on Cuba and uncommon in the Bahamas, Virgin Islands (St John and St Thomas) and Cayman Islands as a non-breeding resident from September to April. Rare in the southern Bahamas and on Barbados; very rare on Puerto Rico and a vagrant on Jamaica,

Hispaniola, Antigua, Dominica, St Lucia, St Vincent and Grenada. It occurs from eastern North America to northern South America.
Comments: A solitary bird of the forest canopy, this vireo may occur more frequently in the West Indies than records indicate. It is likely overlooked due to being difficult to detect and its similarity to more common species.
Habitat: Widespread in many forest types, including natural forests, coastal scrub, woodlands, beach ridge forests and second-growth.

WARBLING VIREO *Vireo gilvus*   Plate 59
Local Name: Vireo Cantor (Cuba)

Identification: 12.5–15 cm (5–5.75"). Note its pale gray upperparts, slightly lighter crown and hindneck and *whitish eyebrow stripe*. Throat to belly is whitish, often with wash of pale or greenish-yellow, particularly in first year birds. **Similar species**: Orange-crowned Warbler lacks a gray crown and has a faint greenish-yellow eyebrow stripe. See also Philadelphia Vireo.
Status and Range: A vagrant in western Cuba and Jamaica during migration in September and October when the species is undergoing its southward migration from Canada and the United States to its non-breeding grounds in Mexico and Central America. Warbling Vireos in the West Indies have strayed from their regular migration route down Mexico's eastern coast. It is widespread in North and Central America south to Nicaragua.

PHILADELPHIA VIREO *Vireo philadelphicus*   Plate 59
Local Name: Vireo de Filadelphia (Cuba)

Identification: 12.5 cm (5"). Field marks are its gray crown, gray-olive upperparts, *pale yellow throat and upper breast*, dark lores, whitish eyebrow stripe, brown iris and no wingbars. **Similar species**: Red-eyed and Black-whiskered Vireos both have a red iris, whitish throat, heavier bill and a black border above the whitish eyebrow stripe. Warbling Vireo has a whiter breast and lacks dark lores. Tennessee Warbler has a more slender bill; in non-breeding plumage, it has a yellowish eyebrow stripe and greenish crown. In breeding plumage, it is much whiter below. Orange-crowned Warbler lacks a gray cap and has a faint greenish-yellow eyebrow stripe.
Status and Range: A rare migrant in the Bahamas, Cuba and Jamaica primarily in October, though birds occur as late as February. A vagrant in the Cayman Islands and Antigua. It is widespread in North and Central America south to Panama.
Comments: Usually forages high in tree foliage for insects, spiders and small fruits, though it sometimes descends to low vegetation. The species is cryptic and easily overlooked.
Habitat: Forests, woodlands and gardens.

RED-EYED VIREO *Vireo olivaceus*   Plate 59
Local Name: Vireo de Ojo Rojo (Cuba)

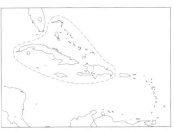

Identification: 15 cm (5.75"). It is distinguished by olive upperparts, a gray cap and *white eyebrow stripe, bordered by a black eyeline and crown stripe. Lacks a black 'whisker.'* **Adult**: Red iris. **Immature**: Brown iris; yellower tints on flanks and undertail-coverts. **Similar species**: Black-whiskered Vireo has a black whisker stripe, buffier underparts and is duller green on the back and paler gray on the crown. Cuban Vireo lacks black facial lines and has a faint eyering. Jamaican Vireo has wingbars. Blue Mountain Vireo lacks facial markings whereas those of Philadelphia and Yucatan Vireos are less sharply defined.
Voice: Usually silent in the West Indies except during its northward migration in April. Call is a nasal, high *chway*. The song consists of abrupt phrases separated by deliberate pauses, repeated many times. Black-whiskered Vireo has a similar song, but with longer phrases.

Status and Range: An uncommon and somewhat irregular southbound migrant through the Bahamas, Cuba, Jamaica and the Cayman Islands (Grand Cayman) from September to November and a rare northbound migrant primarily in April. It is rare on Hispaniola and a vagrant on Puerto Rico, the Virgin Islands, Guadeloupe, Martinique, St Lucia and Barbados. Its range includes North and Central America, and northern South America.

Comments: A relatively sedentary canopy species, easily overlooked because of its similarity to the common Black-whiskered Vireo.

Habitat: Treed areas of both the lowlands and mountains, including dry and wet forests, open woodlands, scrub and gardens.

BLACK-WHISKERED VIREO *Vireo altiloquus*   Plate 59

Local Names: Monkey Bird (Barbados); Chuck (St L); Lady Bird (St V); Greenlet, John Phillip (VI); John-to-whit, John-chew-it (Jamaica, VI); Bien-te-veo (Cuba, PR); Juan Chiví, Julián Chiví (DR, PR); Oiseau Canne, Petit Panache, Pias Kòlèt (Haiti); Bastard Grieve (Grenada); Tchouèque, Cuek (Mart); Tchouenke, Viréo à Moustaches (Guad, Mart); Chouèque, Père Gris, Piade (French LA)

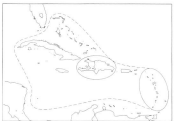

Identification: 15–16.5 cm (5.75–6.5"). *Best identified by its song.* However, the *whitish eyebrow stripe, dark eyeline, black mustache stripe or 'whisker'* and *absence of wingbars* also distinguish this vireo. **Adult**: Red iris. **Immature**: Brown iris, browner plumage and a faint wingbar. **Similar species**: All other vireos in the West Indies lack the black mustache stripe. The somewhat similar Red-eyed Vireo has whiter underparts, a greener back and grayer crown.

Voice: Monotonous song heard through the day, consisting of short, melodious three-syllabled phrases (two syllables in Providencia and San Andrés), each a bit different and separated by a distinct pause. Many of the local names for this bird are renditions of its song, e.g. 'Julián Chiví, Bien-te-veo'. The species also has a thin, unmusical *tsit* and a sharp, nasal note *yeeea*.

Status and Range: Generally a common breeding resident nearly throughout the West Indies. Populations on Hispaniola and the Lesser Antilles are year-round residents, whereas those in the Bahamas (absent from San Salvador), Cuba, Jamaica, Puerto Rico and the Cayman Islands (absent from Grand Cayman) migrate to northern South America in the non-breeding season from September to January. Whether this vireo departs from San Andrés and Providencia outside its breeding season remains to be determined. Also occurs in the extreme southeastern United States and northern South America.

Comments: Normally remains nearly motionless in dense canopy foliage where it goes unnoticed except when singing. Diet includes insects and fruits which it typically gleans from leaves, but occasionally takes while hovering. Migratory forms share more components of their calls with birds of other islands than do non-migratory forms. Non-migratory forms, though year-round residents on a given island, may undergo altitudinal migrations.

Habitat: Forests of all types and at all elevations, woodlands, mangroves, tall undergrowth and gardens.

Nesting: The nest is a cup of grass, covered with moss and pieces of bark and suspended from a branch typically in the canopy of a tall tree. Eggs (2–3) pinkish-white with spots concentrated at the broad end. Breeds primarily in May and June.

YUCATAN VIREO *Vireo magister*   Plate 59

Local Name: Sweet Bridget

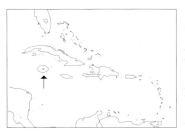

Identification: 15 cm (5.75"). Note its olive-gray crown and back, whitish or buff eyebrow stripe, dark gray eyeline, white underparts with yellowish abdomen, brown iris and absence of wingbars. **Similar species**: Red-eyed and Black-whiskered Vireos both have a red iris, more prominent dark stripes outlining the eyebrow stripe and a gray crown contrasting with the dull green back.

Voice: A two-note whistle *whoi whu* and a three syllabled *sweet, brid-get* (Bradley), very similar to the song of Black-whiskered Vireo.

Status and Range: A fairly common resident on Grand Cayman in the Cayman Islands. Occurs along Beach Bay Road and South Sound Swamp, among other sites. Also occurs in coastal Belize, Honduras and southeastern Mexico.

Comments: Frequents relatively dense vegetation where it slowly moves about foraging primarily on fruits, but also taking insects and spiders. Much more often heard than seen. An endemic subspecies occurs on Grand Cayman.

Habitat: Low elevation woodlands and mangroves.

Nesting: The nest is a deep woven cup built in the fork of a horizontal twig. Eggs (2) with almost no markings. Breeds from April to August.

EMBERIZIDS: FAMILY EMBERIZIDAE

This large and diverse family unites several bird groups such as the wood warblers, tanagers, honeycreepers and orioles along with the blackbirds and other distinctive bird assemblages. It is by far the best represented family in the region, the subfamily of wood warblers alone being better represented than any other group of family status. The subfamilies can be detailed as follows:

Wood Warblers — Wood warblers are tiny, insectivorous birds with thin, pointed bills. Most species actively hop among branches gleaning their prey from leaf surfaces, but some feed on the ground or, like the Redstart, sally after flying insects. The non-breeding plumages of many wood warblers are drab and care must be taken in the identification of these birds. Many species are migratory, breeding in North America and spend the non-breeding season in the Caribbean, Central or South America.

Honeycreepers — The Bananaquit and the Red-legged Honeycreeper are the sole representatives of this tropical Western Hemisphere group in the region. Honeycreepers typically have long, curved bills which they use to probe into flowers for nectar and insects. They have a specially adapted brush-like tongue for extracting the nectar. Soft fruits also form part of their diet.

Tanagers — The tanagers are a large Western Hemisphere assemblage, the males often being beautifully plumaged, but endowed with limited vocal ability (*Euphonia* in this region sing well). Puerto Rican Tanager is atypical because of the male's somber coloration and the lack of sexual dimorphism. Tanagers are generally arboreal forest-dwelling species that feed almost exclusively on fruits.

Grosbeaks — The grosbeaks are characterized by thick, conical bills used for eating seeds. In general appearance they resemble finches, weavers and waxbills.

Blackbirds and Orioles — The birds of this Western Hemisphere group possess pointed, conical bills. Almost all of the species in the region have a substantial amount of black in their plumage and several also show yellow or yellowish-orange coloration.

BACHMAN'S WARBLER *Vermivora bachmanii*   **Plate 62**
Local Name: Bijirita de Pecho Negro (Cuba)

Identification: 11–11.5 cm (4.25–4.5"). Both sexes have yellow eyerings. *Adult male*: Field marks are its *large, black patch on the throat and breast*; black patch on crown and yellow forehead, chin and belly. *Adult female*: Duller than the male, black on breast reduced to fine streaks or absent and crown and hindneck gray. *Immature*: Duller version of the adult. *Similar species*: Oriente Warbler, found only on Cuba, has entirely gray upperparts.

Status and Range: Critically endangered if not extinct, it was formerly an uncommon and local non-breeding resident on Cuba and the Isle of Youth from September to early April. The last widely accepted record was on Cuba in 1964. A 1980 report is dubious. A vagrant in the Bahamas where only recorded from Cay Sal. The cause for its decline is uncertain, but habitat loss is the likely reason both on Cuba, where natural lowland habitats have been converted to sugarcane plantations, and on the breeding grounds in the southeastern United States where canebrakes have been replaced by agriculture.

Habitat: Undergrowth in moist woods, canebrakes and forest edges bordering swamps.

BLUE-WINGED WARBLER *Vermivora pinus*   Plate 63
Local Names: Cigüita Ala Azul (DR); Ti Chit Zèl Ble, Petite Chitte Aile Bleue (Haiti)

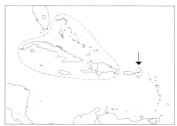

Identification: 12 cm (4.75″). Overall bright yellow with bluish wings, *white wingbars* and a black eyeline. **Similar species**: Prothonotary Warbler lacks white wingbars and the black eyeline.
Status and Range: A rare non-breeding resident in the Bahamas, Cuba, Jamaica, Hispaniola, the larger Virgin Islands and the Cayman Islands. A vagrant on St Barthélemy and Guadeloupe. Occurs primarily from October to March, but recorded as early as August and as late as May. Its range includes eastern North America and Central America south to Panama.
Habitat: Moist forests, trees in the vicinity of Australian Pine (*Casuarina*) and sometimes in bushes.

GOLDEN-WINGED WARBLER *Vermivora chrysoptera*   Plate 64
Local Names: Bijirita Alidorada (Cuba), Reinita Alidorada (PR)

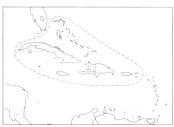

Identification: 12.5 cm (5″). Field marks are the *yellow wing patch* and *gray or black throat and cheek patch*. The forehead is yellow and the underparts whitish. **Adult male**: Throat and cheek patch black. **Female and immature**: Similar to the adult male, but plumage paler and more subdued. Throat and cheek patch gray.
Voice: The call note is a rather strong *chip*.
Status and Range: The species is rare on Puerto Rico and the Virgin and Cayman Islands and very rare in the Bahamas, Cuba, Jamaica and Hispaniola. A southbound migrant in September and October and northbound in April, there are few records during the intervening months. Occurs in the eastern United States, Central America and northern South America.
Comments: This retiring species frequents the tree canopy where it usually probes dead leaves for insects. Easily overlooked.
Habitat: On Cuba, gardens and woodlands. On Puerto Rico, high mountain forests.

TENNESSEE WARBLER *Vermivora peregrina*   Plates 64, 66
Local Names: Bijirita de Tennesse (Cuba); Cigüita de Tenesí (DR)

Identification: 11.5–12.5 cm (4.5–5″). **Adult non-breeding**: Olive-green above, yellowish below with a yellowish eyebrow stripe and noticeable eyeline. **Breeding male**: Bright olive-green above and white below, gray crown, white eyebrow stripe and pale gray line through the eye. **Breeding female**: Similar to the male, but crown duller and greenish; breast with a yellowish wash. **Immature**: Uniformly olive-green above; yellowish-green below except for white undertail-coverts. **Similar species**: Orange-crowned Warbler has faint breast streaks and yellow undertail-coverts.
Voice: A short, fine *tseet-tseet-tseet* ... repeated frequently. Its call can be confused with that of Bay-breasted Warbler with which is sometimes associates.
Status and Range: An uncommon non-breeding resident through the Bahamas, Cuba, Cayman Islands and San Andrés from September to May, it is rare on Jamaica, Hispaniola and Providencia and a vagrant in the Virgin Islands (St John) and Barbados. Occurs through North and Central America, and northern South America.
Comments: Sometimes in small flocks. Primarily feeds on nectar in the West Indies. Frequents the canopies of tall trees, but when foraging regularly, descends to low bushes near the ground.
Habitat: Woodlands, gardens and scrub.

ORANGE-CROWNED WARBLER *Vermivora celata* **Plates 63, 65**

Identification: 11.5–14 cm (4.5–5.5"). Note its unmarked, dull olive-green upperparts, faint *greenish-yellow eyebrow stripe*, thin broken yellow eyering, greenish-yellow *underparts faintly streaked with pale gray* and *yellow undertail-coverts*. **Similar species**: Tennessee Warbler is unstreaked below and has white undertail-coverts. Philadelphia and Warbling Vireos have a white eyebrow stripe and gray cap. Cerulean, Pine, Bay-breasted and Blackpoll Warblers all have wingbars.
Status and Range: A rare non-breeding resident in the northern Bahamas primarily from October to January. A vagrant on Cuba, Jamaica and the Cayman Islands. Occurs through North America south to Guatemala.

NASHVILLE WARBLER *Vermivora ruficapilla* **Plates 62, 66**

Identification: 11.5–12.5 cm (4.5–5"). It has a *conspicuous white eyering* in all plumages and the *grayish head contrasts with the yellowish-green upperparts*. **Adult**: Distinguished by its pale *bluish-gray head* and yellow underparts except for a white belly. **Immature**: Head brownish gray; underparts paler yellow with whitish throat and tan sides. **Similar species**: Oriente Warbler, found only on Cuba, has entirely gray upperparts.
Status and Range: A rare non-breeding resident in the northern Bahamas and Cayman Islands from mid-September to mid-April. A vagrant in the southern Bahamas, Cuba, Jamaica, Hispaniola and Puerto Rico. Occurs from North America south to Costa Rica.

NORTHERN PARULA *Parula americana* **Plate 63**
Local Names: Bijirita Chica (Cuba); Cigüita Parula (DR); Reinita Pechidorada (PR); Ti Chit Ble Pal, Mésange Bleue (Haiti); Paruline à Collier (Guad, Mart)

Identification: 10.5–12 cm (4–4.75"). Grayish-blue above with a *greenish-yellow back*, yellow throat and breast, white wingbars and an incomplete white eyering. **Non-breeding adult and immature**: May have a faint *black and reddish band across the breast*. **Breeding male**: Breast band conspicuous. **Similar species**: Adelaide's Warbler resembles female Northern Parula, but has a yellow eyebrow stripe and lacks a yellowish-green patch on its back.
Voice: Call note is a *toip*. Song an ascending insect-like buzz with a sharp ending note; may be heard before migration from March to May.
Status and Range: Widespread in the West Indies. A common non-breeding resident from August to May in the Bahamas, the Greater Antilles, the Virgin and Cayman Islands and San Andrés. It is generally uncommon in the northern Lesser Antilles from Anguilla to Martinique and is even rarer further south. One of the most common migrant warblers in the West Indies. Occurs from eastern North America south to Guatemala and Belize.
Comments: Parula Warbler is one of six migratory warblers, the entire population of which occurs primarily in the West Indies outside its breeding season. It sometimes joins single and multiple species flocks.
Habitat: Primarily dry forests and scrub of the lowlands, but also moist mountain forests.

YELLOW WARBLER *Dendroica petechia* Plates 63, 65, 66
Local Names: Mangrove Warbler (Jamaica); Yellow Bird (CI, Nevis); Golden Warbler (Jamaica, St V); Canary (Nevis, VI); Banana Bird, Goldfinch (St E, St M); Canario de Mangle (Cuba, DR, PR); Ti Jòn, Sucrier Mangle, Petit Oiseau Mangliers (Haiti); Sucrier Mang (St L); Ti Jaune, Didine; Paruline Jaune (Guad, Mart); Gele Zanger (St E, St M)

Identification: 11.5–13.5 cm (4.5–5.25"). **Adult male**: Yellow overall including patches on outer tail feathers, greenish-yellow upperparts, reddish streaks to breast and sides and yellow crown (Bahamas and Cuba) or with varying amounts of reddish-brown from a tinge (Jamaica, Hispaniola, Puerto Rico and the Cayman Islands) to a distinct cap (most of the Lesser Antilles) to the entire head (Martinique). **Adult female**: Similar to the male, but only faintly streaked below, if at all, and lacking reddish-brown on head. **Immature**: Olive-gray above, grayish-white below, with yellow in the wings. **Similar species**: Female and immature Wilson's Warblers have an eyebrow stripe rather than an eyering, show a more greenish cast to their upperparts and lack tail spots or markings on their underparts. Saffron Finch is larger, has a heavier bill and occurs in grassy habitats. For additional information on distinguishing the Yellow Warbler see: Kaufman, K. 1993. Yellow Warbler and its I.D. Contenders. *American Birds* 45(5): 167–170.

Voice: The song is variable, but typically a loud, clear and rapid *sweet-sweet-sweet-ti-ti-ti-weet*. Call notes include a thin *zeet* and hard *chip*.

Status and Range: A common year-round resident nearly throughout the West Indies, though it is uncommon in the northern Bahamas and does not breed on Saba, Grenada, St Vincent and some of the Grenadines. It is rare on Providencia and a vagrant on Saba. A few migrants which breed in North America occur from October to March particularly in the Greater Antilles. Several populations have declined because of intense brood parasitism by the Shiny Cowbird and the Barbados race is considered endangered due to this threat. It is widespread throughout North and Central America, and northern South America.

Comments: Resident West Indian populations of Yellow Warbler are sometimes considered a distinct species from North, Central and South American birds.

Habitat: Primarily mangroves on most islands, but on some islands found in coastal scrub. On Martinique, ranges into mountain forests. The differing habitat uses of this species among the islands remains an ecological puzzle.

Nesting: A neat, compact, cup-shaped nest of fine grass, fibers and plant down is built in a bush or tree near water, rarely more than 3 m (10') above ground. Eggs (2–3) bluish-white, spotted with brown in a wreath around the large end. Breeds from March to July.

CHESTNUT-SIDED WARBLER *Dendroica pensylvanica* Plates 64, 66
Local Names: Bijirita de Costados Castaños (Cuba); Reinita Castañicostada (PR)

Identification: 11.5–13.5 cm (4.5–5.25"). **Non-breeding adult and immature**: Yellowish-green above, *white eyering*, pale gray underparts and *two yellowish wingbars*. **Breeding adult male**: Note its *yellow cap, reddish band along side*s and white underparts. **Breeding adult female**: Similar to the male, but duller.

Status and Range: An uncommon non-breeding resident on Cuba and rare in the Bahamas, Jamaica, Hispaniola, Puerto Rico and the Virgin and Cayman Islands from September to May. A vagrant in the Lesser Antilles where recorded from Antigua, Dominica, Barbados and St Vincent. Uncommon on San Andrés. It is also widespread in eastern North America through Central America to Panama.

Comments: Sometimes in small single species groups or mixed feeding flocks. Generally forages in low vegetation.

Habitat: Open woodlands and gardens with trees.

MAGNOLIA WARBLER *Dendroica magnolia*   **Plates 61, 65**

Local Names: Bijirita Magnolia (Cuba); Cigüita Magnolia (DR), Reinita Manchada (PR); Ti Chit Ke Blan (Haiti)

Identification: 11.5–12.5 cm (4.5–5"). The *white markings in the tail* are diagnostic in most plumages. Other field marks in most plumages are the white eyebrow stripe and wingbars and the yellow throat and rump. ***Non-breeding adult and immature***: Pale eyebrow stripe, white eyering, gray head and yellow underparts with a buff band nearly across the breast. ***Breeding male***: Cheek black; underparts heavily striped with black. ***Breeding female***: Substantially paler than the breeding male. Cheek gray; underparts moderately streaked. ***Similar species***: All other warblers with yellow rumps lack conspicuous white tail markings. Yellow-rumped Warbler has some white in the tail and has a white, not yellow, throat. Cape May Warbler usually has a noticeable neck mark. Kirtland's Warbler has a dark rump, incomplete eyering and bobs its tail.

Voice: The call note is a hard, sonorous *tseek*.

Status and Range: Generally a fairly common migrant in the Bahamas and Cuba, it is uncommon on Jamaica, Hispaniola, Puerto Rico and the Cayman Islands. This species is rare in the Virgin Islands, Antigua and Barbados and very rare elsewhere in the Lesser Antilles. Magnolia Warbler is common on San Andrés and uncommon on Providencia. It is an infrequent non-breeding resident between migrations, occurring from September to May. It is widespread in North America south through Central America.

Habitat: Open woodlands in the lowlands, swamp edges and bushes. Sometimes gardens during migration.

CAPE MAY WARBLER *Dendroica tigrina*   **Plates 61, 65**

Local Names: Bijirita Atigrada (Cuba); Cigüita Tigrina (DR); Reinita Tigre (PR)

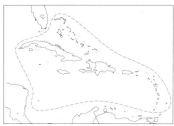

Identification: 12.5–14 cm (5–5.5"). In all plumages, the heavy striping on the breast and yellowish rump help identify this bird. Usually has a diagnostic *yellow neck patch*. ***Adult male***: Reddish-brown cheek; large, white wing patch. ***Adult female***: Duller. Cheek grayish-olive; single white wingbar. ***Immature***: Duller than the female, with a buffy patch behind the cheek and yellowish rump. ***Similar species***: Magnolia Warbler lacks the yellow neck patch. Bay-breasted Warbler lacks the neck patch and yellowish rump and is unstreaked below. **Voice**: Rarely sings its whispery, unmusical single-pitched song, *tseet-tseet-tseet- tseet* before migrating north.

Status and Range: A non-breeding resident throughout the West Indies from October to April though some birds occur as early as August and as late as May. Cape May Warbler is common in the Bahamas, Greater Antilles, Cayman Islands and San Andrés; uncommon in the Virgin Islands and generally rare to very rare in the Lesser Antilles. Occurs through much of North America.

Comments: Often congregates around flowering plants. Primarily feeds on nectar in the West Indies. The West Indies supports almost the entire population of this warbler outside its breeding season.

Habitat: From mountain forests, including shade coffee plantations, to coastal thickets, mangroves and gardens. Occurs almost anywhere plants are flowering.

BLACK-THROATED BLUE WARBLER   **Plates 64, 66**
Dendroica caerulescens

Local Names: Bijirita Azul de Garganta Negra (Cuba); Cigüita Azul con Garganta Negra (DR); Reinita Azul (PR); Petit Chit, Ti Chit Ble Kou Nwa (Haiti); Paruline Bleue (Guad, Mart)

Identification: 12–14 cm (4.75–5.5"). *Male*: *Blue above*, black face and band along sides and *white wing spot*. *Female*: Note the narrow, whitish eyebrow stripe and *white wing spot*, the latter sometimes absent in young females. The upperparts are olive-brown and the underparts dull buffy.

Status and Range: A common non-breeding resident in the Bahamas and Greater Antilles from

September to May, it is fairly common in the Cayman Islands. This warbler is rare in the Virgin Islands and decidedly so in the Lesser Antilles. It is uncommon on San Andrés. Occurs through North America.

Comments: Feeds principally on fruit and nectar, but also takes spiders and insects. Usually forages in low vegetation and infrequently on the ground or high in trees. The sexes show habitat segregation with the males most abundant in tall mature forests and the females most frequent in shrubby second growth. The West Indies supports almost the entire population of this warbler outside its breeding season.

Habitat: Forests, forest edges and woodlands primarily in the mountains, but also in moist to wet lowlands. Infrequently dry forests.

YELLOW-RUMPED WARBLER *Dendroica coronata*   Plates 61, 65

Local Names: Myrtle Warbler (Jamaica); Bijirita Coronada (Cuba); Cigüita Mirta (DR); Reinita Coronada (PR); Paruline à Croupion Jaune (Guad)

Identification: 14 cm (5.5″). In all plumages, the combination of the *yellow rump and patch on the side of the breast,* and the *white throat* are distinctive. Breeding males have the most vivid plumage and immature birds the dullest, but all display these identifying characters. **Adult female and non-breeding male**: Brownish, but with the above field marks. **Breeding male**: Grayish upperparts. **Immature**: Duller than the adult female and non-breeding male. **Similar species**: Magnolia Warbler has a yellow, not white, throat.

Voice: The call note is a hard, characteristic *check.*

Status and Range: A non-breeding resident in the West Indies which typically arrives later than most migrants (November) and leaves earlier (March). However, some birds arrive as early as October and leave as late as April. It varies in status from year to year, but is generally fairly common in the Bahamas, Cuba, Jamaica and San Andrés and uncommon on Hispaniola, Puerto Rico, the Virgin and Cayman Islands and Providencia. It is decidedly rare overall in the Lesser Antilles. Occurs throughout North America.

Comments: Usually in small groups.

Habitat: A wide range of habitats, including gardens, woodlands, thickets and areas with scattered vegetation. Also mangroves and swamp edges.

TOWNSEND'S WARBLER *Dendroica townsendi*   Plate 78

Identification: 13 cm (5″). Note the dark cheek ringed with yellow. **Adult male**: The cheek, chin, throat and heavy side streaks are black; the lower breast and belly are yellow. The outer tail feathers are white. **Adult female**: Slightly duller, with a yellow rather than black chin and throat and with a white rather than yellow belly. **Immature**: Substantially paler than the adult. Olive-green cheeks and underparts may lack black or show only fine streaks. There is less white in the tail. **Similar species**: In all plumages, Black-throated Green Warbler has much paler cheeks with more yellow. The immatures are very similar, but Townsend's Warbler is yellower on the breast and has no yellow on its white undertail-coverts. Townsend's differs from Blackburnian Warbler in its olive-green back with no stripes.

Status and Range: A vagrant in the Bahamas (Grand Bahama and Grand Turk) and also a questionable record from Puerto Rico. Occurs from northwestern North America to Central America.

BLACK-THROATED GREEN WARBLER   Plates 61, 65
Dendroica virens

Local Names: Bijirita de Garganta Negra (Cuba); Cigüita Pechinegro (DR); Reinita Verdosa (PR); Ti Chit Fal Nwa (Haiti); Paruline à Gorge Noire (Guad)

Identification: 12.5 cm (5″). In all plumages, the *yellowish-gray cheeks are surrounded by a characteristic yellow band.* **Adult male**: Black chin, throat, upper breast and side streaks. **Adult female**

and immature male: Duller; chin yellowish. *Immature female*: Duller still. Black absent below except faint streaks on sides. *Similar species*: Immature female Blackburnian Warbler has a yellower throat and breast and whitish back stripes. See also Townsend's Warbler.
Status and Range: A non-breeding resident in the West Indies from September to May. It is common in western Cuba; uncommon in the Bahamas, eastern Cuba, Jamaica and Hispaniola; rare in the Cayman Islands and on San Andrés and very rare on Puerto Rico, the Virgin Islands and the Lesser Antilles where recorded from St Martin, St Barthélemy, Antigua, Guadeloupe, Dominica and Barbados. Occurs through much of North America to Central America.
Comments: Arboreal. Forages actively for caterpillars and insects.
Habitat: Primarily low and mid-elevation forested areas, including shade coffee plantations. Sometimes woodlands and gardens during migration.

BLACKBURNIAN WARBLER *Dendroica fusca* Plates 61, 65
Local Names: Bijirita Blackburniana (Cuba), Reinita de Fuego (PR)

Identification: 13 cm (5"). *Adult female, non-breeding male and immature male*: Bright *orange-yellow throat, breast, eyebrow stripe and sides of neck. White back stripes* and wingbars; dark side stripes. *Immature female*: Paler; orange-yellow replaced by yellowish. *Breeding male*: Brilliant *orange throat and facial markings*. *Similar species*: Immature Black-throated Green Warbler has a buff-colored throat and breast and lacks whitish stripes on its back. See also Townsend's Warbler.
Voice: A fine, weak *tsseek, tsseek*.
Status and Range: Primarily in the West Indies during southbound (September and October) and northbound (April and May) migrations, though a few individuals also occur from November to March. This warbler is uncommon on Cuba; rare in the Bahamas, Jamaica, Hispaniola and the Cayman Islands; very rare on Puerto Rico and the Virgin Islands (St John) and a vagrant in the Lesser Antilles where recorded from Dominica, Barbados and Grenada. Occurs in eastern North America, Central America and northeastern South America.
Comments: Arboreal. On Cuba, it sometimes occurs in fairly large groups.
Habitat: Conifers, high trees and botanical gardens.

YELLOW-THROATED WARBLER *Dendroica dominica* Plate 61
Local Names: Bijirita de Garganta Amarilla (Cuba); Cigüita Garganta Amarilla (DR); Reinita Gargantiamarilla (PR); Ti Chit Fal Jòn (Haiti)

Identification: 13 cm (5"). Note the yellow throat, white eyebrow stripe and *white neck patch*. The distinctive Bahamas race has yellow extending to the breast, belly and abdomen and less white in its facial markings. *Female*: Black slightly reduced. *Similar species*: Olive-capped Warbler lacks the white eyebrow stripe and white neck patch. Kirtland's Warbler bobs its tail and lacks a white neck patch.
Voice: The call note is a soft, high-pitched, slightly metallic *tsip*.
Status and Range: A resident race (*D. d. flavescens*) is common in its limited northern Bahamas range of Grand Bahama and Abaco. Migrants that breed in North America reside in the West Indies primarily from August to March, with some birds arriving as early as July and leaving as late as April. Yellow-throated Warbler is one of the earliest warblers to arrive and depart from the West Indies. These non-breeding birds are generally common in the Bahamas, Cuba and the Cayman Islands and are uncommon on Jamaica, Hispaniola and Puerto Rico. This warbler is a vagrant in the Virgin Islands and the Lesser Antilles where recorded from Montserrat, Guadeloupe and Barbados. Occurs from the eastern United States south through Central America.

Comments: Generally a canopy bird occupying the higher tree branches. The Bahamas race often forages by climbing up pine trunks. This warbler sometimes occurs in mixed species flocks.

Habitat: The Bahamas race primarily inhabits pine forests, while migrants in the Bahamas frequent gardens and developed areas. When in pine woods, migrants occur in the understory. Migrants elsewhere in the West Indies occupy pine forests, Australian pine (*Casuarina*), lowland forests and coconut palms as well as gardens.

ADELAIDE'S WARBLER *Dendroica adelaidae*   Plate 63
Local Names: Christmas Bird, Petit Chitte (LA); Reinita Mariposera (PR)

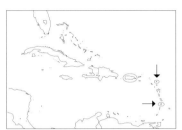

Identification: 12.5 cm (5"). Distinguished by its bluish-gray upperparts, yellow throat and breast, yellow and/or white eyebrow stripe and crescent below the eye variably edged with black. **Female**: Similar to the male, but black edging to crown stripe less pronounced and less white in tail. **Similar species**: Female Northern Parula has a yellowish-green patch on its back and lacks the yellow eyebrow stripe.

Voice: The call note is a *chick* of medium strength. The song typically consists of a loud, variable trill which varies in pitch. It may slow at the end or have other minor modifications. Members of a pair often 'chatter' and sing together.

Status and Range: A common year-round resident in western Puerto Rico (including Vieques off the east coast), Barbuda and St Lucia. It is a vagrant on Martinique. These islands comprise the entire range of the species.

Comments: Arboreal. Forages actively, gleaning insects and spiders from leaves and twigs. Sometimes joins mixed feeding flocks. Endemic races occupy each of the three major islands where this warbler occurs.

Habitat: On Puerto Rico, primarily dry coastal scrubland and thickets and, to a lesser extent, moist limestone forests of the haystack hills. On St Lucia, occurs in forests at all altitudes, but principally at middle and higher elevations. This warbler frequents thickets near wetlands and inland canals on Barbuda.

Nesting: A finely woven, cup-shaped nest is built in a tree or dense thicket from 0.2 m to over 6 m (1–20') above the ground. Eggs (3–4) white, flecked with reddish-brown spots, particularly at the broad end. Breeds from March to June.

OLIVE-CAPPED WARBLER *Dendroica pityophila*   Plate 61
Local Names: Chip-chip (Bahamas); Bijirita del Pinar (Cuba)

Identification: 12.5 cm (5"). The *conspicuous greenish-yellow crown* and *yellow throat and breast bordered by black spots* identify this warbler. Has two whitish wingbars. **Similar species**: Yellow-throated Warbler has a conspicuous white eyebrow stripe and a white patch on the side of the neck.

Voice: A high, melodious whistle-like song, generally of eight quick notes, *wisi-wisi-wisi* ... dropping in pitch in the middle and then rising in pitch on the last note. Sometimes several sing simultaneously, forming a noisy chorus. Also a characteristic *tsip*.

Status and Range: Known only from Cuba and the Bahamas where it is common, but extremely local in distribution. On Cuba, confined to the pine (*Pinus caribaeus*) forests in the western Province of Pinar del Río (Sierra de los Organos, Sierra del Rosario and La Güira) and to the eastern region of Oriente where it occurs in patchy areas of pine (*Pinus cubensis*) forests as found in the Pinares de Mayarí, Cupeyal, Monte Cristo and other zones north of Guantánamo and west of Baracoa. In the Bahamas, it is found only on Grand Bahama and Abaco in pine (*Pinus caribaeus*) forests.

Comments: Usually in treetops, but during the breeding season may descend to the ground to forage. Insects and spiders are its main diet. It combines several foraging methods, as do Yellow-headed and Oriente Warblers. The Bahamas' populations are considered by some experts to be a separate race.

Habitat: A denizen of pine forests, although sometimes in nearby mixed pine-hardwood forests.

Nesting: The nest is cup-shaped and lined with feathers and is usually built high in a pine tree at

2–14 m (7–45') and close to the trunk, so it is very difficult to locate. Eggs (2) variable in shape and color, but generally dull white or gray spotted with brown, most heavily at the broad end. Breeds from March to August.

PINE WARBLER *Dendroica pinus* Plates 61, 65
Local Names: Chip-chip (Bahamas); Cigüita del Pinar (DR); Ti Chit Bwa Pen, Petite Chitte des Pins (Haiti)

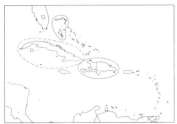

Identification: 12.5–14.5 cm (5–5.75"). *Adult male*: Distinguished by greenish-olive upperparts, *an unstreaked back, two white wingbars*, a very faint yellow eyebrow stripe, variable amounts of yellow on the chin and throat and faint gray to blackish streaking across breast and on upper flanks. *Adult female*: Like the male, but duller. Browner above; grayer below. *Immature*: Duller than adult counterparts. Grayish-brown above, buffy-white below, whitish eyebrow stripe and two white wingbars. Breast streaks may not be noticeable. *Similar species*: White-eyed Vireo has distinct yellow spectacles and lacks streaking below. The adult has a white iris. Orange-crowned Warbler lacks wingbars. Yellow-throated Vireo has distinct yellow spectacles and lacks streaking on the sides. Bay-breasted Warbler has a streaked back in all plumages. See Bay-breasted Warbler citation for additional field marks to distinguish these species.

Voice: Musical trill usually on one pitch. Also a strong *tzip*.

Status and Range: A common year-round resident in the northern Bahamas (Grand Bahama, Abaco, Andros and New Providence) and the Dominican Republic, but considered threatened on Haiti because of widespread habitat destruction. A very rare wanderer to western Cuba and the Cayman Islands during October and November. A vagrant on Jamaica, Mona Island off Puerto Rico and Martinique. It is widespread in the eastern United States.

Comments: Forages from ground level to canopy for insects, spiders, pine seeds and berries. The Bahamas and Hispaniola each support distinct races.

Habitat: Mature pine forests or barrens, particularly in breeding season.

Nesting: A cup-shaped nest is built of pine needles and grass, concealed on a narrow branch, often high in a pine tree. Eggs (3–4) white with brown speckles. Breeds from March to June.

KIRTLAND'S WARBLER *Dendroica kirtlandii* Plates 61, 65

Identification: 15 cm (5.75"). *Habit*: Bobs tail. *Adult*: Bluish-gray above with black streaks on back, two inconspicuous whitish wingbars, *broken white eyering* and *bright yellow throat and belly with black streaks on sides*. *Adult female and non-breeding male*: Forehead and lores dark gray. *Breeding male*: Forehead and lores black and more contrast in plumage. *Immature female*: Brownish-gray above with eyering and flank streaks fainter. *Similar species*: Non-breeding adult and immature Magnolia Warblers have a yellow rump, a *complete eyering* and do not bob their tails. The local race of Yellow-throated Warbler from the Bahamas (Grand Bahama and Abaco) is very similar to Kirtland's, but has a noticeable white neck patch and does not bob its tail. Also, Yellow-throated Warbler forages on tree trunks and in the upper canopy of trees whereas Kirtland's frequents low brush.

Status and Range: A rare non-breeding resident in the Bahamas primarily from October to April. This warbler is widely dispersed in the Bahamas and does not appear to concentrate on a particular island or island group. The species is endangered due to limited breeding habitat and nest parasitism by Brown-headed Cowbirds. It has been suggested that alteration of Bahama's native pine forests may have also negatively impacted this warbler. It also occurs in the north-central United States.

Comments: The Bahamas supports the world population of Kirtland's Warbler for most of the year. This species then migrates to a very local breeding site in the north-central United States (Michigan) where it nests among young jack pines (*Pinus barksiana*). Kirtland's Warbler generally forages low, rarely more than 5 m (16') above the ground.

Habitat: Usually in low broadleaved scrub, thickets and understory. Also, infrequently, in pine forests.

Islands and a vagrant in the Lesser Antilles where recorded from Saba, Dominica, St Lucia and Barbados. Occurs through much of North America.
Comments: Occurs primarily in low vegetation or on the ground. In western Cuba, occurs in single species foraging flocks.
Habitat: Generally brush and bushes near coastal water bodies, including mangroves. Also open areas, including golf courses and fields, with sparse brush, plantation edges and gardens.

BAY-BREASTED WARBLER *Dendroica castanea*　　Plates 64, 65
Local Name: Bijirita Castaña (Cuba)

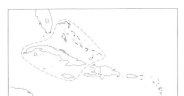

Identification: 12.5–15 cm (5–5.75"). *Non-breeding adult and immature*: Back greenish-gray streaked with black, though sometimes only faintly; unstreaked buffy below, including undertail-coverts; creamy-buff on flanks (some reddish-brown in males), white wingbars and usually blackish legs and feet. *Breeding male*: *Dark reddish-brown cap* and band on chin, throat and sides. Note the black mask and buff patch on side of neck. *Female breeding*: Top of head, breast and sides washed with reddish-brown. *Similar species*: Non-breeding adult and immature Blackpoll Warblers are finely streaked below, have pale legs and white undertail-coverts. Pine Warbler has an unstreaked back. For additional guidance on distinguishing Bay-breasted, Pine and Blackpoll Warblers see: Hough, J. 1996. Pine and 'Baypoll' Warblers — Plumage Variation and Identification Problems. *Birding* 28(4): 284–291; and Votier, S., and C. Bradshaw. 1996. Identification of Blackpoll, Bay-breasted and Pine Warblers in Autumn. *Birding World* 9(8): 313–318. Cape May Warbler has a yellowish rump, often has a yellow patch on the side of the neck and is usually heavily streaked below. Orange-crowned Warbler lacks wingbars.
Voice: A weak *tsee-tsee-tsee* that can be confused with the call of Tennessee Warbler with which it sometimes associates.
Status and Range: A rare migrant in the Bahamas, Cuba, Jamaica, Cayman Islands and San Andrés primarily in October and November and in April and May. A vagrant on Hispaniola, Puerto Rico, the Virgin Islands (St Croix), Antigua, Dominica, Barbados and St Vincent. Occurs through North and Central America, and northern South America.
Comments: A relatively slow-moving warbler, primarily of the canopy, that sometimes forages in single species groups or mixed species flocks with Tennessee and Chestnut-sided Warblers.
Habitat: Forest edges, woodlands, gardens and open areas with scattered trees.

BLACKPOLL WARBLER *Dendroica striata*　　Plates 60, 65
Local Names: Bijirita de Cabeza Negra (Cuba); Cigüita Casco Prieto (DR); Reinita Rayada (PR); Petit Chit, Ti Chit Sèjan, Petite Chitte Rayée (Haiti); Paruline Rayée, Paruline Striée (Guad, Mart)

Identification: 12.5–14 cm (5–5.5"). *Non-breeding adult and immature*: Difficult to identify. Look for white wingbars and undertail-coverts, faint side streaks and pale legs. Generally yellowish-gray above and paler below. *Breeding male*: *Black cap; white cheek patch*. *Breeding female*: Similar to non-breeding adult, but plumage more olive-gray than yellowish-gray. *Similar species*: Non-breeding adult and immature Bay-breasted Warblers are unstreaked below and have buffy, not white, undertail-coverts and black legs. See Bay-breasted Warbler citations for additional guidance on distinguishing these species.
Orange-crowned Warbler lacks wingbars.
Voice: A thin, high-pitched *zeet-zeet-zeet-zeet...*
Status and Range: A migrant throughout the West Indies occurring more regularly southbound (October and November) on Puerto Rico, the Virgin Islands and Lesser Antilles, but more regularly northbound (May) in the Bahamas, Cuba and the Cayman Islands. Blackpoll Warbler is fairly common in the

Bahamas, Cuba, Hispaniola and Puerto Rico and uncommon to rare on most other islands, including Providencia and San Andrés. It occurs in almost equal frequencies during both migrations on Hispaniola. Occurs through much of North America and central South America.

Comments: During October and November virtually the entire world population of Blackpolls migrate southward past the Lesser Antilles on its journey from North America to central South America. The numbers that stop off among these islands may vary dramatically from year to year depending on weather conditions. Primarily forages by gleaning insects, spiders and small fruits from twigs and branches. It regularly joins mixed species flocks.

Habitat: Very varied, including mangroves, brush, scrub forests, open areas with scattered trees and mixed woodlands.

CERULEAN WARBLER *Dendroica cerulea*　　　**Plates 60, 65**
Local Name: Bijirita Azulosa (Cuba)

Identification: 10–13 cm (4–5"). Both sexes have *two white wingbars*. **Adult male**: Field marks are its *light blue head and upperparts,* white underparts with black streaks on sides and a *dark band across breast*. **Adult female and immature male**: *Upperparts grayish-blue,* underparts dull white with yellowish tinge on throat and upper breast and faint streaks on sides. **Immature female**: Olive-green above; yellower below. **Similar species**: Immature female Cerulean Warbler differs from Orange-crowned Warbler by having two white wingbars.

Status and Range: A very rare migrant in the Bahamas, western Cuba, Jamaica and the Cayman Islands (Grand Cayman) primarily in September and October, but also less frequently in April. A vagrant on Mona Island off Puerto Rico and on Barbados. A few birds remain on Grand Cayman as non-breeding residents until April. Occurs from eastern North America to northern South America.

Habitat: Forest canopy, but also low bushes and small trees.

PLUMBEOUS WARBLER *Dendroica plumbea*　　　**Plates 64, 66**
Local Names: Paruline Caféiette, Ti Moulin, Tic-tic (Guad)

Identification: 12 cm (4.75"). **Adult**: Field marks include *plain gray upperparts, white eyebrow stripe,* especially in front of eye, two white wingbars and underparts mostly pale gray with some white through center of breast. **Immature**: Greenish-gray upperparts, eyebrow stripe either white or buffy, underparts buffy and two white wingbars. **Habit**: Flicks tail.

Voice: A musical three-syllabled *pa-pi-a*. Also a loud rattle.

Status and Range: A common year-round resident on Guadeloupe, though uncommon on Marie-Galante and perhaps extirpated from Terre de Haut. Also common on Dominica. These islands encompass the entire range of the species.

Comments: Forages primarily on insects in the understory, but also eats berries.

Habitat: Usually moist mountain forests, but sometimes drier scrub forests and mangroves.

Nesting: The nest is a loosely-constructed cup built low in a bush or bromeliad clump. Eggs (2–3) white to bluish-white, spotted with black concentrated at the broad end. Breeds from March to July.

ARROW-HEADED WARBLER *Dendroica pharetra*　　　**Plates 60, 84**
Local Names: Ants Bird, Ants Picker

Identification: 13 cm (5"). Regularly *flicks tail down*. **Adult male**: *Heavily streaked black and white above and below* and with *two white wingbars*. **Adult female**: Black of male replaced by dark gray. **Immature**: Look for yellowish-olive above, pale yellowish below with fine grayish streaks, wingbars, yellowish eyering and some white in tail. **Similar species**: Adult is similar to Black-and-white Warbler which has a very distinct black-and-white striped head and does not flick its tail. Jamaican Vireo is similar to immature Arrow-headed Warbler, but lacks an eyering, dark eyeline and white in the tail. It also has a pinkish bill and flicks its tail up.

Voice: The call note is a watery '*chip*'. The song is very soft and somewhat variable. Generally it consists of six *tswee* notes, the last rising, followed by a further three *tswee* notes, the last again rising and terminating with either a jumble of notes, the last rising or in their place, three descending notes (Levy).

Status and Range: Endemic to Jamaica where locally common, especially in Blue Mountains, Hardwar Gap, Cockpit Country, Mandeville and Anchovy. Also Fern Gully and Ferry River on the coast.

Comments: Usually gleans insects from leaves high above the ground or beneath the canopy. Arrow-headed, Elfin Woods and Plumbeous Warblers all appear closely related.

Habitat: Moist and humid forests at all elevations. Less frequent in wet lowland forests.

Nesting: A well-concealed cup of plant materials is built in a bush or tree. Eggs (2) white, heavily spotted with reddish-brown and lightly marked with reddish-gray, particularly at the broad end. Breeds in May and June.

ELFIN WOODS WARBLER *Dendroica angelae* **Plates 60, 85**
Local Name: Reinita de Bosque Enano

Identification: 12.5 cm (5"). *Adult: Entirely black and white*, it is distinguished by the *thin, white eyebrow stripe, white patches on ear-coverts and neck, incomplete eyering* and black crown. ***Immature***: Similar in pattern to the adult, but black is replaced by grayish-green on the back and yellowish-green on the head and underparts. ***Similar species***: Black-and-white Warbler creeps along trunks of trees, whereas Elfin Woods Warbler gleans insects from leaves and thinner branches. Black-and-white Warbler also has broad, white crown stripes.

Voice: Song is a series of short, rapidly uttered, rather unmusical notes on one pitch, swelling in volume and terminating with a short series of distinct double syllables sounding slightly lower in pitch. Contact note is similar to the song, but lacks the terminal syllables. The call note, infrequently given, is a single, short, metallic *chip* (Kepler and Parkes).

Status and Range: Endemic to Puerto Rico, where it is uncommon and local. In the east, it is known from Carite and the Luquillo Mountains. In the west, it is restricted to the upper elevations of Maricao State Forest. Elfin Woods Warbler is considered threatened because of its limited habitat.

Comments: Elfin Woods Warbler was not discovered until 1971. An extremely active bird, it often forages for insects in small feeding flocks with other species, particularly Puerto Rican Tanagers.

Habitat: Dense vines of the canopy in humid, mountain dwarf forests on ridges and summits, sometimes ranging to lower elevations.

Nesting: A compact cup, usually close to trunk and well-hidden among epiphytes of a small tree. Eggs (2–3) dull white, moderately to heavily spotted with reddish-brown, concentrated at the broad end. Breeds from March to June.

WHISTLING WARBLER *Catharopeza bishopi* **Plates 64, 86**
Local Names: Whistling Bird, Lesser Soufriere Bird, Black and White Soufriere Bird

Identification: 14.5 cm (5.75"). *Adult: Blackish hood*, upperparts and *broad breast band; broad white eyering and chin* and mark by bill. ***Immature***: Brownish-gray hood, upperparts and breast band; white eyering and mark by bill.

Voice: Rising pattern of notes becoming increasingly loud, ending with two or three emphatic ones.

Status and Range: A rare resident endemic to St Vincent where it occurs primarily at Colonaire and Perserence Valleys and Richmond Peak. Dramatic reduction of forests on St Vincent has led to this bird being threatened. Only about 80 sq. km (31 sq. mi.) of appropriate habitat appear to survive, supporting an estimated 1,500 to 2,500 territorial males in 1986. Eruptions of Mt Soufrière also threaten this warbler's habitat. Two eruptions have occurred since 1900.

Comments: Frequently cocks its tail. Works its way deliberately through vine tangles, undergrowth and the underside of the forest canopy.

Habitat: Primary or secondary mountain forest undergrowth and often the underside of the forest canopy.

Nesting: A cup-shaped nest is built in a shrub or small tree, not far above the ground. Eggs (2). Breeds from April to July.

BLACK-AND-WHITE WARBLER *Mniotilta varia*   **Plate 60**
Local Names: Ants Bird, Ants Picker (Jamaica); Bijirita Trepadora (Cuba); Pega Palo (DR); Reinita Trepadora (PR); Ti Chit Demidèy, Demi-deuil (Haiti); Paruline Noir et Blanc, Mi-deuil, Madras (Guad, Mart)

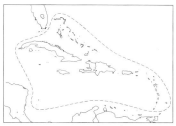

Identification: 12.5–14 cm (5–5.5"). The entirely black-and-white coloration, *black-and-white striped crown* and *habit of climbing on tree trunks* help identify this warbler. **Male**: Black cheek patch. **Female**: Somewhat whiter than the male particularly on cheek, throat and sides. **Similar species**: No other white- and black-plumaged warblers in the West Indies, either migrant or resident, climb trees in the same way or posssess the broad crown stripes.

Voice: May call upon arrival in August and September, rarely before departure. The call is a thin *tee-zee, tee-zee, tee-zee,* tee-zee, varying in length.

Status and Range: A non-breeding resident in the West Indies primarily from August to April, but recorded in all months except June. It is common in the Bahamas, Greater Antilles, the Cayman and Virgin Islands, Providencia and San Andrés, but varies in status in the Lesser Antilles from being common on some islands and very rare on others, likely reflecting habitat availability. Occurs through much of North America to northern South America.

Comments: Climbs trees either upward or downward probing in the bark for insects and spiders. Woodpeckers are only able to climb upward in such an efficient manner.

Habitat: Forests and wooded areas at all elevations.

AMERICAN REDSTART *Setophaga ruticilla*   **Plate 64**
Local Names: Christmas Bird (LA); Butterfly Bird (CI, Jamaica); Bijirita (DR); Candelita (Cuba, DR, PR); Ti Chit Dife, Petite Chitte de Feu (Haiti); Carougette (St L); Paruline Flamboyante, Gabriel du Feu, Carte, Petit du Feu (Guad, Mart)

Identification: 11–13.5 cm (4.25–5.25"). **Adult male**: Note its black upperparts, throat and breast and *large, orange patches in wings and at sides of tail*. **Adult female**: Head gray, upperparts greenish-gray and *large, yellow patches in wings and tail*. **Immature**: Head greenish-gray and yellow patches reduced.

Status and Range: A common non-breeding resident of the Bahamas, Greater Antilles, Cayman and Virgin Islands and northern Lesser Antilles and generally uncommon in the southern Lesser Antilles. It is common on San Andrés and rare on Providencia. Occurs primarily from late August through early May. A few individuals remain throughout the year in the Greater Antilles. There are several recent nesting records for Cuba from both the western and eastern parts of the island. It is widespread in North America through Central and South America south to Brazil.

Comments: Frequently fans its wings and tail. Flits in the air after insects. Redstarts display habitat segregation with older males occuring in tall, mature forests while females and young males occupy scrubby second-growth.

Habitat: Usually forests and woodlands from the coast to the mountains. Also gardens and shrubby areas.

PROTHONOTARY WARBLER *Protonotaria citrea*   **Plates 63, 66**
Local Names: Bijirita Protonotaria (Cuba); Cigüita Cabeza Amarilla (DR); Reinita Anaranjada (PR); Ti Chit Tèt Jòn (Haiti); Paruline Orangée (Guad, Mart)

Identification: 13.5 cm (5.25"). *Male*: *Golden yellow overall except blue-gray wings* and tail. *Female*: Duller, especially on the crown and hindneck. Golden-yellow confined to face, throat and breast. *Similar species*: Blue-winged Warbler has white wingbars and a black eyeline. Saffron Finch is larger with a heavier bill and occurs in grassy habitats. Yellow-headed Warbler has a pale gray belly and abdomen. Oriente Warbler has a gray crown, sharply demarked from its yellow face.

Status and Range: Generally an uncommon migrant both southbound and northbound in the Bahamas, Cuba, Jamaica and Hispaniola primarily from August to October and from March to early April. It is a rare migrant in the Cayman Islands and on Providencia and San Andrés. Prothonotary Warbler is a decidedly uncommon non-breeding resident on Puerto Rico from August to March and a rare one in the Virgin Islands and Lesser Antilles. It occurs from eastern North America to northern South America.

Comments: This warbler is easily overlooked due to its similarity in appearance and choice of habitat to the much commoner Yellow Warbler.

Habitat: In or near mangrove swamps. On Cuba, also gardens and tree clumps.

WORM-EATING WARBLER *Helmitheros vermivorus*   **Plate 64**
Local Names: Bijirita Gusanera (Cuba); Cigüita Cabeza Rayada (DR); Reinita Gusanera (PR)

Identification: 14 cm (5.5"). Field marks are its plain greenish-gray upperparts, wings and tail; buffy head with *black stripes on crown and through eye* and underparts whitish buff, whiter on throat and belly.

Status and Range: A fairly common non-breeding resident in the Bahamas, Cuba, Cayman Islands and San Andrés from September to April; uncommon on Jamaica, Hispaniola, Puerto Rico and Providencia and rare in the Virgin Islands. A vagrant on St Martin, St Barthélemy, Antigua and Guadeloupe. It is widespread in east-central North America through Central America south to Panama.

Comments: Often forages among dead leaves at all levels in the forest. Associates with mixed species flocks.

Habitat: Dense forests at all elevations.

SWAINSON'S WARBLER *Limnothlypis swainsonii*   **Plate 64**
Local Names: Bijirita de Swainson (Cuba); Reinita de Swainson (PR)

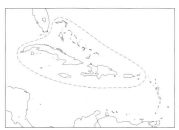

Identification: 14 cm (5.5"). Head brownish-gray with *brown crown*, whitish eyebrow stripe and blackish line through the eye. The back, wings and tail are unmarked olive grayish-brown. Underparts whitish, grayer on sides.

Voice: Call note a sharp, metallic *chip*.

Status and Range: An uncommon non-breeding resident on Cuba and Jamaica and rare in the Bahamas and Puerto Rico. A rare migrant in the Cayman Islands. A vagrant on Hispaniola and the Virgin Islands (St John). Occurs from September to April. It is widespread in southeastern United States to the Yucatan Peninsula and Belize.

Comments: Forages primarily on the ground searching for insects and spiders among the leaf litter. Retiring and extremely difficult to locate. Likely it occurs much more frequently than records suggest.

Habitat: Areas with substantial leaf litter, including canebrakes, thickets, dense woodland understory and wet limestone forests.

OVENBIRD *Seiurus aurocapillus*   **Plate 60**
Local Names: Betsy Kick-up (Jamaica); Señorita del Monte (Cuba); Cigüita Saltarina (DR); Pizpita Dorada (PR); Ti Chit Tè, Petite Chitte Dorée (Haiti); Paruline Couronnée (Guad, Mart)

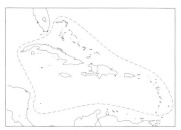

Identification: 14–16.5 cm (5.5–6.5"). Upperparts brownish-olive, *orange crown bordered with blackish stripes, bold white eyering* and white underparts heavily marked with large, dark streaks. *Female*: Slightly duller than the male. *Similar species*: Wood Thrush is larger and lacks the blackish crown stripes.
Status and Range: A fairly common non-breeding resident in the Bahamas and Greater Antilles from August to May, it is uncommon in the Virgin and Cayman Islands and generally rare in the Lesser Antilles south to St Vincent. The species is common on San Andrés and uncommon on Providencia. It is widespread in North America south through Central America.
Comments: Terrestrial. It forages in leaf litter with its tail cocked.
Habitat: Principally woodlands and primary forest floor, often near streams or pools.

NORTHERN WATERTHRUSH *Seiurus noveboracensis*   **Plate 60**
Local Names: Señorita de Manglar (Cuba); Cigüita del Agua (DR); Pizpita de Mangle (PR); Ti Chit Mang, Ti Chit Lanmè, Petite Chitte des Mangliers (Haiti); Paruline des Ruisseaux (Guad, Mart); Noordse Waterlijster (Saba, St M)

Identification: 12.5–15 cm (5–5.75"). Dark olive-brown above and pale buff below with dark brown streaks. Note the *prominent buff eyebrow stripe which narrows behind the eye* and the *fine blackish-brown streaks on throat*. *Habit*: Constantly *bobs and teeters*. *Similar species*: Louisiana Waterthrush is distinguished by its *completely unstreaked throat* and an *eyebrow stripe* which *extends well behind the eye*; this may be buff in front of eye, but widens and is *bright white behind the eye*.
Voice: Call note is a recognizable sharp, emphatic *tchip*.
Status and Range: Generally a fairly common non-breeding resident throughout the West Indies primarily from September to April, but there are records from every month of the year. It is widespread in North America south to northern South America.
Comments: Terrestrial. Fairly tame, it feeds by walking deliberately along the water's edge, bobbing and teetering as it goes, stopping to pick insects or larvae from the mud.
Habitat: Most often the borders of standing water, primarily saline and brackish, in or near mangroves and coastal scrub forests.

LOUISIANA WATERTHRUSH *Seiurus motacilla*   **Plate 60**
Local Names: Señorita de Río (Cuba); Cigüita del Río (DR); Pizpita de Río (PR)

Identification: 14.5–16 cm (5.5–6.25"). Dark gray-brown above and white below with dark brown streaks. Field marks are the *white eyebrow stripe, which broadens behind the eye* and the *absence of streaks on throat*. *Habit*: Constantly *bobs and teeters*. *Similar species*: Northern Waterthrush has fine streaks on the throat and a buffier eyebrow stripe which does not broaden behind the eye.
Voice: Call note a sharp *chink*, similar to that of Northern Waterthrush, but at a slightly higher pitch and with a more ringing quality.
Status and Range: A non-breeding resident in the West Indies from August to March. It is common in the Greater Antilles, uncommon in the Bahamas, rare in the Virgin and Cayman Islands and generally a vagrant in the Lesser Antilles south to St Vincent. Louisiana Waterthrush both departs and returns to the West Indies earlier than the Northern Waterthrush. It is widespread in eastern North America through Central America.
Comments: Terrestrial. It walks and forages in a manner similar to Northern Waterthrush.

Habitat: Edges of flowing fresh water, often at higher elevations. Also sinkhole lakes in karst zones and even standing pools of rain water.

KENTUCKY WARBLER *Oporornis formosus* Plates 62, 66
Local Names: Bijirita de Kentucky (Cuba); Cigüita de Kentuckí (DR); Reinita de Kentucky (PR)

Identification: 12.5–14.5 cm (5–5.75"). *Adult male*: Note the *yellow spectacles, black facial mark and crown* and yellow underparts. *Adult female and immature male*: Similar to adult male, but less black on face and crown. *Immature female*: Black on face absent, replaced by gray on lores.
Status and Range: A rare migrant and very rare non-breeding resident in the Bahamas, Cuba, Jamaica, Hispaniola, Puerto Rico, the Virgin and Cayman Islands and Providencia from late August to April. A vagrant on Antigua and Guadeloupe. Also, it occurs in the eastern United States through southeastern Mexico and Central America south to Panama.
Habitat: Dense undergrowth and thickets in moist forest understory.

CONNECTICUT WARBLER *Oporornis agilis* Plates 62, 66
Local Names: Cigüita de Lentes (DR); Reinita de Connecticut (PR)

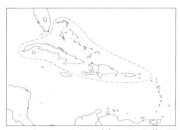

Identification: 13.5–15 cm (5.25–5.75"). A large, terrestrial warbler with a stocky build, *distinctive hood, white eyering* and *dull yellow from belly to undertail-coverts which extend nearly to end of tail*. *Adult male*: Hood bluish-gray. *Adult female and immature*: Similar to the male, but the hood is gray-brown and the throat whitish. *Similar species*: Mourning Warbler sometimes has an eyering, but this is thin and broken in the front. It also has shorter undertail-coverts. For additional guidance on distinguishing Mourning and Connecticut Warblers see: Pyle, P., and P. Henderson. 1990. On Separating Female and Immature *Oporornis* Warblers in Fall. *Birding* 22(5):222–229.
Status and Range: A very rare migrant in the Bahamas, Cuba, Hispaniola, Puerto Rico, the Virgin Islands (St Croix), St Barthélemy and St Martin. Primarily occurs during southbound migration in September and October. There are also records from November through May which suggest that at least some birds irregularly reside as non-breeding residents. Migrates from North America principally to central South America.
Comments: Typically stays on or near the ground. Though there are few records from March and April, the entire world population of Connecticut Warbler is believed to migrate through the West Indies in both directions between North America and South America.
Habitat: Moist woodland understory, usually near water.

MOURNING WARBLER *Oporornis philadelphia* Plates 62, 66

Identification: 13–14.5 cm (5–5.75"). *Adult male*: Identified by its *bluish-gray hood, black breast patch* and lack of an eyering. *Adult female*: Like the male, but *hood is pale gray (sometimes brownish)* and has an incomplete eyering, whitish throat and lacks black on breast. *Immature*: Similar to the female, but throat yellowish. *Similar species*: Connecticut Warbler has a bold white, complete eyering and longer undertail-coverts.
Status and Range: A vagrant as a southbound migrant. Reported from the Bahamas, Cuba, Jamaica, Hispaniola (Dominican Republic), Puerto Rico (including Vieques) and the Virgin Islands primarily in September and October, but also recorded in other months. Occurs in North, Central and northern South America.
Comments: Resides on or near to the ground.
Habitat: Wet thickets, second-growth and swamp edges.

COMMON YELLOWTHROAT *Geothlypis trichas*   Plates 62, 66
Local Names: Caretica (Cuba); Cigüita Enmascarada (DR); Reinita Pica Tierra (PR); Ti Chit Figi Nwa (Haiti)

Identification: 11.5–14 cm (4.5–5.5"). **Adult male**: Note its conspicuous *black facial mask*, edged above by whitish, and its yellow throat and breast. **Adult female**: Similar to the male, but lacks the facial mask. It is also identified by its bright yellow throat and breast contrasting with a whitish belly, the narrow whitish eyering and usually shows a pale, buffy eyebrow stripe. **Immature**: Duller and browner than the adult female. **Similar species**: Bahama Yellowthroat is larger, more lethargic, has a heavier bill and the yellow of the underparts extends to the belly. Crown is gray, rather than tan or olive.

Voice: The distinctive call note sounds like a stone being thrown into a pile of gravel. The clear song *witchity, witchity, witchity, witch* is heard only rarely in May prior to the northward migration.
Status and Range: A common non-breeding resident in the Bahamas, Greater Antilles and Cayman Islands, it is uncommon to rare in the Virgin Islands and a vagrant in the Lesser Antilles where recorded from St Martin, Antigua, Guadeloupe and Dominica. The species is common on San Andrés and rare on Providencia. Occurs primarily from October to early May. It is widespread in North America through Central America.
Comments: Frequents dense vegetation near the ground.
Habitat: Wet grassy and brushy areas usually on the edges of freshwater swamps, ponds or canals.

BAHAMA YELLOWTHROAT *Geothlypis rostrata*   Plates 62, 66, 86
Local Names: Black-eyed Bird, Sage Bird

Identification: 15 cm (5.75"). A relatively large, slow-moving warbler with a relatively heavy bill. **Male**: Field marks are its *black mask, gray cap* and yellow throat, breast and upper belly. The band edging the mask varies in the Bahamas from whitish on Andros and New Providence to primarily yellow on Cat Island and Eleuthera. **Female**: Lacks a mask. Note its yellow throat, breast, and belly; *gray crown* and whitish eyering and eyebrow stripe. **Similar species**: Common Yellowthroat is smaller, more active, has a finer bill, less yellow underparts and has a tan or olive crown, rather than a gray one.

Voice: A loud, rollicking *witchity-whitchity-witchit*, very similar to that of Common Yellowthroat. The call note is a deep, sharp *tchit*, less gravelly than that of Common Yellowthroat. Also a scolding call.
Status and Range: Endemic to the northern Bahamas. It is common on Grand Bahama, Abaco, Eleuthera and Cat Island; uncommon on Andros and rare on New Providence. Possible sight record from Little Inagua.
Comments: Care must be taken in distinguishing Bahama Yellowthroat from Common Yellowthroat which is a common non-breeding resident in the Bahamas from October to early May. Territorial or singing yellowthroats from June through August are likely to be resident Bahama Yellowthroats. Bahama Yellowthroat tends to remain well hidden among dense vegetation and is deliberate in its movements. This species has three distinct races.
Habitat: Scrub, coppice edges and pine woods with an understory of thatch palm.
Nesting: A cup-shaped nest is built near the ground in a dense shrub, vine tangle or tree stump. Eggs (2). Breeds from May to July.

GREEN-TAILED GROUND WARBLER   Plates 64, 82
Microligea palustris
11 Local Names: Cigüita Coliverde, Sigüita (DR); Ti Chit Lasèl (Haiti)

Identification: 12–14 cm (4.75–5.5"). A slender bird with a long tail. **Adult**: Distinguished by its *red iris, incomplete white eyering* and *greenish lower back, rump, wings and tail*. **Immature**: Greener above and tinted olive below; brown iris. **Similar species**: White-winged Warbler has white in its wing, on its tail and in front of the eye; lacks a red iris.

Voice: Rasping notes, similar to typical alarm calls of small song-birds. Song a *sip-sip-sip*.

Status and Range: Endemic to Hispaniola where it is common, but declining in numbers. On Haiti, found at high elevations in the Massif de la Selle where its habitat is dwindling and near sea level in the far northwest. In the Dominican Republic, occurs locally from sea level to high mountains. Also occurs on Beata Island where the local race is considered threatened. The cause of its decline is unknown.

Comments: Secretive; usually feeds alone or in small groups. Rarely found with foraging flocks of migrant warblers. Recent studies suggest closer affinity to tanagers than to wood warblers based on genetic and behavioral data.

Habitat: Dense thickets or disturbed patches of wet broadleaf forests, primarily in mountains. In the Dominican Republic, it is a generalist, occurring in several habitat types, including semi-arid areas. On Haiti, also occasional in transitional scrub between desert thornscrub and more moist woodlands in the northwest, but is found mostly above 1700 m (5525') in wet forests.

Nesting: A cup-shaped nest of plant materials is built in a shrub. Eggs (2) pale greenish, spotted. Breeds in May and June.

YELLOW-HEADED WARBLER *Teretistris fernandinae*   **Plates 63, 80**
Local Names: Chillina, Chillona, Chinchillita

Identification: 13 cm (5"). Gray overall with a *yellowish head and neck*, long and slightly down-curved bill, no wingbars and paler underparts. **Similar species**: Prothonotary Warbler is primarily yellow below, whereas Yellow-headed Warbler has a pale gray belly and abdomen.

Voice: A peculiar, shrill *tsi-tsi-tsi...*, repeated several times and from which several of its local names, such as Chillina (the Shrieker), are derived. Frequently several birds in a flock will call at once. Nearly identical to the call of Oriente Warbler.

Status and Range: This is one of two warbler species endemic to Cuba. It is common in the western and central parts of Cuba, including the Isle of Youth and the Cayo Cantiles in the Archipelago de los Canarreos. Its range extends from Peninsula Guanahacabibes to Itabo (Matanzas Province) in the north to the Zapata Swamp in the south. Oriente Warbler is its counterpart in eastern Cuba.

Comments: Yellow-headed Warbler occurs in pairs only during the breeding season. Typically it forages in noisy flocks of four to fifteen individuals. The flocks are loose, usually attracting migrant warblers and other local species, especially Cuban Vireos and Crescent-eyed Pewees. Yellow-headed Warbler is a generalist feeder that searches for insects, larvae, caterpillars, spiders and small fruits. It seems to occupy the foraging niches of many of the non-breeding warblers and perhaps also the chickadees, a family of birds absent from the West Indies. While foraging, it ranges from the ground to the middle canopy, avoiding only the higher parts of trees. It is an important nuclear species for mixed species flocks.

Habitat: From sea level to mid-elevations. Primarily shrubby areas with plenty of tangled vegetation, bushes and vines. Also open forests. Absent from dense forests, woods and mangroves.

Nesting: The cup-shaped nest of grass, roots and other materials is constructed on a horizontal twig or amid tangled vegetation. Eggs (2–3) white with a light bluish sheen and purplish and brown markings at the broad end. Breeds from April to June.

ORIENTE WARBLER *Teretistris fornsi*   **Plates 62, 80**
Local Names: Pechero, Chinchillita

Identification: 13 cm (5"). *Gray upperparts; yellow underparts.* No wingbars nor white in plumage. Note its *yellow eyering* and long, slightly down-curved bill. **Similar species**: Female Prothonotary Warbler has a less distinctive separation between the yellowish-olive crown and yellow of the face. It also has some white in the tail. Female Bachman's, Nashville, Hooded and Wilson's Warblers have olive-brown back and wings. Female Canada Warbler has a gray rather than yellow cheek and faint black stripes on the breast.

Voice: A shrill *tsi-tsi-tsi...*, repeated several times, practically indistinguishable from call of Yellow-headed Warbler. Differences can be detected only with sonograms.
Status and Range: Endemic to Cuba where it is locally common in the eastern part of the island. It is particularly common in the southern provinces of Granma, Santiago de Cuba and Guantánamo. In the north, it ranges along the coast from western Holguín Province to Camagüey Province, including all of the latter's major cays and westward to Itabo in Matanzas Province. This is also the eastern limit of Yellow-headed Warbler, but the two species do not come into contact, as they are separated by a narrow gap of less than 8 km (5 miles).
Comments: Typically forages in noisy flocks, feeding on a wide array of foods, including small insects, spiders and larvae that it searches for in bark crevices, among vines, on the undersides of leaves and even on the ground. Very similar in behavior to Yellow-headed Warbler.
Habitat: Forests, scrub and borders of swamps from the coast to the highest mountains, including Pico Turquino at 1970 m (6463').
Nesting: A cup-shaped nest of plant materials is constructed on a twig or among dense vegetation. Eggs (2–3) white with a light bluish sheen and markings at the broad end. Breeds in April and May.

SEMPER'S WARBLER *Leucopeza semperi*   Plates 64, 86
Local Name: Pied-blanc

Identification: 14.5 cm (5.75"). Note its long, pale legs and pale feet. *Adult*: *Nearly uniform dark gray upperparts* and whitish underparts. *Immature*: Upperparts including rump gray washed with olive-brown and brownish-buff below.
Voice: A soft *tuck-tick-tick-tuck* scolding call is the only vocalization ever described. Its song is unknown.
Status and Range: Endemic to St Lucia; critically endangered and very possibly extinct. Last certain report was in 1961, though there are reported sightings as recently as 1989 and 1995. Most reports are from the ridge between Piton Flore and Piton Canaries. The cause of its decline is unknown, but the introduced mongoose almost certainly played a role and habitat alteration was probably also a factor.
Comments: Believed to forage on or close to the ground.
Habitat: Primary or secondary moist forests at mid-elevations with thick undergrowth, mountain thickets and dwarf forests.
Nesting: Unknown, but believed to be on the ground.

HOODED WARBLER *Wilsonia citrina*   Plates 62, 66
Local Names: Monjita (Cuba); Cigüita de Gorra Negra (DR); Reinita Encapuchada (PR); Ti Chit Figi Jòn (Haiti); Paruline à Capuchon (Guad, Mart)

Identification: 12.5–14.5 cm (5–5.75"). *Habit*: *Often flicks and fans tail showing white outer tail feathers*. *Male*: Upperparts, wings and tail chiefly olive-green; *forehead and cheeks yellow; black crown, neck and throat form a hood* and breast and belly yellow. *Adult female*: Similar to the male, but variable in the amount of the black hood, ranging from almost complete as in the male to only black markings on the crown. *Immature female*: Lacks black hood. Yellow face sharply demarcated from olive-green crown and hindneck. *Similar species*: Adult female and immature Wilson's Warblers are smaller, have a yellow eyebrow stripe instead of a face patch and lack white in the tail feathers. Oriente Warbler, found only on Cuba, has entirely gray upperparts.
Status and Range: An uncommon to rare non-breeding resident in the Bahamas and Cuba from September to April. It is uncommon only as a migrant on Jamaica. A rare non-breeding resident on Hispaniola, Puerto Rico and the Virgin and Cayman Islands from October to March. A vagrant in the Lesser Antilles south to St Vincent. The species is a common migrant on San Andrés. It is widespread in eastern North America through Central America to Panama.
Habitat: Moist forest undergrowth and mangrove swamps.

WILSON'S WARBLER *Wilsonia pusilla*   **Plates 62, 66**
Local Name: Bijirita de Wilson (Cuba)

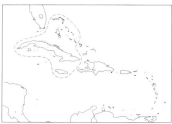

Identification: 11–12.5 cm (4.25–5"). **Adult male**: Upperparts olive-green, underparts yellow, *black cap* and *bright yellow forehead and eyebrow stripe*. **Adult female and immature male**: Similar to adult male, though duller with a hint of the distinctive black cap. **Immature female**: Lacks black on cap. Note the yellow forehead, eyebrow stripe, lores and underparts. **Similar species**: Female and immature Wilson's Warblers have a prominent eyebrow stripe, rather than an eyering, a more greenish cast to the upperparts and lack tail spots of adult female and immature Yellow Warblers. Oriente Warbler, found only on Cuba, has entirely gray upperparts. Adult female and immature Hooded Warblers are larger, have white tail patches and a yellow face patch, rather than an eyebrow stripe.

Status and Range: A very rare migrant and even less frequent as a non-breeding resident in the northern Bahamas, western and central Cuba and Jamaica from September to April. A vagrant on Hispaniola and Puerto Rico (Mona Island). It is widespread in North and Central America.

Habitat: Dense vegetation at all altitudes, but primarily the lowlands.

CANADA WARBLER *Wilsonia canadensis*   **Plates 61, 65**
Local Name: Bijirita del Canada (Cuba)

Identification: 12.5–15.5 cm (5–5.75"). **Adult male**: Note its bluish-gray upperparts, *bold yellow spectacles* and yellow underparts with *black breast stripes forming a necklace*. **Adult female**: Similar to the male, but duller. Necklace fades to gray streaks. **Immature**: Like the adult female, but with an olive-brown wash on the upperparts and virtually no necklace. **Similar species**: Oriente Warbler, found only on Cuba, has yellow cheeks and lacks stripes on the breast.

Status and Range: A very rare migrant and even less frequent as a non-breeding resident in the northern Bahamas and Cuba. It is a vagrant during any season on Jamaica, Hispaniola, Puerto Rico, the Virgin and Cayman Islands, Guadeloupe and St Lucia. Primarily occurs in September and October, but recorded from September to April. It is widespread in eastern North America south to northern South America.

Habitat: Primarily lowlands in moderately open vegetation among scattered trees, usually near swamps or other standing water.

YELLOW-BREASTED CHAT *Icteria virens*   **Plate 63**
Local Name: Bijirita Grande (Cuba)

Identification: 19 cm (7.5"). Upperparts, wings and long tail are olive-green. Note its *black, thick bill* and *white lores and eyering*. The throat, breast and upper belly are yellow; lower belly and undertail-coverts are white.

Status and Range: A very rare migrant and even less frequent as a non-breeding resident in the northern Bahamas, Cuba and the Cayman Islands (Grand Cayman) from late August to early May. It is widespread in southern North America south through Central America.

Comments: Difficult to locate because of its habit of frequenting low, dense vegetation.

WHITE-WINGED WARBLER *Xenoligea montana*   Plates 64, 82
Local Names: Cigüita Aliblanca, Cigüita Cubera (DR); Petit Chitte, Petit Quatre- yeux, Ti Chit Kat Je, Ti Chit Lasèl (Haiti)

Identification: 13.5–14 cm (5.25–5.5"). Distinguished by the *bold white wing patch, white outer tail feathers* and *white line above eye to forehead*. Possesses a heavy bill for a warbler. **Similar species**: Green-tailed Ground Warbler has a red iris and lacks white in wing, tail and in front of eye.
Voice: A low chattering *suit..suit..suit...chir..suit..suit..suit..suit.. chir..chi...* Also a thin *tseep*.
Status and Range: Endemic to Hispaniola. Common very locally only in the Dominican Republic where best found in the Cordillera Central and Sierra de Baoruco. It is very local in the Sierra de Neiba. On Haiti, it is very rare where it occurs in the Massif de la Hotte and Massif de la Selle, though possibly extirpated from the latter. An endangered species throughout its range, it is considered the most endangered bird of Haiti. Its decline appears primarily due to habitat destruction.
Comments: Usually seen in pairs, foraging low to the ground in brush, where it feeds on insects and seeds. It also joins mixed feeding flocks. White-winged Warbler is the only member of its genus.
Habitat: Primarily mature broadleaf forest undergrowth, low trees and thickets and wet shrubs in higher mountains between 1300 and 1800 m (4250 to 6000').
Nesting: Nest and egg unknown. Believed to breed in April and May.

BANANAQUIT *Coereba flaveola*   Plate 67
Local Names: Teasy, Sugar Bird, Beeny Bird (Jamaica); Yellowbreast (LA); Banana Bird (Bahamas, CI, Nevis); See See Bird, Black See-see (Grenada, St V); Cigüita (DR); Reinita (PR); Sucrier (Haiti); Falle Jaune, Sicrié Cage (Guad); Sucrier à Poitrine Jaune, Sucrier à Ventre Jaune (Guad, Mart); Suikerdiefje (Saba, St E, St M)

Identification: 10–12.5 cm (4–5"). Highly variable among islands. **Adult**: In most forms, the *curved bill, white eyebrow stripe and wing spot* and the *yellow breast, belly and rump* identify it. The throat varies from white to black. A black color phase predominates on Grenada and St Vincent. This form has a slight greenish-yellow wash on the breast and uppertail-coverts, black upperparts and lacks the white eyebrow stripe and wing spot. Yellow-breasted phase birds are present in dry areas of the two islands. **Immature**: A pale, washed-out version of the adult. Eyebrow stripe yellowish.
Voice: Variable among islands. In the Bahamas, the song is several ticks followed by a rapid clicking. Jamaican and Hispaniolan birds give a thin, high-pitched *tzi-tzi-tzi-tzi-tziit-tzi* on a single pitch. Birds on Puerto Rico and the Virgin Islands issue a thin, ascending insect-like buzz that tumbles into a short trill. The call note is an unmusical *tsip*.
Status and Range: A very common resident throughout the West Indies with the exception of Cuba where it is a vagrant on a few cays and very locally on the north coast. It also occurs in Central and South America.
Comments: Many nests are built to serve only as sleeping quarters, which are sometimes shared by several birds. Bananaquits alternate between nests on a nightly basis for roosting. The Bananaquit commonly pierces the base of flowers to steal nectar, its primary food. The absence of this generally ubiquitous species from Cuba is an ecological curiosity which remains to be explained.
Habitat: Virtually all habitats, except the highest mountain tops and dryest lowlands. Particularly occurs around flowering plants.
Nesting: A globular nest of grass and fine plant fibers is constructed. Eggs (2–4) whitish with a reddish tint and brown flecks. Breeding peaks from March to June, but occurs in other months. It is directly related to the seasonality of rainfall. Where rainfall is seasonal, the Bananaquit's nesting season is also seasonal.

LESSER ANTILLEAN TANAGER *Tangara cucullata*   **Plate 68**
Local Names: Ci-ci Corossol, Dos-bleu (Grenada); Prince Bird, Golden Tanager, Pawpaw Bird (St V); Soursop Bird (Grenada, St V)

Identification: 15 cm (5.75"). *Male*: *Iridescent orangish-yellow above*, sometimes with a greenish cast. Also identified by its *dark reddish-brown cap* and bluish-green wings and tail. *Female*: Duller than the male, but with greenish upperparts.
Voice: A weak, high-pitched series of single notes followed by a pleasant twitter, *weet-weet-weet-witwitwitwit*.
Status and Range: An uncommon resident known only from St Vincent and Grenada.
Comments: Generally in pairs or small flocks. Congregates at trees in fruit. Formerly referred to as Hooded Tanager.
Habitat: Both moist and dry forests, gardens and second-growth at all elevations.
Nesting: A cup-shaped nest is built in a bush or low tree. Eggs (2) white or bluish, marked with brown and gray. Breeds from April to July.

RED-LEGGED HONEYCREEPER *Cyanerpes cyaneus*   **Plate 67**
Local Names: Aparecido de San Diego, Azulito (Cuba)

Identification: 13 cm (5"). Small in size with a relatively long, slender, down-curved bill. *Breeding male*: Primarily a striking *purplish-blue* with a *light blue crown*; black upper back, wings and tail and *red legs*. Underwing mostly yellow. *Adult female*: Dull olive-green, paler below with faint whitish streaks. Legs and feet dull purple. *Non-breeding adult male*: Similar to the adult female, but wings and tail black. *Immature*: Similar to the adult female, but more lightly streaked.
Voice: The characteristic call is a short, harsh *chrik-chrik*. Other calls are longer and more melodious.
Status and Range: A rather rare and local year-round resident on Cuba, mainly found in the Sierra del Rosario, Sierra de la Güira, Pinar del Río and Sierra Maestra, but also occurs as scattered populations in Zapata Swamp and Havana. Formerly more widespread. May have been introduced to Cuba. There are a few records from Jamaica, probably of escaped cage birds. It also occurs from Mexico through South America.
Comments: Frequents flowering trees or shrubs.
Habitat: Strictly forests and forest edges.
Nesting: The nest is a fine cup of grass and rootlets built in a tree or bush. Eggs (2) white with greenish-blue wash, spotted and blotched with bluish-purple and reddish-brown at the broad end. Breeds in May and June.

JAMAICAN EUPHONIA *Euphonia jamaica*   **Plates 67, 84**
Local Names: Blue Quit, Chocho Quit, Short-mouthed Quit, Cho-cho Quit, Short- mouth Bluequit

Identification: 11.5 cm (4.5"). A *small, drab, compact* bird with a *stubby, dark bill*. *Adult male*: Grayish-blue overall, appearing bright blue in good light, with a yellow belly. *Female and immature*: Two-toned: head and underparts bluish-gray; back, wings and flanks olive-green. *Similar species*: Orangequit is darker below and has a longer, finer bill. Female and immature Orangequits lack bluish on the head.
Voice: A staccato *chur-chur-chur-chur-chur* like a motor being started, sometimes ending in a rising *chip* (Downer and Sutton). Song a pleasant, squeaky whistle.
Status and Range: Endemic to Jamaica where common and widespread.
Comments: Arboreal, feeding primarily on fruits, but also on young shoots, buds and flowers. Mistletoe berries form a major part of its diet, a fruit eaten by few other birds. Consequently, this plant depends heavily on the euphonia for its seed dispersal. Sometimes forages and roosts in flocks.

Habitat: All elevations in open areas with trees, including woodlands, forest edges, shrubbery and gardens. Most common in open secondary forests of the lowland hills.
Nesting: A spherical nest of Spanish moss, with an entrance on the side, is hidden among moss or bromeliads in a tree. Eggs (3–4) white with purplish or lavender-gray speckles sometimes concentrated at the broad end. Breeds from March to May.

ANTILLEAN EUPHONIA *Euphonia musica* Plate 67
Local Names: Christmas Bird (Dominica); Mistletoe Bird, Jilguerillo, Onza de Oro (DR); Canario del País, Jilguero (PR); Louidò, Louis d'or, Oi Seau Grand Père (Haiti); Louis d'Or (Grenada); Avant-Noël, Organiste Louis-d'or, Roi Bois, Carouge (Guad, Mart); Perruche (Guad, Mart, St L)

Identification: 12 cm (4.75"). A small, compact bird with a distinctive *sky-blue crown and hindneck*. **Male**: Variable, from prominently greenish like the female (Lesser Antilles) to primarily dark above and rich yellow below and on the rump and forehead (Puerto Rico), or primarily dark above and orangish-yellow below and on the rump and forehead (Hispaniola). Hispaniolan males have a dark violet chin and throat. **Female**: Duller overall. Greenish above and yellowish-green below. The rump and forehead are yellowish.
Voice: A variety of distinctive call notes, including a rapid, subdued, almost tinkling *ti-tit* (sometimes one or three syllables) and a hard, metallic *chi-chink*. Also a plaintive *whee*, like some *Myiarchus* flycatchers, but more melodious. It also has a jumbled, tinkling song mixed with explosive notes.
Status and Range: A locally common year-round resident on Hispaniola, including Gonâve Island and Puerto Rico. However, the species is now threatened on Haiti due to extensive habitat loss. It is uncommon in the Lesser Antilles, including Barbuda, Antigua, Guadeloupe, La Désirade, Dominica, Martinique, St Lucia, St Vincent and Grenada. A vagrant elsewhere in the Lesser Antilles where known from St Barthélemy, St Christopher, Montserrat and the Grenadines. Believed extirpated from Saba.
Comments: Flits about in the dense vegetation of the canopy where it feeds mainly on mistletoe berries. Sometimes joins in mixed flocks of warblers and tanagers. Roosts in flocks of dozens of individuals during the non-breeding season. This euphonia is easily overlooked despite its colorful appearance. It is most readily located by its call.
Habitat: Dense forests from dry lowlands to wet mountain tops, particularly those with mistletoe.
Nesting: A domed nest with a side entrance, usually well concealed, is built among tree epiphytes. Eggs (4) white, spotted with mauve. Breeds from January to July.

WESTERN STRIPE-HEADED TANAGER *Spindalis zena* Plate 68
Local Names: Stripe-head Tanager (Bahamas); Bastard Cock (CI); Cabrero (Cuba)

Identification: 15 cm (5.75"). The sexes differ dramatically. **Male**: Note the conspicuous *black head striped with white*. Considerable white on the wings and reddish-brown patches on the rump, hindneck and breast. **Female**: Grayish-olive above and whitish below, it has *two whitish facial stripes*.
Voice: The song is variable, but is generally a very high-pitched, thin whistle with some ventriloquial qualities making the bird somewhat difficult to locate by its call.
Status and Range: A common year-round resident throughout most of its range on Cuba and the Bahamas. A fairly common year-round resident on Grand Cayman in the Cayman Islands. It also occurs on the island of Cozumel off Mexico.
Comments: Arboreal. Feeds mainly on berries, but also takes other plant parts. Until recently Western Stripe-headed Tanager was united as a single species with the three other stripe-headed tanagers. They were split into four species based on differences in vocal behavior, coloration, nesting and size. Western Stripe-headed Tanager still contains five subspecies.
Habitat: In the Bahamas, this tanager is found among native and Australian pines during the breeding

season, but at other times it occurs in other habitats, especially coppice. In the Cayman Islands, it breeds in brushlands and woodlands, but forages in all habitats. On Cuba and the Isle of Youth, it occurs from the coast to the mountains in open woods, brushy habitats and mangrove forests. It does not frequent dense forests and is most abundant at middle and high elevations.

Nesting: The nest, constructed of soft materials, can vary in location from quite high in the outer canopy to low in a bush. Eggs (2–3) white covered with brownish dots. Breeds from April to August.

JAMAICAN STRIPE-HEADED TANAGER   Plates 68, 84
Spindalis nigricephalus

Local Names: Mark Head, Goldfinch, Cashew Bird, Champa Beeza, Orange Bird, Silver Head, Spanish Quail, Yam-cutter

Identification: 18 cm (7"). Both sexes display *primarily orangish-yellow underparts*. *Male*: Note the *black head with two bold white facial stripes* and the considerable white on the wings. *Female*: Olive upperparts, with a gray throat and upper breast.

Voice: A soft *seep* often given in flight and other high, fast *chi-chi-chi-chi-chi* notes (Downer and Sutton).

Status and Range: Endemic to Jamaica where it is common and widespread, particularly in the hills and mountains. Occurs locally on the northern and southwestern coasts.

Comments: Arboreal. Feeds on berries, seeds, flowers and leaves. Originally, three species of *Spindalis* were described from the West Indies, but these species were later relegated to subspecific rank with Western Stripe-headed Tanager. Recent studies support a return to multiple species, based on the striking differences in nesting behavior, vocalizations, sizes, plumage patterns and colors.

Habitat: Forests, woodlands and brushy areas.

Nesting: The nest is a loose cup of vegetation, often with fibers of palms and tree ferns, constructed low in a bush or tree. Eggs (3) white with gray and brownish markings concentrated at the broad end. Breeds from April to July.

HISPANIOLAN STRIPE-HEADED TANAGER   Plates 68, 81
Spindalis dominicensis

Local Names: Cigua Amarilla (DR); Moundélé, Bannann Mi Mòn (Haiti)

Identification: 16.5 cm (6.5"). There is a striking difference between the sexes. *Male*: Distinguished by its *black head boldly striped with white*. Underparts are yellow with a reddish-brown wash on the breast. *Female*: Upperparts olive-brown and underparts whitish with fine stripes, it also has a *whitish mustache stripe*.

Voice: A weak, high-pitched *thseep*. The dawn song is a thin, high-pitched whistle.

Status and Range: Endemic to Hispaniola where it is common in mountains and less so on the coast. It also occurs on Gonâve Island.

Comments: Arboreal. Feeds primarily on fruits and flower buds. Until recently it was combined with Western Stripe-headed Tanager as a single species.

Habitat: Pine, hardwood and mixed forests as well as mangroves.

Nesting: A small, cup-shaped nest, poorly made of grass, is constructed at a moderate height in a tree or bush. Eggs (2–3) cream-colored to pale bluish-green, marked with dark brown scrawls and blotches, particularly at the broad end. Individuals breed more than once per year. Breeds primarily from April through June.

PUERTO RICAN STRIPE-HEADED TANAGER
Plates 68, 85
Spindalis portoricensis
Local Name: Reina Mora

Identification: 16.5 cm (6.5"). The male and female differ greatly. *Male*: The distinctive *black head is striped with white*. Underparts are primarily yellow, with a reddish-orange wash on the breast and hindneck. *Female*: Upperparts olive-brown and underparts dull whitish with *gray streaks on the sides and flanks*, it has an inconspicuous white eyebrow stripe and more evident *whitish mustache stripe*.
Voice: A thin, high-pitched whistling song is commonly heard during the breeding season: *zeé-tit-zeé-tittit-zeé*. The *zeé* syllable often seems like an inhaling sound. This basic call has many variations. Two calls heard infrequently are a thin trill like the beating of a tiny hammer and a short, twittering call. The call note is a soft *teweep* with some ventriloquial tendency, so sometimes birds are difficult to spot when singing from high perches.
Status and Range: A common and widespread endemic species to Puerto Rico. It occurs at all elevations.
Comments: Arboreal. Feeds mainly on small fruits and flower buds. Sometimes gathers in flocks where ripe fruit is abundant. Formerly combined with *Spindalis zena* as a single species.
Habitat: Woodlands and forests.
Nesting: The nest is a loose cup of vegetation, including Spanish moss, built low in a bush, tree or palm. Eggs (2–4) pale blue, blotched and scrawled with blackish or dark blue. Breeds primarily from March to June, but sometimes begins as early as December.

SUMMER TANAGER *Piranga rubra*
Plate 67
Local Name: Cardenal (Cuba)

Identification: 18–19.5 cm (7–7.5"). A *large-billed* tanager. *Adult male*: *Entirely red*, brighter below and wings slightly darker. *Female*: Yellowish olive-green above; yellowish-orange below. *Immature male*: Similar to female, but with a reddish tinge. *Similar species*: Male Scarlet Tanager has *black wings;* the female is yellow-green below and lacks an orange tinge. It also has whitish rather than yellow wing linings. Scarlet Tanager also has a smaller bill. For additional information, see citation under Scarlet Tanager.
Status and Range: An uncommon migrant and rare non-breeding resident in the Bahamas, Cuba, Jamaica and the Cayman Islands from September to May. A vagrant on Hispaniola and the Lesser Antilles where recorded from Saba, Guadeloupe, Barbados, the Grenadines (Mustique) and Grenada. It is widespread in southern United States and northern Mexico through Central America to northern South America.
Comments: Singly or in pairs, frequently migrating in the company of thrushes, warblers and vireos.
Habitat: Woodlands, forest edges and gardens primarily at mid-elevations.

SCARLET TANAGER *Piranga olivacea*
Plate 67
Local Names: Cardenal Alinegro (Cuba); Scharlakenrode Tanagra (Saba, St E, St M)

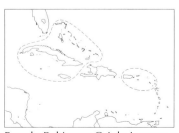

Identification: 18 cm (7"). *Female*: Identified by its overall yellowish-green plumage, distinctive bill shape and white wing linings in flight. *Non-breeding male*: Similar, but with *black wings*. *Breeding male*: Overall *red plumage* and *black wings*. *Similar species*: Non-breeding Scarlet Tanager differs from female Summer Tanager by being greener overall without an orange tint to its plumage, having darker wings, a smaller bill and whitish rather than yellow wing linings. For additional information on distinguishing these species refer to: Kaufman, K. 1988. Notes on Female Tanagers. *American Birds* 42(1): 3–5. Female Baltimore Oriole is more yellowish overall, has a more pointed bill and whitish wingbars.

Status and Range: Much of the West Indies. A rare migrant primarily in September and October and even less frequent from March to May in the Bahamas, Cuba, Jamaica and the Cayman Islands. It is very rare on Puerto Rico, the Virgin Islands and northern Lesser Antilles south to Antigua. Generally a vagrant in the southern Lesser Antilles where it occurs primarily from March to May. It occurs through eastern and central North America south to northwestern South America.

Comments: Often migrates in the company of warblers, vireos and thrushes.

Habitat: Open woods, forest edges and gardens with trees.

BLACK-CROWNED PALM-TANAGER   Plates 68, 82
Phaenicophilus palmarum
Local Names: Cuatro Ojos, Sigua de Cabeza Prieta (DR); Quatre-yeux (pronounced *ka-je*), Ket Je Nò (Haiti)

Identification: 18 cm (7"). ***Adult***: Note its *black crown* and *white throat blending into the gray of the breast* and abdomen. ***Immature***: Duller than the adult. **Similar species**: Gray-crowned Palm-Tanager has a gray crown and sharp contrast between the white throat and gray breast.

Voice: A nasal *pi-au* and a pleasant dawn song (Dod). Call a low *chep*.

Status and Range: Endemic to Hispaniola, including Saona Island, where common in the lowlands, but occurs less frequently to 1800 m (6000'). On Haiti, generally common, but rarely occurs west of Port-au-Prince.

Comments: Feeds on seeds, fruits and insects. Usually found in heavy cover, where it moves about in a slow and deliberate fashion, occasionally twitching its tail. It hops among branches and over huge limbs and hangs on to the bark of large tree trunks. Often serves as the central or 'nuclear' species for mixed species flocks.

Habitat: Most numerous in semi-arid and humid thickets, but occurs wherever there are trees, from towns to dense forests.

Nesting: A deep and frail cup-shaped nest is built in a bush or small tree. Eggs (2–3) whitish to pale greenish, spotted. Breeds from April to June.

GRAY-CROWNED PALM-TANAGER   Plates 68, 82
Phaenicophilus poliocephalus
Local Names: Cuatro Ojos (DR); Quatre-yeux, Kat Je Sid, Oiseau Quatre Yeux de Sud, Kat Je Tèt Gri (Haiti)

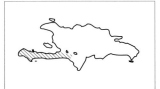

Identification: 18 cm (7"). ***Adult***: Its black mask, *gray crown* and *sharp contrast between the white throat and gray breast* are distinctive. ***Immature***: Duller than the adult. **Similar species**: Black-crowned Palm-Tanager has a black crown and white of throat blends into gray of breast.

Voice: Call a *peee-u*, shorter than the similar note of Black-crowned Palm-Tanager. During courtship, a lovely song and, less often, a canary-like 'whisper song.'

Status and Range: Endemic to Hispaniola. It is common, but local on the southern peninsula of Haiti where it is considered endangered because of habitat destruction. Also common on the satellite islands of Île-à-Vache, Grande Cayemite and Gonâve. In the Dominican Republic, it is rare on the northern and southern slopes of the Sierra de Baoruco down to 1100 m (3500') and on the southern part of Loma de Toro and Hoyo de Pelempito.

Comments: Diet includes seeds, fruits and insects.

Habitat: Forested areas, from sea level to highest mountains, including pine and broadleaf forests. Also open areas and gardens.

Nesting: A frail, deep-cupped nest is built in a dense bush near the ground. Eggs (2–4) pale green to bluish-white, marked with cinnamon and blackish-brown spots and scrawling lines. Breeds in May and June.

CHAT TANAGER *Calyptophilus frugivorus* Plates 68, 82

Local Names: Chirrí, Chirrí de los Baorucos, Patico, Patico Chirrí (DR); Cornichon, Kònichon (Haiti)

Identification: 17–20 cm (6.75–8"). Mockingbird-shaped, with a long, rounded tail. Dark brown above, mostly white below with a *bright yellow spot in front of the eye* and a *yellow fringe on bend of wing*. **Similar species**: The larger La Selle Thrush is also ground-dwelling, but has a red breast and sides. Red-legged Thrush has a red bill and legs.

Voice: One of the finest songsters on Hispaniola. Song an emphatic, clear whistling *chip-chip-swerp-swerp-swerp*, a buzzy *wee-chee-chee-chee-chee* or *chirri-chirri-chirri-chip-chip-chip*, repeated many times. Call note a sharp *chick*.

Status and Range: Endemic to Hispaniola where generally uncommon and local. Found to be locally common on southern Haiti in the higher mountains of Massif de la Selle and Massif de la Hotte, including Pic Macaya and Morne la Viste. The race from Gonâve Island, formerly fairly common, has not been reported in recent years. In the Dominican Republic, the species occurs as disjunct populations in the west, center and spottily in the east on the Samaná Peninsula. The western birds in the Sierra de Baoruco may still be fairly common, though local. The species has undergone a dramatic decline in the Cordillera Central and the race from the Samaná Peninsula has been unrecorded for decades. The Haitian race of the Chat Tanager (*C. f. tertius*) is considered endangered because of extensive destruction of its habitat in the past and continuing threats at present. The species as a whole is also considered threatened due to habitat loss.

Comments: Mainly ground-dwelling, its large, strong feet are adapted for its terrestrial lifestyle and for searching leaf litter for food. Feeds primarily on invertebrates, including centipedes and hairy spiders; also feeds on seeds. Very secretive. Four races are known, each differing in coloration and vocalizations. Chat Tanager is the only member of its genus.

Habitat: Primarily dense undergrowth along streams; in mature, wet broadleaf forests and among overgrown ravines in remote mountains, away from human activity. Infrequently at mid-elevations in eastern portion of range. Also semi-arid scrub on Gonâve Island.

Nesting: A nest believed to be that of Chat Tanager was located in a fern 0.6 m (2') above the ground. Breeding appears to occur from May to July.

PUERTO RICAN TANAGER *Nesospingus speculiferus* Plates 68, 85

Local Name: Llorosa

Identification: 18–20 cm (7–8"). **Adult**: Primarily olive-brown above and white below with pale brownish stripes on the breast and a conspicuous *white wing spot*. **Immature**: Lacks the wing spot and has brownish underparts.

Voice: This noisy bird has a harsh call note *chuck* or *chewp* which is frequently run into a chatter of varying length *chi-chi-chit*. It uncommonly sings a sweet, warbling courtship song with the quality of a hummingbird call. Also a soft, short twitter and a thin sigh like a heavy exhale.

Status and Range: Endemic to Puerto Rico where it is common in higher mountains, but regularly occurs locally at moderate altitudes to slightly below 300 m (1000').

Comments: This tanager typically forms noisy flocks which forage in the dense forest canopy where the bird's feeding methods and general behavior are variable. It appears to be the central bird of mixed species flocks which sometimes contain as many as 12 species. Migrant warblers, particularly Black-throated Blue and Black-and-white Warblers, are regular flock members. At night tanagers retreat to communal roosts in palms or bamboo clumps. Puerto Rican Tanager is the only member of its genus.

Habitat: Primarily undisturbed mountain forests, but also disturbed second growth.

Nesting: The nest is cup-shaped and built from 2 to 10 m (7–33') above the ground. Eggs (2–3) cream-colored and heavily speckled with dark brown. Breeds from January to August.

LESSER ANTILLEAN SALTATOR   *Saltator albicollis*   **Plate 74**
Local Names: Grive Gros-bec (Guad); Gros-bec (Mart, St L)

Identification: 22 cm (8.5"). Upperparts dull green. *Adult*: Note its *whitish eyebrow stripe*, black bill with an orange-white tip, underparts streaked with olive-green and black mustache stripe. *Immature*: Duller facial markings and breast streaks.
Voice: A series of harsh, loud notes that rise and fall.
Status and Range: A common year-round resident on Guadeloupe, Dominica, Martinique and St Lucia. A vagrant on Nevis. These islands comprise the entire range of the species.
Comments: Formerly considered to be of the same species as Streaked Saltator.
Habitat: Thickets, second growth, dry scrub and forest edge undergrowth.
Nesting: A deep cup of twigs and leaves is built in a bush or low tree. Eggs (2–3) light greenish-blue marked with black scrawls and blotches at either end. Breeds from April to July.

ROSE-BREASTED GROSBEAK   *Pheucticus ludovicianus*   **Plate 74**
Local Names: Degollado (Cuba, DR); Piquigrueso Rosado (PR)

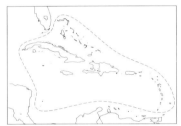

Identification: 19–20 cm (7.5–8"). *Male*: Easily distinguished by its *pinkish-red breast,* black head and back and primarily white belly, rump and wingbars. *Female*: Note its large size, heavy bill, white crown stripes, white wingbars and streaked underparts. *Flight*: The male displays rosy underwing-coverts; the female yellow. The male also shows large white wing and rump patches.
Status and Range: A non-breeding resident in the West Indies from October to April, but most frequent during migration. It is generally uncommon in the Bahamas, Cuba and the Cayman Islands; rare on Jamaica, Hispaniola, Puerto Rico and the Virgin Islands and a vagrant among the larger Lesser Antilles. The species is a common migrant on Providencia and San Andrés. It ranges from sea level to about 600 m (2000'). It occurs through much of North America to northern South America.
Comments: Often migrates in small groups and in association with tanagers, orioles and thrushes.
Habitat: Scrub, woodlands, shade coffee planatations and forest edges. Infrequently gardens.

BLUE GROSBEAK   *Guiraca caerulea*   **Plate 75**
Local Names: Azulejo Real (DR); Azulejo (PR); Azulejón (Cuba, DR)

Identification: 16.5–19 cm (6.5–7.5"). *Male*: *Entirely blue* with *reddish-brown wingbars. Female*: Brown overall distinguished by its *large size, heavy bill* and reddish-brown wingbars. Hints of blue are sometimes present on the wings and rump. *Habit*: Often flicks its tail.
Status and Range: A non-breeding resident from September to April, it is uncommon in the Bahamas and decidedly so in the Cayman Islands; rare on Cuba, Hispaniola and Puerto Rico and very rare on Jamaica and the Virgin Islands. Occurs more frequently during its southbound migration in September and October and its northbound migration in March and April than during the intervening months. It also occurs through the southern United States into Central America.
Habitat: Forest edges, Australian pine (*Casuarina*) groves, rice fields and areas of seeding grass near thickets or woodlands. Also gardens with trees.

INDIGO BUNTING *Passerina cyanea*   **Plate 75**
Local Name: Azulejo (Cuba, DR)

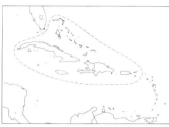

Identification: 14 cm (5.5"). ***Non-breeding male***: Brown overall, but with *traces of blue in the wings and tail*. ***Female***: Entirely dull brown with *very pale breast stripes and wingbars* and no conspicuous markings. ***Breeding male***: Entirely blue, but observed in this plumage only briefly before its northward migration. ***Similar species***: The female's faint breast stripes and wingbars distinguish it from immature mannikins.
Voice: The call note is an emphatic *twit*. Sometimes gives its thin song, usually of paired phrases.
Status and Range: A non-breeding resident in the West Indies from October to early May, Indigo Bunting is common in the Bahamas, Cuba, some of the larger Virgin Islands and on San Andrés; uncommon on Jamaica, Hispaniola and the Cayman Islands and rare on Puerto Rico and Providencia. A vagrant on Saba and Antigua. The species is common on San Andrés and rare on Providencia. It is primarily observed during migration. It also occurs through the eastern United States to Central America.
Comments: Typically flocks.
Habitat: Rice fields, grassy areas bounded by heavy thickets, rows of trees or woodlands, pasture edges and fairly dry scrub.

PAINTED BUNTING *Passerina ciris*   **Plate 75**
Local Names: Mariposa, Verdón, Arco Iris (Cuba)

Identification: 13 cm (5"). ***Male***: Unmistakable with its combination of blue head, red underparts and green back. ***Female and young male***: Green above and yellowish-green below. ***Immature***: Much duller than the female, but with hints of green. ***Similar species***: The female and young male may be confused with vireos, but the bunting's coloration is a brighter green and its bill is much heavier.
Voice: Most frequent call is a loud *chip*. Also a rarely heard thin, sweet song with varied phrases.
Status and Range: A migrant and non-breeding resident in the Bahamas and Cuba primarily from mid-October to the end of April. In the Bahamas, the species is fairly common in November and March as a migrant and uncommon during the months it is a resident. On Cuba, this bunting is uncommon during migration and rare the remaining months. It is a vagrant on Jamaica and the Cayman Islands. It also occurs through the southeastern United States to Central America.
Comments: Typically hidden among dense vegetation close to the ground.
Habitat: Thickets, brush and grassy areas, particularly in semi-arid areas, but often not far from water.

DICKCISSEL *Spiza americana*   **Plate 74**
Local Name: Gorrión de Pecho Amarillo (Cuba)

Identification: 15–18 cm (5.75–7"). Note the *yellowish wash on the breast, dull yellow eyebrow stripe*, thick bill and *reddish-brown bend of wing*. ***Non-breeding male***: A pale, but noticeable *black throat patch*. ***Female***: Black on throat confined to a few streaks. ***Breeding male***: Dark black throat patch. The yellow below is more extensive.
Status and Range: A rare migrant from September to November and again in March and April in the Bahamas, it is very rare on Cuba and Jamaica and a vagrant on Puerto Rico, the Cayman Islands and Barbados. The species is rare on Providencia and San Andrés. It also occurs through the central and eastern United States to northern South America.

Comments: Look for it among flocks of other seed eaters.
Habitat: Open grasslands with scattered trees.

BLUE-BLACK GRASSQUIT *Volatinia jacarina*   **Plate 75**
Local Names: Blue-black See-see; Johnny-jump-up; Prézite; Ci-ci des Herbes Nior

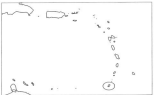

Identification: 11 cm (4.25"). *Adult male*: Entirely glossy blue-black; wingpits sometimes white. **Habit**: The male frequently hops off his perch into the air, typically while singing. *Adult female*: Olive-brown above and yellowish-buff below, heavily streaked with gray on the breast and sides. *Immature*: Similar to the female, but grayer above and more darkly streaked below.
Voice: An emphatic *eee-slick*.
Status and Range: A common breeding resident on Grenada from June to September. Most abundant in the dry southwest. Apparently migrates to South America outside the breeding season. It is widespread both in South and Central America.
Habitat: Shrubby fields, roadsides, low scrubby second growth and farming areas, primarily at low elevations.
Nesting: A cup nest of grass is built on the ground or in a low bush. Eggs (1–3) pale green marked with reddish-brown. Breeds in July and August.

YELLOW-BELLIED SEEDEATER *Sporophila nigricollis*   **Plate 73**
Local Name: White-beak See-see (Grenada, Grenadines)

Identification: 10.5 cm (4.5"). *Adult male*: Note its *black hood, pale blue-gray bill* and yellowish-white underparts. *Female and immature*: Olive-brown above and yellowish-buff below with a dark bill.
Voice: A brief melodious warbling song frequently followed by buzzy notes.
Status and Range: An uncommon and local breeding resident on Grenada and Carriaçou in the Grenadines seasonally from March to November. A vagrant on St Vincent. Outside the breeding season, it likely migrates to South America. The species occurs through South America north to Costa Rica.
Habitat: Shrubby fields and thickets, field edges and roadsides.
Nesting: A deep cup of grass is built in a low shrub or small tree. Eggs (2–3) blue-green or buff marked with dark brown or black. Breeds from March to August.

CUBAN BULLFINCH *Melopyrrha nigra*   **Plate 75**
Local Names: Black Sparrow (CI); Negrito (Cuba)

Identification: 14–15 cm (5.5–5.75"). A small, dark bird with a thick, curved bill and a conspicuous *white band on the edge of the wing*. **Male**: Primarily black. **Female**: Variable. On Cuba, grayish black and lacks glossy sheen of the male. On Grand Cayman, a paler olive-gray. *Immature*: White absent from wing. Bill pale instead of black.
Voice: Most characteristic call is a kind of buzzing *chip*, with some ventriloquial quality. Song is a thin, long, melodious trill that descends and then ascends in pitch, *ti,ti,ti,ti-si-sssiiittt-sssiii*, reminiscent of Western Stripe-headed Tanager, but louder and lower-pitched.
Status and Range: Known only from Cuba and Grand Cayman in the Cayman Islands, it is a common year-round resident. The species is widespread on Cuba, including the Isle of Youth, several cays off the northern coast and only Cayo Cantiles off the southern coast. On Grand Cayman, most abundant at North Side, North Sound Estates and South Sound Swamp.
Comments: Usually found in small flocks and also joins mixed flocks with warblers and vireos. Splits into pairs during the breeding season. Can be found in the upper canopy or close to the ground

while foraging. Mainly eats seeds, buds and fruits. The Grand Cayman race is larger with a much more bulky bill. Believed to have been smuggled abroad for aviculture. Cuban Bullfinch is the only member of its genus.

Habitat: Forests including mangroves, woodlands, brushy areas with bushes and undergrowth in pine country. Found at all elevations.

Nesting: A spherical, bulky nest with a lateral entrance, similar in shape and construction to a grassquit nest, but a bit larger and more compact. The nest is constructed of dried leaves, grass, hairs, rootlets and feathers and is built among bushes or twigs low to the ground. Eggs (3–4) dull white with a greenish tinge and with spots that vary from lilac to brown. Spots more concentrated toward the wider end. Breeds from March to July.

CUBAN GRASSQUIT *Tiaris canora*   Plates 73, 80
Local Names: Tomeguín del Pinar, Senserenico

Identification: 11.5 cm (4.5"). A small bird with a *conspicuous yellow crescent* that *divides the face and breast*. Upperparts olive. **Male**: Black face and breast. **Female**: Yellow less marked and face dark reddish-brown, rather than black. **Similar species**: Male Yellow-faced Grassquit has a yellow throat and eyebrow stripe rather than a yellow crescent edging the face. It also has much less black on the breast.

Voice: A shrill, raspy *chiri-wichi-wichi, chibiri-wichi-wichi* that resembles the song of Bee Hummingbird. Also a common *chip*.

Status and Range: Endemic to Cuba where it is common. Absent from the Isle of Youth. Due to deforestation and illegal exportation of the Cuban Grassquit for the cagebird trade, this bird has declined considerably in numbers and range, though it is still common in some less disturbed areas. Introduced to New Providence in the Bahamas in 1963 where it is fairly common throughout the island.

Comments: Usually in flocks, sometimes with Yellow-faced Grassquits. During breeding season, flocks divide into pairs. Feeds on the ground, mainly on small seeds. A favorite cagebird, it is difficult to breed in captivity.

Habitat: Primarily semi-arid country, particularly near the coast, but also pine undergrowth, edges of woods, bushy areas, shade coffee and citrus plantations and rural farmlands with much shrubbery, from the coast to mid-elevations.

Nesting: A bulky, rough spherical structure with a side entrance and interior lined with soft materials, is built at a low height usually among spiny branches or bushes. Eggs (2–3) white with a grayish-olive cast and with brown and pale purple spots concentrated around the broad end. Believed to breed from March to October.

YELLOW-FACED GRASSQUIT *Tiaris olivacea*   Plate 73
Local Names: Squit (Jamaica); Grass Bird (CI, Jamaica); Tomeguín de la Tierra, Viudito (Cuba); Cigüita de Hierba (DR); Gorrión Barba Amarilla (PR); Petit Z'herbes, Zèbable (Haiti)

Identification: 11.5 cm (4.5"). **Male**: Field marks are its distinctive *yellow throat and eyebrow stripe* and *black breast*. **Female and immature**: Note its yellowish-olive coloration and usually a faint yellowish eyebrow stripe, eyering and chin. **Similar species**: Females and immatures are distinguished from their Black-faced Grassquit counterparts by their more olive coloration and faint facial markings. Cuban Grassquit has a yellow facial crescent. Female Antillean Siskin has a pale yellow bill and yellow wingbars. Male Yellow-shouldered Grassquit has a yellowish back and wings, and the female has a yellow wing mark.

Voice: The call note is usually a soft *tek*, imitated by removing one's tongue from against the upper palate. The song is a distinctive thin trill, sometimes uttered sequentially at different pitches.

Status and Range: A common year-round resident on Cuba, Jamaica, Hispaniola, Puerto Rico and the Cayman Islands. It was introduced to New Providence in the Bahamas in 1963, but the population did not survive. The species also occurs from Mexico to northwestern South America.

Comments: Solitary or in small groups up to five or six. Forages on seeds, usually from grass heads, but sometimes on the ground. Often seen singing from a conspicuous spike of grass or cane.
Habitat: Primarily open grassy areas from the lowlands to moderate elevations, but occurs even into the high mountains where suitable habitat occurs.
Nesting: A domed nest of fine grasses with the entrance in the side is built low off the ground in a clump of grass. Eggs (3) bluish-white, heavily flecked at the broad end. Breeds the year-round.

BLACK-FACED GRASSQUIT *Tiaris bicolor* Plate 73

Local Names: Black Sparrow, Grass Bird (Jamaica); Tobacco Bird (LA); Cheechee Bird, Tobacco Seed (Saba); Sparrow (St E); Groundquit (Grenada, St V); Sinbird, Grass Sparrow (LA, VI); Juana Maruca (DR); Gorrión Negro (PR); Tomeguín Prieto, Barbito (Cuba); Cici-zèb, Mangeur d'herbe (Guad); Sisi Zèb (Haiti); Cici (Mart); Si-si Zeb (St L); Sporophile à Face Noire (Guad, Mart); Zwartkopgrasvink (Saba, St E, St M)

Identification: 11.5 cm (4.5"). *Male*: *Black head and underparts*. *Female and immature*: Drab brownish-olive overall. *Similar species*: Females and immatures are drabber than their Yellow-faced Grassquit counterparts and lack the faint yellowish facial markings. Male Yellow-shouldered Grassquit has a yellowish back and wings, and the female has a yellow wing patch.
Voice: A very emphatic buzz that often receives a second louder effort. The call note is a soft musical *tsip*.
Status and Range: Generally a common year-round resident throughout the West Indies though on Cuba it is rare and very local and found only in the vicinity of Gibara and on Tío Pepe Cayo. Absent from the Cayman Islands. It also occurs in northern South America.
Comments: In urban areas on Puerto Rico and the Dominican Republic, Black-faced and Yellow-faced Grassquits appear to reverse status. Black-faced is the more common in Puerto Rico's urban areas whereas Yellow-faced is more common in urban zones of the Dominican Republic. On Jamaica, the situation is much like that on Puerto Rico.
Habitat: Almost all open areas with grasses and shrubs, including forest clearings, road edges, sugarcane plantations and gardens.
Nesting: The nest is domed with an entrance in the side or bottom. Eggs (3) whitish, heavily flecked with reddish-brown at the broad end. Breeds the year-round.

YELLOW-SHOULDERED GRASSQUIT Plates 73, 84
Loxipasser anoxanthus

Local Names: Yellow-back, Yellow-backed Grass Bird, Yellow-backed Finch, Yellow-shouldered Finch

Identification: 10 cm (4"). *Adult male*: A small two-toned bird with a black head and underparts and *yellowish wings and back*. The undertail-coverts are reddish-brown. *Adult female*: Gray below and yellowish-green above, it has a distinctive *yellow patch on the bend of its wing*. Undertail-coverts are pale reddish-brown. *Immature*: Similar to the female, but yellow reduced on bend of wing. *Similar species*: The slightly smaller Black-faced and Yellow-faced Grassquits lack the yellowish back and wings of adult male Yellow-shouldered Grassquit and the yellow wing mark of adult females. They also lack the reddish-brown undertail-coverts of Yellow-shouldered Grassquit.
Voice: Five notes, descending with an echo-like quality (Levy).
Status and Range: Endemic to Jamaica where it is fairly common and widespread. Most common near Ferry River and in dry limestone woodlands.
Comments: Small groups of two to five birds forage in bushes and low in trees for fruits and seeds. It has the habit of adding material to the exterior of its nest even after the young have hatched. Yellow-shouldered Grassquit is the only member of its genus.
Habitat: Forest edges from wet to dry and at all elevations. Also woodlands and gardens near wooded areas.

Nesting: The nest is a finely woven dome of grass and down, with a side entrance, built in a bush or tree or hidden among vines or epiphytes. Both the male and female assist in nest construction. Eggs (3–4) white, spotted or speckled with cloudy red or dull brown. These markings are sometimes concentrated. Breeds from March to July.

PUERTO RICAN BULLFINCH *Loxigilla portoricensis*   Plates 75, 85
Local Names: Mountain Blacksmith (St C); Comeñame, Come Gandul, Capacho, Gallito (PR)

Identification: 16.5–19 cm (6.5–7.5"). **Adult**: Black with a *reddish-brown throat, undertail-coverts and crown band*. **Immature**: Dark olive-green with only the undertail-coverts reddish-brown. **Similar species**: Greater Antillean Bullfinch has less reddish-brown in the crown and Lesser Antillean Bullfinch nearly lacks this color in the crown altogether.
Voice: A distinctive series of two to ten rising whistles followed by a buzz. The call is much louder and more forceful than the similar call of Lesser Antillean Bullfinch. A second call is a whistle *coochi, coochi, coochi*. The call note is a medium strength *check* like striking two stones together. This bird sings much of the day, particularly from February to June.

Status and Range: Puerto Rican Bullfinch is endemic to Puerto Rico. It is very common though is far more often heard than seen. Curiously, it is absent from the coastal thickets of the extreme eastern tip of the island. Formerly on St Christopher, the last certain record of its occurrence was in the 1920s. There is an unconfirmed sighting of the bird in 1994 from the forest of Stone-fort Ghaut.

Comments: The St Christopher race, substantially larger than the Puerto Rican form, was likely extirpated by the impact of hurricanes on its very locally distributed population confined to the higher elevations of Mt Misery.

Habitat: Particularly dense mountain forests, but also dry coastal thickets and infrequently, mangroves.

Nesting: The nest is either open or domed with an entrance in the side. Eggs (usually 3) dull green with dark spots. Breeds primarily from February to June, but sporadically in other seasons.

GREATER ANTILLEAN BULLFINCH *Loxigilla violacea*   Plate 75
Local Names: Black Sparrow, Jack Sparrow, Cotton-tree Sparrow (Jamaica); Gallito, Gallito Prieto (DR); Petit-Coq, Tchitchi Gwo Bèk, Gros-bec Père-noire, Père-noir (Haiti)

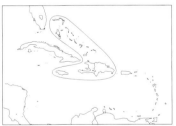

Identification: 15–18 cm (5.75–7"). **Adult male**: A chunky, thick-billed bird with a diagnostic *orange-red eyebrow stripe, throat and undertail-coverts*. **Adult male**: Black overall. **Adult female**: Duller black. **Immature**: Olive-brown with orange-red markings similar to the adults. **Similar species**: Puerto Rican Bullfinch has a reddish-brown crown band.
Voice: Song is a repetition of the shrill, insect-like call note *t'zeet, t'seet, t'seet, tseet, seet, seet, seet, seet, seet*. Alarm note is a thin *spit* (Brudenell-Bruce).

Status and Range: A common year-round resident on most of the larger Bahaman islands, Hispaniola and its satellite islands and Jamaica. These islands comprise the entire range of the species.

Comments: Feeds primarily on fruits and seeds, but also on flower parts and snails. Despite being common and brightly colored, it is difficult to detect due to its habit of keeping to dense vegetation. There are three races.

Habitat: Dense thickets and undergrowth at all elevations from dry coastal scrub to wet mountain forests, including pine woods and gardens.

Nesting: Nest of twigs and leaves, lined with bromeliad, thin bark and other materials, is sometimes cup-shaped, but usually spherical with a side entrance. Nest sites vary widely, including tree branches, tree cavities, shrubs and grass clumps. Eggs (3–4) very pale bluish white with irregular yellowish-brown and reddish-brown streaks concentrated at the broad end. Breeds from March to June.

LESSER ANTILLEAN BULLFINCH *Loxigilla noctis* **Plate 75**

Local Names: West Indian Robin (Nevis); Red-throat See-see (Grenada, St V); Robin, Sparrow, Cheechee Bird (Saba, St E, St M); Gros-bec Rouge-gorge (Guad); Père Noir (male in Mart, St L); Moisson (female in Mart); Sporophile Rouge-gorge (Guad, Mart)

Identification: 14–15.5 cm (5.5–6"). **Male, except Barbados**: All black with red on chin, throat and just in front of eye. Some races have red undertail-coverts. **Female, Barbados male and immature**: Brownish-olive above, gray below and orange undertail-coverts. **Similar species**: Male St Lucia Black Finch has pink legs, a larger bill and bobs its tail; the female has a gray crown. Puerto Rican Bullfinch has a reddish-brown crown band.
Voice: Various sounds from a short, crisp trill to a harsh *chuk*; a thin, wiry *tseep, tseep* and a lengthy twitter.

Status and Range: A common year-round resident through the Lesser Antilles, but absent from the Grenadines. Lesser Antillean Bullfinch expanded its range westward to St John and St Croix in the Virgin Islands in the 1970s where it is now locally common. A vagrant on Puerto Rico.

Comments: A conspicuous and relatively tame species, it sometimes enters human establishments in search of food scraps.

Habitat: Shrubbery, gardens, thickets and forest understory at all elevations. Sometimes mangroves, swamps and dry areas.

Nesting: A domed nest is constructed with a side entrance, usually in a dense bush or tree 1–4.5 m (3–15') above the ground. Eggs (3–4) white, finely spotted with red, especially at the broad end. Breeds from February to August.

ORANGEQUIT *Euneornis campestris* **Plates 67, 84**

Local Names: Long-mouth Quit, Blue Baize, Swee, Long-Month Bluequit, Bluebird, Blue . Badas, Blue Gay

Identification: 14 cm (5.5"). A small bird with a slightly down-curved black bill. **Adult male**: Gray-blue overall, appearing dark in poor light with *orangish-red throat*. **Female and immature**: Crown and hindneck olive-gray; grayish-white below with faint streaks. **Similar species**: Jamaican Euphonia has a shorter, stubbier bill and has much paler underparts. Female and immature Orangequits lack bluish on the head.
Voice: A thin, high-pitched *tseet* or *swee*. Occasionally *fi-swee*.
Status and Range: Endemic to Jamaica where locally common, especially at Newcastle, Hardwar Gap, Mandeville and Anchovy.

Comments: Feeds primarily on nectar and, to a lesser extent, fruits at low to medium heights among vegetation. Sometimes feeds on the sap oozing from tree holes chiseled by Yellow-bellied Sapsuckers. Easily attracted to feeding stations. Orangequit is the only member of its genus.

Habitat: Humid forests and woodlands at all altitudes, but most frequently at mid-elevations.

Nesting: The nest is a moderately deep cup, usually open, of grass and plant fibers and built in a bush or tree. Orangequits sometimes use the abandoned nests of Jamaican Becards. Eggs (2–4) white with reddish-brown and grayish-brown markings concentrated at the broad end. Breeds from April to June.

ST LUCIA BLACK FINCH *Melanospiza richardsoni* **Plates 75, 86**

Local Name: Moisson Pied-blanc

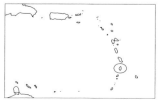

Identification: 13–14 cm (5–5.5"). Note its heavy bill, *pink legs* and *habit of bobbing its tail* up and down. **Adult male**: Plumage entirely black. **Female**: The *gray crown* contrasts with the brown back. Buffy below. **Immature**: Resembles the female. **Similar species**: Both sexes of Lesser Antillean Bullfinch have a smaller bill and lack pink legs; the female has grayish underparts and lacks a gray crown.
Voice: A burry *tick-zwee-swisiwis-you* with the accents on the second and last notes; at a distance similar to song of Bananaquit.

Status and Range: Endemic to St Lucia where it is uncommon and locally distributed.
Comments: Often found in pairs. Primarily terrestrial, it usually forages in leaf litter in dense under-story. Management of its habitat in the plantation forests of La Sorciere and Edmund Forest to maintain ground cover and dense vegetation would contribute to sustaining this species. It is the only member of its genus; its closest living relatives are the Galapagos finches.
Habitat: Found in both moist and semi-arid forests to 700 m (2,300′).
Nesting: A loosely constructed spherical nest of twigs, rootlets, ferns and leaves, with an oval side entrance, is usually built in a shrub or small palm up to 3 m (10′) above the ground. Eggs (2) white with evenly spaced brownish-red spots. Breeds from November to June.

SAFFRON FINCH *Sicalis flaveola*   Plate 74
Local Names: Canary (Jamaica); Gorrión Azafrán (PR)

Identification: 14 cm (5.5″). *Adult*: Medium-sized and *entirely yellow* with an *orange crown*. *Male*: Crown bright orange. *Female*: Crown yellowish-orange. *Immature*: Generally gray, paler below, with yellow undertail-coverts and, with age, a *yellow breast band*. *Similar species*: Distinguished from the somewhat similar Yellow and Prothonotary Warblers by its larger size, thicker bill and occurrence in grassy habitats.
Voice: The call note varies from a soft to a loud, sharp *pink*. Also a whistle *wheat* on one pitch. The song is a fairly loud, melodious, but slightly harsh *chit, chit, chit, chi-chit*, with variations of differing lengths.
Status and Range: Introduced to Jamaica in the 1820s where it is widespread and common and to Puerto Rico about 1960 where it is fairly common, but local in and around San Juan, Río Piedras and Bayamón. There is a l996 record from Cuba. It is native to South America.
Comments: Forages primarily on the ground for seeds. When not feeding, retires to trees.
Habitat: Cultivated lawns on Puerto Rico. On Jamaica, also along roadsides and in farmlands where grasses are in seed.
Nesting: A bulky nest is built among palm fronds or in a building or tree cavity. Eggs (2–3) faint blue and heavily spotted. Reportedly breeds from August to October on Puerto Rico and year-round with a peak from March to July on Jamaica.

GRASSLAND YELLOW-FINCH *Sicalis luteola*   Plate 74
Local Names: Grass Sparrow, Grass Canary (LA); Moisson Jaune (St L); Petit Serin, Sicale des Savanes (Guad, Mart)

Identification: 12 cm (4.75′). *Adult male*: Upperparts pale yellow, heavily streaked with blackish; underparts and rump yellow. *Adult female*: Similar to the male, but duller. *Immature*: Like the female, but blackish streaks on breast.
Voice: A distinctive buzzy trill.
Status and Range: An uncommon and local year-round resident on Antigua, Guadeloupe, Martinique, St Lucia, Barbados, St Vincent and Grenada and a vagrant in the Grenadines (Mustique). Believed introduced to Barbados in 1900 and subsequently to have colonized the other Lesser Antillean islands. It was first recorded on Martinique in 1951 and on Guadeloupe in 1983. The species is native to Central and South America where it is widespread.
Habitat: Open grassy fields and runway edges.
Nesting: A cup of woven grass is built on the ground. Eggs (2–3) white or washed with blue or green, heavily spotted with brown. Breeds primarily from February to June, but may breed year-round.

ZAPATA SPARROW *Torreornis inexpectata*   Plates 74, 80
Local Name: Cabrerito de la Ciénaga

Identification: 16.5 cm (6.5″). A plump sparrow with yellow underparts, white throat and dark mustache stripe. Dark reddish-brown crown and olive-gray upperparts. The wings are short and rounded.

Immature: Darker above and lacks the dark reddish-brown crown. **Voice**: It has four distinct calls, two of which are similar to one another and are only sung during the breeding season. The typical call is a short, somewhat metallic trill, repeated at intervals while a pair forages. It is high-pitched and penetrating, *tziii-tzziii-tzziii...* When hidden, it emits a *tic-tic-tic...* The courtship and territorial calls are similar; both are long and high-pitched, with a series of fluctuating, somewhat raspy notes that end on a deeper note, *tzi, tzi, tziiii-tzzii, zu, zu, zu...* Pairs duet during the breeding season.

Status and Range: Endemic to Cuba where it is very local in distribution. One race, which is uncommon, occurs in Zapata Swamp north of Santo Tomás as far as Maniadero. A second race, even rarer, lives in the coastal areas east of Guantánamo Bay from west of Baitiquirí to Cajobabo. The only common race is restricted to Cayo Coco in the province of Ciego de Ávila. All three races are considered threatened due to the small ranges of their populations making them susceptible to natural threats such as hurricanes and human-caused impacts such as habitat alteration or destruction.

Comments: Usually in pairs that are sometimes accompanied by a third individual. Rarely forms flocks of ten to twelve birds. Pairs appear to defend territories year-round. During the dry season of November through April, appears to feed primarily on seeds and flowers of small plants, but expands its diet in the wet season to include animal matter, such as insects, caterpillars, moths, spiders, *Pomacea* snails (especially their eggs) and even small lizards. It has short, round wings, but can fly as far as 100 m (330'). When the Zapata Swamp becomes drier, the sparrow forages mainly on the ground, scratching and jumping with both feet. Zapata Sparrow is the only member of its genus.

Habitat: Each race occupies very different habitats. The Zapata Swamp population inhabits sawgrass country with scattered bushes. The population east of Guantánamo Bay lives amid very dry vegetation in the most arid part of Cuba. The third population occurs widely on Cayo Coco, from semi-deciduous woods to swampy areas.

Nesting: In Zapata Swamp, the nest is cup-shaped, woven of sawgrass and hidden in the uppermost part of a grass tussock less than 1 m (3') from the ground. Eggs (1–2) white with a greenish tinge and reddish and pinkish spots, more concentrated at the broad end. Breeds primarily from March to June. Also reported to nest in August.

CHIPPING SPARROW *Spizella passerina* Plate 77
Local Name: Gorrión de Cabeza Carmelita (Cuba)

Identification: 12.5–14.5 cm (5–5.75"). ***Non-breeding adult and immature***: Crown brown (immature) or reddish-brown (adult) with black streaks, dark eyeline and buffy or brown cheeks. Underparts gray in adult and buffy in immature. ***Breeding adult***: *Bright reddish-brown crown, gray cheeks* and *white eyebrow stripe*. Note the black line through the eye *all the way to base of the black bill*. It also has a gray rump, is grayish-white below and is lighter on the throat and belly. **Similar species**: Grasshopper Sparrow has a golden spot in front of the eye. See also Clay-colored Sparrow.

Status and Range: A very rare non-breeding resident in the northern Bahamas and Cuba from October to April. A vagrant in the southern Bahamas. It is widespread in North America south through Central America to Nicaragua.

Comments: Forages for seeds on the ground, takes cover among low bushes.

Habitat: Pastures, open areas, grassy fields, bushy thickets and croplands.

CLAY-COLORED SPARROW *Spizella pallida* Plate 77

Identification: 12–13.5 cm (4.75–5.25"). **Adult**: Buff-brown above with bold black streaks on back, *brownish or buffy rump, white median stripe on crown*, wide whitish eyebrow and mustache stripes, *brown cheek patch* outlined by thin, dark lines and *pale lores* and gray hindneck contrasting with back. Underparts are pale buffy-gray. **Immature**: Similar to the adult, but fine streaks on breast. The head pattern is less well-defined than on the adult. **Similar species**: Adult Chipping Sparrow has a reddish-brown crown. Both adult and immature Chipping Sparrows have a dark eyeline through the lores. For additional information on distinguishing Chipping and Clay-colored Sparrows see: Pyle, P.

and S. N. G. Howell. 1996. Spizella Sparrows — Intraspecific Variation and Identification. *Birding* 28(5): 374–387. Grasshopper Sparrow has a golden mark above the lores.

Status and Range: A vagrant in the northern Bahamas and Cuba from October to February. It is widespread in central North America.

Comments: Forages on the ground for seeds.

Habitat: Coastal thickets, borders of salt ponds and bushy areas.

LARK SPARROW *Chondestes grammacus*   **Plate 77**

Identification: 15 cm (5.75″). *Adult*: Note its *bold head and facial pattern,* black breast spot and *large, white patches on the outer corners of the tail*. *Immature*: The head pattern is mostly brown and buff and is less distinct than on the adult. The white underparts are buffy on the breast and heavily streaked and it lacks the black breast spot of the adult. The tail, like the adult's, has conspicuous white outer corners.

Status and Range: A vagrant in the northern Bahamas, Cuba and Jamaica from August to March. It is widespread in central North America.

Comments: Forages on the ground for seeds.

Habitat: Open semi-arid areas with scattered bushes.

SAVANNAH SPARROW *Passerculus sandwichensis*   **Plate 77**
Local Name: Gorrión de Sabana (Cuba)

Identification: 15–19 cm (5.75–7.5″). A slender sparrow with underparts heavily streaked with brown. Eyebrow stripe usually yellowish and conspicuous, though sometimes buff-colored. Also has a pale central crown stripe, dark mustache stripe and pink legs. The tail is short and slightly notched. Typically seen on the ground. **Similar species**: Grasshopper Sparrow has a more golden eyebrow stripe and lacks a mustache stripe. Only immature Grasshopper Sparrow is streaked below and these streaks are much finer and paler than those of Savannah Sparrow. When landing, Savannah Sparrow does not turn slightly to one side as does Grasshopper Sparrow.

Voice: A pleasant, high-pitched, melodious call of three *chips* followed by two wispy notes, the last one shorter and lower, *chip-chip-chip-tisisiiii-tisi.*

Status and Range: Generally an uncommon non-breeding resident in the northern Bahamas and Cuba, including the Isle of Youth. Rare in the Cayman Islands, where only known from Grand Cayman. Occurs from October through April, being most abundant in October and November during southward migration. Occurs through North America into Central America.

Comments: Forages primarily on the ground for seeds.

Habitat: Open fields, pastures, bushy savannas and sparse thickets near the coast.

GRASSHOPPER SPARROW *Ammodramus savannarum*   **Plate 77**
Local Names: Savanna Bird, Grass Dodger, Grass Pink (Jamaica); Chamberguito (Cuba); Tumbarrocío (DR); Gorrión Chicharra (PR); Zwazo Kann, Moineau des Herbes (Haiti)

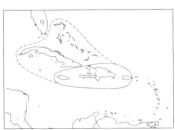

Identification: 12.5 cm (5″). *Adult*: Field marks are the *golden mark on the forward portion of the eyebrow stripe* and the *whitish central crown stripe*. *Immature*: Possesses a paler mark by the bill and has fine streaks on the breast and flanks. **Similar species**: Savannah Sparrow is more heavily streaked than immature Grasshopper Sparrow. Also Grasshopper Sparrow turns slightly to one side upon landing whereas Savannah Sparrow does not. The very similar brown-plumaged Yellow-crowned and Orange Bishops lack the single central crown stripe, whereas Chipping and Clay-colored Sparrows lack the golden mark on the eyebrow stripe. Rufous-collared Sparrow
has a black band on the foreneck, reddish-brown hindneck and a gray crown with black stripes,

and is only found in the mountains on Hispaniola.

Voice: Two distinct songs. A long, thin, insect-like buzz, followed by what sounds like a hiccup *zzzzzzz-hic*. Also a very thin, high-pitched twitter or tinkling song, rather like fairy bells. The call note is a high-pitched, gritty, insect-like *kr-r-it*.

Status and Range: A common, but local year-round resident on Jamaica, Hispaniola and Puerto Rico. Also a non-breeding resident from October through April on Cuba where it is common and in the Bahamas and Cayman Islands where it is rare. It is widespread in North America to northwestern South America.

Comments: Feeds primarily on grass seeds. Very secretive, it is much more often heard than seen. On Cuba, it is disliked by quail hunters because their dogs erroneously point to the sparrow rather than a hoped-for Northern Bobwhite.

Habitat: Weedy fields and pastures with tall grass. Also rice plantations.

Nesting: A domed nest is built in the grass. Eggs (3) white and heavily marked. Breeds primarily from May to August, but also in other months.

LINCOLN'S SPARROW *Melospiza lincolnii*   **Plate 77**
Local Name: Gorrión de Lincoln (Cuba)

Identification: 13.5–15 cm (5.25–5.75"). **Adult**: Upperparts grayish-olive streaked with black. Crown brown, streaked with black. *Central crown stripe, eyebrow stripe, ear patch and sides of neck pale gray*. Note the *narrow and pointed tail feathers, with the outer feathers being the shortest*. Breast buffy, finely streaked with black. **Immature**: Similar to the adult, but eyebrow stripe buffy-white. **Similar species**: Swamp Sparrow has reddish-brown wing patches; buffy flanks; a narrow, pointed tail and, in the adult, a white throat. Immature Swamp Sparrow has a buffy cheek patch.

Status and Range: A rare migrant and perhaps a non-breeding resident in the Bahamas, Cuba and Jamaica from October to April. A vagrant on Hispaniola and Puerto Rico. It is widespread in North and Central America.

Comments: Very shy, but during migration, it is sometimes observed in association with other migrating species including warblers.

Habitat: Usually in moist highland forest thickets, especially around clearings. Also coastal thickets and borders of dense forests.

SWAMP SPARROW *Melospiza georgiana*   **Plate 78**

Identification: 15 cm (5.75"). **Non-breeding adult**: Upperparts generally brown; bright *reddish-brown patches in wing*, including wing-coverts and primaries and back with black and gray stripes. Also note its gray central crown stripe, eyebrow stripe, cheek patch and sides of neck; blackish mustache mark; *white throat* and breast grayish with a few blackish streaks. **Immature**: Very much like the adult, but *breast and throat unstreaked gray; buffy cheek patch* and flanks. **Breeding adult**: Crown reddish-brown. **Similar species**: Lincoln's Sparrow lacks reddish-brown wing patches, buffy flanks and the white throat of adult Swamp or the buffy cheek patch of immature Swamp Sparrow. Lincoln's Sparrow also has a narrow, sharply-pointed tail.

Status and Range: A vagrant in the Bahamas where recorded from New Providence, Exuma and Mayaguana. It is most likely to occur from November to May. Occurs primarily in eastern and central North America.

Habitat: Marshes and brushy areas.

RUFOUS-COLLARED SPARROW *Zonotrichia capensis*   **Plate 77**
Local Names: Cigüita de Constanza, Sigüa de Constanza, Pincha (DR)

Identification: 15–16.5 cm (5.75–6.5"). **Adult**: Identified by its *black neck band, reddish-brown hindneck* and *gray crown with black stripes*. Often displays a slight crest. **Immature**: Duller and spotted below. Lacks black or reddish-brown markings. **Similar species**: Grasshopper Sparrow lacks the black band on foreneck, reddish-brown hindneck and gray on the crown, and does not occur in

mountain forests.

Voice: An accelerating trill *whis-whis-whis-whis-whiswhisu-whiswhis*.

Status and Range: A locally year-round common resident on Hispaniola where known from the Cordillera Central (Constanza to Manabao) and the Sierra de Neiba of the Dominican Republic. It also occurs in Central and South America.

Comments: Shy and retiring in habits. Feeds on seeds, usually in pairs.

Habitat: Mountains above 1000 m (3300') in forest edges and stream-side thickets. Also undergrowth of pine forests.

Nesting: A cup-shaped nest of moss, lichens and pine needles, lined with fine grass, is built in a shrub at low level of 2 m (7'). Eggs (2) pale bluish, heavily spotted. Breeds in May and June.

WHITE-CROWNED SPARROW *Zonotrichia leucophrys*   Plate 77

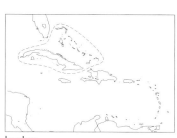

Identification: 18 cm (7"). *Adult*: Note its conspicuously *black-and-white striped crown* and gray underparts. *Immature*: The crown stripes are brown and buff. *Similar species*: Male Western Stripe-headed Tanager has a black-and-white crown, but its underparts are primarily yellow and black rather than gray, and it is rarely found on the ground.

Status and Range: A rare migrant in October and November and rarer still as a non-breeding resident from December to April in the Bahamas and Cuba. A vagrant on Jamaica. Occurs in North America south to southern Mexico.

Comments: Forages on the ground for seeds. Takes cover in bushes.

Habitat: Open woodlands, treed gardens, forest edges and brushy fields.

DARK-EYED JUNCO *Junco hyemalis*   Plate 77

Identification: 16 cm (6.25"). Blackish-gray overall, white belly, *white outer tail feathers* and a *pink bill*.

Status and Range: A vagrant in the northern Bahamas, Jamaica, Puerto Rico and the Virgin Islands. A flock of juncos is known to have hitched a ride on a freighter from New York to the Bahamas and subsequently to the Virgin Islands. It is possible that such human-assisted migration is more frequent than commonly believed, particularly for relatively tame species capable of survival on human food-stuffs. Occurs through North America south to northern Mexico.

Comments: Relatively tame. Forages on the ground for seeds. Takes cover in bushes and trees.

Habitat: Cultivated areas, field edges, hedgerows, lawns and roadsides.

BOBOLINK *Dolichonyx oryzivorus*   Plate 70
Local Names: October Pink, Butterbird, Rice Bird (Jamaica); Chambergo (PR)

Identification: 18.5 cm (7.25"). *Non-breeding adult*: Characterized by its larger size than birds of similar appearance, central buff crown stripe, unmarked buff-colored throat, streaked sides and abdomen and pointed tail feathers. *Breeding male*: Black below with a buff-colored hindneck and white patches on the wings and lower back. *Breeding female*: Similar to non-breeding birds, but with a whitish, rather than buff-colored, throat. *Similar species*: Non-breeding adult Bobolink differs from the various sparrows and bishops by its much larger size and its streaked sides and abdomen.

Voice: A very distinctive *pink*.

Status and Range: Primarily a southbound migrant from as early as August to as late as December in the West Indies, less frequent northbound from February to May. Bobolink is generally common

in the Bahamas, Cuba, Jamaica and the Cayman Islands; uncommon and local on Puerto Rico, the Virgin Islands and Barbados; rare on Hispaniola, St Barthélemy, Antigua and Dominica and very rare among the other islands of the Lesser Antilles. Occurs through much of the Western Hemisphere.
Comments: Typically flocks.
Habitat: Rice fields, pastures and areas where grass is seeding.

RED-SHOULDERED BLACKBIRD *Agelaius assimilis*　　**Plates 70, 80**
Local Names: Mayito de Ciénaga, Chirriador

Identification: 19–23 (7.5–9"). A medium-sized black bird. **Male**: Note its *conspicuous scarlet shoulder patch* edged with yellowish. **Female**: *Entirely black* and a bit smaller than the male. **Immature male**: Shoulder patch reddish-brown. **Similar species**: The very similar Tawny-shouldered Blackbird has a shoulder patch in all plumages, though it is sometimes inconspicuous. Best distinguished by observing the shoulder patch in flight. Male Shiny Cowbird has a noticeable purplish sheen and a heavier bill. Cuban Blackbird is a substantially larger bird and is all black with no shoulder patch. The very similar Red-winged Blackbird of the Bahamas does not overlap in range with Red-shouldered Blackbird.
Voice: A harsh creaking and rather shrill, non-melodious *o-wi-hiiii*, repeated quite often. Also a short *cheap*, *chek-chek-chek* or a single *chek*. When singing, the male drops its wings, exposing the brilliant red shoulder patch, raises its back feathers and spreads its tail.
Status and Range: Endemic to Cuba where confined to the western part of the island. Locally common, it occurs in parts of the Zapata Peninsula, especially Laguna del Tesoro and also at Laguna de Lugones in Guanahacabibes and in swamps north of Itabo, as well as in Lanier Swamp on the Isle of Youth. It has recently been recorded in the vicinity of Ciego de Ávila. The distribution is patchy due to limited habitat.
Comments: Sometimes gathers in large flocks. Periodically forages in the company of Greater Antillean Grackles, Cuban Blackbirds and Tawny-shouldered Blackbirds. Primarily feeds on seeds, but also fruits, insects, small lizards, frogs and even scraps of food which it scavenges from restaurants. Fossil records suggest the species was confined to western Cuba before human settlement. There is debate as to whether or not this bird is a full species or a subspecies of Red-winged Blackbird. It is treated as a separate species based on its somewhat different song and particularly due to the entirely black plumage of the female which in Red-winged Blackbird is brown above and white below with heavy stripes.
Habitat: Swamps and marshes.
Nesting: Nests in colonies or separately in pairs. The nest is woven of dried grass, hair and feathers and is built low among sawgrass and reeds in a swamp. In contrast to the mating system of Red-winged Blackbird, in which each breeding male has several mates, a male Red-shouldered Blackbird has a single mate. Eggs (4) white with a bluish sheen and some brown and pale purple spots. Breeds from April to June.

RED-WINGED BLACKBIRD *Agelaius phoeniceus*　　**Plate 70**

Identification: 19–23 (7.5–9"). A medium-sized black bird. **Male**: Note the *conspicuous scarlet shoulder patch* edged with yellowish. **Female**: Brown above and buffy below, heavily streaked with dark brown. Also has a light buffy eyebrow stripe. **Immature male**: Dark mottled brown with a faint pale eyebrow stripe and a small reddish-brown shoulder patch. **Similar species**: Shiny Cowbird has a heavier bill. Male Shiny Cowbird has a distinct purplish sheen and lacks the red shoulder patch. Female and immature Cowbirds have finer, less distinct streaking on underparts compared with female and immature Red-winged Blackbirds. The very similar Red-shouldered Blackbird does not occur in the Bahamas.
Voice: Song a bubbling, shrill *ok-a-lee*, repeated often. Call a sharp *chek*. Song display consists of the male hunching forward, spreading its tail and drooping its wings to expose brilliant red shoulder patches.
Status and Range: A common resident very locally in the northern Bahamas south to Andros and Eleuthera. A vagrant in the southern Bahamas. Occurs from subarctic Canada south to Central America.

Comments: Social, at times feeding and breeding in large groups. Feeds mainly on grass seeds, but also fruits, insects and small vertebrates. Separated from Red-shouldered Blackbird by differences in song and the entirely black plumage of female Red-shouldered Blackbird. The resident Red-winged Blackbird of the Bahamas is an endemic subspecies.

Habitat: Swamps and marshes.

Nesting: Nests in colonies or separately in pairs. The nest, a woven cup of dried grass, feathers and other materials, is placed low among sawgrass and reeds in a marsh. Eggs (4) white with a bluish sheen and some brown and pale purple spots. Breeds from April to July.

TAWNY-SHOULDERED BLACKBIRD *Agelaius humeralis* Plate 69

Local Names: Mayito, Totí Mayito (Cuba); Merle (Haïti)

Identification: 19–22 cm (7.5–8.5"). A medium-sized bird, black overall, with a tawny shoulder patch, most conspicuous when flying. **Immature**: Shoulder patch much smaller. **Similar species**: The shoulder patch of Tawny-shouldered Blackbird is sometimes not visible in perched birds, particularly immatures, giving them the appearance of female Red-shouldered Blackbird, which lacks a shoulder patch. Greater Antillean Grackle is larger, has a long V-shaped tail and lacks a shoulder patch.

Voice: Sometimes emits a harsh call similar to that of Red-shouldered Blackbird, but softer, shorter and less shrill, *wiii-wiiii-wiiii*. Its typical call note is a strong, short *chic-chic* that resembles the *chip* of Northern Yellowthroat, but is stronger.

Status and Range: Known only from Cuba, where it is a common resident and from Haiti, where it is uncommon and local primarily at the Artibonite River. On Cuba, it also occurs on several cays, including Cantiles which supports an endemic race, but is absent from the Isle of Youth. Habitat loss on Haiti has resulted in declining populations to the point where this blackbird's survival is threatened.

Comments: Usually in flocks, it forms pairs during the breeding season. Locally, Tawny-shouldered Blackbirds form mixed flocks with Red-shouldered Blackbirds, Greater Antillean Grackles and Cuban Blackbirds. Primarily feeds on seeds, but also fruits, pollen, nectar, flowers, small lizards and domestic animal feed in farms and dairies. It sometimes enters open restaurants for food scraps. On Cuba, it is parasitized by the Shiny Cowbird.

Habitat: Woodlands, gardens, rural farms, swamp edges, pastures and rice fields, only in the lowlands.

Nesting: Usually builds a nest among palm fronds, but sometimes in trees or epiphytes. Several pairs sometimes nest simultaneously in the same tree. Cup-shaped, the nest is roughly constructed of dried grass, moss, hair, feathers and twigs. Eggs (3–4) bluish or greenish with brown spots concentrated at the broad end. Breeds in April and May.

YELLOW-SHOULDERED BLACKBIRD Plates 69, 85

Agelaius xanthomus

Local Names: Mariquita, Capitán

Identification: 20–23 cm (8–9"). **Adult**: Entirely glossy black with *yellow shoulder patches*. **Immature**: Duller black than the adult and has a brown abdomen. **Similar species**: Black-cowled Oriole is more extensively marked with yellow. Greater Antillean Grackle is larger, with a long, V-shaped tail and lacks a shoulder patch.

Voice: A wide variety of calls including a raspy *tnaaa*, accented at the beginning; a whistle *tsuu*, starting with an accent and descending the scale; a melodious *eh- up*, the second syllable one note lower and slightly accented; a *chuck* and when disturbed a sharp, nasal, squeaky *chink* and *check*, as well as sharp staccato scolding notes around the nest.

Status and Range: Endemic to Puerto Rico, Yellow-shouldered Blackbird occurs regularly only locally along the southwestern coast and on Mona Island. It is decidedly uncommon elsewhere, including in the mountains where it sometimes wanders during the non-breeding season. Common around the coast until as recently as the 1940s, this blackbird is now critically endangered primarily due to nest parasitism by Shiny Cowbirds, but also as a result of expansive habitat loss. The population is presently estimated at fewer than 1,000 individuals.

Comments: Forages both in trees and on the ground feeding on insects, seeds and nectar. Moths and crickets are a major food. Often probes among epiphytes and crevices in twigs. Caribbean Martins have been known to usurp their nests. Yellow-shouldered Blackbird nests studied from 1973 to 1982 were found to be 95 percent parasitized by Cowbirds. Measures are now underway to control the Cowbird and to provide nest boxes for the Blackbird. Other threats to the Blackbird include rats and the Pearly-eyed Thrasher. The Mona Island population of Yellow-shouldered Blackbird has not been as adversely affected by Shiny Cowbird parasitism because many pairs nest in cliff crevices not visited by Cowbirds.

Habitat: Primarily mangroves and arid scrublands.

Nesting: The nest is cup-shaped and nest sites vary from cliff crevices and hollow stumps to the bases of palm fronds and tree forks. Eggs (2–4) bluish with brown splotches or fine squiggles. Breeds primarily in small colonies from March to September.

JAMAICAN BLACKBIRD *Nesopsar nigerrimus*   Plates 70, 84
Local Names: Black Banana Bird, Corporal Bird, Wild Pine Sargeant

Identification: 18 cm (7"). A medium-sized, entirely *black* bird with a *slender, pointed bill* and a short tail. **Similar species**: Jamaican Blackbird is smaller than Greater Antillean Grackle, which has a longer, V-shaped tail and a yellow or pale brown eye. Shiny Cowbird has a more conical bill and is not strictly arboreal. Male Jamaican Becard is stockier and has a stubbier bill.

Voice: A loud, wheezy *zwheezoo-whezoo whe*. Call note a *check* (Downer and Sutton).

Status and Range: Endemic to Jamaica where decidedly uncommon. Widely distributed, but found mostly in higher elevation forests at Newcastle, Worthy Park, Kew Park, Cockpit Country, and the Blue and John Crow Mountains. One of the most threatened of Jamaica's endemic species, its habitat is being destroyed for coffee plantations, Caribbean pine and illegal cultivation.

Comments: Exclusively arboreal, typically foraging 3–12 m (10–39') above the ground. Looks and acts like an oriole. Seeks insects alone or in pairs in the canopy among ferns and epiphytes, vigorously tossing debris. Pairs occupy large territories. Some birds move to lower elevations outside the breeding season. Jamaican Blackbird is the only member of its genus.

Habitat: Wet mountain forests. Occasionally humid woodlands at lower elevations. Confined to areas with small epiphytic bromeliads or *Phyllogonium* moss. Generally absent from slopes exposed to strong winds.

Nesting: Nest is a bulky cup of plant materials, constructed in a tree. Eggs (2) with a few spots and scrawled markings. Breeds in May and June.

EASTERN MEADOWLARK *Sturnella magna*   Plate 70
Local Name: Sabanero

Identification: 23 cm (9"). Medium-sized, with *yellow underparts* and a conspicuous *black V on the breast*. The *outer tail feathers are white*. Crown and upperparts striped. Has a distinctive call and walk.

Voice: A distinctive, high call on three different tones. Also a peculiar harsh, loud alarm note.

Status and Range: A common resident on Cuba, including the Isle of Youth. Primarily in lowlands, but also at middle and high elevations where habitat is available. Occurs through eastern North America and Central and South America.

Comments: Typically perches on fences and wires to sing and rest. Usually in pairs, but sometimes solitary. Feeds on the ground and mainly eats insects, worms, seeds, lizards and frogs, as well as small fruits. It has a peculiar strutting walk similar to a starling's. Often occurs where Northern Bobwhite or Cattle Egrets are found. Cuba hosts an endemic subspecies, *S. m. hippocrepis*.

Habitat: Open grasslands, savannas, marshes, and pastures with only scattered trees or bushes.

Nesting: The spherical nest is large and bulky, with a side entrance and hidden on the ground among bushes or tall grass. It is built of interwoven grass, straw and dead leaves and lined with rootlets, dried grass and other soft materials. Eggs (4–5) white, spotted with browns and grays, primarily at the broad end. Breeds from January to July.

YELLOW-HEADED BLACKBIRD   Plate 70
Xanthocephalus xanthocephalus

Identification: 21–28 cm (8–11"). **Adult male**: Black overall with an *orange-yellow hood* and *white wing patch*. **Adult female**: Grayish-brown above and yellowish-orange eyebrow stripe, throat, breast and line below cheek.
Status and Range: A vagrant in the Bahamas (Grand Bahama and San Salvador), Cuba and Grand Cayman in the Cayman Islands. It is widespread in central and western North America south to northern Central America.

CUBAN BLACKBIRD *Dives atroviolacea*   Plates 70, 80
Local Names: Totí, Choncholí

Identification: 25–28 cm (10–11"). A grackle-sized black bird, with glossy purplish iridescence, a *dark iris* and a *square tail*. The bill and feet are black. **Similar species**: Greater Antillean Grackle has a yellow iris and a V-shaped tail. Female Red-shouldered Blackbird is smaller in size. Male Shiny Cowbird is also smaller and has a more conspicuous sheen.
Voice: Gives a vast variety of calls; however, most typical is a loud, repetitive *tí-o*, with a metallic tone. Another frequent call is *chon-cho-lí, chon-cho-lí*. Both of these calls give rise to the bird's local names. Also a cat-like *mew* and guttural, complaining and whistling calls.
Status and Range: Endemic to Cuba where common and widespread. Does not occur on the Isle of Youth or any of the cays.
Comments: Commonly walks on the ground. Gathers in flocks, sometimes mixing with Greater Antillean Grackles and Tawny-shouldered Blackbirds. Separates into pairs during the breeding season. Both sexes are alike, but the female is slightly smaller. Although the bird looks black, in good light its feathers have a purplish metallic sheen. Omnivorous, it is a very clever forager, sometimes getting into barns and piercing chicken or cattle feed sacs to feed on the contents. Perches on top of cattle to extract ectoparasites with its tweezer-like bill. Also searches under thatched roofs and follows plows searching for grubs and other insects that are unearthed.
Habitat: Primarily gardens in urban and rural areas, but also woodlands from the lowlands to mid-elevations.
Nesting: The nest is usually built among palm fronds, bromeliads or clusters of palm nuts. It is constructed of dried grass, roots, hair, feathers, vegetable fibers and other soft materials. Eggs (3–4) white with a grayish wash and with dark spots concentrated at the wider end. Breeds from April to June.

GREATER ANTILLEAN GRACKLE *Quiscalus niger*   Plate 70
Local Names: Ching Ching (CI); Cling Cling (Jamaica, CI); Chichinguaco (Cuba); Chinchilín (DR); Mozambique, Chango (PR); Merle Diable, Mèl Diab (Haiti)

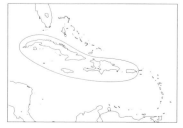

Identification: 25–30 cm (10–12"). Note its fairly large size, dark plumage, long tail and conical, sharply pointed bill. **Adult male**: Has glossy metallic-blue to violet-black plumage and a deep, *V-shaped tail*. Also has a *yellow iris*. **Adult female**: Duller than the male; tail with a smaller V; iris yellow. **Immature**: The plumage is dull brownish black; the tail is flat and the iris light brown. **Similar species**: All other blackbirds within its range lack a V-shaped tail. Male Shiny Cowbird is smaller, without a yellow iris and has a thinner bill. Yellow-shouldered and Tawny-shouldered Blackbirds are smaller with

a yellow or tan (respectively) shoulder patch. Jamaican Blackbird is smaller and has a dark eye.
Voice: Highly variable repertoire, including a high *cling, cling, cling*. Also clear, musical notes and wheezy gasps. Song a four-syllabled phrase. Call note a *chuck*.
Status and Range: A common year-round resident on Cuba (including nearby cays and the Isle of Youth), Jamaica, Hispaniola (as well as Gonâve, Tortue and Beata Islands and Île-à-Vache), Puerto Rico (including Vieques Island) and the Cayman Islands (but absent in Cayman Brac in recent years). Introduced to the Virgin Islands (St Croix) about 1917, but soon died out. These islands comprise the entire range of the species.
Comments: Typically flocks. The smaller Carib Grackle replaces Greater Antillean Grackle in the Lesser Antilles. Often forages around livestock, feeding on insects. Also forages on lawns and commonly scavenges food scraps from humans in parks and around restaurants. Roosts in large flocks and shows a decided preference for using electrical transformer substations for this purpose.
Habitat: Primarily lowlands in every type of open area, including pastures, residential zones, croplands and mangrove forest edges. Uncommon in mountains in unforested localities.
Nesting: Nests as separate pairs, in small groups and in large colonies, low in a bush or high in a tree, including palms. A bulky cup-shaped nest of grass and plant matter is lined with finer plant material. Eggs (3–4) olive-colored with darker markings of various colors. Breeds from February to September, with peaks from April to August.

CARIB GRACKLE *Quiscalus lugubris*   Plate 70
Local Names: Blackbird (Grenada, Nevis, St M); Merle (Grenada, St L); Bequia Sweet (Grenada, St V); Bilbitin, Quiscale Merle, Crédit, Merle, Cancangnan (Guad, Mart)

Identification: 24–28 cm (9.5–11"). *Adult male*: Entirely black with a violet, green or steel-blue sheen; yellowish-white iris and tail long and V-shaped. *Adult female*: Smaller than the male with amounts of glossy black varying among islands from relatively dark on Barbados to quite pale from Montserrat to Martinique. The tail is shorter and less V-shaped than the male. *Immature*: Brownish-black. *Similar species*: Male Shiny Cowbird is much smaller with a finer bill and lacks a V-shaped tail.
Voice: A squeaky pattern of three to seven syllables with a rising inflection. Also various whistles and *chuck* notes.
Status and Range: A common year-round resident on most of the Lesser Antilles from Anguilla to Grenada. Possibly introduced to the Lesser Antilles north of Montserrat, it appears to have extended its range among those islands to Anguilla, St Martin, St Barthélemy, St Christopher, Antigua and Barbuda. It also occurs on adjacent northeastern South America.
Comments: Typically flocks. Very diverse in its feeding habits and foraging strategies. The five Caribbean races have different song dialects.
Habitat: Primarily open areas in the lowlands, including pastures, open scrubland, agricultural fields and residential zones.
Nesting: Often colonial. The nest is a bulky structure of grass, plant fibers and leaves with a deep central cup and constructed in a large bushy tree or palm. Eggs (2–4) greenish-blue with black scrawls. May breed year-round, but primarily February to July.

SHINY COWBIRD *Molothrus bonariensis*   Plate 70
Local Names: Tordo (PR); Pájaro Vaquero (Cuba, DR); Merle Ste Lucie, Vacher Luisant (Mart); Merle de Barbade, Blackbird's Cousin, Corn Bird (St L)

Identification: 18–20 cm (7–8"). A medium-sized dark bird with a conical bill. *Adult male*: Uniformly glossy black with a purplish sheen. *Adult female*: Drab grayish-brown upperparts and lighter brown underparts. Has a faint eyebrow stripe. *Immature*: Resembles the adult female, but underparts are streaked with pale gray and has a light stripe above the eye. *Similar species*: Cuban Blackbird and Greater Antillean and Carib Grackles are much larger with heavier bills. Similar-sized Yellow-shouldered and Tawny-shouldered Blackbirds have a yellow or tan (respectively) shoulder patch. Jamaican Blackbird has a longer and more slender bill. Female Brown-headed Cowbird is slightly grayer than female Shiny Cowbird, has a whitish throat and lacks the faint eyebrow stripe. Male Red-winged Blackbird has a red shoulder patch. Female Red-shouldered Blackbird has a finer bill and lacks the purplish sheen of male Shiny Cowbird.

Voice: Song consists of one or more whistles, followed by a melodious trill. Also a variety of short call notes.

Status and Range: A common year-round resident through much of the West Indies. Since 1891, following widespread habitat modification, this cowbird has extended its range north from South America and Trinidad through the Lesser and Greater Antilles, reaching Barbados in 1916, Puerto Rico in the 1940s, Hispaniola in the 1970s and Cuba in the 1980s. A small population of cowbirds occurs locally in the Bahamas on Andros and there are increasingly frequent records from Jamaica where the bird was first observed in 1993. Recorded for the first time in the Cayman Islands in 1995 on Grand Cayman, a single pair of birds was seen at the north end of the island. Shiny Cowbird is not yet known to have colonized Anguilla to Guadeloupe in the northern Lesser Antilles. It is now becoming established in the southeastern United States. Native to tropical and subtropical zones of South America.

Comments: Shiny Cowbird is a brood parasite and has caused the decline of several West Indian birds, such as Puerto Rican Vireo, Yellow-shouldered Blackbird and Martinique Oriole. The first records of parasitism on Jamaica are of Jamaican Oriole.

Habitat: Primarily lowlands, but also mountains in fairly open country and woodland edges. It favors dairies and agricultural areas where grains are available.

Nesting: A nest is not built. Rather the female lays her eggs in the nests of other species to be hatched and the young are then raised by the foster parents. Eggs vary greatly in color and marking, being white, light blue or light brown in base color and unmarked to heavily speckled with reddish-brown, especially at the broad end. Breeds from March through July.

BROWN-HEADED COWBIRD *Molothrus ater*   Plate 70

Identification: 16.5 cm (6.5"). **Male**: Body black with a metallic greenish sheen and a *brown head*. **Female**: Brownish-gray. **Similar species**: The female is a bit grayer and not so brown as female Shiny Cowbird, has a whitish throat and lacks the faint eyebrow stripe.

Voice: A distinctive, harsh rattle and creaky whistles.

Status and Range: A rare non-breeding resident in the Bahamas primarily from October to February and a vagrant on Cuba. Unknown in the West Indies prior to 1960, the species has only recently expanded its range in the West Indies where it is occurring with increasing regularity. Brown-headed Cowbird has spread dramatically through the eastern United States and most recently into the West Indies by capitalizing on human transformation of the landscape from forests to fields. Occurs through most of North America.

Comments: Brown-headed Cowbird is a brood parasite, laying its eggs in the nests of other birds. If it adjusts to nesting in the subtropical climate of the West Indies, it could become a major threat to local birds as has Shiny Cowbird.

Habitat: Farms, gardens and rural areas.

BLACK-COWLED ORIOLE *Icterus dominicensis*   Plate 69

Local Names: Bahaman Oriole (Bahamas); Banana Bird (Abaco); Coconut Bird (Andros); Solibio (Cuba); Cigua Canaria (DR); Calandria, Calandria Capuchinegra (PR); Banane Mûre, Carouge, Bannann Mi Fran (Haiti)

Identification: 20–22 cm (8–8.5"). **Adult**: Black overall, with distinctive *yellow shoulders, rump and undertail-coverts* extending to the lower breast in Bahamas birds. **Immature**: Upperparts mainly olive, underparts dull yellow, wings black and throat sometimes black or reddish-brown. **Similar species**: The similarly-sized Yellow-shouldered Blackbird has only a yellow shoulder patch.

Voice: The call note is a hard, sharp *keek* or *check* sometimes sounding as if the bird has a cold. The beautiful, but rarely heard, song consisting of exclamatory and querulous high-pitched whistles is given after dawn.

Status and Range: A fairly common year-round resident on Cuba (including the Isle of Youth),

Hispaniola (including Tortue, Gonâve, Île-à-Vache and Saona) and Puerto Rico. In the northern Bahamas, this oriole occurs only on Andros where it is a common year-round resident and on Abaco where it is on the verge of extirpation. The Bahamas race is considered threatened. The cause of the bird's decline on Abaco is unknown. It is feared that the Andros population will soon succumb to the recently arrived Shiny Cowbird. It also occurs in the Gulf lowlands of southern Mexico to western Panama.

Comments: Feeds on fruits, insects, flowers and nectar, often on the undersides of palm fronds. Some populations (e.g. Cuba, Hispaniola and Puerto Rico) have been heavily exploited by the parasitic Shiny Cowbird and may be in decline. Some authorities consider the Bahamas form to be a distinct species.

Habitat: Forests, forest edges, woodlands and gardens from the coast to mid-elevations in the mountains, particularly where palms are available for nest sites.

Nesting: The nest, a finely woven basket of plant fibers, is sewn to the underside of tree leaves, particularly banana or palm fronds. Eggs (3–4) white with a blue hue, spotted. Breeds primarily from March to June, but also irregularly throughout the year.

ST LUCIA ORIOLE *Icterus laudabilis*　　　　　Plates 69, 86
Local Name: Carouge

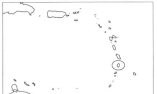

Identification: 20–22 cm (8–8.5"). ***Adult male***: Primarily black except for lower back, rump, shoulder and lower belly which are rich orange or orange-yellow. ***Adult female***: Similar to the male, but orange-yellow is duller. ***Immature***: Mostly greenish with a blackish throat.

Voice: Drawn-out series of melodic whistles.

Status and Range: Endemic to St Lucia where uncommon and becoming scarcer. It is considered threatened probably due to spraying of pesticides, habitat loss and parasitism by Shiny Cowbirds.

Habitat: Woodlands, including both moderately dry and moist forests from near sea level to about 700 m (2300'); often associated with palms.

Nesting: Constructs a hanging nest sewn to leaves or palm fronds, usually well above the ground. Eggs (2–3) white, spotted with dark brown. Breeds from April to July.

MONTSERRAT ORIOLE *Icterus oberi*　　　　　Plates 69, 72
Local Names: Tannia Bird, Blantyre Bird

Identification: 20–22 cm (8–8.5"). ***Adult male***: Mostly black above with a *yellowish lower back, rump, shoulder, lower breast, belly and abdomen*. ***Adult female***: Mainly yellowish-green above and underparts bright yellow. ***Immature***: Similar to the female, but duller.

Voice: A series of loud whistles and a harsh, scolding *chuur* call.

Status and Range: Endemic to Montserrat where rare. Found only in the Soufrière Hills and Centre Hills. Endangered due to habitat destruction, parasitism by Shiny Cowbird and the risk of hurricanes or volcanic activity destroying its limited remaining habitat. The recent eruptions of Mt Soufrière are believed to have had only a limited impact on the habitat of the oriole to date, but the volcano has not yet ceased to be active.

Comments: Contrary to most orioles, the Montserrat Oriole feeds almost exclusively on insects.

Habitat: Mountain forests between 230 m (750') and 800 m (2600') elevation.

Nesting: The basket-shaped woven nest is suspended from and sewn to leaves of a tree or palm frond. Eggs (2–4) white to pale greenish-white, sparingly but boldly spotted with brown and violet-gray. Breeds from April to July.

MARTINIQUE ORIOLE *Icterus bonana*   **Plates 69, 71**
Local Name: Carouge

Identification: 18–21 cm (7–8″). *Adult*: Mostly black with a *reddish-brown hood* and reddish-orange shoulder, rump, lower belly and abdomen.
Voice: A series of clear whistles and a harsh, scolding call.
Status and Range: Endemic to Martinique where uncommon. Most frequent in the semi-arid hills in the southern part of the island and, to a lesser extent, in moist forests in the north central part. The species has declined significantly in recent decades. It is now considered endangered primarily due to brood parasitism by Shiny Cowbirds.
Comments: Shiny Cowbird first colonized Martinique in the late 1940s and by the 1980s was parasitizing about 75 percent of known oriole nests. Clearly it can be expected to cause a further decline of this already scarce oriole. The oriole forages primarily in the canopy on a wide range of insects and a few fruits.
Habitat: Nearly all forests from mangroves and dry coastal to humid forests at higher elevations. Also plantations and gardens with trees. Absent from cloud forests.
Nesting: A pendulum-like, strongly woven nest is suspended from leaves or palm fronds from 2–4 m (7–13′) above the ground. Eggs (2–3) creamy white with a pale bluish tinge, heavily marked with brownish spots at the broad end and lightly spotted overall. Breeds from February to June.

ORCHARD ORIOLE *Icterus spurius*   **Plate 69**
Local Name: Turpial de Huertos (Cuba)

Identification: 16.5–18 cm (6.5–7″). *Adult male*: Primarily black with a *reddish-brown breast, belly, lower back and bend of wing*. *Female*: Grayish olive-green above, brighter on the head and rump and dull yellow below. Note the two white wingbars and bright olive-green tail. *Immature male*: Similar to the female, but with a black chin and throat. *Similar species*: Female Hooded Oriole has a longer, more slender, downcurved bill and a longer tail.
Status and Range: A very rare migrant on Cuba in October and again in April and May. A vagrant in the Bahamas and Jamaica. It is widespread in central and eastern North America south to northern South America.
Habitat: Woodlands and gardens.

HOODED ORIOLE *Icterus cucullatus*   **Plate 69**

Identification: 17.5 cm (7″). *Adult male*: Orangish-yellow with a black throat, breast, wings, back and tail. Two white wingbars. *Female and immature*: Olive-yellow overall; duller and darker above. Two white wingbars, the lower one less conspicuous. *Similar species*: The female and immature are distinguished from female Orchard Oriole by their longer, more slender, down-curved bills and longer tails.
Status and Range: A vagrant on Cuba where it is known from two specimens taken in the 1880s. It occurs primarily in the southwestern United States and Mexico.

TROUPIAL *Icterus icterus*   **Plate 69**
Local Names: Bugler Bird (VI); Turpial (PR)

Identification: 25 cm (9.75″). A large *orange-yellow* and *black* bird, its *extensive white wing patch* is distinctive. *Similar species*: Baltimore Oriole is smaller, has less extensive black on the breast, less white in the wing, and lacks orange on the hindneck.
Voice: A clear series of whistles *troup, troup, troup,* or *troup-ial, troup-ial, troup-ial.*
Status and Range: Believed to have been introduced widely to the West Indies long ago, the Troupial is established on Puerto Rico where it is common in the southwest, but uncommon throughout the rest of the island. The Troupial also occurs in the Virgin Islands where it is found on the south

and east coasts of St Thomas, on Water Island and on St John, where a few individuals have recently been recorded. In the Lesser Antilles, there are recent reports from Antigua, Dominica and Grenada. The birds on Antigua are likely wanderers from the Virgin Islands or escaped cagebirds. Individuals on Grenada and Dominica could possibly be stragglers from Venezuela. It is native to South America.

Comments: Occurs singly or in pairs. A very conspicuous bird, it often gives its loud, distinctive call from the top of a bush or cactus.

Habitat: Principally arid scrublands.

Nesting: Typically a deep cup-shaped nest is built among thorny scrub or cacti. Eggs (3–4) purplish-white, irregularly marked. Breeds from March to June.

JAMAICAN ORIOLE *Icterus leucopteryx*   Plate 69
Local Names: Auntie Katie, Banana Katie (Jamaica); Banana Bird (Jamaica, San Andrés)

Identification: 21 cm (8″). From *bright yellow* (Cayman Islands) to dull *greenish-yellow* (Jamaica) with a *black mask and 'bib'* and a *large, white wing patch*. **Immature**: Shows two wingbars rather than a wing patch. **Similar species**: Immature and adult female Baltimore Orioles have orange-yellow bellies and lack the large, white wing patches.

Voice: Whistled phrases of *you cheat, you cheat*. Sometimes *cheat-you*. Song (October to June) is a melodious *Auntie Atie* (Downer and Sutton).

Status and Range: A common year-round resident on Jamaica and San Andrés. The endemic race (*I. l. bairdi*) from Grand Cayman in the Cayman Islands is apparently extinct (not recorded since 1967). These islands comprise the entire range of the species.

Comments: Forages for insects, its primary food, by prying away bark, a habit not found among other birds of its genus.

Habitat: On Jamaica, found in nearly all forests, woodlands and areas with trees except mangroves, from the coast to the mountains. Also found in gardens.

Nesting: A hanging, open nest of dried bromeliad and grass stalks is attached to a tree branch. Other West Indian orioles sew their nests to leaves. Eggs (3–5) white with a few angular markings and large spots of deep brown. Breeds from March to August.

BALTIMORE ORIOLE *Icterus galbula*   Plate 69
Local Names: Turpial (Cuba); Cigua Canaria Americana (DR); Calandria del Norte (PR)

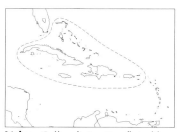

Identification: 18–20 cm (7–8″). **Adult male**: Distinguished by its medium size, *orange and black plumage*, white wingbar and *orange tail patches*. **Adult female and immature**: Brownish above and *orange-yellow below* with *two whitish wingbars*. **Similar species**: Troupial is larger and has a more extensive black bib, an orange-yellow hindneck and much more white in the wing. Jamaican Oriole is greenish-yellow, lacks the black hood and has a large, white wing patch. Female Scarlet Tanager is more greenish overall, has a stubbier bill and lacks wingbars. Male Village Weaver is chunkier with a heavier bill and shorter tail.

Voice: Call a distinctive flute-like, double-noted whistle, infrequently heard in the West Indies.

Status and Range: An uncommon migrant and rare non-breeding resident in the Bahamas, Cuba and Jamaica from September to May. Rarer on Hispaniola, Puerto Rico, the larger Virgin Islands and the Cayman Islands. A vagrant in the Lesser Antilles where recorded from St Barthélemy, St Christopher, St Lucia, Barbados, St Vincent and Grenada. It occurs from eastern Canada to northern South America.

Habitat: All elevations in gardens with trees, semi-arid scrubland, open woodlands, swamps and forest edges.

FRINGILLINE AND CARDUELINE FINCHES AND ALLIES:
FAMILY FRINGILLIDAE

The finches are characterized by a conical bill for eating seeds, although the crossbills have specialized bills for extracting seeds from pine cones. In appearance they resemble the Ploceidae, Estrildidae and the grosbeaks of the Emberizidae. The males of most species are colorful, at least during the breeding season, and many species flock following nesting. The nest is usually cup-shaped. Finches have an undulating flight.

WHITE-WINGED CROSSBILL *Loxia leucoptera*   Plate 74
Local Names: Periquito, Turquesa, Picocruzado, Pico Cruzado (DR); Bèk Kwazé, Bec-Croise, Gros Bec (Haiti)

Identification: 15 cm (5.75"). Note the *crossed tips to the bill* and *two broad, white wingbars on black wings*. **Adult male**: *Pale red overall*. **Adult female**: Yellowish rump and finely-streaked breast. **Immature**: Browner and more heavily streaked. **Voice**: A high-pitched, emphatic, often repeated *chu-chu-chu-chu*. During the breeding season, also a soft, whistling warble. **Status and Range**: An uncommon and local year-round resident in the highest mountains of Hispaniola. May be increasing in numbers on Haiti (Massif de la Hotte), but considered endangered on Hispaniola as a whole. Declining overall due to habitat destruction and brood parasitism by Shiny Cowbirds. A vagrant on Jamaica. Occcurs through northern North America and northern Eurasia.

Comments: Often quiet and secretive, but sometimes in noisy flocks, feeding on pine seeds, which it extracts from cones with its specialized bill. Breeds during colder periods of the year, as do North American populations. Recent studies suggest the Hispaniolan race (*L. l. megaplaga*) may be a distinct species. The resident status of White-winged Crossbill in the West Indies, a species typical of northern coniferous forests, supports the argument that the region was more temperate during the Pleistocene. As the West Indies warmed up during the past few thousand years, this species was 'trapped' in the last cool refugium on the islands, the high peaks of Hispaniola.

Habitat: Pine forests in high mountains.

Nesting: A deep cup-shaped nest of twigs, rootlets, weed stalks, moss, lichens and bark strips which is lined with fine grass, feathers, hair and bark shreds, and is built 2–20 m (6–70') above ground on a pine branch. Eggs (2–5) pale bluish or greenish-white, spotted or blotched with brown or purple. Breeds from December to April.

RED SISKIN *Carduelis cucullata*   Plate 73
Local Name: Cardenalito

Identification: 10 cm (4"). **Male**: Note its small size, *black hood* and extensive *orange-red coloration*. **Female**: Gray above and light gray below. Its identifying characters are its *orange rump, wing markings* and *wash on the breast*. **Voice**: A high-pitched twitter and a distinctive *chi-tit* similar to that of Warbling Silverbill. **Status and Range**: Introduced to Puerto Rico, probably in the 1930s, Red Siskin is rare and local in the area between Coamo, Ponce and Guayama. Illegal collecting threatens the population. Native to Venezuela, Colombia and Trinidad.

Comments: Typically occurs in flocks. Appears to be somewhat nomadic as it searches for food sources. Red Siskin was so heavily collected for the international pet trade in its native northern South America that it is endangered there. Illegal collecting threatens the Puerto Rican population. Red Siskin is not included in the Endangered Species List due to its status as an introduced species.

Habitat: Areas of thick scrub on dry hills.

Nesting: The nest has not yet been described on Puerto Rico. Birds have been seen carrying nesting materials in June. On Trinidad, the nest is reported to be a deep cup in a tree fork. Eggs are a pale greenish-white.

ANTILLEAN SISKIN *Carduelis dominicensis*   Plates 73, 82
Local Names: Canario, Sigüita Amarilla (DR); Petit Serin, Ti Serin (Haiti)

Identification: 11 cm (4.25"). A small, chunky bird with a light yellow bill. **Male**: Distinctive *black head* and *yellowish body;* tail black with two yellow patches. **Female**: Olive-green above and yellowish-white below, with faint pale gray streaks. Also has two yellow wingbars and a pale yellowish rump. **Similar species**: The female resembles female Village Weaver, which is larger and has a darker, more massive bill and an eyebrow stripe. Flat-billed Vireo, which is unstreaked below, has a darker, more slender bill. Female Yellow-faced Grassquit has a dark bill, lacks wingbars and has no streaks on its underparts.
Voice: A soft *chut-chut* when flushed and a higher-pitched *swee-ee*. Also a low, bubbling trill.
Status and Range: Endemic to Hispaniola where common and widespread in the mountains of the western Dominican Republic. On Haiti, a vagrant in the Massif de la Selle and uncommon, but increasing, in the Massif de la Hotte. Declining overall due to habitat destruction.
Comments: Large flocks actively forage from tree to tree and in bushes or grassy patches.
Habitat: Pine forests and associated grassy clearings and forest edges in mountains, but may wander to other habitats at lower altitudes outside the breeding season, including agricultural areas bordered by dry scrub forest
Nesting: The nest is a small mossy cup, usually in a bush or sometimes a pine. Eggs (2–3) light greenish-white, spotted with brown. Breeds in May and June.

AMERICAN GOLDFINCH *Carduelis tristis*   Plate 73

Identification: 11–12 cm (4.25–4.75"). **Non-breeding adult and immature**: Brownish or grayish above, *black wings with white wingbars*, light gray to whitish below, whitish rump and *often with some yellowish on the face*. **Breeding male**: Bright yellow overall with a *black cap, wings and tail*. **Breeding female**: Olive above, yellowish below, black wings with white wingbars and white rump.
Status and Range: A vagrant in the Bahamas (Grand Bahama, Abaco and Eleuthera) and on Cuba. Recorded from mid-October through December and also in April. It occurs from southern Canada to northern Mexico.
Habitat: Weedy fields, roadsides, thickets and second growth.

YELLOW-FRONTED CANARY *Serinus mozambicus*   Plate 74
Local Name: Verdón Cantador (PR)

Identification: 11.5 cm (4.5"). Identified by its yellowish breast, rump and eyebrow stripe, thick bill and dark mustache stripe.
Voice: A clear, whistled warble.
Status and Range: Introduced to Puerto Rico arround 1960, this finch is very rare and local along the north coast. Small numbers were recorded from Vacia Talega, Punta Mamayes and Ramey, but there are no recent records. Native to much of Africa.
Comments: Observed on the ground and in bushes and trees.

Relatively tame.
Habitat: Coastal sea grape forests.

OLD WORLD SPARROWS: FAMILY PASSERIDAE

A family of drab birds with conical finch-like bills represented in the Western Hemisphere only by introduced species.

HOUSE SPARROW *Passer domesticus*   **Plate 74**

Local Names: English Sparrow (Cuba); Gorrión (Cuba, DR); Gorrión Doméstico (DR); Gorrión Ingles (PR)

Identification: 15 cm (5.75"). *Male*: Distinguished by its *black bib, gray crown* and *pale cheek*. *Female* and *immature*: Buff-colored eyebrow stripe and underparts; brown upperparts streaked with black.
Voice: The call note is a distinctive *chirp*.
Status and Range: Introduced to the West Indies probably as an incidental passenger on grain and tour ships, the species is very common and widespread on Cuba. It is locally common in the northern Bahamas and on Great Inagua in the southern Bahamas, in all urban areas of the Dominican Republic and on Puerto Rico where it has spread in the past two decades from Ponce in the southwest to the entire coastal plain and is currently colonizing towns at high elevations. This sparrow has recolonized St Thomas and recently colonized St John in the Virgin Islands. Introduced on Jamaica in 1903, the species flourished in the 1920s, declined in the 1940s and appeared to have died out in the 1960s. However, there is a 1994 sighting from south-central Jamaica. Introduced virtually around the world. Native to Eurasia and Africa.
Comments: Primarily feeds on the ground. Typically flocks. It is extremely tame.
Habitat: Urban areas.
Nesting: Generally builds a bulky nest with a small interior cup. It nests in trees of gardens, parks and town plazas, but also on roofs or in any natural or artificial cavity in urban areas. Eggs (3–5) white with spots, speckles or small splotches of gray or brown. Breeds year-round, but primarily from March to September.

WEAVERS: FAMILY PLOCEIDAE

This is a large Eastern Hemisphere family that consists primarily of heavy-billed, seed-eating birds similar to the finches. Many species are very colorful and make popular pets. As a result of extensive importation into the Western Hemisphere, individuals of several species have escaped and become established. Ploceids generally build domed nests.

VILLAGE WEAVER *Ploceus cucullatus*   **Plate 74**

Local Names: Madam Sagá, Cigua Haitiana, Chichiguao (DR); Madame Sara (Haiti)

Identification: 17 cm (6.75"). Chunky and heavy-billed. *Male*: A distinctive *orange-yellow* overall, with a *black hood* and red iris. *Female*: Generally yellowish-green on the face and breast with yellow wingbars. *Similar species*: Adult male Baltimore Oriole is also black and orange-yellow, but is slimmer and with a longer bill and tail. Female Antillean Siskin is smaller, has a paler and less massive bill and lacks an eyebrow stripe.
Voice: A steady high-pitched chatter with musical whistling calls.
Status and Range: Introduced to Hispaniola and Saona Island where common and widespread. First discovered on Haiti in 1796, it apparently arrived during the early colonial era. Introduced to Martinique in the 1970s, it is now common very locally on the northern end of the island. Native to Africa.
Comments: Often flocks. During breeding, male performs a spread-wing, flapping display at nest, sometimes hanging head down. This is a spectacular sight when several males display simultaneously. Feeds on seeds and grain, including cultivated rice, where large flocks cause great damage. Its nest is frequently parasitized by Shiny Cowbirds.

Habitat: Mostly lowlands in rice fields, vegetation near water and open woodlands and scrub. Also plantings around human dwellings.

Nesting: In noisy colonies with up to 100 pairs in one tree. The woven spherical nest with a spout-like entrance is often in association with stinging wasps. Eggs (2–4) variable in color, ranging from light, medium or dark blue-green; lightly or moderately spotted. Breeds from December to June.

ORANGE BISHOP *Euplectes franciscanus*   **Plates 76, 77**
Local Names: Obispo Colorado (PR); Grenadier (Guad, Mart)

Identification: 12.5 cm (5"). ***Breeding male***: The *orange-red plumage* and the *black belly and crown* are distinctive. ***Female and non-breeding male***: Mottled brown above and buff-colored below with a buff-colored eyebrow stripe. The breast and crown are finely striped. ***Immature***: Like the female, but more buffy. ***Similar species***: Female and non-breeding males differ from the similarly-plumaged Yellow-crowned Bishop by the paler cheek patch; pale brown, rather than dark brown, eyeline and by the absence of yellow in the eyebrow stripe. Grasshopper Sparrow has a golden spot near the bill and a single, central whitish crown stripe.

Voice: Breeding males sing a sputtering series of *sweet* notes interspersed with a few harsh *chuck* notes while in their bobbing nuptial flight or while perched in the open.

Status and Range: Introduced to the West Indies. Introduced to Puerto Rico, probably in the 1960s, it is uncommon locally from San Juan to Arecibo. The species is rare elsewhere in the lowlands. First recorded on Martinique in 1983, Orange Bishop now breeds there and on Guadeloupe. It is uncommon and local on both islands, though flocks of 30 to 40 birds are sometimes observed. The species was recently reported for the first time from Jamaica and on St Croix in the Virgin Islands. The bird's status on both islands is unknown. Native to Africa.

Comments: Forms tight flocks outside the breeding season or when foraging away from their nesting territories. Feeds on seeds both on the ground and from grass stems. Inconspicuous outside the breeding season, but easily found when breeding males are performing territorial displays. The species is potentially a pest to rice, sorghum and other grain crops. Introduction of this species in the West Indies was likely the result of pet birds escaping or being released.

Habitat: Primarily sugarcane fields bordered by grassy edges.

Nesting: A bulky, poorly constructed spherical nest with a side entrance is built in dense cane or reeds, often near water. Eggs (2–4) glossy blue. Males may have several mates. Breeds from March to November.

YELLOW-CROWNED BISHOP *Euplectes afer*   **Plate 76**
Local Names: Golden Bishop, Napoleon Bishop (Jamaica); Napoleon Weaver, Napoleon Tejedor (PR)

Identification: 11.5–12.5 cm (4.5–5"). ***Breeding male***: Identified by its *yellow rump and crown* and entirely *black underparts*. ***Female and non-breeding male***: Mottled brown above and buff-colored below with a *yellowish eyebrow stripe* which contrasts sharply with the *dark brown eyeline*. The breast and crown are finely striped. ***Similar species***: Female and non-breeding male Orange Bishops have a paler cheek patch; a pale, rather than dark brown, eyeline and lack yellow in the eyebrow stripe. Grasshopper Sparrow has a whitish central crown stripe.

Voice: A series of *sweet* and *chuck* notes similar to the call of Orange Bishop.

Status and Range: Recently introduced, it is uncommon and very local on Puerto Rico in marshes around San Juan, at Cartagena Lagoon and east of Ponce and introduced to Jamaica at Caymanas Pond and near Hellshire sewage ponds. Native through much of Africa.

Comments: Typically flocks. Conspicuous during the breeding season when males are displaying in the reeds along pond edges. It was first reported from Puerto Rico in the 1970s and from Jamaica in 1989. Both introductions likely resulted from the escaping or release of caged pets.

Habitat: High grass and reeds near fresh water.

Nesting: The nest has not yet been found in the West Indies. Males seen defending territories in cattails of pond borders suggest breeding occurs sometime between June and October.

ESTRILDID FINCHES: FAMILY ESTRILDIDAE

This Eastern Hemisphere family of finch-like birds is represented in the West Indies only by introduced species.

ORANGE-CHEEKED WAXBILL *Estrilda melpoda*   **Plate 76**
Local Name: Veterano

Identification: 10 cm (4″). *Adult*: Note the reddish bill and uppertail-coverts and particularly the *orange cheek patch*. *Immature*: Has a pale pinkish bill, lacks the orange cheek. *Similar species*: Black-rumped Waxbill lacks the red uppertail-coverts and has a red stripe through the eye rather than an orange cheek. Immatures of both species lack diagnostic facial markings and appear similar for a brief period after fledging. However, at this stage they are usually in association with adults.

Voice: The call note is a clear *pee* singly or in a series. Flocking birds have a characteristic twittering call. The song is rarely heard and apparently is quite variable.

Status and Range: A common resident of Puerto Rico's coastal plain likely resulting from several introductions, the first coincident with the early colonial era. That introduction appears to have established this waxbill in the southwest corner of the island to which the bird was confined apparently until the 1960s. The species' abrupt expansion around the entire coastal plain in the 1970s suggests a second introduction. These new individuals were likely escaped cage birds. There are also recent records of this species from Guadeloupe and Martinique. Native to central West Africa.

Comments: Typically flocks. Feeds on seeds, primarily from grass heads. Usually forages near dense cover.

Habitat: Tall seeding grass at agricultural stations, sugarcane borders and road edges.

Nesting: A domed nest with a funneled entranceway and lined inside with fine grass is usually constructed at ground level. Eggs (3–4) white. Appears to breed from June to August.

BLACK-RUMPED WAXBILL *Estrilda troglodytes*   **Plate 76**
Local Names: Red-eared Waxbill, Veterano Orejicolorado (PR); Bengali (Guad); Astrild Cendré (Mart)

Identification: 10 cm (4″). *Adult*: The *red eyeline* is diagnostic. The bill is red; uppertail-coverts gray. *Immature*: Lacks the red eyeline and has a pale pink bill. *Similar species*: Orange-cheeked Waxbill differs by having an orange cheek patch and reddish uppertail-coverts. Immatures of both species are indistinguishable shortly after fledging. Female and non-breeding male Red Avadavats possess white wing spots and a dark, not red, eyeline.

Voice: Call notes include a *pit, cheww* or *chit-cheww*, the latter sounding like a bullet ricocheting off a rock. Also a nervous twittering call.

Status and Range: Introduced to Puerto Rico and Guadeloupe. This is a widespread, but uncommon exotic on Puerto Rico. An escapee, probably in the 1960s, it occurs spottily along the entire coastal plain. First observed on Guadeloupe in 1975, it is now locally common and has been found breeding. The species was recently introduced on Martinique where it is presumably uncommon and local. There are recent records from St Thomas in the Virgin Islands of only a few individuals. Native to central Africa.

Comments: Typically flocks. Feeds primarily by perching on grass stems and taking seeds from grass heads. Usually forages only a short distance from cover. Introduction of this species in the West Indies was likely the result of pet birds escaping or being released.
Habitat: High grass by sugarcane fields.
Nesting: The nest has not yet been found in the West Indies. Observations of young birds suggest breeding occurs around September to November.

RED AVADAVAT *Amandava amandava*   Plate 76
Local Names: Strawberry Finch, Chamorro Fresa (PR); Bengali Rouge (Guad, Mart)

Identification: 10 cm (4"). ***Breeding male***: Primarily *deep red* overall with *white spots on the wings, flanks and sides*. ***Adult female and non-breeding male***: Brown above, paler below. Note the red uppertail-coverts and bill, *white spots on the wing* and the dark eyeline. ***Immature***: Similar to the adult female, but lacks red and the wing spots are buff-colored. Immatures typically associate with adults. ***Similar species***: Female and non-breeding males are distinguished from similar Black-rumped Waxbill by the white wing spots and the nearly black, rather than red, eyeline.
Voice: The call notes are a musical *sweet* and *sweet-eet*. The species has a variety of appealing songs including melodious whistles and warbles.
Status and Range: Introduced to Puerto Rico, probably in the late 1960s, it is now locally common in the lowlands. Introduced to and recorded for the first time on Guadeloupe in l965 and on Martinique in 1970, it is now common on both islands. A flock was reported from the Dominican Republic in 1997. Native from Pakistan through South-East Asia to Indonesia.
Comments: Typically flocks. Usually feeds on the ground under tall grass, making it more difficult to observe than other small seedeaters. Its introduction in the West Indies likely resulted from pet birds escaping or being released.
Habitat: Primarily grassy margins of freshwater swamps, but also borders of sugarcane fields and along weedy drainage canals.
Nesting: The nest has not yet been found in the West Indies, but breeding apparently occurs from June to November.

WARBLING SILVERBILL *Lonchura malabarica*   Plate 76
Local Names: Indian Silverbill, Gorrion Picoplata (PR)

Identification: 11.5 cm (4.5 "). Distinguished by its overall light brown upperparts, *white underparts* and rump and dark tail. The heavy bill is bluish.
Voice: A medium strength *chit* singly or in series, but usually a quick, two-syllabled *chit-tit*. Rarely a loud, musical song.
Status and Range: Introduced to Puerto Rico, probably in the 1960s, it is common in metropolitan San Juan, occurring locally west to Dorado. It is abundant on the southwestern coast. There are recent records from the Virgin Islands (St Croix). Native to India, Sri Lanka, the Arabian Peninsula and central Africa.
Comments: Typically flocks. Tamer than most other introduced finches. Feeds on seeds on the ground, from grass heads and possibly in trees.
Habitat: Arid scrub, pastures and gardens where grass is seeding.
Nesting: A domed grass nest with a side entrance is built in a tree or on a window ledge. Eggs (4–6) white. Breeds primarily from June to November, but also in other months.

BRONZE MANNIKIN *Lonchura cucullata*   Plate 76
Local Names: Hooded Weaver, Diablito (PR)

Identification: 10 cm (4"). ***Adult***: Note the *black hood*, dark grayish-brown back and *white belly* with scalloped pattern confined to the sides and flanks. ***Immature***: The hood is either faint or lacking. The back is dark, similar to that of the adult. Lacks scalloped markings on sides. ***Similar species***:

Immature Bronze Mannikin is darker and smaller than other mannikin species.
Voice: The call note is a coarse *crrit*. There is much chattering within flocks.
Status and Range: A common resident on Puerto Rico, probably introduced during the early colonial era. A small flock was reported in the late 1970s from St Croix in the Virgin Islands. It is less common with increased elevation and is rare over 300 m (1000'). Widespread in Africa.
Comments: Typically flocks. Quite tame. Feeds on seeds both on the ground and from grass heads.
Habitat: Fields, lawns and virtually wherever grass is in seed.
Nesting: A loose, domed nest is built with an entrance hole in the side. Eggs (3) white. Breeds from March to October.

NUTMEG MANNIKIN *Lonchura punctulata* Plate 76
Local Names: Spice Finch, Gorrión Canela (PR); Capucin Damier, Capucin Ponctué (Guad)

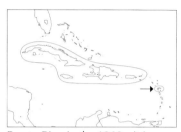

Identification: 11.5 cm (4.5"). **Adult**: The *cinnamon-colored hood* and *scalloped underparts* are diagnostic. **Immature**: Lacks adult markings. Cinnamon-colored above; paler below. **Similar species**: The immature can be confused with several other species. Its heavy, blackish bill and light cinnamon coloration distinguish it. It is not as pale below as immature Chestnut Mannikin.
Voice: A soft, plaintive, whistle *peet* dropping in pitch and fading away at the end.
Status and Range: Introduced to Cuba, Jamaica, the Dominican Republic, Puerto Rico and Guadeloupe. Introduced to Puerto Rico in the 1960s, it is common from Ceiba to Vega Baja and occurs less frequently throughout the island, though primarily in the lowlands. First recorded in the Dominican Republic in 1978 and from St Croix, Virgin Islands in the 1980s, these were likely both range expansions from Puerto Rico. Its present status in the Virgin Islands is unknown, while in the Dominican Republic, it is locally common. The species was first observed on Guadeloupe in 1984 where it now breeds and is locally common. Nutmeg Mannikin is decidedly uncommon and local on Cuba in the vicinity of Guantánamo where it is known to breed. Flocks of up to 40 birds were recently reported on Jamaica where the bird's range is expanding and includes Rio Cobre, St Catherine, Windsor and the west end. The species is uncommon and local on Martinique where it was first recorded around 1995. Native from India to southeastern Asia, Taiwan and the Philippines.
Comments: Typically flocks. Forages for seeds on the ground and from grass heads. The introduction of this species in the West Indies likely resulted from cage birds escaping or being released.
Habitat: Lowland open areas with seeding grass, such as the borders of sugarcane plantations, agricultural areas, road edges and parks in urban areas.
Nesting: A bulky, domed nest with an entrance hole in the side is built at a moderate height in a tree. Eggs (6) white. Breeds primarily from June to October.

CHESTNUT MANNIKIN *Lonchura malacca* Plate 76
Local Names: Black-headed Nun, Monja Tricolor (PR)

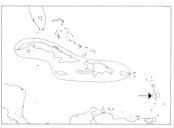

Identification: 11.5 cm (4.5"). **Adult**: The *black hood* and cinnamon-colored back are good field marks. Underparts vary from white with a black belly patch to pale brown with a black belly patch. **Immature**: Cinnamon-brown above and buffy below. **Similar species**: All immature mannikins are very similar. This species is more cinnamon-colored and has a paler bill and underparts than Nutmeg Mannikin. It is not so small and dark as Bronze Mannikin.
Voice: The call note is a thin, nasal honk *neat*, less plaintive, clear and melodious than that of Nutmeg Mannikin.
Status and Range: Introduced to Cuba, Jamaica, Hispaniola, Puerto Rico and Martinique. Introduced

to Puerto Rico probably in the 1960s, it is uncommon around the entire coast. First recorded from Hispaniola and Martinique in the 1980s and Cuba and Jamaica in the early 1990s, the species was already present in relatively large numbers when discovered on each of these islands. It is now locally common on Cuba in the southern Havana Province and at a number of localities along the south coast and on Hispaniola where it frequents agricultural areas. It is uncommon and very local on Jamaica (Caymanas and on the north coast near Priory and St Ann) and Martinique. Native from India through southeastern Asia to Taiwan, Indonesia and the Philippines.

Comments: Typically flocks. It is a potential pest to various grain crops. Forages on seeds both on the ground and from grass heads. Appears dominant to the other species of its genus where they come in contact. Introduction of this mannikin on Puerto Rico, Jamaica and Martinique was likely the result of locally escaped or released cage birds. The populations on Cuba and Hispaniola may have resulted through range expansions from the other islands.

Habitat: High grass bordering sugarcane, swampy areas, croplands with seeding grass, and canals.

Nesting: A bulky nest with a side entrance is built 1 to 3 m (3–10') in dense sugarcane. Eggs (4–5) white. Breeds primarily from June to September.

JAVA SPARROW *Padda oryzivora* Plate 76
Local Names: Java Finch, Gorrión Arrocero (PR)

Identification: 15–16.5 cm (5.75–6.5"). **Adult**: Primarily gray above and below, recognized by its broad, *pinkish-red bill, white cheek patch* and *black crown*. **Immature**: Similar to the adult, but has a duller bill, buff-colored cheeks and a brownish body.

Voice: The call note is a very hard, metallic *chink*.

Status and Range: Introduced to Puerto Rico probably in the 1950s or early 1960s, it is fairly common in the San Juan metropolitan area. The species was introduced on Jamaica around 1903 near Castleton and Thomasfield where it was recorded until 1946 and then appeared to die out. There are recent reports from Jamaica, likely a new introduction. Native to Java, Sumatra and Bali.

Comments: Typically flocks. A potential pest to grain crops. Forages primarily on the ground for seeds. Its introduction likely resulted from cagebirds escaping or being released.

Habitat: Primarily urban areas with short grass, such as athletic fields and large lawns where grass is seeding.

Nesting: The nest, usually of grass, is built in a crevice or on a window ledge. Eggs (4–6). Breeds from July to as late as February.

PIN-TAILED WHYDAH *Vidua macroura* Plate 76
Local Name: Viuda Colicinta (PR)

Identification: Breeding male: 30–33 cm (12–13"); female and non-breeding male: 11.5 cm (4.5"). **Breeding male**: The *long tail plumes, black and white coloration* and *red bill* identify it. **Female and non-breeding male**: Mottled reddish-brown above, *red bill* and *black-and-white facial stripes*. **Immature**: More grayish-brown and with a buff-colored, rather than white, eyebrow stripe. The bill is blackish, but has pinkish red at the base.

Voice: A distinctive twittering call sometimes intermixed with loud, chattering notes and plaintive whistles. The call note is an emphatic *sweet*.

Status and Range: Probably introduced in the 1960s to Puerto Rico, Pin-tailed Whydah occurs uncommonly and locally around the entire coast and, to a lesser extent, inland well into the mountains. Native to much of Africa.

Comments: Flocks outside the breeding season. Forages for seeds, primarily on the ground. Likely introduced as a result of cage birds escaping or being released.

Habitat: Lawns and fields with short grass.

Nesting: A nest is not constructed, but rather the female lays her eggs in the nests of other birds, primarily those of waxbills of the genus *Estrilda*. Breeds as early as April through November.

VAGRANTS

This list presents vagrants recorded too infrequently in the West Indies for inclusion in the species accounts. Vagrants described in the main text have been documented by a minimum of two specimens or photographs or six separate sight records.

Red-necked Grebe *Podiceps grisegena*: New Providence, Bahamas
Black-browed Albatross *Diomedea immutabilis*: Martinique
Northern Fulmar *Fulmarus glacialis*: Virgin Islands; New Providence, Bahamas
Bermuda Petrel *Pterodroma cahow*: Crooked Island, Bahamas
Herald Petrel *Pterodroma arminjoniana*: Culebra, Puerto Rico
Bulwer's Petrel *Bulweria bulwerii*: Barbados
Little Shearwater *Puffinus assimilis*: Puerto Rico
Little Bittern *Ixobrychus minutus*: Barbados
Striated Heron *Butorides striatus*: St. Vincent
White Stork *Ciconia ciconia*: Antigua; Barbuda
Jabiru *Jabiru mycteria*: Grenada
Brant *Branta bernicla*: Barbados
Garganey *Anas querquedula*: Puerto Rico; Barbados
Common Goldeneye *Bucephala clangula*: Eleuthera, Bahamas
Bald Eagle *Haliaeetus leucocephalus*: Puerto Rico; St. John, Virgin Islands
White-tailed Hawk *Buteo albicaudatus*: St. Vincent
Eurasian Kestrel *Falco tinnunculus*: Martinique
Bat Falcon *Falco rufigularis*: Grenada
Yellow Rail *Conturnicops noveboracensis*: Grand Bahama, Bahamas
Spotted Crake *Porzana porzana*: St. Martin
Collared Pratincole *Glareola pratincola*: Barbados
Common Ringed Plover *Charadrius hiaticula*: Barbados
Eurasian Curlew *Numenius arquata*: Eleuthera, Bahamas
Black-tailed Godwit *Limosa limosa*: St. Christopher
Bar-tailed Godwit *Limosa lapponica*: St. Croix, Virgin Islands
Little Stint *Calidris minuta*: Antigua; Barbados
Jack Snipe *Lymnocryptes minimus*: Barbados
Slender-billed Gull *Larus genei*: Antigua
Little Gull *Larus minutus*: Puerto Rico
Sabine's Gull *Xema sabini*: Cuba
Large-billed Tern *Phaetusa simplex*: Cuba
Common Cuckoo *Cuculus canorus*: Barbados
Dark-billed Cuckoo *Coccyzus melacoryphus*: Grenada
Long-eared Owl *Asio otus*: Cuba
White-necked Jacobin *Florisuga mellivora*: Carriacou, Grenadines; Grenada
Rufous Hummingbird *Selasphorus rufus*: Grand Bahama, Bahamas
Ruby-topaz Hummingbird *Chrysolampis mosquitus*: Grenada
Least Flycatcher *Empidonax minimus*: Grand Cayman, Cayman Islands
Indian House Crow *Corvus splendens*: Barbados
Fish Crow *Corvus ossifragus*: Grand Bahama, Bahamas
Marsh Wren *Cistothorus palustris*: Cuba
Wagtail *Motacilla* sp: Barbados
Sprague's Pipit *Anthus spragueii*: Bahamas: Grand Bahama, Eleuthera, Exuma
Loggerhead Shrike *Lanius ludovicianus*: Bahamas: Grand Bahama, Great Exuma, Andros
Yellow-Green Vireo *Vireo flavoviridis*: Providencia
Virginia's Warbler *Vermivora virginiae*: Cuba; Grand Bahama, Bahamas
Golden-cheeked Warbler *Dendroica chrysoparia*: St. Croix, Virgin Islands
Western Tanager *Piranga ludoviciana*: Cuba; New Providence, Bahamas
Swallow-Tanager *Tersina viridis*: Grand Cayman, Cayman Islands
Northern Cardinal *Cardinalis cardinalis*: Cayman Brac and Grand Cayman, Cayman Islands
Lazuli Bunting *Passerina amoena*: Cuba
Green-tailed Towhee *Pipilo chlorurus*: Cuba
Vesper Sparrow *Pooecetes gramineus*: Grand Bahama, Bahamas
Black-throated Sparrow *Amphispiza bilineata*: Andros, Bahamas
Song Sparrow *Melospiza melodia*: Bahamas: New Providence, Grand Bahama, Great Abaco; Dominican Republic
White-throated Sparrow *Zonotrichia albicollis*: Puerto Rico
Snow Bunting *Plectrophenax nivalis*: Cat Island, Bahamas
Yellow-hooded Blackbird *Agelaius icterocephalus*: Barbados
Rusty Blackbird *Euphagus carolinus*: Grand Bahama, Bahamas
Brewer's Blackbird *Euphagus cyanocephalus*: Grand Bahama, Bahamas
Common Grackle *Quiscalus quiscula*: Andros, Bahamas
Yellow-tailed Oriole *Icterus mesomelas*: Cuba
Yellow Oriole *Icterus nigrogularis*: Grenada
Black-headed Oriole *Icterus graduacauda*: Puerto Rico
Common Redpoll *Carduelis flammea*: Jamaica; Eleuthera, Bahamas

SELECTED REFERENCES: ISLAND AVIFAUNAS

Barbour, T. 1923. *The Birds of Cuba*. Memoirs of the Nuttall Ornithological Club No. IV, Cambridge.

— 1943. *Cuban Ornithology*. Memoirs of the Nuttal Ornithological Club No. IX, Cambridge.

Benito-Espinal, E. 1990. *Birds of the West Indies*. Les Editions Latanier, St Barthelemy. [Principally the French-speaking Lesser Antilles.]

Blankenship, J.R. 1990. *The Wildlife of Monserrat — Including an Annotated Bird List for the Island*. Monserrat National Trust, Montserrat.

Bradley, P. 1995. *Birds of the Cayman Islands*. (Revised edition.) Caerulea Press, Italy.

Brudenell-Bruce, P.G.C. 1975. *The Birds of the Bahamas*. Taplinger Publishing Company, New York.

Burden, D.W. 1987. *The Birds of the Southern Bahamas*. BOU Check-list No. 8. British Ornithologists' Union, London.

Clark, A.H. 1905. Birds of the Southern Lesser Antilles. *Proceedings of the Boston Society of Natural History*, Vol. 32(7): 203–312.

Devas, Fr. R.P. 1970. *Birds of Grenada, St Vincent and The Grenadines*. (Second edition.) Privately printed, Port-of-Spain, Trinidad.

Dod, A.S. 1978. *Aves de la Republica Dominicana*. Museo Nacional de Historia Natural, Santo Domingo.

Downer, A. and R. Sutton. 1990. *Birds of Jamaica — A Photographic Field Guide*. Cambridge University Press, Cambridge.

Evans, P.G.H. 1990. *Birds of the Eastern Caribbean*. Macmillan Education Ltd., London.

Garrido, O. and A. Kirkconnell (in prep.) *Birds of Cuba*.

Hilder, P. 1989. *The Birds of Nevis*. Nevis Historical and Conservation Society. Charlestown, Nevis.

Hutt, M.B., H.F. Hutt, P.A. Buckley, F.G. Buckley, E.B. Massiah and M.D. Frost (in press). *The Birds of Barbados*. BOU Check-list. British Ornithologists' Union, London.

Keith, A.R. 1997. *The Birds of St Lucia, West Indies*. BOU Check-list No. 15. British Ornithologists' Union, London.

Lack, D. 1976. *Island Biology — Illustrated by the Land Birds of Jamaica*. Studies in Ecology —Volume 3. University of California Press, Berkeley and Los Angeles.

Pinchon, Fr. R. 1976. *Faune des Antilles Françaises — Les Oiseaux*. (Second edition.) Privately printed, Fort-de-France, Martinique.

Raffaele, H.A. 1989. *A Guide to the Birds of Puerto Rico and the Virgin Islands*. Princeton University Press, Princeton.

Siegel, A. 1983. *Birds of Montserrat*. Montserrat National Trust, Montserrat.

Voous, K.H. 1983. *Birds of the Netherlands Antilles*. De Walburg Press, Curaçao. (English version.)

Wetmore, A. and B.H. Swales. 1931. *The Birds of Haiti and the Dominican Republic*. Smithsonian Institution, US National Museum, Bulletin 155. Washington, DC.

White, A. W. (in prep.) *Birders Guide to the Bahamas and Turks & Caicos*.

SELECTED REFERENCES: BIRD FAMILY AND REGIONAL IDENTIFICATION GUIDES

Adolfsson, K. and S. Cherrug. 1995. Bird Identification — A Reference Guide. *Anser*, Supplement 37 (379 pp.). Lund, Sweden.

Alström, P. and P. Colston. 1991. *A Field Guide to the Rare Birds of Britain and Europe*. HarperCollins, London.

Byers, C., J. Curson and U. Olsson. 1995. *A Guide to the Sparrows and Buntings of North America and the World*. Houghton Mifflin Company, Boston.

Chantler, P. and G. Driessens. 1995. *Swifts — A Guide to the Swifts and Treeswifts of the World*. Pica Press, Sussex.

Clement, P. 1993. *Finches and Sparrows —– An Identification Guide*. A & C Black, London.

Curson, J., D. Quinn and D. Beadle. 1994. *New World Warblers — An Identification Guide*. A & C Black, London.

Grant, P. J. 1986. *Gulls — A Guide to Identification*. Buteo Books, Vermillion, South Dakota.

Harris, A., L. Tucker and K. Vinicombe. 1993. *The Macmillan Field Guide to Bird Identification*. Macmillan Press, London.

Hayman, P., J. Marchant and T. Prater. 1986. *Shorebirds — An Identification Guide to the Waders of the World*. A & C Black, London.

Howell, S. N.G. and S. Webb. 1995. *A Guide to the Birds of Mexico and Northern Central America*. Oxford University Press, Oxford.

Jonsson, L. 1993. *Birds of Europe with North Africa and the Middle East*. A & C Black, London.

Kaufman, K. 1990. *A Field Guide to Advanced Birding*. Houghton Mifflin Company, Boston.

Olsen, K. M. and H. Larsson. 1995. *Terns of Europe and North America*. A & C Black, London.

Rising, J. D. 1996. *A Guide to the Identification and Natural History of the Sparrows of the United States and Canada*. Academic Press, London.

Rosair, D. and D. Cottridge. 1995. *Photographic Guide to the Waders of the World*. Hamlyn, London.

Turner, A. and C. Rose. 1989. *A Handbook to the Swallows and Martins of the World*. A & C Black, London.

Wheeler, B. K. and W. S. Clark. 1995. *A Photographic Guide to North American Raptors*. Academic Press, London.

LOCALITY CHECKLIST

This checklist presents the status of each bird species by island or island group. Status categories are consolidated for simplicity from those used in the main text:

C = Common or Fairly Common — one or more seen daily
U = Uncommon — not seen on every trip, but seen at least twice per year
R = Rare — occurs less than twice per year, but with at least one record every five years
V = Very Rare or Vagrant — occurs less frequently than once every five years
E = Extinct or Extirpated
? = Status Uncertain

Islands are presented generally from northwest to southeast. Their codes are:

BAH	=	Bahamas
T/C	=	Turks and Caicos
CUB	=	Cuba
CAY	=	Cayman Islands
JAM	=	Jamaica
HIS	=	Hispaniola
PR	=	Puerto Rico
VI	=	Virgin Islands
ANG	=	Anguilla
ST M	=	St Martin
ST B	=	St Barthélemy
SABA	=	Saba
ST E	=	St Eustacius
ST C	=	St Christopher and Nevis
A/B	=	Antigua and Barbuda
MON	=	Montserrat
GUA	=	Guadeloupe
DOM	=	Dominica
MAR	=	Martinique
ST L	=	St Lucia
BDS	=	Barbados
ST V	=	St Vincent and the Grenadines
GRE	=	Grenada
PRO	=	Providencia
ST A	=	San Andrés

SPECIES OF BIRD	BAH	T/C	CUB	CAY	JAM	HIS	PR	VI	ANG	ST M	ST B	SABA	ST E
Common Loon			V										
Least Grebe	C	C	C	R	C	U	U	R					
Pied-billed Grebe	C	C	C	C	C	C	C	U	U	R	C		
Black-capped Petrel	R		V	V	V	R	V	V					
Jamaican Petrel					E?								
Cory's Shearwater	U		V										
Greater Shearwater	U			V		V	U	V					
Sooty Shearwater	R		V		V		V						
Manx Shearwater			V			V	V						
Audubon's Shearwater	C	U	R		V	R	U	U		U	R	C	U
Wilson's Storm-Petrel	U		R			U	R	R		R	V	R	
Leach's Storm-Petrel	R		R			V	R	R			V	R	
Band-rumped Storm-Petrel			V										
White-tailed Tropicbird	C	C	R	C	C	C	C	C	U	U	C	C	U
Red-billed Tropicbird			V		V	V	U	C	U	U		C	U
Masked Booby	V	V	V	V	R	V	R	R	U	V	V	V	
Brown Booby	C	U	U	C	C	C	C	C	C	U	C	U	U
Red-footed Booby	R		V	C	V	R	U	U	R	V		V	V
Northern Gannet	V	V	V										
American White Pelican	V		V	V	V		V			V			
Brown Pelican	C	C	C	U	C	C	C	C	C	U	C	R	C
Double-crested Cormorant	C	V	C	R	V	R	V	V		V			
Neotropic Cormorant	C	U	C		V		V	V			V		
Anhinga	V		C	V	V	V							
Magnificent Frigatebird	C	C	C	C	C	C	C	C	C	U	C	C	U
American Bittern	U	V	U	V	V	V	V	V					

SPECIES OF BIRD	ST C	A/B	MON	GUA	DOM	MAR	ST L	BDS	ST V	GRE	PRO	ST A
Common Loon												
Least Grebe				V								
Pied-billed Grebe		C	R	R	V	R	V	U	V	R		R
Black-capped Petrel					R							
Jamaican Petrel												
Cory's Shearwater		V		V		V		V				
Greater Shearwater				R	V	R	V	R				
Sooty Shearwater						V	V	V				
Manx Shearwater									V			
Audubon's Shearwater	V	V	V	R	V	R	V	R	R	R		
Wilson's Storm-Petrel		V		R		R		U	R	R		
Leach's Storm-Petrel		V		R		R		R				
Band-rumped Storm-Petrel		V										
White-tailed Tropicbird	R	V	U		U		U	R	R	R		
Red-billed Tropicbird	R	C	U	U	R	U	U	R	R	R		
Masked Booby	V	R		V	V	V	V	R	V	V		
Brown Booby	C	C	C	C	C	C	C	U	C	C		
Red-footed Booby		V	V	R	V	V	R	R	R	R		
Northern Gannet												
American White Pelican												
Brown Pelican	C	C	C	U	U	R	R	R	R	U	R	R
Double-crested Cormorant												
Neotropic Cormorant					V							
Anhinga							V			V		
Magnificent Frigatebird	C	C	C	C	C	C	C	C	C	C		U
American Bittern			V	V		V		V				

SPECIES OF BIRD	BAH	T/C	CUB	CAY	JAM	HIS	PR	VI	ANG	ST M	ST B	SABA	ST E
Least Bittern	U	R	C	C	C	U	C	V					
Great Blue Heron	C	U	C	C	C	C	C	C	U	R	R		
Gray Heron													
Great Egret	C	C	C	C	C	C	C	U	U	R	C	V	
Little Egret							V						
Snowy Egret	C	C	C	C	C	C	C	C	U	R	C	V	V
Western Reef-Heron							V						
Little Blue Heron	C	U	C	C	C	C	C	C	U	U	C	R	R
Tricolored Heron	C	C	C	C	C	C	C	C	R	R	R		
Reddish Egret	C	C	C	U	U	R	V			V			
Cattle Egret	C	C	C	C	C	C	C	C	C	C	C	C	C
Green Heron	C	C	C	C	C	C	C	C	C	C	C	U	U
Black-crowned Night-Heron	U	U	U	U	U	R	U	U	R	V	R		
Yellow-crowned Night-Heron	C	C	C	C	C	C	C	C	U	R	C	U	U
White Ibis	R		C	R	U	C	V						
Scarlet Ibis			V		V								
Glossy Ibis	U	R	U	R	U	U	R	V					
Roseate Spoonbill	C	R	U	V	V	U	V	V		V	V		
Wood Stork	V		R		V	V							
Greater Flamingo	C	C	C	V	R	C	R	V		V			
Fulvous-Whistling Duck	R	R	C	R	V	C	U	V			R		
West Indian Whistling-Duck	U	U	C	U	R	U	R	R					
White-faced Whistling-Duck			V			V							
Black-bellied Whistling-Duck	V		V	V	V		V	V			V		
Tundra Swan			V				V	V					
Greater White-fronted Goose			V										
Orinoco Goose					V								

456

SPECIES OF BIRD	ST C	A/B	MON	GUA	DOM	MAR	ST L	BDS	ST V	GRE	PRO	ST A
Least Bittern				U	R			V				
Great Blue Heron	U	U	V	U	U	U	U	C	U	U		
Gray Heron			V			V		V				
Great Egret	U	C	U	C	U	U	U	C	U	R	U	U
Little Egret				V		V	R	U				
Snowy Egret	U	C	R	C	U	C	U	C	U	R		U
Western Reef-Heron							V	V				
Little Blue Heron	U	C	R	U	C	U	C	C	C	U	C	U
Tricolored Heron		U		R	R	R	V	U	V			C
Reddish Egret		V	V		V							
Cattle Egret	C	C	C	C	C	C	C	C	C	C	C	C
Green Heron	U	C	U	C	C	C	C	C	C	C	U	U
Black-crowned Night-Heron		U		R	V	R	U	U	R	R		
Yellow-crowned Night-Heron	C	C	U	R	U	R	U	U	U	U	C	U
White Ibis					V							
Scarlet Ibis					V					V		
Glossy Ibis	V	V	R	V	V	V	V	R				R
Roseate Spoonbill				V								
Wood Stork					V							
Greater Flamingo	V	E										
Fulvous-Whistling Duck	V	R		V	V	V	V	R	V	V		
West Indian Whistling-Duck	V	R			V	V		V		V		
White-faced Whistling-Duck								V				
Black-bellied Whistling-Duck				V	V	V	V	R	V	V		
Tundra Swan		V										
Greater White-fronted Goose												
Orinoco Goose								V				

SPECIES OF BIRD	BAH	T/C	CUB	CAY	JAM	HIS	PR	VI	ANG	ST M	ST B	SABA	ST E
Snow Goose	R		R				V	V					
Canada Goose	V	V	V	V	V	V	V						
Wood Duck	R		U	V	V	V	V			V		V	
Green-winged Teal	U	R	R	R	R	R	R	R			R		
American Black Duck	V	V					V						
Mallard	V	V	V	V	V	V	V	V			V		
White-cheeked Pintail	C	C	C	V	V	U	U	C	U	R	U		
Northern Pintail	R	U	U	V	V	U	U	R		V	R		
Blue-winged Teal	C	C	C	C	C	C	C	C	C	R	C		
Cinnamon Teal	V		V		V		V	V					
Northern Shoveler	U	U	C	U	R	U	U	V			V		
Gadwall	R	R	V		V	V							
Eurasian Wigeon						V	V						
American Wigeon	U	U	C	U	R	C	U	U	R	V	R		
Canvasback	V		V		V	V	V						
Redhead	V	V	V		V	V							
Ring-necked Duck	C	R	C	V	U	U	U	U			R		
Greater Scaup	V				V			V					
Lesser Scaup	C	U	C	U	U	U	U	R	R		U		
Bufflehead	V		V		V		V						
Hooded Merganser	V	V	V			V	V	V					
Red-breasted Merganser	V		V	V		V	V						
Ruddy Duck	U	C	C	V	C	C	C	R					
Masked Duck	V	V	C	V	U	U	R	V					
Black Vulture	V		V		V								
Turkey Vulture	C		C	R	C	C	C	V					
Osprey	C	C	C	C	C	C	C	C	U	U	U	R	U
Hook-billed Kite													
Cuban Kite			V										

SPECIES OF BIRD	ST C	A/B	MON	GUA	DOM	MAR	ST L	BDS	ST V	GRE	PRO	ST A
Snow Goose								V				
Canada Goose												
Wood Duck												
Green-winged Teal	V	V	V	V	V	V	V	R	V			
American Black Duck												
Mallard		V		V		V			V			
White-cheeked Pintail	V	C		V		V		R				
Northern Pintail		V		V		V	V	R	V			
Blue-winged Teal	U	C	U	U	U	U	C	C	U	U		R
Cinnamon Teal		V						V				
Northern Shoveler		U		R	V	R	V	U	V			
Gadwall				V			V					
Eurasian Wigeon		V						V				
American Wigeon		V		R	R	R	V	R				
Canvasback		V										
Redhead								V				
Ring-necked Duck				V		V	V	R				R
Greater Scaup								V				
Lesser Scaup	V	V		V	U	V	V	R				R
Bufflehead												
Hooded Merganser						V		V				
Red-breasted Merganser												
Ruddy Duck	V	V		V			V	R	V	V		
Masked Duck		V		R	V	R	U	R				
Black Vulture										V		
Turkey Vulture												
Osprey	R	U		U	U	U	U	U	U	U		
Hook-billed Kite										R		
Cuban Kite												

459

SPECIES OF BIRD	BAH	T/C	CUB	CAY	JAM	HIS	PR	VI	ANG	ST M	ST B	SABA	ST E
Swallow-tailed Kite	V		R	V	V								
Snail Kite			C										
Northern Harrier	U	U	U	R	V	U	U	R	R	R			
Sharp-shinned Hawk	U	R	C		V	C	C	V					
Gundlach's Hawk			R										
Common Black-Hawk			C				V						
Ridgway's Hawk						C	V						
Broad-winged Hawk			C		V		R						
Red-tailed Hawk	C	R	C		C	C	C	C		E	C	C	R
Crested Caracara			R		V								
American Kestrel	C	C	C	C	C	C	C	C	U	R	C	C	U
Merlin	C	C	U	U	U	U	U	U	R	U	U	R	R
Peregrine Falcon	U	U	U	U	U	U	U	U	R	V	U		
Rufous-vented Chachalaca													
Red Junglefowl						R	R						
Ring-necked Pheasant	C		C				V	V					
Common Peafowl	C												
Crested Bobwhite													
Northern Bobwhite	C		C			U	R	R					
Helmeted Guineafowl			R			C	R	R		R			
Black Rail	V		R		V	R	V						
Clapper Rail	C	C	C		C	C	C	C					
King Rail			C		V								
Virginia Rail	R		V				V						
Uniform Crake					E								
Sora	C	R	C	U	U	U	U	U	U	V	R		
Yellow-breasted Crake			U		U	R	U						
Zapata Rail			R										

SPECIES OF BIRD	ST C	A/B	MON	GUA	DOM	MAR	ST L	BDS	ST V	GRE	PRO	ST A
Swallow-tailed Kite												
Snail Kite												
Northern Harrier		V		V	R	V	V	R		?		
Sharp-shinned Hawk												
Gundlach's Hawk												
Common Black-Hawk							V		U	V		
Ridgway's Hawk												
Broad-winged Hawk	U	C			C	C	C	V	C	U		
Red-tailed Hawk	C		R	V			V	E				
Crested Caracara												
American Kestrel	C	U	C	C	C	C	U	V	R	R		R
Merlin	V	V		R	R	R	U	R	R	R	U	U
Peregrine Falcon	V	R	R	R	R	R	R	R	R	R		
Rufous-vented Chachalaca									U			
Red Junglefowl									R			
Ring-necked Pheasant												
Common Peafowl												
Crested Bobwhite									?			
Northern Bobwhite												
Helmeted Guineafowl	R	R										
Black Rail		V										
Clapper Rail	R	C		R		R		V				
King Rail												
Virginia Rail												
Uniform Crake												
Sora	R	U	R	R	R	R	R	U	R	R		R
Yellow-breasted Crake												
Zapata Rail												

SPECIES OF BIRD	BAH	T/C	CUB	CAY	JAM	HIS	PR	VI	ANG	ST M	ST B	SABA	ST E
Spotted Rail			R		V	R							
Purple Gallinule	R	R	C	U	U	C	U	V			R		
Common Moorhen	C	C	C	C	C	C	C	C	C	U	C	V	
American Coot	C	C	C	C	C	C	C	U	R		U		
Caribbean Coot			V		R	U	U	R	U	R	R		
Limpkin	C	R	C		C	U	E						
Sandhill Crane			R										
Double-striped Thick-Knee						U							
Northern Lapwing	V						V						
Black-bellied Plover	C	C	C	C	C	C	C	C	U	U	C	V	
American Golden-Plover	R	U	R	R	V	R	R	R	R	V	V		V
Pacific Golden-Plover													
Collared Plover										V			
Snowy Plover	C	C	V	V	V	C	U	U	C	U	U		
Wilson's Plover	C	C	C	U	C	C	C	C	R	C	C		
Semipalmated Plover	C	C	U	C	C	C	C	C	U	U	C		
Piping Plover	C	R	R		R	R	R	R					
Killdeer	C	C	C	U	C	C	C	U	R	U	C		R
American Oystercatcher	C	C	R		V	R	C	C	R	R	R		
Black-necked Stilt	C	C	C	C	C	C	C	C	U	C	C		
American Avocet	V	V	V	V	V		V	V					
Northern Jacana			C		C	C	V						
Common Greenshank							V						
Greater Yellowlegs	C	C	C	C	C	C	C	C	U	U	C		
Lesser Yellowlegs	C	C	C	C	C	C	C	C	U	U	C	V	
Spotted Redshank													
Wood Sandpiper													
Solitary Sandpiper	U	U	C	U	R	C	C	U	U	U	C		
Willet	C	C	C	C	C	C	C	U	R	U	C		

SPECIES OF BIRD	ST C	A/B	MON	GUA	DOM	MAR	ST L	BDS	ST V	GRE	PRO	ST A
Spotted Rail												
Purple Gallinule		V	R	R	V	R	V	R	V			U
Common Moorhen	C	C	C	C	U	C	U	C	R	R		U
American Coot	V	V		R		R		V	V	V		U
Caribbean Coot	R	R	U	R	R	R	R	R	R	R		
Limpkin												
Sandhill Crane												
Double-striped Thick-Knee												
Northern Lapwing						V		V				
Black-bellied Plover	U	C	R	C	R	C	C	C	U	U		U
American Golden-Plover	V	R	R	U	R	U	R	C	R	R		
Pacific Golden-Plover								V				
Collared Plover	V						V	R	?	U		
Snowy Plover	R	V		V				V				
Wilson's Plover	C	C	R	R		V		R	U	R		
Semipalmated Plover	C	U	R	C	U	C	C	C	U	U		U
Piping Plover	V	V						V				
Killdeer	V	R	R	R	V	V	V	U	V	V		U
American Oystercatcher	V	V		R		V	V	R				
Black-necked Stilt	R	C	U	U	R	R	V	R	V	V		
American Avocet		V						V				
Northern Jacana												
Common Greenshank								V				
Greater Yellowlegs	U	U	U	C	U	C	C	C	U	U		R
Lesser Yellowlegs	U	C	U	C	C	C	C	C	U	U		U
Spotted Redshank								V				
Wood Sandpiper								R				
Solitary Sandpiper	U	U	R	U	C	U	R	U	R	R		
Willet	R	U	R	C	R	C	R	U	V	R	C	U

463

SPECIES OF BIRD	BAH	T/C	CUB	CAY	JAM	HIS	PR	VI	ANG	ST M	ST B	SABA	ST E
Spotted Sandpiper	C	C	C	C	C	C	C	C	U	U	C	V	V
Upland Sandpiper	R	V	V	V	V		R	V		V	R		
Eskimo Curlew							V						
Whimbrel	R	U	V	R	U	R	R	V	U	R	C		
Long-billed Curlew			V		V		V	V					
Hudsonian Godwit	V	V	V			V	V	V		V	V		
Marbled Godwit			V	V	V	V	V	V					
Ruddy Turnstone	C	C	C	C	C	C	C	C	C	C	C		V
Red Knot	R	R	R	R		R	U	R	R		R		
Sanderling	C	C	U	C	C	C	C	R	U	U	R		R
Semipalmated Sandpiper	C	C	C	C	C	C	C	U	U	U	C		V
Western Sandpiper	U	C	U	R	C	U	C	R		R	C		
Least Sandpiper	C	C	C	C	C	C	C	C	U	R	C	V	
White-rumped Sandpiper	R	U	R	C	U	R	U	U	R	V	U		
Baird's Sandpiper				V				V					
Pectoral Sandpiper	U	U	R	U	U	U	C	C	R	R	C		
Dunlin	R	R	V	V	V		V	V					
Curlew Sandpiper							V	V					
Stilt Sandpiper	U	C	U	U	U	C	C	C	U	U	R		
Buff-breasted Sandpiper	V		V		V	V	V	V			V		
Ruff					V		V	V					
Short-billed Dowitcher	C	C	U	C	C	U	C	U	U	R	R	V	
Long-billed Dowitcher		V	V	R	V			V					
Common Snipe	C	C	C	U	U	C	U	U	U	U	U		
Wilson's Phalarope	V			R	V	V	V	V					
Red-necked Phalarope	V		V		V	V	V						
Red Phalarope			V					V					
Pomarine Jaeger	U		V			R	V	V		R	R		
Parasitic Jaeger	R		V		V	R		V					
Long-tailed Jaeger	V		V	V	V	V							

SPECIES OF BIRD	ST C	A/B	MON	GUA	DOM	MAR	ST L	BDS	ST V	GRE	PRO	ST A
Spotted Sandpiper	C	C	U	C	C	C	C	C	U	U	U	U
Upland Sandpiper			R	R	R			R	V	V		
Eskimo Curlew				V				V	V	V		
Whimbrel	R	C	R	U	U	U	U	U	R	R		U
Long-billed Curlew		V										
Hudsonian Godwit		V		V	V	V	V	U				
Marbled Godwit	V			V		V		V	V	V		
Ruddy Turnstone	C	C	R	C	U	C	C	C	U	U		C
Red Knot	R	U	R	V	V	V	V	C		V		
Sanderling	C	U	R	U	U	U	U	C	U	U		C
Semipalmated Sandpiper	C	C	R	C	C	C	U	C	U	U		C
Western Sandpiper	R	R		U	R	U	R	C	U	R		U
Least Sandpiper	C	U	R	C	R	C	R	C	R	R		C
White-rumped Sandpiper	R	R	R	U	R	U	R	U	V			
Baird's Sandpiper					V		V	V	V			
Pectoral Sandpiper	U	R	R	U	U	U	R	C	R	R		
Dunlin	V				V			V				
Curlew Sandpiper		V			V			V	V	V		
Stilt Sandpiper	U	C		U	R	U	R	U	R	R		
Buff-breasted Sandpiper		V		V			V	R	V	V		
Ruff		V	V	V			V	R	V	V		
Short-billed Dowitcher	R	U	R	U	R	U	R	C	R	R		
Long-billed Dowitcher	V							R				
Common Snipe	V	U		U	U	U	U	U	V	R		
Wilson's Phalarope		V		V		V		V		V		
Red-necked Phalarope												
Red Phalarope		V										
Pomarine Jaeger		V		U	R	U	V	R	V			
Parasitic Jaeger				R	V	R		R	V	V	V	
Long-tailed Jaeger				V	V	V		V				

SPECIES OF BIRD	BAH	T/C	CUB	CAY	JAM	HIS	PR	VI	ANG	ST M	ST B	SABA	ST E
Skua			V				V	V			V		
Laughing Gull	C	C	C	C	C	C	C	C	C	C	C	R	C
Franklin's Gull						V	V				V		
Black-headed Gull	V	V	V				R	R					
Bonaparte's Gull	U	R	U			V	V						
Ring-billed Gull	C	U	R	U	R	R	C	R	R	R	R		
Herring Gull	U	U	U	U	R	R	R	R		V	V	V	
Lesser Black-backed Gull	V						V	V		V	V		
Great Black-backed Gull	V		V			V	R				V		
Black-legged Kittiwake	V		V		V	V		V					
Gull-billed Tern	U	U	R	R	R	U	U	U	U	V	R		
Caspian Tern	R	R	R	V	R	R	V	V					
Royal Tern	C	C	C	C	C	C	C	C	C	C	C	R	C
Sandwich Tern	C	C	C	V	C	U	U	U	U	U	U		V
Roseate Tern	U	R	R		R	U	U	C	U	U	U	R	
Common Tern	R	U	R	R	V	U	C	U	U	R	U	R	
Arctic Tern			V				R	V					
Forster's Tern	R		R	R		V	V	V					
Least Tern	C	C	C	C	C	C	U	U	U	C	U		R
Bridled Tern	C	C	C	R	U	C	C	C	C	U	U	R	R
Sooty Tern	C	C	C	R	C	C	C	C	C	U	C	R	R
Whiskered Tern													
White-winged Tern	V							V					
Black Tern	R	R	R	V	C	R	C	V					
Brown Noddy	C	C	C	V	C	C	C	C	C	C	C	C	
Black Noddy							V	V	V				
Black Skimmer	V	V	V	V	V	V	V	V					
Dovekie	V	V	V										
Rock Dove	C	C	C	C	C	C	C	C	C	C	C	C	C
Scaly-naped Pigeon			U	V	C	C	C	C	C	R	C	C	R
White-crowned Pigeon	C	C	C	U	C	C	C	C	U	R	U	V	V

SPECIES OF BIRD	ST C	A/B	MON	GUA	DOM	MAR	ST L	BDS	ST V	GRE	PRO	ST A
Skua				V								
Laughing Gull	C	C	U	C	C	C	U	C	C	C		U
Franklin's Gull				V								
Black-headed Gull		V		R			V	R		V		
Bonaparte's Gull		V				V		R				
Ring-billed Gull	V	V		R	R	R	V	U	V			
Herring Gull	V			V	R	V	V	R				
Lesser Black-backed Gull		V						R				
Great Black-backed Gull									V			
Black-legged Kittiwake				V			V					
Gull-billed Tern		U		R	R	R	V	R	V			
Caspian Tern	V	V			V	V	V	R				
Royal Tern	C	C	U	C	C	C	U	C	U	C		C
Sandwich Tern	V	C		U	R	U	R	U	R	R		
Roseate Tern	R	U		U	U	U	U	U	R	U		
Common Tern	R	U	R	U	R	U	R	U	R	R		
Arctic Tern												
Forster's Tern		V	V						V			
Least Tern	U	C		U	R	U	V	U	V	V		
Bridled Tern	R	R	R	C	U	C	C	C	U	U		
Sooty Tern	R	U		C	R	C	C	C	U	U		
Whiskered Tern								V				
White-winged Tern								V				
Black Tern		U		V	V			U	V	V		
Brown Noddy	R	C	U	C	U	C	C	U	C	C		
Black Noddy								V				
Black Skimmer										V		
Dovekie												
Rock Dove	U	C	C	C	C	C	C	U	C	C		
Scaly-naped Pigeon	U	R	C	C	C	C	C	C	C	C		
White-crowned Pigeon	V	C		R	V	V	V		V		C	C

SPECIES OF BIRD	BAH	T/C	CUB	CAY	JAM	HIS	PR	VI	ANG	ST M	ST B	SABA	ST E
Plain Pigeon			R		R	C	R						
Ring-tailed Pigeon					C								
Eurasian Collared-Dove	C		C	C									
Spotted Dove								?					
White-winged Dove	C	C	C	C	C	C	U	R				V	
Zenaida Dove	C	C	C	C	C	C	C	C	C	C	C	C	C
Eared Dove													
Mourning Dove	C	C	C	C	C	C	C						
Passenger Pigeon			E										
Common Ground-Dove	C	C	C	C	C	C	C	C	C	C	C	C	C
Grenada Dove													
Caribbean Dove	U			U	C								
Key West Quail-Dove	C	U	C			C	U						
Bridled Quail-Dove							V	U			C	R	R
Gray-headed Quail-Dove			U			R							
Ruddy Quail-Dove			C		C	C	C	V					
Crested Quail-Dove					C								
Blue-headed Quail-Dove			R										
Budgerigar				R			V						
Monk Parakeet				U			C	V					
Black-hooded Parakeet							R						
Hispaniolan Parakeet						C	V						
Cuban Parakeet			C										
Olive-throated Parakeet					C								
Orange-fronted Parakeet							U						
Brown-throated Parakeet							?	C				U	
Cuban Macaw			E										

SPECIES OF BIRD	ST C	A/B	MON	GUA	DOM	MAR	ST L	BDS	ST V	GRE	PRO	ST A
Plain Pigeon												
Ring-tailed Pigeon												
Eurasian Collared-Dove	V		V	C	V	C						
Spotted Dove												
White-winged Dove											C	C
Zenaida Dove	C	C	C	C	C	C	C	C	U	C		
Eared Dove						V	C	R	C	C		
Mourning Dove												
Passenger Pigeon												
Common Ground-Dove	C	C	C	C	C	C	C	C	C	C		
Grenada Dove									V			
Caribbean Dove												C
Key West Quail-Dove												
Bridled Quail-Dove	U	R	U	U	R	U	R					
Gray-headed Quail-Dove												
Ruddy Quail-Dove		U		U	U	U	U		U	U		
Crested Quail-Dove												
Blue-headed Quail-Dove												
Budgerigar				V								
Monk Parakeet				R								
Black-hooded Parakeet												
Hispaniolan Parakeet												
Cuban Parakeet												
Olive-throated Parakeet												
Orange-fronted Parakeet												
Brown-throated Parakeet				V	U	V						
Cuban Macaw												

SPECIES OF BIRD	BAH	T/C	CUB	CAY	JAM	HIS	PR	VI	ANG	ST M	ST B	SABA	ST E
Green-rumped Parrotlet					C								
Canary-winged Parakeet						V	C						
Rose-throated Parrot	C		C	C									
Yellow-billed Parrot					C								
Hispaniolan Parrot						C	C						
Puerto Rican Parrot							R						
Black-billed Parrot					C								
Red-crowned Parrot							R						
Orange-winged Parrot							U						
Yellow-headed Parrot							R						
Red-necked Parrot													
St Lucia Parrot													
St Vincent Parrot													
Imperial Parrot													
Black-billed Cuckoo	V		R	V	V	R	V						
Yellow-billed Cuckoo	C	C	C	U	U	C	C	R	R	R	R		R
Mangrove Cuckoo	C	C	U	U	C	C	C	C	C	R	C	V	
Great Lizard-Cuckoo	U		C										
Puerto Rican Lizard-Cuckoo							C	V					
Hispaniolan Lizard-Cuckoo	`					C							
Jamaican Lizard-Cuckoo					C								
Chestnut-bellied Cuckoo					C								
Bay-breasted Cuckoo						R							
Smooth-billed Ani	C	C	C	C	C	C	C	C				V	R
Barn Owl	U	U	C	U	C	C	V						
Ashy-faced Owl						C							

SPECIES OF BIRD	ST C	A/B	MON	GUA	DOM	MAR	ST L	BDS	ST V	GRE	PRO	ST A
Green-rumped Parrotlet								R				
Canary-winged Parakeet												
Rose-throated Parrot												
Yellow-billed Parrot												
Hispaniolan Parrot												
Puerto Rican Parrot												
Black-billed Parrot												
Red-crowned Parrot												
Orange-winged Parrot						U						
Yellow-headed Parrot												
Red-necked Parrot					C							
St Lucia Parrot							U					
St Vincent Parrot									U			
Imperial Parrot					U							
Black-billed Cuckoo		V			V		V	V				
Yellow-billed Cuckoo	R	V	R	U	U	U	R	U	V			
Mangrove Cuckoo	C	R	C	C	C	C	C		C	C	C	R
Great Lizard-Cuckoo												
Puerto Rican Lizard-Cuckoo												
Hispaniolan Lizard-Cuckoo												
Jamaican Lizard-Cuckoo												
Chestnut-bellied Cuckoo												
Bay-breasted Cuckoo												
Smooth-billed Ani		V	U	U	C	U	R		C	C	C	R
Barn Owl					C				R	R		
Ashy-faced Owl												

SPECIES OF BIRD	BAH	T/C	CUB	CAY	JAM	HIS	PR	VI	ANG	ST M	ST B	SABA	ST E
Puerto Rican Screech-Owl							C	V					
Bare-legged Owl			C										
Cuban Pygmy-Owl			C										
Burrowing Owl	C		C			C							
Stygian Owl			R			V							
Short-eared Owl	V	V	C	R		C	U	V			V		
Jamaican Owl					C								
Common Nighthawk	U	U	?	R	?	V	?	R		?	R		
Antillean Nighthawk	C	C	C	C	C	C	C	C		?	R		
Jamaican Poorwill					E?								
Least Poorwill						C							
Chuck-will's-widow	U	R	U	R	U	C	R	R		V	V	U	
Rufous Nightjar													
Greater Antillean Nightjar			C			C							
Whip-poor-will			V		V								
Puerto Rican Nightjar							C						
White-tailed Nightjar							V						
Northern Potoo					C	R	V						
Black Swift			R	V	C	C	U	V			V		
White-collared Swift			C		C	C	V					V	
Chimney Swift	U	R	V	U	V	V		V					
Short-tailed Swift							?	V					
Gray-rumped Swift						V							
Lesser Antillean Swift													
Alpine Swift							V						
Antillean Palm Swift			C		C	C	V						
Rufous-breasted Hermit													
Green-breasted Mango													
Jamaican Mango					C								

SPECIES OF BIRD	ST C	A/B	MON	GUA	DOM	MAR	ST L	BDS	ST V	GRE	PRO	ST A
Puerto Rican Screech-Owl												
Bare-legged Owl												
Cuban Pygmy-Owl												
Burrowing Owl	E	E		E								
Stygian Owl												
Short-eared Owl												
Jamaican Owl												
Common Nighthawk		?	?	?	?	?	V	?	?	?		R
Antillean Nighthawk	V	?	U	?	?	?	?	?	?	?		
Jamaican Poorwill												
Least Poorwill												
Chuck-will's-widow		V										
Rufous Nightjar							C					
Greater Antillean Nightjar												
Whip-poor-will												
Puerto Rican Nightjar												
White-tailed Nightjar						V		V				
Northern Potoo												
Black Swift	V	V	R	C	C	C	U	R	U	R		
White-collared Swift	V					V				U		
Chimney Swift												
Short-tailed Swift								V	C	?		
Gray-rumped Swift										C		
Lesser Antillean Swift	V			U	C	C	C		C			
Alpine Swift				V			V	V				
Antillean Palm Swift												
Rufous-breasted Hermit										C		
Green-breasted Mango											C	C
Jamaican Mango												

473

SPECIES OF BIRD	BAH	T/C	CUB	CAY	JAM	HIS	PR	VI	ANG	ST M	ST B	SABA	ST E
Antillean Mango						C	C	R					
Green Mango							C						
Purple-throated Carib								V			C	C	U
Green-throated Carib							C	C	C	C	C	C	C
Antillean Crested Hummingbird							C	C	C	C	C	C	C
Cuban Emerald	C		C										
Brace's Hummingbird	E												
Hispaniolan Emerald						C							
Puerto Rican Emerald							C						
Blue-headed Hummingbird													
Black-billed Streamertail					C								
Red-billed Streamertail					C								
Bahama Woodstar	C	C											
Ruby-throated Hummingbird	R		R	V	V	V	V						
Vervain Hummingbird					C	C	V						
Bee Hummingbird		V	R										
Cuban Trogon			C										
Hispaniolan Trogon						C							
Cuban Tody			C										
Broad-billed Tody						C							
Narrow-billed Tody						C							
Jamaican Tody					C								
Puerto Rican Tody							C						
Ringed Kingfisher							V						
Belted Kingfisher	C	C	C	C	C	C	C	C	U	U	C	R	U
Antillean Piculet						C							
Guadeloupe Woodpecker													

SPECIES OF BIRD	ST C	A/B	MON	GUA	DOM	MAR	ST L	BDS	ST V	GRE	PRO	ST A
Antillean Mango												
Green Mango												
Purple-throated Carib	U	U	U	C	C	C	C	V	C	C		
Green-throated Carib	C	C	U	C	C	C	C	U	C	C		
Antillean Crested Hummingbird	C	C	U	C	C	C	C	U	C	C		
Cuban Emerald												
Brace's Hummingbird												
Hispaniolan Emerald												
Puerto Rican Emerald												
Blue-headed Hummingbird					C	C						
Black-billed Streamertail												
Red-billed Streamertail												
Bahama Woodstar												
Ruby-throated Hummingbird												
Vervain Hummingbird												
Bee Hummingbird												
Cuban Trogon												
Hispaniolan Trogon												
Cuban Tody												
Broad-billed Tody												
Narrow-billed Tody												
Jamaican Tody												
Puerto Rican Tody												
Ringed Kingfisher			V	U	C	U						
Belted Kingfisher	U	U	C	U	U	U	U	C	U	U	U	C
Antillean Piculet												
Guadeloupe Woodpecker		V		C								

SPECIES OF BIRD	BAH	T/C	CUB	CAY	JAM	HIS	PR	VI	ANG	ST M	ST B	SABA	ST E
Puerto Rican Woodpecker							C						
Hispaniolan Woodpecker						C							
Jamaican Woodpecker					C								
West Indian Woodpecker	C		C	C									
Yellow-bellied Sapsucker	C	C	C	U	U	U	R	R		V	V		
Cuban Green Woodpecker			C										
Hairy Woodpecker	C	V					V						
Northern Flicker			C	C									
Fernandina's Flicker	V		R										
Ivory-billed Woodpecker			V										
Jamaican Elaenia					U								
Caribbean Elaenia				C			C	C	C	C	C	C	C
Yellow-bellied Elaenia													
Greater Antillean Elaenia					C	C							
Western Wood-Pewee			V		V								
Eastern Wood-Pewee	R	R	R	R	V			V					
Crescent-eyed Pewee	C		C										
Hispaniolan Pewee	V					C	V						
Jamaican Pewee					C								
Puerto Rican Pewee							C						
Lesser Antillean Pewee													
St Lucia Pewee													
Yellow-bellied Flycatcher			V		V								
Acadian Flycatcher	R		R	V									
Willow Flycatcher			V		V								
Euler's Flycatcher													

476

LOCALITY CHECKLIST

SPECIES OF BIRD	ST C	A/B	MON	GUA	DOM	MAR	ST L	BDS	ST V	GRE	PRO	ST A
Puerto Rican Woodpecker												
Hispaniolan Woodpecker												
Jamaican Woodpecker												
West Indian Woodpecker												
Yellow-bellied Sapsucker					V							U
Cuban Green Woodpecker												
Hairy Woodpecker												
Northern Flicker												
Fernandina's Flicker												
Ivory-billed Woodpecker												
Jamaican Elaenia												
Caribbean Elaenia	C	C	U	C	C	C	C	C	C	C	R	R
Yellow-bellied Elaenia									C	C		
Greater Antillean Elaenia												
Western Wood-Pewee												
Eastern Wood-Pewee								V			R	R
Crescent-eyed Pewee												
Hispaniolan Pewee												
Jamaican Pewee												
Puerto Rican Pewee												
Lesser Antillean Pewee	?			C	C	C						
St Lucia Pewee							C					
Yellow-bellied Flycatcher												
Acadian Flycatcher												
Willow Flycatcher												
Euler's Flycatcher										E?		

477

SPECIES OF BIRD	BAH	T/C	CUB	CAY	JAM	HIS	PR	VI	ANG	ST M	ST B	SABA	ST E
Eastern Phoebe	V		V										
Sad Flycatcher					C								
Great Crested Flycatcher	V		R			V	V						
Grenada Flycatcher													
Rufous-tailed Flycatcher					C								
La Sagra's Flycatcher	C		C	C									
Stolid Flycatcher					C	C							
Puerto Rican Flycatcher							C	U					
Lesser Antillean Flycatcher													
Tropical Kingbird			V										
Western Kingbird	V		V										
Eastern Kingbird	R	V	U	R	R		V						
Gray Kingbird	C	C	C	C	C	C	C	C	C	C	C	C	C
Loggerhead Kingbird	C		C	C	C	C	C						
Giant Kingbird	E	E	R										
Scissor-tailed Flycatcher	V		V			V	V						
Fork-tailed Flycatcher			V	V	V					V	V		
Jamaican Becard					C								
Purple Martin	U	U	C	C	V	V	V	V					
Cuban Martin	V		C										
Caribbean Martin	V	V		V	C	C	C	C	C	C	C	C	C
Tree Swallow	U	V	C	C	U	R	R	R					
Golden Swallow					V	U							
Bahama Swallow	C		V										
Northern Rough-winged Swallow	R	R	R	R	R	R		V					
Bank Swallow	U	U	U	U	R	R	U	U					
Cliff Swallow	R	R	R	U		V		R			V	V	
Cave Swallow			C	R	C	C	C	R					
Barn Swallow	C	C	C	C	C	C	C	C	C	C	C	C	C

SPECIES OF BIRD	ST C	A/B	MON	GUA	DOM	MAR	ST L	BDS	ST V	GRE	PRO	ST A
Eastern Phoebe												
Sad Flycatcher												
Great Crested Flycatcher												
Grenada Flycatcher									C	C		
Rufous-tailed Flycatcher												
La Sagra's Flycatcher												
Stolid Flycatcher												
Puerto Rican Flycatcher												
Lesser Antillean Flycatcher	C	C		C	C	C	C					
Tropical Kingbird										R		
Western Kingbird												
Eastern Kingbird	V				V							R
Gray Kingbird	C	C	C	C	C	C	C	C	C	C		
Loggerhead Kingbird												
Giant Kingbird												
Scissor-tailed Flycatcher												
Fork-tailed Flycatcher							V	V	V	V		
Jamaican Becard												
Purple Martin												
Cuban Martin												
Caribbean Martin	U	U	U	C	C	C	C	C	C	C		
Tree Swallow												
Golden Swallow												
Bahama Swallow												
Northern Rough-winged Swallow				V								
Bank Swallow	R	V		R	R	R	V	U	V	V		U
Cliff Swallow	V	V		R	R		R	U	V			U
Cave Swallow						V	V		V			
Barn Swallow	C	C	U	C	C	C	C	C	C	C	C	C

SPECIES OF BIRD	BAH	T/C	CUB	CAY	JAM	HIS	PR	VI	ANG	ST M	ST B	SABA	ST E
Cuban Palm Crow			R										
Hispaniolan Palm Crow						C							
Cuban Crow		C	C										
White-necked Crow						C	E						
Jamaican Crow					C								
Brown-headed Nuthatch	V												
Zapata Wren			R										
House Wren	V		V										
Ruby-crowned Kinglet	V		V		V	V							
Blue-gray Gnatcatcher	C	C	C	U									
Cuban Gnatcatcher			C										
Northern Wheatear	V		V				V						
Eastern Bluebird	V		V					V					
Cuban Solitaire			C										
Rufous-throated Solitaire					C	C							
Veery	R		R	V	R	R		V					
Gray-cheeked Thrush	?	?	R	?	?	?	?	?					
Bicknell's Thrush	?	?	R	?	R	U	V	V					
Swainson's Thrush	V		R	R	R								
Hermit Thrush	V		V										
Wood Thrush	V		R	V	V	V	V						
Cocoa Thrush													
Bare-eyed Robin													
White-eyed Thrush					C								
American Robin	R	V	R		V	V	V						
La Selle Thrush						U							
White-chinned Thrush					C								
Grand Cayman Thrush				E									
Red-legged Thrush	C		C	C		C	C						

SPECIES OF BIRD	ST C	A/B	MON	GUA	DOM	MAR	ST L	BDS	ST V	GRE	PRO	ST A
Cuban Palm Crow												
Hispaniolan Palm Crow												
Cuban Crow												
White-necked Crow												
Jamaican Crow												
Brown-headed Nuthatch												
Zapata Wren												
House Wren				E	C	E	R		U	C		
Ruby-crowned Kinglet												
Blue-gray Gnatcatcher												
Cuban Gnatcatcher												
Northern Wheatear								V				
Eastern Bluebird												
Cuban Solitaire												
Rufous-throated Solitaire					C	C	C		C			
Veery	V										V	V
Gray-cheeked Thrush						V					?	?
Bicknell's Thrush												
Swainson's Thrush												
Hermit Thrush												
Wood Thrush												
Cocoa Thrush									C	C		
Bare-eyed Robin						C	C		C	C		
White-eyed Thrush												
American Robin												
La Selle Thrush												
White-chinned Thrush												
Grand Cayman Thrush												
Red-legged Thrush					C							

SPECIES OF BIRD	BAH	T/C	CUB	CAY	JAM	HIS	PR	VI	ANG	ST M	ST B	SABA	ST E
Forest Thrush													
Gray Catbird	C	C	U	C	U	R	V		V				
Northern Mockingbird	C	C	C	C	C	C	C	C					
Tropical Mockingbird													
Bahama Mockingbird	C	C	C		C								
Brown Thrasher	V		V										
White-breasted Thrasher													
Scaly-breasted Thrasher											C	C	E?
Pearly-eyed Thrasher	C	C			V	C	C	C	C	C	C	C	C
Brown Trembler								V				C	V
Gray Trembler													
American Pipit	V				V								
Cedar Waxwing	V	V	U	R	R	V	V	V					
Palmchat						C							
European Starling	C	V	R	V	C		V	V					
Hill Myna							U						
White-eyed Vireo	U	R	U	U	R	V	R	V					
Thick-billed Vireo	C	C	U	C		C							
Mangrove Vireo													
St Andrew Vireo													
Jamaican Vireo					C								
Cuban Vireo			C										
Puerta Rican Vireo							C						
Flat-billed Vireo						U							
Blue Mountain Vireo					U								
Blue-headed Vireo	V		V		V								
Yellow-throated Vireo	U	R	C	U	V	V	V	U					
Warbling Vireo			V		V								
Philadelphia Vireo	R	R	R	V	R								

SPECIES OF BIRD	ST C	A/B	MON	GUA	DOM	MAR	ST L	BDS	ST V	GRE	PRO	ST A
Forest Thrush			C	U	U		R					
Gray Catbird											C	U
Northern Mockingbird												
Tropical Mockingbird		C		C	C	C	C		C	C		C
Bahama Mockingbird												
Brown Thrasher												
White-breasted Thrasher						R	R					
Scaly-breasted Thrasher	C	E?	U	C	C	C	C	E?	V	R		
Pearly-eyed Thrasher	C	C	C	C	C	U	C	V				
Brown Trembler	U	V	U	C	C	R	U		U	R		
Gray Trembler						C	C					
American Pipit											V	V
Cedar Waxwing				V	V							
Palmchat												
European Starling												
Hill Myna												
White-eyed Vireo												
Thick-billed Vireo												
Mangrove Vireo											?	
St Andrew Vireo												C
Jamaican Vireo												
Cuban Vireo												
Puerta Rican Vireo												
Flat-billed Vireo												
Blue Mountain Vireo												
Blue-headed Vireo												
Yellow-throated Vireo		V			V		V	R	V	V		
Warbling Vireo												
Philadelphia Vireo		V										

SPECIES OF BIRD	BAH	T/C	CUB	CAY	JAM	HIS	PR	VI	ANG	ST M	ST B	SABA	ST E
Red-eyed Vireo	U	U	U	U	U	R	V	V					
Black-whiskered Vireo	C	C	C	C	C	C	C	C	C	R	C	U	U
Yucatan Vireo				C									
Bachman's Warbler	E?		E?									∘	
Blue-winged Warbler	R	R	R	R	R	R		R			V		
Golden-winged Warbler	V		V	R	V	V	R	R					
Tennessee Warbler	U	R	U	U	R	R		V					
Orange-crowned Warbler	R		V	V	V								
Nashville Warbler	R	V	V	R	V	V	V						
Northern Parula	C	C	C	C	C	C	C	C	U	U	C	U	U
Yellow Warbler	C	C	C	C	C	C	C	C	C	C	C	V	C
Chestnut-sided Warbler	R	R	U	R	R	R	R	R					
Magnolia Warbler	C	C	C	U	U	U	U	R		V	V		
Cape May Warbler	C	C	C	C	C	C	C	U	U	R	V	R	R
Black-throated Blue Warbler	C	C	C	C	C	C	C	R		V	V		
Yellow-rumped Warbler	C	C	C	U	C	U	U	U					V
Townsend's Warbler	V	V											
Black-throated Green Warbler	U	U	C	R	U	U	V	V		V	V		
Blackburnian Warbler	R	V	U	R	R	R	V	V					
Yellow-throated Warbler	C	C	C	C	U	U	U	V					
Adelaide's Warbler							C						
Olive-capped Warbler	C		C										
Pine Warbler	C		V	V	V	C	V						
Kirtland's Warbler	R	R											
Prairie Warbler	C	C	C	C	C	C	C	C	R	R	U	R	R
Vitelline Warbler				C									
Palm Warbler	C	C	C	C	C	C	U	R				V	

SPECIES OF BIRD	ST C	A/B	MON	GUA	DOM	MAR	ST L	BDS	ST V	GRE	PRO	ST A
Red-eyed Vireo				V		V	V	V				
Black-whiskered Vireo	C	C	U	C	C	C	C	C	C	C	U	U
Yucatan Vireo												
Bachman's Warbler												
Blue-winged Warbler				V								
Golden-winged Warbler												
Tennessee Warbler									V		R	U
Orange-crowned Warbler												
Nashville Warbler												
Northern Parula	R	C	R	U	R	U	V	R	V	R		C
Yellow Warbler	C	C	U	C	C	C	C	C	U	U	R	C
Chestnut-sided Warbler		V			V			V	V			U
Magnolia Warbler		R		V	V			R			U	C
Cape May Warbler	R	R	R	R	V	V	V	R	V	V		C
Black-throated Blue Warbler	V	V		R	R			R	V			U
Yellow-rumped Warbler	V	V		R	R		V	R	V		U	C
Townsend's Warbler												
Black-throated Green Warbler		V		V	V			V				R
Blackburnian Warbler					V			V		V		
Yellow-throated Warbler			V	V				V				
Adelaide's Warbler		C				V	C					
Olive-capped Warbler												
Pine Warbler						V						
Kirtland's Warbler												
Prairie Warbler	R	V	R			V		R		V		
Vitelline Warbler												
Palm Warbler					V		V	V				U

SPECIES OF BIRD	BAH	T/C	CUB	CAY	JAM	HIS	PR	VI	ANG	ST M	ST B	SABA	ST E
Bay-breasted Warbler	R	R	R	R	R	V	V	V					
Blackpoll Warbler	C	C	C	U	R	C	C	U	R	R	R	V	
Cerulean Warbler	V		V	V	V		V						
Plumbeous Warbler													
Arrow-headed Warbler					C								
Elfin Woods Warbler							U						
Whistling Warbler													
Black-and-white Warbler	C	C	C	C	C	C	C	C		R	C	V	V
American Redstart	C	C	C	C	C	C	C	C	U	R	C	R	R
Prothonotary Warbler	U	U	U	R	U	U	U	R	R	V	R		
Worm-eating Warbler	C	C	C	C	U	U	U	R		V	V		
Swainson's Warbler	R		U	R	U	V	R	V					
Ovenbird	C	C	C	U	C	C	C	U	R	V	R	V	
Northern Waterthrush	C	C	C	C	C	C	C	C	U	U	C	R	R
Louisiana Waterthrush	U	U	C	R	C	C	C	R		V	V		
Kentucky Warbler	R	R	R	R	R	R	R	R					
Connecticut Warbler	V	V	V			V	V	V		V	V		
Mourning Warbler	V	V	V		V	V	V	V					
Common Yellowthroat	C	C	C	C	C	C	C	R		V			
Bahama Yellowthroat	C												
Green-tailed Ground Warbler						C							
Yellow-headed Warbler			C										
Oriente Warbler			C										
Semper's Warbler													
Hooded Warbler	U	U	U	R	U	R	R	R		V	V	V	
Wilson's Warbler	V		V		V	V	V						

SPECIES OF BIRD	ST C	A/B	MON	GUA	DOM	MAR	ST L	BDS	ST V	GRE	PRO	ST A
Bay-breasted Warbler		V			V		V	V				R
Blackpoll Warbler	R	R		U	C	U	R	U	R	R	R	R
Cerulean Warbler									V			
Plumbeous Warbler				C	C							
Arrow-headed Warbler												
Elfin Woods Warbler												
Whistling Warbler									U			
Black-and-white Warbler	C	C	R	C	C	C	V	U	V		C	C
American Redstart	C	C	R	U	U	U	R	U	R	R	R	C
Prothonotary Warbler	V		V	R	R	R	V	R	V	R	R	R
Worm-eating Warbler		V		V							U	C
Swainson's Warbler												
Ovenbird	V	V	R	R	V	R	V	R	V		U	C
Northern Waterthrush	R	C	U	U	U	R	U	U	R	R	C	C
Louisiana Waterthrush	R	V	R	R	R	R	V		V			
Kentucky Warbler		V		V							R	
Connecticut Warbler												
Mourning Warbler												
Common Yellowthroat		V		V	V						R	C
Bahama Yellowthroat												
Green-tailed Ground Warbler												
Yellow-headed Warbler												
Oriente Warbler												
Semper's Warbler							E?					
Hooded Warbler	V	V	V	R	V	V			V	V		C
Wilson's Warbler												

SPECIES OF BIRD	BAH	T/C	CUB	CAY	JAM	HIS	PR	VI	ANG	ST M	ST B	SABA	ST E
Canada Warbler	V		V	V	V	V	V	V					
Yellow-breasted Chat	V		V	V									
White-winged Warbler						C							
Bananaquit	C	C	V	C	C	C	C	C	C	C	C	C	C
Lesser Antillean Tanager													
Red-legged Honeycreeper			R										
Jamaican Euphonia					C								
Antillean Euphonia						C	C				V	E?	
Western Stripe-headed Tanager	C	C	C	C									
Jamaican Stripe-headed Tanager					C								
Hispaniolan Stripe-headed Tanager						C							
Puerto Rican Stripe-headed Tanager							C						
Summer Tanager	U	U	U	U	U	V						V	
Scarlet Tanager	R	R	R	R	R		V	V	V	V	V	V	V
Black-crowned Palm-Tanager						C							
Gray-crowned Palm-Tanager						C							
Chat Tanager						U							
Puerto Rican Tanager							C						
Lesser Antillean Saltator													
Rose-breasted Grosbeak	U	U	U	U	R	R	R	R					
Blue Grosbeak	U	U	R	U	V	R	R	V					
Indigo Bunting	C	C	C	U	U	U	R	C				V	
Painted Bunting	C		U	V	V								
Dickcissel	R		V	V	V		V						
Blue-black Grassquit													
Yellow-bellied Seedeater													

SPECIES OF BIRD	ST C	A/B	MON	GUA	DOM	MAR	ST L	BDS	ST V	GRE	PRO	ST A
Canada Warbler				V			V					
Yellow-breasted Chat												
White-winged Warbler												
Bananaquit	C	C	C	C	C	C	C	C	C	C	C	C
Lesser Antillean Tanager									U	U		
Red-legged Honeycreeper												
Jamaican Euphonia												
Antillean Euphonia	V	U	V	U	U	U	U		U	U		
Western Stripe-headed Tanager												
Jamaican Stripe-headed Tanager												
Hispaniolan Stripe-headed Tanager												
Puerto Rican Stripe-headed Tanager												
Summer Tanager				V				V	V	V		
Scarlet Tanager	V	U	V	R	V	V	V	R		V		
Black-crowned Palm-Tanager												
Gray-crowned Palm-Tanager												
Chat Tanager												
Puerto Rican Tanager												
Lesser Antillean Saltator	V			C	C	C	C					
Rose-breasted Grosbeak		V		V	R	V	V	V	V		C	C
Blue Grosbeak												
Indigo Bunting		V									R	C
Painted Bunting												
Dickcissel								V			R	R
Blue-black Grassquit										C		
Yellow-bellied Seedeater									U	U		

SPECIES OF BIRD	BAH	T/C	CUB	CAY	JAM	HIS	PR	VI	ANG	ST M	ST B	SABA	ST E
Cuban Bullfinch			C	C									
Cuban Grassquit	C		C										
Yellow-faced Grassquit			C	C	C	C	C						
Black-faced Grassquit	C	C	R		C	C	C	C	C	C	C	C	C
Yellow-shouldered Grassquit					C								
Puerto Rican Bullfinch							C						
Greater Antillean Bullfinch	C	C			C	C							
Lesser Antillean Bullfinch							V	C	C	C	C	C	C
Orangequit					C								
St Lucia Black Finch													
Saffron Finch			V		C		C						
Grassland Yellow-Finch													
Zapata Sparrow			U										
Chipping Sparrow	V	V	V										
Clay-colored Sparrow	V		V										
Lark Sparrow	V		V		V								
Savannah Sparrow	U		U	R									
Grasshopper Sparrow	R		C	R	C	C	C						
Lincoln's Sparrow	R		R		R	V	V						
Swamp Sparrow	V												
Rufous-collared Sparrow						C							
White-crowned Sparrow	R	R	R		V								
Dark-eyed Junco	V				V		V	V					
Bobolink	C	U	C	C	C	R	U	U		V	R	V	
Red-shouldered Blackbird			C										
Red-winged Blackbird	C												
Tawny-shouldered Blackbird			C			U							

490

SPECIES OF BIRD	ST C	A/B	MON	GUA	DOM	MAR	ST L	BDS	ST V	GRE	PRO	ST A
Cuban Bullfinch												
Cuban Grassquit												
Yellow-faced Grassquit												
Black-faced Grassquit	C	C	U	C	C	C	C	C	C	C	C	C
Yellow-shouldered Grassquit												
Puerto Rican Bullfinch	E?											
Greater Antillean Bullfinch												
Lesser Antillean Bullfinch	C	C	C	C	C	C	C	C	C	C		
Orangequit												
St Lucia Black Finch							U					
Saffron Finch												
Grassland Yellow-Finch		U		U		U	U	U	U	U		
Zapata Sparrow												
Chipping Sparrow												
Clay-colored Sparrow												
Lark Sparrow												
Savannah Sparrow												
Grasshopper Sparrow												
Lincoln's Sparrow												
Swamp Sparrow												
Rufous-collared Sparrow												
White-crowned Sparrow												
Dark-eyed Junco												
Bobolink	V	R		V	R	V	V	U	V	V		
Red-shouldered Blackbird												
Red-winged Blackbird												
Tawny-shouldered Blackbird												

SPECIES OF BIRD	BAH	T/C	CUB	CAY	JAM	HIS	PR	VI	ANG	ST M	ST B	SABA	ST E
Yellow-shouldered Blackbird							U						
Jamaican Blackbird					U								
Eastern Meadowlark			C										
Yellow-headed Blackbird	V		V	V									
Cuban Blackbird			C										
Greater Antillean Grackle			C	C	C	C	C						
Carib Grackle									C	U	C		
Shiny Cowbird	U		C	V	R	C	C	R					
Brown-headed Cowbird	R	V	V										
Black-cowled Oriole	C		C			C	C						
St Lucia Oriole													
Montserrat Oriole													
Martinique Oriole													
Orchard Oriole	V		V		V								
Hooded Oriole			V										
Troupial							C	U					
Jamaican Oriole				E	C								
Baltimore Oriole	U	U	U	R	U	R	R	R			V		
White-winged Crossbill					V	U							
Red Siskin							R						
Antillean Siskin						C							
American Goldfinch	V		V										
Yellow-fronted Canary							V						
House Sparrow	C		C		V	C	C	R					
Village Weaver						C							
Orange Bishop					V		U	V					
Yellow-crowned Bishop					U		U						
Orange-cheeked Waxbill							C						
Black-rumped Waxbill							U	V					

SPECIES OF BIRD	ST C	A/B	MON	GUA	DOM	MAR	ST L	BDS	ST V	GRE	PRO	ST A
Yellow-shouldered Blackbird												
Jamaican Blackbird												
Eastern Meadowlark												
Yellow-headed Blackbird												
Cuban Blackbird												
Greater Antillean Grackle												
Carib Grackle	C	C	C	C	C	C	C	C	C	C		
Shiny Cowbird				C	U	C	U	C	C			
Brown-headed Cowbird												
Black-cowled Oriole												
St Lucia Oriole							U					
Montserrat Oriole			R									
Martinique Oriole						U						
Orchard Oriole												
Hooded Oriole												
Troupial		V		V						V		
Jamaican Oriole												C
Baltimore Oriole	V						V	V	V	V		
White-winged Crossbill												
Red Siskin												
Antillean Siskin												
American Goldfinch												
Yellow-fronted Canary												
House Sparrow												
Village Weaver						C						
Orange Bishop				U		U						
Yellow-crowned Bishop												
Orange-cheeked Waxbill				V		V						
Black-rumped Waxbill				C		U						

SPECIES OF BIRD	BAH	T/C	CUB	CAY	JAM	HIS	PR	VI	ANG	ST M	ST B	SABA	ST E
Red Avadavat						V	C						
Warbling Silverbill							C	V					
Bronze Mannikin							C	V					
Nutmeg Mannikin			U		R	C	C	V					
Chestnut Mannikin			C		U	C	U						
Java Sparrow							C						
Pin-tailed Whydah							U						

LOCALITY CHECKLIST

SPECIES OF BIRD	ST C	A/B	MON	GUA	DOM	MAR	ST L	BDS	ST V	GRE	PRO	ST A
Red Avadavat				C		C						
Warbling Silverbill												
Bronze Mannikin												
Nutmeg Mannikin				C		V						
Chestnut Mannikin						U						
Java Sparrow												
Pin-tailed Whydah												

INDEX OF ENGLISH AND SCIENTIFIC NAMES

Figures in bold refer to plate page numbers

INDEX OF LOCAL NAMES

502